THE YALE EDITIONS OF

The Private Papers of James Boswell

RESEARCH EDITION

Volume 1 THE CORRESPONDENCE OF JAMES BOSWELL AND JOHN JOHNSTON OF GRANGE, edited by Ralph S. Walker, 1966

Volume 2 THE CORRESPONDENCE AND OTHER PAPERS OF JAMES BOSWELL RELATING TO THE MAKING OF THE 'LIFE OF JOHNSON', edited by Marshall Waingrow, 1969

Volume 3 THE CORRESPONDENCE OF JAMES BOSWELL WITH CERTAIN MEMBERS OF THE CLUB, edited by Charles N. Fifer, 1976

Volume 4 THE CORRESPONDENCE OF JAMES BOSWELL WITH DAVID GARRICK, EDMUND BURKE, AND EDMOND MALONE, edited by Peter S. Baker, Thomas W. Copeland, George M. Kahrl, Rachel McClellan, and James Osborn, with the assistance of Robert Mankin and Mark Wollaeger, 1986

Volume 5 THE GENERAL CORRESPONDENCE OF JAMES BOSWELL, 1766–1769, Vol. I: 1766–1767, edited by Richard C. Cole, with Peter S. Baker and Rachel McClellan, and with the assistance of James J. Caudle, 1993.

THE GENERAL CORRESPONDENCE

OF

James Boswell

1766–1769

Vol. I: 1766–1767

edited by

RICHARD C. COLE

with

PETER S. BAKER AND RACHEL MCCLELLAN

and with the assistance of

James J. Caudle

EDINBURGH UNIVERSITY PRESS

Edinburgh

YALE UNIVERSITY PRESS

New Haven and London

© Yale University 1993

Edinburgh University Press
22 George Square, Edinburgh

Set in Linotron Goudy
by Koinonia Ltd, Bury, and
printed in Great Britain by
Alden Press Ltd, Oxford.
Bound in Great Britain by
Hunter and Foulis Ltd, Edinburgh

A CIP record for this book is available
from the British Library

Edinburgh University Press
ISBN 0 7486 0403 0

Yale University Press
ISBN 0-300-05803-9

Library of Congresss Catalog Card Number
93-60351

The paper in this book meets the guidelines for permanence and durability of the Committee on the Production Guidelines for Book Longevity of the Council on Library Resources.

Published by Yale University Press with the assistance of the Annie Burr Lewis Fund.

Boswell's Correspondence, Volume 5

General Editor: Claude Rawson

THE GENERAL CORRESPONDENCE OF
JAMES BOSWELL

1766–1769

Vol. I: 1766–1767

The preparation of *The General Correspondence of James Boswell,* *1766–1769* (Vol. I: *1766–1767*) was generously supported by the National Endowment for the Humanities.

Editorial Committee

Advisory Committee

General Editorial Note

The research edition of the Private Papers of James Boswell will consist of three co-ordinated series: Boswell's journal in all its varieties, his correspondence, and the *Life of Johnson*. The undertaking is a co-operative one involving many scholars, and publication is proceeding in the order in which the volumes are completed for the press. It is expected that the whole edition will consist of at least thirty volumes.

The journal and its related notes and memoranda will be presented in one chronological sequence.

The correspondence is appearing in three kinds of volumes: *subject* volumes of letters relatable to a topic or theme, such as *The Correspondence of James Boswell with Certain Members of The Club*, ed. C. N. Fifer, and its companion volume, *The Correspondence of James Boswell with David Garrick, Edmund Burke, and Edmond Malone*—the three members of The Club not included in the Fifer volume—ed. P. S. Baker and others. The forthcoming volume of Boswell's Estate Correspondence, 1762-95, ed. N. P. Hankins and John Strawhorn, is another volume in this category. Then there are *single-correspondence* volumes, as between *James Boswell and John Johnston of Grange*, ed. R. S. Walker, and the soon-to-be-published correspondence between James Boswell and William Johnson Temple, ed. Thomas Crawford. The final group consists of *general correspondence* volumes each spanning a period of time, of which this volume, which covers the years 1766 to 1769, is the first to be published.

The *Life of Johnson* will be presented in an arrangement which will show the method and progress of its composition. Entitled *An Edition of the Original Manuscript of Boswell's 'Life of Johnson'*, it is edited by Marshall Waingrow, who also edited its companion volume, *The Correspondence and Other Papers Relating to the Making of the 'Life of Johnson.'*

The parallel 'reading' or 'trade' edition, which began publication in 1950, is now complete. Whereas the annotation of this edition turned inwards towards the text, the annotation of the research edition turns outwards from the text and is intended to relate the documents to the various areas of scholarship which they are capable of illuminating: history (literary, linguistic, legal, medical, political, social, local), biography, bibliography, and genealogy. The comprehensiveness and coherence of the papers that Boswell chose to preserve make them highly useful for such exploitation.

Acknowledgements

It is unfortunately impossible to acknowledge the assistance of everyone who has helped in the preparation of this edition or to specify the exact nature of their contributions. We can, however, list the names of those, not always mentioned in the notes, to whom we are particularly indebted for their co-operation and generosity.

Uppermost in the minds of the editors who have worked on this edition is the image of Frederick A. Pottle wearing his green eye-shade, working long hours in 'the Boswell Factory' in Sterling Library, always willing to halt his own work and answer a question or suggest a solution for a student in difficulties. He was Chairman of the Editorial Committee until ill health forced his retirement from that position in 1983. Of equal presence was his successor as Chairman, Frank Brady, without whose insightful suggestions and ever-present editorial skills this volume would have been much longer in the making. We are also indebted to Marion S. Pottle, whose *Catalogue* of the Papers was so helpful, Marshall Waingrow, and Claude Rawson, who is now Chairman in place of Martin Price, and General Editor in place of Marshall Waingrow.

We are particularly grateful to members of the office staff, past and present: Irene Adams, Susan Bianconi, Caterina Bosio, Harriet Chidester, Tulin Duda, Jessica Francis, Marcia W. Levinson, and Eve Sterne. Also deserving of mention are the Warnock fellows who have spent the summer months working in the Boswell Office on this edition: Heather Barkley, Jessica Branch, Margaret Conable, John Eglin, Bernard Schlager, and Marion Wells. From among the number of helpers, we would like to single out three: Liliane Greene, Managing Editor, *Yale French Studies*, for her reading and correction of the transcriptions of the French correspondence, Ian Duncan, assistant professor, Department of English, Yale University, for his assistance with the translations of the Italian letters, and finally, Andrew Elfenbein, assistant professor, Department of English, University of Minnesota, for his invaluable close reading of the notes for accuracy and consistency.

For other assistance, we are greatly obliged to Michael Behen, Janet Dick-Cunyingham, Viscountess Eccles, Lady Eliott of Stobs, Margaret Boswell Eliott of Redheugh, Marena Fisher, Edith Hallo, David G. Herrmann, A. E. M. Hibberink, Sally Hofmann, R. D. Ireland, J. G. Kerkhoven, Jean Munro, Kevin Pacelli, S. R. Parks, W. Schmitz, Francis Sheppard, and Gordon Williams; The

Hyde Collection, Somerville, New Jersey, the Pierpont Morgan Library, the Bodleian Library, the British Library, the Houghton Library, the New York Public Library, the Bibliothèque Publique et Universitaire, Neuchâtel, the Maine Historical Society, the Public Record Office (London), the Auchinleck Boswell Society, and the staffs of Beinecke and Sterling Libraries at Yale.

Mr. Cole is appreciative of the grants which have made it possible for him to work on this edition. They include the Robert Warnock Fellowship, 1975–76, research grants from Davidson College, the American Council of Learned Societies, the Procter and Gamble Fund, the Piedmont University Center of North Carolina, and the Board of Higher Education of the Presbyterian Church of the United States.

Our thanks must go to the late Robert Warnock, not only for the bequest from which we derive funds for our summer interns and grants for our editors, but for the basic research he performed in the archives of the countries Boswell visited on the Grand Tour. He was a fine linguist, and his notes and the biographical registers he compiled of notable people in Europe still provide a base for our annotation of letters sent and received by Boswell on his foreign travels.

Lastly, we are grateful to the National Endowment for the Humanities, without whose support the publication of this volume would not have been possible, and to gifts from the James J. Colt Foundation and the L. J. Skaggs and Mary C. Skaggs Foundation, which will be put towards the matching funds needed.

Contents

Acknowledgements   xiii

List of correspondents   xvi

Preface   xxiii

James Boswell—curriculum vitae to 1767   xxiv

Editorial procedures   xxv

Cue titles and abbreviations   xxviii

Introduction   xxxiii

Correspondence   1

Appendices   269

Index   271

List of Correspondents

From, 13 Nov. 1767
AGNEW, Alexander
†To, 16 June 1766
AITKEN, Edward
†To, 31 July 1766
†From, c. early Aug. 1766
ASHBURY, Francis
From, 3 May 1767
To, 4 June 1767
BARETTI, Giuseppe
From, 24 Nov. 1766
To, 5 Jan. 1767
From, 20 Jan. 1767
†To, betw. late spring and early autumn, 1767
From, 7 Nov. 1767
BOSVILLE, Godfrey
†To, 31 Mar. 1766
†From, c. late Apr. 1766
From, 24 June 1766
†To, 8 July 1766
From, 12 Aug. 1766
From, 25 Dec. 1766
From, 5 June 1767
†To, c. Aug. 1767
From, 4 Oct. 1767
†To, c. late Nov. or early Dec. 1767
From, 19 Dec. 1767
BROWN, James
From, 21 Aug. 1767
BROWN, Robert
From, 3 Mar. 1766
†To, 8 May 1766
†From, c. late Oct. 1766
†To, 5 Jan. 1767
From, 27 Jan. 1767
To, 28 Apr. 1767

From, c. late June 1767
†To, c. early Oct. 1767
From, 22 Oct. 1767
BROWN, William
To, c. 18 May 1767
From, 18 May 1767
To, between 18 and 22 May 1767
BURNABY, Andrew
†To, c. early 1767
†To, c. 13 June 1767
From, 10 Aug. 1767
From, 21 Sept. 1767
†To, 16 Oct. 1767
From, 25 Oct. 1767
BUTTAFOCO, Matteo
†To, 24 Apr. 1766
CARDROSS, Lord
From, 19 June 1766
†To, 5 Jan. 1767
From, 4 Oct. 1767
CHALMER, John
†To, c. mid-Apr. 1767
From, 22 Apr. 1767
CHATHAM, Lord
To, 15 Feb. 1766
From, 16 Feb. 1766
To, 19 Feb. 1766
To, 18 Sept. 1766
To, 3 Jan. 1767
From, 4 Feb. 1767
To, 8 Apr. 1767
CLARKE, Godfrey
†To, 31 Mar. 1766
COCHRANE, Basil
†To, 31 Mar. 1766
From, 7 Apr. 1766
†To, 24 Apr. 1766

(Letters marked with a dagger (†) are known from various sources to have existed, but the manuscripts are not reported and no printed texts of them have been found.)

xvi

†To, 10 May 1766
From, 14 May 1766
†To, 19 Aug. 1766
From, 19 Aug. 1766
To, 18 May 1767
From, 20 May 1767
†To, c. 14 Aug. 1767
From, 14 Aug. 1767
COCHRANE, Lady
†To, 31 May 1766
From, 27 June 1767
COLE, Charles
From, 7 Nov. 1767
CRAUFURD, James
From, 16 May 1766
DAVEL, Theodore
From, 7 Mar. 1767
DAVIES, Thomas
†To, 11 Aug. 1766
From, 21 August 1766
†To, 7 Oct. 1766
From, 15 Nov. 1766
†To, c. early Jan. 1767
From, 17 Jan. 1767
From, 28 Apr. 1767
From, 18 June 1767
†To, 4 Sept. 1767
From, 15 Oct. 1767
†To, c. early Dec. 1767
From, 12 Dec. 1767
DELEYRE, Alexandre
From, 1 Mar. 1766
To, 15 Oct. 1766
From, 8 Dec. 1766
†To, 30 July 1767
From, 25 Sept. 1767
DEMPSTER, George
†To, 7 Mar. 1766
†From, c. late Mar. 1766
†To, 31 Mar. 1766
†From, c. mid Apr. 1766
†To, 8 May 1766
†From, c. mid-May 1766
†To, 3 June 1766
†To, 11 Aug. 1766
†From, c. mid Sept. 1766
†To, 7 Oct. 1766
To, 1 Jan. 1767
DICK, Sir Alexander
From, 22 Aug. 1766
To, 23 Oct. 1766
From, 1 Nov. 1766
To, 9 Dec. 1766
From, 13 Dec. 1766

From, 17 Dec. 1766
From, 10 Apr. 1767
To, 16 Apr. 1767
From, 17 May 1767
To, 15 Aug. 1767
From, 15 Aug. 1767
To, 21 Aug. 1767
From, c. 27 Aug. 1767
To, [31 Aug. 1767]
From, 1 Sept. 1767
To, 2 Sept. 1767
To, 3 Sept. 1767
From, 3 Sept. 1767
To, 3 Nov. 1767
DICK, Sir John
From, 25 Feb. 1766
†To, 10 Apr. 1766
†To, 24 Apr. 1766
From, 30 May 1766
From, 18 June 1766
†To, 27 Aug. 1766
†To, 7 Sept. 1766
From, 26 Sept. 1766
From, 6 Oct. 1766
From, 24 Oct. 1766
From, 31 Oct. 1766
†To, 9 Dec. 1766
From, 7 Jan. 1767
From, 23 Jan. 1767
From, 6 Feb. 1767
From, 6 Mar. 1767
To, 14 Mar. 1767
To, 22 Apr. 1767
From, 11 May 1767
†To, 6-13 June 1767
From, 17 June 1767
From, 28 June 1767
†To, 18/20 July 1767
From, 29 July 1767
From, 10 Aug. 1767
†To, c. 11 Aug. 1767
†To, c. 15 Aug. 1767
From, 20 Aug. 1767
From, 21 Aug. 1767
From, 27 Aug. 1767
†To, c. late July or early Aug. 1767
From, 1 Sept. 1767
†To, 15 Sept. 1767
From, 26 Sept. 1767
†From, between 18 and 24 Oct. 1767
From, 29 Oct. 1767
DILLY, Edward
†To, c. early July 1767
From, 28 July 1767

From, 1 Aug. 1767
From, 4 Aug. 1767
To, 6 Aug. 1767
†To, c. early Aug. 1767
†To, 9 Aug. 1767
From, 10 Aug. 1767
From, 15 Aug. 1767
†To, 20 Aug. 1767
From, 31 Aug. 1767
†To, 4 Sept. 1767
From, 10 Sept. 1767
†To, c. mid-Sept. 1767
From, 24 Sept. 1767
†To, 5 Oct. 1767
From, 13 Oct. 1767
†To, c. late Oct. 1767
From, 4 Nov. 1767
To, c. early Nov. 1767
From, 10 Nov. 1767
†To, c. mid Nov. 1767
From, 19 Nov. 1767
DODDS, Mrs.
†To, 19 Aug. 1766
†From, c. late Aug. 1766
†From, c. mid September 1766
†To, 20 Sept. 1766
†From, c. late Sept. 1766
From, c. Apr. 1767
DONALDSON, Alexander
†To, 24 Apr. 1766
DOUGLAS, Duchess of
To, 13 Cct. 1766
DRUMMOND, William
†To, 30 May 1767
From, 1 June 1767
DUN, John
From, 15 Mar. 1766
†From, c. early June 1766
†To, c. mid July 1766
From, 29 July 1766
†To, c. mid to late Nov. 1766
From, 19 Dec. 1766
'DUN TAYLOR'
†To, 26 June 1766
DUNCAN, James
From, 20 Dec. 1766
DUNDAS, Robert
To, c. early Apr. 1767
From, 10 Apr. 1767
To, 18 Apr. 1767
DUPONT, Pierre Loumeau
From, 23 Apr. 1766
†To, c. late March or early Apr. 1767
From, 7 Apr. 1767

EDWARDS, Richard
From, 24 Apr. 1767
From, 26 June 1767
From, 30 Nov. 1767
EGLINTON, Lord
†To, 7 Mar. 1766
†From, c. late Mar. 1766
†To, 19 Apr. 1766
ERSKINE, Andrew
†From, c. mid April 1766
†To, 8 May 1766
†From, c. early June 1766
†To, 3 June 1766
FARQUHAR, Alexander
From, 30 Mar. 1767
FERGUSSON, Joseph
†To, 10 May 1766
†To, 3 Oct. 1766
From, 20 Dec. 1766
FITZHERBERT, William
From, 17 Apr. 1767
FLEXNEY, William
†To, 18 June 1766
FRAZER, George
†To, 29 Mar. 1766
From, 4 Apr. 1766
FROMENT, Marie de
From, 9 July 1767
GAYOT, Félix-Louis
From, 1 Jan. 1767
GENTLEMAN, Francis
From, 26 Apr. 1766
From, c. late July 1766
†To, c. early 1767
From, 23 June 1767
GILKIE, James
From, 4 Apr. 1767
GORDON, John
†To, 10 May 1766
GRAHAM, Janet
From, 9 June 1766
GRAHAM, William
†To, 10 May 1766
†To, 3 Oct. 1766
HADDOW, JAMES
To, 13 Oct. 1766
HAY, Robert, a friend of
From, 20 Feb. 1767
HUNTER, Mrs. James
†To, 16 June 1766
†To, 3 Oct. 1766
JOHNSTON, Archibald
†To, 3 Oct. 1766
JOHNSTON, Daniel

From, 1 Dec. 1766
JOHNSTOUN, John
  †To, c. early Nov. 1766
  From, 20 Nov. 1766
KAMES, Lady
  †To, 10 May 1766
  From, 21 May 1766
KINLOCH, David
  To, 28 Apr. 1767
LE VASSEUR, Thérèse
  †To, 11 Aug. 1766
LEVEN, Lord
  From, 23 Nov. 1767
LOCKHART, Alexander
  To, ?Summer 1766
LOVE, James
  †To, 26 June 1766
  From, 27 June 1766
MACDONELL, Alexander
  From, 26 Aug. 1766
MACFARLANE, Lady Elizabeth
  †From, c. early July 1766
  †To, 18 June 1766
  †From, c. 1 Aug. 1766
  †To, 12 Aug. 1766
  †From, c. mid Aug. 1766
  From, 13 Feb. 1767
  From, 14 Feb. 1767
MACKINTOSH, Anne
  From, 12 May 1767
MACONOCHIE, Alexander
  †To, c. early to mid Dec. 1767
  From, 25 Dec. 1767
MAITLAND, James
  From, 18 May 1767
MARISCHAL, Lord
  From, 30 Apr. 1766
  †To, 19 Aug. 1766
  From, 2 Oct. 1766
  To, 12 Mar. 1767
  From, 14 Apr. 1767
  From, c. 1 June 1767
  From, 10 July 1767
  †To, 20 July 1767
  †To, c. mid-Aug. 1767
  From, 1 Sept. 1767
  From, 12 Sept. 1767
  †To, c. early Oct. 1767
  From, 24 Oct. 1767
  †To, c. late Dec. 1767 or early Jan. 1768
MAXWELL, Beatrix
  †To, 18 June 1766
McCLURE, David
  †To, 6 June 1767

†To, 9 June 1767
From, 13 June 1767
McQUHAE, William
  †To, 7 Oct. 1766
  See REID, George
McQUHAE, William, and George Reid
  From, 14 July 1766
MITCHELL, Alexander
  From, 25 July 1767
MONTGOMERIE, Mary
  From, 27 Mar. 1766
  †From, c. 8 Apr. 1766
  †To, c. mid-Apr. 1766
  From, 22 Apr. 1766
MONTGOMERIE-CUNINGHAME,
    Alexander
  From, 11 May 1767
MONTGOMERIE-CUNINGHAME,
    Elizabeth
  From, 18 Sept. 1767
MONTGOMERY, James
  †To, 30 May 1767
  ·From, 4 June 1767
MOUNTSTUART, Lord
  †To, mid-March or 31 Mar. 1766
  From, 29 May 1766
  †To, 16 June 1766
  From, 25 June 1766
  To, 6 Aug. 1766
  †From, c. Dec. 1766
  To, 1 Jan. 1767
MUIR, George
  To, 18 Mar. 1767
  From, 23 Mar. 1767
PAOLI, Pasquale
  †To, 24 Apr. 1766
  †From, c. early to mid-June 1766
  †From, c. 20 Oct. 1766
  †To, 9 Dec. 1766
  †To, c. early Feb. 1767
  †To, c. 13 June 1767
  To, 28 Aug. 1767
  From, 1 Nov.-14 Nov. 1767
  †From, 13 Nov. 1767
  From, 15 Dec. 1767
PICCOLOMINI, Girolama
  From, 23 Feb. 1766
  †From, c. early Apr. 1766
  †To, 10 May 1766
  From, 20 Mar. 1767
  To, 25 Mar. 1767
  From, 3 May 1767
  †To, c. mid-Oct. 1767
  From, 16 Nov. 1767

PITT, William: See CHATHAM
PLESS, Baron von
  From, 19 Nov. 1766
PRESTON, Lady
  †To, 10 Oct. 1766
  From, 16 Oct. 1766
PRESTON, Patrick
  From, 8 May 1767
  From, 19 Sept. 1767
PRINGLE, Sir John
  †To, 31 Mar. 1766
  From, 10 June 1766
  From, c. early Jan. 1767
  To, c. Jan. 1767
  From, 10 Feb. 1767
  †To, c. Aug. 1767
  From, 4 Dec. 1767
QUEENSBURY, Duke of
  †To, 19 Dec. 1767
RAMSAY, Robert
  †To, 11 Aug. 1766
REID, George, and William McQuhae
  To, 23 July 1766
  See McQUHAE, William
REID, John
  From, 13 Nov. 1766
RIVAROLA, Count
  †To, 24 Apr. 1766
  From, 19 Sept. 1766
  †To, 9 Dec. 1766
  †From, c. early Feb. 1767
  To, 14 Mar. 1767
  From, 18 Mar. 1767
  From, 2 May 1767
ROUSSEAU, Jean-Jacques
  †From, c. mid Mar. 1766
  To, 25 Mar. 1766
  †To, c. late June 1766
  From, 4 Aug. 1766
  †To, 11 Aug. 1766
ROWAND, John
  From, 24 Nov. 1766
SCOTT, Robert
  From, 21 Sept. 1767
SEROOSKERKEN, Isabella van Tuyll van
  †To, c. mid to late July 1767
  †From, c. late Oct. 1767
SEROOSKERKEN, Willem van Tuyll van
  †To, mid-Oct. 1766
  From, 11 Nov. 1766
SMITH, Andrew
  †From, c. early Apr. 1766
SMITH, James
  †From, c. mid-Apr. 1766

  †From, c. late Aug. 1766
SMITH, Mungo
  From, 18 Nov. 1766
SMITH, Thomas
  From, 1 July 1767
SOMMELSDYCK, Heer van Aerssen van
  From, 14 Mar. 1766
  †To, 6 Apr. 1766
  †To, 8 May 1766
  From, 1 July 1766
  To, 21 Mar. 1767
  †From, c. July or Aug. 1767
SPAEN, Baroness von
  †To, 20 Apr. 1766
  From, 22 July 1766
  †To, before 31 Mar. 1767
STEUART, Sir James
  †To, c. mid-Sept. 1767
  †From, c. mid-Sept. 1767
STEWART, Archibald
  †To, 11 Aug. 1766
  †From, c. mid-Sept. 1766
  From, 5 Dec. 1766
  †To, c. Summer 1767
STOBIE, John
  †To, 10 Oct. 1766
STRANGE, Robert
  To, 16 Mar. 1767
  From, 16 May 1767
SYMONDS, John
  †From, 1766
  From, 3 Oct. 1767
TAIT, John
  To, 28 Mar. 1767
  From, 7 Apr. 1767
VOLTAIRE, François-Marie-Arouet de
  To, 29 Mar. 1767
WALLACE, William
  From, 26 Aug. 1766
WATERS, John
  To, 10 May 1766
WIDDRINGTON, John
  †From, between 24 and 29 Aug. 1767
WILKES, John
  To, 6 May 1766
WILKIE, John
  †To, 31 Mar. 1766
  †To, 18 Sept. 1766
  From, 30 Dec. 1766
  To, 28 Apr. 1767
  From, 7 May 1767
  To, c. 21 July 1767
  From, 28 July 1767
  †To, c. late Oct. 1767

†To, c. early Nov. 1767
WOODFALL, Henry
†To, c. early Nov. 1767
WYVILL, Christopher

†To, c. mid-Sept. 1767
From, 3 Oct. 1767
ZUYLEN, Heer van
†To, 8 May 1766

Preface

This volume is the first of two containing Boswell's correspondence with more than 200 correspondents in the period from 1766 to 1769. They include Pitt, Rousseau, Paoli, John Wilkes, Sir Alexander Dick, Baretti, the Earl Marischal, and various women friends, to name but a small fraction of them. Excluded are those members of The Club whose correspondences with Boswell are to be found in a previous volume: *The Correspondence of James Boswell With Certain Members of The Club*, ed. C. N. Fifer, and its companion volume, *The Correspondence of James Boswell with David Garrick, Edmund Burke, and Edmond Malone*, those being the three members of The Club omitted for considerations of space and significance from the Fifer volume. This last was edited by P. S. Baker and others. We print the texts of 233 letters, 54 from Boswell and 179 to Boswell. A hundred and eighty-five additional letters (57 to Boswell, 128 from him), of which no texts are known to be extant, receive notice under their proper dates, with as much information about their contents as could be gathered.

The editing was done by Richard C. Cole, and was revised in the later stages by the late Frank Brady, Peter S. Baker, and Rachel McClellan, with assistance from James J. Caudle.

CLAUDE RAWSON
Chairman

James Boswell —
curriculum vitae to 1767

1740   29 October: Born.

1753   Autumn: Matriculated at University of Edinburgh.

1759   Autumn: Matriculated at University of Glasgow.

1760   Spring: Ran away to London with intention of becoming a Roman Catholic.
Published A *View of the Edinburgh Theatre … Summer Season 1759*.
Published *Observations … on … 'The Minor'*.

1761   Published *An Elegy on the Death of an Amiable Young Lady*.
Published *An Ode to Tragedy*.

1762   Published poems in *A Collection of Original Poems by Scotch Gentlemen*.
7 March: Signed a deed in which he consented to be put under trustees of his father's choosing in case he succeeded to Auchinleck.
Published *The Cub at Newmarket*.
30 July: Passed his trials in Civil Law and received permission to go to London to try to obtain a commission in the Foot Guards.
15 November: Left for London.

1763   Published *Critical Strictures on the New Tragedy of 'Elvira'*.
Published *Letters between The Honourable Andrew Erskine and James Boswell, Esq.*
16 May: Introduced to Samuel Johnson.
August: Travelled to Utrecht for further study of law.

1764   June: Left Utrecht for tour through Germany, Switzerland, Italy, Corsica, and France.

1766   11 January: His mother died while he was in Paris.
12 February: Returned to London from the Continent.
11 July: Passed examination in Scots Law.
26 July: Passed advocate, printed thesis *De Supellectile Legata*.

1767   Volunteer in the Douglas Cause, about which he published a number of works: *The Douglas Cause, Dorando, The Essence of the Douglas Cause, Letters of Lady Jane Douglas*.
Published *Prologue for thc Opening of the Theatre Royal*.

Editorial Procedures

The Texts

Choice and Arrangement of Letters
The copy-text has been the MSS. of letters sent, whenever such MSS. are available; failing letters sent, we have used MS. drafts and copies.

'Not reported' in the head-notes means that, though there is evidence that the letter in question was sent, we have no evidence that any kind of MS. of it survived the sender and the recipient. 'Missing' bears the ordinary narrow sense 'not in the place where one would expect it to be', as 'the lower half of the second leaf is missing'.

Transcription
In conformity with the plan of the research edition as a whole, the manuscript documents in this edition have been printed to correspond to the originals as closely as is feasible in the medium of type. A certain amount of compromise and apparent inconsistency seems unavoidable, but change has been kept within the limits of stated conventions. A few clear inadvertencies have been made right without notice, but no change that could affect the sense has been made silently.

The editorial conventions governing the presentation of the text and annotation are many, complex, and minute; only the most important of them have been stated here. The writers' paragraphing and capitalization is retained, as is spelling, except for certain inadvertencies which are corrected in the text and recorded in the notes.

Editorial intervention has been more active in formulary and mechanical elements than elsewhere. The following editorial conventions are imposed in the volume as a whole without notice:

Addresses. Elements appearing on separate lines in the MS. are run together and punctuated according to modern practice. Handwriting is that of the sender unless otherwise specified.

Headings. Headings are in the hand of the writer or, in the case of copies, that of the copier, unless otherwise specified.

Datelines. Places and dates are joined at the head of the letter regardless of their position in the MS., and the punctuation regularized.

Salutations. Abbreviations are expanded. Commas and colons after salutations are retained; when the manuscripts show other punctuation, colons are substituted. The first word following the salutation is capitalized.

Complimentary closes. The punctuation of complimentary closes and signatures is regularized. Elements appearing on separate lines in the MS. are run together. Complimentary closes separately paragraphed in the MS. are printed as continuations of the last line of text. Abbreviations are expanded.

Postscripts. The punctuation of the symbol P.S. is regularized, and the postscript is treated as a separate paragraph of the text.

Endorsements. Unless otherwise specified, handwriting in the case of originals is that of the recipients, in the case of drafts or copies that of the writer.

Punctuation. Periods are supplied at the end of sentences, unless sentences are concluded with a dash. Following a period, a sentence always begins with a capital. Some nonsensical periods have been read as commas, and vice versa. Where the end of a line stands in place of punctuation in the MS., commas or other punctuation have occasionally been supplied to clarify meaning. Periods following cardinals have been removed, as have periods following ordinals except in datelines, where they serve as punctuation separating elements of the date. Punctuation in lists is regularized. Question marks are read as exclamation points when required by sense.

Interlineations and marginalia. The insertion of interlineations and marginalia is explicitly indicated only in unusual cases.

Changes. Substantive additions and deletions are recorded in the notes in all cases for originals, and for drafts or copies when originals are unavailable. They are recorded only if significant in drafts or copies when originals are available.

Lacunae. Words and letters missing through a tear or obscured by a blot are supplied within angular brackets. Inadvertent omissions by the writer are supplied within square brackets.

Abbreviations, contractions, and symbols. The following abbreviations, contractions, and symbols, and their variant forms, are expanded: abt (about), acct (account), affecly (affectionately), agst (against), Bp (Bishop), cd (could), compts (compliments), Dr (Dear), evng (evening), ed (editor), edn (edition), humb (humble), Ld (Lord), Lop (Lordship), Ly (Lady), Lyship (Ladyship), obt (obedient), p (per), Q (query), r (read), recd (received), sd (should), sert (servant), Sr (Sir), wc (which), wd (would), wt (with), witht (without), ye (the), yr (your), yt (that), & (and), &c (etc). All retained abbreviations are followed by a period.

Superior letters. Superior letters are lowered, except in foreign postmarks.

Quotations. Primary quotation is indicated by single quotation marks, secondary by double. Quotation marks repeated at the beginning of each line of a paragraph are deleted, as are quotation marks around wholly italicized passages. Omitted quotation marks are supplied where one is indicated and the other missing at the beginning or end of a passage.

Brackets. Parentheses replace square brackets in the text, brackets being reserved for editorial use.

Devices of emphasis. Underlinings for purposes of emphasis are printed in italics. Words written in particularly large letters or those doubly underlined are printed in small capitals. Underlinings which seem to be meaningless flourishes are ignored.

The Annotation

Headnotes. Where more than one text is cited, the first mentioned is the one reproduced. Former printings are mentioned only if the original remains untraced. Where an address is not given, usually the letter was sent 'under cover'.

Footnotes. Reference titles in the footnotes are sufficiently complete for ready identification. Except where the works have been directly quoted, no source is given when the information is available in the DNB, an encyclopaedia, or other general reference works, such as gazetteers, the *British Library Catalogue of Printed Books*, Joseph Haydn and Horace Ockerby's *Book of Dignities*, and H. B. Wheatley and Peter Cunningham's *London Past and Present*. When an abbreviated source is given, the full citation either appears in a preceding note or is found in the list of cue titles which follows.

Cue Titles and Abbreviations

This list omits familiar abbreviations of such standard works of reference and periodicals as DNB, OED, and N & Q.

Note: All manuscripts referred to in the notes without mention of a repository are in the Yale Collection. Catalogue numbers are supplied in some instances to facilitate identification.

ADB: *Allgemeine Deutsche Biographie*, 56 vols., 1875–1912.

Adelsarchief: D. G. van Epen, 'Het Geslacht van Aerssen,' *Adelsarchief, Jaarboek voorden Nederlanden Adel*, vol. iii, [1902].

Alum. Cantab: John Venn, *Alumni Cantabrigienses*, 1922–27.

Army List: *A List of the Officers of the Army, etc.*, 1756–.

Ayr and Wigton: James Paterson, *History of the Counties of Ayr and Wigton*, 3 vols. in 5 parts, 1863–66.

Ayrshire: *Ayrshire at the Time of Burns*, Ayrshire Archaeological and Natural History Society, vol. v, 1959.

Baker: *The Correspondence of James Boswell with David Garrick, Edmund Burke, and Edmond Malone*, ed. P. S. Baker, T. W. Copeland, G. M. Kahrl, Rachel McClellan, and J. M. Osborn, 1986.

Baronage: Sir Robert Douglas, *The Baronage of Scotland*, 1798.

Beawes: Wyndham Beawes, *Lex Mercatoria Rediviva*, 6th edition, 1773.

Bell: Robert Bell, *A Dictionary of the Law of Scotland*, 2 vols., 1807–08.

Bettany: Lewis Bettany, *Diaries of William Johnston Temple*, 1929.

Biog. Dict. Actors: *A Biographical Dictionary of Actors, Actresses, Musicians, Dancers, Managers & Other Personnel in London, 1660–1800*, ed. P. H. Highfill, Jr., K. A. Burnim, and E. A. Langhans, 12 vols., 1973–.

Boswell's Paoli: Joseph Foladare, *Boswell's Paoli*, 1979.

Boswelliana: *Boswelliana: The Commonplace Book of James Boswell*, ed. Charles Rogers, 1874.

BP: *The Private Papers of James Boswell from Malahide Castle in the Collection of Lt.-Colonel Ralph Heyward Isham*, ed. Geoffrey Scott and F. A. Pottle, 18 vols., 1928–34.

BSSC: *Bulletin de la société des sciences historiques et naturelles de la Corse*, 529 fascicules, 1881–1937.

BU: *Biographie universelle, ancienne et moderne*, with supplement, 85 vols., 1811–62.

Burke's Commoners: John Burke, *A Genealogical and Heraldic History of the*

Commoners, 4 vols., 1834–38.

Burke's Landed Gentry: John Burke and others, *Burke's Genealogical and Heraldic History of the Landed Gentry*, various years.

Burke's Peerage: John Burke and others, *Burke's Genealogical and Heraldic History of the Peerage, Baronetage, and Knightage*, 1826–.

Burnaby: Andrew Burnaby, *Journal of a Tour to Corsica in the Year 1766*, 1804.

BW: A. J. Van der Aa, *Biographisch Woordenboek der Nederlanden*, 12 vols., 1852–78, reprinted 1969.

Cal. Merc.: *The Caledonian Mercury*, 1720–1867.

Chatham Corres.: William Pitt, Earl of Chatham, *Correspondence*, ed. W. S. Taylor and J. H. Pringle, 4 vols., 1838–40.

College of Justice: George Brunton and David Haig, *An Historical Account of the Senators of the College of Justice*, 1832.

Comp. Bar.: G. E. C[okayne], *Complete Baronetage*, 5 vols., 1900–06.

Comp. Peer: G. E. C[okayne], *Complete Peerage*, ed. Vicary Gibbs, H. A. Doubleday, and others, 13 vols., 1910–40.

Consultation Book: MS. consultation (fee) book of James Boswell, 1766–72, National Library of Scotland.

Corres. HW: *The Yale Edition of Horace Walpole's Correspondence*, ed. W. S. Lewis and others, 48 vols., 1937–83.

Corres. Rousseau: *Correspondance complète de J.-J. Rousseau*, ed. R. A. Leigh, 40 vols., 1975–.

Corsica: James Boswell, *An Account of Corsica, The Journal of a Tour to that Island, and Memoirs of Pascal Paoli*, 1st ed., Glasgow, 1768.

Crane and Kaye: R. S. Crane and F. B. Kaye, *A Census of British Newspapers and Periodicals, 1620-1800*, 1927.

CSD: *The Concise Scots Dictionary*, ed. Mairi Robinson, 1985.

Cuthell: E. E. Cuthell, *The Scottish Friend of Frederic the Great*, 2 vols., 1915.

DBF: *Dictionnaire de Biographie Française*, 1933–.

Dennistoun: James Dennistoun, *Memoirs of Sir Robert Strange, Knt., … and of His Brother-in-Law Andrew Lumisden*, 2 vols., 1855.

Dibdin: J. C. Dibdin, *The Annals of the Edinburgh Stage*, 1888.

Dict. Nob: *Dictionnaire de la Noblesse*, ed. de la Chesnaye-Desbois et Badier, 19 vols., 1863–76.

Dict. of Printers: H. R. Plomer, G. H. Bushnell, E. R. McC. Dix, *A Dictionary of the Printers and Booksellers Who Were at Work in England, Scotland, and Ireland from 1726–1775*, 1932.

Douglas Cause: *The Douglas Cause*, ed. A. Francis Steuart, 1909.

Earlier Years: F. A. Pottle, *James Boswell, The Earlier Years, 1740–69*, 1966.

Edin. Adv.: The Edinburgh Advertiser, 1764–1824.

Edinburgh Directory: Peter Williamson, *Directory for the City of Edinburgh, Canongate, Leith, and Suburbs*, 1773–96.

Edin. Even. Cour: *The Edinburgh Evening Courant*, 1718–1859.

Eur. Mag.: *The European Magazine*, 1782–1826.

Fac. Adv.: The Faculty of Advocates in Scotland, 1532–1943, ed F. J. Grant, 1944.

Fasti Angl.: John LeNeve and T. D. Hardy, *Fasti Ecclesiae Anglicanae*, 3 vols., 1854.

Fasti Scot.: Hew Scott, *Fasti Ecclesiae Scoticanae*, 7 vols., 1915–28.

Fortunes of a Family: Lady Macdonald of the Isles, *The Fortunes of a Family (Bosville of New Hall, Gunthwaite,and Thorpe) Through Nine Centuries*, 1927.

Gent. Mag.: *The Gentleman's Magazine*, ed. Edward Cave and others, 1731–1907.

Godet: Philippe Godet, *Mme. de Charrière et ses amis*, 2 vols., 1906.

Grand Tour I: *Boswell on the Grand Tour: Germany and Switzerland,1764*, ed. F. A. Pottle, 1953.

Grand Tour II: *Boswell on the Grand Tour: Italy, Corsica, and France, 1765–1766*, ed. Frank Brady and F. A. Pottle, 1955.

Grant: James Grant, *Cassell's Old and New Edinburgh*, 3 vols., 1882.

Hardenbroek: G. J. van Hardenbroek, *Gedenkschiften*, 1747–88, ed. F. J. L. Krämer, Amsterdam, 1901.

Hebrides: *Boswell's Journal of a Tour to the Hebrides with Samuel Johnson, LL.D., 1773*, ed. from the original MS. by F. A. Pottle and C. H. Bennett, new ed., 1961.

Hendy: J. G. Hendy, *History of the Early Postmarks of the British Isles*, 1905.

Hist. Ayr: James Paterson, *History of the County of Ayr*, 2 vols., 1847.

Holland: *Boswell in Holland, 1763–1764*, ed. F. A. Pottle, 1952.

Horn: D. B. Horn, *British Diplomatic Representatives, 1689–1789*, 1932.

JB: James Boswell.

JHC: *Journals of the House of Commons*.

JHL: *Journals of the House of Lords*.

Journ: JB's fully written journal. Transcribed conservatively from the MS.

Letters JB: *Letters of James Boswell*, ed. C. B. Tinker, 2 vols., 1924.

Letters DG: *The Letters of David Garrick*, ed. D. M. Little and G. M. Kahrl, 3 vols., 1963.

Letters DH: *Letters of David Hume*, ed. J. Y. T. Greig, 2 vols., 1932.

Letters SJ: *The Letters of Samuel Johnson, with Mrs. Thrale's Genuine Letters to Him*, ed. R. W. Chapman, 3 vols., 1952.

Lettres Zélide: *Lettres de Belle de Zuylen (Madame de Charrière) à Constant d'Hermenches, 1760–1775*, ed. Philippe Godet, 1909.

Life: *Boswell's Life of Johnson, Together with Boswell's Journal of a Tour to the Hebrides and Johnson's Diary of a Journey into North Wales*, ed. G. B. Hill, rev. L. F. Powell, 6 vols., 1934–50; vols. v and vi rev. 1964.

Lillywhite: Bryant Lillywhite, *London Coffee Houses*, 1963.

'List of Ages': a typed list made from a notebook of Boswell's, now missing, which once belonged to C. B. Tinker.

Lit. Anec.: John Nichols, *Literary Anecdotes of the Eighteenth Century*, 9 vols., 1812–15.

Lit. Car.: F. A. Pottle, *The Literary Career of James Boswell, Esq.*, 1929; reprinted 1965, 1967.

Lond. Chron.: *The London Chronicle*, 1757–1823.

Lond. Mag: *The London Magazine*, 1732–85.

Lond. Stage: *The London Stage, 1660-1800*, ed. William van Lennep and others, 5 parts in 11 vols., 1960–68.

Maxted: Ian Maxted, *The London Book Trades, 1775–1800*, 1977.

Mem: JB's memoranda. Transcribed conservatively from the MS.

Morison: W. M. Morison, *Decisions of the Court of Session*, 1801–1805.

Namier and Brooke: Sir Lewis Namier and John Brooke, *The History of Parliament, The House of Commons 1754–1790*, 3 vols., 1964.

NBG: *Nouvelle biographie générale*, ed. J.-C.-F. Hoefer, 46 vols., 1853–66.

NCBEL: *The New Cambridge Bibliography of English Literature*, ed. George Watson and I. R. Willison, 5 vols., 1971–77.

New Hume Letters: New Letters of David Hume, ed. Raymond Kiblansky and E. C. Mossner, 1954.

New Stat. Acct.: *The New Statistical Account of Scotland*, 15 vols., 1845.

NGHN: *Neue Genealogisch-Historische Nachrichten*, ed. Michael Ranfft, 27 vols., 1750–77.

NLS: National Library of Scotland.

MNBW: *Nieuw Nederlandsch Biografisch Woordenboek*, ed. P. C. Molhuysen and P. J. Blok, 10 vols., 1911–37.

Notes: JB's condensed journal. Transcribed conservatively from the MS.

NUC: *National Union Catalog, Pre-1956 Imprints*, 1968–.

Ominous Years: Boswell: The Ominous Years, 1774–1776, ed. Charles Ryskamp and F. A. Pottle, 1963.

Pol. Car: Frank Brady, *Boswell's Political Career*, 1965.

Polvliet: C. J. Polvliet, *Genealogie van let Geslacht van Tuyll van Serooskerken*, 1894.

Pub. Adv: Public Advertiser, 1752–94.

Reg. Let: JB's register of letters sent and received.

Renfrew: George Crawfurd, *A General Description of the Shire of Renfrew ... continued to the present period by George Robertson*, 1818.

Roy. Kal: Royal Kalendar, 1767–?1893.

S. of L.: Survey of London, 52 vol., 1900–.

Scotland and Scotsmen: John Ramsay, Esq. of Ochtertyre, *Scotland and Scotsmen in the Eighteenth Century*, ed. Alexander Allardyce, 2 vols., 1888.

Scots Charta Chest: Curiosities of a Scots Charta Chest, 1600–1800, with the Travels and Memoranda of Sir Alexander Dick, Baronet of Prestonfield, Midlothian, Written by Himself, ed. the Hon. Mrs. Atholl Forbes, 1897.

Scots Gazetteer: Ordnance Gazetteer of Scotland, ed. Francis H. Groome, 1901.

Scots Mag.: The Scots Magazine, 1739–1817.

Scots Peer.: Sir James Balfour Paul, *The Scots Peerage*, 9 vols., 1904–14.

Sea Officers: D. B. Smith, *Commissioned Sea Officers of the Royal Navy*, 1660–1815, 3 vols., 1954.

Search of a Wife: Boswell in Search of a Wife, 1766–1769, ed. Frank Brady and F. A. Pottle, 1956.

SHS: Scottish Historical Society.

SJ: Samuel Johnson.

SND:*The Scottish National Dictionary*, ed. William Grant and D. D. Murison, 10 vols., 1941–76.

SRO: Scottish Record Office .

SRS: Scottish Record Society.

Stat. Acct. Scot: Sir John Sinclair, *The Statistical Account of Scotland*, 21 vols., 1791–99.

Stodart: R. R. Stodart, 'Sir William Dick of Braid, Knight', *The Herald and Genealogist* (1874) viii. 257–269.

Strawhorn: John Strawhorn, *Ayrshire: The Story of a County*, 1975.

Talbot Papers: Boswell materials supplied by Lord Talbot de Malahide, 1960–64.

Thieme-Becker: Ulrich Thieme and Felix Becker, *Allgemeines Lexikon der Bildenden Künstler*, 37 vols., 1907–50.

Thrasher: Peter A. Thrasher, *Pasquale Paoli*, 1970.

Tommaseo: Niccolo Tommaseo, 'Lettere di Pasquale Paoli', *Archivio storico italiano*, 1846.

Walker: *The Correspondence of James Boswell and John Johnston of Grange*, ed. R. S. Walker, 1966.

Wheatley and Cunningham: H. B. Wheatley and Peter Cunningham, *London, Past and Present*, 3 vols., 1891.

Works SJ: *The Yale Edition of the Works of Samuel Johnson*, A. T. Hazen and J. H. Middendorf, General eds., 1958–.

Writers to the Signet: A History of the Society of Writers to her Majesty's Signet, with a List of the members of the Society from 1594 to 1890 and an Abstract of the Minutes, 1890.

Introduction

The correspondence in this edition begins with James Boswell's return from the Grand Tour in February 1766 and ends in December 1769, shortly after his marriage to Margaret Montgomerie. During this period, the Boswell who longed to be grew into the Boswell who had become: the law student became the practising advocate, the literary hopeful a best-selling author, the pursuer of heiresses the family man, the feudal dreamer, a landowner in his own right as Laird of Dalblair. By the end of 1769, he had achieved some measure of success in every area where he had wanted to succeed: even in politics, where success would finally elude him, his prospects seemed good. Potential and forward motion brighten these pages: the years 1766 to 1769 were the happiest of Boswell's life.

'General correspondence' is what remains after certain individual correspondences – those extensive enough to warrant separate publication – have been extracted. While some important correspondents are missing from this edition (e.g. Garrick, Burke, Johnson, Temple, Johnston of Grange, members of Boswell's immediate family), 'general' in no way implies 'minor': among the correspondents represented here are Giuseppe Baretti, Thomas Davies, Lord Lyttelton, Catherine Macaulay, Lord Marischal, James Oglethorpe, Pasquale Paoli, William Pitt the Elder, Sir John Pringle, Jean-Jacques Rousseau, and John Wilkes. Minor figures also are here in abundance: in fact, one of the most pleasing aspects of a 'general correspondence' is that in it, the noble and powerful are jostled by tradesmen, farmers, even felons, in a manner that recalls more life's own disorder than the artificial tidiness of biographical synthesis. A 'selected correspondence' is already like a biography: in it, the raw material of life has been sifted and everything irrelevant to the editor's own interests discarded.

'General correspondence' in a sense encompasses biography. If the biographer uses letters as raw material, the reader of biography returns to them as a traveller might revisit a place glimpsed from a tour bus. Like Boswell's journals, these letters fill in much of the detail that the biographer must discard, but their detail is of a different kind. Where the journals present only Boswell's point of view, the letters add the perspectives of others: they show us not only how Boswell felt about himself, but also how others felt about Boswell, not only how he presented himself to the world, but also how the world presented itself to him. Biography and journal introduce most characters with quick sketches. Godfrey Bosville, for example, is a minor character both historically and biographically: he is now remembered, if at all, chiefly for his son William's famous dinner-parties (see DNB), and while he was a good friend, he had little involvement in the business of Boswell's life. Boswell's journal introduces Bosville as a 'plain-looking man, but a judicious, knowing, worthy gentleman' (15 Feb. 1766), and Boswell's biographer F. A. Pottle mentions him only once as 'a shrewd, solid, hearty squire of engaging manners and considerable parts'.[1] These are attractive qualities, but having been informed of them, we can hardly claim an acquaintance with Godfrey Bosville. From his letters, though, we learn his opinions on politics, architecture and gardens, the last an essential index of character, as Jane Austen's Elizabeth Bennett understood. We take the precise measure of his affection for his family, and we almost hear his voice in his informal style; in short we get to know him well, and most readers will grow rather fond of him.

The utility of this pair of volumes to scholars researching eighteenth-century topics should be immediately apparent. Source materials to be found within them cover a vast array of subjects: high society, low society, landownership, politics, gender, crime, theatre, industry, agriculture, domestic life, religion, law, philosophy, Britain's relations with the Continent, with India, with North America, to mention but a few of the matters of interest to an historian. If literature is the primary interest, the scholar will find rare views of the world of publishing and bookselling, of literary hacks and the often humiliating search for patronage, and glimpse the literary tastes of the time. Readers will also find as rich a sampler of the many styles of letter-writing as practised by both sexes in this age as exists anywhere, ranging from the self-consciously literary to the barely literate. In short, the editors have every reason to hope that these first volumes of General Correspondence will be read with pleasure as well as for information.

The major issues in Boswell's life at this time – and the topics around which Pottle organizes his biography – are Corsica, the law, and marriage. Since an introduction must be organized in one way or another, we here adopt Pottle's scheme. However, this collection of letters resists this, or any other such treatment: and so the sections of this introduction will overlap, and it will frequently wander by the way. What follows is a guide for the reader who wishes to revisit some Boswellian places.

Corsica

For Boswell, the Corsican cause was not only a matter of justice and liberty; he saw in it a chance to forge a way to political prominence and literary fame. He had 'opened his campaign' almost as soon as he returned from Corsica to the mainland, getting his visit noticed in the Genoese gazettes, lobbying the British Consul there, and sending articles about Corsica and – not incidentally – himself to the *London Chronicle*.[2] This correspondence opens with a letter to William Pitt (later Lord Chatham) requesting an audience 'to acquaint you with some things which past between Signor De Paoli and me'; and the Corsican theme continues to the end of 1769, after Paoli, defeated and in exile, has taken up residence in London.

The immediate aim of Boswell's correspondence with Pitt was to bring about the repeal of a Proclamation of 1763 that forbade British subjects 'to give and furnish aid, assistance, countenance, or succour' to the Corsican rebels.[3] The

1. *Earlier Years*, p. 284.
2. *Earlier Years*, pp. 261–268.
3. *Annual Register*, 1763, p. 213.

failure of this effort (see From Chatham, 4 Feb. 1767) foreshadows the ultimate failure of the Corsican cause, despite the support of Enlightenment intellectuals and political theorists. But if Boswell could do little for Corsica, there is no overestimating the good that Corsica did for him: the benefits were not only literary, but also personal.

This correspondence shows Boswell carrying on research for his *Account of Corsica*. While his first major book does not achieve the depth and accuracy characteristic of the *Life of Johnson*, we trace through these letters the beginnings of the research skills he would perfect in his great work. Boswell solicited and received materials from six correspondents in Italy and Corsica: Consul John Dick, Richard Edwards, and the Rev. Andrew Burnaby, all from the British consulate in Leghorn; Count Antonio Rivarola, a Corsican serving as Sardinian consul in Leghorn and John Symonds, historian and writer on agriculture (Symonds and Burnaby, like JB, had recently visited the island and recorded their observations). These correspondents supplied information and forwarded materials supplied by others. The booksellers Edward Dilly and Thomas Davies also laboured on Boswell's behalf, procuring for him printed materials on Corsica that could be had in London. Despite imperfections in Boswell's secondary research, his rich source materials do justify the boastful claim he made in his preface: 'I am thus enabled to lay before the world such An Account of Corsica, as I flatter myself will give some satisfaction; for, in comparison of the very little that has been hitherto known concerning that island, this book may be said to contain a great deal' (p. xii). The importance of Boswell's *Account* lies, then, in his first-hand observations of Paoli and the Corsican republic at its height.

The Thomas Davies who sent materials on Corsica is the one who introduced Boswell to Samuel Johnson. He declined to publish *Corsica* (a business decision he must later have regretted), predicting that it would be 'dry and unentertaining' (From Davies, 15 Nov. 1766). *Corsica* was published by Edward and Charles Dilly, whose firm would later publish the *Journal of a Tour to the Hebrides* and the *Life of Johnson*. Perhaps these booksellers – liberal and non-conformist – were first attracted by the subject-matter, for they were enthusiastic admirers of John Wilkes, Catherine Macaulay, the North American Patriots, and Liberty. But they soon became great friends with the Tory Boswell, who, from 1769, frequently stayed with them in London. A more interesting pair than the brothers Dilly one rarely meets. One astonished visitor to their lodgings in the Poultry recalled Edward as 'one of the greatest talkers I ever met with, tongue, hands, and head all moving at a time with so much rapidity that I wonder how his lungs sustain it'; Charles, on the other hand, was 'a modest, genteel-behaved man, and I suppose is now so much inured to hear his brother talk that he scarce thinks of speaking himself'.[4] John Nichols claimed that Edward was 'so fond of conversation, that he almost literally *talked himself to* death';[5] Boswell found Charles 'a good tall smartish civil bowing young man, quite of the city form' (Journ. 23 Mar. 1768).

Edward Dilly carried on most of the correspondence for the firm; his breathless epistolary style probably gives a good impression of what it must have been like to

4. S. H. Bingham, 'Publishing in the Eighteenth Century with Special Reference to the Firm of Edward and Charles Dilly', unpub. diss. Yale, 1937, p. 6.
5. *Lit. Anec.* iii. 191.

hear him talk. On Tuesday 28 July 1768 he wrote agreeing 'To Pay Mr. Boswell One Hundred Guineas for the Copyright of his Account of Corsica' and pressed for a publication date around the end of November (the beginning of the Parliamentary season). Boswell could not possibly have received this letter before Friday the 31st, but on Saturday 1 August Dilly, already impatient, wrote again, 'I sent you a Letter a few Days ago. intimating my agreement to your Proposal for the Purchase of the Copy right of your History of Corsica. It is necessary on your Part to send me something Counter to that, of your acceptance of the same.' Dilly's technique, and that of his brother who carried on the business after Edward's death, was to push his authors: from 28 July to the following February, when *Corsica* was published, Dilly wrote at least twelve letters, all urging speed. 'I acknowledge,' he wrote, 'that I am a Friend to Punctuality and dispatch, and have Often Wish'd that I had more of both' (From Dilly, 24 Sept. 1767). Dilly also encouraged Boswell – though he needed no encouragement – to promote his book in the newspapers, but he declined to call the practice puffing: 'I own I am no friend to what is called *Puffing* in the common acceptation of the Word; but surely Sir when the Truth is spoken of anything that is deserving of Praise, it cannot be call'd by that Name. Merit deserves applause and Justice requires it to be given' (ibid.).

The Dillys' significance in Boswell's life goes far beyond their involvement with his Corsica project. The same is true of John Dick, already mentioned as a supplier of materials for the book. Boswell thought Dick a 'Genteel, good man' (Notes, 13 Aug. 1765); his sober, cautiously phrased letters betray his diplomatic habit of mind. Their friendship originated in their common interest in Corsica, and much of their correspondence concerns Corsican affairs; but soon Boswell was embarked on the more personal project – closely tracked in these letters – of securing for Dick the dormant baronetcy of Braid. Perhaps Boswell himself had suggested, either in Italy in 1765 or in a lost letter of 27 Aug. 1766, the possibility that the baronetcy could be revived. However the idea came up, Dick was enthusiastic about the claim, though perhaps a little doubtful of its validity: 'Circumstanced as I am, without Children, the succeeding in making out my right to this Title, is of very little importance' (From Dick, 6 Oct. 1766). If the claim is a fiction, he seems to be saying, it is harmless enough, since it affects only one generation. If Dick had doubts, Boswell did not share them; neither did Sir Alexander Dick, Boswell's old friend and John Dick's distant cousin, whom he enlisted in the cause. Together they were acting out the plot, well known in story, in which, as Sir Alexander put it, 'The male family Head' is 'recoverd' (From Sir A. Dick, 15 Aug. 1767). The romance of it was irresistible.

Sir Alexander was to supply genealogical materials from his library, where he kept a hogshead stuffed with family papers; Boswell would supply legal expertise, specifying the kind of evidence he needed and working though the intricacies of 'serving' an heir; John Dick himself would leave Leghorn in March 1767 to spend the next seventeen months in England and Scotland working to substantiate his claim. They never did find positive evidence that Sir William Dick, from whom both John and Sir Alexander were descended, was actually a baronet – rather, the evidence suggests a knighthood. And if he had been a baronet, John Dick probably could not have inherited the title, since he was descended from Sir William's fifth son. Charles Dick of Frackafield, who was descended from Sir William's first son, contested John Dick's claim and lost.[6] But the exertions of Boswell, Sir Alexander and John Dick on behalf of the sacred principle of Family were conspicuously successful, and as he reported to Sir Alexander, Boswell himself presented the news to the Dicks with characteristic dramatic flair:

> I was a great man, for I came laden with valuable things. I produced the Retour which I read in English with an audible voice. I then displayed the magnificent Burgess Ticket which was much admired, and I give you my word that my heart beat with real gladness as I read it also aloud. I next displayed the portrait of the venerable Sir William, and then my worthy Baronet's letter made the *Bonne Bouche*. You may figure me quite at home, and in high spirits investing your Cousins with their titles! 'Sir John Dick my service to you, Lady Dick I have the honour to drink your Ladyships good health.' So it went and I know not when I was happier (Boswell to Sir A. Dick, 18 April 1768).

Later Boswell had the brass plate on the new baronet's door changed to read *Sir John Dick* (To Sir A. Dick, 28 Apr. 1768). He remained friends with Dick until the end of his life.

Boswell went to Ireland in May-June 1769 to court Mary Ann Boyd, a sixteen-year-old heiress. The trip as originally conceived was doomed from the start: Mary Ann, he soon decided, was too childish to suit him, and in any case he had discovered on the journey over that he was in love with his first cousin and travelling companion, Margaret Montgomerie. Instead of wooing, he spent the trip promoting the cause of the Corsicans, whose situation was now desperate. Irish newspapers of the time show that Boswell was already well known as the leading British apologist for the Corsican rebellion;[7] he now found that he was a celebrity:

> The Irish are zealous friends to Corsica, and on that account I found myself treated with a distinction that has been very flattering to the blood of Auchinleck. Though my book has told allmost every thing that I knew, there is still a great curiosity to hear many little particulars, which different minds are eager to ask. And you know how communicative I am. So that you may imagine me in all companies, and relish by reflection the pleasure I enjoyed. (To Sir A. Dick, 29 May 1769)

Boswell replicated in Ireland the campaign he had conducted on behalf of the Corsicans in Britain. In June and July an advertisement headed 'Corsican Contribution' appeared repeatedly in the *Freeman's Journal* and the *Dublin Journal* over Boswell's name; it was similar to advertisements he had placed in English and Scottish papers, though tailored to an Irish audience: 'Having had the pleasure to find that a generous Zeal for the Corsicans prevails in Ireland, I have been encouraged to hope that a contribution may be raised here in Support of the Cause of Liberty, in which this Country has on so many Occasions so gloriously distinguished herself.' To enhance the appearance of local support, he wrote as 'A Free Hibernian' in the *Freeman's Journal* for 17–20 June, urging his 'Countrymen to contribute towards a scheme, which will be attended with so many good Consequences'. And in early June, the Dublin newspapers announced the found-

---

6. Stodart.

7. See Richard C. Cole, 'James Boswell and the Irish Press, 1767-1795', *Bulletin of the New York Public Library* (1969) lxxiii. 581–88.

ing of a Corsican Club 'to support the Cause of Liberty and Paoli'[8] Boswell began the campaign and, on his return to Scotland, left enthusiasts behind him to carry it on; but the news of the fall of Corsica arrived before it could gather momentum (From Andrew Caldwell, 25 Aug. 1769).

Even after the cause was lost, Boswell could not resist boasting about his triumph in Ireland. He wrote a story for the *Public Advertiser* stating that he had met Viscount Townshend, Lord Lieutenant of Ireland, and James Fitzgerald, Duke of Leinster, and describing his early success in raising money (7 July). He sent the same piece to George Faulkner's *Dublin Journal*, but the Irish newspapers would mention neither the Lord Lieutenant nor the Duke of Leinster without permission; though Boswell said he had 'not met a firmer or keener Corsican', the Lord Lieutenant had the story killed.[9] As late as 1791, when he published his memoirs in the *European Magazine*, Boswell regarded his Irish tour as a spectacular success; the Boyds, on the other hand, were infuriated by his neglect.[10]

The Law

Many of the letters in this volume have to do with Boswell's law practice. He often described himself as having been 'pressed' into the law, but he seems to have gone about his work with diligence , sometimes with enthusiasm, and he soon recognized that the law might lead him to his most treasured goal, a seat in the House of Commons. His friend George Dempster, who had followed that route, stated the matter plainly:

> Were you never so much bent upon getting into Parliament you should only apply so much the harder to the practice and Study of Law. It is the best school for acquiring eloquence, and the best Education for a Legislator is that of a Lawyer ... Ply the Bar as a qualification for Parliament, and then keep that Object as closely in view as You like, It will make your Study on a more enlarged plan, and will lead you to know not only what is the Law in every Question, but why it is so. (From Dempster, 13 Apr. 1769).

There was no shortage of friends to remind Boswell that the law could be a means of advancement; Lord Marischal recommended, rather, that he look at it as a means of doing good: 'Now I am persuaded that an advocat who should never accept the management of a cause but where equity was clear, would not only gain great honor but also advantage when his reputation on that head was once established, tho in the beginning he might have less practice than others' (From Marischal, 2 Oct. 1766). Boswell replied, 'It is said that a Lawyer can never plead contrary to his conscience, because a Lawyer has no title to judge, so cannot say whether a cause be right or wrong' and dismissed the matter with a witticism about his fading conscience being like a woman's fading beauty (To Marischal, 12 Mar. 1767). But Lord Marischal had touched an issue that troubled Boswell deeply. He brought it up to Johnson in 1768:

> I had longed much to see him as my great Preceptour to state to him some

---

8. Advertisements began to appear in the *Freeman's Journal, Dublin Journal,* and *Dublin Mercury* on 10 June; see From Andrew Caldwell, 25 Aug. 1769.
9. From Caldwell, 25 Aug. 1769; To Sir A. Dick, 28 May 1769.
10. 'Memoirs of James Boswell, Esq.', *European Mag.* (1791) xix. 404; reprinted in *Lit. Car.* p. xxxvii. For the Boyds' anger, see To James Boyd, 20 June 1769 and *Earlier Years,* p. 408.

difficulties as a moralist with regard to the Profession of the law, as it appeared to me that in some respects it hurt the principles of honesty and I asked him if it did not. 'Why no Sir' said he, 'if you act properly. You are not to deceive your clients with false representations of your opinion. You are not to tell lies to a Judge.' 'But' said I 'what do you think of pleading a cause which you know to be bad.' 'Sir you dont know it to be bad, till the Judge determines it. ... An argument which does not convince you yourself may convince the Judge before whom you plead it; and if it does convince him, why then Sir you are wrong and he is right.' ... At once he satisfied me as to a thing which had often and often perplexed me.[11]

Boswell was rarely selective about his causes; he followed at least so far the dictum that 'a Lawyer has no title to judge'. But the causes most likely to figure in the surviving correspondence are those he took on for friends or those he cared about deeply. We know little, for example, about most of the causes listed in his 'Consultation Book,' presumably because he did not care enough to keep any record of them. But he carefully preserved a number of papers relating to John Reid (his first criminal client, accused of stealing sheep), including several of the letters in this edition: From Reid, 13 Nov. 1766, From John Johnstoun, 20 Nov. 1766, and From John Rowand, 24 Nov. 1766.[12] Boswell does not seem to have found the cause of Sir Alexander Dick v. the Earl of Abercorn intrinsically interesting; it comes into this edition because Boswell preserved Sir Alexander's correspondence as that of a personal friend. He kept no legal papers concerning that cause, a boundary dispute that arose because the shoreline of Duddingston Loch, which formed the boundary between Dick's and Abercorn's estates, had shifted as the water level subsided (From Sir A. Dick, 10 Apr. 1767 and n. 7). Similarly, Lord Marischal v. the York Buildings Company, in which Boswell represented the old ex-Jacobite in a long-running dispute over the repurchase of his forfeited estates, is only glanced at in the correspondence (From Marischal, 14 Apr. 1767); Boswell does not seem to have thought the papers worth keeping.

Boswell may not have been selective about his causes (though Pottle points out that he was reluctant to serve as prosecutor in criminal cases[13]); he may indeed have been willing to take on causes that he suspected were wrong. But the paper record itself shows us which causes he passionately believed to be right. Certainly the trials of the rioters at Garlieston, Wigtownshire, and Stewarton, Ayrshire, fall into this category: in these towns, as in much of Scotland, people were starving because those who traded in meal found it more profitable to export it than to sell it locally. Boswell defended these rioters, who had seized the grain and forced its sale at a just price.[14] He had a continuing interest in the plight of those whom economic changes in Scotland had displaced, economically or socially. His

---

11. Journ. 26 Mar. 1768. The entry was adapted for *Life* ii. 47. When the subject came up again in 1773, Johnson offered the same argument (*Life* v. 27) .

12. For accounts of Reid's encounters with Scottish law, see *Earlier Years*, pp. 298, 308-09, and Frank Brady, *James Boswell: The* Later Years, 1769–1795, 1984, pp . 96–104 .

13. *Earlier Years*, pp. 309–10.

14. The Stewarton trials are treated in this edition: see From Alexander Montgomerie-Cuninghame, 11 May 1767, From William Brown, 18 May 1767, From James Maitland, 18 May 1767, To William Brown, 18–22 May 1767. For both trials, see *Earlier Years*, pp. 328, 538-39. Many legal papers relating to the trials are at Yale, Lg 8 and Lg 9.

interest, far from radical, was reactionary: Boswell longed to see the restoration of relationships that had once existed between the gentry on the one hand and townspeople and tenants on the other. He believed those relationships were being destroyed by the greed of the merchant class, a group which had no place in the 'feudal' system for which he felt such romantic enthusiasm. His 'feudal' sentiments are even more evident in his attempt to prevent the eviction of Ranald and Alexander Macdonnell from the estate on which they were tenants. The estate had once belonged to a Highland Chief, attainted after the '45, and was now in the hands of an avaricious English clergyman, who wished to use the land for sheep-rearing. If Boswell deplored 'an attempt to turn the ancient possessors of these estates out of their possessions without any reason', he deplored equally the disruption of the ancient hierarchy of the Chief and his dependents.[15] In April 1772, Boswell 'argued warmly for the old feudal system' with Johnson and Sir Alexander Macdonald (well remembered from the *Journal of a Tour to the Hebrides* as a Hebridean Chief who disappointed Boswell and Johnson with his modernity);[16] in the Macdonnell cause he was making the same argument in a different forum.

Another cause about which Boswell felt strongly enough to preserve a record was Mackenzie v. Mackenzie, in which he defended an heir against his father's attempt to provide for children from a subsequent marriage by setting aside the entail that prescribed the order of inheritance.[17] In the printed plea Boswell argued,

> An entail is materially useful in a political view because it is the means of preserving ancient families, which are like beams in the constitution, are the firmest security against tyrannical incroachments, and, in this state, must ever hold the balance between the sovereign and the people. Ancient families too contribute to the happiness of society, founded on just subordination. (*Information*, p. 5)

That 'subordination' is necessary to 'the happiness of society' will be familiar to readers of Boswell as a favourite notion – one that he discussed extensively with Johnson. Equally familiar will be Boswell's statement that the Mackenzie entail 'is in perfect consonance with the ideas of the ancient feudal system, of which, while the form is decayed through the vicissitudes of time, the spirit remains as a noble incentive to manly and generous conduct' (*Information*, p. 7). But this cause did not merely engage Boswell's abstract principles; it echoed his own situation, for, like his young client, Boswell would one day inherit an estate, and although the inheritance was protected by an entail, his father had often threatened to disinherit him.[18] In defending the Mackenzie inheritance, he was defending his own as well.

The great Douglas Cause was also about inheritance: the pursuers (plaintiffs) charged that Archibald Douglas, heir to one of the largest fortunes in Scotland, was not the child of the woman who claimed him as her son, but instead the child

---

15. Quotations are from the *Petition* of Ranald and Alexander Macdonnell, 30 June 1770—Houghton Library, Harvard University. The cause is discussed in From Alexander Macdonnell, 26 Aug. 1766 and From Anne Mackintosh, 12 May 1767.
16. *Life* ii. 177. For Boswell and Johnson's disappointment with Macdonald in Skye, see *Life* v. 147–56.
17. The cause is discussed in From John Tait, 7 Apr. 1767 and 31 Aug. 1768. Yale has Boswell's copy of the printed *Information for Hector Mackenzie*, 1 July 1767 – Lg 10.
18. *Earlier Years*, pp. 80–81.

of a French peasant and thus not entitled to inherit. Boswell was not employed by either side, but was a violent Douglas partisan, and published three short books (*Dorando*, *Essence of the Douglas Cause*, and *Letters of the Right Honourable Lady Jane Douglas*), as well as a ballad in broadside and numerous newspaper pieces.[19]

The Cause is a pervasive topic in these letters, and offers interesting sidelights: Boswell's outrage when John Wilkie, publisher of the *Essence*, tacked another tract onto the end of the book (Boswell had an author's concern for the integrity of his text, even when it was only a pamphlet); the agitation of Edward Dilly (who saw there was money to be made from the cause) to publish the speeches of the Lords of Session; or Boswell's public controversy with Margaret Primrose over the accuracy of her testimony at the trial.[20]

Love and Marriage

The title of this section is appropriate only if one defines 'love' rather broadly, for here we take in matters as diverse as certain of Boswell's nocturnal romps, which by 1767 produced effects that should have been predictable; Girolama Piccolomini, his Siena conquest; Mrs Dodds, mother to his first daughter Sally; and the heiresses he sampled before marrying his first cousin, Margaret Montgomerie.

Those romps appear in this edition mainly by implication: the activities themselves are mentioned less often than their results. In summer 1767, spring 1768, and spring 1769 references to Boswell's bouts of gonorrhoea are frequent. In general Boswell tells his correspondents of his illness in vague terms, and receives from them equally vague condolences: 'I am so unlucky as to be confined to the house by indisposition' (To Lord Hardwicke, 18 Apr. 1768); 'am very sorry to hear of your Indisposition' (From Edward Dilly, 10 Aug. 1767). With Sir Alexander Dick he is more frank. He writes from London, indulging in the classical banter that he and Sir Alexander delighted in:

> Notwithstanding all my wise resolutions, I must confess that since I last came to London, I have been if possible more extravagantly fond of the Ladies than ever. Vixi puellis nuper idoneus – Et militavi non sine gloria [21] But the consequence has been fatal. Infandum Regina jubes renovare dolorem.[22] (18 Apr. 1768).

Boswell also confided in Sir John Pringle, the eminent physician whom he had long been in the habit of consulting for advice on every matter. He thought of Pringle as kind and steady, if somewhat 'sour' in his manner (Journ. 15 Sept. 1769), and wrote of him, 'As Sir John has witnessed many of my weaknesses and follies, and been allways like a Parent to me, I cannot help standing much in awe of him' (Journ. 2 Sept. 1769). Pringle was all the more like a parent in that he could be counted on to echo Lord Auchinleck's opinion on every issue, though

19. *Lit. Car.* pp. 27–50, 236–65.
20. From Alexander Maconochie, 25 Dec. 1767; From Dilly, 1, 10, 15 Aug., 10 Sept. 1767; From Margaret Primrose, between 22 June and 18 July, c. 18 July; To Primrose, c. 5–10 Aug.; From Primrose, 19 Aug.
21. 'Till recently I lived fit for Love's battles and served not without renown' (Horace, *Odes* III. xxvi. 1–2 – Loeb ed., trans. C. E. Bennett).
22. 'O Queen, you bid me renew an unspeakable sorrow' (Virgil, *Aeneid* ii. 3).

typically in kinder and more sympathetic tones. Pringle favoured marriage as a means of attaining both happiness and virtue:

> I would advise you to look out for a wife, and to make such a match as [Lord Auchinleck] and the whole world shall approve of ... I am persuaded that you would have a great deal of satisfaction in following that plan; for your temper is good, you would have joy in children; and I believe I may add that You have had too much experience of the vague and vitious pleasures, not to relish the confined and virtuous ones, as soon as you will make the comparison. (From Pringle, 10 Feb. 1767)

Having made the suggestion, Pringle could hardly withhold advice about particular prospects, even though in such matters 'a man, after asking the opinion of twenty friends, will either do or omit doing just as if he had no friends at all' (From Pringle, 4 Dec. 1767). Catherine Blair, an heiress from a neighbouring estate, would be a fine match, he says, but adds with admirable prescience, 'I could lay a bett that in this very affair you will meet with a disappointment' (ibid.). On the subject of Zélide he wavers: she has 'too much vivacity', is too much the *bel esprit*; her being a foreigner is a problem; but finally Boswell's going to Utrecht to explore the possibility seems a good plan.[23]

Pringle seems to have known nothing about Girolama Piccolomini – at least, he understood the reference to 'sweet Siena' in *Corsica* in only a general way (From Pringle, 20 Feb. 1768) – but Boswell confessed to him fully about his whoring, his gonorrhoea, and Mrs. Dodds's pregnancy. Pringle intimated that, if the illness was the physical result of his visit to a prostitute, it seemed the moral result of his corrupting one of the weaker sex. He counselled repentance: 'If You have not repented, and with great compunction too, be assured that your misfortunes are not at an end, and that Providence, for your amendment will not cease to chastise You till you cry *peccavi*' (From Pringle, 4 Dec. 1767). Unfortunately, Boswell was far better at repenting than he was at reforming. As Pringle foresaw, he was bad at taking advice as well.

Lord Auchinleck and Pringle favoured Catherine Blair, but Boswell's Dutch friends and relations busied themselves with promoting a marriage with Zélide. Her father was receptive, though there was the matter of another suitor, the Marquis de Bellegarde, to be settled first; Robert Brown, the Scottish minister in Utrecht, passed word when the Marquis was out of the picture and intimated that Zélide was interested; the Baroness von Spaen suggested that Boswell bring Lord Auchinleck to Utrecht to look at her for himself.[24] Zélide kept an amused distance from the issue, as she wrote in reply to what must have been one of Boswell's flightier letters:

> Celui que vous proposez depuis si longtems sur notre sort si nous etions mariés est la preuve de ce gout: je vous le laisse à mediter mon cher Boswell, outre que je ne suis pas assez habile pour decider je trouve peu de plaisir à discuter une question aussi oiseuse. Je ne connois pas votre Ecosse ... j'en ai vu sortir des maris asses despotiques et d'humbles bonnes femmes qui rougissoient et regardoient leurs epoux avant que d'ouvrir la bouche.

23. To W. J. Temple, 4 Mar. 1767; From Pringle, 20 Feb. 1768; To Zélide, 26 Feb. 1768; Journ. 24 Mar. 1768.
24. From M. de Zuylen, 30 Jan. 1766; From Robert Brown, 27 Jan., 22 Oct. 1767; From Baroness von Spaen, 12 July 1766.

Her implication, of course, is that she could not be one of those 'humbles bonnes femmes'; she would probably agree with Lord Auchinleck and Sir John Pringle that she was too much the *bel esprit*. In the end, the courtship foundered on the rocky shores of *Corsica*, which she admired tremendously and had begun to translate. She wanted to make some alterations and abridgements; he refused to allow that, whereupon she decided that she would neither translate his book nor marry its author. He decided she was a 'termagant' – or would be one when she was forty.[25] Both Boswell and Zélide no doubt recognized in the ruction over *Corsica* a prefigurement of the sexual politics that would accompany a marriage between them. She did not have it in her to follow his text to the syllable, as a humble, simple wife would do. Yet, though that was not precisely what he wanted in a wife, it was what he had decided to demand of her – perhaps, as Pottle hints, by way of sabotaging the match, which had begun to look like a real possibility. And so, like *Corsica*, he remained for her 'un livre interressant que j'aime, mais que je ne traduis plus'.[26]

Boswell and George Dempster, another bachelor, confided their matrimonial perplexities to each other. Boswell's letters to Dempster are some of the liveliest in this edition; their style recalls that of the London Journal of 1762-63. In February 1769, while Boswell was rhapsodizing about his Irish heiress Mary Ann Boyd, he undertook (with or without permission is not clear) to woo on Dempster's behalf one 'B' – possibly Margaret Crauford, a mining heiress. Whether attracted by B herself or by the romantic plot-device of the go-between falling for the lady he means to win for another, he fancied himself in love:

> Dempster you dog why did you allow me to aproach the mines? I went into the basket, thinking to amuse myself by going down a little way and looking at the Spars etc. But before I had time to recollect myself away went the Pullies, and I found myself two hundred fathoms below ground, where a candle would not burn and where I could hardly breathe. (To Dempster, 23 Feb. 1769)

It was an agony, he declares, to plead for Dempster, yet he soldiered on: he told B he had received a letter from a gentleman who loved her; how (he almost asked outright) should this man approach her? Would she be offended by a go-between? (She would – and so revealed the magnitude of the error Dempster had made the year before in sending a friend to state his case.) 'Come over,' Boswell cries, 'or write to her, or give her up. And let me set myself at rest, one way or other. If she is for you, God bless you both. If not, I will ask her, and then we shall be *Companions*' (To Dempster, 24 Feb. 1769). She finally refused Dempster, who did not marry until 1774; Boswell seems not to have pursued her further.

During and after his Irish jaunt, Boswell wrote to Dempster in a more serious vein, telling him that he was in love with Margaret Montgomerie, and, in fact, always had been. The only other correspondent to whom he wrote so frankly was Temple. Mary Ann Boyd was an angel, a charming child with £500 a year. Margaret was 'a heathen goddess painted alfresco on the cieling of a palace at Rome'.[27] He begged for advice: should he marry for love, or for money? Dempster wisely declined to

---

25. Zélide to Baron Constant d'Hermenches, 2 June 1768 (Isabelle de Charrière, *Oeuvres complètes*, ed. Jean-Daniel Candaux *et al.*, 1979--84 ii. 87); To Temple, 14 May 1768.

26. Ibid. For Pottle's summing up of the courtship, see *Earlier Years*, pp. 383--87.

27. To Dempster, 4 May ('la belle Irlandoise l'ange l'enfant charmant'), 21 June 1769 (£500, 'heathen goddess').

answer, but once Boswell had made up his mind for Margaret, said 'that his only surprise was how I could do so rational a thing' (Journ. 2 Aug. 1769).

Two Last Correspondents

Boswell's other important or interesting correspondents include Giuseppe Baretti, the irascible Italian scholar and friend of Johnson; Basil Cochrane, Boswell's kinsman and old friend; Alexandre Deleyre, Rousseau's disciple; the Rev. Pierre Loumeau Dupont, a Huguenot pastor in Edinburgh; Francis Gentleman, an unctuous hack writer who hoped to enlist Boswell as a patron; William Julius Mickle, aspiring poet, and later, distinguished translator, who sought Boswell's help in getting his tragedy performed;[28] Lord Mountstuart, whom Boswell alternately flattered and fought with; Heer van Sommelsdyck, a noble relation in Holland; and the Rev. Christopher Wyvill, once a schoolfellow and later a Parliamentary reformer. Of these and many of the two hundred or more correspondents represented here it is perhaps enough to say that they will reward the browser's curiosity. But two correspondents deserve special mention: Sir Alexander Dick and Lord Marischal.

Dick was sixty-two years old at the beginning of the period covered here. A student of Boerhaave, he had already enjoyed a distinguished career in medicine, which he continued as a gentlemanly avocation after inheriting his baronetcy in 1746. The pattern of Boswell's friendship with him was settled long before he wrote from Rome on 22 May 1765:

> You write to me in a stile that strongly revives the agreable ideas with which you inspired me in my earliest days. I cannot think of Sir Alexander Dick without thinking of elegant learning and arts, of the cordial freindship between our familys, and of that easy cheerfullness which makes life a blessing.

When in Edinburgh, Boswell used to walk the mile from James's Court in the Old Town to Dick's seat at Prestonfield each Saturday, and he often noted how happy he was there. After one such visit he wrote, 'I dont believe there ever existed a man more continually amiable than Sir Alexander' (Journ. 16 Jan. 1768). Dick's letters confirm that he had a great talent for happiness, and particularly for adopting the happiness of others as his own.

Unlike Sir John Pringle, whose role was always that of mentor and adviser, Dick had by 1766 already put Boswell on the footing of an equal, and in matters of law at least, that of a superior: just a week after Boswell put on the gown of an advocate Dick became one of his first clients and addressed him as 'Counsellor'.[29] He could be counted on to give delighted approval to all of Boswell's activities. On the publication of *Corsica*, which Pringle disapproved of: 'the Bishop and Mr. Spence . . . heartily wishd you would proceed to favor the world, them, and all your freinds, with your account of Corsica and your history of the Hero, which I told them you propos'd soon to present to the Publick'.[30] On the prospect of Boswell's

---

28. For a detailed account of Mickle's quarrel with Garrick, see Frank Brady, 'Mickle, Boswell, Garrick, and *The Siege of Marseilles*', *Transactions of the Connecticut Academy of Arts and* Sciences (1987) xlvi. 235–97.

29. The cause was Sir Alexander Dick *v.* the Earl of Abercorn, mentioned above. See From Dick, 22 Aug. 1766.

30. From Dick, 22 Aug. 1766. For Pringle's opinions on *Corsica*, see From Pringle, 10 Feb., 4 Dec. 1767.

publishing an offhand though clear enough reference to Girolama Piccolomini, his lover in Siena: 'You must know I fancyd you (when you had got your Sienna Innamorata into the Journal) as young Hercules . . . balancing betwixt the soft endearments of Sienna and the Rude virtuous paths to paoli at Corsica'.[31] When Boswell told him of his gonorrhoea, he did not scold; when Boswell decided to marry Margaret Montgomerie, he seems to have given his blessing.[32] In the matter of John Dick's baronetcy, he was more than approving: he expended as much energy in the cause as Boswell himself. Boswell's way of talking about Dick's projects—for example, the Duddingston Loch lawsuit and the Forth-Clyde Canal—sounds very much like the way Dick talked about Boswell's.

Under the 'elegant learning' and classical polish of their letters, we perceive in this relationship a significant element of play: Jamie and Sir Alexander, young rascals, conspiring in each other's mischief, egging each other on, and together cheering the success of their exploits. Boswell liked to call his friend *Corycius senex*, the 'old man of Corycus' whom Virgil held up as the model of a contented rustic farmer; but he had in him much of the child as well—an excellent match, in fact, for the child in Boswell.

George Keith, 10th and last Earl Marischal of Scotland, had accompanied Boswell from Utrecht to Germany in 1764 and had shown him the German courts. Attainted and later pardoned for his participation in the Jacobite uprising of 1715, Lord Marischal had spent much of his life in Germany, France, and Spain. He had long been a close friend of Frederick the Great, serving under him as governor of Neuchâtel and spending the last years of his long life in a small house adjacent to Sans Souci. Cosmopolitan, generous, broad-minded, fanciful, and blessed with a 'composed and mild' temper (Journ. 17 Nov. 1764), he was such a man as Boswell could wish to be. The genial and tolerant tone of his letters, and the jocularity of Boswell's letters to him (almost all earlier than the period covered here), call to mind the correspondence with Sir Alexander Dick. But there is a major difference: Boswell rarely asked Dick for advice, and Dick rarely volunteered it. But almost from the moment when Boswell began his travels with Lord Marischal, he solicited and received his advice on matters of all kinds.[33] The subjects dealt with in the Marischal correspondence include Corsica, finance, the Douglas Cause, David Boswell, Rousseau, illegitimate children, and marriage. The last two subjects are worth a closer look, for here Marischal's advice was characteristically pointed.

When Mrs. Dodds became pregnant, Boswell proposed to name the child, if a boy, George Keith, and asked what country he should live in. The compliment to Marischal was seriously intended, the question about a country less so, and Marischal's reply ('let him be a Spaniard') was suitably light (From Marischal, 1

---

31. From Dick, c. 27 Aug. 1767. Compare From Pringle, 20 Feb. 1768: 'The other indelicacy is that You are pleased to insinuate that You had been too much the man of gallantry at Siena, which had relaxed you so much'.

32. Boswell's letter telling Dick of his gonorrhoea is quoted above. Dick's opinion of Margaret Montgomerie is inferred from To Dick, 29 May, 12 Sept. 1769. Dick did oppose one of Boswell's matrimonial schemes, his pursuit of Mary Ann Boyd. He seems to have feared that Boswell might move to Ireland (From Dick, 1 Oct. 1768).

33. See Journ. 25 Aug. 1764 (on melancholy); 6 Sept. 1764 (on the choice of occupation); 23 Sept. 1764 (on travel). See also the advice quoted above on the practice of law.

Sept. 1767). Marischal's next letter (12 Sept.) is weightier than it at first seems. His opening, 'Bonny wark, Colonel, getting the lassys wi' bairns', looks congratulatory, but his next words, 'and worse to your sel', take back the congratulations, reminding Boswell that he will have to face some practical consequences. He continues, 'what sais Mes. John?'—what does the minister say?—a glance at the morality of the situation; and concludes resignedly, 'whats done is done.' Marischal goes on to say that 'George Keith' should become a nabob in India—far more practical advice than urging him to become a Spaniard, though again he disguises it as a joke: 'He slays a Nabob, gets upon his Elephant, and becomes himself Nabob; amen.'

On the subject of marriage, Lord Marischal was a reluctant adviser:

> I wish you a good and happy marriage, you do me too much honor to seem to wish my advice, every one must choose for himself after well examining his own and the Lady temper, neither of which is easy to do; and in all cases much indulgence must be reciprocally given to any little humors may arise in life (From Marischal, 26 Jan. 1768).

Boswell persevered, and at length obtained Marischal's opinion of most of his prospects. On Zélide: 'take a scots lass, I insist on it that there is less risk with one of our Country than of any other' (29 May 1768); 'a Lady *bel esprit* must govern as an absolute monarch, and the husband must blindly obey' (12 Sept. 1768). On Mary Ann Boyd: 'I have no objection to your union with the Irish Lady, and wish you good luck; the Irish are either (commonly speaking) exceeding good or exceeding bad, I do not like luke warm folks' (18 Apr. 1769). And on Margaret Montgomerie: 'consult your father a wise and good man (so he be not in love with your mistress for in that case I would not take his word) but as I see you are, I can not entirely count on all the fine things you say of the Lady. . . . I can not take a lover's word for the character of his mistress' (26 Aug. 1769).

Perhaps Boswell asked Lord Marischal's advice—as he did Pringle's—*because* he knew it would echo that of his father. Perhaps, too, he neglected to seek Sir Alexander Dick's advice because he knew it would not. By now it is almost a cliché that he sought out father figures among his older friends, but the father figures he was drawn to did not actualize the common childhood fantasy of a permissive parent, though he could easily have chosen men who would do so; instead they replicated Lord Auchinleck in the most essential ways, even if their edges were smoother and their corners softer than his. Their function in Boswell's life was to persuade him to repress the man he felt he was and become the man he knew he ought to be. Sometimes he listened to them. He did become an advocate, after all, not an army officer or a diplomat. But when it came to the choice of a wife, the advice Boswell sought out most assiduously was precisely that which he was least likely to follow. Here, though, some instinct drew him to the one woman who would love and honour him, with humour and forbearance, throughout her life. Without her strength and her enduring love, his life would have lacked meaning.

From John Symonds, 1766

Not reported. The only evidence for this letter is in From Symonds, 3 Oct. 1767: 'Agreeably to Your Desire, I wrote to You last Year.' We cannot date this letter more precisely.

In Genoa on 2 Dec. 1765 Symonds (1730–1807) had told JB how 'he rode over europe to study agriculture', and on 5 Dec. had shown him his journal (Journ. 3, 6 Dec. 1765). While in Genoa, Symonds gave JB historical notes he had made on the cities JB would pass through on his way to Paris (C 2633), but there is no evidence that his account of Calabria which, according to Symonds's letter of 3 Oct. 1767, he sent to JB, at his request, with an accompanying letter, written 'last year', ever reached him. On the death of Thomas Gray in 1771 Symonds succeeded him as Professor of Modern History at Cambridge.

To William Pitt,[1] Saturday 15 February 1766

MS. Yale (*L 364.1). Sent 15 Feb. (Reg. Let.).[2] A draft of this letter survives, in JB's hand, with the heading 'To The Right Honourable William Pitt, Esq.' (L 364); the three substantive changes in the draft are noted below. JB enclosed his correspondence with Chatham (1766–67) in a wrapper endorsed 'Letters To and From Mr. Pitt—Earl of Chatham'.

ENDORSEMENT (in the hand of Lord Cardross)[3]: 1766 Feby. 15th.

St. James's Street,[4] Saturday 15 Febry. 1766

SIR: I am just arrived from Corsica,[5] where I had several[6] conversations with Signor De Paoli, who wished much that I could see you on[7] my return to Britain.[8]

If you can give me an audience I shall be very happy to pay you my respects, and to acquaint you with some things which past between Signor De Paoli and me. If not, I have done my duty in complying with the desire of that great Man. I am with the highest esteem, Sir, your Most Obedient and Most Humble Servant,

JAMES BOSWELL

[1] After serving as Prime Minister during the Seven Years' War, William Pitt (1708–78), the Great Commoner, had resigned from the government in 1761, but he still retained his seat in the House of Commons. On 7 July he would be asked to form a ministry and on 4 Aug. he would be created first Earl of Chatham with the official position of Lord Privy Seal (Namier and Brooke iii. 290, 298).

[2] Listed by error in the column for letters received.

[3] David Steuart Erskine (1742–1829), Lord Cardross, later (1767) eleventh Earl of Buchan. He founded the Society of Antiquaries of Scotland in 1780 and was a man of considerable talents, but eccentric and immensely vain. As William Pitt's secretary he was present at JB's interview with Pitt on 22 Feb. (To Pitt, 19 Feb. n. 2). JB and Cardross were distant cousins, both being descended from John Erskine, seventh Earl of Mar (Ominous Years, Gen. Chart iv).

[4] We do not know where or with whom JB had lodgings in St. James's Street.

[5] Draft, 'making a tour in the Island of' deleted before 'Corsica'. JB had arrived in London from the Continent on 11 Feb. (Journ. 12 Feb.).

[6] Draft, 'several' written above deleted 'many'

[7] Draft, 'Sir' deleted before 'on'

[8] Neither Paoli nor JB could have known how little influence Pitt had with the Cabinet at this time; but JB did know that for Paoli and the Corsicans Pitt was the champion of freedom, opposed to the Government that had issued the offensive Proclamation of 1763, in which the Corsicans had been described as 'rebels' (Boswell's Paoli, p. 41). Paoli urged JB to present a more accurate report of the Corsicans: "'Only undeceive your court. Tell them what you have seen here. They will be curious to ask you. A man come from Corsica will be like a man come from the Antipodes'" (Corsica, p. 320).

From William Pitt, Sunday 16 February 1766

MS. Yale (C 785).
ADDRESS: To James Boswell Esqr., in St. James's Street.

Hayes,[1] Sunday Feb. 16, 1766

SIR: The honour of your letter reach't me here, where I have been some days detaind with a fit of the gout. My present situation puts it out of my power to receive the favour you are so good to intend me: when I return to London I shall be very proud to see you. In the mean time allow me, Sir, to suggest some doubts of the propriety of a simple Individual, as I am, (in all respects, but that of a Privy Counsellor which adds to the difficulty,) receiving any communication from an Illustrious Personage circumstanced as General de Paoli is.[2] Under these considerations, might not a Communication to His Majesty's Secretary of State answer better the views of the able Corsican Cheif?[3]

In the mean time, Sir, I desire to assure you that I shall esteem myself fortunate in the opportunity of being introduced to your acquaintance. I have the honour to be with great esteem and Consideration, Sir, Your most obedient and most humble Servant,

WILLIAM PITT

[1] Hayes Place, Pitt's estate, was in north-west Kent, four miles south-east of Beckenham.
[2] Pitt had been a Privy Councillor since 1746. The 'difficulty' arising from his anomalous position at this time is explained in To Pitt, 19 Feb. n. 2.

[3] After a long military and Parliamentary career, Lt.-Gen. Henry Seymour Conway (1719–95) became Secretary of State for the Southern Department and leader of the House of Commons in 1765 under the Rockingham Administration (Namier and Brooke ii. 244–45).

To William Pitt, Wednesday 19 February 1766

MS. Chatham Papers, P. R. O., London. Sent 22 Feb. (Reg. Let.). JB's copy (L 365) bears the heading 'To The Right Honourable William Pitt Esq.' and differs slightly from the letter in capitalization and punctuation.
ENDORSEMENT (in the hand of Lord Cardross): 1766 Feby. 19th.

St. James's Street, 19 Febry. 1766

SIR: I have had the honour to receive your most obliging letter, and can with difficulty restrain myself from paying you compliments on the genteel manner in which you are pleased to treat me: But I come from a People among whom even the honest arts of insinuation are unknown.

However you may by political circumstances be in one view 'a simple Individual', yet, Sir, Mr. Pitt will allways be the Prime Minister of the Brave, the Secretary of freedom and of spirit; and I hope I may with propriety talk to him of the views of illustrious Paoli.[2]

Be that as it may, I shall very much value the honour of being admitted to your Acquaintance. I am With the highest esteem, Sir, Your Most Obedient and Most Humble Servant,

JAMES BOSWELL

¹ JB drafted this letter with the help of W. J. Temple, who told JB he wrote 'in too swelling a stile'. He and Temple 'consulted on writing to Mr. Pitt and you threw out many bouncing sallies which Temple represt. At last you gave him a clean neat short letter which pleased and was sent' (Notes, 17 Feb.).

² At JB's interview with Pitt on 22 Feb. Pitt was cordial but pointed out the difficulty of his position: "'Now Sir I will explain to you how I cannot properly recieve communications from General De Paoli for I am a Privy Counselor and have taken an oath to hear nothing from any foreign power that may concern Great Britain without declaring it to the King and Council.'" But Pitt continued: "'Sir I should be sorry that in any corner of the world however distant or however small it should be suspected that I could ever be indifferent to the cause of liberty'" (Journ. 22 Feb.). Also present at the beginning of the interview was Pitt's secretary, Lord Cardross, who years later wrote that JB appeared in Corsican garb with a letter from Paoli, but JB's full account of the interview does not give these details (To Cardross, 5 Jan. 1767).

From Girolama Nini Piccolomini,¹ Sunday 23 February 1766

MS. Yale (C 2258). Received 11 May (Reg. Let.).
ADDRESS: A Monsieur, Monsr. Giacomo Bossnell,² Scozia.

Siena, 23 Febro. 1766

La vostra lettera del 29 scaduto fece in me lo stesso effetto, che suol fare un fulmine quando cade addosso. La nuova della perdita³ della vostra cara Madre mi ha veramente afflitta per il dispiacere, che indubitatamente reca a voi, ed io prendo troppa parte in tutto quello che puo dispiacervi, e siccome non mi è ignoto il vostro buon cuore, e il dolore, che porta la morte di una Madre cosi vedo con tutta la chiarezza la vostra mestizia; e permettetemi Caro Boswell di unire le mie lagrime a quelle che voi spargete, e di esservi compagna nelle disgrazie. L'altro punto della vostra lettera, che mi ha turbata⁴ ancora, e' l'essere voi tornato in Iscozia, e tuttochè voi mi avesse scritto di non tornare più in Italia tanto mi pareva di nutrire una certa speranza di rivedervi finche voi erei in viaggio; ma ora che il caso e disperato non vedo altra resurza, che abbandonarmi in preda della disperazione, sollievo,⁵ che non è inteso che da chi si trova nella mia situazione.

Voi non mi dite come devo farvi l'indirizzo; e se mai fosse per impedirmi di scrivermi, voi vedete che non avete ottenuto il vostro intento poichè avventuro questa lettera al caso, ed imploro la giustizia della mia causa, che velà faccia recapitare. Ditemi se vi è stata recapitata una seconda lettera scrittavi a Parigi, dove vi manifestavo gli miei sentimenti con della libertà. Non crediate, che per essere tornato in Patria io non voglio il vostro ritratto, anzi lo voglio sicuramente, e potrete indirizzarlo al Sigre. Crocchi con pregarlo di rimettermelo con tutta la segretezza.

Non azzardo spiegarvi il mio cuore per non sapere qual debba essere il destino di questa lettera, e solo vi prego di ricordarvi di una persona, che vi ama con sincerità, e che desidera delle fortunate occasioni, per le quali vi possa chiaramente dimostrare almeno quel tanto, che non gli è stato permesso di offrire al vostro infinito merito nel breve spazio della vostra dimora in Siena; onde sappiate, che troverete sempre in me una onesta donna, una vera amica, e una costante amante in me riunita in sieme; adesso prevaletevi Caro Boswell di questa mia dichiarazione se vi fa piacere, e datemi così delle riprove di una vera corrispondenza; di grazia fatemi il piacere di credere, che con tali sentimenti io vivo per voi, e che la lontananza, ne il tempo non⁶ può farmi variare da quella, che io sono, giacchè i miei sentimenti per voi saranno indelebili, perchè l'opinione del vero merito non si p⟨erde⟩ mai, ed ho vissuto più stando un momento con voi, che ne lunghissimi giorni che ho passati lontani da voi e le vostre nuove ravvivano[7] questi dolci momenti, e sono i soli che conti nel sistema della mia vita, però sollevatemi con le vostre lettere, ed assicuratevi, che io vi amo, e vi stimo. Sigillo questa lettera e pretendo che voi l'avrete, ma chi sa in che mani andrai?

[Your letter of the 29th of last month struck me like the fall of a thunderbolt. The news of the loss of your dear mother has truly afflicted me because of the grief it undoubtedly is causing you. I enter only too deeply into everything that can make you unhappy; and as I well know the goodness of your heart and the grief that a mother's death brings, I see your sorrow with perfect clarity. Permit me, dear Boswell, to mingle my tears with yours, and to be your companion in distress.[8] The other part of your letter, which upset me further, is the fact that you have returned to Scotland.[9] Although you had written me that you would not come back again to Italy, I still cherished a hope of seeing you again as long as you were on your travels. But now that the case is hopeless, I have no other recourse but to abandon myself to despair. It is a relief that can be understood only by someone in my situation.

You did not let me know your address. If by any chance that was to prevent me from writing, you can see that you did not attain your end, for I commit this letter to chance, and implore the justice of my cause to see that it is delivered to you. Tell me if you received another letter addressed to you at Paris, in which I revealed my feelings for you with a degree of freedom.[10] Never think, because you have returned to your native land, that I do not wish for your portrait. On the contrary, I certainly want it, and you can send it to Signor Crocchi, asking him to deliver it to me with the greatest secrecy.[11]

I dare not risk explaining to you the state of my heart, not knowing what may be the fate of this letter, I only beg you to remember one who loves you with all her heart; one who longs for opportunities to make that offering, due to your great merit, which the brief period of your stay in Siena would not allow. Be certain that you will always find in me an honourable woman, a true friend, and a constant lover, all united in one. Dear Boswell, accept this declaration of mine, if it gives you any pleasure, and in so doing give me fresh proof that you sincerely reciprocate my affection. Do me the kindness of believing that, having such feelings, I live for you; and that neither time nor distance can make me change from what I am. My feelings for you will be indelible, for the impression of real merit is never lost. I have lived more during one moment with you than in the longest days that I have spent far from you. Hearing from you revives these sweet moments, the only ones worth anything in the whole of my life. So make things easier for me with your letters, and rest assured that I love and esteem you. I seal this letter and pretend to myself that you will receive it, but who knows into what hands, my letter, you will fall!][12]

[1]Girolama Nini Piccolomini (1728–92) had married Orazio Piccolomini, Capitano del Popolo of Siena, in 1748 and was now the mother of four children (MS. Nati e Batazzati, Maschi e Femmine, di Famiglie Nobili Senesi, 1700–1852, Bibliotheca Communale, Siena; MS. Archivio di Stato, marriage and death records; A. Lisini and A. Liberati, Genealogia dei Piccolomini de Siena, 1900, Tavola iv). The records listed above make this marriage date certain, though Girolama herself told JB that she had been married at sixteen (To Rousseau, 3 Oct. 1765). JB, who called her

'Moma', became her lover in Sept. 1765, and they enjoyed three weeks of happy intimacy until JB left Siena at the end of the month (*Grand Tour II*, pp. 130, 134–38). Girolama's letter bears no postmark; it was probably sent in another wrapper to JB's banker in Paris, John Waters, and forwarded to him in Edinburgh from there.

[2] MS. 'Bossnell' here and wherever the name appears in the text.

[3] MS. 'vostra' deleted before 'perdita'

[4] MS. 'turbuta'

[5] MS. 'sollie-sollievo'. Girolama wrote 'sollievo' as the first word of a new page, evidently having forgotten that she had started the word at the foot of the previous page.

[6] MS. 'mi' altered to 'non'

[7] MS. 'ravvivano' written above deleted 'rinnovano'

[8] JB first learned of his mother's death from a notice in *St. James's Chron.* (16–18 Jan. p. [3]), which he had read at Wilkes's lodgings in Paris

on 27 Jan., the day before he received his father's letter informing him that his mother had died unexpectedly on 11 Jan. (Journ. 27–28 Jan.; From Lord Auchinleck, 11 Jan.).

[9] JB arrived back in Scotland shortly after 6 Mar. (To W. J. Temple, 6 Mar.).

[10] Girolama had written to JB on 14 Feb., but he did not receive the letter until 9 Mar. (Reg. Let.); it had been forwarded to him from Paris. The letter is printed in translation in *Grand Tour II*, pp. 303–06; in it Girolama reminded JB of his promise to send her his portrait.

[11] JB described Abate Pietro Crocchi, who had taught JB Italian in Siena in 1765, as a learned man with an excellent disposition, who had pleased all his English students ('Riflessioni Scritte in Siena 1765', no. 6—M 108; From Crocchi, 2 Jan. 1769).

[12] Translation by F. A. Pottle and Ian Duncan.

From John Dick,[1] Tuesday 25 February 1766

MS. Yale (C 1004).

Leghorn, 25 February 1766

Mr. Dick presents his Compliments to Mr. Boswell and sends him the Inclosed papers which he has receiv'd for that purpose from Count Reverola, who is lately gone to Sardinia, but is expected back soon.[2]

[1] JB met John Dick (1720–1804), British Consul at Leghorn (1754–76), in Florence on 13 Aug. 1765 (Notes). The meeting was the beginning of a lifelong friendship and a regular correspondence, their common interests being the Corsican struggle for independence and the establishment of Dick's claim to the dormant baronetcy of Braid. For an account of JB's relationship with Dick and his involvement in the baronetcy claim, see *Scots Charta Chest*, pp. 216–23.

[2] Count Antonio Rivarola (1719–95), a Corsican by birth and son of a Corsican general, was now Sardinian chargé d'affaires at the court of Tuscany and residing in Leghorn, where his

house became a rendezvous for supporters of Paoli and the Corsican cause. From Leghorn he moved to the governorship of Villafranca in Piedmont. He was married to a niece of Paoli's (BU, Suppl.). In *Corsica* JB gives a lengthy account of this family of Corsican patriots, describing Rivarola as 'my very good friend' and, in the Preface, acknowledging his aid in writing the book (*Corsica*, pp. xiii, 97–100). The enclosures are unidentified but probably were Corsican newspapers or other materials for *Corsica*. Rivarola's secret reports to the King of Sardinia on commercial and Corsican affairs and on JB's activities in Corsica survive in the Archivio di Stato, Turin.

From Alexandre Deleyre,[1] Saturday 1 March 1766

MS. Yale (C 926). Received 10 Apr. (Reg. Let.).

À Parme, ce 1er mars 1766

Vous avés fait une perte bien sensible, Monsieur, et je vois au ton dont vous m'en parlés que vous avés grande raison de vous en affliger.[2] Mais vous recevés ce coup d'une main qui console ceux qu'elle frappe, et vous êtes à cet égard moins à plaindre que les ames qui n'ayant point d'espérance, restent sans dédommagement dans leurs afflictions. Je vous envie le bonheur de votre façon de penser. On en reconnoît le prix et l'avantage dans la situation douloureuse où vous êtes. La raison et la Philosophie nous convainquent de la triste nécessité de souffrir, mais n'apportent point de baume aux playes de notre coeur. Heureux qui peut trouver du reméde à ses maux dans la source du bien! Ne craignés pas que je veüille jamais ôter à personne une ressource si désirable. Ce n'est pas l'idée d'un Etre Suprême qui doit déplaire à l'honnête homme; mais les qualités incompatibles et les volontés injustes ou déraisonnables que des méchans, des fourbes ou des ambitieux lui attribuent pour dominer eux-mêmes sur le genre humain. Eh! mon cher Ecossois, qui a plus d'intérêt à souhaitter une autre vie, que le juste malheureux dans celle-cy! Qui mieux que moi, sans me flatter d'être ce juste, sent le besoin de se reposer dans le sein d'un pere et d'un consolateur universel qui répare le mal Physique et passager par des trésors éternels de félicité! Non, je ne connois point de dévot qui dans le fond de son coeur, implore plus ardemment cette bonté paternelle, et la cherche avec plus de bonne foy. Hélas! qu'est-ce qui pourrait m'empêcher de l'aimer et de l'invoquer?

Vous tâchés d'adoucir vos peines par de bonnes actions; c'en est la voye la plus sûre et la plus satisfaisante pour une belle ame. Je vous applaudis et vous félicite d'avoir amené Mlle. Levasseur à Mr. Rousseau.[3] J'aurois bien voulu me trouver à votre place. Mais je n'éspére plus de revoir cet ancien et déplorable ami. L'espace et le sort qui nous traversent, nous ont comme séparés pour toujours. Se porte-t-il bien? Souffre-t-il de ses infirmités habituelles? A t-il du moins l'esprit[4] plus tranquille dans la Patrie des ames libres, et loin de sa République qui se déchire aujourd'huy les entrailles, en punition, ce semble, des outrages qu'elle a faits à l'un de ses plus vertueux citoyens?[5]

Mais vous-même, cher Ecossois, êtes-vous content dans la maison paternelle? La douceur d'y consoler un pere respectable et tendre dont vous êtes maintenant le plus cher appui, vous rend-elle plus agréable un séjour où de sinistres[6] impressions de jeunesse vous faisoient craindre de rentrer? Oüi, je me persuade que le deüil même où vous aurés trouvé votre famille, effacera des sensations plus lugubres encore dont votre imagination était noircie. La douleur qui vient de la tendresse est naturelle et porte avec elle je ne sçai quoi de doux qui flatte l'ame et la tourne vers le bien; au lieu que la tristesse et la mélancolie d'un esprit effaré des dogmes révoltans d'une Religion mal entendüe, ne sont propres qu'à rendre l'homme féroce, ennemi de lui même, de ses semblables et presque du Dieu qui le poursuit et l'obséde de cruels phantomes. Pensés mieux de cet Etre, et haïssés ceux qui se disent ses ministres, plutôt que l'espéce humaine en général qui seroit bien mieux l'image de la Divinité, si les méchans ne l'y défiguroient par de fausses idées et des actions barbares.

Parlés-moi, je vous prie, en détail de votre voyage en corse. On m'ècrit que la Gazette de Lugano en a fait mention; mais je ne l'ay point lüe.[7] Marqués moi, s'il vous plaît, si le climat de cette Isle vous a paru fort chaud, si le terroir en est bien varié pour les productions et les perspectives; s'il est arrosé, d'une maniere utile et agréable? Les montagnes arides dont la Corse est couverte, ne sont-elles pas entrecoupées de quelque vallon habitable ou fraix; ou sont-elles bordées de plaines riantes et propres à la fécondité: En un mot, si vous étiés le maitre de votre sort, iriés-vous le fixer dans cette Isle. Je sçais que les moeurs des habitans sont encore

6

grossieres et sauvages; mais ce n'est pas ce qui m'effrayeroit. Je crains seulement que là comme ailleurs, la noblesse n'ait toutes les terres, et le peuple que du fer pour travailler et de la paille pour dormir. Si les païsans n'y ont pas un petit domaine, jamais la liberté ne s'y soutiendra. La révolution a t-elle occasionné un nouveau partage des terres? Je crois que des loix agraires devoient faire le fond du code de Législation dont les corses avoient besoin. Mais comment les nobles auront-ils voulu se dépoüiller, pour céder quelque chose à des laboureurs qui ne sont que des hommes? A-t-on surtout eu la précaution de laisser[8] peu de pouvoir au clergé, dangereux dans tous les Etats mais plus encore dans une Démocratie; car c'est pour cela qu'on a dit de tout tems que la Religion catholique ne convenoit pas à l'État populaire. Quelle est la nourriture des corses? Est elle saine, abondante, à bon marché? Y a t-il des cantons où l'air soit pur et sérein? Le centre du païs vaut-il mieux que les côtes? Les corses doivent-ils devenir un peuple commerçant et navigateur? Enfin donnés moi sur ce sujet toutes les lumieres que vous avés acquises; ce que vous m'en avés dit me donne la curiosité d'en apprendre davantage.[9]

Ecrivés moi souvent et fort au long, soit en Français, soit en anglois. J'espére vous entendre. Je me familiarise avec votre Langue dans le beau Poëme de Milton que je lis tous les soirs avec ma femme.[10] O le sublime génie, cher Ecossois, que l'auteur du Paradis perdu! Nous ne le connoissons pas en France, malgré deux traductions assez exactes.[11] C'est qu'il faut être Poëte, pour traduire des poëtes. La traduction me laisse froid et l'original m'enflame. Les François disent que Milton est fou d'avoir fait battre les Diables[12] avec des canons. Mais y a-t-il une plus belle idée que celle d'avoir attribué l'invention de la[13] poudre aux[14] Démons?[15] Les hommes veulent donc en avoir la gloire. Il est vrai qu'on trouve bien assez l'Enfer sur la terre, sans le placer ailleurs. Mais c'est nous peindre tels que nous sommes, que d'imputer[16] nos méchancetés à des Diables. J'ay déjà lû la moitié de ce magnifique Poëme et je n'y ai trouvé que deux ou trois idées que j'eusse voulu en retrancher, encore sont-elles bien courtes et peu importantes. Il faut avoüer que si les anglois ont honoré leurs grands hommes en général, il y en a deux qu'ils ont négligés, ou traités injustement, *Bacon et Milton*. Vous ne les avés connus qu'après leur mort. Il est vrai que le premier est venu dans un tems d'ignorance où l'on ne pouvoit pas encore l'entendre, et le second dans un tems de révolution où le Fanatisme échauffoit les têtes et bouchoit tous les yeux.[17] Mais ces beaux génies n'en sont pas moins restés sans gloire et sans nom durant leur vie. Que leur importe aujourd'huy l'ádmiration du monde où ils ne sont plus? Tel est le partage de l'homme. Mettons donc, cher Ecossois, notre mêrite et notre récompense dans nos vertus publiques ou privées. Elles nous suivent partout et leur voix se fait entendre au fond de nos coeurs, au lieu que les éloges prodigués au génie, viennent tard, de bien loin et ne vont qu'à l'oreille. Devenés un bon pére de famille, si vous ne voulés pas être un grand magistrat, et vous trouveres plus de satisfaction et de véritables joüissances de l'ame dons vos propres foyers, que dans les clameurs du Barreau et dans le vil encens de la multitude, si chêrement vendu, quoique d'un prix si vain.[18] Adieu, cher Ecossois. Ma famille vous salüe et vous aime. Je vous embrasse pour elle,

DELEYRE

P.S. Addressés moi vos lettres, je vous prie, par la voye de l'ambassadeur d'angleterre en France, ou de celui de France en angleterre,[19] sous l'enveloppe de Mr. Charay, commis à l'un des Bureaux des affaires étrangeres à versailles.[20]

[1] Alexandre Deleyre (1726–97), French *philosophe* and disciple of Rousseau, was librarian to the Duke of Parma and in charge of the education of the Duke's young son when JB met him on 29 Jan. 1765 (Journ.). His publications included books on Bacon and Montesquieu and translations of two of Goldoni's plays (NBG; DBF). In Italy JB had found him 'a genteel, amiable Frenchman with a simplicity of manners that charmed me' and later had taken him for confessor and counsellor (Journ. 29 Jan. 1765; Notes, 3–6 Aug. 1765). In *Corsica* JB described Deleyre as 'a man who unites with science and genius the most amiable heart and most generous soul' (p. 138).

[2] JB's mother had died on 11 Jan. (From G. Piccolomini, 23 Feb. n. 8).

[3] JB had escorted Marie-Thérèse Le Vasseur (1721–1801), mistress of Jean-Jacques Rousseau (1712–78), from Paris to Chiswick, near London, where she was reunited with Rousseau on 13 Feb. (Journ.); she and JB had had an affair in the course of the journey (*Earlier Years*, pp. 277–79).

[4] MS. 'l'esprit' superimposed upon an illegible erasure.

[5] Rousseau had been forced to leave Switzerland for various reasons: the doctrines expressed in *Emile*, the attacks on the ruling oligarchy of Geneva in *Lettres écrites de la montagne*, and above all, Voltaire's exposure of his private life in his pamphlet, *Sentiment des citoyens*, issued anonymously on 27 Dec. 1764 (*Earlier Years*, p. 167). Rousseau had found asylum in England through the efforts of David Hume, and at the moment he was satisfied with his situation in England though his habitual sense of persecution soon reasserted itself (From Baroness von Spaen, 22 July, n. 6). He suffered from a chronic congestion of the urethra, which caused him pain and necessitated 'a chamber-pot every minute', as he told JB at the end of their third interview in Môtiers (Journ. 5 Dec. 1764).

Geneva was in a ferment over the mistreatment of Rousseau. Calm was restored only in 1768 when the government issued an edict limiting the powers of the aristocracy and substantially increasing those of the burghers (Wilhelm Oechsli, *History of Switzerland, 1499–1914*, trans. E. and C. Paul, 1922, pp. 280–81).

[6] MS. 'de sinistres' superimposed upon an illegible erasure.

[7] At JB's request, Padre Pio Clemente Vasco, Dominican at Bologna, had inserted a paragraph about JB's tour of Corsica in the Bologna *Gazette*; the notice was copied by other Italian newspapers, the Lugano *Gazette* presumably being one of them (From Vasco, 1 May 1774).

[8] MS. 'laisser' superimposed upon an illegible word.

[9] JB answered Deleyre's queries on Corsican climate, topography, and government in *Corsica* (pp. 11–54, 144–57), but he does not indicate whether he would like to live there. He does not discuss land reform, and none appears to have taken place as a result of the rebellion (which had been going on intermittently since 1729) until Paoli took over as General of the Nation in 1755. Paoli did much to bring order to Corsica: he abolished the power of the feudal lords, stamped out the vendetta, and encouraged agriculture, which JB notes was still in a primitive state (p. 190). JB writes that although the Corsican people were Roman Catholic, they had got rid of their bishops because of their Genoese sympathies (pp. 163–68). He says little about the diet; he observes that chestnuts were eaten (p. 48), but he fails to report that the staple food was bread made from ground chestnuts and more rarely from millet (Paul Arrighi, *La Vie quotidienne en Corse au xviii*^{e} *siècle*, 1970, pp. 56–57). In 1765 Rousseau had worked on a constitution for Corsica but had been forced to abandon it when he fled from Switzerland (From Marischal, 30 Apr. n. 4).

[10] Caroline-Alexandrine Deleyre, *née* Loiseau (b. c. 1728), Deleyre's wife since 1760 (DBF). JB found her good-tempered and well-bred (Journ. 1 Aug. 1765).

[11] The prose translation by Nicolas-François Dupré de Saint-Maur, as revised by Claude-Jean Chéron de Boismorand (1729) was used in all of the many French editions of *Paradise Lost*, until a new translation by Louis Racine, son of the dramatist, was published in Paris in 1755 (NUC ccclxxxv. 324–25). Racine also translated parts of the poem into verse and wrote a life of Milton (*Life of Milton, together with Observations on 'Paradise Lost'*, ed. Katherine John, 1930, pp. 79, 82).

[12] MS. 'Diables' superimposed upon 'anges'

[13] MS. 'avoir fait l'inventer la poudre' changed to 'avoir attribué l'invention de la poudre'

[14] MS. 'par' deleted before 'aux' superimposed upon 'des'

[15] Attribution of the discovery and proliferation of gunpowder to the Devil was traditional. For documentation, see J. R. Hale, 'Gunpowder and the Renaissance', *From the Renaissance to the Counter-Reformation: Essays in Honor of Garrett Mattingly*, ed. C. H. Carter, 1965, pp. 113–44. The best known passage in English is perhaps *Paradise Lost*, bk. vi, ll. 496–598.

[16] MS. 'd'imputer' written over deleted 'd'attribuer'

[17] Deleyre's *Analyse de la philosophie du chancelier François Bacon* (1755) consists of two small volumes of extracts in French translated from Bacon's writings. Deleyre includes no commentary, nor does he mention the English reaction to Bacon.

[18] JB was preparing for his examination in Scots Law and writing his thesis. He was admitted to the Faculty of Advocates on 26 July.

[19] The British ambassador to France was Charles Lennox (1735–1806), third Duke of Richmond (D. B. Horn, *British Diplomatic Representatives, 1689–1789,* 1932, p. 22); the French ambassador to Great Britain was Claude-Louis-François Régnier (1715–67), Comte de Guerchy (*Angleterre, 1698–1791,* ed. Paul Vaucher, 1965, iii. 405, 425 in *Recueil des instructions données aux ambassadeurs et ministres de France, 1884–1969,* xxv-2).

[20] François Charray (b. 1720) was *commis des affaires étrangères,* 1757–67 (Jean-Pierre Samoyault, *Les Bureaux de secrétariat d'état des affaires étrangères sous Louis XV,* 1971, p. 279).

From Robert Brown,[1] Monday 3 March 1766

MS. Yale (C 590). Received 8 Apr. (Reg. Let.).

ADDRESS: To James Boswel Esquire, at The Rt. Honourable The Lord Auchinleck's [Edinburgh *deleted*] by Air.

POSTMARK: [London] MR 31.

Utrecht, 3d March 1766

DEAR SIR: As I have seen by the newspapers that you are safely returned to your native Country, I take this opportunity of congratulating you upon it.[2] You say you have travelled agreeably; and I know you sufficiently both in point of abilities and disposition, to be assured you have done it to advantage:—the reflection upon which gives me much pleasure; for I pretend to be, and desire you shou'd account me as deeply interested in whatever concerns you. How happy would it make me to enjoy your Company for a few days, and to share in the observations you have made on Things, Men and Manners since you left us. You give me hopes that one day or other you may visit Utrecht once more. 'Twas kind in you to say so; but alas! I'm afraid we have seen our last of you on this side the water.[3]—Mr. Peterson has given me a note of what you are due him; amounting to six hundred Gilders of principal, and twenty four Gilders interest, at the rate of four pr. Ct. for one year; viz. the year sixty five; your note of hand bearing that payment should be made in sixty four. When you are pleased to send me either a draught on Holland for the money, or orders to draw on London for it (which perhaps may be more convenient for you, and will be indifferent to Mr. Peterson) I shall retire your Note and send it to you discharged.[4] I shall also send you soon the books you left with me, according to the list made of them at your departure by the trusty Francois, who has lived since that time with Mr. Wishart.[5]—Mrs. Brown and Miss Kinloch are perfectly well, and desire their kindest Compliments to you.[6] The Summer you left us, I purchased the old mansion where we lived; and ever since have been occupied in repairing it; which has cost me a deal of money. However, I endeavour to make it turn to account, having at present no less than seven boarders. Things go well; and I flatter myself will continue so. I'm happy in the best of wives; which is the highest blessing a man can enjoy in this world. The Child you was pleased to do so much honour to, at her birth, is extremely promising, in all respects, and the darling of her mother and me.[7] There have been no changes in our University of late, except that Mr. Hennert (who succeeded Mr. Castillon) is become ordinary instead of extraordinary professor; on which occasion he delivered an harrangue, which I shall send you a Copy of along with your books, not doubting but 'twill amuse you as it has done us.[8] Trotz has had very full Classes this year. He often makes enquiry about you with expressions of much regard.[9] The prince of Orange is expected here against the beginning of June, to be solemnly installed in his high Dignity of Stadholder;[10]—on which occasion, our very dull Town will, 'tis said, be very brilliant.[11]

Let me beg, Sir, that if there is any thing in which I can be serviceable to you in this place, you will honour me with your commands; and that you will ever please to look upon me as most sincerely Yours,

ROBERT BROWN

[1] The Rev. Robert Brown (1728–77), Scottish minister of the English (Presbyterian) Church in Utrecht, 1757–77, and British agent at Utrecht, 1763–77 (Fasti Scot. vii. 555; Hardenbroek, i. 390). JB, who found Brown 'a very good man in his way' (Notes, 28 Nov. 1763) but at other times 'vulgar and rude' and 'too free' (Journ. 31 Jan., 5 Apr. 1764), dined at his house regularly in 1763, where Brown tutored him in French and Greek (Mem. 15 Oct. 1763; Notes, 7 Apr. 1764). Brown was a good friend of the van Tuyll family and a confidant of Zélide (From Willem van Tuyll, 11 Nov.; P.-E. Godet, Madame de Charrière et ses amis, 1906, i. 111 n. 1).

[2] Brown could have seen the notice of JB's arrival in London in Lond. Chron. (13–15 Feb.) xix. 160, or in Lloyd's Evening Post, (12–14 Feb.) xviii. 157.

[3] JB's letter, which has not been reported, was sent on 7 Feb. (Reg. Let.). JB never returned to the Continent.

[4] Henry Peterson, an Englishman who became a citizen of Utrecht in 1760, was settled in that city by 1758. He worked as bookkeeper for a merchant, Abraham Renaud, and in 1764 took over Renaud's business (Lijst der Nieuwe Burgers, 1701–1828, Gemeente Archief, Utrecht; Utrechtsche Courant, 25 May 1764). JB bought cloth from Peterson at least once (Mem. 11 June 1764), which may account for the 600 guilders (51 guineas at the par of exchange—Beawes, p. 397) he owed him.

[5] François Mazerac (d. 1790—Death Register, Gemeente Archief, Utrecht) was engaged as valet by JB in Utrecht on 8 Sept. 1763 (Mem.) and served him 'honestly and well' until JB's departure on 18 June 1764 (Journ.). Before serving JB Mazerac had been valet to William Thomas Wishart (d. 1799), to whose service he returned after JB left Utrecht (From Brown, 11 Sept. 1764). Wishart, son and grandson of principals of the University of Edinburgh, lived with the Browns while studying in Utrecht, 1763–67. He owned the estate of Foxhall, Linlithgowshire, and in 1768 was served heir to his father in the

estate of Carsebonny, Stirlingshire (Charles Rogers, Life of George Wishart, 1876, pp. 96–98). JB found him 'stupid and insensible' (Notes, 14 Nov. 1763).

[6] In 1763 Brown had married Catharine Kinloch (b. 1736), fourth daughter of the expatriate Sir James Kinloch, Bt. and his Swiss wife (Henry Wagner, 'Descendants of Sir James Kinloch, Bart.', The Genealogist [1898], n.s. xiv. 200). Mrs. Brown and her sister Marguerite Susanne (1742–1813) had helped JB with his French ('Dialogues à La Haye', 22 Dec. [1763]—M 91).

[7] Ann Elizabeth Brown (1764–1842) was baptized on 17 June 1764 with the Earl Marischal as her godfather and JB in attendance (Journ.). In 1786 she married her cousin the theologian William Brown, who became Principal of the University of Aberdeen in 1796 (Fasti Scot. vii. 360–61).

[8] Johan Frederik Hennert (1733–1813), German professor of mathematics at Utrecht, 1764–1802, and author of Elementa Matheseos Purae et Applicatae, 9 vols. 1760–75. He delivered the oration, Oratio Inauguralis de Matheseos Studio cum Solida Educatione Conjugendo, in November 1765 (BW; G. W. Kernkamp, De Utrechtsche Universiteit, 1636–1936, i. 336–37). JB had found his earlier inaugural oration 'lively and eloquent' (Notes, 7 Feb. 1764). Hennert succeeded J. F. Salvemini de Castillon (Castiglione, Castilioni—1709–91), Italian professor of mathematics at Utrecht, 1755–64, and at Berlin, 1764–91 (BW; De Utrechtsche Universiteit i. 333–36). At Dutch universities, 'hooglehraar' (ordinary professor) was—and still is—the highest rank and a lifetime appointment. 'Buitengewoon hooğlehraar' (extraordinary- or deputy-professor) was a step lower and did not carry permanence. The concept of a tenured position was unknown in the 18th-century Dutch university, and it remains unknown in the 20th. Most professors are near retirement before they are appointed to a hooglehraarsambt (professorship) (information kindly supplied by Mrs. Edith Hallo). JB met

Castillon soon after arriving in Utrecht (Mem. 19 Sept. 1763) and made him a model for his studies (Mem. 7 Oct. 1763). They renewed acquaintance in Berlin, but at the end of JB's stay there, he had changed his opinion of Castillon: 'I was not sorry to leave *him*. He is a peevish Being, and if he has knowledge it does himself little good and others far less' (Journ. 19 Sept. 1764).

[9] Christian Heinrich Trotz (d. 1773), German professor of law at Utrecht, 1755–72 (NNBW ii.

1453–55; *De Utrechtsche Universiteit* i. 320–22). In one of his Dutch themes (c. 29 Feb. 1764—M 92, p. 18) JB praised Trotz's lively mind and his learning.

[10] Willem V (1748–1806) succeeded his father as Stadtholder in 1751 but did not attain full power until he reached his majority in 1766 (NNBW i. 1556).

[11] MS. 'brillant'—possibly the French usage.

To George Dempster, Friday 7 March 1766

Not reported. Sent 7 Mar. (Reg. Let.). George Dempster (1732–1818), JB's friend and fellow advocate, was highly respected and effective as M.P. for Perth Burghs, 1761–90 (Namier and Brooke ii. 313–17). His estate of Dunnichen in Forfarshire was about twelve miles north of Dundee.

To Lord Eglinton, Friday 7 March 1766

Not reported. Sent 7 Mar. (Reg. Let.). Alexander Montgomerie (1723–69), tenth Earl of Eglinton, was a Representative Peer for Scotland and a neighbour of the Boswells' in Ayrshire. For JB's relationship with Eglinton, see *Earlier Years*, pp. 47–51 and passim.

From Heer van Sommelsdyck,[1] Friday 14 March 1766

MS. Auchinleck Boswell Society. Received 23 Mar. (Reg. Let.).

ADDRESS: To James Boswell Esq., at Lord Auchinlech's, By London [Edinburgh *deleted; added in another hand*] by Air.

POSTMARK: [London] MR 18.

De La haye, ce 14 Mars 1766

MONSIEUR ET TRES CHER COUSIN: J'ai recu dans son temps celle que vous m'avés ecrite de paris dans laquelle il vous a plu de me donner connoissance de la mort inopinée de madame votre mere;[2] j'ai l'honneur de vous en faire mon tres sincere compliment de condoleance aussi bien qu'a Monsieur votre pere que j'asseure de mes tres humbles respects dememe que mon epouse,[3] et vous proteste que cette nouvelle nous a fait une double peine, d'un coté pour la grande perte que vous avés faite, et de l'autre parce que nous nous sommes veu privés par la du plaisir de vous posseder ici dans les circonstances presentes; nous esperons cependant que nous serons plus heureux dans une autre occasion et que vous voudrés bien nous venir voir encore: j'espere que vous aurés eu un voyage heureux et que vous aurés trouvé monsieur votre pere en meilleure santé qu'il ne l'etoit lorsque vous m'avés ecrit. Je languis d'en apprendre des nouvelles, et vous prie de me marquer dans quelle situation vous vous trouvés l'un[4] et l'autre actuellement: aureste, mon cher Cousin, j'ai un milion d'excuses a vous demander de ce que j'ai tant tardé a vous repondre, ne l'attribués cependant a aucune negligence, mais a une grande etourderie de ma part; comme nous etions deja dans les grands embaras lorsque j'ai recu votre lettre,[5] je l'ai lu a la hate et ai negligé de tourner le feuillet, ce qui a été cause que j'ai cru que vous aviés oublié de m'envoyer votre addresse pour l'ecosse, et que ne sachant comment vous repondre, j'ai laissé votre lettre sur ma table, et ce n'a été que ce matin que l'ayant trouvé sous ma main je me suis avisé de tourner le feuillet, et a ma grande confusion ai trouvé l'addresse; j'espere donc que vous voudrés bien me pardonner, vous promettant que je prendrai mieux garde a l'avenir, j'attendrai donc de vos nouvelles avec la plus vive impatience, et si je puis vous etre ici de quelque utilité je vous prie de disposer librement de celuy qui a l'honeur d'etre avec la consideration la plus distinguée, Monsieur et tres cher Cousin, Votre tres humble et tres obeissant Serviteur,

F. C. VAN AERSSEN VAN SOMMELSDYCK

Ma femme et mon fils[6] vous asseurent de leurs respects.

[1] François Cornelius van Aerssen (1725–93), Heer van Sommelsdyck, was JB's distant cousin: Sommelsdyck's greataunt Veronica had married Alexander Bruce, second Earl of Kincardine, and their daughter Elizabeth married James Boswell of Auchinleck, JB's grandfather. His death brought the Sommelsdyck branch of the van Aerssen family to an end (*Adelsarchief* iii. 176–77; *Ominous Years*, Gen. Chart iii). JB found his cousin 'amiable soft genteel' when he met him in The Hague, 23 Dec. 1763 (Notes, 24 Dec. 1763). For his military career, see From Sommelsdyck, 1 July, n. 7.

[2] JB's letter, telling Sommelsdyck that his mother had died on 11 Jan., was sent 29 Jan. (Reg. Let.); it has not been reported.

[3] Sommelsdyck married Everdina Petronella (1730–92), Countess van Hagendorp, in 1761 (*Adelsarchief* iii. 176–77).

[4] MS. 'l'an'.

[5] Perhaps on account of preparations for the festivities surrounding the coming of age of Willem V on 8 Mar. (From Sommelsdyck, 25 Jan.—MS. Auchinleck Boswell Society; From Robert Brown, 3 Mar. and n. 10).

[6] The Sommelsdycks' only child François Johan, born in Aug. 1764, shortly after JB left Holland for Germany; he died, unmarried, in 1784 (*Adelsarchief* iii. 176–7; From Sommelsdyck, 22 Aug. 1764; 29 Jan. 1785—MSS. Auchinleck Boswell Society).

From John Dun,[1] Saturday 15 March 1766

MS. Yale (C 1123). Received 15 Mar. (Reg. Let.).

Auchinleck Manse, 15th March 1766

DEAR SIR: The kind sympathising Letter I had from you when my heart was in deep distress for the loss of a dear relation calls on me now, tho' there were no other reason, to feel for and sympathise with you.[2] You have lost one of the best parents ever lived—lost at present to you, tho nothing is lost that is become immortal and happy. The 'Power that guards the just'[3] takes particular care of such when they get into his more immediate presence. It is his delight and perhaps will[4] be part of his employment thro Eternity to make them happy by a constant communication of good.—Happy they, who tread those paths of Religion which lead to Heaven whatever their denomination on earth be. There they shall spend an Eternity together—where all is harmony, where all is love. For there is no darkness ignorance weakness pride passion selfishness superstition sin idleness nor folly there. O preclarum diem, says Cicero, cum ad illud divinum animorum concilium coetumque profisciscar, cum ex hac turba et colluvione discedam.[5]

My Lord Auchinleck is greatly to be pitied and needs to be encouraged. This I dare say will now be much your study and you have it more in your power to encourage and comfort him than any mortal.—I need not tell you that true politeness consists partly in doing even what is not agreeable to ourselves to oblige and promote the happiness of others and if we are bound to act in this manner for a stranger, surely we ought to go very far for a parent. My strong affection for you makes me entreat you to listen to his advices.[6] The world acknowledges his wisdom, it is enlightned by experience, and sure you cannot doubt his friendship. I should ever think myself concerned in your wellfare tho we were to live at a thousand miles distance from one another.—Providence has timed this heavy trial well for you, when your imagination has been filled with the gayest images, your body is in its vigour and blood warm with youth—timed it well I say, to keep you from forgetting you are mortal.—It may admonish daily like Philips' boy.[7]—And I hope it will be for your good by making serious and lasting impressions on your mind at that time of life, when the human mind, I say it from experience, is ready to build castles upon froth and is an easy prey to the pleasures of sense or useless ones of imagination.

It is as natural for youth and health to forget death as it is for us when the sun is ascending to his meridian height to forget that the evening approaches.

I take also this opportunity of congratulating you on your safe return to your native country. May you ever be an honour to it and it a pleasure to you. I am glad of the near prospect of seeing you again and am, Dear Sir, Yours sincerely,

JOHN DUN

I expect your coming here soon is to prevent any return to this letter.

[1] Rev. John Dun (1723–92) entered the Boswell household in 1748 or 1749 as tutor to JB. He calmed JB's fears about religion, taught him Latin, and introduced him to the Roman poets and the English classics. In 1752 he was ordained and became minister of Auchinleck Parish, where he remained until his death (JB's 'List of Ages'; *Earlier Years*, pp. 18, 20, 24, 28; *Fasti Scot.* iii. 4).

[2] JB's letter has not been reported; it was perhaps written on the death of Dun's first wife Mary Wilson, who died in 1762.

[3] Quotation unidentified.

[4] MS. 'employment' deleted before 'will'

[5] Cicero, *Cato Maior, De Senectute*, 84: 'O praeclarum diem, cum in illud divinum animorum concilium coetumque proficiscar cumque ex hac turba et conluvione discedam!': 'O the happy Day, when I shall leave this tainted Medley of Things, and join that glorious and divine Assembly of Souls above!' (William Massey's translation, 1753).

[6] The Court of Session rose on 11 Mar., and JB accompanied his father to Auchinleck shortly after receiving this letter. He wrote to John Johnston of Grange on 31 Mar. (Walker, p. 211): 'I am studying Scots Law and conforming entirely to the inclinations of my worthy Father.'

[7] Philip of Macedon (382–336 B.C.) employed a servant to remind him daily of his mortality. Dun may have read the story in Claudius Aelianus, *Varia Historia* (bk. viii, ch. 15); it also appears in Thomas Leland's *History of the Life and Reign of Philip, King of Macedon*, 1758.

From Jean-Jacques Rousseau, c. mid-March 1766

Not reported. For a reply (in which JB denies that he has neglected Rousseau) see To Rousseau, 25 Mar.

To Lord Mountstuart, c. mid-March or 31 March 1766

Not reported. The evidence for the dating of this letter comes from Mountstuart himself: 'I receiv'd a letter from you so long ago, as the 25th of March' (From Mountstuart, 29 May). Reg. Let. shows that JB sent letters to Mountstuart on 20 Jan. and 31 Mar. but not in between, hence the indecisive heading.

John Stuart (1744–1814), Viscount Mountstuart, later (1792) fourth Earl and (1796)

first Marquess of Bute, was the eldest son of the former Prime Minister, John Stuart, third Earl of Bute. JB first met him in Rome on 25 Feb. 1765 (Notes) and, at Mountstuart's invitation, they had travelled together until Mountstuart was called home while they were in Venice (Notes, 3 June–27 July 1765). They quarrelled frequently, but shortly before they parted Mountstuart admitted that he would miss JB 'on the road' (Notes, 23 July 1765). For an account of JB's relationship with Mountstuart, see *Pol. Car.*, pp. 23–27.

To Jean-Jacques Rousseau,[1] Tuesday 25 March 1766

MS. Yale (L 1120). Sent 31 Mar. (Reg. Let.).

ADDRESS: A Monsieur, Monsieur Rousseau.

HEADING: *Extrait*, A M. Rousseau

Auchinleck, ce 25 Mars 1766

Cher et singulier Philosophe ne croyez pas que Je vous *neglige* (comme vous m'avez accusé de faire) depuis que vous eťes venu en Angletêrre.

C'est vraye qu'au plupart des hommes la presence de ce qu'ils ont admirés le plus leur en ote l'admiration. Si par[2] hazard le Soleil tomberoit sur la terre, il n'y seroit pas dix jours avant qu'on en feroit une boule pour jouer aux quilles. Mais Je ne suis pas comme la plupart des hommes.

[1] JB had become a disciple of Rousseau's as the result of five interviews with the great philosopher in December 1764 at Môtiers. His sense of discipleship had gradually lessened, however, and by 12 Feb. when he delivered Thérèse Le Vasseur to Rousseau in England, he could write of his former master: 'He seem'd so oldish and weak you had no longer your enthusiasm for him' (Journ. 13 Feb.).

[2] MS. 'par' superimposed upon 'le'

From Mary Montgomerie,[1] Thursday 27 March 1766

MS. Yale (C 752).

ADDRESS: To James Boswell Esqr., at Auchinleck, By Air.

Doura, 27 March 1766

DEAR SIR: It gave me great pleasure to hear You were arived safely in Your native Country more so that You had attended Your worthy Father to Auchinleck—God grant You may long be a comfort to him. What a blank must the loss of Your good Mama make to him You and every one concerned. For my own part I never knew the want of a Mother as long as her Life was spared but Gods will be done. He called her out of this World to inherit everlasting happiness with the blessed above for never was a greater Saint I dare say in this World. I wish we may be enabled to follow her good example and be entitled to the great reward promised to the faithfull.

I had this day a letter from Bristoll. Mrs. Montgomerie sayes she thinks my Brother rather better that he has a better stomach since he drunk the waters.[2] It revived my spirits a little. We are alwayes ready to grasp at the least shadow of hope. I expect to hear from Mrs. Cuninghame who is gon there next week. She wil be a better judg as it is a good while since She saw him.[3]

I beg you'l offer my Duty to my Unckle. Tel him I return him thanks for the Cloak I hear his Lordship has made me a present of. It shall be highly esteemed by me for the sake of the worthy owner—may I beg the favor of a line to let me know particularly how my Lord stood his journey and how his health and spirits are.

The Capt. and my Sister went of in such a hast that they had not time to give proper orders to any but me which confines me here,[4] els I would have waited on my Lord and You at Auchinleck.— I hope Davie is in good health and pray write me if Johnie be stil at Newcastle and if he be behaving better.[5] God grant he may. Your Father ⟨has⟩ much need of simpathy and comfort fr⟨om⟩ You all. He has been an indulgent Paren⟨t⟩ and his late loss to be sure will mak any thing improper in his Childrens behavior sit much heavier upon him. Forgive me for this long epistle. I hope You know me so wel it is meant out of friendship. Believe me to be, Dear Sir, Your affectionate Cousine and obedient Servant,

MARY MONTGOMERIE

[1] Mary Montgomerie (d. 1777), daughter of Lord Auchinleck's sister Veronica and David Montgomerie of Lainshaw. In 1768 she married, as his second wife, James Campbell of Treesbank (*Ayr and Wigton* i. 656); in 1769 her younger sister Margaret married JB.

[2] James Montgomerie (d. 1766) was married to Jean Maxwell, daughter of Sir John Maxwell of Nether-Pollok, Bt. (*Ayr and Wigton* iii. 598). JB described his cousin as looking 'very ill' when he called on him in London on 14 Feb. (Notes, 15 Feb.); he died on 16 Dec. (*Gent. Mag.* 1766, xxxvi. 600).

[3] Elizabeth Montgomerie-Cuninghame (d. 1776), eldest of the Montgomerie sisters, succeeded her brother James as laird of Lainshaw (*Ayr and Wigton* iii. 592). Her husband, Capt. Alexander Montgomerie-Cuninghame (d. 1770), son and heir of Sir David Cuninghame of Corsehill, Bt., served in the army until he inherited the estate of Kirktonholm from his maternal aunt Anne Montgomerie in 1761; it was at this point that he added Montgomerie to his own surname. He died shortly before his father, and the baronetcy passed to his eldest son Walter

(*Ayr and Wigton* iii. 592).

[4] Mary Montgomerie is writing from a farm at Doura, Stewarton Parish, belonging to her brother-in-law (Journ. 23 Sept. 1776). Presumably she was looking after the Cuninghame children while their parents were in Bristol.

[5] JB's younger brothers, John (1743–c. 1798) and David (1748–1826): birthdates of both brothers taken from the 'List of Ages'. John was a lieutenant in the army and stationed at Plymouth when he suffered the first of recurrent fits of insanity (*Army List*, 1765, p. 74; Journ. 26 Oct. 1762; Walker, p. 44 and n. 3); he had been on half pay since Apr. 1765 (Walker, p. 249 and n. 1). He was now in Newcastle under the care of the Rev. Edward Aitken, a dissenting clergyman who had once been tutor to Lord Auchinleck (*Earlier Years*, pp. 286, 528–29; Journ. 18 Mar. 1768); JB had visited John there on his way north from London and found him well (To W. J. Temple, 6 Mar.). David had been an apprentice in the banking firm of John Coutts and Co., Edinburgh since 1763 (Walker, p. 58 and n. 6); he and JB were close and had corresponded regularly while JB was on the Continent.

From George Dempster, c. late March 1766

Not reported. Received 23 Mar. (Reg. Let.).

From Lord Eglinton, c. late March 1766

Not reported. Received 23 Mar. (Reg. Let.).

To George Frazer, Saturday 29 March 1766

Not reported. JB invited Frazer to Auchinleck (From Frazer, 4 Apr.).

To Godfrey Bosville, Monday 31 March 1766

Not reported. Sent 31 Mar. (Reg. Let.). JB wrote that he had not taken Bosville's book about King David (From Bosville, 24 June).

To Godfrey Bagnall Clarke, Monday 31 March 1766

Not reported. Sent 31 Mar. (Reg. Let.). JB had known Clarke (c. 1742–74), M.P. for Derbyshire, 1768–74, in Italy (Namier and Brooke ii. 216; Notes, 15 Apr.–8 June 1765; From Clarke, 17 Aug. 1765). Presumably JB gave Clarke an account of his meeting with the Hon. Alexander Murray in Paris; Clarke had sent JB a letter of introduction to him (Journ. 17 Jan.; From Clarke, 17 Aug. 1765).

To Basil Cochrane, Monday 31 March 1766

Not reported. Sent 31 Mar. (Reg. Let.). Basil Cochrane (1701–88—'List of Ages'), brother of JB's maternal grandmother, Euphemia Erskine, and of Thomas Cochrane, eighth Earl of Dundonald. After a long military career he was appointed Commissioner of Excise in 1761 and a Commissioner of Customs in Scotland in 1764 (Scots Peer. iii. 349). JB characterized his greatuncle as 'a Man of great common sense and Prudence' (Journ. 30 Oct. 1762). In this letter he told Cochrane that he had reached Auchinleck safely from Edinburgh and that he was studying law with his father (From Cochrane, 7 Apr.).

To George Dempster, Monday 31 March 1766

Not reported. Sent 31 Mar. (Reg. Let.).

To John Pringle, Monday 31 March 1766

Not reported. Sent 31 Mar. (Reg. Let.). JB asked Pringle to persuade Lord Auchinleck to allow him a separate residence (From Pringle, 10 June).

To John Wilkie, Monday 31 March 1766

Not reported. Sent 31 Mar. (Reg. Let.). John Wilkie (d. 1785) had been publisher of Lond. Chron. since its beginning in 1757 (Gent. Mag. 1785, lv. 573). In 1767 he published JB's Dorando, The Essence of the Douglas Cause, and Letters of Lady Jane Douglas. Throughout 1766 JB sent Wilkie articles, both 'fact' and 'invention', for Lond. Chron. (Lit. Car. pp. 236–37). Presumably JB was sending him Corsican items for insertion (Lit. Car. pp. 236–37).

From Girolama Nini Piccolomini, c. early April 1766

Not reported. Received 11 May, 'La Signora' (Reg. Let.).

From Andrew Smith, c. early April 1766

Not reported. Received 10 Apr. (Reg. Let.). The writer is almost certainly the Rev. Andrew Smith (1741–89), in July of this year ordained minister of Langton Parish, Berwickshire (Fasti. Scot. ii. 23). An Andrew Smith was a classmate of JB's at the University of Edinburgh; their names appear on the Matriculation Roll of John Stevenson's class for Mar. 1757, which shows that Smith was in his second year, JB in his fourth (Account Book, University of Edinburgh Library).

From George Frazer,[1] Friday 4 April 1766

MS. Yale (C 1322).

Edinbr. 4 April 1766

DEAR SIR: After congratulating you on your safe Arrival from your Travels in your Native Country again, I beg leave to acknowlege the receipt of your favors of the 29th Ulto.—And should be extremely happy that my present situation would admit of my waiting on My Lord and you.—But I hope to have it in my power to do it some days before his Lordship set out on the Circuit.[2]

I should have been very happy to come in Company with your Cousin Mr. Boswell who brings you this.[3]—But it was not in my power for the reasons I have mentioned to His Lordship.

I am with the greatest regard, Dear Sir, Your most Obedient, humble Servant,

GEO. FRAZER

[1] George Frazer (c. 1701–74) served fifty years as deputy-auditor of excise in Edinburgh (*Scots Mag.* 1774, xxxvi. 559). JB described him as 'a most ingenious agreable man' (Journ. 28 Oct. 1762).

[2] Lords Auchinleck and Coalston were assigned by the Court of Justiciary to the northern circuit; they held court in Perth, Aberdeen, and Inverness, on 8, 16, and 24 May respectively (*Scots Mag.* 1766, xxviii. 279).

[3] Claud Irvine Boswell (1742–1824), son of Lord Auchinleck's uncle, John Boswell of Balmuto, arrived at Auchinleck some time after 5 Apr. and was now studying law with Lord Auchinleck, as was JB (From David Boswell, 5,

29 Apr.). On 29 Apr. 1769 JB contrasted his own temperament with his cousin's: 'I observed that she [Margaret Montgomerie] and I had more enlarged views as we had fancy to look beyond what really is ours. Like one whose house has a prospect not only of his own lands, but of many beautiful objects at a distance. That Balmuto saw nothing but what was solid, and substantially his own. That he had thick high stone walls built round that extent and had that only in his view; except when I surprised him by sometimes taking a hammer and beating a hole in his walls so as to give him a peep of the fields of fancy which made him caper; but his mother and sisters took care to build all up again directly' (Journ.).

To Heer van Sommelsdyck, Sunday 6 April 1766

Not reported. For date and contents, see From Sommelsdyck, 1 July.

From Basil Cochrane,[1] Monday 7 April 1766

MS. Yale (C 799). Received 20 Apr. (Reg. Let.).
ADDRESS: To James Boswell Esqr. att Auchenleck house, per Air.
POSTMARK: [Edinburgh] AP 7.

Edinburgh, April 7th 1766

DEAR JAMES: Last week I had your's and am glade to find you gott all well Hom and in good Health that you are goeing with your Studies gives me Sincer Joy. Continue to doe So and be assured that by that means you will make both your Father and your Self happy while you[2] are in this World.

I send you a letter[3] which this Moment came to my hand. I am, My Dear James, Your Sincer Friend,

BASIL COCHRANE

² MS. 'your'

From Mary Montgomerie, c. Tuesday 8 April 1766

Not reported. Received 10 Apr. (Reg. Let.).

To John Dick, Thursday 10 April 1766

Not reported. See From Dick, 30 May: 'The pleasure I purposed to myself in hearing from you, was greatly diminished, when I learnt by your obliging letter of the 10th past, that You had lost your Mother.'

From George Dempster, c. mid-April 1766

Not reported. Received 19 Apr. (Reg. Let.).

From Andrew Erskine, c. mid-April 1766

Not reported. Received 20 Apr. (Reg. Let.). Andrew Erskine (1740–93), third son of the fifth Earl of Kellie, was at this time a lieutenant in the 24th Regiment of Foot, Gibraltar, though he had been in Edinburgh at least since early April (*Army List*, 1766; From John Johnston, 26 Apr.). JB and Erskine had been the principal contributors to *A Collection of Original Poems by Scotch Gentlemen*, vol. 2, 1762, and together had published *Letters Between the Honourable Andrew Erskine and James Boswell, Esq.*, 1763 (*Lit. Car.* pp. 10–14, 19–24).

To Mary Montgomerie, c. mid-April 1766

Not reported. See From Mary Montgomerie, 22 Apr.: 'I was favoured with Your kind epistle happy to hear such good accounts of You and my Unkle.'

From James Smith, c. mid-April 1766

Not reported. Received 20 Apr. (Reg. Let.). Presumably the writer was James Smith (d. 1788), writer in Edinburgh and JB's schoolfellow at Mundell's School (*Scots Mag.* 1788, p. 623; *List of Scholars Educated by the Late James Mundell*, 1789, p. 14).

To Lord Eglinton, Saturday 19 April 1766

Not reported. Sent 19 Apr. (Reg. Let.).

To Baroness von Spaen, Sunday 20 April 1766

Not reported. Sent 8 May (Reg. Let.). See From Baroness von Spaen, 22 July: 'En revenant d'une petite coursse que j'avois fait. . . j'ai trouvé votre lettre monsieur qui a eté plus de deux mois en chemin, elle est datée du 20 Avril, et n'est arrivée ici, que le 26 Juin'. It is likely that JB began this letter on 20 Apr. and did not finish it until 8 May; such would explain both the discrepancy in dates and a part of the delay in the letter's reaching the Baroness.

18

From Mary Montgomerie, Tuesday 22 April 1766

MS. Yale (C 753). Received 25 Apr. (Reg. Let.). This letter is a postscript to Margaret Montgomerie's letter to JB of 22 Apr., which will be printed in a forthcoming volume of family correspondence.

[Doura, 22 April 1766]

DEAR SIR: I was favoured with Your kind epistle happy to hear such good accounts of You and my Unckle. I take this opportunity to thank You for the favour of writing which I hear You dislike much. I am not very fond of writing and never writes to any body but those I esteem and wishes to hear of their welfare. Peggy has mentioned in her Letter the accounts from Bristoll so I need not tire Your patience with any more.[1] I am, Dear Sir, Your affectionate Cousine,

MARY MONTGOMERIE

[1] Margaret Montgomerie reported that their brother James was not benefitting from the wa- ters at Bristol (From Margaret Montgomerie, 22 Apr. 1766).

From Pierre Loumeau Dupont,[1] Wednesday 23 April 1766

MS. Yale (C 1162). Received 25 Apr. (Reg. Let.).
ADDRESS: To James Boswell Esqr. at Auchinlec, To the care of the Post Master at Air.
POSTMARK: [Edinburgh] AP 23.

A Edimbr. le 23d Avril 1766

MONSIEUR: Vous me trouverez sans doute de la dernière hardiesse, puisque je prend la liberté de vous détourner de vos études, mais la bonté que vous m avez temoignée me fait espérer, que vous ferez cette grace a celui qui est penetré d'estime pour votre rare mérite qui ne peut que frapper les ésprits au dessous du médiocre. Je puis ajouter pour me servir de justification au sujet de ma hardiesse cest le desir extreme que j'ay d'aprendre l'état de la santé de My Lord votre illustre Père et de la votre Monsieur, objets qui me touchent beaucoup.

Vous savez Monsr. la mort de My Lord justice Clerc,[2] qui a passé subitement, il avoit pris un vomitif, et par les efforts quil a faits un vaisseau dans le Cerveau s'est rompu et lui a causé la mort et c'est la une conjecture qui n'est pas tout á fait, sans quelque vraisemblance, il faudra reparer cette brèche, mais y en est de plus capable sur lequel la Cour puisse jetter les yeux, que sur My Lord L'Aristide Chretien le Mécenas de Mr. Chais,[3] et je voudrois l'apeler le mien si j'étois digne d'un tel honneur. Le public se trouveroit heureux, si l'on faisoit choix d'un si grand sujet, Madame Scott, Mademoiselle sa fille et moy le souhaitons ardemment,[4] et quand nous aurons apris cette nouvelle nous nous en réjouirons avec le bon Docteur Bosewel au quel nous sommes infiniment obligé des soins empresses qu'il a eut la bonté de se donner pour le retablissement de Madame Scott, elle se porte beaucoup mieux par la grace de dieu, elle prend de la nourriture et elle peut lier conversation avec ceux qui la voient, et elle lit dans son Lit de bons Livres, et les nouvelles publiques pour se délasser, et j'espere que les forces lui reviendront avec le beau tems, elle n'oubliera jamais la maniere genereuse avec laquelle My Lord pendant quelle a eté en danger s'est interressé pour elle, je puis dire qu'avec la benediction de Dieu, l'habi[li]té du Docteur et les prieres de My Lord l'ont mises dans l'état ou elle se trouve presentement, son sang est rénouvellé et dans sa maladie, il a eté fort corrompu, nous souhaitons un heureux succes a Mr. votre Oncle, dans son dessein puisse s'il obtient la robe de Professeur, il en est digne, il est bon Physicien, et fort heureux dans la pratique de la Medecine, et tres capable de faire de bons Ecolliers.[5]

J'ay dessein aujourdhui de souscrire pour cette fameuse Taille douce, ou la famille de Calas est representée dans une triste situation,[6] c'est une Satyre tres piquante contre le Parlement de Thoulouse, et apropos du Parlement de Thoulouse Mr. Graham Avocat fils de Mr. Graham de Gathmore[7] avec lequel j'ay l'honneur de me promener quelques fois sur la croix me dit y est un bon mot de Madame la Duchesse D'anville,[8] au sujet de la condanation du pauvre Calas a un des Juges du Parlement de Thoulouse qui étoit a Paris, elle lui temoigna sa surprise au sujet de ce qu'un cors sage et éclairé ait commis une telle faute en condamnant un homme innocent a une si cruelle mort la dessus il lui fait réponce, 'Madame vous savez qu'il n'est point de bon Cheval qui ne bronche quelques fois,' la dessus elle lui replique 'il est vrai Monsieur mais on n'a jamais vû que toute une Ecurie ait bronché,' vois bien qu'elle compare le Parlement de Thoulouse dont les Chevaux bronchent, voici un bon mot de Madame la Maréchalle de Maillebois;[9] Mr. de Maillebois etant fort pauvre a èpousé la fille d'un riche Marchand qui lui a aporté en mariage de grandes richesses un Seigneur etant a la Table de Mr. le Maréchal lui dit sans doute que vous ferez quelques uns de Messieurs vos fils Chevaliers de Mode, Mr. ma femme a fermé la porte, il voulait dire par la que M'rs. les Chevaliers ne voudroient pas le[s] recevoir dans leur Societé paree, parce que les jeunes Messieurs etoient fils d'une Mere qui n'étoit pas noble, la bonne Dame picquée de ce bon mot, lui fait une réponce, 'il est vrai que j'ay fermé cette porte, mais j'ay fermé une autre c'est celle de l'hôpitale'; voulant dire par la que sans son mariage, il aurait eté obligé d'aller y passer ses jours. Mr. Graham m a dit que proche de Nimes ou il y a beaucoup de Protestans il s'etat fait une assemblée de pres de 13000 ames,[10] qu'on y avoit preché, et chanté les Pseaumes, a coté d'un Convent de Capucins, ces bons Peres, scandalisés de voir cette assemblée, et d'entendre le chant des Pseaumes on[11] font leurs plaintes au Gouverneur de la Province de Languedoc, et pour toute satisfaction il leur dit 'mes Pères tenez vous en repos ils ne vous font point de mal,' vous voiez par la Monsieur qu'avec le tems on se defera en France de cet esprit bigot[12] et persécuteur.[13]

Voyla une lettre bien longue et assommante, il est tems de finir en vous demandant pardon de ce que j'ay abusé de votre patience jespere que vous continuerez Monsieur de votre bienveillance et de me croire avec le plus sincer attachement, et en devouement le plus parfait, Monsieur, Votre tres humble et bien obeissant Serviteur,

P. L. DUPONT

Madame Scott et Mademoiselle sa fille font bien leurs complimens a My Lord et prient Dieu pour sa santé et pour sa conservation et pour vous aussi et pour tout ce qui vous interesse. Je vous prie d'assurer My Lord de mes profonds respects, et de lui faire ressouvenir de ces curiosites qu'il a eut la bonté de me promettre pour Mr. Chais.

[1] The Rev. Pierre Loumeau Dupont (1699–1786), son of a Huguenot minister who had fled from France in 1685 and established a French church in Edinburgh. Dupont studied in Geneva for seven years before succeeding his father as pastor of the French congregation in 1725; he held the post until his death, by which time his flock had virtually ceased to exist. In 1774 he petitioned the Town Council for an augmentation of his stipend, but the petition was unsuccessful, as was his subsequent petition, drawn up by JB in 1777 (Dupont to Hailes, 21 Feb. 1777; John Hamilton to F. A. Pottle, 5 Sept. 1938). Dupont was an old friend of Lord Auchinleck's, and JB had known him well since childhood.

[2] Sir Gilbert Elliot (1693–1766), Lord Minto, had died on 16 Apr. He was succeeded as Lord Justice Clerk, not by Lord Auchinleck as Dupont had hoped, but by Thomas Miller of Barskimming, Lord Advocate since 1760 (*College of Justice*, pp. 500, 530).

[3] Dupont had written a letter of recommendation for JB, c. Nov. 1763, to Rev. Charles Chais (1701–85), Swiss theologian, Professor of Theology at Geneva, where Dupont made his acquaintance, and minister of the French church at The Hague, 1728–78 (J. P. de Bie and J. Loosjes, *Biographisch Woordenboek van Protestantsche Godgeleerden in Nederland*, 1919–49; NNBW vii. 295–96). Chais wrote voluminously on subjects ranging from theology to English customs, but his chief claim to remembrance is his founding of the House of Charity at The Hague (BU). He was a close friend of the Sommelsdyck family (From Lord Auchinleck [c. 26 Oct. 1763]). In likening Lord Auchinleck to Aristides 'the Just', and Maecenas, famous as a literary patron, Dupont is presumably referring respectively to Lord Auchinleck's skill as a jurist and his gifts to Chais of curiosities for his 'cabinet' (From Lord Auchinleck, 10 Dec. 1763). On one of his frequent visits to Chais in 1764 JB noted that the objects in his cabinet were 'very numerous' (Notes, 5 Jan. 1764). See also the postscript to this letter.

[4] Magdalen Scott (d. 1770), widow of William Scott, Professor of Greek, 1708–29, and Moral Philosophy, 1729–34, at the University of Edinburgh (*Scots Mag.* 1770, xxxii. 168; Sir Alexander Grant, *The Story of the University of Edinburgh*, 1884, ii. 322–23, 336). Magdalen le Mercier, a Frenchwoman, was Scott's second wife; the 'Miss Scott' mentioned here is their daughter, Magdalen, who was housekeeper to Dupont in his old age and was named sole heir in his will, which JB and Johnston witnessed on 20 May 1777 (Journ.; John Hamilton to F. A. Pottle, 5 Sept. 1938).

[5] John Boswell (1710–80), M.D., Lord Auchinleck's younger brother, practised medicine in Edinburgh; he was later President of the Royal College of Physicians. JB wrote to Johnston that he and his uncle were 'quite hand and Glove' and praised his hospitality, affectionate nature, and generosity (To John Johnston, 20 July 1763—Walker, p. 93). The professorship of chemistry sought by Dr. Boswell went to Joseph Black, formerly Professor of Chemistry at Glasgow (Grant ii. 395–97). Dr. Boswell told JB that he had not expected to obtain the professorship and that he was more disturbed that Miller had become Lord Justice Clerk instead of Lord Auchinleck (From Dr. John Boswell, 24 May).

[6] After Jean Calas (1698–1762) was executed on 9 Mar. 1762 for the murder of his son, his family, spurred on by efforts on its behalf by such writers as Voltaire, Grimm, and Diderot, appealed to higher courts, and his innocence was confirmed on 9 Mar. 1765. Friedrich Grimm organized a subscription in Apr. 1764 to raise money throughout Europe for the family by employing Louis Carmontelle and Jean-Baptiste-Joseph de la Fosse to design and engrave a print of the family to be sold to subscribers for six francs. The engraving appears in N. Weiss, 'A Propos de Calas, histoire de l'estampe de Carmontelle', *Bulletin de la société de l'histoire du protestantisme français* (1913) lxii. 261. On 31 Dec. 1766 Grimm presented the Calas family with just over 4,070 francs. The subscription was even more successful in Britain, where 1,200 engravings were sold and 16,338 francs (approx. £672 at the par of exchange—Beawes, p. [399]) sent to the Calas family through a Swiss banker, who received the money from English agents. A Mr. Balfour headed the drive in Scotland (Weiss, p. 264). For a description of the print, an account of the subscription, and a partial list of subscribers, see *Correspondence littéraire, philosophique et critique par Grimm, Diderot, Raynal, Meister, etc.*, ed. Maurice Tourneux, 1877–82, xvi. 352–63.

[7] Dupont's walking companion at the Cross was William Graham (d. 1775), eldest son of Nicol Graham of Gartmore and an advocate since 1756 (*Fac. Adv.* p. 87). JB met him by chance in Lausanne in Dec. 1764: 'I flew to see him and happy we were to meet. He was quite gay. It pleased me to see that an Advocate may be made a fine fellow' (Journ. 21 Dec. 1764). In a letter to Johnston, written the same day (Walker, p. 151), JB described Graham as 'a fine bold Highlander learned lively cordial'. Graham could have heard the story about the Duchesse d'Anville in France, where he had spent some months before going to Switzerland (Journ. 21 Dec. 1764).

[8] The Duchesse d'Anville, formerly Marie-Louise-Nicole de la Rochefoucauld (b. 1716), was the widow of Jean-Baptiste-Louis-Frédéric de la Rochefoucauld de Roye, Duc d'Anville, 1709–46 (*Dict. Nob.* xvii. 358–59, 365–66).

The Duchess was one of the prime movers in the Calas subscription and the largest contributor with 1,200 francs (*Correspondence littéraire* xvi. 356, 363).

⁹ Madame la Maréchale de Maillebois, formerly Marie-Emmanuelle d'Algère (b. 1692), was the widow of Jean-Baptiste-François Desmarets, Seigneur de Maillebois, a Marshal of France. Since the Maréchale's father was a nobleman, the Marquis d'Algère, Dupont may have confused her with her mother-in-law, Madeleine Béchameil, who came of a wealthy but untitled family. Mlle. Béchameil married Louis XIV's minister of finance, Nicolas Desmarets, who purchased the marquisate of Maillebois (*Dict. Nob.* vi. 834–35; DBF).

¹⁰ MS. 'mille' deleted before 'ames'

¹¹ MS. 'on on'

¹² MS. 'big' deleted before 'bigot'

¹³ Large assemblies of Protestants were held in defiance of the law throughout the Languedoc during the first half of the eighteenth century, many of them in Nîmes, particularly after Paul Rabaut, perhaps the best known fighter for the Protestant cause, was appointed pastor there in 1743. Around 1760 the persecution subsided, and religious assemblies became more regular and were held more openly (G. de Félice, *History of the Protestants of France*, trans. Henry Lobdell, 1851, pp. 474–81, 505–23). For a general account of Protestantism in eighteenth-century France, see Félice, bk. 4; for details of the religious assemblies held between 1743 and 1748 and the numbers attending them, see 'Un journal du désert, 1743–48', *Bulletin de la société de l'histoire du protestantisme français*, 1883, xxxii. 361–67.

To Matteo Buttafoco, Thursday 24 April 1766

Not reported. Sent 24 Apr. (Reg. Let.). Matteo Buttafoco (fl. 1731-94) was colonel of the French Royal-Corse Regiment; in 1764 he corresponded with Rousseau in an attempt to bring him to Corsica to 'be that wise man who should illuminate their minds' (*Corsica*, pp. 361–64; Joseph Foladare, 'James Boswell and Corsica', diss. Yale, 1936, p. 598 n. 1). JB met Buttafoco during his tour of Corsica, and thought he possessed 'the incorrupted virtues of the brave islander, with the improvements of the continent' (*Corsica*, p. 361). He showed JB his correspondence with Rousseau and allowed him to copy part of one of Rousseau's letters (M 6, p. 61; *Corsica*, pp. 362–63). We know nothing of the content of the present letter; very likely JB asked permission to print his extract from Rousseau's letter.

To Basil Cochrane, Thursday 24 April 1766

Not reported. Sent 24 Apr. (Reg. Let.).

To John Dick, Thursday 24 April 1766

Not reported. Sent 24 Apr. (Reg. Let.). David Boswell wrote to JB on 29 Apr. that he had forwarded the letter to Dick by way of Herries and Co., bankers in London.

To Alexander Donaldson, Thursday 24 April 1766

Not reported. Sent 24 Apr. (Reg. Let.). JB had asked Donaldson to order books for him from London (From David Boswell, 21 May). Alexander Donaldson (d. 1794) ran a bookshop in the Strand; he previously (1750–63) had sold books in Edinburgh, and kept his shop open there when he moved to London (see To Lord Mountstuart, 1 Jan. 1767, n. 1). Donaldson issued cheap reprints of books on which he considered the copyright expired, and campaigned against perpetual copyright (Maxted, p. 68; *Lit. Car.*, pp. 10–12, 92–101). JB described him as 'a man of uncommon activity and enterprise in Business, who has a smattering of humour and a tollerable Address. He is very obliging and entertains like a Prince' (Journ. 27 Oct. 1762).

To Pasquale Paoli, Thursday 24 April 1766

Not reported. Sent 24 Apr. (Reg. Let.). Count Antonio Rivarola forwarded the letter to Paoli (From Rivarola, 19 Sept.).

To Count Rivarola, Thursday 24 April 1766

Not reported. Sent 24 Apr. (Reg. Let.). Answered in From Rivarola, 19 Sept.

From Francis Gentleman,[1] Saturday 26 April 1766

MS. Yale (C 1365).

ADDRESS: To James Boswell Esqr.

Malton, Yorkshire, April the 26th 1766

SIR: Had I known your particular address I should have been much earlier to acknowledge the Honour of yours from Berlin, and to congratulate your safe arrival from those diversified scenes of travel which Mr. Boswell's sprightly Genius and solid Judgement, must make as profitable to his intellects hereafter as they were gratefull to particular feelings upon the different spots—per favour of Mr. Love[2] I endeavour to communicate a Poetical Epistle of mine to your perusal, and shall rejoice if it is found worthy your approbation[3]—there is a set of Fables in verse near finished at press, they are designed for his Royal Highness the Prince of Wales; if I am honoured with your direction a Copy of them shall also be laid before you.[4] Believe me to be, Sir, in the fulness of Respect and esteem, very much and faithfully, your most Humble Servant,

FRANCIS GENTLEMAN

[1] Francis Gentleman (1728–84), Irish actor, dramatist, and journalist, acted in Dublin, Edinburgh, and the English provinces before going to Glasgow at the end of the 1758–59 Edinburgh season. In Glasgow he met JB, who was attending the University, and dedicated to him his adaptation of Southerne's Oroonoko, published in Glasgow in Feb. 1760 (Lit. Car. pp. [284]–93). JB wrote to Gentleman from Berlin, 19 Sept. 1764, declining his offer to dedicate the second volume of his A Trip to the Moon to him, but he lent him money in later years (Journ. 30 July 1774). Constantly in debt, he 'struggled under sickness and want, to a degree of uncommon misery' for the last years of his life (Gent. Mag. 1784, liv. 958–59). For a detailed account of Gentleman's life and career, see Biog. Dict. of Actors vi. 138–53.

[2] James Dance alias Love (1722–74), comic actor and theatre manager—'the best Falstaff since Quinn', according to John Jackson, who was responsible for bringing him from Edinburgh to Drury Lane in 1762 (John Jackson, The History of the Scottish Stage, 1793, pp. 41–42; Lond. Stage

pt. 4, iii. 948). Love remained with the Drury Lane company till his death (Lond. Stage, Index). JB had known him well since 1758, and saw him frequently in London in 1762–63 (Journ. 21 Nov. 1762–28 July 1763 passim); earlier he was JB's 'second best friend' (To W. J. Temple, 16 Dec. 1758—MS. Pierpont Morgan). Mrs. Love was JB's mistress at least during 1761–62 (Earlier Years, pp. 77, 82, 98).

[3] Gentleman's 'Poetical Epistle' was published this year by T. Becket and P. A. de Hondt as Characters, an Epistle Inscribed to the Earl of Carlisle (see From Gentleman, c. late July, n. 2; From James Love, 27 June, n. 2). Gentleman had written to W. J. Mickle on 8 May and again on 7 Dec. 1764 (Osborn Collection) asking if he knew of JB's whereabouts. Presumably Mickle did not answer Gentleman's inquiries, and he relied upon Love to forward the Epistle to JB.

[4] Becket and de Hondt also published Gentleman's Royal Fables, which was sent to JB by messenger (From Gentleman, c. late July).

From Godfrey Bosville, c. late April 1766

Not reported. Received 2 May (Reg. Let.).

From Lord Marischal,[1] Wednesday 30 April 1766

MS. Yale (C 1953). Received 25 May (Reg. Let.).
ADDRESS: Mr. Boswell.
ENDORSEMENT: From The Earl of Marischal at Berlin,—received at Moffat 25 May 1766.

30 Avrile

SIR: I congratulate you on your safe arrival at home, after your agreable travels. I saw in the news papers that you was a Minister from England to the Corsicans, and also an Emissary from P. E—d; I believed neither,[2] but supposed you intended to make a present of that Iland to the Infanta:[3] now I learn you are to employ your time in the Law, which will be agreable to my Lord your father and I hope so to yourself, as well as profitable, being with the greatest regard your most humble and obedient servant,

M.

It was spread about, that the Corsicans did not apply to Mr. Rousseau for a Code of Laws, and that it was a trick of Mr. de Voltaire to give to Rousseau a needless trouble, and ridicule also. Please let me know the truth.[4] My humble service and best compliments to Lord Auchenlec.

[1] George Keith (?1693–1778), tenth Earl Marischal, was attainted for his participation in the Jacobite Rebellion of 1715 and spent many years in Spain before entering the service of Frederick of Prussia c. 1748. Pardoned by George II in 1759, he bought back his Scottish estates in 1763, only to sell them again when Frederick begged him to return to his service in Feb. 1764 (Cuthell i. 132; ii. 182–83, 187–88, 199–200). JB was in Utrecht when he received letters telling him that his father had arranged for him to travel with Lord Marischal, who would pass through Utrecht before continuing on his way to Potsdam (From Marischal, 25 May 1764; Journ. 18 June–2 July 1764). JB was overjoyed by the news: 'Never was a Man happier than I this morning. I was now to travel with a venerable Scots Nobleman who . . . had known intimately Kings and great men of all kinds, and could introduce me with the greatest advantage at courts' (Journ. 4 June 1764). JB and Marischal travelled together to Potsdam by way of the courts of Hanover and Brunswick (Journ. 18 June–2 July 1764).

[2] Marischal must have seen reprints of London newspaper items inserted by JB himself as part of an elaborate propaganda campaign designed to enlist sympathy for the Corsican cause (Earlier Years, pp. 266–68). One such paragraph

(Lond. Chron. 7–9 Jan. xix. 32) hinted that JB may have been sent as ambassador to Corsica; another (Lond. Chron. 21–23 Jan. xix. 73) that JB's intention had been to procure 'some kind of establishment of sovereignty' for Prince Charles Edward (1720–88), now in Rome. The paragraphs appearing in the Lond. Chron. between 7 Jan. and 15 Feb. are printed in Grand Tour II, Appendix D.

[3] Marischal told JB much about Spain on their journey to Potsdam, and had jokingly suggested that JB might become a colonel in the Spanish service, conquer Portugal, and marry a Portuguese infanta (Journ. 23 June, 2 July 1764; To Marischal, 2 Sept. 1764). The Portuguese Infanta at the time was Maria of Braganza, daughter of King Joseph Emanuel. She became Queen of Portugal in 1777 (Kings, Rulers, and Statesmen, ed. E. W. Egan, C. B. Hintz, and L. F. Wise, 1976, pp. 378–79).

[4] According to JB (Corsica, pp. 292, 361–62) Matteo Buttafoco, a Corsican officer in the French army, sent the original invitation to Rousseau to assist the Corsicans 'in forming their laws' after reading Rousseau's praise of Corsica in the Contrat social (bk. ii, ch. 10). Rousseau accepted the invitation and worked on a constitution for Corsica in 1765 but abandoned it when he was forced to leave Switzerland; the fragments

were not published until 1861. For an account of the negotiations between Buttafoco and Rousseau and the complexity of Buttafoco's motives in issuing the invitation to Rousseau, see *Boswell's Paoli*, pp. 24–28. Voltaire's friends believed that the letters from Corsica to Rousseau were written by Voltaire himself (Ernestine Dedeck-Hery, *Jean-Jacques Rousseau et le projet de constitution pour la Corse*, 1932, pp. 61–64), but Paoli denied Voltaire's claim 'that the invitation was merely a trick which he had put upon Rousseau' (*Corsica*, pp. 292, 364–66; L. G. Crocker, *Jean-Jacques Rousseau*, 1968–73, ii. 257–59). The question is still unresolved: see F. G. Healey, 'Rousseau, Voltaire, and Corsica; Some Notes on an Interesting Enigma', *Studies on Voltaire and the Eighteenth Century*, 1959, x. 413–19. As Frederick the Great's Governor of Neuchâtel, Marischal had granted Rousseau's appeal for asylum in 1762, and they had become close friends (Cuthell ii. 128–45).

To John Wilkes,[1] Tuesday 6 May 1766

MS. British Library, Add. MS. 30. 877. Sent 10 May (Reg. Let.). The draft, which is in JB's hand and signed (MS. Yale L 1290) differs slightly as noted below.

ADDRESS in draft: To Mr. Wilkes Esq., Paris.

HEADING in draft: To Mr. Wilkes.

Auchinleck, 6 May 1766

DEAR SIR: I shall never forget your humane and kind behaviour to me at Paris, when I received the melancholy news of my mother's death. I have been doing all in my power to comfort my worthy Father, and I thank God He is now greatly recovered. You suggested to me a very just reflection that it was lucky for My Father that He received the severe stroke when I was absent; for, had I been with him, He would have had nothing strong enough to divert his attention from an irreparable loss: Whereas my return from my Travels would be a new Object to him, and help to compensate for his great Misfortune. I have found the truth of what you said, and for once in my life have been of considerable use. I know you will not like me the worse that I have been doing my duty. I have often thought of you with affection. Indeed[2] I never admired you more than when you tried to alleviate my affliction; for whether it be from self interest or not, I set a higher value on the qualitys of the heart than on those of the head. I hope you are better, and am anxious to hear particularly every thing that concerns you.[3] I have a great deal to say to you: But you forgot to give me your address, and I think it would be[4] improper for me to write to you with our usual freedom, till I am sure that my letters can go safe. I inclose this under cover to Mr. Foley.[5] If you receive it, pray write to me immediatly. My Address is at The Honourable Lord Auchinleck's by Edinburgh North Britain. Believe me, Dear Sir, Yours as ever,

JAMES BOSWELL

P. S. I beg you may put[6] John Wilkes at the end of your letters, that they may not look like unsigned Title-Deeds.[7]

[1] Following his arrest for libel in 1763 John Wilkes (1725–97) withdrew to France, was expelled from the House of Commons, and spent almost five years in exile on the Continent. JB first met him at the Beefsteak Club in 1762 (Journ. 27 Nov. 1762), and they had seen much of each other in Italy and France, 1765–66; it was at Wilkes's lodgings in Paris that JB first heard of his mother's death (From G. Piccolomini, 23 Feb. n. 8). JB's notes for 30 Jan. record Wilkes's sympathy with his grief.

[2] Draft, 'Indeed' written above deleted 'for'

[3] Wilkes's correspondence reveals considerable mental anguish but no physical illness at this

time. On 15 Feb. he complained to Humphrey Cotes of his 'cruel situation' and the lack of 'one friendly star' to guide him (John Almon, *Correspondence of the Late John Wilkes*, 1805, ii. 224–25, 229). He was deeply in debt and convinced of the injustice of his exile (Almon, pp. 222–27). With the advent of the Rockingham administration in July 1765 Wilkes's hopes for a pardon had risen, and he arrived in England on 12 May to put his case before the Government. His efforts were unsuccessful, however, and he returned to France on 31 May (Charles Chenevix Trench, *Portrait of a Patriot: A Biography of John Wilkes*, 1962, pp.

199–201).

[4] Draft, 'not' deleted before 'be'

[5] Robert-Ralph Foley (c. 1727–82), later (1767) created Baronet, was head of the banking-house Foley et Cie in Paris until c. 1767 and banker in Paris for both JB and Wilkes (Herbert Lüthy, *La Banque protestante en France*, 1959–61, ii. 317; Almon, pp. 222–23, 225; Journ. 28 Jan.).

[6] Draft, 'put' written above deleted 'print'

[7] Wilkes had not signed his previous letters and continued to send them unsigned. In the draft an illegible deletion follows JB's last sentence.

To Robert Brown, Thursday 8 May 1766

Not reported. Sent 8 May (Reg. Let.).

To George Dempster, Thursday 8 May 1766

Not reported. Sent 8 May (Reg. Let.).

To Andrew Erskine, Thursday 8 May 1766

Not reported. Sent 8 May (Reg. Let.). Erskine wrote to John Johnston on 2 June that he had received JB's letter, but said nothing about its contents (Walker, p. 219 and n. 12).

To Heer van Sommelsdyck, Thursday 8 May 1766

Not reported. Sent 8 May (Reg. Let.).

To Heer van Zuylen, Thursday 8 May 1766

Not reported. Sent 8 May (Reg. Let.).

To Basil Cochrane, Saturday 10 May 1766

Not reported. Sent 10 May (Reg. Let.). Answered in From Cochrane, 14 May.

To Joseph Fergusson, Saturday 10 May 1766

Not reported. Sent 10 May (Reg. Let.). Fergusson (?1719–91) succeeded John Dun as tutor to the Boswell children in 1752 (*Earlier Years*, p. 20). In his 'Ebauche de ma vie', written for Rousseau, 5 Dec. 1764, JB described him as 'un fort honnet homme, mais dure et sans aucune connoissance de lesprit humain. . . . Il etoit dogmatiste sans jamais douter' (L 1107). In 1761 Fergusson was ordained and presented to the parish of Tundergarth, Dumfriesshire (*Fasti Scot.* ii. 223).

To John Gordon, Saturday 10 May 1766

Not reported. Sent 10 May (Reg. Let.). The Rev. John Gordon (d. 1777) since 1752 had been Principal of the College for Scottish Catholics in Paris (J. F. S. Gordon, *Ecclesiastical*

Chronicle of the College for Scotland, 1867, iv. 249). JB had seen him several times in January (Notes, 13–30 Jan.).

To William Graham, Saturday 10 May 1766

Not reported. Sent 10 May (Reg. Let.). William Graham (d. 1773) of Shaw, Dumfriesshire, was a close friend of John Johnston (Walker, p. 72, 2nd n. 2). JB saw Graham and his daughter Janet on his visit to Moffat in late May and early June (From Johnston, 21 May; From Janet Graham, [9] June).

To Lady Kames, Saturday 10 May 1766

Not reported. Sent 10 May (Reg. Let.). Answered in From Lady Kames, 21 May.

To Girolama Nini Piccolomini, Saturday 10 May 1766

Not reported. Sent 10 May (Reg. Let.). A reply to her letter of 14 Feb. which JB received 9 Mar. (Reg. Let.).

To John Waters, Saturday 10 May 1766

Not reported. Sent 10 May (Reg. Let.). John Waters (d. 1771), JB's banker in Paris, his elder brother George, and their nephews George and Laurent Woulfe, were members of an Irish Catholic family which founded a group of banks in Paris between 1740 and 1760. The Waters family was strongly Jacobite in sympathy: Charles Edward Stuart borrowed money from them to purchase arms for his 1745 invasion of Britain, and John Waters witnessed Clementina Walkinshaw's 1767 affidavit that she and Charles had never been married (David Daiches, *Charles Edward Stuart*, 1973, pp. 102, 299–300). The decline of the Waters banking-house coincided with the fading of the Jacobite cause. The house of George Woulfe, the last representative of the Waters family, was dissolved in 1772 (Herbert Lüthy, *La Banque protestante en France*, 1961, ii. 316–17).

From Basil Cochrane, Wednesday 14 May 1766

MS. Yale (C 800). Received 15 May (Reg. Let.).

ADDRESS: To James Boswel Esqre. att Moffat.

POSTMARK: [Edinburgh] MY 14.

Edinburgh, May 14th 1766

DEAR SIR: This Moment I had a letter from your Father who I am glade to know holds well out upon his Journey.[1] Inclosed you have a letter that came under Cover to me. I hope the Water Agrees with you.[2] I am, Dear Sir, Your most Humble Servant,

BASIL COCHRANE

[1] The letter has not been reported. Lords Auchinleck and Coalston held court in Aberdeen on 16 May after having been in Inveraray, Dumfries, Perth, and Stirling (*Scots Mag.* 1766, xxviii. 279).

[2] JB had been in Moffat, a well-known spa in Dumfriesshire, since 8 May (To John Johnston, 4 May—Walker, p. 215). He had taken the mineral waters there for his health when he was eleven and again when he was sixteen (*Earlier Years*, pp. 4, 21–22, 33).

From George Dempster, c. mid-May 1766

Not reported. Received 20 May (Reg. Let.).

From James Craufurd,[1] Friday 16 May 1766

MS. Yale (C 850). Received 25 May (Reg. Let.).

ADDRESS: James Boswell Esqr., Att the House of Lord Anchinbecks, [Edinburg *deleted; added in another hand*] by Air, Nh. Britain.

POSTMARK: [London] MA 20.

Rotterdam, 16 May 1766

DEAR SIR: I had in cource the pleasure of yours of 2d Febr. from Calais, I have recd. the three small cases sent me by Mr. Dick for you by Amsterdm. and have reshipt the Same in Capn. George Tod for Leith whose bill of loading for Same you have inclosed, as by the shape [of] some of the cases, they appear to be arms, you may find some difficulty to gett them enter'd, and they are now very strict att Leith, have therefore recommended to the Captain to take particular care of them, and you'll doe well to see him yourself immediately on his arrival, or make some friend att Leith speak to him, to gett them saved if possible.[2] He left this Some day's ago, and may Soon be with you, if the wind comes fair.[3] I have not yet recd. from Amsterdm. the accot. of charge of freight and duty inwards, when I doe shall send you Same, and draw on you for the value, it will always give me pleasure to doe you any Service in this country. I beg you'll offer my respects to your father and am with regard, Dear Sir, Your most Obedient, humble Servant,

JAMES CRAUFURD

James Boswell Esqr. Edinbr.[4]

[1] James Craufurd (d. 1766), merchant in Rotterdam since c. 1745 (*Doopregister der Engelsch Episcopaalsche Kerk, 1708–1818*), younger brother of Patrick Craufurd of Auchenames, who was M.P. for Ayrshire, 1741–54, and for Renfrewshire, 1761–68. The family was distantly related to the Boswells (From Lord Auchinleck, 23 July 1763; *Renfrew*, pp. 366–68). After James Craufurd's death, in July, three of his sons carried on his business until 1780, when the eldest, Patrick, sold his interest to his brother James, British agent in Rotterdam, for 40,000 guilders (*Gifte Boek* 102, Gemeente Archief, Rotterdam). At the par of exchange, 40,000 guilders were worth approximately £3,600 sterling (Beawes, p. 397).

[2] John Dick's letters of 22 Oct., 22 Nov., 22 Dec. 1765 show that the shipment originally consisted of books and two gun barrels; then a gun and a picture were added, and finally a gun barrel from Paoli. The first two gun barrels were made in the Spanish fashion by Francesco Leoni at Rosina, near Pistoia, Italy, and sold to JB for nineteen zecchini (M 107). Zecchini were Venetian gold coins, and nineteen, at the par of exchange, were worth about £9 sterling (William Gordon, *The Universal Accountant and Complete Merchant*, 2 vols. 2nd ed. 1765, p. 339). Paoli added this third gun barrel to the two pistols he had given JB in Corsica (*Corsica*, p. 317). The bill of lading has not been recovered. Importing arms without a licence was forbidden (Thomas Daniel, *The Present State of the British Customs*, 1752, pp. 5, 61), but presumably this prohibition did not extend to gun barrels alone. John Dick valued the original shipment at 278. 19. 9 Genoese lire (22 Oct. 1765), which, at the par of exchange, amounted to approximately £13 sterling (Gordon, pp. 371–72). George Tod (fl. 1766–69) was a shipmaster in Leith (*Edinburgh Directory*, 1774–79).

[3] Captain Tod's ship, the *Janet*, had arrived in Leith 'from Rotterdam with goods' by 26 May (*Edin. Even. Cour.* 26 May p. [2]).

[4] This appears to be a direction for the employee of Craufurd's firm who addressed the letter.

From Lady Kames,[1] Wednesday 21 May 1766

MS. Yale (C 1646). Received 25 May (Reg. Let.).

ADDRESS: To James Boswell Esqr., at Moffat, by Edinburgh.

POSTMARK: ⟨D⟩UNS⟨E⟩.[2]

Kames, may 21st[3]

SIR: Last nights Post brought me yours, my Daughter and I are very much honored by your kind rememberence of us, we have lived here in a state of widowhood ever since Lord Kames went upon the Circuit, he carryd allong with him Heron and my Son,[4] and we hope to see them all this Day, we should have been happy in our pleasent solitude had not[5] Mrs. Herons bad state of health distresd both of us, about ten Days ago she was endeed so bad, that I judged it necessary to carry her to Town, for Cullens advice,[6] and have his derections in my pocket, he seems positive she should derectly set out upon a long Ride not less then two stages a Day and would have her after that give Harrowgate watter a tryal, especially as she will probably travel in to England and that road is as convenient as any other, Doctor hunter I believe wishes her to drink Moffat watter,[7] which I am persueaded would do well, and I doubt not but she will encline some time of the Season to give it a tryal—but am afraid it may not be while you are there, you are I think lucky in haveing so good people as Doctor and Mrs. Hunter in such a place, I hope you do not ail any thing, and yet I can not guess what else should carry you to Moffat.[8]

That you are reading Law with an intention to apear at our Bar, gives me real pleasure, both as I am certain it must delight good Lord Auchenleck, and am[9] convincd you will do honor to your self and your country—I never did think you did very much ill, and I ever believd you would some, time or other, do a great deal of good.

I am busie in my Garden and in my House, makeing what I think improvements upon both, in particular I have fitted up what was my nursrey, in a very Cliver Room for my Husband, I have likeways made George a convenient apartment, and am happy in haveing them both to show upon there arival. Mrs. Heron begs you will accept of her gratefull complements, I hope I need not assure you that you possess the best regards of all my family and that I am with very much real good will, Dear Sir, Your obliged and obedient, humble Servant,

AGATHA HOME

Remember Mrs. Heron and me to Doctor and Mrs. Hunter. etc.

Thursday morning, since Mr. Herons arival Mrs. Herons rout seems to be alterd and you may possibly see them at Moffat I can not say when nor how long—all our Gentlemen salute you, young Percie and Oswald are to be with us to Day.[10]

[1] Agatha Drummond (1711–95), Lady Kames, daughter of James Drummond of Blair Drummond, succeeded to her father's estates on the death of her nephew in May of this year (William Fraser, *The Red Book of Menteith*, 1880, i. 468–69). In 1741 she married Henry Home (1696–1782) of Kames, Berwickshire, Scots advocate, raised to the bench of the Court of Ses- sion, with the style Lord Kames, in 1752, and appointed to the Court of Justiciary in 1763 (*College of Justice*, pp. 515–16). On 16 Oct. 1762 JB had characterized Lady Kames as 'a woman of good understanding and very well bred. Regulates her family with accuracy, and has in her house and at her table a remarkable degree of elegance. She has a great fund of humour, and a peculiar

turn of strong and brillant propriety of Expression' (Journ.).

[2] Dunse (Duns), Berwickshire, is a few miles north of Kames.

[3] MS. '22d'. Dated in error; Lady Kames added the postscript on Thursday 22 May.

[4] Patrick Heron (c. 1732–1803) of Kirroughtree had married Jean Home-Drummond (c. 1745–after 1782), daughter of Lord and Lady Kames, in 1761; JB had an affair with her in 1762 and Heron divorced her in 1772 (*Earlier Years*, pp. 78–79). In 1769 Heron was one of the founders of the ill-fated Ayr Bank, Douglas, Heron and Co., and from 1795 he was M.P. for Kirkudbright Stewartry (P. H. M'Kerlie, *History of the Lands and Their Owners in Galloway*, 1878, iv. 429–30; Joseph Foster, *Members of Parliament, Scotland*, 2nd ed. 1882, p. 179). Lord and Lady Kames's son was George Home (1743–1819) who, after a career as a merchant, succeeded his mother as sixth laird of Blair Drummond in 1796 (Fraser i. 469).

[5] MS. 'not' superimposed upon 'had'

[6] William Cullen (1710–90), appointed Professor of Chemistry at the University of Edinburgh in 1755, Professor of Physiology in 1766, and Professor of Medicine in 1773.

[7] James Hunter (d. 1792) M.D., appears twice in the register of sasines for Dumfriesshire during the period 1767–78 as 'doctor of medicine, Moffat, afterwards doctor, Edinburgh'. He is probably the Dr. Hunter who dined with JB on 8 July 1774 (Journ.); from that year he practised at

several addresses in Edinburgh until his death (S.R.O., *Index to Particular Register of Sasines for Sheriffdom of Dumfries and Stewartries of Annandale and Kirkcudbright*, No. 51, 1961, v. 76; *Edinburgh Directory*, 1774–92; Scots Mag. 1792, liv. 103).

[8] JB wrote to W. J. Temple on 17 May that he had come to Moffat 'to wash off a few scurvy Spots which the warmer climates of Europe had brought out on my skin'. JB was taking the waters somewhat ahead of the regular summer season (W. R. Turnbull, *History of Moffat*, 1871, p. 99).

[9] MS. 'am' superimposed upon 'that'

[10] Presumably Algernon Percy (1750–1830) and James Townshend Oswald (1748–1814), both students at the University of Edinburgh (*Selections from the Family Papers Preserved at Caldwell*, ed. William Mure, 1885, II. ii. 105; Namier and Brooke iii. 240, 269). Percy, second son of Hugh Percy (formerly Smithson), second Earl (later this year, first Duke) of Northumberland, made the Grand Tour of Europe the following year under the supervision of Louis Dutens, whom JB had known in Turin in 1765 (Journ. 9, 11 Jan. 1765); Dutens gives an account of the tour in his autobiography, *Mémoires d'un voyageur qui se repose*, 1806 (i. 240–353). Oswald succeeded his father, James Oswald of Dunnikier, close friend and correspondent of Lord Kames, as M.P. for Dysart Burghs in 1768 (Namier and Brooke iii. 240; A. F. Tytler, *Memoirs of the Life of Lord Kames*, 1814, i. 100–17).

From Lord Mountstuart, Thursday 29 May 1766

MS. Yale (C 717). Received 5 June (Reg. Let.).

ADDRESS: To James Boswell Esqre., of Auchinleck, at Edinburough, N. B.

FRANK: FREE, Mountstuart.

London, May 29th 1766

MY DEAR BOSWELL: I receiv'd a letter from you so long ago, as the 25th of March, which though I have neglected answering till now, yet was determin'd to do it from the minute I read it: You seem so desirous to keep up an acquaintance with me that I begin to think that you like me as well as you say, yet I think, the strange incoherency of your temper makes it dangerous to render that acquaintance intimate, you have fine old noble ideas, as I us'd to tell you; but the least thing alters you the last man you see, of whom you have an opinion carries away yours, add to that, I think you a little dangerous to trust, for you are glad to exult whenever you can lay hold of an opportunity and then every thing comes out to render that exultation the greater; but to lay aside this nonsense, I am much oblig'd to you for those expressions of warmth towards me in your letter and receive them as you desire I should; and be assur'd that in spite of your oddities I take you to be a most excellent good hearted man and as such, will do every thing in my power (without shew and affectation) to oblige you and whatever you may do, I shall always have that regard and friendship for you I had at Rome.[1] Sincerely yours,

MOUNTSTUART

[1] Lord Auchinleck had written to Dr. John Pringle informing him that he would permit JB to stay 'but one month in all at Paris' on his way home and asking Pringle to transmit the news to JB. Pringle did so and at the same time asked Mountstuart to write to JB urging him to obey his father's instructions as his 'patience was almost worn out' (From Pringle, 28 Jan.). JB received the letter from Mountstuart on 12 Jan. (Reg. Let.). He wrote what in Pringle's opinion was an ill-tempered reply to Mountstuart complaining of his lack of sympathy and saying that he would never ask a favour of him again (From Pringle, 28 Jan.). Pringle then advised JB to apologize to Mountstuart for his bad manners. When JB and Mountstuart met on 14 Feb. JB came close to an apology: he told Mountstuart he 'was sorry he had been offended' and asked him not to be angry any longer (Journ. 15 Feb.). He may have made a fuller apology in one of his March letters.

From John Dick, Friday 30 May 1766

MS. Yale (C 1005). Received 18 June (Reg. Let.).

ADDRESS: To James Boswell Esqr. at Messs. Harries Cochrane and C., London.[1]

POSTMARK: [London] IU 14.

NOTE in Dick's hand at foot of first page: James Boswell, Esq.

Leghorn, 30 May 1766

MY DEAR SIR, The pleasure I purposed to myself in hearing from you, was greatly diminish'd, when I learnt by your obliging Letter of the 10th past, that You had lost your Mother. Notwithstanding, these misfortunes are certain, yet when ever they happen Nature will shew it self, and in Spight of all our Philosiphy we cannot help grieving. As I cannot help interesting myself in everything that concerns you,[2] I most sincerely condole with You on this Melancholy Event.

The judgement You have had in conferring with none but the great Patriot on the Subject of our worthy Heroe, confirms me in the high opinion I had conceived of You, patience, and time bring about great events, if that Gent. comes again into play, as I doubt not he will, I hope You will by his means be able to assist these friends to Liberty, He must simpathise with poor Paoli—one great Genius must love another when situated in different Countrys, and both ingaged in the same Cause, that is one Strugling to preserve and the other to recover Liberty. I hope if You have any further Conferences with him, You will make a humble Offer of my poor Services, my Situation may enable me to be usefull, without being known or Suspected but by the Partys.[3] I own it would give me a real pleasure to be of the least use to these brave people.

Count Riverola is not yet returned from Sardania, Your Letter has been safely deliverd to his Secretary,[4] and I have sent You by a Mr. Vail who sett out yesterday,[5] another Copy of the book publish'd at Coltellini's,[6] also two Maps, but as yet I have not been able to find the one publish'd by Padre Lionardo, but have employ'd One to write to different places and make all imagionable enquierys about it. If I succeed in getting it, you may depend on my Endeavours to have it

Convey'd to Mess. Harries as soon as possible, the other book and the Maps are addressed to them.[7]

I hope you have receiv'd your things which I sent by way of Holland consigned to Mr. Craufurd.[8]

I have wrote to Mr. Hollford as you desire, praying him to enquire after your Letters, which you suppose laying there.[9]

Look into the 4th. Edition of the *Present State of Europe* page 411—where Tuscany is Treated of, and you'l find the Article about Mr. Dudley,[10] which is all I know about it.

I have only time to add Mrs. Dicks kindest Compliments to You,[11] and to Assure You, that I am always, with unalterable Regard, and true Esteem, My dear Sir, Your most affectionate Friend and Servant,

JOHN DICK

[1] The London branch of Coutts' bank from Dec. 1762–Jan. 1766. Robert Herries (1730–1815), a wine merchant with interests in Barcelona, Montpellier, and Valencia, and William Cochrane (fl. 1761– after 1778—E. H. Coleridge, *The Life of Thomas Coutts, Banker*, 1920, i. 116), the Coutts' uncle, formerly a woollen-draper in Edinburgh, were taken into the firm as partners resident in London in 1762. Cochrane, an old friend of Lord Auchinleck's, acted as JB's banker in London in 1762–63 (Journ. 26 Nov. 1762; 28 Mar., 28 May 1763). The firm retained the name of Herries, Cochrane, and Company until Jan. 1766, when Cochrane was forced to withdraw from the partnership because of insufficient financial experience (Sir William Forbes, *Memoirs of a Banking-House*, 1860, pp. 14–23). Herries, knighted in 1774 and M.P. for Dumfries Burghs, 1780–84, instituted the idea of 'circular notes', an early form of the traveller's cheque, to be used abroad. In 1770 he set up his own banking-house in St. James's Street (F. G. H. Price, *A Handbook of London Bankers*, 1876, reprinted 1970, pp. 74–75).

[2] MS. 'you' superimposed upon 'one'

[3] JB had no further conferences with William Pitt.

[4] JB's letter has not been reported but was sent on 24 Apr. (Reg. Let.). For Rivarola, see From John Dick, 25 Feb. and n. 2. His secretary and vice-consul in Leghorn was Giuseppe Balbi, whose signature appears on many of the reports of the Sardinian consul (Archivio di Stato, Turin).

[5] Unidentified. In the MS. 'Vail' seems to be written over 'Viel' or 'Veel'.

[6] The book is unidentified. Marco Coltellini (1719–77) owned the most important press in Leghorn and wrote librettos for operas by Gluck, Traetta, Mozart, and others (*The New Grove Dictionary of Music and Musicians*, ed. Stanley Sadie, 1980, iv. 586; Alfred Loewenberg, *Annals of Opera*, 1955, i. 272–345 passim).

[7] One map was probably that facing p. 1 of the *Histoire de l'isle de Corse*, 1749, attributed to J. F. Goury de Champgrand; JB acknowledged his indebtedness to this work in *Corsica* (p. xi). The map in JB's *Corsica* facing p. 1 is a large folding map engraved by Thomas Phinn of Edinburgh in 1768 from an unknown source. The two maps are the same size and alike in most respects, though certain topographical details such as mountains and forests are indicated with greater precision in the *Histoire* map. The map by Padre Leonardo Grimaldi da Campoloro (fl. 1764–90), whom JB had met in Corsica and whose *Discorso Sacro-Civile* JB commended in *Corsica* (pp. 177, 358), is not identified. Padre Leonardo may have prepared the large foldout map in *Giustificazione della rivoluzione di Corsica*, 1764; following the 607 pp. of text and preceding the map is a letter written from the parish of Campoloro by an anonymous Corsican, possible Padre Leonardo. Padre Leonardo, friend and confidante of Paoli, was made professor of philosophy and mathematics at the new university of Corte in 1764 and appointed theologian of the nation in 1790 (Louis Villat, *La Corse de 1768 à 1789*, 1925, i. 6 n. 7; Tommaseo, I. xi. 66, 329).

[8] See From James Craufurd, 16 May, n. 2.

[9] James Holford or Hollford (d. 1788), British consul in Genoa, 1761–77, with whom JB had discussed the Corsican cause in Dec. 1765 (*Gent. Mag.* 1788, lviii. 84; *Court and City Register*, 1761–77; Notes, 1 Dec. 1765). JB's letters have not been reported.

[10] JB quoted the passage from [John Campbell] *The Present State of Europe*, 1750, in *Corsica* (p. 20), citing Sir Robert Dudley's work as an example of what might be done with the harbour of Porto Vecchio, Corsica: 'The country about Leghorn was formerly a vile morass or rather quagmire, the noxious steams of which, rendered the air unwholesome; but by the skill and pains of an Englishman, Sir Robert Dudley son to Queen

Elizabeth's potent favourite, the Earl of Leicester, the soil was rendered habitable, the air much less unwholesome, and the port improved, so as to become the best in Italy.' The 4th edition, where the passage, with a few variations, appears on p. 411—p. 407 in the 1st ed.—(see JB's notes in *Corsica*, p. 20) was published in 1753.

[11] Dick married Anne Bragg (1720–81), daughter of Joseph Bragg of Somerset, c. 1746 (*Comp. Bar.* ii. 449; *Scots Charta Chest*, p. 285).

To Lady Grizel Cochrane, Saturday 31 May 1766

Not reported. Sent 31 May (Reg. Let.). Lady Grizel Cochrane (b. 1727) was the daughter of Thomas Cochrane, eighth Earl of Dundonald, and his first wife, Elizabeth Ker of Mariestoun (*Scots Peer.* iii. 360); thus she was JB's first cousin once removed.

From John Dun, c. early June 1766

Not reported. Received 3 June (Reg. Let.).

From Andrew Erskine, c. early June 1766

Not reported. Received 8 June (Reg. Let.). Erskine told Johnston he would answer JB's letter of 8 May before leaving England to join his regiment in Gibraltar (Andrew Erskine to John Johnston, 2 June).

From Pasquale Paoli, c. early to mid-June 1766

Not reported. Received 10 July (Reg. Let.). The letter was forwarded by John Dick (From Dick, 18 June).

To George Dempster, Tuesday 3 June 1766

Not reported. Sent 3 June (Reg. Let.).

To Andrew Erskine, Tuesday 3 June 1766

Not reported. Sent 3 June (Reg. Let.).

From Janet Graham,[1] Monday 9 June 1766

MS. Yale (C 1387). Received 9 or 10 June (Reg. Let.).

ADDRESS: To James Boswell esq'r. at Moffat.

NOTE (in the hand of John Johnston): Memorandum to buy Mr. Newal a Copy of Shenstones works Lond. Edition and send it out by the return of the Chaise to Moffat.[2]

Shaw, June, Munday th [9th]

DEAR SIR: I had not a face to tell you nor have I words to express the gratitude I feel for your kind visit and friendly behaviour, it gave me great pleasure bothe on enjoyment and reflection and I fancy was somthing like the joy that wou'd have warmed the Motherly breast of my worthy aunt had her eyes been blest with[3] the sight of you after so long an absence.[4] I found a strong inclination to stay a day or two longer at Moffat but for that and other reasons I suspected it was my duty to go home so you see how I have profited by your sense of duty Doctrine. I should certainly be ane adept in your reasonable systam had I the happiness to be some times with you, but I can see no chance for that till you come to Moffat again but alas I can see many chances I[5] may never see you. Honest Mr. Christipher is very happy at the tho'ts of seeing you[6] please my Complements to Grange if he don't write me John Dunwoody shall be informed[7] sister Joins in best complements to you[8] excuse improprietys from, Dear Sir, your sincere friend and much obliged,

JENNY GRAHAME

[1] Janet Graham (c. 1724–1805) was the eldest daughter of William Graham of Shaw (d. 1773), whose estate was in Dumfriesshire, near Heithat, a farm belonging to John Johnston of Grange (Walker, p. 72 n. 2). She wrote verse in Scots dialect, her best known composition being The Wayward Wife (To Johnston, 28 May 1763; Walker, p. 76 n. 1).

[2] JB and Johnston were together in Moffat from about 27 May till at least 9 or 10 June, when JB received this letter (From John Johnston, 21 May—Walker, pp. 216–17). Johnston is reminding JB to buy Shenstone's Works, probably in the two-volume London edition of 1764, when he returns to Edinburgh, and send the books back by the post-chaise, which left for Moffat from Pollock's, Cowgate-head every Friday (Edin. Almanack, 1767, p. 105). 'Mr. Newal' may be Adam Craufurd Newall (d. 1790—Scots Mag. 1790, lii. 362) of Polquhairn, who was JB's neighbour and dined with him at least twice at Auchinleck the following year (Journ. 13 Apr., 30 May 1767; Ayrshire, p. 287), or John Newall (d. 1793—Scots Mag. 1793 lv. 620), of Barskeoch, Kirkcudbrightshire, to whom JB was related through the Montgomerie-Cuninghames (information from N. S. Curnow; P. H. M'Kerlie, History of the Lands and Their Owners in Galloway,

1870-79, iv. 81), and whom he described as his 'good acquaintance' (Journ. 1 Oct. 1776).

[3] MS. 'with with'

[4] The aunt was probably Janet Anderson (d. 1763), sister-in-law of Janet's mother. Mrs. Anderson used to sit opposite JB in the New Church, Edinburgh (From Johnston, 28 Apr. 1763; Walker, p. 73 n. 3).

[5] MS. 'to that' deleted before 'I'

[6] Christopher Carruthers (d. 1811—Scots Mag. 1811, lxxii. 718) was a friend of both JB and Johnston (To Johnston, 28 May 1763—Walker, pp. 76–77). His father was John Carruthers, who inherited Hardriggs, near Annan, Dumfriesshire. He married Elizabeth Graham, possibly a relation of the Grahams of Shaw (A. S. Carruthers and R. C. Reid, Records of the Carruthers Family, 1934, pp. 26, 145–46). Johnston engaged JB as advocate for a member of the Carruthers family in 1768 and for Christopher Carruthers in 1779 (To Johnston, 14 Jan. 1768—Walker, p. 236; Consultation Book, 26 Jan. 1768; Journ. 17 July 1779).

[7] Unidentified. Dunwoody and its variations was an old family name in Dumfriesshire (C. L. Johnstone, Historical Families of Dumfriesshire, 1889, pp. 76, 121).

[8] Margaret Graham (From Johnston, 28 Apr. 1763; Walker, p. 72 n. 2).

From Sir John Pringle,[1] Tuesday 10 June 1766

MS. Yale (C 2295). Received 14 June (Reg. Let.).
ADDRESS: To James Boswel Esquire.

London, 10 June 1766

DEAR SIR, You have long known me a bankrupt in point of correspondence, and therefore if I have lately failed you in payment of epistolary debt, you can have properly no action against me. I acknowledge your letter, which you favoured me with some time ago. In answer to which, I think I may assure you that your father, my worthy friend, will do every thing for you that can be expected of an indulgent parent, so long as you continue to act such a part, as I flatter my self you have done since your return to Scotland. If he should not incline to your living separate from him, I dare say that he has good reasons for his so doing, tho' he has not yet communicated them to me: indeed as you have never to him mentioned any such scheme, I could not well have heard him express himself on the subject. It is likely that he inclines to have you under the same roof with himself not only for the comfort that a parent has in the more frequent company of his son which he enjoys by that means, but that the world may thereby see that he has not only freely forgiven all your youthful offences against him, but that he has a real satisfaction in your company, which he cannot express towards all his children.[2] Another advantage will be the opinion that all the world will have[3] of your improvement under so able a master in the Law. And I may add a fourth, the regaining of your character as a good natured man and a dutiful son, in keeping company with a father, who is one of the best of men, and who has lately laboured under grievous afflictions of different kinds.[4] I long to hear of your appearance at the bar.[5] You know how little I flatter, and yet how much I commended your talent for speaking. You know that in this country they are bewitched with eloquence.[6] Make first a figure at the bar at Edinburgh, that will get you employed in appeals, and if then you can acquit your self well at the bar of the House of Lords, you need not doubt of gaining high reputation, and rising high in your profession. If ever you get into Parliament, it will be a great advantage to have the character of being an eminent lawyer at home. I heartily wish you all happiness, Dear Sir, Your most affectionate, humble Servant,

JOHN PRINGLE

[1] Sir John Pringle (1707–82), Fellow, later (1772–78) President, of the Royal Society, best remembered as a pioneer in the reform of military medicine and sanitation. He had been physician to the Queen since 1761 and was created Baronet on 5 June. Pringle was a close friend of Lord Auchinleck's but was also kindly disposed towards JB and frequently served as intermediary between them.

[2] For Lord Auchinleck's younger sons, John and David, see From Mary Montgomerie, 27 Mar. n. 5. Lord Auchinleck was frequently impatient with John and had complained to JB the previous year that he was 'full of pride and illnature and disposed to follow no sort of Business that he is capable for' (From Lord Auchinleck, 16 Sept. 1765). David, for his part, wrote to JB, c. 12 Aug., complaining of his father's ill-treatment: 'I am afraid he seldom bestows a thought upon me. . . . I think it is hard I should be refused a small trifle to pay for learning musick as a small relaxation.'

[3] MS. 'imagine' deleted before 'have'

[4] Lord Auchinleck's most recent affliction was the death of his wife, 11 Jan. The previous year he had begun to suffer a suppression of urine, or strangury, which was to plague him for the rest of his life (From Lord Auchinleck, 16 Sept. 1765; John Ramsay, *Scotland and Scotsmen*, ed. Alexander Allardyce, 1888, i. 176 and n. 2; Journ. 2 Jan. 1768); in February David described his father as being 'in a Declining state of health' (From David Boswell, 3 Feb.).

[5] JB passed advocate on 26 July (*Fac. Adv.*).

[6] MS. 'eloquence' written above deleted 'speaking'

To Alexander Agnew, Monday 16 June 1766

Not reported. Sent 16 June (Reg. Let.). Alexander Agnew (d. 1768) of Dalreagle, Wigtonshire, advocate since 1754, was appointed Judge Advocate in March (*Fac. Adv.*; P. H. M'Kerlie, *History of the Lands and Their Owners in Galloway*, 1906, ii. 231). JB had met him while visiting the Herons of Kirroughtrie on 2 Oct. 1762 and dined with him the following day (Journ.).

To Mrs. James Hunter, Monday 16 June 1766

Not reported. Sent 16 June: 'Mrs. Hunter Moffat' (Reg. Let.). Mrs. Hunter was the wife of Dr. James Hunter, physician in Moffat (From Lady Kames, 21 May).

To Lord Mountstuart, Monday 16 June 1766

Not reported. Sent 16 June (Reg. Let.). Answered in From Mountstuart, 25 June.

From John Dick, Wednesday 18 June 1766

MS. Yale (C 1006). Received 10 July (Reg. Let.).
NOTE in Dick's hand at foot of first page: James Boswell Esquire.

Leghorn, 18 June 1766

MY DEAR SIR, I had the pleasure to write You the 30 May, since which, we have been enjoying a little quiet at Pisa, and return'd yesterday morning, soon after Capitano Santi sent me the Inclosed Letter from our Heroe,[1] who I find had not a few days ago, receiv'd Your Letter which I sent to Reverola's Secretary, as a Monsieur Nani of Bruxelles a sensible clever young man has been there,[2] and the General said he had not heard from you since you left Italy, but Captn. Santi says, I may depend your Letter will reach his hands safely. Riverola is not returned, but is expected soon.

I lately thought you would have had an Opportunity of talking again to the great Patriot, about the Corsican Affairs, but find as yet he does not come into the Ministry,[3] I own I heartily wish some thing could be done for these poor people, was that Proclamation only annulled,[4] it would be a great thing, they then would undoubtedly have englishmen engage with them, and take their Colours to Cruize, and Command their Privateers.

I have no news to send you from hence worthy your notice. Mrs. Dick's best Compliments wait on you, and I ever am with unalterable Regard and Esteem, My dear Sir, Your most Affectionate Friend and Servant,

JOHN DICK

[1] Apparently Captain Santi worked in Leghorn with Count Rivarola for the Corsican cause. He may have been Captain Santi of Vannina, who in 1763 had fought against the Genoese at Ajaccio ('Osservazioni storiche sopra le Corsica dell'Abbate Ambrogio Rossi', ed. L'Abbe Letteron, BSSC, 1902–03, fasc. 260–65, p. 97). Neither Dick's letter of 30 May nor Paoli's letter has been reported.
[2] Unidentified.
[3] The King asked Pitt to form a ministry on 7 July (To Pitt, 15 Feb. n. 1).
[4] For the proclamation, see To Pitt, 15 Feb. n. 8.

To William Flexney, Wednesday 18 June 1766

Not reported. Sent 18 June (Reg. Leg.). Flexney (c. 1731–1808), bookseller in London, had published *Letters between the Honourable Andrew Erskine and James Boswell, Esq.* in 1763 (*Dict. of Printers*; Journ. 12 Apr. 1763).

To Beatrix Maxwell, Wednesday 18 June 1766

Not reported. Sent 18 June: 'Miss Maxwell at Pollok' (Reg. Let.). Beatrix Maxwell (1716–95), daughter of Sir John Maxwell of Nether-Pollok, Bt. and his first wife, Lady Anne Carmichael, lived at Pollok House, Eastwood parish, Renfrewshire (William Fraser, *Memoirs of the Maxwells of Pollok*, 1863, i. 94–99). Her half-sister, Jean, was married to JB's cousin, James Montgomerie of Lainshaw (From Mary Montgomerie, 27 Mar. n. 2).

From Lord Cardross, Thursday 19 June 1766

MS. Yale (C 672). Received 23 June (Reg. Let.).
ADDRESS: To Mr. Boswell at Lord Auchinleck's at Edinburgh.
POSTMARK: BATH 2 ?0 IV.
ENDORSEMENT: From My Lord Cardross.
NOTE at the foot of the letter: *Mr. Boswell.*

Walcot near Bath, June 19, 1766[1]

Lord Cardross, continued in London after he had the Pleasure of Seeing Mr. Boswell—till the Beginning of May. Since that time he has been at this Place. The Embassy to Poland he Believes is delayed for Some time and Perhaps Altogether, nothing at present Seeming to be Attended to but the Domination of Particular Parties or of Individuals.[2]

Lord Cardross will keep in Peto, till Another Occasion his Conversation with Mr. Boswell—a few months may bring About Events that may Alter the face of things.[3] My Lord Desires his best Compliments to Lord Auchenleck and all friends at Edr. He goes to Burton Mr. Pitts[4] Soon upon a Visit who left Bath about a Month ago as he Could not Drink the Water.[5]

[1] The family was staying at Walcot, Somerset, where Cardross's father, the tenth Earl of Buchan, died the following year (*Chatham Corres.* ii. 426).

[2] The post of resident in Poland went to Thomas Wroughton (*Roy. Kal.*, 1767, p. 97). Factions in the Commons and the lack of a strong leader to bring order to the government had undoubtedly caused the delays in such appointments. For a summary of the political turmoil at this time, see Steven Watson, *The Reign of George III, 1760–1815*, 1960, pp. 117–20. Later this year Cardross was offered the post of secretary to the embassy in Spain but declined it because the newly appointed ambassador was a commoner (*Chatham Corres.* ii. 426 n. l; *Life* ii. 177).

[3] Presumably Cardross was keeping *in petto* JB's request for government assistance to Corsica (To Pitt, 19 Feb. and n. l).

[4] MS. 'Pitts;'

[5] Pitt was at Burton Pynsent, the estate in Somerset bequeathed to him by Sir William Pynsent (*Chatham Corres.* ii. 303 and n. l). One of Pitt's titles on being raised to the peerage on 4 Aug. was Viscount Pitt of Burton Pynsent.

From Godfrey Bosville,[1] Tuesday 24 June 1766

MS. Yale (C 172). Received 27 June (Reg. Let.). One of a group of letters from Bosville found with a discarded wrapper on which JB had written, 'Godfrey Bosville Esq.'
ADDRESS: To James Boswell Esqr. at Lord Auchinlecks, near Edinburough, Scotland.
POSTMARK: WAKEFIELD.

Gunthwait, 24th June 1766

DEAR SIR: I ought to make you the Earliest Acknowledgements and beg your Pardon, for I dare say The Man after Gods own heart has troubled you more than he did the Philistians: I thought you might inadvertantly have packd him up in your Portmanteau, but to my great Confusion, in looking over some things to bring here and others to lock up, I found him layd Snug in the Dust upon the Top of the Bureau in the Room next the Garden: I examind my Servants, but Nobody, that Wicked Varlet, had receivd him, and carefully layd to rest instead of giving him to me.[2] One of Mrs. Bosvilles Sisters that you have not seen a Miss Wentworth from

Bath has been at my House in Great Russel Street about three weeks, and Sir Thomas Wentworth returnd with her and took my Daughter along with him, they are got to Bretton, for about 5 miles from hence we met 5 returnd Post horses and having askd at the Turnpike house who they had carryd, we were surprisd to hear it was them for I expected Sir Thomas would have stayd longer:[3] We lengthend out our Journy by going to Cambridge, where I was educated, so that we got home only last Saturday.[4] I expect William down as soon as the Muster is over, for the 21st of next Month he will be of Age,[5] it is likewise Miss Julias Birthday.[6] As we come down late we shall stay late: and I wish you woud visit this Old Mansion in your way to London, if you are a Lover of Antiquities it will please you.[7] What a different Life one leads here from London, there one hears all the News and Politics in Abundance, not that I mind them much I have seen such Revolutions: I remember when the King of Prussia was the Greatest Rogue breathing, and when afterwards we were to spend Millions for him: I remember when we were in the Same generous humour to the Queen of Hungary, and we are not yet convincd that all these Kings and Princes our Faithful Allies value us no more than we do a Coal Pitt, for what we can get out of it to bear our Expences.[8] I coud wish for just such another man to be Prime Minister of England as your friend Paschal Paoli. All our Family desire their best Compliments to you and to Lord Auchinleck. Mr. Wilks who made so much noise has been in Engld. and went as Quietly out of it as I coud have done: Nay, it is said he thot. it, if not the pleasantest, at least the Safest way to be gone.[9] Billy is still desirous to be a Captain in North America.[10] I am, Dear Sir, Your most obedient Servant,

GODFREY BOSVILLE

[1] Godfrey Bosville (1717–84) of Gunthwaite, near Wakefield in the West Riding of Yorkshire, whom JB regarded as his 'chief', though no connection between the families has ever been proved. JB first met Bosville and his family at Bosville's house in Great Russell Street, London, on 15 Feb. and described him as a 'plainlooking Man but a judicious knowing worthy Gentleman' (Notes, 16 Feb.). They corresponded regularly; in 1768 JB remarked that Bosville 'talked quite like one of his letters' (Notes, 15 May 1768). For an account of the Bosvilles, see The Fortunes of a Family, 1927.

[2] The misplaced book was the anonymous History of the Man after God's Own Heart, first published by Robert Freeman, London, in 1761 and variously attributed to Peter Annet, Archibald Campbell, John Noorthouck, and David Mallet; though the phrase appears elsewhere in the Bible, the title is almost certainly taken from I Samuel 13: 14. The work was denounced generally for its scathing attack on King David, and in 1766 a two-volume defence of him was published: Samuel Chandler, A Critical History of the Life of King David.

[3] Bosville's wife Diana (1722–1795) was a member of the Wentworth family of Bretton,

Yorkshire. Passages from her 'Book of Extracts', ranging in date from 1758 to 1793, which show her to have been a well-read woman with a wry sense of humour, are printed in A. M. W. Stirling, A Painter of Dreams, 1916, pp. 7–62. Diana Bosville's sister Annabella (1742–c. 1781), formerly of Bath, now lived in London; her wealthy brother Sir Thomas Wentworth (1725–92), Bt. was Sheriff of Yorkshire, 1765–66. The Bosvilles's elder daughter Elizabeth Diana, or 'Di' (1748–89), whom JB had much admired in February and praised in a letter to W. J. Temple on 17 May as 'extremely sensible', married Sir Alexander Macdonald of Sleat, Bt. in 1768 ('Pedigree of Wentworth, of Elmsall, Bretton, and Baron Wentworth of Nettlesed' in Joseph Foster, Pedigrees of the County Families of Yorkshire, 1874, ii; Fortunes of a Family, pp. 119–21, 126–30; Notes, 16 Feb.).

[4] After studying at Westminster School Bosville had been admitted pensioner at St. John's, Cambridge, in 1734 and matriculated in 1735. He left in 1737 before completing his degree to study at the Inner Temple (Alum. Cantab. I. i. 183).

[5] Bosville's elder son William (1745–1813), whom JB had met on 18 Apr. 1763 (Journ.). He

served in the Coldstream Guards from 1761 until his father's death, when he retired from the army to manage the family estates. Preferring life in London to life as a country squire, he spent most of his time at his house in Welbeck Street and gained a reputation as a *bon vivant* (*A Painter of Dreams*, pp. 70–115; *Army List*, 1762–75). On 20 Aug. the 1st and 2nd battalions of the Coldstream Guards were moved out of their headquarters at St. James's and dispersed among barracks in various parts of London (Daniel Mackinnon, *Origin and Services of the Coldstream Guards*, 1833, ii. 437).

6 Bosville's younger daughter Julia (1754–1833) married, in 1780, William Ward, later (1788) third Viscount Dudley and Ward of Dudley (*Fortunes of a Family*, pp. 143–44).

7 The Bosvilles acquired the manor of Gunthwaite in the fourteenth century through the marriage of Thomas Bosville to Alice, heiress of John de Gunthwaite; it had existed in some form since very early times (Joseph Hunter, *South Yorkshire: The History and Topography of the Deanery of Doncaster*, 1828–31, ii. 343–50). In Godfrey Bosville's day the house was built of stone below, black and white timbers above, and in his own 'Memoirs of the Bosville family', written in 1765, Bosville notes the motto 'Try and Tryst' over the door and a crest—a bird on one foot—presumably that of the Gunthwaite family, on the hall chimney. After Bosville inherited the manor of Thorpe in the East Riding in 1773 the family moved to the more comfortable Thorpe Hall, leaving Gunthwaite to tenants. In the nineteenth century the old manor-house was almost entirely pulled down, though the enormous tithe barn—said to be a sixteenth-century structure—for which Gunthwaite is still famous, survived and stands behind the farmhouse built on the site of the old Hall (*Fortunes of a Family*, pp. viii, 23–27, 51, 110; *A Painter of Dreams*, pp. 68–69). In 1981 Gunthwaite still belonged to the Macdonald family.

8 In the War of the Austrian Succession (1740–48) England supported Maria Theresa, with £300,000, against Frederick the Great, but in the Seven Years' War (1756–63) England supported Frederick with both troops and money. By a treaty of 11 Apr. 1758 George II agreed to pay Frederick £670,000 (*Gent. Mag.* 1742, xii. 66; *Annual Register*, 1758, i. 40).

9 See To Wilkes, 6 May, nn. 1, 3.

10 William got his wish: he served as a captain with the Coldstream Guards in North America from Apr. 1776 to May 1777 (Mackinnon ii. 26).

From Lord Mountstuart, Wednesday 25 June 1766

MS. Yale (C 718). Received 30 June (Reg. Let.). 'London', in Mountstuart's hand, on a fold of the wrapper.

ADDRESS: To James Boswell Esqre. of Auchinleck at Edinburgh, N.B.

POSTMARK: [London] FREE [2]6 IV.

FRANK: Mountstuart.

London, june 25, 1766

My Dear Boswell: I am very glad to find that we are at last come to a good understanding once more and thank you very much for your many expressions of regard and friendship, for your dedication also, I take it very kindly that you should think of me, shall leave it entirely to your judgement wheither you think me great enough personnage for such a thing but still am always mindful of your friendly attention. With regard to arms I have got no print of them my seal is the best thing to copy if you should want them and besides you may find my fathers arms in any book of Peerage and there is only the difference of a Viscount's Coronet.[1] You know I hate writing so without Ceremony I shall leave off, only begging you first before you dedicate your Theses to me to[2] consider wheither you had not better give this publick testimony of your regard to some of those many great men in various ways, your Friends; such as a Statesman Mr. Pitt. a great Warriour, Genl. Paoli. a great Genius Rousseau. a larn'd man Johnson.[3] a Compound of them all, L'abbatè Barretti I believe his name is, I mean your Venetian hero.[4] and some of those worthy Domenican Fryers would not[5] be amiss,[6] but I shall leave you to your stately meditations walking up and down the room, and tell you that I have a great regard for you and will shew it on all occasions. Yours sincerely,

MOUNTSTUART

[1]JB dedicated his printed law thesis—*Disputatio Juridica Ad Tit. X. Lib. XXXIII. Pand. De Supellectile Legata*—one of the requirements for admission to the Faculty of Advocates, to Mountstuart. The dedication, which describes Mountstuart as 'viro nobilissimo, ornatissimo . . . atavis edito regibus, excelsae familiae de BUTE spei alterae', 'a man most noble, most illustrious . . . sprung from royal pregenitors, second hope of the exalted family of Bute' is surmounted by the engraved arms of the Earls of Bute, with the coronet of a viscount (Mountstuart's courtesy title) substituted for that of an earl (*Lit. Car.* pp. [22]–26).

[2]MS. 'wheither' deleted before 'to'

[3]MS. 'Johnson' superimposed upon 'Johnston', which was corrected from 'Johtnson'

[4]Giuseppe Marc'Antonio Baretti (1719–89), critic and miscellaneous writer, friend and trans-lator of Johnson, was a controversial figure in Italy by the time JB first met him in Venice on 8 July 1765 (*Earlier Years*, p. 230; Notes, 8 July 1765). He left Venice shortly afterwards (Baretti to Johnson [c. 18 July 1765]), and by the autumn of 1766 had settled in London, where he had become well known for his *Dictionary of the Italian and English Languages* in 1760.

[5]MS. 'not' superimposed upon 'be'

[6]JB wrote to John Johnston on 11 May 1765 that he had 'travelled through Italy under the Protection of the Dominican Friers'. In Milan he had met Padre Guiseppe Allegranza, a Domini-can of the Convent of Saint-Eustorgue, who had made arrangements for JB to visit convents in the course of his travels through Italy (Walker, pp. 165–66, 165 n. 9). JB had been especially friendly with some Irish Dominicans in Rome (From Michael Brenan, 31 July 1768).

To James Love, Thursday 26 June 1766

Not reported. Sent 26 June (Reg. Let.). Possibly this letter had to do with the poem Francis Gentleman had asked Love to send to JB (From Gentleman, 26 Apr.).

To 'Dun Taylor', Thursday 26 June 1766

Not reported. Sent 26 June (Reg. Let.). The recipient has not been identified. He may have been either James or Alexander Dun, Edinburgh tailors who were admitted burgess in 1736 and 1737 respectively (*Roll of Edinburgh Burgesses or Guild-Brethren, 1701–1760*, ed. C. B. B. Watson, 1930, p. 60).

From James Love, Friday 27 June 1766

MS. Yale (C 1788). Received 2 July (Reg. Let.).

ADDRESS: To James Boswell Esqr., at Lord Auchinleck's, Edinburgh.

POSTMARKS: ISLEWORTH, 28 IV.[1]

Richmond, June 27th, 1766

DEAR SIR: The enclos'd came to my hand some time ago, but I hope there will be no mischeif ensue from my having suffer'd a multiplicity of Business to delay your receiving it.[2] I hop'd to have giv'n you some Account of Captain Mant but have never seen him since—You may depend upon it when he appears I will execute your Orders.[3]

You see, by the papers, the King has honour'd me with Authority to perform here—indeed I have receiv'd the greatest indulgence from him—and as the new Palace here will soon be built and the Court reside at Richmond there is no doubt but my Theatre will flourish abundantly—We have now no reason to complain.[4]

I wish You Sir, most ardently a vast portion of good health—there is little more to be added to your present possessions—good Sense and good fortune.

Remember me always as a Being that sincerely prays for your peace and happiness—and ever must remain Your unalterable friend and most obedient, humble Servant,

JAMES LOVE

[1] Isleworth, where Love had been living since the inception of his theatre (see n. 4), is two or three miles west of Richmond. JB visited him there on 18 Sept. 1769 (Journ.).

[2] Love's letter is written on the wrapper of Francis Gentleman's *Characters, an Epistle Inscribed to the Earl of Carlisle* (From Gentleman, 26 Apr. n. 3).

[3] Presumably Thomas Mante (b. c. 1733—MS. Baptismal Register, St. Faith's Havant, Hants.), adventurer, writer of military works, double agent for the French and British governments in the 1770s, and candidate for the identity of Junius (Frank Monaghan, 'A New Document on the Identity of "Junius"', *Journal of Modern History*, 1932, iv. 68–71; H. B. Bates, 'Some Notes on Thomas Mante', ibid. pp. 232–34). He served as lieutenant in the 77th Highland Foot in North America from 1762–64, and was put on half-pay when the regiment was disbanded (*Army Lists*, 1763–85); in 1772 he published a *History of the Late War in America*, the work for which he is best known and on the title page of which he described himself as 'Assistant Engineer during the Siege of the Havanna, and Major of a Brigade in the Campaign of 1764'. James Love was not Mante's only theatrical connection: he was acquainted with Garrick, and carried letters between him and Jean Monnet, director of the Opéra-Comique, on several occasions in 1767 (*Letters DG* ii. 561 n. 4; *Private Correspondence of David Garrick*, ed. [James Boaden] 1831–32, ii. 508, 512, 515–21). We do not know where or how well JB knew Mante, nor what JB's 'Or-

ders' were. After 1769 Mante spent much of his time in France as sheep-farmer and spy, mistrusted by both the French and the British. For Mante's activities in France after 1769 and his connections with Benjamin Franklin, see C.-L. Lopez, 'Benjamin Franklin and William Dodd: A New Look at an Old Cause Célèbre', *Proceedings of the American Philosophical Society*, 1985, ciiix. 260–67.

[4] The New Theatre (sometimes called the Theatre Royal or the Theatre on the Green) was modelled after the Theatre Royal, Drury Lane. It attracted many of the most distinguished players of the day and brought prosperity to the town, though George III seems not to have attended a performance there until 1791 (H. M. Cundall, *Bygone Richmond*, 1925, pp. 55–56). The opening of the theatre, 'by Authority', had taken place on 15 June 1765 (*St. James's Chron.* 15–18 June 1765, p. [4]) with Love speaking a Prologue written by Garrick for the occasion, though Love did not obtain a licence from the Lord Chamberlain until 5 July (*Letters DG* ii. 446 and n. 1; *Lond. Chron.* 3–5 July, xx. 22). The old palace, built by Henry VII and enlarged and embellished by succeeding sovereigns, was allowed to fall into decay after the Civil War and, although George III commissioned Sir William Chambers to draw up plans for a new palace at Richmond in 1769, the town authorities refused to sell the King land for the purpose, so the palace was never built (Janet Dunbar, *A Prospect of Richmond*, 1966, pp. 62, 90 and passim).

To Sir John Pringle, c. late June 1766

Not reported. JB congratulated Pringle on the baronetcy he had received on 5 June (From Pringle, 10 Feb. 1767).

To Jean-Jacques Rousseau, c. late June 1766

Not reported. See David Hume to Rousseau, 22 July: 'I send you a Letter from Mr Boswel, which came to my hand about three Weeks ago. He complains to me very much of your Silence' (*Letters DH* ii. 68).

From Heer van Sommelsdyck, 1 July 1766

MS. Auchinleck Boswell Society. Received 31 July (Reg. Let.)

Gorcum,[1] ce i[er] Juillet 1766

MONSIEUR ET TRES CHER COUSIN: Ma femme m'a envoyé ces jours passés de la haye celle que vous m'avés fait l'honeur de m'ecrire le 6 d'avril dernier, et que j'ai recu dans le temps que je desesperois de recevoir jamais plus de vos nouvelles; je vous remercie du detail de vos voyages, et suis ravi de vous savoir echappé aux *stilettos* et au poison a genes, car j'avoue que vous avés joué gros jeu, pour satisfaire votre curiosité:[2] vous me faites tort de me croire faché contre vous j'avoue que j'ai été choqué du mepris avec lequel vous traities ma nation, car sur cet article je suis aussi fier qu'on ecossois, mais c'est sans rancune contre vous, car it est libre a chacun de penser comme il veut, par exemple vous n'aimés pas mon pays, ce qui est ordinaire a votre nation, et moy j'ai tres mauvaise opinion de vos montagnes d'ecosse, mais nous n'en devons pas etre moins bons amis pour cela.[3] Je suis extremement charmé d'apprendre que monsieur votre digne pere se porte mieux que vous ne l'avés trouvé a votre arrivée, j'espere que cela continuera longtemps et vous prie de l'asseurer de mes tres humbles respects; recevés mes tres sinceres complimens de felicitation sur la charge de conseiller que vous allés remplir,[4] j'espere que vous y gouterés tous les agremens et la satisfaction que vous en pouvés desirer, mais j'avoue que c'est une vocation qui ne seroit pas de mon gout quoique j'aye etudié pour cela. A present nous avons chacun des vocations si differentes, et si fixes chacun dans notre pays que je crains que nous ne nous revoyons de longtemps; vous serés sans doute surpris de l'endroit d'ou je date ma lettre, mais c'est que je suis a mon poste; et pour vous mettre au fait apprenés les changemens qui se sont fait parmy nous a la majorité du prince,[5] le comte de degenfeldt a été fait colonel commandant d'un des bataillons allemands d'orange,[6] et moy colonel commandant du regiment de villegas hollandois, en gardant ma compagnie aux gardes jusqu'a ce que l'on puisse me donner un equivalent dans le regiment ou je suis, et comme le regiment est en garnison ici, je commande dans la ville;[7] Monsieur de maasdam a cedé sa compagnie des gardes dragonds a son fils ainé qui par la se trouve lieutenant colonel, et le cadet de ses fils le petit henry vient d'etre fait enseigne a la suite dans le regiment des gardes hollandoises.[8] Je vous aurai beaucoup d'obligation de m'envoyer l'arbre genealogique que vous me promettés, et serois tres charmé si je pouvois faire connoissance avec le parent ecoissois que vous m'anoncés;[9] mais s'il vient ce été je crains qu'il aura tout le loisir de s'ennuyer, car la cour n'y etant pas la haye est deserté, et il n'y trouvera personne de la famille; il n'y a a la haye que ma femme et mon enfant, encore n'y seront ils pas longtemps; puisque dans trois ou quatre jours je vais les chercher pour aller en zelande; et je serai tout l'eté en zelande, ou a la campagne, ou au regiment;[10] madame de wilhem est a sa campagne avec tous ses enfans, et son mary est a aix la chapelle,[11] Monsieur pieck de roslen suit le prince dans tous ses voyages,[12] et monsieur et madame de maasdam sont avec tous leurs enfans a son gouvernement de breda,[13] ainsi vous voyés que toute la famille est eparpillée voila tout ce que je puis vous mander d'un endroit aussi solitaire que celuy ou je me trouve. je suis tres sensible a votre attention pour ma femme et mon enfant, mais je ne les ai pas veu de deux mois, cependant par les lettres que j'en recois j'aprends qu'ils se portent bien: il ne me reste plus que de me recommander dans la continuation de votre amitié, vous priant de me croire avec la plus parfaite estime et consideration, Monsieur et tres cher Cousin, votre tres humble et tres obeissant Serviteur,

F. C. VAN AERSSEN VAN SOMMELSDYCK

[1] Gorkum or Gorinchem, in South Holland province, was the headquarters of Sommelsdyck's battalion (see n. 7).

[2] On 9 Dec. 1765 (Walker, p. 193) JB had written to John Johnston describing his reception in Genoa: 'I have had my own fears at Genoa for being just arrived from Corsica where I was very intimate with their terrible Ennemy Paoli. I am pretty certain that the Noble Merchants of this despicable Republic would have been very well pleased to have had a Stiletto slipt into my back, or to have got me into Prison and very quietly given me a little poison.'

[3] In his letter of 25 Jan. (MS. Auchinleck Boswell Society) Sommelsdyck complained that JB, in a letter written from Venice, 21 July 1765, had insulted Holland and his Dutch kinsmen deeply.

[4] JB passed advocate on 26 July (Earlier Years, p. 292).

[5] See From Sommelsdyck, 14 Mar. and n. 5.

[6] Friedrich Christoph (1721–81), Count von Degenfeld-Schomburg, was a German general in the Dutch army and Dutch envoy to Vienna, 1767–81. He was married to Louise Susanna, Countess van Nassau, whom JB had found 'Sweet and handsom amiable' when he dined at her house in The Hague (NGHN, [1764–65] 3rd ser. iii. 726–27; [1768–69] viii. 171, 770; De Nederlandsche Heraut [1890] vi. 177; Notes, 23 Dec. 1763). The Dutch army at this period consisted largely of German troops and other foreign mercenaries (Simon Schama, Patriots and Liberators, 1977, p. 57).

[7] Since 21 May 1762 Sommelsdyck had been colonel-commander of the Regiment de Villegas, an infantry regiment in the Dutch service consisting of two battalions, garrisoned at Gorkum and Schoonhaven respectively. He was appointed major-general in Aug. 1772, and retired from the army in June 1781 (information supplied by Dr. J. G. Kerkhoven, Royal Dutch Military Museum, Leiden). In Mar. 1772, shortly after he had been inscribed in the nobility of Holland with the title of Baron van Aerssen (14 Jan.—Adelsarchief iii. 176–77), Sommelsdyck purchased the regiment from General de Villegas (From Sommelsdyck, 11 Dec. 1772).

[8] Aarnout Joost (1718–85), Baron van der Duyn, Heer van Maasdam, trusted councillor of Willem V, and Governor of Breda. He had been colonel of the Regiment Gardedragonders (Dra-goon Guards) since 1744, and was promoted to general on 10 May 1771 (information supplied by Dr. J. G. Kerkhoven, Royal Dutch Military Museum, Leiden). The eldest son of his marriage to Anna Margaretha van Aerssen, Sommelsdyck's eldest sister, was Adam François (1745–93), who had reached the rank of major-general at the time of his death from wounds suffered at the Battle of Meenen in Flanders. Maasdam's youngest son, Willem Hendrik (1755–1832), joined the Dutch Guards as ensign at the age of eleven and rose to the rank of lieutenant-general (NNBW iv. 540, 542, 544–46). JB spent much time with Maasdam in 1764 and enjoyed his company: 'I dined at Maasdam's quite the gay foreign Cousin. He has taken a great liking to me' (Journ. 4 June 1764).

[9] JB's genealogical chart has not been reported. See From Sommelsdyck, 14 Mar. n. 1 for their relationship; To Sommelsdyck, 21 Mar. 1767 for records at Auchinleck. The relative may have been JB's uncle, Dr. John Boswell.

[10] Perhaps Sommelsdyck's regiment moved to Ecluse, Zeeland, for the summer, as it did two years later (From Sommelsdyck, 8 Feb. 1768). In any case, the Sommelsdyck family owned the Castle of Graayestein on the island of Schouwen, one of the larger islands in the Schelde estuary in the province of Zeeland; presumably the family spent the summers there (information supplied by A. E. M. Hibberink, Director, Algemeen Rijksarchief, The Hague).

[11] Maria Philippina Jacoba (b. 1735), daughter of Willem Hendrik Pieck, Heer van Zoelen, and Elisabeth Louise van Aerssen (1714–40), Sommelsdyck's late sister, was married to Daniel Adriaan le Leu de Wilhem de Bantousel, Heer van Besoyen, counsellor in the court of feudal tenure of Brabant and director of the Surinam Company (W. de Haas, 'Het Geslacht Pieck', Heraldieke Bibliotheek, [1882] n.s. iv. 172; Nieuwe Nederlandsche Jaarboeken, 1766, p. 1258). They had three daughters: Pauline, Elisabeth, and Henriette (b. 1759, 1761, 1764—Hague Archives), and their country-house was 'une demie lieue' (about one and a half miles) 'de la haye' (From Sommelsdyck, 25 Sept. 1764). JB had been 'easy and happy' at their house (Notes, 1 Jan. 1764).

[12] Anne Frans Willem Pieck (1736–?75), Heer van Zoelen, brother of Mme. de Wilhem and chamberlain to the Prince of Orange (NNBW ix. 800). Always prone to make a fool of

himself (From Sommelsdyck, 25 Sept. 1764), Pieck gambled away his fortune and estates, took ship for the Indies in 1775, and was never heard from again (W. de Haas, 'Het Geslacht Pieck', *Heraldieke Bibliotheek* [1882] n.s. iv. 173). JB was amused by his 'inclinations errantes' (To Sommelsdyck, 10 Sept. 1764).

[13] In addition to the sons cited in n. 8 the Maasdam children included Anna, Cornelia, and Willem (NNBW iv. 540).

From Lady Elizabeth Macfarlane, c. early July 1766

Not reported. Received 8 July (Reg. Let.). Lady Elizabeth Macfarlane (1735–94), sister of Andrew Erskine and Thomas Erskine, sixth E. of Kellie, was the wife of Walter Macfarlane of Macfarlane, the eminent antiquary. The year following Macfarlane's death in June 1767 she married Alexander Colville, seventh Lord Colville of Culross. JB found her 'a woman of noble figure and majestic deportment, uncommon good sense and cleverness' (Journ. 30 Oct. 1762), and later told her that he had once thought seriously of marrying her (Journ. 23 Nov. 1776). She remained JB's constant and helpful friend throughout his years of residence in Edinburgh (see, for example, Journ. 19 July 1769, 25 June 1774).

To Godfrey Bosville, Tuesday 8 July 1766

Not reported. Sent 8 July (Reg. Let.).

From William McQuhae and George Reid,[1] Sunday 14 July 1766

MS. Yale (C 1885). Received 15 July (Reg. Let.). The letter is in McQuhae's hand.
ADDRESS: To James Boswell Esqr., at Lord Auchinlecks, Edinr.

Barwharry, 14 July 1766

DEAR SIR, Mr. Reid and I have been much importun'd to apply to you in favour of a young man in Ochiltree parish who wants to get into the Excise. His name is Hugh Morton[2] he has been bred a Mason and is now employed at Auchencruive house.[3] He has always had a good Character, and we are both perswaded he would be honest and faithful in any office in which he was Employed. If your acquaintance with any of the Commissioners of Excise can Without too much trouble to yourself be of any use to him in getting him put on the List for being instructed— it would be a great favour to us both.[4] We are, Dear Sir, your most Obedient and humble Servants,

WILLIAM MCQUHAE, GEORGE REID

[1] Rev. William McQuhae (1737–1823) succeeded Joseph Fergusson as tutor to the Boswell boys. McQuhae was only slightly older than JB, and for a time, JB regarded him as one of his closest friends, writing his 'Journal of My Jaunt, Harvest 1762' for him as well as for John Johnston (*Earlier Years*, p. 83); but the friendship did not survive JB's three years of Continental travel (Journ. 16 Feb. 1763; Walker, p. 13 n. 7). McQuhae was now minister of St. Quivox parish, Ayrshire, where he remained for the rest of his life (*Fasti Scot.* iii. 66–67). Rev. George Reid (1696–1786) had been Lord Auchinleck's tutor and was married to Lord Auchinleck's first cousin, Jean (or Jane) Campbell. He was now minister of Ochiltree parish, which included much of the Auchinleck estate. Barwharry (or Barquharie) was his farm (*Fasti Scot.* iii. 62, Walker, p. 32 n. 3; *Ayrshire*, p. 145).

[2] MS. ?'Mot' deleted before 'Morton'

[3] Hugh Morton may have been a relative of the stone masons Andrew Morton and his son James who lived in the village of Auchinleck; Andrew died in 1784 of injuries suffered while working in a quarry (From James Bruce, 3, 24 May, 1784). The mansion at Auchencruive, St. Quivox parish, was nearing completion (*Ayrshire*, p. 271); it belonged to the eminent London

merchant Richard Oswald, who, in 1782, was principal British commissioner at the peace conference ending the American Revolution.

[4] JB's granduncle, Basil Cochrane, though now a commissioner of customs, had formerly been a commissioner of excise (To Cochrane, 31 March). JB also knew George Frazer, deputy auditor of the excise (From Frazer, 4 Apr. n. 1), but he recommended that Morton remain a mason (To Reid and McQuhae, 23 July).

To John Dun, c. mid-July 1766

Not reported. See From Dun, 29 July: 'I was favoured with yours and had the pleasure soon after of learning that you are quite well.'

To Lady Elizabeth Macfarlane, Friday 18 July 1766

Not reported. Sent 18 July (Reg. Let.).

From Baroness von Spaen,[1] Tuesday 22 July 1766

MS. Yale (C 2522). Received 26 Aug. (Reg. Let.).

ADDRESS: To James Boswell Esq., at The Honourable Mylord Auchinleck, by Edinburgh, Great Britain.

POSTMARK: [London] AV 16.

a belle vue, ce 22 Juillet 1766

En revenant d'une petite coursse que j'avois fait, pour aller voir une de mes Amies, avec laquelle j'ai passé quelque tems j'ai trouvé votre lettre monsieur qui a eté plus de deux mois en chemin, elle est datée du 20 Avril, et n'est arrivée ici, que le 26 de Juin, si celle si a le meme sort il faudra convenir que notre correspondance, n'est guere exacte, et que les nouvelles que nous nous mandons, n'aurons pas le merite de la nouveaute, il faut esperer mon Ami, qu'une fois notre commerce epistolaire bien etabli, que les contrarietes diminueront, et que nos lettres voyageront avec plus de celerité, je le desire, car sans vous dire une fadeur, ou un Complimen je serois bien aise d'avoir de tems en tems de vos nouvelles.

Vous voila donc revenú de toute vos coursses, et etabli aupres de Mr. votre pere, c'est penser en bon fils, que de rester aupres de lui pour le consoler autant qu il depend de vous, de la perte d'une epouse dont le portrait que vous m'en faites, me fait croire qu'il est aussi affligé que merite qu'on soit apres se voir separé d'une femme qui avoit un juste droit, sur tous les Sentiments, du plus tendre attachement et la plus haute estime et veneration, je vous sai bien bon gre que vous regrettez une mere aussi respectable, et si digne de vivre dans votre memoire, imitez mon ami son exemple vous vivrez heureusement, et votre fin Sera comme le Sien[2]—un Commencement d'une heureuse eternité. C'est une belle perspective que cette esperance mais ne suis je pas trop grave? Non, mon Ami, ne veut pas etre philosophe seulement, mais aussi philosophe Chretien, la mort de sa bonne Mere lui a donné ce desir, du moin j'espere que j'ai deviné juste.

La peintúre que vous me faites de la Campagne ou vous vivez six mois de l'année, me donneroit envie d'y aller, si les circonstances me favorisoient, mais mille petits riens, qui font un grand, joints ensemble, me contrarient, ce ne seroit pas seulement vous mon ami que je voudrois y aller voir, non, Mr. votre pere y auroit bien sa part, un homme comme vous me le depeignez, merite qu on desire de le connoitre, un homme que preche le vertu, par son exemple merite bien plus qu'on fasse un voyage, pour lui rendre hommage et profiter de ces leçons, que les hommes de ce siecle, qui ne font aimer les vertús ni par leurs écrits, ni par leurs exemple, ils font briller leurs esprit et leurs amour propre au depens[3] de leur jugement, et souvent qu'en faveur, de l envie d'ecrire, et de paroitre singulier, et monte plús haut que le reste des humain! Que leurs chute sera grande! Qu'un jour ils[4] seront humilie, sur tout sils ont ecrit contre leurs propre conviction, dites moi[5] mon Ami que dois je penser de Mr. Rousseau, la lettre que Mr. hume a ecrit en france a son sujet, donne une idée bien meprisable, de cet ecrivain![6] Commant! Il n'auroit pas respecte les liens de l'amitie, il auroit mal agi avec Son ami, et son protecteur, au point qu'il le nomme un Serpent nouri dans le sein, j'avoue mon ami que j ai la plus grande curiosite de savoir le fonds de cette histoire faites moi le plaisir de me l'ecrire, je vous en aurez une obligation infinie.

Vous etes bien aimable mon ami de nous laisser une petite lueur d'esperance de vous revoir un jour, je puis vous dire avec verite, que je serois enchantée de pouvoir causer quelque tems avec vous ainsi, je serois bien aise que vous vintes a la Campagne, la lesprit est plus libre que dans la foule des villes, on y est moins dissipé, on court moin de risque de voir interompre une conversation. Enfin mon ami, il y auroit bien des choses que vous aurez vu dans vos voyages, avec un oeuil, philosophique un peu critique sur lesquels je voudrois vous questionner, je vous croise asse impartial ami de la verité, pour pouvois penser apres vous, sur tout apres que nous aurions fait quelques discutions sur le sujet, venez donc mon Ami encor une fois revoir ce païs, engagez Mr. votre pere de vous accompagner, ce petit voyage mattra quelque distraction a sa douleur, qu'il vienne voir Zelide, qu'il juge si c est un caractere qui convient a son fils, si L'esprit de Zelide peut faire le bonheur de ce fils, (le coeur de cette aimable personne est bon) j'en suis sure![7] Si vous etes capable de lui faire sentir la superiorite, et la Solidite de votre esprit, qu'elle en soit convincue, qu'elle en agisse en consequence, alors, elle pouvoit vous rendre heureux. Voila mon ami ce que j'en pense, son mariage avec le marquis Italien n aura pas lieu, la religion y met obstacle, dans son païs, le mariage ne pouroit jamais etre legitime.[8]

Le Comte de Degenfelt va a vienne en qualité d'envoye extraordinaire de leurs hautes puissances, il partira avec sa femme le mois prochain. Je suis tres faché de ce depard, c est la plus proche parente que jai a la haye, et nous etions lie d'amitie, ainsi j'y perds beaucoup.[9]

Mr. Reynst a ete fait Lieutenant Collonel.[10] Il est loge ici, et me prie de le rapeller a votre Souvenir, Mr. de Spaen est tres sensible aux assurances d'amitie dont vous l'honnorez, et vous prie d'agreer les siens,[11] mon fils vous assure de ces respects, il ira au mois de Septembre a l'accademie a Utrecht, nous y avons loue une maison pour lui ou il tiendra manage avec deux de ces Cousins, sous le Gouvernement de Mr. Linder, son Gouverneur, qui a l honneur d etre connu de vous,[12] adieu mon Ami soyez heureux, soyez content, et n oubliez pas vos Amis, sur tout pas celle qui a l honneur d etre, Monsieur, Votre humble et obeissante Servante,

B. DE SPAEN NEE C. DE NASSAU

¹ Elisabeth Agnes Jacoba (1724–98), Baroness von Spaen, daughter of Willem Hendrik, Count van Nassau La Lecq. She married Alexander Sweder (1703–68), Baron von Spaen, a German officer in the Dutch army, as his second wife in 1749 (BW, 1969 ed. vi. 273). The von Spaens had entertained JB several times at their house in The Hague, 1763–64 (Notes, 30 Dec. 1763, 24 Apr. 1764; To Baroness von Spaen, 28 Mar. 1764). He also dined with them at their country estate of Bellevue when he and Lord Marischal stopped in Cleves on their way to Berlin (Journ. 19 June 1764). JB corresponded regularly with the Baroness between 1764 and 1773.

² MS. 'la Sienne' changed to 'le Sien'

³ MS. final 'd' of 'depend' changed to 's'

⁴ MS. 'il'

⁵ MS. 'n' of 'mon' changed to 'i'

⁶ Rousseau's paranoid suspicions of his patron Hume had burst into the open in a letter dated 23 June 1766. Hume felt he must take steps to protect his reputation, so in late June and early July he denounced Rousseau's eccentric behaviour and ingratitude to the Baron d'Holbach in two letters intended for dissemination to their friends (Hume to Mme. le Présidente de Meinières, 25 July 1766, *New Hume Letters*, p. 150). Not only did d'Holbach read out extracts from these letters in his own salon (*Corres. Rousseau* xxix. 306) but, according to Mme. du Deffand, d'Alembert also circulated extracts from them around Paris (Mme. du Deffand to Walpole, 9 July 1766, *Corres. HW*, iii. 89). In early July d'Alembert and his friend, Julie de Lespinasse, had jointly asked for and received a detailed account of the quarrel from Hume, and this had been read aloud at Mlle. de Lespinasse's salon the day she and d'Alembert received it (From Mlle. de Lespinasse and d'Alembert to Hume, 6 July 1766, in *Letters DH* ii. 408–9; From Hume to d'Alembert, 15 July 1766, *New Hume Letters*, pp. 136–41; From d'Alembert to Hume, 21 July 1766, *Letters DH* ii. 412–15). It seems clear then that the news of the quarrel quickly spread far and wide; see also, for example, a letter from La Condamine to l'Abbé Trublet, written from the château de Bassy on 13 July 1766: 'Il y a à Paris (et, dit-on, entre les mains du baron d'Holbach) une lettre de M. Hume, j'ai parlé à gens qui l'ont vue' (*Corres. Rousseau* xxx. 85). For JB's role in the Rousseau-Hume quarrel, see F. A. Pottle, 'The Part Played by Horace Walpole and James Boswell in the Quarrel between Rousseau and Hume', *Horace Walpole: Writer, Politician, and Connoisseur*, ed. W. H. Smith, 1967.

⁷ Isabella Agneta Elisabeth van Tuyll van Serooskerken (1740–1805), familiarly known as Belle de Zuylen, or Zélide, the pseudonym she adopted for her writing, had been one of JB's matrimonial possibilities since their first meeting in Utrecht in Oct. 1763 (Journ. 30–31 Oct. 1763; *Holland*, pp. 293–97). Although JB was strongly attracted to Zélide, he had equally strong reservations about her. He had written to John Johnston on 11 May 1765 (Walker, p. 166 and n. 12) that she was 'well looked and has £8000', but was also 'an universal Genius and rather too learned', and this ambivalence is reflected in their correspondence.

⁸ Among her many suitors was François-Eugène Robert (1720–90), Comte de Bellegarde, Marquis des Marches et de Cursinge, a French officer in the Dutch army with an estate in Savoy. His mother was English, a sister of Gen. James Edward Oglethorpe (Godet i. 71, 97). Belle was willing to marry Bellegarde, but as Protestants her family objected to his Roman Catholicism, and Belle would not marry without their approval. In 1771 she married her brothers' former tutor, Charles-Emmanuel de Charrière (Godet, pp. 75–85, 166–171).

⁹ From Sommelsdyck, 1 July, n. 6. The Countess von Degenfeld-Schomburg and the Baroness von Spaen were distant cousins since both were descended from Willem Hadriaan, Count van Nassau (NNBW i. 1368–69; A. W. E. Dek, *Genealogie van het Vorstenhuis Nassau*, 1970, pp. 151–52, 158–60).

¹⁰ Jean Lucas Reynst (1730–92), army officer in the Dutch Footguards who reached the rank of colonel in 1774 and major-general in 1787 (information supplied by J. G. Kerkhoven, Director, Royal Dutch Army Museum, Leiden). He was a close friend of the von Spaens' from 1760 until his marriage in 1769 (J. E. Elias, *De Vroedschap van Amsterdam*, 1905, i. 371; From Baroness von Spaen, 9 Apr. 1770). JB thought him 'un Homme du monde tout à la mode, tout du ton' when he dined with him in Lucca (To Baroness von Spaen, 3 Oct. 1765).

¹¹ JB had great respect for von Spaen, having been impressed by his account of his involvement in a plot to free Frederick the Great from his father's control, for which he had been imprisoned briefly in Potsdam before entering the Dutch army in 1732 (BW, 1969 ed. vi. 273; Notes, 30 Dec. 1763; *Holland*, pp. 97 n. 5, 111 n. 3; To Baroness von Spaen, 28 Mar. 1764).

¹² The von Spaens' son, Willem Anne (1750–1817) later became an important Dutch official and historian (NNBW v. 781–83). In his letter of 7 June 1764 to the Baroness JB mentioned meeting Willem's tutor but did not identify him.

To George Reid and William McQuhae, Wednesday 23 July 1766

MS. Yale (L 1097). A copy. Sent 24 July (Reg. Let.). JB sent the letter to James Bruce, the Auchinleck overseer, who delivered it to Reid at Mauchline on 28 July (From James Bruce, 29 July).

HEADING: To the Reverend Messrs. George Reid and William McQuhae.

Edinburgh, 23 July 1766

REVEREND SIRS: I have received your letter of the 14 Currt. asking me to use my interest towards getting Hugh Morton into the Excise. I dare say He is a very deserving young man; but as your letter informs me that He is allready a mason, I think He has a much better business than the one He wishes for. I would therefore have you translate for him Horace's excellent Satyre

> Qui fit Maecenas ut nemo quam sibi sortem
> Seu ratio dederit, seu Fors objecerit illa
> Contentus vivat? etc.[1]

In so doing You will serve the young man more than in making Him a Gauger.[2] I am, Reverend Sirs, etc.

[1] Horace, *Satires* I. i. 1–3. trans. Philip Francis, 1746:
> Whence is it, Sir, that none contented lives
> With the fair Lot, which prudent Reason gives.

[2] In Scotland, where smuggling was carried on regularly with impunity and confidence by people in all walks of life from bakers to Justices of the Peace, the excise officer, or 'gauger', was held in contempt, and outwitting him was an honourable exploit (H. G. Graham, *The Social Life of Scotland in the Eighteenth Century*, 5th ed. 1969, pp. 526–30; see also Burns, *Epistle to Dr. Thomas Blacklock*, ll. 19–24 and *The De'il's Awa wi' th' Exciseman*). At this time the salary of an officer of the lowest rank was £35 a year (*Edin. Almanack*, 1767, pp. 81–82).

From John Dun, Tuesday 29 July 1766

MS. Yale (C 1124). Received 31 July (Reg. Let.).

ADDRESS: To James Boswell younger of Auchinleck, Esqr., at Edinr.

Auchinleck Manse, 29th July 1766

DEAR SIR: I was favoured with yours and had the pleasure soon after of learning that you are quite well.[1] Afflictions are useful, especially to young men, in many respects. I heartily wish you Joy of the Gown which I suppose you have put on by this time of this Day[2]—the utile et dulce may you find in it.[3] Providence, kind to you, determined your grandfather in opposition to much discouragemt. to commence Lawyer and by integrity application and skill of the Law attended with Prudence forthought and a becoming regard for Religion your family is become great.[4] May it by the same means become greater and greater still; and I hope it will, when a lively imagination and eloquence too, always captivating and productive of esteem but never more so than now shall have proper opportunities of displaying themselves.

May that wisdom which is from above guide my dear friend in everything. He[5] will be so good as to make my respectful Compliments to Lord Auchinleck and tell His Lordship that the box, its key, and contents came safe to hand.[6] Health dwells in my little family at present. I am, Dear Sir, Your affectionate, humble Servant,

JOHN DUN

[1] A letter to JB from James Bruce, overseer at Auchinleck, dated 19 July, identifies the affliction as JB's 'Corsican trouble (the Ague)', a recurrence of the malaria he had contracted in Corsica (*Corsica*, pp. 352–75). Bruce's letter of 29 July mentions JB's restoration 'to some considerable State of health'.

[2] JB passed his examination in Scots Law on 11 July and the public examination on his thesis on 26 July; he put on his advocate's gown on 29 July (*Earlier Years*, pp. 291–92, 529–30). The ceremony of putting on the gown was held at noon, as it still is (information supplied by Sheriff Ronald Ireland, Q.C.).

[3] 'useful and pleasurable'. In the eleven days before the Court rose at the end of the Summer Session JB earned eight guineas for his work on ten causes (Consultation Book).

[4] Having attended the University of Glasgow, JB's grandfather, James Boswell (1672–1749), 'with great difficulty' and chiefly through the intercession of his mother's cousin Lord Whitelaw, one of the judges of the Court of Session, obtained his father's consent to study Civil Law at Leiden. After his years there (1695– 98), 'Old James' passed advocate and under Lord Whitelaw's auspices built up one of the most extensive practices of the day. He married Lady Elizabeth Bruce, daughter of the second Earl of Kincardine, in 1704. Together, through frugal living, they did much to restore the family's fortunes, clearing off the debts with which the estate had been encumbered when James succeeded to it in 1713 and making considerable additions to the property (information from the unpublished second volume of J. J. Boswell's *History and Genealogical Tables of the Boswells*, gen. table 23, Fondazione Sella, Biella, Italy). See also *Earlier Years*, p. 9.

JB described his grandparents' strong regard for religion in the first draft of the 'Ebauche de ma vie' ([5 Dec. 1764]) which he sent to Rousseau. His grandfather served as a ruling elder in the General Assembly of the Church of Scotland (Journ. 19 Sept. 1778), and Lord Auchinleck always showed a decent respect for religion.

[5] MS. 'Plea' deleted before 'He'
[6] We know nothing about the box or its contents.

From Francis Gentleman, c. late July 1766

MS. Yale (C 1366). Received 25 July (Reg. Let.).
ADDRESS: To James Boswell Esqr.

[Malton, Yorkshire]

SIR: I take the opportunity of a Person going from hence to send as a small token of my respect a copy of *Royal Fables* lately Published by me; they have been extremely well received at Court and I hope will prove acceptable to Mr. Boswell's delicate Taste and Judgement[1]—I did myself the Honour to transmit thro' favor of Mr. Love, about two Months since, a Poetical Epistle of mine to the Earl of Carlisle[2]—shall I not be troublesome? If I am impute it to my desire of shewing that perfect esteem I have Sir for your many amiable Qualifications—I should be happy, as I know not his address if my respectfull compliments might pass through you to Mr. Hamilton of Airshire your fellow student at Glasgow:[3] believe me to be, sir, with unflatt'ring esteem, your most obliged and obedient, Humble Servant,

FRANCIS GENTLEMAN

[1] Gentleman's *Royal Fables* was published by T. Becket and P. A. deHondt in June, and one of the fables, 'The Cynic and Fashion', was reprinted in the June issue of *Gent. Mag.* (xxxvi. 284, 287). On the fly leaf of the copy Gentleman sent him JB wrote: 'James Boswell, 1766. A present from the Authour Vide the Contents', the last presumably referring to Gentleman's inscription, which appears at the end of the Table of Contents, and reads: 'The Author of these Fables as a mark sincere tho' small, of most respectfull Esteem presents this Copy to James Boswell, Esqr. of North Britain.' JB's copy of the *Fables* is now at Yale.

[2] Frederick Howard (1748–1825), fifth Earl of Carlisle, whose seat, Castle Howard, was five miles from the town of Malton, in the North Riding of Yorkshire, where Gentleman lived for four years, c. 1764–c. 1768. Gentleman was always in search of noble patrons, but the dedication of this piece, the first he signed his name to, went unrewarded (*Biog. Dict.* vi. 144–45).

[3] John Hamilton (1739–1821) of Sundrum, Convenor of Ayrshire for thirty-six years and Vice-Lieutenant of the county for several years (Ayr and Wigton I. i. 247–48). He and JB had been college mates at the Universities of Edinburgh and Glasgow (University of Edinburgh Matriculation Lists; W. I. Addison, *Matriculation Albums of the University of Glasgow*, 1913, p. 59). The estates of Auchinleck and Sundrum were not more than ten miles apart, but JB and Hamilton were not close friends. In 1767 there was 'a kind of aukwardness' when he and JB 'who had formerly travelled pretty much in the same way, and had now taken so very different roads, met again' (Journ. 16 Apr. 1767).

To Edward Aitken, Thursday 31 July 1766

Not reported. Sent 31 July (Reg. Let.). The Rev. Edward Aitken (c. 1695–1771), minister in Castlegarth, Newcastle, 1736–71 (*Fasti Scot.* vii. 516; *Scots Mag.* 1771, xxxiii. 559). He had been Lord Auchinleck's tutor at one time, and JB's brother John had been placed under his care in Newcastle earlier in the year (From John Boswell, 10 Feb.; From Mary Montgomerie, 27 Mar. n. 5). John was now at a house kept by Dr. John Hall, just outside Newcastle (From David Boswell, 30 May).

To Alexander Lockhart,[1] ?Summer 1766[2]

MS. Yale (L 390). A draft.
HEADING: To Alexander Lockhart Esquire.

[Edinburgh]

SIR: I am very sorry I was out of town when you was good enough to send me[3] an invitation to dine with you. I returned only last night.

I beg leave to assure you and hope you will not look upon it as a ceremonious compliment which means nothing that I shall be proud to be known to Mr. Lockart and to deserve his regard.[4]

I have sought the acquaintance of great and distinguished men wherever I could. To be near such is of infinite advantage to a young man who has any fire[5] of Ambition and were there no advantage to be gained from it the pleasure of contemplating Human Nature in a degree of dignity would be sufficient to me. Now when I am returned to my own Country and from a variety of circumstances am thrown[6] into the Forum I am very desirous to put myself under the Protection of so able an Orator as The Dean of Faculty.[7]

I hope Sir you will excuse this liberty. I know I lay myself open to the imputation of forwardness and perhaps of vanity. But I would lye under the imputation of these and of worse qualitys rather than be prevented from telling you the high admiration with which I have the honour to be, Sir, your most Obedient, Humble Servant.

[1] Alexander Lockhart (c. 1700–82), advocate since 1722 and a man of prodigious energy with an extensive practice at the bar. When JB passed advocate in July Lockhart was Dean of the Faculty of Advocates, a post he held from 1764 until he was raised to the bench of the Court of Session, as Lord Covington, in 1775 (*College of Justice*, p. 533). Noting the great number of causes Lockhart heard in a morning, JB described him as 'a Brownie in business' (Journ. 16 Jan. 1768), and later, speaking of his skill in grasping a cause quickly, JB called him 'a Prodigy in his profession'

(Journ. 29 July 1774).

When Lockhart was raised to the bench the next year JB thought of writing his life (Journ. 20 Feb. 1775), and actually contributed a brief memoir of Lockhart to the *Lond. Mag.* for March 1775 (xliv. 142–43). Here he says that Lockhart 'may be recorded as one of the first barristers, if not the very first that ever appeared in any country', and says that Lockhart's Jacobitism had held up his appointment to the Court of Session for many years.

[2] JB heard his first cause as an advocate on 29 July and his last for the Summer Session on 7 Aug. (Consultation Book). Presumably he left Edinburgh for Auchinleck soon after the court rose on 12 Aug. (see From David Boswell, [c. 12] Aug.).

[3] Draft, 'was good enough to send me' written above deleted 'did me the honour of'.

[4] Draft, 'Protection' deleted before 'regard'

[5] Draft, 'of the' deleted before 'fire'

[6] Draft, 'I find myself' with 'find myself' deleted and replaced with 'I am returned to my own Country and from a variety of circumstances am' before 'thrown'

[7] Lockhart was noted for his eloquence as an orator (*Scotland and Scotsmen* i. 133–35), though JB later came to view Lockhart's appearance of earnestness on behalf of his clients in a less favourable light: 'Mr. Alexander Lockhart . . . very readily shed tears when he pleased, whether from feeling or from a weakness in his eyes was disputed. He was also very fond of getting his fees. I applied to him a *part* of a fine passage in Shakspere,

He hath a *tear* for pity, and a *hand*
Open as the day'
(*Boswelliana*, p. 279).

From Lady Elizabeth Macfarlane, c. Friday 1 August 1766

Not reported. Received 1 Aug. (Reg. Let.).

From Edward Aitken, c. early August 1766

Not reported. Received 4 Aug. (Reg. Let.).

From Jean-Jacques Rousseau, Monday 4 August 1766

MS. Yale (C 2420). A draft in the Neuchâtel Library (MS. Rousseau 283, fol. 15) containing possibly significant differences is printed below.[1]

ADDRESS: To James Boswell Esqr., at the Honourable My Lord Auchinleck's, Edinburgh, Scotland.

POSTMARKS: ASHBORNE, 4 AV.

ENDORSEMENT in an unidentified hand: Letter from Rousseau, 1766

A Wootton,[2] le 4 Aoust 1766

Vos lettres, Monsieur, me paroissent difficiles à entendre.[3] Je vous remercie, cependant, de l'intérêt que vous voulez bien prendre à ma santé et à celle de Mlle. le Vasseur. A un mal d'yeux près, elle s'est bien portée depuis son arrivée; j'en voudrais pouvoir dire autant de moi.[4] Permettez que je vous recommande à mon tour le soin de votre santé, et Surtout de vous faire saigner de tems à autre; je crois que cela pourroit vous faire du bien.[5] Recevez, Monsieur, je vous prie, mes très humbles salutations.

J.- J. ROUSSEAU

Vos lettres, venues toutes deux par M. Hume, ont souffert de très grands retards. La prémiére à peu près ouverte, et la seconde, qui ne m'est parvenue qu'un mois après sa date, pouvoit l'avoir été aisément; vû la forme de son enveloppe.[6]

[1] The draft reads: 'Wootton. A M. Boswell le 2 Aoust 1766. Recevez mes remercimens, Monsieur, de votre bon souvenir et de l'intérest que vous voulez bien prendre à ma santé et à celle de Mlle. le Vasseur. Elle n'a été incomodée que d'un mal d'yeux depuis son voyage et je voudrois me porter aussi bien qu'elle. [Je vous recomma: *deleted*] Mon cher Monsieur Boswell je vous recommande aussi le soin de votre santé, et surtout de vous faire saigner de tems à autre. Je crois que cela vous seroit fort bon. Je vous fais Monsieur mes tres humbles salutations.'

[2] Rousseau and Thérèse Le Vasseur were living at Wootton Grange, Staffordshire, an estate belonging to Richard Davenport, who had offered it as a refuge to Rousseau at the suggestion of David Hume. Davenport (?1705–71) was a country gentleman of Derbyshire and Staffordshire. He corresponded with Hume and Rousseau, and most of what is known about him comes from their letters. He was also a friend of Garrick's and Sterne's (*New Hume Letters*, p. 132 n. 3).

[3] JB's letters of 25 Mar. and c. late June. Rousseau's paranoid suspicions of Hume (see From Baroness von Spaen, 22 July, n. 6) had no doubt coloured his view of all his British acquaintance. But the difference in tone between the draft of 2 Aug. and the letter as sent, as well as the addition of this sentence, suggests that something specific occurred in this short period to make him more uneasy about JB, who was baffled by this letter. He wrote to Temple (1 Feb.–8 Mar. 1767): 'You must know that Rousseau quarrelled with me too [as well as Hume], and wrote me last summer a peevish letter with strong marks of frenzy in it. For he has never yet told me the cause of his offence.'

[4] Davenport wrote to Hume, 29 July: Rousseau 'has been a deal out of order lately in his health, and I found him but very poorly, tis his old complaint which has returned upon him with great violence. He looks much worse than when I saw him last, nor has he at all his usual spirits' (*New Hume Letters*, p. 216). For Rousseau's complaint, see From Deleyre, 1 Mar. n. 5.

[5] R. A. Leigh comments on this suggestion for blood-letting: 'Thérèse avait sans doute raconté à sa manière ce qui s'était passé entre elle et Boswell, en faisant valoir sa résistance héroïque aux assauts du jeune Ecossais' (*Corres. Rousseau* xxx. 204). JB had conducted an affair with Thérèse when he had accompanied her from Paris to London the previous winter.

[6] Rousseau suspected Hume of opening his letters; in a very long letter to Hume (10 July), in which he accused him of conspiring with d'Alembert and Walpole to dishonour him, Rousseau mentions that when he received JB's letter of 25 Mar. its seal was in very bad condition (*Corres. Rousseau* xxx. 37).

To Lord Mountstuart, Wednesday 6 August 1766

MS. Yale (L 344). Sent 11 Aug. (Reg. Let.). A draft.

HEADING: To My Lord Mountstuart.

Edinburgh, 6 August 1766

MY DEAR LORD: I am very happy that you have allowed me to dedicate my Theses to your Lordship.[1] Receive the Dedication Copy and pray let it be honoured with a place in the noblest Library[2] that any Subject ever possessed. Your Lordship jokes me on my many great friends to whom I might have written a Dedication.[3] But My Lord I have the honour to know your Lordship very[4] well and I know that Heaven has blest you with remarkable abilitys so that it will be your own fault if you are not as great a man as any of them[5] all and[6] therefore My Lord I have inscribed my Theses to John Lord Mountstuart in full expectation that all his Countrymen will one day be as fond to dedicate to him as I am now and therefore My Dear Lord remember You have accepted of my Dedication as earnest that you are to distinguish yourself in the service of your Country and I maintain that like one[7] who has taken the King's money,[8] your[9] Lordship cannot draw back. I hope the Dedication will please you for I am pleased with it myself and it has been approved of by the few Gentlemen now remaining amongst us who know what it is to have good blood in their veins.[10] I think the Print of your Lordship's Arms is very well done. I[11] had it engraved by a Mr. Phinn of this City a very deserving ingenious man.[12] If your Lordship likes the engraving I will have your name put[13] on below, and send you the Plate from which you may have Impressions for your Books.[14]

I am now fairly called to the Bar and begin to know a little of the labours and rewards the[15] bitter and the sweet of my Profession.[16] Time[17] will I trust reconcile me to my duty. My Father was allways anxious to have me a Lawyer so that I have been[18] prest into the service. But I have observed that Prest Men both by Sea and Land after a little while, do just as well as Volunteers.[19] I have no doubt of your Lordship's kind intentions to befriend me in whatever I shall undertake and[20] therefore I shall upon every occasion of consequence, most freely apply to you. By Study and experience I hope to be in a capacity of being able to do Your Lordship service. I earnestly wish to keep alive our friendship, to[21] be as much with you as possible to advise with you in all my schemes and for all your indolence I must flatter myself with the hopes of hearing from You frequently. I have the honour to remain, My Dear Lord, etc.

[1] See From Mountstuart, 25 June and n. 1.

[2] Draft, 'one of' deleted before 'the' and 'Librarys' changed to 'Library'

[3] SJ wrote to JB on 21 Aug.: 'Why did you dedicate it [the thesis] to a Man Whom I know you do not Much love?' (Life MS. Paper Apart for p. 318.) For the printed Life (ii. 20) JB deleted everything in that sentence following the first three words.

[4] Draft, 'I believe as well as any Body does' deleted before 'very'

[5] Draft, 'the' changed to 'them'

[6] Draft, 'whom You have mentioned' deleted before 'and'

[7] Draft, 'one' written above deleted 'Him'

[8] To take the King's money—or 'the King's shilling', which is the more usual expression—means to enlist as a soldier by accepting money from a recruiting officer.

[9] Draft, 'I maintain that' deleted before 'your'

[10] See From Mountstuart, 25 June, n. 1 for the first five lines, with translation, of the Dedication. The entire twenty-nine-line Latin Dedication is reprinted in Life ii. 20–21. SJ did not approve much of its Latin (Life ii. 20–25).

[11] Draft, 'It is' deleted before 'I'

[12] Presumably Thomas Phinn, or Phin (fl. 1746–68), who engraved various maps of Scotland between 1746 and 1759 (G. H. Bushnell, Scottish Engravers, 1949). Phinn engraved a Perth burgess-ticket (a diploma of citizenship) for JB's brother John in 1764 (C 2244.5) and the large folding map facing p. 1 of Corsica in 1768 (see From John Dick, 30 May, n. 7).

[13] Draft, 'added to the Plate' deleted before 'put'

[14] We have found no evidence that Mountstuart asked for the plate of the engraving.

[15] Draft, 'the sweet and' deleted before 'the'

[16] JB earned eight guineas for his work on ten causes between 29 July and 7 Aug.

[17] Draft, JB originally wrote 'Time and application', changed the phrase to 'Time and experience', and finally settled on 'Time'

[18] Draft, 'have been' written above deleted 'am'

[19] 'After putting on the gown he [JB] said with great good humour to his brother advocates, "Gentlemen I am prest into the service here; but I have observed that a prest man, either by sea or land, after a little time does just as well as a volunteer"' (Boswelliana, p. 242). 'Pressed' into the law was a favourite expression of JB's to describe his submission to his father's wishes: he used it in describing himself to George III in 1781 (Journ. 27 May 1781) and in his own character sketch in the Journal of a Tour to the Hebrides (Life v. 52).

[20] In the draft, JB first wrote 'undertake I hope to put' ['put' written above deleted 'render'] 'myself in such a situation that I may have the satisfaction to be' [changed from 'of being'] 'of some use to you' ['and perhaps to my' deleted] 'so that I shall deserve your' ['attention and I shall most freely apply to you till I find you fail me' deleted] all deleted before 'and'

[21] Draft, 'alive' deleted before 'to' and inserted before 'our' in the same sentence.

To Thomas Davies, Monday 11 August 1766

Not reported. Sent 11 Aug. (Reg. Let.). After a long career on the stage, Davies (c. 1712–85) became a bookseller in London in 1762. It was in the back room of Davies's shop in Russell Street, Covent Garden, that JB met SJ for the first time on 16 May 1763 (Journ.).

For an answer to this letter, see From Davies, 21 Aug.

To George Dempster, Monday 11 August 1766

Not reported. Sent 11 Aug. (Reg. Let.).

To Robert Ramsay, Monday 11 August 1766

Not reported. Sent 11 Aug. (Reg. Let.). Ramsay (d. 1778), physician in Edinburgh, graduated M.D. from the University of Edinburgh in 1757 and was appointed Professor of Natural History in 1770 (*Graduates in Medicine in the University of Edinburgh from 1705 to 1866*, 1867, p. 7; *Catalogue of the Edinburgh Graduates in Arts, Divinity, and Law*, 1867, p. xxiii; *Scots Mag.* 1778, xl. 686). JB had met him in Nice on 15 Dec. 1765 (Journ.).

To Jean-Jacques Rousseau, Monday 11 August 1766

Not reported. Sent 11 Aug. (Reg. Let.).

To Archibald Stewart, Monday 11 August 1766

Not reported. Sent 11 Aug. (Reg. Let.). Stewart (d. 1779), a merchant in Rotterdam, had befriended JB in 1763 and treated him with great kindness during a particularly severe bout of hypochondria (To W. J. Temple, 16 Aug. 1763; To John Johnston, 23 Sept. 1763). In 1770 he purchased an estate in Tobago and came into possession of a fortune of about £20,000; he died while defending his estate against a band of American privateers (*Renfrew*, p. 414; Journ. 29 Mar. 1772). For an answer to this letter, see From Stewart, 5 Dec.

To Thérèse Le Vasseur, Monday 11 Aug. 1766

Not reported. Sent 11 Aug. (Reg. Let.).

From Godfrey Bosville, Tuesday 12 August 1766

MS. Yale (C 173). Received 18 Aug. (Reg. Let.).

ADDRESS: To James Boswell, Esqre. at Lord Auchinlecks near [Edinborough in Scotland *deleted, and direction altered to*] by Air.

POSTMARK: WAKEFIELD.

Gunthwait, near Wakefield, August 12th 1766

DEAR SIR: Your Letter dated last Month came very duly to hand, and I deferrd answering it till I coud give you some account of Billys birth day; he came of Age the 21st of July, but[1] it was not of the same Consequence to him as a day of the same Nature had formerly been to me because there happend not to be a Vacancy:[2] however the Gentlemen of the Neighbourhood came in and we dind above 40 in my Old Hall and drank his Health and likewise his Sister Julias for it happens to be her Birthday too, Di's was the thursday before[3] and Sir Tho. Wentworth made an Entertainmt. at Bretton upon the occasion. The 22d I invited my Tenants and their wives, and the workmen about the House, they were about 300, in the Evening came whole Sholes of Ragamuffins, that I neither askd nor desird to see and it was past 12 o'Clock before I coud get rid of them all which you know was very wrong, for a Birthday never extends to a day and a half: About one Sir T. Wentworth woud have some Sky Rockets let of,[4] much Contrary to my Inclinations for I was afraid it would have brot. them all back again, but it did not. The night before I had illuminated a little wood near the house with above 70 lamps, which they heard of and expected it would have been done again. William went the friday following to Hull to meet Major Alderton and they embarkd for Hamborough, from whence they are gone to Berlin to see the King of Prussia review his Troops;[5] when William will come back again I do not know but it cannot be long for his leave of absence is but for two Months, and Lord Tyrawley supposes him in Yorkshire all the time.[6] I am pretty certain I shall not hear from him till he comes. Though I had not been to wait on Lord Strafford, yet he very genteely sent his Compliments to me and Billy and some very fine Carp the 21st in the Morning.[7] Venison I had from Sir T. W. and Mr. Spencer.[8] I have just now Half[9] a Buck sent me by a Countryman of yours Lord Bute[10] who has a Park at Wortley[11] 5 miles of, and I am to send word when I chuse to have another Half and they will kill another Buck. I had fed a very fine Ox, and very fine Calf some Sheep and a Pig for Williams Birthday, they had got a Silly Notion that I intended to roast the Ox whole. We shall be exceedingly glad if you will favor us with your Compy. here and see what kind of a habitation your Ancestors livd in when they were Ancestors both to you and me: It is individually the same and I verily believe is ante Conquestum.[12] Mrs. Bosville and Julia desire their best Respects to you, Di is gone to Buxton bath[13] with Miss Annabella[14] and Sir Thomas, T. is at school[15] and Billy with the K. of P. I beg You will present my Compliments to Lord Auchinleck. I should be very glad to see him too. I am, Dear Sir, Your Kinsman and most Humble Servant,

GODFREY BOSVILLE

[1] MS. 'but' superimposed upon '&'

[2] Bosville's father died in 1724 when Godfrey was seven. During Bosville's long minority his estates were well managed, and by the time he succeeded to them at the age of twenty-one in 1738, all encumbrances had been cleared from the property (*Fortunes of a Family*, pp. 99–100).

[3] 17 July.

[4] By an Act of 1698 (*Statutes at Large*, 1763, iii. 693–94), which remained in effect until 1860, the making, selling, and letting-off of fireworks was prohibited in Britain, but the Act was only sporadically enforced, and the threat of fines or imprisonment did not prevent their widespread manufacture (A. St. H. Brock, *Pyrotechnics: The History and Art of Firework Making*, 1922, pp. 57–67).

[5] William Bosville's companion was Maj. William Alderton, on half pay from 1764 on (*Army Lists*). Bosville and Alderton presumably went to view the autumn manoeuvres of Frederick's army, 'which, in process of time, became so celebrated, as to attract military and other foreigners of distinction from every country

in Europe'. Customarily manoeuvres were held in September. ([Frederic Shoberl] *Frederick the Great, His Court and Times*, ed. Thomas Campbell, 2nd ed. 1842, ii. 318–19; Cuthell ii. 268, 270).

[6] James O'Hara (1690–1773), second Baron Tyrawley, Field Marshal, and Colonel of William Bosville's regiment, the Coldstream Guards (Daniel Mackinnon, *Origin and Services of the Coldstream Guards*, 1833, i. 394; see also *Life* ii. 211 and n. 4).

[7] William Wentworth (1722–91), second Earl of Strafford. The Wentworths of Bretton, Bosville's wife's family, were a cadet branch of the Wentworths of Wentworth-Woodhouse from which the Earls of Strafford were directly descended (John Wentworth, *The Wentworth Genealogy*, 1878, i. xvi–xix, xxv).

[8] John Spencer (1718–75), friend and neighbour of the Bosvilles (*Fortunes of a Family*, p. 159). His seat, Cannon Hall, was in the village of Cawthorne, some two miles from Gunthwaite.

[9] MS. 'Half' superimposed upon 'a Sid'

[10] The Wortley estates belonged to Lord

Bute's wife, the former Mary Wortley Montagu, who inherited them from her father, Edward Wortley Montagu, and was created Baroness Mount Stuart of Wortley in 1761. Lady Bute's mother was the celebrated Lady Mary Wortley Montagu.

[11] MS. 'Wantley'

[12] Bosville wrote to JB on 21 Jan. 1781: 'I take it that both my Ancestor Anthony, and your Ancestor Richard, were old enough to be with their father Martin at the Battle of Hastings.' He is referring to Sir Martin de Bosville (d. 1092), who came over with William the Conqueror, and Martin's two sons: Anthony, the elder, heir to his father's English estates, and Richard, who went to Scotland either with Queen Margaret in 1068 or, perhaps more likely, in the reign of her son David I (Fortunes of a Family, pp. 5–6). JB's own account of the Boswells (MS. 'Boswell of Auchinleck'—Hyde Collection) begins with the Sieur de Boseville, who came to England with the Conqueror, and continues with Robert de Boseville (fl. 1165–88), 'the undoubted ancestor of this family', according to Douglas (Baronage, p. 307), whose account of the Boswells is very similar to JB's. For the manor-house, see From Bosville, 24 June, n. 7. J. J. Boswell gives a thorough account of the origins and history of the Boswell family in History and Genealogical Tables of the Boswells, 1904.

[13] Buxton, Derbyshire, about twenty-three miles south-west of Gunthwaite, had been famous for its baths since Roman times.

[14] For Annabella Wentworth, see From Bosville, 24 June, n. 3.

[15] Thomas Bosville (c. 1756–93) served as an officer in the Coldstream Guards from 1775 until his death at the battle of Lincelles (Mackinnon ii. 492). He was now studying at Cheam School in Surrey (Fortunes of a Family, pp. 112–15).

To Lady Elizabeth Macfarlane, Tuesday 12 August 1766

Not reported. Sent 12 Aug. (Reg. Let.).

From Lady Elizabeth Macfarlane, c. mid-August 1766

Not reported. Received 18 Aug. (Reg. Let.).

From Basil Cochrane, Tuesday 19 August 1766

MS. Yale (C 801). Received 26 Aug. (Reg. Let.).

ADDRESS: To James Boswell Younger of Auchenleck, Advocate, Esqr., att Auchenleck, pr. Air.

POSTMARK: [Edinburgh] AU 19.

Edinburgh, August 19th, 1766

Dear Sir: I hope My Lord and you gott Safe to Auchenleck.[1] Inclosed you have a letter from John.[2] When you have look'd over the Papers you carryd with you pray Return them to me.[3]

We have fine weather the Hearvest is begun and if Rain keeps off dayly Cutting we shall have which I believe will produce plenty for the Poor who are att Present in great Want of Meal.[4] My Compliments to all with you. I am, Dear Sir, Your most Obedient, Humble Servant,

BASIL COCHRANE

[1] Lord Auchinleck and JB had left Edinburgh for Auchinleck when the Summer Session ended on 12 Aug. (From David Boswell, [c. 12] Aug.).

[2] JB's brother John (From Mary Montgomerie, 27 Mar. n. 5). John's letter to JB, dated 13 Aug., mentions a severe illness from which he is well on the way to recovery.

[3] The papers have not been identified.

[4] Harvests were in fact poor this summer, and there was a shortage of wheat and corn throughout Great Britain during the autumn. The price of grain rose steadily following the expiration of the Act that prohibited exportation of corn, which had been passed during the last session of Parliament. As a result, there were widespread riots in England in September and October

(Gent. Mag. 1766, xxxvi. 414–15, 436–37, 493–94). On 26 Sept. the King, using the royal prerogative, issued a Proclamation forbidding the export of grain and its use for distilling purposes, and the embargo was to remain in effect until Parliament reopened on 11 Nov. The embargo was renewed on 12 Nov. (ibid. pp. 398–99, 547–48). For riots in Scotland the following year, see From James Maitland, 18 May 1767.

To Basil Cochrane, Tuesday 19 August 1766

Not reported. Sent 19 Aug. (Reg. Let.).

To Mrs. Dodds, Tuesday 19 August 1766

Not reported. Sent 19 Aug.: 'Mrs. ———' (Reg. Let.). JB had written to W. J. Temple on 17 May that he had taken a mistress in Moffat. The only record of her name is in Journ. 3 Mar. 1767.

To Lord Marischal, Tuesday 19 August 1766

Not reported. Sent 19 Aug. (Reg. Let.). Answered in From Lord Marischal, 2 Oct.

From Thomas Davies, Thursday 21 August 1766

MS. Yale (C 896). Received 2 Sept. (Reg. Let.).
ADDRESS: To James Boswell Esqr. of Auchinleck, in the County of Ayr, North Britain.
POSTMARKS: TW;[1] 21 AV.

London, Augt. 21st

DEAR SIR: I did not receiv your obliging letter with the present of your Thesis till within these few days.

I and all your friends rejoice that you are now in the true path to Honour and preferment, Such as your birth, and merit in your profession, will justly claim in due time.

Your Latin is pure and elegant, but pardon me if I object to that mixture of verse and prose, with some times a Cento of one Author and sometimes of another;[2] This is a fault not peculiar to yourself but common to allmost[3] all the Writers of modern latin—Erasmus and Buchanan[4] are among the few who are entirely free from it.[5]

I am pleased to see you to acquit yourself so handsomely in your Thesis—It Appears that you have not been idle.

I should be glad to know what you demand for the whole or half of the copy of your book[6]—Please to let me know and will consider of it, and give an immediate answer—Dr. Johnson is out of Town. I hope to see him very soon and will chide him for his neglect—I am sure he has a true respect for you, but you know the Indolence of his temper. I sent your Thesis to him and to Dr. Goldsmith.[7]

I return my sincere thanks for your promise to employ me to furnish a Library to General Paoli—Such a Commision is honourable as well as advantagious.[8]

I should advise the printing of your book at Edinburgh—It will certainly be more correct and at least as well printed—The great number of periodical performances of all kinds, is the ruin of the art of Printing in this Town.[9]

Mrs. Davies desires her best respects.[10] I am, Sir, Your most obedient, humble Servant,

THOMAS DAVIES

[1] Presumably 'posted at the receiving house of Thomas Wheeler' (J. G. Hendy, *The Story of Early Postmarks of the British Isles*, 1905, p. 60), but lacking the bullet customarily printed between the initials.

[2] In presenting his eight theses concerning legacies of household furniture JB quotes prose passages among his five pages of text from such Roman jurists as Paulus, Florentinus, and Papinianus. In his two-page proem JB quotes lines of verse lamenting the decline of Rome, without identifying the source as Juvenal (*Satires* vi. 291–92, 297–99).

[3] MS. 'all' deleted before 'allmost'

[4] George Buchanan (1506–82), Scots historian and poet, was a notable scholar. SJ said of him: 'He not only had great knowledge of the Latin language, but was a great poetical genius' (*Life* ii. 96). Today he is best remembered as a leading figure of the Scottish Reformation.

[5] MS. 'it' written above deleted 'this fault'

[6] Davies declined the opportunity to publish JB's *Corsica*; see From Davies, 15 Nov.

[7] SJ spent July, August, and September at Streatham (*Works* SJ i. 111), though a letter from him to William Drummond, 13 Aug., is dated from Johnson's Court, Fleet St., and one to JB, 21 Aug., is dated simply from 'London'. JB says in the *Life* that he had written twice to SJ since receiving a letter from him dated 10 May 'without being able to move his indolence; nor did I hear from him till he had received a copy of my inaugural Exercise, or Thesis in Civil Law'. SJ's letter of 21 Aug., which comments at length on JB's thesis, begins, 'The reception of your Thesis put me in mind of my debt to you' (ii. 20). If Goldsmith, whom JB had met at Davies's table on Christmas Day 1762 (Journ. 25 Dec. 1762), made a comment on the thesis, it has not survived.

[8] In 1765 JB had been amused by the meagreness of Paoli's English library and had promised to augment it (*Corsica*, pp. 297–98). For a complete list of the books that Davies, who was known as a buyer and seller of libraries (Maxted, p. 62), shipped to Paoli at JB's request, see From Davies, 15 Oct. 1767, n. 3.

[9] JB chose Robert and Andrew Foulis of Glasgow to print *Corsica* for Edward and Charles Dilly, booksellers in London. The Foulis brothers, whose output exceeded 600 volumes between 1742 and 1776 (Philip Gaskell, 'Printing the Classics in the Eighteenth Century', *Book Collector*, 1952, i. 104), were especially noted for their classical editions, several of which were included among the books sent to Paoli (From Davies, 17 Jan. 1767, 28 Apr. 1767). For Robert and Andrew Foulis and the Glasgow Press, see From Thomas Davies, 17 Jan. 1767, n. 3.

[10] Susannah Yarrow Davies (c. 1723–1801), an actress who played with her husband at Drury Lane, 1752–62 (*Lond. Stage* pt. 4, i. 318, 376, 436; ii. 494–882 passim). She was well known for her beauty, which Charles Churchill paid tribute to in his *Rosciad* (l. 320) in 1761: 'That Davies hath a very pretty wife!' She was also known for her virtue, and JB commented on Davies and his wife: 'Their strict conjugal union secretly reproached my licentiousness' (Journ. 1 Apr. 1776).

From Sir Alexander Dick,[1] Friday 22 August 1766

MS. Yale (C 957). Received 2 Sept. (Reg. Let.). In the hand of an amanuensis (presumably Janet Dick, see n. 2), except for the complimentary close and signature. The letter and Sir Alexander's poem on Durham Cathedral (C 956), along with other letters from Sir Alexander, are enclosed in a wrapper endorsed in JB's hand, 'Sir Alexander Dick'.

Durham Colledge, Augst. 22, 1766

According to my promise, Most worthy Counsellor, and freind; I write you from this place, how we have spent our time since we left you[2]—The finest weather, that ever man saw, has attended us the whole way, and since we came hay making and hay makers on all sides, of which there are immense crops, which perfumd the Air, as it was extremly green and well got.—

We found our worthy freind the Prebend, stout, and well, at our arrival;[3] in spite of the Alarming paraletic stroke he had, six weeks before, were immediately surrounded with a number of venerable well fed Prebends, and their plump wives, and we reckond ourselves from that moment, part of the great body of the church and Ecclesiastical consistory, and can't but say, that In the clerical spirit of christian Epicurism, we have livd devoutly, soberly, and righteously, as in duty bound.[4]—

We had a most obliding invitation from Dr. Lowth, the now Bishop of Oxford, and his Lady to dine with them at Sedgefield seven miles off, where we spent a most agreeable day he is Mr. Spences most intimate freind, and by his emminence both for knowledge and elecution, and the great favor he is in at Court, if he lives, bids very fair to be Archbishop of Canterbury,[5] Lady Dick and my daughter, were charmd with his little wife, and agreeable little family.[6]—

The great Pasquali Paoli, your heroic freind's story, came naturaly in, in the course of conversation; and on my opening to him, some of the scenes, which you was pleas'd to communicate to me, of your interviews with that Hero, in Corsica, the Bishop and Mr. Spence highly applauded you for undertaking that voyage, and heartily wishd you would proceed to favor the world, them, and all your freinds, with your account of Corsica and your history of the Hero, which I told them you propos'd soon to present to the Publick.[7]—

Doctor Armstrong only joind us within these two days and we proceed to make pleasant excursions, evry other day round the City of Durham[8]—Lord Strichen and Governor Wemyss were here with us at dinner and all yesterday examining the antiquitys and beautys of the Place—You may, with all our best Compliments to My Lord, your father, acquaint him, that his brother judge is very well, and going to Halifax for a jaunt and returns by Carlile.[9]—

We live here much as it were in the Castle of Indolence,[10] employing ourselves decently, and soberly, as seemeth good unto our own hearts—to show you, I have not been quite idle, here you have the effusions of the spirit rudely composd, directly from the pen without dressing,[11]—We shall sett out on Teusday the 26. and rejoice to see you, on your return from the West,—The Bishop of Oxford and his Lady dine here tomorrow, with us, and Pasquali Paolis health is to be drunk,—if it was possible, I could wish there was a solemn service sung for his sucess, in this Cathedral, in which I dare say were you here you would asisst with the most pious and fervent prayr's.—As I enclose these flowers of my fancy, such as they are, I have got the Bishop of Oxford to frank the same, you see he does it under the title of St. Davids, having not yet been install'd according to forms.[12]—

Our whole circle, in a chorus salute you, and all Paolis freinds—Your, Dear Counceller and friend,

ALEXANDER DICK

[1] Sir Alexander Dick (1703–85) of Preston-field, Bt., son of Sir William Cunyngham of Caprington and Janet Dick, heiress of Sir James Dick of Prestonfield, was a distinguished physician and one of the founders of the Royal Society of Edinburgh. On the death of his brother William in 1746 Alexander succeeded to the baronetcy of Dick, assumed his mother's name, and gave up the practice of medicine. He took up residence at Prestonfield House, which lies at the foot of Arthur's Seat, some two miles south-east of the centre of Edinburgh. JB frequently walked to Prestonfield from James's Court.

[2] Dick was accompanied to Durham by his second wife, the former Mary Butler (d. 1820), of Pembrokeshire, Wales, whom he had married in 1762, and Janet (1749–1806), the elder of his two daughters by his first wife (Scots Mag. 1749, xi. 150; 1806, lxviii. 488). Janet, or Jessie as she was usually called, often acted as her father's secretary

(see To Sir Alexander Dick, 23 Oct.; *Scots Charta Chest*, pp. 186, 198–99).

³ Joseph Spence (1699–1768), miscellaneous writer and friend of Pope and James Thomson. He was Professor of Poetry at Oxford, 1728–38, and was appointed Regius Professor of Modern History at the same university in 1742. He had been a prebendary of Durham Cathedral since 1754 (William Hutchinson, *History and Antiquities of the County Palatine, of Durham*, 1785–94, ii. 200). The literary work for which he is best remembered—*Anecdotes, Observations, and Characters of Books and Men*, first published in 1820—includes in an Appendix to the edition by S. W. Singer (1820, pp. 458–70) four letters to Spence from Dick.

⁴ 'Teaching us that, denying ungodliness and worldly lusts, we should live soberly, righteously, and godly, in this present world' (Titus 2: 12). Since the granting of a Foundation Charter to Durham Cathedral by Henry VIII in 1541, the Cathedral establishment had consisted of a dean, twelve prebendaries, and a number of minor officials, all of whom, with the bishop, were housed within the precincts of the old monastery 'according to the dignity of the prebends, which are reputed more richly endowed than any other church' (Hutchinson ii. 102–110). The 'clerical spirit of Christian Epicurism' to which Dick refers is an allusion to the blatant pursuit of material comfort and pleasure by the 'well fed Prebends'. For the more serious implications of the encounter of Epicureanism and Christianity in the eighteenth century, see Peter Gay, *The Enlightenment: An Interpretation*, i. (*The Rise of Modern Paganism*) 100–02, 304–08.

⁵ Robert Lowth (1710–87), D.D., prebendary of Durham Cathedral and rector of Sedgefield since 1755, was consecrated Bishop of St. David's, Pembrokeshire, in June, translated to Oxford in October and to London in 1777, when he was also appointed Dean of the Chapel Royal and a Privy Counsellor. In 1783 he was offered the Archbishopric of Canterbury, but declined it because of failing health. Lowth gained a wide reputation as a Hebrew scholar—his influential *Praeleciones Academicae de Sacra Poesi Hebraeorum* were first published in Oxford in 1753 (trans. G. Gregory as *Lectures on the Sacred Poetry of the Hebrews* in 1787)—and was well known as a formidable antagonist in controversy. JB owned a copy of his *Short Introduction to English Grammar*, published in 1762 ('A Catalogue of Books belonging to James Boswell, Esq.' [c. 1770]

MS. NLS).

⁶ Lowth and his wife Mary (d. 1803) had seven children, only two of whom survived him: his second son, Robert, and his daughter Martha.

⁷ JB's *Account of Corsica* was first published in Feb. 1768.

⁸ John Armstrong (1709–79), M.D., Scots poet, physician, and essayist, best known for his didactic poem, *The Art of Preserving Health*, which was first published in four books in 1744 and had run into at least nine editions by 1766 (NUC). He had served as physician to the army in Germany during the Seven Years' War and remained on half pay, after the army's return to England, until he died. His friendship with Dick and Spence is mentioned in Dick's letter to Spence, 25 Aug. 1765 (*Anecdotes*, Singer ed. pp. 467–69).

⁹ Sir Alexander's dinner companions were Alexander Fraser (1699–1775), Lord Strichen, and John Wemyss (d. 1786), lieutenant-governor of Edinburgh Castle, 1763–81 (*Army Lists*). Lord Strichen had been a judge of the Court of Session since 1730 (*College of Justice*, p. 503). He was returning to his estate in Aberdeenshire by way of Halifax in Yorkshire and Carlisle in Cumberland. Wemyss was married to Lady Catherine Lindsay, daughter of John Lindsay, nineteenth Earl of Crawford, and half-sister of Lord Strichen, whose mother had married Lord Crawford after the death of her first husband, Alexander Fraser of Strichen (*Scots Peer.* iii. 38–39; *Memorials of the Family of Wemyss of Wemyss*, ed. Sir William Fraser, 1888, i. 154–55).

¹⁰ Dick's alluding to Thomson's poem in this context strongly suggests that he was aware that Thomson was generally supposed to have had Armstrong in mind as the 'One shyer still, who quite detested Talk' (I. lx. 3), and that Armstrong had contributed, at Thomson's request, the final four stanzas of Canto I (see *James Thomson: 'The Castle of Indolence' and Other Poems*, ed. A. D. McKillop, 1961, pp. 193–94, 197–98). Armstrong, a close friend of Thomson's, was characterized by a fellow physician as a man of 'considerable abilities in his profession . . . but indolent and inactive, and therefore totally unqualified . . . to elbow his way through a crowd of competitors' (*Lit. Anec.* ii. 311).

¹¹ Dick encloses his 'Thoughts after viewing the Cathedral of Durham and the Country around it', some sixty lines of blank verse, much of it in praise of Spence.

¹² The cover, with Lowth's frank, is missing.

From Alexander Macdonnell,[1] Tuesday 26 August 1766

MS. Yale (C 1841). Received 2 Sept. (Reg. Let.).

Tullochcrom, August the 26, 1766

DEAR SIR: I am ashemed not to have Sent your Terier Sooner be assuerd it was nither the want of memory or will keept him So Long from you but that I was much from home sence I had the pleasour of Seeing you, otherwise would send him Immediatly as I cam home he is of the True kind and Thorowly broak or taught and have no fault with him but being reather Small, and if you think so I can get a Larger kind one or more as youll have occeassion, for any time you want of the kind or any thing Ells from the highlands you have any fancy for and I am hopefull youll honour me with your Comands in Leting me know any thing you want from the Country and in So Dowing nothing can give me more happyness than to oblidg.[2] The Civility and friendship you Showd me and your kind Concern for me and my Brother when last at Edinr. renders me uncapable to Express my thankfullness for the troubles and pains you was pleased to take to forward our Intrests which will at Least be Reported to the best of our friends but in Such a way as not to Let our Enimys know who were our friends.[3] Ill god willing be at Edinr. in November as our Buisiness is not yet finally made out the Containuance of your Friendship in making my friends[4] till I goe up I greatly Rely upon and Belive me Sincerly without flatery not Doubting but you will Easily be Convinced that you was most thorowly possessed of my best wishes as befor I had Such Strong prooffs as you was pleased to Show me Liatly by Interesting and Excerting yourself in Interseeding so much with the Barrons and other Nobelmen in my Behalff it is uncertain but Providence might order it So without prjdows[5] to your Intersts as that I or Som friend of mine might yet Serve or obldg you or yours. I Shall Say no more at Present but that I beg pardon for writting you in so bad and Confeuesed a Style. I beg Leve to trouble you with my best Respects and in Presenting my Complements to Lord Achenleck,—and Ever am, Dear Sir, Yours sincerely while,

ALEXANDER MDONELL

The Teriers Name is Syder.[6] When you honoure me with yours Derect to me to the care of John McDonald merchout at Fortwilliam[7]—in a month or Two I shall send you som birds worth while but at Present its Stormy here and could send but few.

[1] Alexander Macdonell, or Alastair Bàn, of Tullochrom, Inverness-shire, is listed twice in the Register of Sasines for Inverness in the period from 1748 to 1765 (SRO, *Index to Particular Register of Sasines for Sheriffdoms of Inverness, Ross, Cromarty, and Sutherland*, no. 64, 1967, iii. 56, 62). His first wife, Grisel Mackintosh of Balnespick, bore him four children, his second wife, Jessie Macdonald of Keppoch, five more. He and his elder brother, Ranald Macdonell of Aberarder (d. c. 1771), were Roman Catholics and had been active Jacobites in the service of Prince Charles Edward (Alexander Macdonald and Archibald Macdonald, *The Clan Donald*,

1900–04, iii. 443–44, 448–49; Robert Forbes, *The Lyon in Mourning*, ed. Henry Paton, 1895–96, iii. 182). JB had met Ranald Macdonell at Ruthven, Inverness-shire, on 13 May 1761 and had found him 'not so much of a Gentleman—but much friendship and Veracity—quite an untamed Highlander' (Journ.).

[2] JB's brother David wrote to JB on 30 Aug. that the dog had arrived in Edinburgh along with Macdonell's letter. Claud Boswell would bring the letter to Auchinleck, and eventually the carrier from Edinburgh would deliver the dog, which was being kept for the moment by a chairman named Alexander McDonald. In a letter of 10

Sept. to JB David discussed other means of bringing the dog to Auchinleck.

[3] JB's legal services to the Macdonell brothers between 1766 and 1770 are summarized in his final *Petition* on their behalf to the Court of Session, 30 June 1770 (*Petition* of Ranald and Alexander Macdonells, Tenants in Aberarder, Tullochromb, etc., 30 June 1770—Houghton Library, Harvard University). Ranald and Alexander Macdonell and their ancestors had, for more than a century, leased farms on the estates, in southern Inverness-shire, of Evan Macpherson of Clunie (or Cluny). Clunie was attainted on 12 July 1746 (*Celtic Mag.* 1876–77, ii. 422), and his lands annexed automatically by the Crown. In 1766 management of the Clunie estates rested with the Barons of the Scottish Exchequer, and they, through their factor, an unscrupulous Englishman named Henry Butter, had leased the Clunie estates to the Rev. Robert Macpherson, an avaricious and impecunious clergyman who wished to use the lands for sheep-rearing. JB managed to delay the Barons' order for the eviction of the Macdonells and their households from Clunie for three years (Consultation Book, 1, 6 Dec. 1766—NLS; *Memorial* for Ranald and Alexander Macdonells, etc., 19 July 1768—Signet Library, no. 124:9), and in his *Petition* of 1770 he argued that the Barons had been superseded and power of management of forfeited estates was now vested in trustees appointed by the Crown. His *Petition* was refused on 3 July 1770 on the grounds that the transfer of power had not yet taken place. In fact, the Clunie estate was not returned to Evan Macpherson's son Duncan until 1784—Evan having died before that date (*Statutes at Large*, 1784, c. 57, xiv. 597). Alexander Macdonell was permitted to keep his farm of Inverwidden, but most of the other tenants (about eighty in number) emigrated to America. For a detailed account of the Macdonells' struggle to keep their lands, and their subsequent fate, see Charles Fraser-Mackintosh, 'The Depopulation of Aberarder in Badenoch, 1770', *Celtic Mag.* ii. 418–26; for JB's part in this cause, see R. C. Cole, 'Young Boswell Defends the Highlanders', *Studies in Scottish Literature*, ed. G. R. Ross, 1985, xx. 1–10.

[4] Possibly, 'providing for my kinsfolk'. Among the meanings for 'friend' given in the *Scot. Nat. Dict.* are 'relative, blood-relation, kinsman'.

[5] i.e., 'prejudice'

[6] Gaelic *saighdear*. David Boswell wrote to JB on 10 Sept.: 'Syder's name in English is Soldier.'

[7] Unidentified. In 1791 the twin towns of Fort William and Maryburgh, some twenty miles west-south-west of Aberarder and Tullochrom, had a population of about 1,200, including two merchants (*Stat. Acct. Scot.* viii. 427–29).

From William Wallace,[1] Tuesday 26 August 1766

MS. Yale (C 3057). Received 2 Sept. (Reg. Let.).
ADDRESS: To James Boswell Esqr., Advocate, at Auchinleck, by Ayr.
POSTMARK: [Edinburgh] AU 26.

Edenr. 26 August 1766

DEAR SIR: Prefixed, I send you a Copy of a Letter I have received from Mr. Adam Wood, in consequence of what I wrote him at your desire—I am sorry it does not turn out agreeable to expectations—If my Lord chuses to write Mr. Wood himself, he will please direct for him 'in Mark Lane'—[2]

I beg you'l offer my most respectful complements to his Lordship and beleive me to be most sincerely and affectionately yours,

WIL. WALLACE

I shall leave this, on thursday next and hope we shall meet in Airshire.

[1] William Wallace (d. 1786), of Cairnhill, son of Robert Wallace of Holmston, W.S., and Anne Fullarton (whose genealogy he showed JB on 23 July 1769—Journ.), had been admitted advocate in 1752. He had been Professor of History at Edinburgh University since 1755, and Professor of Scots Law since 1765. He later (1775) became Sheriff of Ayr (*Fac. Adv.*; *Writers to the Signet*, p. 210). In June he had presented JB with Louis-Amand Jaussin's *Mémoires historiques, militaires et politiques, sur les principaux événemens arrivés dans l'isle et royaume de Corse, 1758–59*, describing it 'as a small, but sincere token of Love and Esteem' (C. B. Tinker, *Young Boswell*, 1922, p. 191).

[2] Adam Wood was a merchant at no. 68, Mark Lane, Tower Street (*Kent's Directory*, 1768). JB had asked Wallace, presumably before

leaving Edinburgh for Auchinleck at the end of the Summer Session, to propose to Wood that he accept David Boswell as a partner; on or about 12 Aug. David asked JB 'to write Mr. Wallace a line to know his Success' (From David Boswell, c. 12 Aug.). David was perhaps impatient: Wallace had written only on 10 Aug., and Wood did not reply until 19 Aug. Wallace prefixed to the present letter a transcript of Wood's reply, in which he says that he carries on only a small amount of trade (unspecified) on commission, and unless David had 'an almost certain prospect' of bringing in more business he could not take him as a partner. David was not discouraged by this letter; on 10 Sept. he sent JB a long list of Scots peers, 'Gentlemen of Fortune', and others whose business he thought he could bring to Wood's firm, and as late as 12 May 1767 he was still considering the scheme (From David Boswell, 31 Oct. 1766; 12 May 1767). But in late 1767 he left Britain to become a merchant in Spain (From Lord Marischal, 26 Jan. 1768). We do not know why David settled on Wood as a prospective partner, or what the connection was between Wallace and Wood.

To John Dick, Wednesday 27 August 1766

Not reported. See From Dick, 6 Oct.: 'this day I am favour'd with your very kind and obliging Letter of the 27 August, which ought to have been here long ago.'

From Mrs. Dodds, c. late August 1766

Not reported. Received 2 Sept.: 'Mrs. ———' (Reg. Let.).

From James Smith, c. late August 1766

Not reported. Received 2 Sept. (Reg. Let.).

To John Dick, Sunday 7 September 1766

Not reported. Sent 7 Sept. (Reg. Let.). Dick may never have received this letter; he does not acknowledge it in any of his extant ones.

From George Dempster, c. mid-September 1766

Not reported. Received 16 Sept. (Reg. Let.).

From Mrs. Dodds, c. mid-September 1766

Not reported. Received 16 Sept.: 'Mrs. ———' (Reg. Let.).

From Archibald Stewart, c. mid-September 1766

Not reported. Received 16 Sept. (Reg. Let.).

To Lord Chatham, Thursday 18 September 1766

MS. Collection of Sir Timothy Hoare of Annabella, Bt., on deposit in the Public Record Office, London (PRO 30/70). The Yale MS. (L 366) is a draft, and a third MS. in the Chatham Papers, Public Record Office, is a copy[1] that JB enclosed with To Chatham, 3 Jan. 1767. The three texts are virtually identical. Sent 18 Sept. (Reg. Let.).[2]

Auchinleck, County of Ayr, 18 Sept. 1766

MY LORD: When, (to use your own words) you was 'William Pitt a plain Member of Parliament' you exprest[3] a high regard for the Corsicans and their illustrious Chief. I have ever remembered that conversation which Mr. Pitt honoured me with[4] and I own my hopes of relief to the brave Islanders have been very great. May[5] I presume to ask the Earl of Chatham if He will befriend a noble and unfortunate little nation whom I have seen with the enthusiasm of liberty and for whom I shall be interested while my blood is warm.[6] Pardon me My Lord if I intrude upon you, and believe me to be, With the highest consideration, Your Lordship's most Obedient and most Humble Servant,

JAMES BOSWELL

[1] Both draft and copy have the heading, 'To the Earl of Chatham.'

[2] JB first sent the letter to W. J. Temple, who forwarded it to Chatham, but not until November (From Temple, 20 Nov.).

[3] Draft, 'exprest' changed to 'expressed'

[4] The conversation is described in To Pitt, 19 Feb. n. 2.

[5] In both draft and copy 'May' begins a new paragraph.

[6] The previous summer Pitt had formed a government with himself as Lord Privy Seal, accepting a peerage as first Earl of Chatham.

To John Wilkie, Thursday 18 September 1766

Not reported. Sent 18 Sept. (Reg. Let.).

From Count Antonio Rivarola, Friday 19 September 1766

MS. Yale (C 2389).

ADDRESS: Mr. Boswell, a Auchinlech.

Livorno, 19 7mbre. 1766

ILLUSTRISSIMO SIGNORE SIGNORE PADRONE COLENDISSIMO: Ero in Sardegna in un viaggio importante allorchè ebbi la gratma sua de' co. Aprile scorso; e poichè colà mi fù mandata intatta, ho dovuto trattener meco anche quella che andava al Sigr. Generale, la quale gli ho fatta ultimamente avere cauta come spero, e ne aspetto risposte.

Ora che Mr. Pitt è alla testa degli affari di codesto Regno, spero vedere avverato quanto Ella predice, e lo bramo a bene della Gran Brettagna e della mia Patria, giacchè questo è stato sempre il maggiore de miei desideri.

La sua gita in Corsica vi ha richiamato altri de suoi Nazionali: sapra che Mr. Harvey e Mr. Barneby vi sono stati ultimamte., e sento che son tornati molto contenti.

Vorrei che cominciasse da costì ad illuminarsi il mondo sulla mia Patria, giacchè Londra è oggidì quella, che puol dar legge all' Europa; ma mi rincresce che sento che codeste gazette portano sulla data di Livorno una infinità de corbellerie: Io credo che in vece della data di Livorno potrebbe senza scrupolo mettersi quella di Genova.

Ho procurato de rispondere all meglio ai suoi quesiti: quelli su i quali sapevo qualche cosa di più mi ci sono più esteso; ma quel che vanto si è la certezza di non averle detto nulla di più del vero.

Io la pregherei di non far parola di me in conto alcuno nella storia che vuol dare alla luce. Son troppo piccolo, onde non merito di esser posto sul candeliere, e soprattutto non vorrei vergognarmi di essere stato strumento inutile a servirla nella mia Patria. La prego perciò a non toccar cos' alcuna delle lettere da me datele per Corsica non per altro, sennon che per essere questo di tanto poco momento, che non vedo meritino di farsene menzione. Di vero cuore sono a sarò sempre e senza riserva, Di Vostra Signoria Illustrissima, Devotissimo, Obbligatissimo Servitore,

RIVAROLA

[MOST ILLUSTRIOUS LORD, WORSHIPFUL MASTER: I was in Sardinia on an important journey when I received your most welcome letter of last April. Since it was sent to me unopened, I had to keep with me also the letter addressed to the General. I have finally forwarded this to him, I trust with the proper caution, and I await a reply.[1]

Now that Mr. Pitt is at the head of the affairs of your kingdom, I hope that what you predict will come true. This has always been my fondest wish for the good of Great Britain and of my country.

Your trip to Corsica has brought other citizens from your country; you probably know that Mr. Hervey and Mr. Burnaby have been there recently, and I hear that they returned very well satisfied.[2]

I wish that these travellers would begin to enlighten the world about my country, since London nowadays may legislate to all Europe; but it grieves me to hear that your newspapers are reporting a great deal of nonsense dated from Leghorn. I believe that one could without scruple replace the dateline of Leghorn with that of Genoa.[3]

I have tried as best I can to answer your inquiries. I have dealt at greater length with those I know more about; in any case I take pride in the assurance that I have not told you anything more than the truth.

I beg you not to mention my name in the account that you are about to publish. I am too minor a figure, unworthy of being placed in the limelight, and above all I do not wish to be ashamed of the uselessness of the service I rendered you in my country. I beg you, therefore, not to refer in any way to the letters I have given you about Corsica, since they are of so little consequence as not to be worth mentioning.[4] With all my heart I am and always will be unreservedly, your most illustrious lordship's most devoted and obliged servant,

RIVAROLA][5]

[1] This paragraph suggests that JB's letter to Paoli of 24 Apr. was enclosed in this letter. Since Rivarola was in Sardinia when he received JB's letter, he was unable to forward the letter to Paoli until he got back to Leghorn.

[2] The Rev. Frederick Augustus Hervey (1730–1803) and the Rev. Andrew Burnaby (c. 1734–1812) had visited Paoli in Corsica for eight days in August (W. S. Childe-Pemberton, The Earl Bishop, 1924, i. 79–80). Hervey became Bishop of Cloyne, in Ireland, in 1767, and Bishop of Derry in 1768; in 1779 he succeeded his brother as fourth Earl of Bristol. JB had met Hervey in Genoa on 1 Dec. 1765 and described

him as a 'neat little Clergyman talking of the fine characters of the Swiss Pasteurs' (Notes, 2 Dec. 1765). Though Burnaby had been chaplain to the British factory at Leghorn since about 1762, JB did not meet him until 22 Sept. 1769 (Journ.). Burnaby kept a journal of his trip to Corsica and gave JB a copy of it (Corsica, pp. xiii–xiv); in 1804, he published it as Journal of a Tour to Corsica in the Year 1766.

[3] Rivarola may have read reports unfavourable to the Corsicans in Lond. Chron. The issue for 29–31 May (xix. 514), for example, reported that Corsicans had plundered the coast of Naples and kidnapped several people, and the issue for

5–7 June (xix. 544) reported that Corsican manifestos had denounced French oppression, though Paoli's policy was to avoid antagonizing the French.

[4] Nevertheless JB mentioned Rivarola's letters in the Preface to Corsica (p. xiii). Perhaps Rivarola's reluctance to have JB acknowledge his help in Corsica arose from the fact that while acting as the official Sardinian chargé d'affaires at the Court of Tuscany, he was also supplying the King of Sardinia with secret reports on JB's activities in Corsica (From John Dick 25 Feb. n. 2) and was therefore playing something of a double game.

[5] Translation by Caterina Bosio and Ian Duncan.

To Mrs. Dodds, Saturday 20 September 1766

Not reported. Sent 20 Sept.: 'Mrs. ———' (Reg. Let.).

From John Dick, Friday 26 September 1766

MS. Yale (C 1007).

NOTE in Dick's hand at foot of first page: James Boswell, Esq.

Leghorn, 26 Septr. 1766

MY DEAR SIR, I had the pleasure to write You the 30 May last, since which I have not receiv'd any of your kind Letters. I told You in my last, that I had carefully deliver'd your inclosed to Count Reverola's Vice Consul,[1] the beginning of the last month, or rather the middle of it. Mr. Hervey, and Mr. Burnaby took a trip to Sparta, to see Licurgus.[2] I desired Mr. Burnaby to enquire if Your Letter had reached his hands, and found on his return that it had not, I was then at Pisa, this gave me some uneasiness, I therefore wrote to Riverolas Vice Consul, who answer'd me that he had carefully forwarded it, this very answer I sent to the General, and wrote him about it, that he might not think you wanting. I have since learned, that it was sent to Riverola who is yet in Sardania, that it had been returned hither, and was safely forwarded to Sparta, and this very day, the inclosed has been deliverd to me for you, which probably may be the Answer. I have also some prints to forward you, but shall send them by a Ship which sails in a day or two, not to occasion you expence in Postage.[3]

Now our great Patriot is att the head of the Ministry, I hope he will be able to afford this heroe some assistance, was it only to annul the Proclamation, it would be of great Consequence,[4] I cannot help thinking the Genoes did not merit so much kindness from us, for they certainly did us all the harm they[5] could during the last War.[6] I hope you'l Endeavour to Serve these poor people, if so, I heartily wish you Success—I think we might open a Trade with the Island, that, might be of consequence to us.

We have nothing new here worthy your notice, Mrs. Dick desires your acceptance of her best Compliments, and I ever am with the most perfect Regard and true Esteem, My dear Sir, Your most Faithfull and most Assured Servant,

JOHN DICK

[1] Giuseppe Balbi (From John Dick, 30 May, n. 4).

[2] Dick used code names for Corsica and Paoli because, as a government official, he was not permitted to interfere in the affairs of foreign states. The analogy between Lycurgus and Paoli, as well as between Sparta and Corsica was developed more fully in Burnaby's journal (quoted in Corsica, pp. 32–33); JB returned to this analogy later in the book (p. 342).

³ The prints have not been identified.

⁴ For Chatham's attitude towards British intervention in Corsican affairs, see From Chatham, 4 Feb. 1767. The Proclamation of 29 Dec. 1762 that forbade British subjects 'to give or furnish aid, assistance, countenance or succour, by any ways or means whatsoever, to any of the inhabitants of the island of Corsica' was not rescinded (*Lond. Chron.* 1–4 Jan. 1763, xiii. 9).

⁵ MS. 'the'

⁶ Although the Genoese were not official combatants in the Seven Years' War, they were bound by treaty to France and provided port facilities to French naval vessels in the campaigns against Minorca and other British naval bases (René Boudard, *Gênes et la France dans la deuxième moitié du xviiième siècle (1748–1797)*, 1962, pp. 58, 67–68). JB wrote, 'It is notorious, that without its [Genoa's] assistance, the French could not have fitted out that fleet at Toulon, which enabled them to take Minorca; that the Genoese continued building ships for them, during the whole of the last war, and constantly supplied them with seamen' (*Corsica*, pp. 189–90).

From Mrs. Dodds, c. late September 1766

Received 27 Sept.: 'Mrs. ———' (Reg. Let.).

From Lord Marischal, Thursday 2 October 1766

MS. Yale (C 1954). Received 21 Oct. (Reg. Let.).
ADDRESS: To James Boswell Esqr., of Auchenlek, [Edenburgh *deleted; added in another hand* by Air, en Ecosse; fr[anco] *amsterdam*, par Londres [*added*].
POSTMARK: [London] OC 13.

Potsdam, 2 October 1766

SIR: I am glad you are become advocate; first, as you say, from the pleasure it gives your worthy father, and next that it will be to you an honorable occupation, for idlenesse is a severe evil. I dont know but it may possibly happen to my good freind and fellow traveller the Spanish Collonel¹ as it did to Maréchal Catinat; he was an advocate, and having pleaded, as he verily believed, well in a just cause, on hearing it decided against him, he went home, burnt his advocate's gown, sold his books, and went into the army.² It is presumption in me to offer advice to you; your own mind, and your father are better advisers; but there is one thing to be considered in law suits which lawyers do not allways, the difference betwixt law and equity; for ignorance of form in a deed may make law and equity clash. Now I am persuaded that an advocat who should never accept management of a cause but where equity was clear, would not only gain great honor but also advantage when his reputation on that head was once established, tho in the beginning he might have less practice than others.³ I know your honorable sentiments are such, that I dare swear you⁴ are of my opinion. I wish you and my Lord your father all health and happyness, being with the greatest regard your most obedient, humble servant,

MARISCHAL

You undertake, my good freind, not an easy task in writing an account of Corsica; how can you inform your self of what both sides have to say? If you take your relation only from Paoli, how different will it be from that of the Genoese: tho I am persuaded that the Corsicans are in the right, yet no doubt they will, as all men, be partiall to their cause, and induce you into error. I am ever faithfully yours.

¹ For JB's nickname 'the Spanish Collonel,' see From Marischal, 30 Apr. n. 3.

² Nicolas de Catinat de la Fauconnerie (1637–1712) after leaving the law had a brilliant military career culminating in his being named a marshal of France (NBG).

³ A couple of years later, JB asked SJ whether it was unethical for a lawyer to argue for a bad cause, and SJ told him to leave the determination of what was a bad cause to the judge. JB said he was satisfied with this answer (Journ. 26 Mar. 1768; see *Life* ii. 47, v. 26–27).

⁴ MS. 'your'

To Joseph Fergusson, Friday 3 October 1766

Not reported. Sent 3 Oct. (Reg. Let.). Answered in From Fergusson, 20 Dec.

To William Graham, Friday 3 October 1766

Not reported. Sent 3 Oct. (Reg. Let.).

To Mrs. James Hunter, Friday 3 October 1766

Not reported. Sent 3 Oct.: 'Mrs. Hunter at Moffat' (Reg. Let.).

To Archibald Johnston, Friday 3 October 1766

Not reported. Sent 3 Oct. (Reg. Let.).

From John Dick, Monday 6 October 1766

MS. Yale (C 1008). On the verso of the 2nd leaf is a copy of Dick's letter to Paoli of the same date.

NOTE in Dick's hand at foot of first page: James Boswell Esq.

Leghorn, 6 October 1766

MY DEAR SIR, I had the pleasure to write You the 26 of last Month, and since that sent You by Sea two Examplairs of the 2d Nos. of the Ragualio dell' Isola de Corsica,¹ this day I am favour'd with your very kind, and obliging Letter of the 27 August, which ought to have been here long ago. I therefore sitt down to acquaint You of it's coming to hand, and what I have already done in concequence thereof. I immediately went to Riverola, but found he was sett out for Turin. I then waited on Capt. Santi, who has promised me to procure me as many notices of the particulars which you mention as possible, when I gett them, shall immediately Transmit them to You. Mr. Burnaby who desires your acceptance of his best Compliments, Say's that he will give me a Copy of his Journall to send to You and that You are welcome to make what use of it You please. You may expect to hear from me again in about a fortnight after You receive this. You ask my Opinion about publishing the Generals Letter. I cannot think it right to do it without his Consent, I therefore to save time have wrote him a few lines Copy of which You have here inclosed.² I have also order'd You some Corsican Wine, both red and White, which is Excellent, we shall drink the General's and Your health by and by in it. I wish Your Letter to Lord C. may be productive of the desired Effect,³ sure a Trade with that Island must be advantagiouse to us—as they would in Time take of great quantitys of our Fish and Manufactures. I am much obliged to Sir Alexander Dick, pray present him my best Compliments, and offers of Services in these parts. I have not a perfect knowledge of my own Family, but look on myself as The only Male descendent of Sir William Dick, by his fourth son Louis. I have neglected making any claim to the Title, as have no Children, and to be plain with You, when I was in Trade, I thought it most prudent to avoid everything that might cause extraord. Expences. That reason now Subsisting no more, perhaps I may think about it. I fancy Sir Wm. must have died about the Years 1650 or 1660—if You can Send me this Geniology You will do me a pleasure, it is not impossible but I may make you a Visset some time or other, as I want much to see Scotland, and should be glad to make acquaintance with some of my relations, for in England I have none.[4]

Mrs. Dick desires Your acceptance of her best Compliments, and I ever am with the most perfect Regard, and true Esteem, My dear Sir, Your most Affectionate Friend and Faithfull Servant,

JOHN DICK

(Copy)   6 October 1766

I have the Honour to inform You, that I have just received a Letter from Mr. Boswell dated 27 Aug. acknowledgg. the receipt of the Corsican Gazettes, accompanied with Your Excellencys Letter, which I transmitted to him in Spring last. He mentions an Intention he has form'd of publishing a relation of the present Situation of Corsica, and desires me to procure him any information which may be curous and which I may imagine he may not be informed of. Amongst other things he desires to be informed of the particulars relative to the Greek Colony settled at Ajaccio: to have sent him some Specimens of the Corsican Poetry; particularly he mentions those of Your Excellencys Father, and the Pater Noster paraphrased against the Genoese. He should be glad also to be permitted to publish Your Excellencys first Letter to him, and wishes to be informed of some of the most striking Anecdotes relative to the bravery and Heroism of the Corsicans, during the late Troubles, in short he desires to gett all the intelligence he can concerning the[5] Affairs of Corsica.[6]

I intend to speak to the Abbot Gigli upon these points[7] but have thought it necessary also to write to Your Excellency, particularly to know your pleasure concerning the makg. publick your Excellency's Letter.

Mr. Boswell also mentions moreover his intentions of writing to Lord Chatham (late Mr. Pitt) to endeavour to obtain a revocation of the Kings Proclamation of 1763 and to interest himself as much as possible in the Affairs of Corsica etc.

[1] The *Ragguagli per l'Isola di Corsica* is said to have been published in Campoloro between 1760 and 1767 and also at certain periods in Bastia. According to one source, this weekly periodical was published at Corte and was also read avidly in Italy (Carmine Starace, *Bibliografia della Corsica*, 1943, p. 983). The copies sent by Dick have not been preserved.

[2] In his letter to Dick of 6 Dec. (see n. 6), Paoli granted JB permission to publish his letter of 23 Dec. 1765. It is included, with JB's translation, in *Corsica* (pp. 376–81).

[3] To Chatham, 18 Sept. JB had informed Dick that he would ask Chatham to follow up their conversation of 22 Feb. (Dick to Paoli, 6 Oct., printed at the end of this letter).

[4] In his unreported letter of 27 Aug. JB presumably had raised the possibility that Dick could claim a baronetcy which he believed to have been held by Sir William Dick of Braid (1580–

1655), and which had lapsed since Sir William's death. As later letters make clear, Sir Alexander Dick was to provide, from his charter chest, genealogical and legal documents to substantiate John Dick's claim (From Sir Alexander Dick, c. 27 Aug., 1 Sept., 3 Sept. 1767; early Apr., c. 17 July 1768). See App. I for the Dick of Braid genealogy.

⁵ Copy, 'thee'

⁶ JB succeeded in obtaining from Corsican sources most of the information he needed for *Corsica*. For his account of the settlement of the Greek colony in Corsica he made use of three documents: one sent to him by John Dick (From Dick, 24 Oct. n. 2) and two sent by Paoli (From Paoli to Dick, 6 Dec., printed in BP vii. 216–17, 254–55). JB also included his own translation of one of the many sonnets by Paoli's father Giacinto (*Corsica*, pp. 213–14) and, as an example of one of the Corsicans' 'essays of grave humour ... a curious paraphrase of the Lord's Prayer, where all the petitions are strangely turned into severe accusations against the Genoese' (p. 215). On Paoli's advice, he did not attribute the Pater Noster to the elder Paoli (From Paoli to Dick, 6 Dec.). For Paoli's first letter to JB, see n. 2, above.

⁷ L'Abate Gili was secretary and adviser to Paoli ('Lettere inedite di Pasquale de' Paoli', *Archivio Storica Italiano*, ed. Giovanni Livi, 1890, 5th ser. v. 236, 239).

To Thomas Davies, Tuesday 7 October 1766

Not reported. Sent 7 Oct. (Reg. Let.). Answered in From Davies, 15 Nov.

To George Dempster, Tuesday 7 October 1766

Not reported. Sent 7 Oct. (Reg. Let.).

To William McQuhae, Tuesday 7 October 1766

Not reported. Sent 7 Oct. (Reg. Let.).

To Lady Preston, Friday 10 October 1766

Not reported. Sent 10 Oct. (Reg. Let.). Answered in From Lady Preston, 16 Oct.

To John Stobie, Friday 10 October 1766

Not reported. Sent 10 Oct. (Reg. Let.). John Stobie (d. c. 1792) was Lord Auchinleck's law clerk and, after Lord Auchinleck's death in 1782, factor to his widow. He was also enrolled by the Court of Session as an 'agent or solicitor', 1755–92 (*Edin. Almanack*, 1792, p. 44). JB sent funds to Stobie to assist his old nurse (From Lady Preston, 16 Oct., n. 3).

To the Duchess of Douglas,¹ Monday 13 October 1766

MS. Yale (L 441). A copy, with signature, in the hand of John Boswell of Knockroon,² with one correction by JB, noted below.

ENDORSEMENT by John Boswell of Knockroon: Copy Letter Mr. Js. Boswell To the Dutches of Douglas 1766.

Ayr, 13th Octr. 1766

MADAM: I know it is unnecessary for me to use any arguments with your Grace in behalf of the bearer of this Letter³ your generous humanity I have no doubt of and your Spirit and activity⁴ are known to all the world. But as I was one of the Council for his unfortunate son, and have had occasion to talk with the Poor old Man, I am so much Concerned to think of the deep affliction of good and creditable people that I cannot but beg leave to trouble your Grace with a few lines.

The young man has had a very fair tryal, and I must say that he has been Convicted of Crimes most destructive to society; for two repeatted acts of House-breaking have been proved upon him.[5] But as he was always a lad of remarkable good Character 'till lately he fell in with bad Company and as he is very young and very Simple I think he has a Strong claim for mercy add to this that his poor old parent is like to break his heart and has even some little reflection against himself for having treated his son rather too harshly and being in some measure the Occasion of his joining himself with wicked Company. I must add that I have the Strongest reason to believe that my Lord Advocate himself moved by the misery of the aged Father positively told him that his son should get off for transporta-tion.[6] I own that what has happened is to me most astonishing, after assurances I had to the contrary. If it be really true that my Lord Advocate gave his word to the old man that his sons life Should be saved, and desired that his parents should set their minds at ease, I should with all submission think his Lordship, bound in humanity I will even say in honour to make good what he has said if there is still a possibility of doing it. And I should hope that an[7] application made by his Majesty's advocate himself to whom the Crown entrusts the whole Charge of Criminal bussiness in Scotland, I should hope that a Strong application made by him cannot be refused. Let me then earnestly entreat of your grace to lose No[8] time in prevailling with his Lordship to write up for a transportation pardon to James Haddow, which I cannot but think will not be thought unreasonable. Your Grace will Consider how Cruel it must be upon the poor Family; if after being assured from the highest authority that his son's life should be saved, the young man should yet be brought to the Gallows. I would write to Lord Advocate, and I would speak to the Judges were it not that it is thought improper in ane advocate,[9] who is to do his duty in defending a pannell before a Court but ought not to Sollicite the officers of the Law. The Duke of Queensberry being Justice's general is a very lucky Circumstance[10] and I would hope the Justice Clerk would not be too Severe.[11] I offer my respectabl. compliments to Mr. Douglass and hope he will join in Endeavouring to relieve a worthy Tennant from the greatest misery.[12] For god's sake my lady Dutches be earnest and forgive this trouble from your Graces most obedient and faithfull, humble servant,

/signed/ JAMES BOSWEL

[1] Margaret Douglas (d. 1774), Duchess of Douglas, was the widow of Archibald Douglas, first Duke of Douglas (1694–1761), whom she had married in 1758. In 1762 JB entertained thoughts of marrying the Duchess (*Earlier Years*, pp. 81, 479–80). For further information about her, see *Life* v. 43 n. 4.

[2] John Boswell (1741–1805), younger of Knockroon, was a 'writer' practising in Ayr. Both his parents were descended from John Boswell, third Laird of Auchinleck, and he was heir to his mother's estate of Knockroon (Walker, p. 251 n. 1).

[3] James Haddow's father. See n. 5 below and To James Haddow, 13 Oct.

[4] Copy, JB has written 'activity' above deleted 'alacrity'

[5] James Haddow, *alias* Blackwood, son of James Haddow in Longhouse, Douglas parish, Lanarkshire, had been found guilty on 11 Oct. by a jury in Ayr of two counts of housebreaking and theft; on 13 Oct. he was sentenced to be hanged in Ayr on 14 Nov. Patrick Murray, Advocate Depute, appeared for the prosecution; Charles Brown, Claud Boswell, and JB for the defence. The judges were the Lord Justice Clerk (see n. 11 below) and Lord Coalston (*Earlier Years*, pp. 299–300, 532).

[6] The Lord Advocate was James Montgomery (1721–1803). In the spring of this year he had

succeeded Thomas Miller both as Lord Advocate and as M.P. for Dumfries Burghs through the influence of the Queensberry family interest. In 1775 he became Chief Baron of the Scottish Exchequer and in 1801 was created a baronet (Namier and Brooke iii. 159–60).

[7] Copy, 'our' altered to 'an'

[8] Copy, 'to' altered to 'No'

[9] Copy, 'in ane advocate' (a dittography) deleted before 'who'

[10] Charles Douglas (1698–1778), third Duke of Queensberry, was titular head of the Court of Justiciary as Lord Justice General. His paternal grandmother was Isabel Douglas, daughter of William Douglas, first Marquess of Douglas, great-grandfather of the first Duke of Douglas. The Duke of Queensberry and the Duchess of Douglas were guardians of Archibald Douglas (1748–1827), principal in the Douglas Cause, which was soon to come before the Court of Session (William Fraser, *Douglas Book*, 1885, ii. 524).

[11] The Lord Justice Clerk was Thomas Miller (1717–89), Lord Barskimming, whose promotion to that office earlier this year JB and his brothers had resented (*Earlier Years*, pp. 292, 530). In 1761–66 he had been M.P. for Dumfries Burghs, a seat procured for him by the Duke of Queensberry. His appointment as Lord Justice Clerk may also have been due to Queensberry's influence (Namier and Brooke iii. 139–40).

[12] Nine-tenths of Douglas parish, Lanarkshire, belonged to the Douglas family (*New Statistical Account of Scotland*, 1845, vi. 487). For 'Mr. Douglass', see n. 10 above.

To James Haddow, Monday 13 October 1766

MS. Yale (L 595). A copy, with signature, in the hand of John Boswell of Knockroon.

ENDORSEMENT by John Boswell of Knockroon: Copy Letter Mr. Boswell To James Haddow 1766.

Ayr, 13th Octr. 1766

DEAR JAMES: Inclosed you have a letter for the Dutches of Douglass in which I have said all I can to make her Grace earnest in endeavouring to get your Son's sentence changed to Transportation.

The Judges would not allow him any more than the usual time, but if transportation can be granted there is time enough for Procuring it. I would have written to my Lord Advocate but I find that it is not proper for one of my Profession to Sollicite the officers of the law. So you will excuse me not writting to his Lordship. I can assure you I have said every thing to my Lady Dutches which I could have written to him.

I would advise you not to have great hopes of obtaining a Change of the Sentence, which I am affraid it will be difficult to get done. Above all beware of giving your Son any hope. If he should live the more dismal his situation is at present, the deeper impression will be made on his mind in order to his reformation. And if he must die it is proper that his mind should be tottally fixed on a preparation for another world, in which I hope the poor simple young man who is very penitent will be better than he has been in this. May god in his great Mercey comfort you and his afflicted mother.[1] I am, Dear James, Your sincere wellwisher,

/signed/ JAMES BOSWELL

[1] On 12 Nov. the Provost of Ayr presented to the Ayr Council a royal respite of three weeks dated 29 Oct. (Ayr Council Book, 1759–67—information kindly supplied by Sir James Fergusson of Kilkerran, Bt.). Though there is no further record of the cause, the absence of any notice of Haddow's execution either in JB's papers or in the legal records suggests that his sentence was commuted to transportation (*Earlier Years*, p. 532).

To Alexandre Deleyre, Wednesday 15 October 1766

MS. Yale (L 413). An extract copied from the original letter, which was sent to David Boswell for his perusal; David Boswell forwarded the letter to M. Charray[1] in Paris (From David Boswell, 31 Oct.).

HEADING: Extrait A M. De Leyre.[2]

á Auchinleck, ce 15 dOctobre 1766

J'ai une idée que M. Rousseau aurroit eté assez content de prendre une pension. Mais Il souhaitoit de l'avoir sur un pied que Jamais un Homme peut avoir une pension. Il a des idées d'independance qui sont tout á fait visionnaires, et qui ne conviennent pas á un Homme de son etat.[3] Car dites moi Je vous en prie, comment Jean Jacques Rousseau peut vivre independant, excepté á l'egard á son esprit, les ressorts duquel ne dependeront jamais que de cette force singuliêrre que la Nature lui a accordée. Mais a l'egard de sa situation exterieure, il faut bien qu'il soit dependant. Si Jean Jacques etoit jeune, et robuste, et rude, comme un de ces Sauvages qu'il veut nous faire tant admirer, alors il pourroit se mocquer de tout le Genre humain, et courant par les Bois, s'ecrier *Vivo et regno*.[4] Mais Jean Jacques est veritablement un Homme d'une certaine age, et un Homme qui a vecu. Il est foible, malade, et delicat á un point que Je ne croirois jamais sans l'avoir vu. C'est un Homme qui aime la friandise même, et qui seroit tres mecontent si on lui otoit la bonne chêre, et un lit doux. Il peut avoir les idées d'un Hercule. Mais voila l'Homme qu'il est; et dites moi si un tel Homme n'a pas besoin de beaucoup d'attention et beaucoup d'amitié de ses semblables, et par consequent ne dependera pas d'eux comme nous dependons tous l'un de l'autre?

XXXXXXX——

En quel etat que Je serai, soyez persuadé que Je conserverai toujours pour vous un affection la plus vive. C'est vraye qu'actuellement Je n'ai pas besoin de vos secours á mon Ame melancolique, comme J'avois autrefois á Parme; mais la memoire en m'est tres douce, et Je souhaitrois presque d'etre encore triste, pour avoir encore le plaisir d'etre consolé par M. DeLeyre.[5]

XXXX——

Les Anglois sont bien lents á determiner si un auteur est veritablement un Beau Genie; et par cette principe ils accordent trop tard á leurs Hommes celêbres la reputation qu'ils meritent, á peur de ne l'accorder a ceux qui ne la meritent pas.

[1] François Charray (1720–after 1795) served as clerk in the Foreign Affairs Office in Versailles from 1757 until 1767, when he was dismissed following a general review of the department (*Corres. Rousseau* xxxi. 266).

[2] The three paragraphs, copied by JB from his original letter, are concerned with three of several subjects discussed in From Deleyre, 1 Mar.: Rousseau, JB's state of mind, and the English neglect of Bacon and Milton.

[3] Refusing to recognize his dependence on the good will of David Hume, Richard Davenport, and others, Rousseau had initially declined the pension of £100 a year awarded him by George III (*New Hume Letters*, pp. 149–50, 160). He finally decided to accept it in May 1767, just before leaving England (*Corres. Rousseau* xxxiii. 66).

[4] Horace, *Epistles* I. x. 8: 'I live and reign' (trans. H. R. Fairclough, Loeb ed.); the poem is about living in the country according to nature. Here JB is referring to Rousseau's Second Discourse (*Sur l'origine et les fondements de l'inégalité parmi les hommes*, 1755). JB uses the same phrase (*vivo et regno*) in his Memorabilia ([1767] p. 3—M 175) under the heading,

Inscription to be put over the door of a Little House. Quid pueris? vivo et regno.

[5] For JB's relationship with Deleyre while visiting Parma in 1765, see From Alexandre Deleyre, 1 Mar. and n. 1.

To Willem van Tuyll van Serooskerken, c. mid-October 1766

Not reported. Answered in From van Tuyll, 11 Nov.

From Lady Preston,[1] Thursday 16 October 1766

MS. Yale (C 2282). Received 21 Oct. (Reg. Let.).
ADDRESS: To James Boswell Esqr., Auchinleck.

Valliefield, Octr. 16

DEAR SIR: I had yours by Gordon and you may belive shall very willingly execute the Comision you give me, ore any other in my powre.[2] I yesterday receved from Mr. Stobie two and fifty shilings which you had orderd for your Nurse, and imeadiatly sent to inquire about her situation that the ten shilings now due might be laid out to the best advantage, and find that she was in such want of some nesesery pairts of Clothing which are now to be provided for her, and made the ten shilings Come in a very sesonable time, and belive you know that she is non of the best managers, I shal indevour that your bounty to her shal be from time to time given in the best maner.[3]

All in this house Joyn me in our best Complements to Lord Auchinleck and your self, and belive me ever to be your most affectionat Aunt and Humble servant,

ANN PRESTON

[1] Lady Preston (d. 1779), née Anne Cochrane, was a sister of JB's maternal grandmother, Euphemia Cochrane, and wife of Sir George Preston, Bt., of Valleyfield, Fife (*Ominous Years*, gen. chart V). There were nine Preston children, of whom five sons and two daughters were still living (William Stephen, *History of Inverkeithing and Rosyth*, 1921, pp. 79–80). Lady Preston had helped to bring up JB's mother (*Earlier Years*, pp. 11–12), and JB said some time after his marriage that she and Sir George 'had really been like parents' to him and his wife Margaret 'for these several years' (Journ. 30 Dec. 1775).

[2] Gordon may have been the carrier who brought the mail from Edinburgh to Culross on Tuesdays (*Edin. Almanack*, 1767, p. 104). Valleyfield was one and a half miles from the town of Culross.

[3] Presumably Lady Preston is referring to the wet-nurse who suckled JB as an infant. We do not know the nurse's name, but it seems likely that since 'Mr. Harrower at Torryburn' was responsible for delivering her weekly one-shilling pension (Journ. 17 Mar. 1780), she lived in Torryburn, a village two and a half miles from Culross and about half that distance from Valleyfield House. Lady Preston died in Nov. 1779, and before her death she transferred the 'commission' to deliver the 'shilling a week' JB had been allowing his nurse since he was admitted to the bar, to Mrs. Boswell and Lady Preston's daughter Agnes (*Laird*, p. 191 and n. 8; From Lady Preston, 4 Jan. [1779]).

From Pasquale Paoli, c. Monday 20 October 1766

Not reported. See from John Dick, 24 Oct. On 22 Nov. James Bruce wrote to JB that 'sixteen quarto pages from General Paoli' had arrived at Auchinleck. For the contents of this letter, see To George Dempster, 1 Jan. 1767, and To Lord Chatham, 3 Jan. 1767.

To Sir Alexander Dick, Thursday 23 October 1766

MS. New York Public Library.

Auchinleck, 23 Octr. 1766

My Dear Sir: I return you a thousand thanks for your most obliging letter from Mr. Spence's. The lively description you give me of the happiness which you enjoyed during your late agreable Tour, has made me enjoy it with you. And this is what you wish to do with all good things,—to share them with your Friends. Perhaps I whom you have done the honour to make your Counsellor, have a title to put in my claim in a double capacity.[1] You seem to think so, and it is not my business to call it in question. I may however very safely affirm that all the Counsel I can give you these seven years will not be equivalent to the pleasure which your last has given me. You used to call yourself the Corycius Senex. I am sure We must all address you as fortunate Senex.[2] You have brought home with you all the fine spirits, and *piaccevole* temper of an Italian;[3] and I hope to see you like Cornaro the old Venetian Nobleman gayer and happier in the last stage than others are in[4] the first: And this too without living by weight and measure as Signor Cornaro did.[5] The best praise I can give your verses is to tell you that I began to read them before I read your letter, and from their boldness and manly expression I concluded that they were a Sally of Doctor Armstrong who I knew was of your Party. This was praise without partiality, for I never knew that my esteemed Friend courted the Muse in his own language.[6] I hope I shall see more of such Sallys. I have had three or four returns of the ague this Autumn; but am now quite well, and I hope a little of the Bark has braced me up beyond further danger.[7] I was at two different Circuits, where I did my best for some poor Pannels.[8] So that I have some excuse for delaying so long to answer your favour from Mr. Spence's. I am going on with my Account of Corsica, and hope to make it a tollerable Book. I would wish to do the brave Islanders no harm by relating what I saw while I was among them; and I would wish to have old Plutarch at Auchinleck for a month or two, were it probable that He would condescend to assist me: And indeed I imagine He would not be averse to it. I could tell him of Souls equal in sentiment and bravery to any He has pourtrayed in his immortal Biography. You remember Mr. Pitt applyd to General Paoli what the Cardinal de Retz said of the great Duke of Montrose 'C'est un de ces Hommes qu'on ne trouve plus que dans les vies de Plutarque.'[9] I am delighted with your idea of having a solemn service performed for Paoli in the Cathedral of Durham.[10] I offer my best Compliments to Lady Dick, and to your fair Secretary who I dare say were very happy with your pleasant Tour. After my long silence I can hardly expect a letter from you while I am here. Tho' as I find my friends so much better than myself, I will presume to flatter myself with the hopes of hearing from you again before the Session sits down. Ever yours,

James Boswell

[1] JB had represented Sir Alexander before the Court of Session on 4 Aug. in his controversy with James Hamilton, eighth Earl of Abercorn, over Duddingston Loch (Consultation Book) and would be involved in the same controversy for the next three years (From Sir Alexander Dick, 10 Apr. 1767 and n. 7).

[2] Dick felt he resembled Virgil's old Corycian farmer who *regum aequabat opes animis*—

'matched in contentment the wealth of kings' (*Georgics* iv. 132, trans. H. R. Fairclough, Loeb ed.). See To Sir Alexander Dick, 22 May 1765. 'Fortunate senex' is Virgil, *Eclogues* i. 46: 'Happy old man!' (trans. H. T. Fairclough, Loeb ed.).

[3] Like JB, Sir Alexander loved ancient Rome and modern Italy, and he had kept a journal during his Italian travels in 1736–37 (*Scots Charta Chest*, pp. 104–22). His letters reveal that

he was indeed *piacèvole* or 'good-humoured'.

[4] MS. 'in' written above deleted 'at'

[5] Luigi Cornaro (1467–1566) was the author of an extraordinarily popular work, *Discorsi della vita sobria*, describing his own mental and physical history. Near death at forty, Cornaro embarked upon a rigorous programme of physical culture, severe dietary restrictions, and spiritual discipline, which brought him health, happiness, and a long life. Numerous English translations were published throughout the eighteenth century, including one called *Sure Methods of Attaining a Long and Healthful Life*, brought out in 1753 by R. and A. Foulis in Glasgow.

[6] For notice of the verses, see From Sir Alexander Dick, 22 Aug. n. 11. Dick also wrote verses in Latin (*Scots Charta Chest*, p. 123).

[7] David Boswell had written to JB on 30 Aug. that Peter Adie, an Edinburgh surgeon, advised JB to use the bark, 'not in Tincture, but the Solid Bark', to relieve a recurrence of the malaria he had first contracted in Corsica (Journ. 28 Oct.

1765).

[8] JB's first criminal client, John Reid, was brought to trial on a charge of sheep-stealing 13 Sept. in Glasgow, on the Western Circuit (From John Reid, 13 Nov. n. 1); another client, James Haddow, was convicted of housebreaking 11 Oct. in Ayr, on the Southern Circuit (To the Duchess of Douglas, 13 Oct. and n. 5; *Earlier Years*, pp. 299–300, 532).

[9] Although JB did not record it, William Pitt must have paid this tribute to Paoli at his interview with JB on 22 Feb., and JB used it to conclude *Corsica*. Jean-François-Paul de Gondi (1613–79), Cardinal de Retz, described James Graham (1612–50), first Marquess of Montrose as 'le seul homme du monde qui m'ait jamais rappelé l'idée de certains héros que l'on ne voit plus que dans les Vies de Plutarque' (*Mémoires*, 1828, ii. 66).

[10] See From Sir Alexander Dick, 22 Aug. There is no evidence that such a service was held.

From John Dick, Friday 24 October 1766

MS. Yale (C 1009).

Leghorn, 24 October 1766

DEAR SIR, I had the pleasure to write You the 6 Instant, since which have endeavd. to put together as many materials relating to Corsica as I could possibly gett, herewith I send You Copy of Mr. Burnaby's Journal which he permitted me to take and send You, and wishes it may be of any use to You.

Amongst my old papers I found the Resolution of the Corsicans on de Paoli's first arrival amongst them, Copy of which I also send You.[1]

You will also find an account of the Greek Colony,[2] and a Letter which came to my hands yesterday from the General—he had not receiv'd that which I wrote him last concerning You,—but I beleive I may expect his answer soon, when shall not fail to Transmit it to You, and in about eight days hence, shall send You a Packett of Poetry, they are now transcribing, indeed had the person not disapointed me, they would have gone in this, I am sorry that I have no way of Conveying this Packett to You to save You the Postage,[3] but as you talkd of Publishing this winter, I did not think it prudent to wait, especially as I perceiv'd by the Papers, that there is a Man in France who is about publishing a History of Corsica.[4]

Mrs. Dick desires Your acceptance of her best Compliments, and I ever am with the most perfect Regard and unalterable Esteem, My dear Sir, Your most Assured Friend and Faithfull Servant,

JOHN DICK

P.S. I had forgott to Congratulate You, on your becoming a Patronus Causarum,[5] and have not the least doubt of your making a figure in your Profession.

[1] The Proclamation, issued by the General Council of the Kingdom of Corsica and dated 15 July 1755, declared Paoli to be elected General of the Nation. JB printed the enclosed English translation of the Proclamation (C 826), with some verbal changes and without the last paragraph, in *Corsica* (pp. 127–30).

[2] JB made some use in *Corsica* (pp. 84–90) of this manuscript, 'Nottizia intorno Allo Stabilimento di una Collonia Grecca nel Regno di Corsica' (C 830), concerning the Genoese grant of a part of Corsica to a group of Greeks fleeing the oppression of the Turks. For the other documents relating to the Greek Colony, which JB received from Paoli—an account by Dr. Stefanopoli, a Greek refugee living in Sartene and another by a Greek living in Ajaccio—see From John Dick, 6 Oct. and n. 6; 7 Jan. 1767.

[3] The package presumably contained the materials mentioned in Dick's letter to Paoli, 6 Oct. (From Dick, 6 Oct. and n. 6). See also From Dick, 31 Oct. and n. 1.

[4] Perhaps *Description géographique et historique de l'isle de Corse*, Paris, 1769, by Jacques-Nicolas Bellin.

[5] *Patronus Causae* is a Latin legal term meaning 'advocate' (Adolf Berger, *Encyclopedic Dictionary of Roman Law*, 1953, pp. 352, 623).

From Robert Brown, c. late October 1766

Not reported. For contents of this letter, see From Brown, 27 Jan. 1767.

From John Dick, Friday 31 October 1766

MS. Yale (C 1010).

NOTE in Dick's hand at foot of first page: James Boswell Esq.

Leghorn, 31st October 1766

My DEAR SIR, I hope my Letters of the 6th and 24th of this month, will have reached You, I trouble You with this to cover the Corsican Poetry, which I have not been able to gett Copied untill this moment.[1] I have spent in all three Zechines for you, which is placed to your debit.[2]

I hope when You publish your book You will contrive to send me a Couple by the first Ship, in the mean while should You have any further Commds. for me, pray favour me with them, You can't possibly make me more happy than by Employing me. If ever You see Jimmy Ferguson, or Capt. Napier present my most Affectionate Compliments to them.[3]

Mrs. Dick begs your acceptance of her kindest Compliments, and I ever am with the most unalterable Regard, and true Esteem, My dear Sir, Your most affectionate Friend and Faithfull Servant,

JOHN DICK

[1] For the Corsican poetry, see From John Dick, 6 Oct. and n. 6.

[2] The zechine or sequin was a Venetian gold coin worth just under 10s. sterling at the 1753 rate of exchange (*Gent. Mag.* 1753, xxiii. 7).

[3] Presumably James Ferguson (1735–1820), younger of Pitfour, and the Hon. Charles Napier (1731–1807). Young Pitfour, JB's fellow advocate (*Fac. Adv.* p. 69), had announced his intention, in Nov. 1757, of 'going to Italy with a Leghorn fleet of merchant-men' (*Letters of George Dempster to Sir Adam Fergusson, 1756–*

1813, ed. James Fergusson, 1934, p. 43), and it must have been at this time that he became acquainted with Dick. He later served as M.P. for Aberdeenshire, 1790–1820 (Namier and Brooke ii. 419). In Mar. 1767 Dick asked Ferguson to help him substantiate his claim to the Braid baronetcy (From John Dick, 6 Mar. 1767). Napier, second son of Francis Napier, fifth Lord Napier, had been a Captain in the Royal Navy since 1762, but was no longer on active service by 1766 (*Court and City Register*, 1766, p. 208).

From Sir Alexander Dick, Saturday 1 November 1766

MS. Yale (C 958).

Prestonfield, November 1, 1766

MY DEAR SIR, I have been fancying, You (during the long tract of good weather) circulating with a variety of the Judges in different Circuits, sometimes viewing the Nakedness of our Native land, At other times admiring the Nobly rude prospects of nature, which dignify and adorn us, and make us justly held to be the Classic ground of Ossian and Fingal.[1]— I often painted you in my mind a *Doctissime Trebate*[2] in defending the causes of the poor, and miserable pannels, who from a Ray springing from your Eloquence at the Barr, have from Dungeons, been at lenth extricated, and restord to human Society. In these last excellent scenes I find by your Notable and freindly letter of Octr. 23d. you have been last engagd. These are deeds Worthy of yourself!

To tell you the truth, I did not expect a return to my Letter, sooner then it came, but I no sooner read it over, (which I did with a peculiar degree of pride and pleasure,) than I put pen to paper to send you this. Lord! what a degree of strenth and stability, you have given to the Crutches of an Old man, who last week, climd to the very top of the[3] grand Climaterieal hill, which had three score and three small hills, to pass, before we arrive at its summit.[4] In passing in some of these, my journey has been very much chequerd with a variety of uncommon adventures. And I now consider myself at liberty to smoak the pipe of Old age, alongst with some Veterans, such as my brother Sir John and Mr. Keith,[5] who have made the same journey with me, with this small difference of having sett out a little earlier.— By those freindly Crutches you have given me, and the philosophic interviews I hope often to have with you, my descent down-hill, will give me immense pleasure and satisfaction.—

Your progress in relating the Deeds of the great Pasquale Paoli, gives me the highest pleasure, I beleive you will at lenth, bring[6] me to worship the Shrine of that Hero. At any rate I resolve to have a place for him in my garden among the *Remarkables*, which I call Muses, because they set people a musing, upon what is either great good or Eloquent.— There are to be lines cut out but[7] few in number, on stone, but on very large stones and these stones are to be Whin some rude, some regular, from Arthurs Seat, to speak to Posterity a language they ought to hear which may come to make their Ears tingle.[8]— I remember forty years ago, when Old Allan Ramsay and I were taking a pleasing pastoral Walk, along my hill at Clermiston, near Corstorphin,[9] in the midst of a little wild Glen, we were surprisd with an uncommon sight which was, a big hercules of a mason, driving off chips from a very large whin stone which lay below, with uncommon attention and as it were fury. My freind Allan, askt him calmly; 'what are you about honest man? you seem very warmly employd'.— 'Employd' says he, 'I am engagd in a dreadfull attempt No less then carving a King Robert the Bruce and since I begun his image is staring me thro the stone as if it wants to burst out and he becomes so odd like and God like, I am almost frighted out of my Senses, and the gentleman who employd me expects to put him up at Bruce hill this night'[10]—thus, ends my Anecdote: and my paper. My Dear Sir, I and all my family wish you well and long to see you and drink paoli's health. Yours most affectionatly,

ALEXANDER DICK

¹ James Macpherson (1736–96) had published *Fingal* in 1762 and *The Works of Ossian* in 1765.

² 'Most learned Trebatius'. C. Trebatius Testa, a distinguished jurist, is Horace's interlocutor in *Satires* II. i., where he is addressed as *docte Trebati*—'learned Trebatius' (l. 78). Cicero, a close friend, dedicated his *Topics* to him.

³ MS. 'the' superimposed upon 'this'

⁴ Sir Alexander had reached the age of 63 on 23 Oct. (William Baird, *Annals of Duddingston and Portobello*, 1898, ii. 124).

⁵ Sir John Cunningham (c. 1696–1777) of Caprington, Bt., eldest brother of Sir Alexander, had succeeded to the title and estates of their father, Sir William Cunningham of Caprington, Bt., in 1740; for Sir Alexander's change of name and his title, see From Sir Alexander Dick, 22 Aug. n. 1. Robert Keith (d. 1774) was husband of Sir Alexander's sister Margaret. Generally known as 'Ambassador' Keith, he had served as British Minister in Vienna, 1748–58, and Ambassador to St. Petersburg, 1758–62, before settling in the Hermitage at Leith Links, where, like his brother-in-law, he devoted himself to gardening (*Letters of David Hume*, ed. J. Y. T. Greig, 1932, ii. 208 and n. 1; DNB).

⁶ MS. 'bring' superimposed upon 'cause'

⁷ MS. 'but' superimposed upon 'out'

⁸ The charming grounds of Prestonfield House had been laid out by Sir Alexander's grandfather, Sir James Dick, and improved by Sir Alexander (*Annals of Duddingston* ii. 123, 125–29), who took a keen interest in horticulture and was at great pains to maintain and improve his lands (ibid. pp. 125–29). His plan to have carved the sayings of great men called for stone of the Markle basalt type found at the summit and on the northern slope, called Whinny Hill, of Arthur's Seat, which overlooked his estate (B. N. Peach, et al., *Geology of the Neighbourhood of Edinburgh*, 1910, pp. 318–19). There is no evidence that he carried out this plan.

⁹ Allan Ramsay (1686–1758), the poet, and Sir Alexander were close friends for many years (*Scots Charta Chest*, pp. 90. 163–71). Sir Alexander owned an estate to the west of Edinburgh at Clermiston (*New Stat. Acct.* i. 215).

¹⁰ 'Brucehill', where the statue was to be set up that night, was the old name for Belmont, one of three estates on the south side of Corstorphine Hill. Belmont was originally leased by Charles Bruce, a glazier in Edinburgh (information and the reference to the *New Stat. Acct.* i. 213, 215–16, kindly supplied by Dr. Jean Munro). No evidence connects Brucehill to Robert the Bruce.

To John Johnstoun, c. early to mid-November 1766

Not reported. See From Johnstoun, 20 Nov.: 'I have Communed with John Reid Several times upon what You Wrote me but have not as Yet been able to Learn any thing further from him to the purpose.'

From Willem van Tuyll van Serooskerken,¹ Tuesday 11 November– Thursday 4 December 1766

MS. Yale (C 3013).

ADDRESS: Monsieur, Monsieur Boswell d'Auchinleck à Auchinleck en Ecosse; [*added notations, from top to bottom*] Pr. Strange; Not Found In; Return'd from; try Cork [*deleted*]; Scotland.

POSTMARKS from top to bottom: Dublin; [Dublin] Cork; I•A 14; [London] 27 IA.²

à Utrecht, ce 11 Novembre 1766

J'ai eu trop de plaisir Monsieur à recevoir une Marque d'amitié et de Souvenir d'un Ami pour n'y pas répondre avec empressement. Je reçois dans cet instant votre lettre et je l'ai à peine achevée de lire. Je vous felicite de tout mon coeur de la situation d'esprit ou vous êtes. Je relis volontiers cette phrase: 'Je crois que je serai capable de passer par cette vie assés bien.' Cette esperance en est un sur garand.

Vous parlés de votre long silence. On fait bien aisement sa paix avec moi sur cet article la une lettre racomode tout. Les lettres sont un agrement dans l'amitié. Mais elles n'en sont pas la marque essencielle. Dites moi aprés un long silence jai souvent pensé à mon ami et je vous[3] tiens quitte de ce que vous auries[4] pu me dire dans l'intervalle. Mais je crains que cette regle ne tire à consequence. Souvenèz vous donc Monsieur je vous prie quelle n'est que pour racommoder le passé. Vous me parlés de ce que je vous disois à Paris au sujet de mon pere vous avés on ne peut pas mieux deviné.[5] Nous sommes je crois aussi bien ensemble quil soit possible de l'etre je profite autant que je le puis de ses conoissances. Je ne le connois bien que depuis mon retour. Je voudrois avoir retenu toutes ses conversations instructives elles le sont beaucoup. Ma soeur est plus prés de vous que vous ne l'imaginés elle est à londres elle y à passé bien près d'un mois mon frere l'y à conduite et il l'y à laissé il avoit des affaires ici. Il est avancé il est actuellement Commendeur de Vaisseau.[6] Il pense a se marier. Il à demandé Mlle. de Reede soeur de Lord Athlone. Elle ne l'a pas refusé mais elle exige absolument qu'il quitte le Service elle à la dessus des prejugés invincibles. Cela met mon frere dans un grand embaras. Mon pere seroit faché quil quittat. Il est beaucoup combattu. Je ne sais pas encore ce que cela deviendra.[7] Mais avant que de passer outre je dois vous avertir monsieur que cest aujourdhuy le 4 Decembre jai ete obligé de discontinuer notre conversation du 11 de Novembre et je n'ai pu renouer qu'aujourdhuy. J'ai beaucoup chassé.[8] Apresent que la chasse est fermée je suis tout a mes amis, et je no regrette pas les forets. Que nous sommes loin l'un de l'autre jadmire comment nos idees bravent les elements, franchissent les mers et les montagnes et nous parviennent sans avoir rien perdu par une si etrange course. Aves vous apris les demelés de Rousseau et de Mr. Hume. Quels etranges procedés. Rousseau est il encore votre ami après une conduite aussi deraisonnable est on genereux est on homme quand on trouve insuportable le poids de la reconnoissance quand on se fait volontairement illusion pour en secouer le joug?

Je me porte mieux qua Paris beaucoup mieux. J'ai ete obligé d'avouer à mon Pere ma maladie. Vous en avés vu le comencement à Paris.[9] J'ai ete oblige de passer les grands remèdes. J'etois fort malade j'espérois toujours de me guerir sans en venir la mais jempirois tous les jours. J'ai pensé à vous quand ma mere et ma soeur etoient près de mon lit me plaignoient et se doutoient bien peu du sujet de mes meaux.[10] J'ai admiré comment mon Pere s'est conduit dans cette affaire. Pas un mot de reproche pas un moment d'humeur, toujours donnant les meilleurs conseils et menageant ma delicatesse en ne s'y melant qu'indirectement. J'ai eu longtems des inquietudes sur mon etat. Jai ete gueri a Aix la chapelle et je n'ai pas rencontré de bons medecins.[11] J'ai consulté de loin Monsieur Tissot de Suisse, et un autre chez nous.[12] J'ai cru longtems netre pas gueri mais enfin je le suis. Et je me porte mieux d'esprit et de corps. Que puis encore vous dire qui vous interesse. Je suis dans ce moment avec Mon pere et ma mere, l'un ecrit et l'autre travaille. J'ai causé longtems avec mon pere je leur tiens beaucoup compagnie à tous deux. Je lis l'Histoire de Hume en francois à Ma mere.[13] Je serois heureux sans une imagination qui court les champs sans m'en demander la permission. Mais il faut bien que tout le monde s'amuse. Je n'ai pas perdu l'esperance de vous voir un jour dans votre patrie elle est un des païs ou je me plais à promener mes idées. Mais je n'en suis pas encore la je suis plus loin[14] de l'Ecosse à Utrecht que je n'en etois à Paris ou en Suisse. Adieu Monsieur continués a etre heureux et rendèz moi comte quelquefois de votre bonheur. Il contribuera au mien. Vos anciens amis d'Utrecht se portent bien. Le Dom est toujours le plus respectable le plus melancolique et le plus vanteux de tous les batiments possibles j'oubliois de dire le plus gothique ce seroit dire tout en un mot.[15] Monsieur Brouun et sa maison se portent fort bien aussi. Je dis fort bien en general, mais jai tort. Monsieur Broun[16] est souvent très incomodé, et sa santé est chancelante cest en verité un homme trés estimable.[17] Mr. de guiffardiere demande à etre troisieme Ministre avec Messieurs Rambonnet et Huet conoissés vous ces ennuieux et tristes personnages?[18] Leur[19] eglise n'est plus quun *Church-Jard* je veux dire un cimetiere.[20]

[1] Willem René van Tuyll van Serooskerken (1743–1839), younger brother of Belle de Zuylen (Zélide). He became a member of the first chamber of the States-General, commander of the Order of the Netherlandish Lion, and was created Baron in 1814 (Ch. J. Polvliet, *Genealogie van het Geslacht van Tuyll van Serooskerken*, 1894, pp. 32–34). At JB's meeting with him in Paris on 13 Jan. they had discussed the possibility of JB's marrying Belle (Notes, 14 Jan.).

[2] The reconstruction of the address and postmarks is conjectural. 'Pr.' in the address is an abbreviation for 'Per'. 'Return'd from' may be meant to precede 'Cork', though the conjunction of handwriting and stamp has not been observed elsewhere. 'I A 14' seems to be a stamp of the Dublin Post Office (R. C. Alcock and F. C. Holland, *Postmarks of Great Britain and Ireland* [1940], p. 126). Evidently this letter strayed to Dublin and Cork; we do not know when it reached JB.

[3] MS. 'vous' written above deleted 'te'

[4] MS. 'que vous auries' written above deleted 'quil aurait'

[5] JB had written to Willem's father, Diederik Jacob van Tuyll van Serooskerken (1707–76), Heer van Zuylen, a wealthy nobleman of Utrecht (Polvliet, pp. 32–33) on 16 Jan. to ask for Belle's hand in marriage. His proposal was hedged about with conditions, among them an oath to be taken by Belle and witnessed by her father and brothers that she would always remain faithful to him, and a virtual guarantee that she preferred him to all others, including the Comte de Bellegarde with whom JB was aware that she was considering marriage (From Baroness von Spaen, 22 July, nn. 7, 8). JB received a friendly reply from van Zuylen, dated 30 Jan., saying that he could not consider JB's proposal seriously until a decision had been made about Bellegarde.

[6] Diederik Jacob van Tuyll van Serooskerken (1744–c. 1773), Belle's favourite brother (she called him 'Ditie'), whom she described as 'le plus joli garçon et l'homme le plus indolent du pays' (Godet i. 106), joined the Dutch navy at the age of seventeen (ibid. i. 54). He became a lieuten-ant, though he also served three years on an English warship. JB noted how easily father and sons got along with one another (Dutch theme for [6 or 7] Feb. 1764—*Holland*, p. 138). Diederik escorted Belle to England towards the end of the year. She spent six months there, mostly in London, where she was entertained by Garrick, doctored by Sir John Pringle, and charmed by David Hume (Godet i. 127–34). JB did not hear from her during that visit (To Temple, 4 Mar. 1767—*In Search of a Wife*, p. 35).

[7] Maria Frederica, Baroness van Reede-Ginckel (1748–1807), sister of Frederik Christiaan van Reede-Ginckel (1743–1808), fifth Earl of Athlone, was lady-in-waiting to Wilhelmina of Prussia, consort of the Stadtholder, Willem V (NNBW iii. 1014–15, v. 224; A. W. J. Mulder, *Het Kasteel Amerongen en zijn Bewoners*, 1949, p. 129, pedigree opposite p. 156). Maria Frederica demanded that Diederik resign his naval commission before she would consider marrying him; he refused, and the engagement was broken off in Sept. 1767 (*Lettres Zélide*, p. 320).

[8] Belle described her brother William as 'toujours à la chasse, à moins qu'il ne soit malade pour avoir trop chassé' (Godet i. 149).

[9] In his letter of 30 Jan. van Zuylen had thanked JB for his kindness to his son when Willem was in Paris and suffering from his first venereal infection (*Earlier Years*, p. 281).

[10] Helena Jacoba van Tuyll van Serooskerken (1724–68), daughter of René de Vicq, a wealthy merchant of Amsterdam, married van Tuyll in 1739 (Polvliet, p. 32). JB had cultivated an acquaintance with her while in Holland (Notes, 17 Dec. 1763, 18 Mar. 1764).

[11] Books on the wonders of Aix-la-Chapelle by François Blondel in 1685 and by [K. L. Pollnitz] in 1736 recommended the waters for most illnesses but did not mention venereal diseases. William Fordyce's popular *Review of the Venereal Disease* in 1767 attributed some value to the waters but stressed the usual mercurial ointments and a newer remedy from sarsaparilla root

(pp. 132–33).

[12] Simon-André Tissot (1728–97), M.D. and noted as a medical writer, especially for his *Avis au peuple sur sa santé* (1761). If Willem means by 'un autre' not merely 'another doctor' but 'another Tissot', then presumably he is referring to Louis Tissot—no relation of his Swiss namesake—who had practised medicine in Utrecht since 1739 (*Strichtsche Almanach*, 1763) and was also Director of the Dolhuis, or insane asylum, until 1773 (J. P. T. van der Lith, *Geschiedenis van het Krankzinnigen-Gesticht te Utrecht*, 1863, p. 54). JB met him in Utrecht and found him 'a true Original, a shrewd lively little fellow of sixty. . . . A great sceptic' (Journ. 25 May 1764); he also visited the Dolhuis with Tissot (Journ. 29 May 1764).

[13] Part of David Hume's *History of England*, 1754–62, was published in French translation in Amsterdam in 1765 (NUC cclx. 145–46).

[14] MS. 'loige' deleted before 'loin'

[15] The Domkerk or Cathedral, built 1254–67, dominated the city of Utrecht with its great Gothic tower 364 feet high standing apart from it. Much of the Cathedral itself was in ruins by 1764. JB climbed the tower on 28 Mar. 1764 (Notes, 29 Mar. 1764). For a description of the ascent of the tower, see *Holland*, p. 201 and n. 6.

[16] MS. illegible spelling of Brown('Bro——') partially erased and crossed out before 'Broun'

[17] For Robert Brown and his family, see From Brown, 3 Mar. n. 1; for his illness, see From Brown, 27 Jan. 1767 and n. 2.

[18] JB knew all three at Utrecht: Charles de Guiffardière (c. 1740–1810—Gent. Mag. 1810, lxxx. i. 93), Jean-Jacques Rambonnet (d. 1768), and Daniel-Théodore Huët (1724–95). Guiffardière was about to leave for a career in England marked by his ministry in the French chapel at St. James's Palace (Edgar Sheppard, *Memorials of St. James's Palace*, 1894, ii. 239), his post as French reader to Queen Charlotte, and his friendship with Fanny Burney, in whose diary he appears as Mr. Turbulent (*Diary and Letters of Madame d'Arblay*, ed. Charlotte Barrett and Austin Dobson, 6 vols., 1904–05, ii. 391–92, iii. 79, 92–93 and passim). Following twenty years as minister in Kampen, Rambonnnet became pastor of the Walloon church in Utrecht in 1752 and was joined there as co-pastor by Huët in Feb. 1763 (F. H. Gagnebin, 'Liste des églises wallones des Pays-Bas et des pasteurs qui les ont desservies,' in *Bulletin de la commission pour l'histoire des églises wallones*, [1888] iii. 116, 220, 229; BW). For JB's opinions of Guiffardière and Rambonnet, see French themes, no. 12, c. 28 Sept. 1763—extract in *Holland*, p. 49 n. 5—and no. 144, 5 Feb. 1764—both M 87.

[19] MS. 'cette' deleted before 'leur'

[20] Van Tuyll alludes, of course, to Gray's *Elegy*.

From John Reid,[1] Thursday 13 November 1766

MS. Yale (C 2350). The letter is in the hand of John Johnstoun[2] except for the signatures of the witnesses and the direction, 'to mr. James Boswell, Advocat edr.' which may be in Reid's hand, as is his signature.

ADDRESS: To Mr. James Boswell, Advocate, at Lord Auchinlecks, Edinburgh.

ENDORSEMENT: Letter from John Reid asking Banishment, with a Letter from John Johnstoun, His Agent at Glasgow, Received 22 Novr. 1766.[3]

Glasgow, 13 Novemr. 1766

SIR: Having now long been confined in a Dungeon of this prison Where I possibly may remain Starving all this Winter, A thing hard for humane nature to bear— And tho' I am Conscious of my Innocence rather than be thus punished for so long a Space but at Same time very unwilling to part with my wife and three Infant children I am inclined from mere necessity to Apply for Banishment.[4] And As You was So very kind to be Counsel for me at Glasgow not to mention other favours I have Again taken the Liberty to intreat You will be so good as undertake an Additional piece of trouble for me, that is, To Apply to My Lord Advocate for his Consent to my being banished Who I am told is a very humane Gentleman So that I flatter My self He will by your influence give his Consent If he is petitioned for that effect And in so doing You will Add another very high favour to former ones bestowed by You on me.[5] And I am with the greatest esteem, Sir, Your most humble Servant,

JOHN REID

to Mr. James Boswell, Advocat edr.
Signed In presence of
John Johnstoun Witness
?John ?   Witness[6]

[1] John Reid (c. 1725–74), flesher of Muiravonside, Stirlingshire, had been charged on 16 Aug. with stealing 120 sheep during the autumn of 1765 from Robert Laidlaw of Craig Kingledoors, Peeblesshire. Reid was imprisoned first in Stirling and then in Glasgow while awaiting trial. In Glasgow on 12 Sept. JB and his fellow advocate Bannatyne MacLeod were able to get the trial moved to Edinburgh on the grounds that Reid was not assigned counsel in time to collect evidence, that his witnesses lived too far away to be brought to court, and that the jury in Glasgow was hostile because of Reid's bad reputation. In November Reid was also charged with stealing twenty-seven sheep in 1763 in Lanarkshire; presumably he thought he had no chance of escaping two charges, and petitioned for banishment. At the trial before the Court of Justiciary on 15 Dec. the jury found the two charges not proven. JB's argument was that the twenty-seven sheep had not actually been stolen in 1763 and that the 120 sheep stolen in 1765 could not have been carried off by Reid in such numbers (Lg 4:1–10, 24:4; Process H. M. Advocate v. John Reid, Edinburgh,

15 Dec., Justiciary Papers, S.R.O.). Although JB was able to get Reid off in 1766, he was not successful in 1774, when Reid was sentenced to death by the Court of Justiciary for sheep-stealing and hanged on 21 Sept. 1774 (Journ.).
[2] John Johnstoun or Johnstone (fl. 1766–81), writer in Glasgow, registered testaments on 22 Mar. 1779 and 28 Feb. 1781 in the Commissary Court of Glasgow (SRS, *Commissariot Record of Glasgow, Register of Testaments, 1547–1800*, ed. F. J. Grant, 1901, p. 251). No links between Johnstoun and JB have been reported apart from this case.
[3] Reid's letter was sent to JB with Johnstoun's letter of 20 November.
[4] Reid's family included his wife Janet, a daughter Janet aged about seven, a son Benjamin aged about three, and a child who presumably had died by the time JB listed the children on 20 Sept. 1774 (Journ.).
[5] For the Lord Advocate, see To the Duchess of Douglas, 13 Oct. n. 6.
[6] The surname of the second witness is not legible.

From Thomas Davies, Saturday 15 November 1766

MS. Yale (C 897).

London, Novr. 15th, 1766

DEAR SIR: I am to beg your pardon for not answering your very obliging letter sooner. I heartily wish it were consistent with my interest to be the Purchaser of Mr. Boswells History of Corsica as I have not the least Doubt of its being written with the greatest skill and accuracy.— You seem to be doubtful of its making more than a 4to. book.— As the subject is of such a nature as to excite chiefly the curiosity of Antiquarians and readers of particular History I really do not think you will sell more than ⟨100⟩ 0 or 1500 copies;[1] This will certainly not reward the Purchaser sufficiently[2] who ventures 100l for the copy, and must be at all expences which will certainly be very considerable.— You must at the same time deduct 20 or 25 pr. Cent, the usual allowance to the trade.

This is not a work of wit and humour but in its nature (for the most part) dry and unentertaining.— They are a brave and generous People it is confess'd but their Wars with the Genoese and their other military achievements, I fancy may be comprehended in a small Number of sheets.

I heartily wish you success in your undertaking and am, Dear Sir, with the truest respect, Your most obedient, humble Servant,

THOMAS DAVIES

P.S. Dr. Johnson and Mrs. Davies beg their compliments.

[1] 3,500 copies, octavo rather than quarto, were printed of the first edition, which sold out within six weeks. For this and subsequent edi- tions, see *Lit. Car.* pp. 50–62.
[2] MS. 'for' deleted before 'sufficiently'

To John Dun, between mid-November and mid-December 1766

Not reported. See From Dun, 19 Dec.: 'I had the pleasure of yours and am glad to find you got all safe to Town.' Presumably JB arrived in Edinburgh in time for the start of the Winter Session on 12 Nov., and was certainly there by 17 Nov., when he was retained for two causes (Consultation Book).

From Mungo Smith,[1] Tuesday 18 November 1766

MS. Yale (C 2494).

ADDRESS: To James Boswell Esqr., Advocate, Edinburgh.

Lochmark,[2] 18th Novr. 1766

SIR: I am sorry I had it not in my Power to fulfil the Promise I made when I had the Pleasure of seeing You at Logan of waiting on You at Auchinleck which was owing to my being at Glasgow at the Time You left the Country not Thinking You was to leave it so soon.[3] You'll remember at that Time we talk'd of an Appearance of Limestone in the Trabboch Barony of which I wish'd to see a proper Tryal.[4] I think You said You imagined Lord Auchinleck would not chuse to make any Tryal of that kind himself but that You did not doubt he would give any Person inclining to try it proper Encouragement which makes me trouble You with this that You may if You think proper speak of it to his Lordship and if he will give me Liberty to try in any Part of the Trabboch Lands I please and in Case of finding a workable Lime Quarry will give me a Tack of it for Thirty Years for giving his Lordship (or his Tennants) One Half of all the Lime I may raise and take the other Half to myself his Lordship and me being at the joint Expence of working it and not to be lyable for any Damage for the Surface or proper Roads to the Quarry. I will try it and in Case of not finding a workable Lime Quarry I shall be at the Expence of the Tryal myself. If these Proposals are acceptable to his Lordship and he'll take the Trouble to write me so I will Immediately set about making a Tryal but if his Lordship chuses rather to make Tryal himself I should be glad to see it soon as many People think the Appearance good. It would be much for his own Interest if it succeed a general good to this Part of the Country and a particular One to me as it would be a new Customer for Coals.[5] Should take it as a Favr. if You'll write me his Lordship's Opinion of this Proposal[6] excuse the Freedom I have taken and give me leave to assure You that I am very respectfully, Sir, Your most obedient, humble Servant,

MUNGO SMITH

[1] Mungo Smith (d. 1814—*Scots Mag.* 1814, lxxvi. 319) appears as 'Mungo Smith of Drongan' in the list of members of the assize at the trial of the Garlieston rioters, May 1767 (Lg 8:1), making it likely that he had taken over management of the Drongan estate from his father John before that date (*Ayrshire*, p. 289). He began a serious improvement of his land in 1770; he built a road to enable him to bring manure for enriching his lands, and he was a firm advocate of the use of lime as fertilizer. At the same time, he actively promoted mining the coal on his estate, which was his main interest (Janet Retter, *Drongan: The Story of a Mining Village*, 1978, pp. 24, 26, 77).

[2] Lochmark, a farm on the Drongan estate some four miles south-west of Auchinleck House, was occupied by both John and Mungo Smith. It was incorporated into a new Drongan House some time before 1775 (Retter, pp. 23, 74). See also Armstrong's *Map of Ayrshire*, 1775 (4EE).

[3] Logan was an estate near Auchinleck belonging to Hugh Logan, the celebrated 'Laird of Logan' (*Ayrshire*, p. 304–05). JB was at Auchinleck on 6 Nov. (To SJ, *Life* ii. 22–25) and at Dalziel on 8 Nov. (J 11.1—Memoranda at

Auchinleck . . . and Dalzell, p. 13); from here presumably he went to Edinburgh for the opening of the Winter Session on 12 Nov.

[4] Trabboch barony was part of the Auchinleck estate and was situated in Ochiltree parish. In 1792 the *Stat. Acct. Scot.*, reprint 1982, vi. 504, reported that there was no limestone in Ochiltree that could be quarried to advantage. However, by 1778, on the estate of Drongan in the neighbouring parish of Stair, Mungo Smith used the spreading of lime 'at the rate of 160 bolls of five Winchester bushels of lime in powder per acre' as a way of improving his lands (Retter, p. 77).

[5] Coal had been mined at Drongan on a small scale since the 17th century (Retter, p. 23). There was an extensive colliery on the lands of Drongan, which yielded the 'abundance of coal' needed to burn limestone, which was widely used as fertilizer (*Stat. Acct. Scot.*, reprint 1982, vi. 98, 575).

[6] Lord Auchinleck's attitude towards Smith's proposal to determine whether there was limestone worth quarrying in Trabboch has not been reported.

From Baron Cuno Burchard von Pless,[1] Wednesday 19 November 1766

MS. Yale (C 2271).
ADDRESS: à Monsieur, Monsieur Boswell, à London.

Bronsvic, le 19 9br. 1766

MONSIEUR: J'ai pas voulû faire passer cette bonne occasion, sans Vous assurer des mes très sinceres et très humbles Sentiments de L'amitié. Pensez Vous bien encore quelquefois â votre ami Plesse mon cher Monsieur Bosswell. Je Vous assure que je Vous oublie et oublierai jamais. Nous avons eû des aventures assès egales dans le monde, qui rongent naturellement le coeur â L'un et L'autre. Souvenez Vous bien des nos Promenades sous les arquades du Chateau? Adieu mon cher Monsieur Boswell. Je regrette infiniment mon ami Graham,[2] qui Vous portera cette lettre. C'est un homme de grande merite, et qui s'est acquis L'e⟨sti⟩me de tout le monde. Je suis avec une e⟨sti⟩me particuliere, Monsieur, Votre très humble et très obeissant serviteur,

PLESSE

[1] When JB met Cuno Burchard, Baron von Pless, he was a major-general in the Brunswick infantry—having served as a regimental commander during the Seven Years' War—and an aide-de-camp to Prince Ferdinand of Brunswick (*Fortgesetzte Neue Gen.-Hist. Nachrichten* xiii. [1763], 63). JB described him as 'a brave, worthy, amiable young man' (Journ. 8 Aug. 1764). They quickly became friends, JB explaining melancholy to him and von Pless confessing that 'he had lived with a *danceuse* an Italian Girl', and that he intended never to marry (Journ. 19 Aug. 1764). Later they corresponded briefly, von Pless sending JB some specimens which he had asked for of Brunswick coins minted that year (To von Pless, 15 Oct. 1764; From von Pless, 20 Oct. 1764).

[2] For William Graham of Garthmore, see From Pierre Loumeau Dupont, 23 Apr. n. 7.

From John Johnstoun, Thursday 20 November 1766

MS. Yale (C 1643). The letter is written on the third side of John Reid's letter of 13 Nov.

Glasgow, 20th Novemr. 1766

SIR: I have Communed with John Reid Several times upon what You Wrote me but have not as Yet been able to Learn any thing further from him to the purpose. Only he tells me and I believe it is true that his wife and friends are in Diligence to find out the person he says Gave him the sheep as he assures me that his wife Went home of late for that purpose.[1] But to be plain with You from the first time I Conversed with him I could not allow my self to think otherways than that he is Actually the Guilty person. If any thing new occurrs to me that may be of any Service to him I shall Write You. Meantime on the other Side is a Request by him to You to apply to The Lord Advocate for Banishment which I see he earnestly Wishes may be Granted. I am informed he makes Closs Application to his books and prays frequently fervently[2] which Show's he fears what he as well as many others would wish to Avoid.[3] Mean time I remain respectfully, Sir, Your most obedient and very humble Servant,

JOHN JOHNSTOUN

Would have wrote you Sooner But have been much from home.

[1] Johnstoun's memorandum (Glasgow, 1766 —Lg 4:2) identifies the person who gave Reid the sheep to drive to Glasgow as James Wilson, drover in Chapplehill, Dumbartonshire. Reid claimed that Wilson had stolen the sheep from Robert Laidlaw. Wilson did not appear to claim the sheep in Glasgow, and Reid did not see him again until some four years after his trial, when he saw him in a public market and tried to have him seized. Wilson evaded capture, and Reid never saw him again (*The Last Speech, Confession, and Dying Words of John Reid* [1774]—Lg 24:4).

[2] MS. 'ver' deleted before 'fervently'

[3] One of the books may have been a book of devotion JB had given Reid at some time, presumably during his trial. A scrap of paper among the Boswell papers at Yale bears an unfinished draft of an inscription: 'To John Reid an unhappy Prisoner From James Boswell one of his Council Who if He cannot save him from punishment in this world hopes to assist him in obtaining mercy in the world which is to come and hea . . .' (M 125).

To Thomas Davies, between 20 November 1766 and 15 January 1767

Not reported. JB told Davies of his intention to put his name to a forthcoming advertisement for *Corsica* (From Davies, 17 Jan. 1767).

From Giuseppe Marc'Antonio Baretti, Wednesday 24 November 1766

MS. Yale (C 74).

NOTE at foot of letter: at the Prince of Orange's Coffee House in the Hay-market[1]

Londra, li 24 Novre. 1766

E che fa il mio Signor Jacopo? Come sta Egli? quando verrà Egli? Ohimé! Due intieri Mesi sono passati dacchè riposi il piede sulla britannica spiaggia, ed eccomi pur fraudato tuttavia del diletto di trovare il mio Boswell in questa Metropoli! E nessuno sa dirmi se sia sua intenzione o no di lasciare cotesto suo Paese per questo. Ditemelo almeno voi per lettera giacchè nessuno mel sa dire in voce.

O che lunghi discorsi vorremmo fare se foste quì, Signor Jacopo mio! Voi mi direste mille cose de' vostri viaggi fatti dacchè ci separammo, e specialmente di quello di Corsica, che fu pure una bella bravura, e degna d'una mente inquisitiva come la vostra, ed io vi direi della mia partenza da Venezia, del mio lungo soggiorno in Ancona, in Monferrato, e in Genova. Se foste quì, e amante ancora della Lingua nostra vi regalerei una copia di tutto quello che ho scritto col titolo di Frusta Letteraria, e ve ne leggerei de' pezzi, spianandovi que' passi che ve potessero riuscir difficili, e faremmo cent' altre cose buone. Ma voi siete lontano moltissime miglia, e Dio sa quando avro' il piacere di raccozzarmi con Voi. Tuttavia sarà quando sarà. Intanto favoritemi se v'aggrada di qualche novella di voi onde io m'assicuri che no avete ancora dimenticato quello che si protesta cordialmente, Vostro buon Servitore ed Amico,

GIUSEPPE BARETTI

[And what is my Signor James doing? How is he? When will he appear? Alas! Two whole months have passed since I set foot on the British shore, and now I find myself cheated of the pleasure of meeting my Boswell in this metropolis! And no one can tell me whether or not you are planning to leave your own country for this one. Let me know, at least, by letter, since no one can tell me here.[2]

What long conversations we would have if you were here, my Signor James! You would tell me a thousand things about the trips you have undertaken since we last parted, and especially about your Corsican tour—such a bold adventure, worthy of an inquiring mind like yours! I would tell you about my departure from Venice and my long stay in Ancona, Monferrato, and Genoa.[3] If you were here, and still a lover of our language, I would give you a copy of all that I have written under the title of Frustra Letteraria.[4] I would read you extracts, explaining those passages that might prove difficult, and we would do hundreds of other fine things. But you are so many miles away from here, and God only knows when I shall have the pleasure of meeting with you again. However, be that when it may. Meanwhile, please do me the favour of sending me some news of you, so I may be sure you have not yet forgotten him who professes to be, with all cordiality, your true servant and friend,

GIUSEPPE BARETTI][5]

[1] The Prince of Orange Coffee-house had been in the Haymarket since c. 1700 (Lillywhite, p. 457). Baretti lived in Queen Anne Street, near Portland Chapel (From Baretti, 4 Mar. 1768), but received his mail at the coffee-house until at least 16 Aug. 1769 (Giuseppe Baretti, Epistolario, ed. Luigi Piccioni, 1936, i. 410).

[2] JB did not return to London until 22 Mar. 1768.

[3] Baretti had been in Ancona from Aug. 1765 until January of this year, in Monferrato—his native state—in March and April, and in Genoa until August. He was in Paris on 19 Sept., and his next surviving letter is this one to JB (Epistolario i.

256–347).

[4] Baretti brought out the first of his periodical reviews, issued fortnightly as Frusta letteraria ('Literary Scourge') under the pseudonym 'Aristarco Scannabue', in Oct. 1763. He continued them until Feb. 1765 (thirty-three numbers in all), when the authors and scholars whom Baretti had attacked so outspokenly succeeded in having the publication suppressed, and Baretti was forced to seek asylum in England (Lacy Collison-Morley, Giuseppe Baretti, 1909, pp. 152–79).

[5] Translation by Caterina Bosio and Ian Duncan.

From John Rowand,[1] Wednesday 24 November 1766

MS. Yale (C 2422).

ADDRESS: To James Boswel Esqr., Adevocate, In Edinburgh.

ENDORSEMENT: Letter From John Rowand Jailer at Glasgow Concerning John Reid Received 25 Novr. 1766.

Glasgow, Nobmr. 24th, 1766

Septmr. 15th receed from James Boswel, for Aliment to John Reid to 22d of
    Nomber. Currtt both Days Inclusive at 3d pr Deam is 69[2] ———— £0.17.3
                  To Cash Delivred to John Reid ———— 0.10.9
                                        £1. 8.0

SIR: You delivred to me Twenty Eight shillings storling for aliment of John Reid. I paid the remendars in my hand to him at his departur which you see by the above acompt wass 10/9. He meid some reflections becaus he wass not enterd ass a Comon prisioner and that The Lords[3] had recomended and ordained him the Liberty of the Goall which is falce. If that Liberty had been Granted you wold had no ocetion for his Trayel now. I wish him a happy Exectn. and shutabel preperation. I am, Sir, Your Most Humbel and obedient Sarvant,

JOHN ROWAND

N.B. he had the same alownce from The Town that you wass so Good ass Gave him.[4]

[1] John Rowand (c. 1702–c. 1783) had been a merchant in Glasgow before taking up the post of gaoler in 1762. He resigned the post in 1774 because of advanced years and was voted an annual pension of £20 (*Extracts from the Records of the Burgh of Glasgow*, ed. Robert Renwick, 1912–13, vii. 112, 423–24; viii. 105).

[2] Presumably prisoners were allowed 3d. a day for maintenance.

[3] Rowand is referring to Lords Auchinleck and Pitfour, the judges serving on the Western Circuit at the time of Reid's trial.

[4] During the period from 29 Aug. 1766 to 30 Sept. 1767 Rowand received £4. 10s. from the magistrates of Glasgow 'for mentaining poor prisoners' (*Extracts* vii. 254).

From Lord Mountstuart, c. December 1766

Not reported. See To Mountstuart, 1 Jan. 1767, where JB quotes a part of this letter: 'though in the course of things with your odd way many quarrels may happen betwixt us, yet my Friendship shall never be wanting to give you all the assistance it can whenever you shall have the least occasion for it.'

From Daniel Johnston,[1] Thursday 1 December 1766

MS. Yale (C 1613).

ADDRESS: To James Boswell Esqr., att Lord Auchenlecks, Parlament Closs, Edr.

Cumnock, Decmr. 1st, 1766

WORTHY SIR: Your kind and friendly Inquery for my Health I received from Jas. Bruce with all the Gratefullness of Heart; I am capable of[2]—and returns you my most sincere thanks therefore, I Esteem it as a Very singular favour, and wants words to Express how much I think myself Oblidged to you, for this Mark of your concern and trouble you have put your self too, by this Inquery.

I wish it were in my Power to Testify how much I think my self Oblidged to the good family for the many favours, and the Countinance I have for some time been favoured with, I have been much in my Ordinary Health ever since I saw you and was happy in[3] Discovering that Night, the Cause of my Disorder—it was owing to a pair Strait Boots which pinched My feet and legs so Much as Stoped in part the Circulation and rendered my feet as cold as Death.— Upon getting home and my self therrowly warmed I became quite easy and feelt a happyness, and An Agreeable sensation threw my whole Body, that nearly Compensate the Distress, I had before feelt—only the trouble I put the family into was to me an Overballane to all.

permitt me ser in the Next place, to make Inquery how his Lordship and you have keept your Health since ye went to Edr.—and if ye keep free of your Ague.

My most Dutyfull Compliments to his Lordship, mr. Claud Boswell which please Acceptt off from, sir, your much Oblidged and Very Humble servant.

DANIEL JOHNSTON

[1] Daniel Johnston (d. 1779), surgeon in Cumnock, near Auchinleck (SRO, *Commissariat Record of Glasgow, Register of Testaments, 1547–1800,* ed. F. J. Grant, 1901, p. 250). JB saw Johnston several times in 1767, both socially and for treatment of urethritis, and in Apr. 1769 just before setting out for Ireland (Journ. 28 Mar.–3 June 1767 passim, 25 Apr. 1769; W. B. Ober, 'Boswell's Clap' in *Boswell's Clap and Other Essays,* 1979, pp. 13, 40).

[2] James Bruce (1719–90), gardener and overseer at Auchinleck (*Earlier Years,* p. 289).

[3] MS. 'is'

From Archibald Stewart, Friday 5 December 1766

MS. Yale (C 2566).

ADDRESS: To James Boswall Esqre., At the House of Lord Achinlect In Edinburgh.

Rottm. 5th Decr. 1766

DEAR SIR: I was very Sorry, I had not the pleasure of meeting with you when in Scotland, but it was not in My Power, to be at Achinlect, Tho I was in hopes I Should have Seen you, at Ardgowan, which would have Made us all very Happy.[1]

When last in Scotland, I Spent Some days in Perth and Dundee, Soliciting the Merchants there for a Share, of their orders for flax and flax-seed, etc. which they Import from this place.[2] Some particular friends of mine then told me it was a great pity, I had not got Letters to Some of their folks from Mr. George Demster who they assured me had more to Say in their Town than any body in Scotland.[3]—Now as I am no Stranger to the Great Intimacy, that is 'twixt you and that Gentleman, besides Mr. Demster's natural Inclination to do Good, which I have had occasion to know in Several Instances, more of which you, yourself was Consern'd, I take the liberty, to beg of you, to write that Gentleman, to be So Good as recommend me to All those he has any Influence with in Dundee etc., the first time he happens to be in that Country, and in order that he May not be at the trouble to recommend me to those who can be of No use to me, Mr. James Craufurd, of Dundee will point out to your friend Mr. Demster all in[4] Said[5] place that Import Goods from this Country and are Safe to Deal with,[6] This if you can bring it about will be doing me a most Essential Service, of which I Shall ever retain a Gratefull Sense. My Compliments to all friends and believe me with Most Distinguished regard, Dear Sir, yours etc.,

ARCHD. STEWART

P.S. If you wuld find time to Write me a letter Now and then, in the Stile of a Domestick Newspaper it would be very obliging,—[7]

[1] The principal seat of Sir Michael Stewart of Blackhall, Bt., situated on the coast of Renfrewshire, at Inverkip Bay. Admitted advocate in 1735, Sir Michael was an accomplished scholar and had studied widely at home and abroad. Archibald (killed in Tobago, 1779—*Burke's Peerage*, 1978) was his third son (*Renfrew*, pp. 58, 413–14).

[2] Raw flax imported from Holland or through Dutch ports was much in demand in eastern Scotland for use in the linen industry (Henry Hamilton, *An Economic History of Scotland in the Eighteenth Century*, 1963, pp. 30, 261–62, 283, 285).

[3] See To George Dempster, 7 Mar. Demp-

ster's Parliamentary constituency included Perth and Dundee.

[4] MS. 'of them' deleted before 'in'

[5] MS. 'tha' altered to 'Said'

[6] James Crawford (d. 1783—*Scots Mag.* 1783, xlv. 671), merchant in Dundee, became a partner in the Dundee Banking Company some time between 1765 and 1777, when the company was enlarged. Dempster was one of the original partners of the bank, which was founded in 1763 (C. W. Boase, *A Century of Banking in Dundee*, 1867, 2nd ed. pp. xvii–xviii).

[7] No letters from JB to Stewart after 2 Jan. 1764 have been reported.

From Alexandre Deleyre, Monday 8 December 1766

MS. Yale (C 927).

à Parme, ce 8 decembre 1766

Enfin, cher et brave Ecossois, je reçois de vos nouvelles, et telles que je pouvois les souhaitter; puis que vous m'annoncés une tranquillité d'esprit que je n'osois guéres espérer de votre caractere.[1] Mais vous avés pris un parti sage et courageux, le seul peut-être qui pût fixer vos irrésolutions et calmer vos peines. Le choix d'un etat est comme essentiel dans la société, pour y trouver du repos; sans quoi l'on risque d'en porter les chaines, sans en gouter les douceurs. Que peut attendre de ses semblables, celui que ne vit point comme eux, ni d'une manière propre à leur rendre les services qu'ils en exigent? Traverses, contradictions, mépris ou même persécutions de toute espéce. J'avoüe qu'il me paroît presqu'aussi difficile de servir les hommes et de ne pas s'avilir en se polissant dans leur commerce, que de vivre loin d'eux et sans leur secours. Mais une ame forte comme la votre, quand elle a pû se vaincre et se plier contre ses goûts aux volontés d'un pere, doit trouver en elle-même des ressources pour résister à la contagion des vices et des passions qui semblent infecter et même animer la plûpart des états et des professions de la vie civile. Je dis animer, mon cher ami, parce que sans un peu d'ambition je crois qu'on ne se résout point à embrasser une carriere longue, pénible, épineuse, comme celle de l'étude des loix et de la jurisprudence. Aussi me dites vous franchement que vous êtes prêt à recevoir des guinés en plaidant des causes bonnes ou mauvaises. Vous avés encore de la bonne foy, parceque vous êtes novice dans la chicane, et je vous rends la justice de vous croire le plus honnête fripon que je connoisse parmi les avocats.

Un des plus surs moyens d'étouffer les remords qui pourroient vous troubler dans votre métier, c'est de vous marier. Désque vous aurés des enfans, les scrupules s'évanoüiront insensiblement devant la tendresse paternelle, et vous ne sçauriés prévoir actuellement combien elle vous palliera d'injustices, et vous fera dévorer de faux[2] raisonnemens. Munissés vous d'une excellente Dialectique et d'un triple airain,[3] contre les sophismes de l'amour propre et les pleurs d'une famille qui vous demandera d'abord du pain, et puis des terres, et puis des chateaux, et puis des honneurs et des dignités soit à la cour, soit à la ville.[4] Vous avés un Patrimoine assez riche pour vous garantir des tentations du besoin extrême: mais ne sçavés-vous pas que ce sont les moins dangereuses, et qu'il n'en coute peut-être pas autant de résister à la nécessité qu'à la vanité? Il vous reste d'ailleurs, si je ne me trompe, un principe capable de vous séduire et d'imposer silence à l'équité sévère; c'est d'imaginer qu'il y a des hommes nés pour commander aux autres, et qui sont autorisés par la nature à tout faire pour dominer.[5] Avec cette doctrine, vous iriés loin, mon cher ami, dans le chemin du crime. Je croirois au contraire que la nature n'a pas plus destiné l'homme que les autres espèces, pour asservir la sienne; et s'il en arrive autrement, c'est que l'ètat actuel de la société met les individus à peu prés dans la situation où se trouveroient des Lions affamés qu'on lâcheroit dans un cirque, et qui seroient forcés de s'entredévorer, faute d'autre proye. Mais il ne s'ensuit pas que tandis qu'un homme peut vivre avec ses talens et ses forces, il ait le droit d'ètendre ses desirs et ses facultés aux dépends du genre humain, ni même d'aspirer à le gouverner sous prétexte de le conduire plus sûrement à son bonheur. Car le terme est fort incertain, et la route scabreuse pour la probité. Combien de crimes à hazarder, pour opérer ce qu'on appelle mal à propos un grand bien?

J'ai sçu et même lû la querelle de M. Hume avec M. Rousseau. J'y vois avec douleur que notre ami se rend malheureux par ses vertus mêmes qui lui font exagérer dans l'homme des excés, soit en bien, soit en mal, dont peu de gens sont capables. Il a traité l'amitié, ce me semble, comme on traite ordinairement les premieres amours, et sa derniere Lettre à son nouvel ami renferme tous les ombrages, les soupçons, et les reproches dont un jeune amant pourroit accabler une maitresse plus réservée ou moins vive que lui.[6] Je sens même que sa foiblesse n'est pas exempte de délire, ni des noirceurs qui entrent dans l'imagination d'un malheureux. Mais toutes ces injustices partent cependant d'une sensibilité qui ne doit point lui faire tort dans l'estime des ames honnêtes. S'il pêche et s'il erre, c'est par de faux supposés qu'il établit en principes d'où son esprit raisonneur tire les plus funestes conséquences. J'avoüe que les apparences son à son desavantage, et qu'il y a trés peu de personnes qui puissent lui pardonner de s'être livré à ses préventions défavorables contre l'homme qui devoit lui etre le moins suspect. Il y en a même qui ne lui sont suggérées que par cet amour propre dont les grands génies ne peuvent jamais se dépouiller, quelques vertus qu'ils aient d'ailleurs. L'imprudence de M. Rousseau, c'est qu'avec un caractere trés difficile et délicat en fait d'amis, il se soit abandonné sans aucune réserve aux prévenances et aux offres d'un homme qu'il devoit estimer par ses ouvrages, mais dont il no connoissoit pas assez intimément l'humeur[7] ni la façon de vivre et d'agir, pour se mettre entierement entre ses mains et comme dans sa dépendance. Il n'y a peutetre rien de si antipathique dans la nature que les gens froids et les gens vifs et boüillans. J'en ai fait l'expérience à mes dépends. M. Rousseau a tort encore de vous imputer de mauvais procédés. Mais je le connois trés prompt à accuser et même à provoquer. Cependant malgré ses défauts, je m'estimerois encore heureux de pouvoir le servir, le consoler et surtout le ramener des écarts où l'a fait tomber une imagination aigrie par les malheurs. Je l'aime toujours.

Revenons à vous, mon digne Ecossois. Vous avés donc travaillé sur la corse. Je vous en félicite et vous en remercie, par l'intérêt que je prends à tout ce qui peut vous honorer et contribuer à la gloire d'une République naissante. Envoyés moi votre livre, avant qu'il paroisse en public, afin que je ne sois pas prévenu dans la traduction par des écrivains de Paris ou de Hollande. Si votre ouvrage est bon, comme je le présume; je me ferai honneur et plaisir de le faire passer dans notre langue, et de lui donner par cette voye encore plus de publicité qu'il n'en peut avoir dans sa langue originale, moins connüe en Italie que le François.[8] Je suis réellement impatient de voir cet Ecrit; d'autant plus qu'il trouvera mon esprit dans des despositions trés propres à profiter des lumieres que vous y donnerés sur l'état actuel des corses. J'ai même intérêt à sçavoir ce qui se passe chez eux, et depuis un an je roule des idées qui ne me laissent point indifférent sur la destinée de ce peuple. Ainsi ne tardés pas, je vous prie, à satisfaire mon empressement, dussieés-vous m'envoyer une copie de votre manuscrit, si l'imprimé ne paraissait pas encore. Ce seroit même le moyen le plus court et le plus sûr de remplir votre projet et mes desirs sur la traduction dont vous m'offrés d'avance les honneurs.

Finissons, cher ami, par vous souhaitter de la constance et de la prospérité dans le nouvel état que vous avés embrassé. Que je vous estime heureux de contribuer au bonheur d'un pere tendre, sage raisonnable et privé d'une épouse qu'il devoit extrémement chérir! Je crois bien qu'il ne vous faut qu'une occupation forte pour vous délivrer des vapeurs d'une imagination noire. Pourvû que vous puissiés suivre une genre d'ètude et de travail, vous deviendrés aussi heureux que vous pouvés l'être: car vous sçavés qu'avec une certaine sensibilité, qui donne quelquefois de grands plaisirs, on ne doit pas s'attendre à beaucoup de bonheur.

Je vous adresse, brave Ecossois, une Lettre pour un homme que nous aimons vous et moi, sans trop sçavoir s'il nous le rend. Voilà la quatriéme que je lui écris depuis un an, dans l'attente de trois réponses.[9] Faites en sorte qu'il reçoive celle-cy par la voye la plus sûre et la moins couteuse. Adieu Monsieur le conseiller. Ma femme vous remercie et vous salüe affectueusement. Tout à vous,

DELEYRE

---

[1] For an extract from JB's letter, see To Deleyre, 15 Oct.

[2] MS. 'faux' superimposed upon ?'rais'

[3] An allusion to Horace's 'aes triplex', *Odes* I. iii. 9: 'triple bronze' (trans. C. E. Bennett, Loeb ed.).

[4] Deleyre may be remembering JB's comment at their meeting in Parma on 4 Aug. 1765: 'Je veux quon vient m'accab[ler] de honneurs' (Notes, 5 Aug. 1765).

[5] Just as he had informed Caroline Kircheisen on 10 Sept. 1764 and Rousseau on 15 Dec. 1764 (Journ.), JB may have told Deleyre that he loved to have power over others.

[6] In October, Hume had published Rousseau's long, wild letter to him of 10 July 1766 in his *Exposé succinct de la contestation qui s'est élévée entre M. Hume et M. Rousseau, avec les pièces*

justicatives (see E. C. Mossner, *The Life of David Hume*, 2nd ed., 1980, pp. 528–30; From Baroness von Spaen, 22 July n. 6; From Rousseau, 4 Aug.).

[7] MS. 'l'humeur' superimposed upon an illegible word.

[8] If Deleyre prepared a translation of *Corsica* in French, he does not seem to have published it. Two French translations of *Corsica* were published in 1769, one by a certain S. D. C. and the other by J. P. I. Du Bois. Mme. du Deffand mentions two other French translations, but apparently they were never published. The translator of *Corsica* into Italian is unidentified, but presumably Deleyre would have prepared his translation in his primary language rather than in Italian. See *Lit. Car.* pp. 63–75 for a full account of the translations of *Corsica*.

[9] In his letter to Rousseau of 13 Dec. Deleyre

assures Rousseau that neither his friendship for him nor his sympathy with him in his quarrel with Hume have diminished, despite the fact that he has had no response to the three letters he has written to him during the past year. In the postscript to this letter Deleyre tells Rousseau that JB will forward the letter to him (*Corres. Rousseau* xxxi. 264–66).

To Sir Alexander Dick, Tuesday 9 December 1766[1]

MS. Hyde Collection

ADDRESS: To Sir Alexander Dick, Baronet, Prestonfield.

[Edinburgh]

MY DEAR SIR: You are continually adding to the many favours I have received from you. Mr. Ainslie called on me yesterday, and is so good as to carry all our Packets for Leghorn and Corsica.[2] Mr. Fergusson has taken a copy of your Account of the Family of Dick with the Act of Parlt. and is to return both to me this forenoon, and I shall send them to you on monday, after looking again to see if I can find any little expressions which A friend may point out for alteration.[3]

We live in a strange World where we cannot often have many good things at once. You have done me a great favour in procuring me the opportunity of Mr. Ainslie to carry my dispatches. But you have at the same time deprived me of the pleasure I had in view of being with you today; for now that I have this opportunity, I cannot but write very fully to the illustrious Chief,[4] the gallant Count (Rivarola) and the worthy Baronet. So that I shall exist for half a day in the character which when I was abroad I had a great ambition to be—a foreign minister.[5]

Had I the forenoon free; I might perhaps have the happiness of being with you. But I have no less than seven Causes in the Outerhouse,[6] and the great Cause of Cairncross before the Lords. This is the cause I was attending with so much anxiety when you did me the honour to call upon me. I am for the Descendant of an ancient family who after an obscurity of several generations lays claim to the estate of his Forefathers.[7] You know my old feudal Soul and how much a Cause of this kind must interest me. Besides John Reid my Glasgow Client is to stand his Tryal on Monday before the High Court of Justiciary, so that I have really a great deal to do. I wish you would come in on Monday and hear a little of the Tryal. I have made John Reid of importance to my Friends. I shall just dedicate this afternoon to labour. Mr. Ainslie does not set out till the evening. I am sorry to lose a Saturday with you: but I comfort myself by reflecting that I am now a sort of established Man at Prestonfield, and can come and go as if I had a claim to the Place. So should all Friends live. But there are very few who deserve to be called Friends. My best respects to Lady Dick and Compliments to all your young Family. I hope the young Knight does not forget me.[8] I ever am, With unfeigned esteem and Affection, My Dear Sir Alexander, ever yours,

JAMES BOSWELL

P.S. I shall send you your account of the Family on Tuesday.

[1] The date of this letter is fixed by references to John Reid's trial on 15 Dec. and to JB's letters to John Dick, Rivarola, and Paoli; the replies from Dick and Rivarola show that these letters were written on 9 Dec. (From John Dick, 6 Mar. 1767; From Rivarola, 18 Mar. 1767).

[2] Presumably Robert Ainslie (c. 1730–1812), merchant in Bordeaux and youngest son of George Ainslie, whose estate of Pilton was just outside Edinburgh. Ainslie was later Ambassador to Turkey (1775–92), knighted (1775), M.P. for Milborne Port (1796–1802), and created baronet (1804). Ainslie and Sir Alexander were distant cousins: Ainslie's great-grandfather, John Ainslie of Newbottle, and Sir Alexander's grandfather, Sir James Dick, had married daughters of Andrew Paterson of Dunmore (*Baronage*, pp. 272–73, 301–02).

[3] Since both Sir Alexander and John Dick were descended from Sir William Dick of Braid, Sir Alexander's family archives were helpful in establishing John Dick's claim to the vacant baronetcy of Braid; see Introduction and App. I. The *Baronage* account of the Dicks of Braid cites Sir Alexander's records five times (pp. 269–70, 274). The *Acts of the Parliaments of Scotland, 1124–1707*, 12 vols. 1814–75, often mentions Sir William Dick of Braid. JB may be referring specifically to acts concerning Sir William Dick's loans to the government (*Acts* VI. i (1643–47), 558–59, 643–44, 769–71, 811). The money was never repaid, and Sir William died in a London gaol in 1655 (*Baronage*, p. 270); counsel may have used this to argue that something was owed to John Dick as a descendant.

[4] Paoli.

[5] While abroad, JB several times mentions the idea of becoming an envoy, and in his despatches to the *Lond. Chron.* after his stay in Corsica he drops hints that he was an emissary to Paoli from the British government or from Prince Charles Edward Stuart (*Pol. Car.* p. 22 and nn. 1, 2; *Grand Tour II*, App. D).

[6] Each week in turn one of the fifteen judges of the Court of Session presided over the Outer House in the Parliament Hall, where the old Scots Parliament had met before the Union of 1707. JB's causes in the Outer House for the period 4–16 Dec. included Ker *v.* Thomsons before Lord Barjarg; Allan and Co. *v.* Stephenson before Lord Coalston; Gemmil *v.* Brown, Wilson and Co. *v.* Heastie [Hastie], Clark *v.* Bell, and Paxton *v.* Johnston, all before Lord Auchinleck; and Durham *v.* Edington before Lord Elliock (Consultation Book).

[7] On 4 Dec. JB had appeared before the Court of Session in Cairncross *v.* Heatly (Consultation Book). The Cairncross family had been settled in Hillslap, Roxburghshire, since at least the late sixteenth century (*Baronage*, p. 219; J. F. Hunnewell, *The Lands of Scott*, 1871, pp. 324–25). The estate was now in the hands of William Heatly, who had succeeded through the female line. On 8 Aug. 1765 William Cairncross, who claimed to have descended through the male line, had petitioned the Court for permission to study family papers in Heatly's possession. Hugh Cairncross (presumably William's son), a mason in Galashiels, was claiming to be the rightful heir to the estate. On 8 Aug. 1767 the Court denied his claim (*Supplement to the Dictionary of the Decisions of the Court of Session*, ed. M. P. Brown, 1826, v. 912), and on 9 Mar. 1769 its decision was upheld in the House of Lords (*Journals of the House of Lords*, 1768–70, xxxii. 285). Only a few rough notes of this cause survive among JB's papers (Lg 5.5, p. 5).

[8] William Dick (1763–96—*Gent. Mag.* 1763, xxxiii. 45, correcting date of birth in *Comp. Bar.* iv. 446), son of Sir Alexander by his second wife, succeeded his father in 1785. He joined the 1st Foot Guards at the age of sixteen, and by the time of his death he was a major in the Midlothian Fencible Cavalry (*Scots Charta Chest*, pp. 279, 313, 328–29; *Comp. Bar.* iv. 446).

To John Dick, Tuesday 9 December 1766

Not reported. See From Dick, 6 Mar. 1767: 'Yesterday Mr. Ansley deliver'd me Your very kind and obliging Letter of the 9th of December last'.

To Pasquale Paoli, Tuesday 9 December 1766

Not reported. Enclosed in To John Dick, 9 Dec. Dick forwarded the letter from Leghorn by two Capuchins who were in Paoli's confidence. See From John Dick, 6 Mar. 1767.

To Count Antonio Rivarola, Tuesday 9 December 1766

Not reported. See From Rivarola, 18 Mar. 1767: 'I received your very welcome letter of 9 December last with the Leghorn post; I cannot think how it can have taken so long to reach me.'

From Sir Alexander Dick, Saturday 13 December 1766

MS. Yale (C 959).

ADDRESS: James Boswell Esqr., advocate.

[Prestonfield] Sat. 11, forenoon[1]

MY DEAR FRIEND: Excuse hurry when your servt. came being in the Garden directing some new works.

I must regret the loss of this Saturday; but you are so excellently well employd[2] I submit your propriety of Language accuracy[3] of reasoning and modest deportment good[4] adress and action in Your Long and first Speech before the whole Lords I did not know of when I got near you tother day but at Dinner at Clerhues where many of your brethren dind I had the Joy of hearing you fully approvd of:[5] in this I feelt with your father those delicate emotions of his friend and yours.

An Engagement keeps Me here on Monday else I had attended.

Give me all the Saturdays you can, and come[6] and go as you like, Dear Sir, Yours,

A. DICK

P.S. I am glad I thot of any time for you.[7]

[1] '11' in the dateline refers not to the date but to the time of day when Dick would have been in the garden.

[2] JB was obliged to cancel his Saturday visit to Prestonfield because he was preparing a criminal cause; presumably the document he stayed at home to write was the speech he delivered in defence of John Reid on the following Monday (From John Reid, 13 Nov. n. 1).

[3] MS. '&' deleted before 'accuracy'

[4] MS. '&' deleted before 'good'

[5] The Star and Garter Tavern in Writers' Court adjoining the Royal Exchange was kept by a man named Cleriheugh. It was a favourite gathering place for lawyers, magistrates, and town councillors (Grant i. 184, 187). There is a description of Cleriheugh's in Scott's Guy Mannering (2nd ed. 1815, ii. 260–64).

[6] MS. 'come' is uncertain; it is superimposed upon an illegible word.

[7] Presumably Dick is referring to his invitation to JB to 'come and go as you like'.

From Sir Alexander Dick, Wednesday 17 December 1766

MS. Yale (C 960).

ADDRESS: James Boswell Esqr., Advocate, Edr.

Prest. Wed. noon

I am overjoyd my Dear Sir at your success in Reids affair. The Glascow delay was all and all.[1] If you go on this way you will have all the World at your Knocker daily and you must keep a Swiss to do justice to first comers.[2]

I got the papers safe and shall be happy to bring you out with me on Saturday to dinner.[3] Lord president having engagd me to attend betwixt 12 and one at the meeting he has calld of the Gentlemen of the Supply about the City of Edr. scheme for extending the Royalty over the new north City: it will be worth your while to hear the discussion of that point it wont be long.[4] I shall meet you at the outer house. I am glad you interpone tuis interdum Gaudia Curis[5] a Saturday and Sundays relief is a great healing Balsam to the soul for a top Lawier like you, Dear Friend. Yours,

ALEXR. DICK

95

¹ The letter was written after JB's successful defence of John Reid on Monday 15 Dec. The 'Glasgow delay' could well have been instrumental in bringing about the not proven verdict (From Reid, 13 Nov. and n. 1).

² Presumably Dick had seen the Swiss mercenaries guarding the Pope during his visit to the Vatican on 29 Nov. 1736 (*Scots Charta Chest*, p. 113).

³ Papers relating to the Dicks of Braid (To Sir Alexander Dick, 9 Dec. n. 3).

⁴ The bill for extending the boundaries of the royal burgh of Edinburgh beyond the original walls of the old city was proposed in 1759 but was set aside because of opposition from landowners. The North Loch had been drained, however, and a bridge was being built across it to what would become the New Town (Royal Commission on the Ancient Monuments of Scotland, *An Inventory of the Ancient and Historical Monuments of the City of Edinburgh*, 1951, pp. lxxii– lxxviii). Like

Sir Alexander, Robert Dundas of Arniston (1713–87), Lord President of the Court of Session, was one of the Commissioners of Supply, a body appointed by the Crown for each county from among the greater landholders, originally to collect the land-tax or 'cess'. Eventually, the commission had grown in numbers to include every landholder of the county and all burgh officials of importance, and the Commissioners came to share with the Justices of the Peace the supervision of roads, bridges, and ferries (J. D. Mackie and G. S. Pryde, *Local Government in Scotland*, 1935, pp. 8–9). Presumably a scheme for any extension of royalty would have fallen within their jurisdiction, and a bill for this purpose was passed in Apr. 1767 (*Statutes at Large*, 1765–70, c. 27, x. 298–300).

⁵ Dionysius Cato, *Distichorum de Moribus ad Filium*, III. vii. 1, trans. by James Logan, 1735: 'By turns with Pleasure soften anxious Care'.

From John Dun, Friday 19 December 1766

MS. Yale (C 1125).

ADDRESS: To James Boswell Esqr. younger of Auchinleck, Advocate, Edinr.

Auchinleck Manse, 19th Decr. 1766

MY DEAR SIR: I had the pleasure of yours and am glad to find you got all safe to Town. I hope Balmuto was not the worse of the severe pelting he got by the Storm.¹ My respectful Compliments to him, tell him all things are for good, it will have taught him what his Clients may frequently suffer in attending their Causes and engage him to give dispatch.— 'Every man to his post',² is the way to be useful and happy in Life. Such are the solid sterling Coins, the rest are but counterfeits, mock-men, feathers that know not where to fly, where to rest.— I thought our modern philosophers had been ALL CHARITY, or if conscious they are not in earnest themselves would have been SO GENEROUS as to allow others to wear the mask with applause as well as themselves.³ Will David Hume now say that there cannot be a reality in that of which some pretenders have put on the mask? Let him look upon the picture of Rousseau drawn by himself and he will not say so.⁴ Or if Philosophy as well as the Religion of Jesus is a dream, let him, FOR THE SAKE OF TRUTH, give us an eloquent and learned Dissertation on the UN-reality of philosophy and the hypocrisy of its PROFESSORS.⁵— It is certainly necessary now that either Mr. Hume for the honour of modern Philosophy, or Mr. Rousseau in self defence, should show that Ungratitude, lying, and backbiting are as lawful as fornication, provided the object be 'past CHILD-bearing' or past child-getting. A propos, your Client of modern philosophick virtue, Clomfort, has entailed his Estate on his Bastards.⁶— There is truth and sweetness both in Religion and philosophy where the streams are kept pure what a pity is it that men for selfish ends should have mudied either of them. What ruined the credit of Romish Christianity is ruining that of modern Philosophy the granting Indulgences.— My little family and I are well.[7] Is Mr. David well?[8] My best compliments to him. I am, with great respect and no small affection, My Dear Sir, Yours,

JOHN DUN

Decr. 20th. Clomfort is dead.

[1] We have no further information concerning the storm at Balmuto.

[2] Presumably a military phrase.

[3] Dun may be alluding to Hume's *Enquiry Concerning the Principles of Morals* (1751), Section II, pt. i: 'No qualities are more intitled to the general good-will and approbation of mankind than beneficence and humanity, friendship and gratitude, natural affection and public spirit, or whatever proceeds from a tender sympathy with others, and a generous concern for our kind and species' (David Hume, *Enquiries Concerning Human Understanding and Concerning the Principles of Morals*, ed. L. A. Selby-Bigge, 3rd ed. rev. P. H. Nidditch, 1975, p. 178) and to Rousseau's claim in Part I of his *Discours sur l'origine et les fondements de l'inégalité parmi les hommes* (1755) that pity is innate in all men.

[4] On the quarrel between Rousseau and Hume, see From Baroness von Spaen, 22 July, n. 6, From Rousseau, 4 Aug. Dun had presumably seen the English translation of Hume's *Exposé succinct de la contestation qui s'est élevée entre M. Hume et M. Rousseau*, 1766, published on 18 Nov. under the title *A Concise and Genuine Ac-* count *of the Dispute between Mr. Hume and Mr. Rousseau* (W. B. Todd, 'David Hume. A Preliminary Bibliography', *Hume and the Enlightenment*, ed. W. B. Todd, 1974, p. 202), and reprinted in *Edin. Even. Cour.* 29 Nov., 1, 3 Dec.

[5] Perhaps an allusion to Hume's *Natural History of Religion* (1757) where Hume expounds his theory that the religious doctrines most men espouse are 'sick men's dreams' or 'the playsome whimsies of monkies in human shape' (ed. with an Introduction, by H. E. Root, 1956, p. 75). In 1774 Hume defined a clergyman, for Temple's benefit, as 'a person appropriated to teach hypocrisy and inculcate vice' (From W. J. Temple, 15 Feb. 1774).

[6] Unidentified; possibly Clonford, the owner of 'Clonfords', a farm in Sorn parish, some six miles north-east of Auchinleck House (*Ayrshire*, p. 327). See also Armstrong's *Map of Ayrshire*, 1775 (4FE).

[7] Dun's family included two daughters, Elizabeth (b. 1758) and Isabella (b. 1760); his wife had died in 1762 (*Fasti Scot*. iii. 4).

[8] David Boswell.

From James Duncan,[1] Saturday 20 December 1766

MS. Yale (C 1131.1).

ADDRESS: To Mr. James Boswell of Achenleck, Advocate, att The Honble. Lord Achenlecks Lodging, Edinburgh.

ENDORSEMENT in Duncan's hand: with a Bundle.

Moffatt, 20th Decr. 1766

SIR: Mr. James Little Informs me that he had the Pleasure of Seing you when he was in Town Last week.[2] I understand he made ane Apolegie for my not having got a wife to keep Up the Character of the place in Sending a Burgish Ticket to So valuable a friend to the Brugh of moffatt[3] but I hope your goodness will Excuse me and accpt of the present from a Batcholer who will Esteem it a great honour Done.[4] Meantime wishing you the Compliments of the Season, and beleive me to be, Dear Sir, your most Humble Servant,

JAMES DUNCAN

[1] James Duncan (fl. 1761–80) appears as a feuar or burgess of Moffat in the register of sasines, 1761–72 and 1778–80 (SRO, *Index to Particular Register of Sasines for Sheriffdom of Dumfries and Stewartries of Annandale and Kirkcudbright*, no. 51, 1961, v. 45). Since Duncan was presenting a burgess ticket to JB, making him a burgess and guild brother of Moffat, presumably Duncan was a town official.

[2] James Little (fl. 1766–83) appears as vintner

of Moffat in the Register of Sasines, 1767–72 and 1778–80. He was married to Elizabeth Graham, daughter of John Graham, burgess and postmaster of Moffat (*Index to Sasines, Dumfries* v. 63, 97). In 1783, while in Moffat, JB 'invited Mr. Little, the Landlord, to sup with us' and described him as 'my old acquaintance and my Client' (Journ. 14 Mar. 1783); according to Grange Little kept 'the best publick house' in Moffat (From Johnston, 26 Apr.—Walker, p. 213).

[3] JB had been sent to Moffat, a noted spa, for his health at least twice, as a boy and again as a young man, and he felt comfortable there (*Earlier Years*, pp. 4, 21–22, 33). His most recent visit had been made in May of this year for a reunion with Grange after three years' absence on the Grand Tour, but we do not know why Moffat considered JB so valuable a friend; for example, there is no evidence that he had represented the burgh in court.

[4] We have been unable to discover whether it was customary for women to make the burgess tickets.

From Joseph Fergusson, Saturday 20 December 1766

MS. Yale (C 1243.9)

ADDRESS: To James Boswell younger of Auchinleck, Advocate, Edinburgh.

Tundergarth Manse, 20 Decemr. 1766

DEAR SIR: A few days ago I was honoured with your short but kind and emphatick letter, dated above two months by post. As you said nothing to the Contrary I hope that Lord Auchinleck is in good health.

The reason that I did not fulfill my promise of paying you a visit at Auchinleck in the end of the last harvest, was owing to a course of very bad weather that we had here at that time, which continued about six week during which time we had very few good days.[1]

I congratulate you, on your commensing Advocate and I hope you will shine at the Bar in the defence of the civil rights of your country men; I think that it is a most honourable and agreeable employment, especially to such as you, who have reason to hope that you will be advanced higher in the study of the Law, as my Lord has been before you.

As to the horse you speak of, I think you are freed from your promise, upon several accounts, as you was a Minor when you made it, and as I did not keep mine to you etc. etc.—so I would not have you to mind him any more[2]—but Sir if you would be so good as to procure one of Lord Dundonalds Burces for my Nephew Jeamie Fergusson it would be a very great favour done both to me and him.[3]

How is my friend Grange, did you ever see him laugh more than that night that you and he was at the Shaw, and I hope he was equally well pleased when paddocked up in the Chaise next day, with Miss Jenny graham. Shaw is threatning to prosecute him for breaking the back of a chair when he was seised with the convulsive fit of laughter, but I cannot see how you can honourably undertake Shaws cause against grange when you provoked him to[4] laugh to that excess, as to fall back and breake the Chair; except you argue the more mischief the more gain to[5] the Lawyer.

Sir if ever you are so good as to write me again, direct to the Care of the post Master in Lochmaban, for your letter was put into a wrong bag.[6]— Please make my most respectfull Compliments to Lord Auchinleck and to my good friend Mr. David.[7] I am, Dear Sir, your very Humble Servant and Sincere wellwisher,

JOS. FERGUSSON

P.S. Please let me know how Mr. John Boswel your brother is, and where he is, for I propose to write him very soon.

[1] On 22 Nov. James Bruce reported that the weather at Auchinleck had been 'very uncertain the ground vastly wet and dirty' and again on 28 Nov.: 'the Late storme has done Much harm among plantings etc'.

[2] Nothing further has been reported about the promised horse.

[3] Fergusson hoped JB would urge his granduncle, Thomas Cochrane (1691–1778), eighth Earl of Dundonald (*Ominous Years*, Gen. Chart V), to provide a burse (O. Sc. *burse, burs, burce*—*Scot. Nat. Dict.*) or scholarship for young James Fergusson. Dundonald's ancestor, William Cochrane, first Earl of Dundonald, had founded the 'Dun-

donald bursaries' at the University of Glasgow in 1672. Originally there were four bursaries, one in Philosophy and three in Divinity, but there is no record of a James Fergusson ever having been a bursar (information kindly supplied by Michael S. Moss, Archivist at the University of Glasgow). Fergusson's nephew later became a successful planter in Virginia, and named his son James Boswell (From Fergusson, 24 July 1786).

[4] MS. 'so much' deleted before 'to'

[5] MS. 'for' deleted before 'to'

[6] Lochmaben, Dumfriesshire, six miles west-north-west of Tundergarth.

[7] David Boswell.

From Godfrey Bosville, Thursday 25 December 1766

MS. Yale (C 174).

ADDRESS: To James Boswell Esqr. at the House of Lord Auchinleck in Edinborough.

POSTMARK: [London] 25 DE.

London, Decr. 25th 1766

DEAR SIR: We are now all of us safely arrivd in Great Russel Street, we just Missd of Governor Wentworth who is gone to America and I receivd a Letter from him the day after I got here from Bridgewater in his way to Portsmouth, he seems to leave England with some Regret.[1] Sir Thomas and Miss Annabella are still at Bretton. I think you have judgd extreamly right to apply to the Study of the Law, which must be much more agreeable in Scotland than in England as you have not occasion for a long dull train of Acts of Parliament contradictory one to another to load your Memory with. There is warm work expected after the Hollidays, whoever gets uppermost we shall be certain of Places and Pensions to them and Debts and Taxes to us. Lord Talbot is exceeding angry, he savd forty thousand a year in the Oeconomy of the Houshold for which he incurrd much Personal Ill will, and it is now given away in Pensions.[2] You will find much pleasure in what you are about as you have a father to help to instruct you and likewise to help you on when you are instructed, both very material Considerations: if I had had the same Advantages I am very certain I should have studyd the Law my self. The first Grand Jury I ever was upon Sir Hugh Smithson now Duke of Northumberland was High Sherrif, I was then at the Temple and I followd the Lawyers the Circuit as far as Newcastle, I was by that time very heartily tird and turnd back again: I had but few Acquaintance and those I did not like.[3] In our way to London We calld upon an Acquaintance and stayd a Day or two with him at Darfield which was the Ancient Estate of our Family and of which I have the Skeleton; The Mannor, the Old Mansion house called[4] Newhall moated round and a porters lodge, some Demesne Lands, and a Quire in the Church with a Marble Knight in it and his Lady who I am obligd to keep in repair as well as their habitation: there is a Chappel too at the end of the bridge to pray for the Souls of our family, but as the

99

family chuses to pray for themselves I let it for a Cottage. There is a Pillar in the Quire which seemd hollow and may lead to a subterraneous passage and I intend to have it opend. The Knight as far as I can trace was Thomas son to another Thomas and Alicia Gunthwait and his wife was the daur. of his Uncle Sir Robert Constable of Pomfret Castle this was in Edw. 3ds. time his name upon the Newhall seat is Thomas Bosswell.[5] If you come to my house from Doncaster you go through this town,[6] but there is a nearer way from Scotland through Leeds. We all desire our best Respects to you and likewise to Lord Auchinleck. I am glad that firebrand of Sedition Mr. Wilks is not to return, he is in France in the Latitude 45 and I hope he will be obligd to stay there.[7] I hope we shall see you in Town this winter and that you will soon write again to, Dear Sir, Your most Obedient Servant,

GODFREY BOSVILLE

A merry Christmas we wish you and a happy new year.

[1] John Wentworth (c. 1737–1820), a native of New Hampshire, had been sent to England in 1766 as an agent for the province to present a petition against the Stamp Act at Court. While in England he spent time in Yorkshire making the acquaintance of the Wentworth families and the Marquess of Rockingham, who arranged for Wentworth's appointment as Governor of New Hampshire on 11 Aug. He reached New Hampshire in March and took up his post on 13 June 1767, remaining as Governor until 1775. He spent the next several years in America and England, finally settling (1783) in Nova Scotia, where he served (1792–1808) as Lt.-Governor of the province. He was created baronet in 1795 (Jeremy Belknap, *The History of New Hampshire*, 1831, pp. 335–36, 357–58 and n.; *Comp. Bar.* v. 302). Wentworth shared a common ancestor with Bosville's wife Diana, née Wentworth (John Wentworth, *The Wentworth Genealogy*, 1878, i. xv–xxv).

[2] William Talbot (1710–82), first Earl Talbot, was Lord Steward of the Royal Household, 1761–82, and as such had 'sole direction of the Royal Household below stairs' (W. J. Thoms, *The Book of the Court*, 1844, p. 298). Speaking before the House of Lords in 1777, Lord Talbot recalled the 'endless clamour' that had arisen when he tried (unsuccessfully) to reduce the expenses of the Household by cutting off those who held sinecures (e.g. an M.P. who was 'one of the *turnspits* in his Majesty's kitchen'—a duty which brought him £5 a year) while menial servants performed the actual labour (*Gent. Mag.* 1777, xlvii. 156). Protests against the awarding of sinecures and undeserved pensions abounded in the newspapers and periodicals of the time, e.g. *Gent. Mag.* Aug. 1766, xxxvi. 351–52; *Lond. Chron.* 21–23 Oct. xx. 393, 1–4 Nov. xx. 433.

[3] Sir Hugh Smithson (c. 1714–86) of Stanwick, Bt., had changed his name to Percy in 1750 when he succeeded his father-in-law as Earl of Northumberland; he had been created first Duke of Northumberland on 22 Oct. of this year. He was High Sheriff of Yorkshire in 1738 when Bosville was studying law at the Inner Temple (From Bosville, 24 June, n. 4).

[4] MS. 'call'

[5] The Bosvilles (there are many variant spellings) seem to have settled at Darfield in the thirteenth century. This Thomas (fl. c. 1383), son of Thomas Bosville (d. c. 1362) and Alice de Gunthwaite, married Alice, daughter of William Monk of Chevet, not a daughter of the son Thomas's greatuncle, Robert Bosville (d. 1362), Constable of Pontefract Castle. Joseph Hunter states that New Hall passed out of the Bosvilles' hands in 1639—according to *Fortunes of a Family*, p. 81—but was bought back again by Godfrey Bosville (d. 1714), greatuncle of our Godfrey Bosville, in 1713. Hunter continues, 'Mr. Bosvile [the writer of the present letter], the grandfather of Lord Macdonald, in some memoirs of his family, says that what his uncle bought was but the skeleton of the antient New Hall estate, namely the manor, the mansion house, and demesne lands, certain chief rents in Darfield, Wombwell, Hill, Ederthorpe, Milnehouse, and Middlewood, with a quire in the church' (*South Yorkshire*, 1828–31, ii. 109–114, quotation on p. 114; J. J. Boswell, *History and Genealogical Tables of the Boswells*, [c. 1906], pp. 72–75; *Fortunes of a Family*, pp. 19–23, 29–30, 233–34).

[6] Darfield.

[7] Wilkes was an exile in Paris, latitude 49°, but of course Bosville is referring to his notorious *North Briton* no. 45. After spending some five years on the Continent in poverty and frustration, Wilkes returned to England in Feb. 1768 (Namier and Brooke iii. 639–40).

From John Wilkie, Tuesday 30 December 1766

MS. Yale (C 3110).
ADDRESS: To James Boswell Esqr., Edinburgh.

London, 30 Decemr. 1766

Sir: I have this day the favor of your letter inclosing some little peices for the Chronicle[1] for which and your former favors of the same kind I am very greatly obliged to you, I shall Sir with the greatest pleasure undertake your Commission of forwarding the Newspapers to General Paoli; in the manner desired, and you may depend on my sending them regular as opportunity by shiping Offers. Your puting my[2] name to your Intended History of Corsica will do me great honour[3] and conferr a further Obligation on, Sir, Your most obedient, humble Servant,

JOHN WILKIE

[1] The pieces JB had sent to Wilkie were presumably those marked in his own file of *Lond. Chron.* for 1, 3, 6, and 8 Jan. 1767: an epigram by a banker, a request for a translation of Seneca's epigrams on Corsica, and two articles on the Hume-Rousseau quarrel (*Lit. Car.* p. 237).
[2] MS. 'my' deleted before 'my'
[3] Presumably JB had asked Wilkie about publishing *Corsica*; however, it was published by Edward and Charles Dilly.

To Andrew Burnaby, c. early 1767

Not reported. See From Burnaby, 10 Aug.: 'The letter You honoured me with, did not arrive till long after the time it was due'.

To Francis Gentleman, c. early 1767

Not reported. See From Gentleman, 23 June: 'I should much sooner have acknowledged the last Honour you indulged me with; had I any thing to say which might compensate an intrusion upon Time so importantly devoted as yours is at present'.

To Thomas Davies, c. early January 1767

Not reported. Answered in From Davies, 17 Jan.

To Sir John Pringle, c. January 1767

Not reported. See From Pringle, 10 Feb.: 'I received some time ago your kind and, I am assured, sincere congratulations on the late honour conferred upon me by His Majesty'. Pringle had been created baronet on 5 June 1766, but Pringle's not mentioning the matter in his letter of early Jan. rules out dating this letter earlier than that.

To George Dempster, Thursday 1 January 1767

MS. Yale (M 175). An excerpt from JB's Memorabilia for 1767.

[Edinburgh]

To *Dempster* 1 Janry. 1767. Your Picture of me is better than Signor Georgio's.[1] It is truly poetical. I shall therefore in time coming allways prefer Poetry to Painting.

Poetry has certainly this advantage, that you may flatter a Man much more than you can do as a Painter. Had you Dempster instead of so many amiable qualitys, given me a fine complexion, an elegant forehead, and a beautifull symetry of features,—it would not have done. Every body even myself must have said it was not a bit like.

I had lately a letter of sixteen quarto pages from General Paoli.[2] It is impossible for me not to be proud. The old Castle of Auchinleck seems to receive me with the cordiality of other times; and the venerable Trees of my Ancestors nod, as I talk of Corsica under their shade.[3]

I speak well I think; and I am content though my voice should never be heard in England, but in Appeals. Perhaps indeed I may yet be a Parliament man as well as the best of you. But my views now are such that I would not wish it soon, and at any rate shall hardly think of it, except it be first thought of by my noble Fellow Traveller and Patron My Lord Mountstuart.[4]

Were you to come in to the Parliament House, and see me gravely walking about, you might address me from Buchanan's Franciscanus.

> Unde novus rigor in vultu? tristisque severis
> Frons caperata minis? tardique modestia gressus?
> Illaque fraenatae constans custodia linguae?
> Quo lepor et risus abiere salesque venustae?[5]

You see how finely I adapt my mind to my objects. I am like a man who has been used to wear large Buckles, and can now have only small ones. No doubt the tongues of my small Buckles will not answer the large holes. I therefore pierce another part of my latchet with the small tongues, and walk about with my shoes as well buckled as a Gentleman need do. Whenever it shall please the King to order me a pair of magnificent Buckles, I have holes for them.

[1] Though Dempster dabbled in poetry (both he and JB had contributed to A *Collection of Original Poems by Scotch Gentlemen*, 1762), his poetical portrait of JB has not been reported. George Willison (1741–97) was first cousin to Dempster, who had sent him to Rome to study art; it was there, in 1765, that he painted JB's portrait (*Earlier Years*, pp. 221–22). The painting, which now hangs in the National Portrait Gallery, Edinburgh, is described by C. B. Tinker and F. A. Pottle in A *New Portrait of James Boswell*, 1927; it is reproduced as the frontispiece in *Earlier Years*.

[2] Presumably the 'sixteen quarto pages from General Paoli' which James Bruce reported as having arrived at Auchinleck in Nov. 1766 (From Paoli, c. 20 Oct. 1766; From John Dick, 24 Oct. 1766 and n. 2).

[3] The Old Castle, the first of the three Boswell residences at Auchinleck, was replaced by the Old House in which JB lived as a boy. The replacement occurred before 12 Feb. 1531–32, the date on which the lands and barony of Auchinleck were confirmed by charter to David Boswell, second laird of Auchinleck (information supplied by Sir James Fergusson of Kilkerran, Bt., in letters to F. A. Pottle, dated 17 Feb. 1954 and 4 Mar. 1956, on deposit in the Boswell Office, Yale). The castle ruins were allowed to remain. The New House built by Lord Auchinleck was occupied by Aug. 1762 (*Earlier Years*, p. 454).

[4] Lord Mountstuart had been M.P. for his mother's family borough of Bossiney, Cornwall, since Jan. 1766, and his father controlled other seats in Parliament (Namier and Brooke i. 166-67, iii. 502). For JB's relations with Mountstuart, see *Pol. Car.* pp. 23–27; From Mountstuart, 29 May 1766; To Mountstuart, 1 Jan.

[5] The passage from *Franciscanus et Fratres* I. 1–4, by George Buchanan (1506–82), was translated by George Provand in 1809:

> Why, with a slow and solemn pace advance,
> To mortals round scarce deign a passing glance,
> Beneath the fretted vault and sculptur'd dome,
> With downcast and delusive aspect roam?

From Félix-Louis Gayot,[1] Thursday 1 January 1767

MS. Yale (C 1360).
ADDRESS: To Sir James Boswell, At Auchinleck in Scottland, Angleterre.
POSTMARK: [London] 17 IA.

A Strasbourg, Le 1er Janvier 1767

DEAR SIR: Je suis trôp flatté de vivre dan vôtre souvenir pour ne pas oublier que vôtre Silence m'a donné Lieu de craindre Le contraire; Les asseurances flatteuses que vous vouléz bien m'en donner me penetrent de La plus vive reconnoissance. Ce Sentiment pretieux vis a vis de vous sera inviolable pour moy, mon coeur aura toujours interêt de Le conserver.

Si'il suffisoit de meriter d'être heureux pour L'être en effet j'aurois eté tranquille sur Le sort que La fortune vous destinoit; je vois avec un vray plaisir que vous vous êtes fixé a un etat Libre. Vous étiés sans doute fait pour aller loin dans Les fonctions publiques, mais plus on merite de parvenir dans La voye de L'ambition moins on est capable de prendre Les moyens necessaires pour parvenir ils repugnent à une ame vertueuse. C'est donc de tout mon coeur que je vous felicite sur Le choix d'un etat où vous pourréz faire Le bien et Le bien faire, chose aussy rare dans ce siecle qu'il est commun de voir Le mieux être L'ennemy du bien.

J'ay eû occasion de parler beaucoup de vous avec Mr. Wilks dans un voyage que j'ay fait à Paris L'eté dernier et j'ay eû ces jours cy Le même plaisir avec Mr. Le Chev. Echlin, homme trés estimable.[2]

J'espere que vous voudrés bien me faire part de l'ouvrage auquel vous travaillés sur La corse; je pense bien comme vous que Les citations des classiques enrichissent, ornent un ouvrage mais comme j'ay toujours regardé avec pope L'etude et La connoissance du coeur humain, comme La plus digne de Lhomme, quelsques satisfaisantes que soyent Les Remarques physiques D'Adisson sur Litalie, j'aurois desiré quil eû plus donné aux considerations morales sur Le genie et Les moeurs des hommes dont il à parlé celà eût ajouté un grand interet à La curiosité.[3] Au reste je m'en rapporterois bien plus à vôtre decision qu'a mon avis.

Oseroi je vous demander si Les deux Exemplaires des fetes de strasbourg que j'ávois addressé à Paris[4] pour vous vous ont ete remis et si vous avés eû La bonté d'en donner un a mon Respectable ami Armstrong.[5]

Ma compagne et Le professeur Schoepfflin sont trés sensibles à Lhonneur de vôtre souvenir et me chargent de vous faire agreer Leurs obeissances.[6]

Je suis trés flatté de L'esperance que vous voulez bien me donner d'entretenir nôtre correspondance. Je continueray si vous Le Vouléz bien dans ma Langue et vous dans La vôtre. I am for ever, Dear Sir, your faithfull humble Servant,

GAYOT FILS

[1] Félix-Louis Gayot (c. 1735–69)—JB refers to him as Gaio (Journ. 21, 22 Nov. 1764)— served as one of six 'sénateurs nobles' of Strasbourg from 1762 to 1765 (Jacques Hatt, Liste des membres du grand sénat de Strasbourg . . . du XIIIe siècle à 1789, 1963, pp. 368–70, 436). 'Ein damals 33 jähriger vielversprechender Mann', he succeeded his father, François-Marie Gayot, as Royal Praetor (Governor of the city) in 1768 (Ingeborg Streitberger, Der Königliche Prätor von Strassburg, 1685–1789, 1961, p. 204). He was already ailing, however, and died in March of the following year (ibid. pp. 205, 280 n. 18). JB found him 'a genteel black little man, much of the Gentleman and the man of the World', who 'spoke good english, tho' his accent was foreign

... a noble fellow' (Journ. 21, 22 Nov. 1764). Gayot is mentioned in two anecdotes in *Boswelliana* (p. 234).

[2] JB had met and dined with Sir Henry Echlin (1740–99), Bt., at Wilkes's house in Paris on 21 Jan. 1766 (Notes, 22 Jan. 1766).

[3] Gayot is referring to the opening lines of *An Essay on Man*, Epistle II, perhaps as translated by L'Abbé du Resnel in the Strasbourg edition of 1762:

Ne sonde point de Dieu l'immense profondeur;
Travaille sur toi-même, et rentre dans ton coeur,
L'étude la plus propre à l'Homme, est l'Homme même.

However, since Gayot 'spoke good english' and this is a polyglot edition of English, Latin, Italian, French, and German, he might very well have read Pope's poem in English.

Gayot had already noted in his letter to JB of 7 Jan. 1766 that the interest in human nature for which he is praising Pope in this letter was lacking in Addison's *Remarks on Several Parts of Italy etc. in the Years 1701, 1702, 1703, 1705*. JB had carried Addison's book with him in Italy in 1765 and also pointed out its deficiencies ('Addison's Remarks on Italy', 16 Aug. 1765, M 102).

[4] Louis XV, after recovering from a near-fatal illness in Metz, was fêted for five days as ostensible deliverer of Alsace from the Imperial armies of Maria Theresa, on his triumphal entry into Strasbourg in Oct. 1744 (Rodolphe Reuss, *Histoire de Strasbourg*, 1922, pp. 310–13). Mme. Gayot, 'a young pretty sweet creature without any airs' (Journ. 21 Nov. 1764), had presented JB with a memorial of the festival, an album of prints, *Représentation des fêtes données par la ville de Strasbourg pour la convalescence du Roi, à l'arrivée et pendant le séjour de Sa Majesté*, engraved in 1744 by J. M. Weis (Journ. 22 Nov. 1764; Thieme-Becker xxxv. 330). Presumably Gayot was forwarding copies of this album to JB in Paris (From Gayot, 7 Jan. and 5 Feb. 1766).

[5] Gayot had known Dr. John Armstrong well when Armstrong was serving as physician to the army in Kassel (for Armstrong, see From Sir Alexander Dick, 22 Aug. 1766, n. 8). Gayot described his friend and correspondent to JB: 'C'est un Homme Hypochondre, chez qui la physique influ beaucoup sur la morale. Avant diner il est tout abattu. Mais quand il a eu un Bouteille de bon vin il commence de se sentir; il etend les ailes il s'eleve comme un Aigle. Quand il etoit comme cela, Je le mena dans ma voiture hors de Cassel. Nous nous sommes mis sur l'herbe a notre aise, et il haranguoit d'une maniere la plus vive avec un feu celeste' (Journ. 21 Nov. 1764); for his part Armstrong characterized Gayot in *A Day: An Epistle to John Wilkes*, 1761 (concluding section):

Yet *Cassel* else no sad Retreat I find,
While good and amiable *Gayot*'s my Friend,
Generous and plain, the Friend of Humankind;
Who scorns the little-minded's partial View.

[6] Jean-Daniel Schoepflin (1694–1771) had been Professor of History at Strasbourg since 1720 and Royal Historiographer to Louis XV since 1740. His numerous publications included *Alsatia illustrata* (1751–61) and *Historia Zoeringo-Badensis* (1763–66), an 'elegant latin History of the Principality of Baden' (Journ. 21 Nov. 1764). Meeting Schoepflin at dinner with the Gayots, JB had found him 'a tall figure, full of knowledge, healthy and lively' (ibid.). JB had also been much impressed by his massive library, one of the great private libraries of the time; Schoepflin bequeathed it to the city (NBG).

To Lord Mountstuart, Thursday 1 January 1767

MS. Yale (L 345). A draft, unsigned.

HEADING: To My Lord Mountstuart.

Edinburgh, 1 January 1767

MY DEAR LORD: It is impossible to tell you how much I am surprised and vexed to find that You have not received my Thesis. I sent it in the month of August by Mr. John Donaldson Bookseller in the Strand who promised to take particular care of it.[1] What He has done with it I cannot comprehend but I beg your Lordship may immediatly send one of your Servants with the inclosed note and[2] bid him wait for an Answer. You must indeed have thought me a very odd man and You cannot beleive how much I am touched with your last very kind letter to a man who could not but appear to you in a strange light. It shews me My Dear Lord that You have a real regard for me which the greatest odditys cannot destroy. You write to me with the dignity of a Philosopher and the generosity of a Friend 'though in the course of things with your odd way many quarrels may happen betwixt us, yet my Friendship shall never be wanting to give you all the assistance it can whenever you shall have the least occasion for it'. My Dearest Lord I thank you from my Soul: and be assured I shall not abuse your goodness. I am not so odd a man now as you knew me. I shall be every day less so. And in this affair[3] of my Thesis You will find I am not to blame.[4] I hope Donaldson will find the Packet I sent by him. If he does not, pray let me know and I will immediatly send another. In the mean time I inclose You the Dedication and as I kept[5] a Copy of theLetter which I wrote when I sent you my Thesis I likeways beg leave to send that to your Lordship.

I sincerely wish you joy on your marriage which I have the satisfaction to hear is most[6] agreable in every respect.[7] How[8] noble is your Lordship's lot in life! and how happy are you in being Philosopher enough to know it[9] and to relish it. 'Di tibi divitias dederant artemque fruendi' says Horace.[10] The ars fruendi is of infinite importance in all advantages.

Did not I sometimes mention to your Lordship my youngest Brother David whom with true[11] feudal authority I put[12] to be Banker?[13] He is a very diligent pretty young man and makes me very happy. I must tell you an Anecdote of him which will please you. Just before I left[14] Paris a Bill of mine came over which my Father was much displeased with and went so far as to refuse to pay it. David in great concern for his Brother prevailed with the Banker on whom it was drawn to delay protesting it and He[15] immediatly wrote a very earnest letter to your Lordship intreating you to save the honour of an absent Friend. Before his letter was sent off my Father discovered that the Bill was no more than what He had ordered and accordingly payed it.[16] But my Brother's conduct was admirable. He shewed his affection for me and He shewed his just ideas in addressing himself[17] to your Lordship. There[18] was then indeed an unlucky difference[19] between Your Lordship and me. But that would have been of no consequence. I know you would have instantly shewn your generosity. I like to think of this Anecdote. My Brother intends to settle in London about a year hence. I will beg leave to recommend him to Your Lordship. Your countenance will greatly support him. I have the honour to remain etc.

[1] John Donaldson (c. 1730–?82) took over the family linen manufactury at Drumsheugh, Edinburgh on the death of his father in 1754, while his younger brother Alexander became a bookseller in Edinburgh (See To Alexander Donaldson, 24 Apr. 1766). The brothers went to London in 1763, opened a booksellers' establishment at the corner of Arundel Street in the Strand, and remained in partnership until 1773, when Alexander removed to St. Paul's Churchyard (R. T. Skinner, A Notable Family of Scots Printers, 1927, pp. 1, 3–5, 13, 45).

[2] Draft, 'to him' deleted before 'and'

[3] Draft, 'last instance' deleted before 'affair'

[4] Draft, 'am not to blame' written above deleted 'have acted with the greatest exactness'

[5] Draft, 'luckily' deleted before 'kept'

[6] Draft, 'a' deleted before 'most'

[7] On 12 Nov. 1766 Mountstuart had married Charlotte Jane Windsor, daughter and heir of Herbert Hickman Windsor, Viscount Windsor and Baron Mountjoy. JB found Lady Mountstuart 'civil and obliging' (Journ. 17 Mar. 1776); Horace Walpole thought her ugly (Corres. HW x. 237).

[8] Draft, 'What great advantages are you born with' deleted before 'How'

[9] Draft, 'the' deleted before 'it'

[10] Horace, Epistles I. iv. 7, trans. Philip Francis, 1746:

To thee the Gods a large Estate
In Bounty gave, with Skill to know
How to enjoy what they bestow.

Although several 18th-century editions read 'dederunt', the Foulis edition of 1760 reads 'dederant', as did presumably their edition of 1750, which was in JB's library ('A Catalogue of

Books belonging to James Boswell Esq.'—MS. NLS).

[11] Draft, 'true' written below deleted 'the'. JB then tried to change 'the' to 'true', realized he only had room for 'tr' and ended by writing 'true' below the deletion, all before 'feudal'

[12] Draft, 'feudal authority of an elder made a' written above 'put to be Banker' with 'of an elder made a' deleted before 'put'

[13] For David Boswell's banking career, see From Mary Montgomerie, 27 Mar. 1766, n. 5.

[14] Draft, 'left' written above deleted 'came from'

[15] Draft, 'in' deleted before 'He'

[16] Lord Auchinleck had written to JB on 30 Jan. 1766 making it clear that he considered he had already advanced more money to JB than he had intended and that he would pay no more of his bills 'either for one purpose or another'. Written shortly after Lord Auchinleck's, David Boswell's letter of 3 Feb. 1766 informed JB that 'a Bill for £100 from Paris has come down most unexpectedly as it is the full extent of your Credit; your Father has paid it with Reluctance'. Presumably, the banker on whom the bill was drawn was Robert-Ralph Foley (To Wilkes, 6 May 1766, n. 5); both the letters mentioned above reached Paris after JB had left for London and they remained at Foley's bank until JB was able to have them sent to him.

[17] Draft, 'addressing himself' written above deleted 'applying'

[18] Draft, 'you and I My Lord were then indeed' deleted before 'There'

[19] Draft, 'coldness' written above 'difference'

From Sir John Pringle, c. 1 January 1767

MS. Yale (C 2296)

ADDRESS: To James Boswell Esqr.

[London]

DEAR SIR: Not satisfied with including You in the Compliments of the season, which by this post I send to Your father, I thought proper to write You this line apart to convey to You my best wishes of a new year and congratulations on the good appearances which I have heard You have made, at the bar, and that soon after You were called to it.[1] If You will but continue Your application I make no doubt of hearing more and more commendations of You, and a compleat justification of myself, for having always told You, that by that means You had the best chance for becoming eminent. I have seen your friend Lord M. since his marriage, and was glad to find that all Your quarrels were made up, and that after the coldness which had some time subsisted between You, there was nothing[2] more of that kind likely to happen.[3] Believe me to be with affection and truth, Dear Sir, Your most obedient, humble Servant,

JOHN PRINGLE

[1] Between his first cause after passing advocate (29 July 1766) and his last cause of the Winter Session (9 Mar. 1767), JB earned eighty-four guineas (Consultation Book).

[2] MS. 'likely' erased before 'nothing'

[3] For the quarrels between JB and Mountstuart and their subsequent reconciliation, see From Mountstuart, 29 May 1766, n. 1 and 25 June 1766.

To Lord Chatham, Saturday 3 January 1767

MS. Chatham Papers, Public Record Office, London. JB's unsigned draft (L 367) bears the heading 'To The Earl of Chatham' and differs from the original letter primarily in capitalization and punctuation, but also in a few instances in wording.

ENDORSEMENT (in the hand of Lord Cardross): 1767 Jany. 3rd.

Edinburgh, 3 January 1767

My Lord: It is now more than three months since I took the liberty to write Your Lordship a short letter in behalf of the Corsicans, of which a Copy is herewith[1] transmitted, lest the original[2] should not have come to your hands.

I have received a letter from General Paoli, in which He thus talks of Mr. Pitt. 'La pubblica fama esalta fino alle Stelle Li Talenti del Signor Pitt; ma la Relazione che Ella mi fa della Conversazione avuta con esso Lui, mi riempie ancora di maggior ammirazione e di attaccamento per la buonta del Cuore di questo Pericle della Gran Bretagna.'[3]

My Lord, I wrote to General Paoli the many strong and noble expressions which you uttered in a private conference to me,[4] with as much eloquence as ever Mr. Pitt displayed[5] in the fullest Assembly: And My Lord I trust[6] you will now shew a generous sincerity.

I would[7] recommend to Your Lordship Mr. Dick His Majesty's Consul at Leghorn as a Gentleman of great information and Judgment as to every thing that concerns the Mediterranean;[8] and I would[9] recommend him as a Man of worth and spirit who is warmly attached to the brave Corsicans. He will give[10] your Lordship all the light you can desire as to the advantages which Great Britain might derive from an alliance with Corsica, either in the way of trade, or for the conveniency of war, and will faithfully execute whatever commands Your Lordship may lay upon him.

Your Lordship knows that a Proclamation stands in force by which the Subjects of Great Britain are prohibited from holding any intercourse with the Malecontents of Corsica.[11] If Your Lordship would only[12] get us that[13] Proclamation annulled, it would be of great consequence in the mean time. Corsica seems to be particularly unlucky. The Swiss and the Dutch had powerfull assistance in recovering their libertys. But the gallant Islanders for whom I am concerned have now been in arms for the glorious cause nine and thirty years, and not a State[14] in Europe has interposed in their behalf.[15]

Let me plead with Your Lordship for Corsica. Let me put you[16] in mind of the People animated with the spirit of liberty whom the Romans[17] stood forth and protected against the great King of Asia,[18] and in so doing gained more real honour than by the most extensive Conquests.[19] And let[20] me recall to your Lordship the excellent old Fable of The Lion and the Mouse.[21] Far be it from me to attempt pointing out any measures to be taken by the Government of my Country. But surely a great free Nation may befriend a small one. Is Great Britain now affraid of France? or does She owe any thing to Genoa?

As an Advocate for Corsica I look up to the Earl of Chatham, and I cannot but hope for a favourable return.[22] I have the honour to remain[23] with the highest Consideration Your Lordship's Most Obedient and Most Humble Servant,

James Boswell

My Address is at Lord Auchinleck's Edinburgh.

[1] Draft, 'now'
[2] Draft, 'it'. Both the original and the copy survive in the Chatham Papers (To Chatham, 18 Sept. 1766, headnote).
[3] 'Public report exalts Mr. Pitt's talents to the stars, but the report you give me of the conversation you had with him fills me with even greater

admiration and love for the goodness of heart of this Pericles of Great Britain.' For Paoli's 'letter', see To Dempster, 1 Jan. n. 2. JB uses Paoli's description of Chatham as 'the Pericles of Great Britain' in *Corsica* (p. 382).
[4] Draft, 'to me in a private conference', with 'in a private conference' inserted above the line.

⁵ Draft, 'displayed' written above deleted 'used'

⁶ Draft, 'trust' written above deleted 'would hope that'

⁷ Draft, 'would' written above deleted 'can'

⁸ See From John Dick, 30 May 1766 for Dick's offer to supply Chatham with information about Corsica.

⁹ Draft, 'would' written above deleted 'can'

¹⁰ Draft, 'faithfully' deleted before 'give'

¹¹ To Pitt, 15 Feb. 1766, n. 8.

¹² Draft, 'only' inserted above the line.

¹³ Draft, 'that' superimposed upon 'this'

¹⁴ Draft, 'Power' deleted before 'State'

¹⁵ In 1648, by the Treaty of Westphalia (the name given to the two treaties which brought an end to the Thirty Years' War), both Switzerland and the United Netherlands won formal recognition of their independence from the Holy Roman Empire. The Swiss and the Dutch had been aided in the struggle for independence by the rising power of France and the break-up of the Empire, which came about as a result of constitutional changes effected by the treaties of Westphalia. Corsica had been fighting for its independence since the French invasion of 1738; JB describes their struggle in *Corsica* (pp. 110–43).

¹⁶ Draft, 'your Lordship' altered to 'you'

¹⁷ In the draft, JB first wrote 'of those whom the Romans', leaving a space between 'those' and 'whom' for later revision. He then changed 'those' to 'the' and inserted 'People animated with the spirit of liberty'

¹⁸ Draft, 'against the great King of Asia' inserted above the line.

¹⁹ The Jews' appeal to the Romans for aid against the Assyrians is related in 1 Maccabees: 8. JB transcribed the chapter, omitting two verses and condensing others, in *Corsica* (pp. 322–36); he thought that 'Paoli's favourite story . . . very well applies to Great Britain and Corsica, is told with great eloquence, and furnishes a fine model for an alliance' (p. 322).

²⁰ Draft, 'And' inserted before 'Let'

²¹ JB alludes to one of Aesop's fables, no. xxxi in the popular translation by Samuel Croxall (first published 1722, and reprinted often thereafter).

²² Draft, 'answer'

²³ Draft ends 'remain, &c'

To Giuseppe Marc'Antonio Baretti, Monday 5 January 1767

MS. Yale (L 31). An excerpt from JB's Memorabilia for 1767 (M 175). The original letter has not been reported, but Baretti's response shows that it was sent; see From Baretti, 20 Jan.

[Edinburgh]

To Signor Baretti 5 Janry. 1767. I am now entered on the profession of the law, which you know is one great road of ambition in this Country. I am an Advocate at the Scots Bar, which is a very good field for me. The labours indeed of my Profession are great. But so are the rewards. A Counsellor not only gets guineas, but he obtains the confidence of his fellow-creatures, and an insensible superiority over them; and at last he arrives at high honours. Such is my career, and in thus advancing I am chearfull and happy.

You and I are connected by the strong attachment which both of us have to the illustrious Philosopher of this age Mr. Samuel Johnson.[1] After all that I have seen I feel my veneration for him increased. I feel how little all other men are when compared with that wonderfull Genius.

> Illustrious Johnson! when of thee I think
> Into my distant self abash'd I shrink.
> With all my soul thy genius I admire;
> Thy strength of Judgment thy poetic fire,
> Thy knowledge vast, thy excellence of mirth,
> And all thy moral and religious worth.

I dare say you now pass many a noble hour with him. O noctes coenaeque Deum!²—He has done me more service than I can express. He has tempered my soul with genuine steel; though indeed I too often allow it to be softened. I remember you told me at Venice, that by being at a distance from him, you was becoming absolutely good-for-nothing; your lamp had long been dim and was gradually extinguishing.[3] By this time You will have got a large supply of oil and some Johnsonian fire added to your own.

[1] At the time of Baretti's trial for murder in 1769 SJ testified that he had first met him 'about the year 53 or 54' (H. W. Liebert, *A Constellation of Genius*, 1958, p. 16).

[2] Horace, *Satires* II. vi. 65. Philip Francis translated the passage in the 7th ed., 'revised and corrected' (1765), as:

O joyous nights! delicious feasts!

At which the gods might be my guests.
JB quotes the phrase in *Corsica*, p. 297 and in *Life* i. 2.

[3] Baretti may very well have made this remark on the morning of 8 July 1765 while he was showing JB 'some letters of Johnson's' (Notes, 9 July 1765).

To Robert Brown, Monday 5 January 1767

Not reported. See From Brown, 27 Jan.: 'Yours of the 5th of January I received last post; and from it understand you have not had my last dated about three months ago.'

To Lord Cardross, Monday 5 January 1767

Not reported. In his edition of JB's *Life of Samuel Johnson*, 1835, x. 122, John Wilson Croker notes that the letter was from the Buchan MSS. of William Upcott; attached to the letter was a note by Lord Cardross concerning JB's interview with William Pitt, later Earl of Chatham, on 22 Feb. 1766 (To Pitt, 19 Feb. 1766, n. 2). The note became separated from the letter and was acquired by the Bodleian Library in 1864 (Montagu d. 6, fol. 191). It reads in part: 'In consequence of this letter I desired him to call at Mr. Pitts and took care to be with him when he was introduced, Mr. Pitt was then in the D. of Grafton's house in G. Bond Street. Boswell came in the Corsican dress and presented a letter from Paoli. Lord Chatham Smiled but received him very graciously in his Pompous manner. Boswell had genius but wanted ballast to counteract his Whim. He preferred being a Shew man to keeping a Shop of his own' (Reproduced with permission of the Bodleian Library).

From John Dick, Wednesday 7 January 1767

MS. Yale (C 1011)

NOTE in Dick's hand at foot of first page: James Boswell Esq.

Leghorn, 7th January 1767

While every one is gone to the Opera,[1] I stay at home to write You this, in order to convey to You Copy of a Letter, which I have this afternoon receiv'd from the General, I am sorry his answer has been so long in reaching me, but the extreem bad Weather we have had for some time past, together with the few opportunitys he has of conveying Letters safe are the Causes of it.[2] You also have here the two papers he refers to in his Letter. I wish they may reach You in time, for your book, which I realy long to see.[3]

I have been very uneasy of late at my not having had the pleasure of hearing from You, fearing therefrom, that my Letters may not have reached You, they were dated the 26 Septr. 6 and 24 October, pray lett me know if You have receiv'd them.

The poor Islanders have now a fine Schiabec[4] at Sea, Commanded by Count Peris,[5] I think it's likely he may have success.

We have nothing new stirring here worthy your notice, which leaves me only to add Mrs. Dick's Compliments, and to assure You, that, I ever am with the most perfect Regard, and true Esteem, My dear Sir, Your most Affectionate and Faithful Servant,

JOHN DICK

I hope My dear Sir, You will give all proper attention to that part of the Generals letter which I have lined, how happy would You make these brave people could You succeed.[6]

[1] There was an opera house in Leghorn by 1709 (J. A. F. Maitland, *The Oxford History of Music*, 1902, iv. 282).

[2] For Dick's letter to Paoli, see From John Dick, 6 Oct. 1766.

[3] For these papers, see From John Dick, 6 Oct. 1766, n. 6.

[4] A *sciabecco* or xebec was a three-masted vessel of varying size used in the Mediterranean, usually as a man-of-war.

[5] Comte Jean-Baptiste de Pérez, a Chevalier of Malta and French expatriate, was in charge of Corsican naval affairs in 1760—JB styles him 'High Admiral of Corsica' in *Corsica* (p. 185)—

but towards the end of 1768, six years after becoming a naturalized Corsican and gaining the confidence of Paoli, he went over to the French (Joseph Foladare, 'James Boswell and Corsica', Yale diss. 1936, ii. 424; J.-M. Jacobi, *Histoire générale de la Corse*, 1835, ii. 281, 346–47; Louis Villat, *La Corse de 1768 à 1769*, 1925, i. 84–87).

[6] Paoli expressed the hope that JB would urge Chatham to get the Proclamation revoked that forbade British subjects to aid the Corsicans. The letter from Paoli to Dick, dated 6 Dec. 1766, is printed in BP vii. 216, 254. See also To Pitt, 15 Feb. 1766 and n. 8.

From Thomas Davies, Saturday 17 January 1767

MS. Yale (C 898).

London, Janry. 17th 1767

SIR: I am extremely obliged for your intention to put my name to your Advertizemt. of the History of Corsica[1]—I generally destroy the letters of my Friends about business least by mistake or neglect they should fall into improper hands—Unless there is a particular reason to preserve them. Yours was certainly burnt, for which I am sorry as you apprehend it might be of service to you.

I return my sincere thanks for the Comission of Paoli's books and will execute it faithfully[2]—The Glasgow Edition[3] of the Classicks is[4] not to be had here compleat: The Herodotus and Thucidides (the first espescially), are not easy to get in London—I wrote to the Foulis's and desired a List of all the Classicks they had printed, but have not as yet been favoured with an Answer. I heartily wish you would negotiate a corrispondence for me with those very eminent Printers—I should be glad to have duplicates of all the greek Classicks they have printed these three years—[5]

I really doubt whether you should call Mr. Johnson reverend, tho' I think his character venerable—He is only Doctor of Laws, not of Divinity[6]—I write this while Mr. Murphy is talking to me and Mrs. Davies; so must beg you to excuse inaccuracies. A Play of Murphys is acting this Night for the 5th time at Covt. Garden called the *School for Guardians*.[7] It met with opposition the first night, but has since[8] gone on very glibly—Mr. Garrick has treated the good people of London with a Shew, or what he calls, a Dramatick Romance—He knows it is much easier to feed the eye than the Understanding, and has given a most gaudy exhibition of fine Scenery, bad musick and flimsy writing—So says the General review—I have not seen it. The Authur wisely conceals himself, 'tis universally said to be very well acted.[9]

Mrs. Davies joins in wishing you many, many happy new years. I am, Sir, Your most obedient, humble Servant,

THOMAS DAVIES

P.S. Pray don't forget the Glasgow Classicks.

[1] The advertisement for *Corsica*, which appeared in *Lond. Chron.*, 6–8 Oct. (xxii. 339), noted only that the work was being printed for Edward and Charles Dilly; Davies had declined the opportunity to publish it himself (From Davies, 15 Nov. 1766).

[2] For more about the books JB was having Davies send to Paoli for the Corsican Academy, see From Davies, 18 June and 15 Oct.

[3] MS. 'Ant' deleted before 'Editions'

[4] MS. 'is' written above deleted 'are'

[5] The Foulis brothers, Robert (1707–76) and Andrew (1712–75) were especially noted for the quality and binding of their classical editions, and the 'Glasgow Editions', as they came to be known, were valued widely, not only for their beauty but also for their accuracy and the 'thought, pains, and care' that went into their production (David Murray, *Robert and Andrew Foulis and the Glasgow Press*, 1913, pp. 26–28). As Philip Gaskell pointed out in his 'Printing the Classics in the Eighteenth Century', *Book Collector*, 1952, i. 106, the secret of the Foulis' success may have lain in their emphasis on accommodating their readers even if it meant a break with tradition: simplicity of text was their prime concern. Among their classical editions, the four-volume Homer was the most renowned, the *Iliad* appearing in 1756, the *Odyssey* in 1758. Their publications of the classics included the works of Thucydides in 1759 (8 vols.) and of Herodotus in 1761 (9 vols.) among others, but their classical

editions in the past three years had been limited to Xenophon's *Anabasis* (4 vols.) and a new edition of Epictetus's *Manual* (Philip Gaskell, *A Bibliography of the Foulis Press*, 1964).

[6] Johnson was awarded the degree of LL.D. by Trinity College, Dublin, on 8 July 1765 (*Life* i. 488–89).

[7] *The School for Guardians* by Arthur Murphy, an amalgam of three of Molière's plays: *L'Ecole des femmes*, *L'Etourdie*, and *L'Ecole des maris*, was first presented at Covent Garden on 10 Jan. and played four more times that month (*Gent. Mag.* 1767, xxxvii. 34; *Lond. Stage* IV. ii. 1210–12).

[8] MS. 'since' written above deleted 'seen'

[9] *Cymon*, by David Garrick (1717–79), 'A Dramatic Romance' in five acts, with music composed by Michael Arne, opened at Drury Lane on 2 Jan. and was presented almost every night in January thereafter (*Lond. Stage* IV. ii. 1208–17). The play was based on Dryden's tale of Cymon and Iphigenia and made much use of stage machinery and other decorations. Genest summed up the prevailing opinion of it: 'Cymon was acted with great success . . . as a first-piece it is contemptible—if it had been brought out in 2 acts as a mere vehicle for songs, scenery, &c., it might have passed without censure' ([John Genest] *Some Account of the English Stage, from the Restoration in 1660 to 1830*, 1832, v. 121). For a long act-by-act review of *Cymon*, see *Gent. Mag.* 1767, xxxvii. 28–32.

From Giuseppe Marc'Antonio Baretti, Tuesday 20 January 1767

MS. Yale (C 75).

London, Janry. 20th 1767

DEAR SIR: I wish it may be in my power to come next Summer to see Scotland.[1] I do not however long to see it as much as to see you again; for I cannot Know whether I shall like Scotland or no, as I never saw it; but I positively Know that I should like to see you because I have seen you already. I have shown Johnson your Letter, and he said you are a clever fellow and will one day or other cut a good figure in this Kingdom. He thanks you for the continuation of your love to him. So much for that solemn Man, whose fire, as you say, begins to warm my soul again. I do not question but that I should be much pleased in the Acquaintance of your

Father. The question is whether he should like such a little queer outlandish Man as I am. Yet for a short while I will indulge myself so far as to say that I am pretty lucky that way, and that I have a pretty good hand at ingratiating myself with Men of worth. I say that for a little while I hope he would not be displeased with my company. But few Men have the talent of pleasing long, and I am afraid that is my case as well as the case of the greatest part of mankind. But I am running on in English, and I ought to remember that you bid me to write you in Italian. Let me therefore change my tone, and speak Italian.

Ho caro che abbiate intenzione di stampare un Ragguaglio della Corsica e del suo Eroe. Se però fosse possibile avrei pur caro di vedere l'opera vostra prima che vada sotto il Torchio, perchè a dirvi il vero ho paura vi lasciate trasportare dall' affetto che avete concepito pel Paoli, e che diciate qualche cosa de' Genovesi che non ista[1] alla mia coppella, essendo io da un canto netto d' ogni avversione a i Corsi, ma dall' altro inclinato molto a i Genovesi, essendo stato ultimamente da molti Signori di quella Republica trattato con tanta gentilezza e con tanta urbanità, che no ho potuto far a meno di non porre molto amore ad essi e alle cose loro. Ricordateri dunque nel parlar di Genova che Genova è la più colta Città d'Italia, e non vi lasciate vincere dalla tenerezza per Paoli a dire alcuna cosa che possa dispiacere a molti degni Uomini di Genova, dove tutti i Signori della Gran Bretagna ricevono costantemente ogni sorte di buon trattamento da molti anni, malgrado quelle tante insolenze che un mondo di Scrittoracci birboni vanno tutto di scarabocchiando contr' essi in queste Carte Ebdomadarie.[2] Scusate se ardisco offerirvi un cenno intorno all' opera vostra senz' esserne richiesto, conservatemi il vostro affetto, e credetemi con ogni rispetto, Vostro affettuósissímo ed obbediéntissímo Servitóre,

GIUSEPPE BARETTI

[I am pleased to hear that you are planning to publish an account of Corsica and its hero. If it were at all possible, I should be happy to see your work before it goes to press, because, to tell you the truth, I am afraid that you will let yourself be carried away by your affection for Paoli and say something about the Genoese that will not meet with my approval, as on the one hand I am free from any prejudice against the Corsicans and on the other I am favourably inclined toward the Genoese. I have recently been treated with so much kindness and courtesy by so many gentlemen of that Republic, that I cannot find it in myself to regard them and their interests with anything less than affection. Remember then, when you are writing about Genoa, that it is the most cultured city in Italy. Do not let your affection for Paoli prevail upon you to say anything that might be offensive to the many worthy persons of Genoa, where for many years now all gentlemen from Great Britain have been treated with every courtesy, notwithstanding the constant spate of insults scrawled against them in the weekly papers by a tribe of rascally scribblers.[2] Forgive me for having been so bold as to offer you these unsolicited comments about your work; continue to think kindly of me, and believe me to be, with all due respect, your most affectionate and obedient servant,

GIUSEPPE BARETTI][3]

[1] There is no evidence to suggest that Baretti ever visited Scotland.

[2] For JB's feelings about Genoa, expressed in a letter he wrote from Genoa to John Johnston, 9 Dec. 1765 (Walker, p. 193), see From Sommelsdyck, 1 July 1766, n. 2. In *Corsica* JB does at times show his hostility towards Genoa; see, for example, his censure of Louis-Amand Jaussin, whose *Mémoires historiques* he used as one of his main sources of information for his favourable attitude towards Genoa (*Corsica*, pp. xi, 116). For Baretti's defence of Genoa after he had read *Corsica*, see From Baretti, 4 Mar. 1768. Baretti's letters from Genoa are dated from 20 Apr. to 21 Aug. 1766. His favourable reception there, however, was outweighed by his disgust with Italy as a whole (see his letter from Genoa to Vincenzo Bujovich, 25 July 1766—*Epistolario*, ed. Luigi Piccioni, 1936, i. 341). JB had a chance to observe Genoese treatment of British and foreign notables during his brief stay in Genoa: he met, among others, Henry Ellis, the explorer, the Rev. Frederick Hervey, and James Hollford, the British consul (Notes, 1–10 Dec. 1765).

[3] Translation by Caterina Bosio and Ian Duncan.

From John Dick, Friday 23 January 1767

MS. Yale (C 1012).

ADDRESS: To James Boswell Esqr. of Auchenleck, to the Care of Messrs. Haries and Comp., Merchants, London.[1]

POSTMARK: [London] FE 12.

NOTE in Dick's hand at foot of first page: James Boswell Esq.

Leghorn, 23 January 1767

DEAR SIR, I had the pleasure to write You the 26th Septr. 6th and 24th October, and 7th Instant, and altho' am not yet favour'd with any of your Letters, venture to trouble You again, as I long to know if all the papers which I sent You have reached Your hands, and if they have been of any use to You.

In looking over your Letters the other day, I observ'd in one of them (which I had not noticed before,) that you seem'd to have an inclination to mention me in your book, as a friend to the General, I cannot help thinking that, I think it would be improper, and perhaps prevent my being able to render him any Services, neither would it be proper on other Considerations, seeing the Proclamation Subsists, therefore pray My dear Sir, don't lett your good wishes, lead you into a thing, that may be prejudicial to me.[2]

We have no news from the Island since I wrote you last, save that I believe you will soon hear of their having sent a very clever stout Privateer to Sea.[3]

Mrs. Dick presents You her best Compliments and I ever am with the most unalterable Regard, and true Esteem, My dear Sir, Your most Obliged and most Affectionate Friend,

JOHN DICK

[1] For Herries and Co., bankers, see From Dick, 30 May 1766, n. 1.

[2] Dick is mentioned only briefly in the Preface to *Corsica* as one of five men whose help JB acknowledges in erecting his 'little monument to liberty' (*Corsica*, p. xiv).

[3] For the privateer, see From Dick, 7 Jan. and n. 4.

From Robert Brown, Tuesday 27 January 1767

MS. Yale (C 591).

ADDRESS: To James Boswell Esqre. Younger of Auchinleck, at Edinburgh.

POSTMARK: [London] FE 2.

Utr. 27th Janry. 1767

DEAR SIR: Yours of the 5th of January I received last post; and from it understand you have not had my last dated about three months ago. 'Twas wrong in me not to have sent it by the post, at least not to have wrote you by that conveyence soon after; for my letter was rather a volume than a missive, and concluded with a long shred of an old sermon. I sent it with several others in a box to a friend, who I suppose was gone for America before the box arrived; for by what I find, not one of my letters have been forwarded. I'm extremely sorry for this, because it has put you in pain with respect to your Books, papers etc., which are all very safe and entire at this present moment, being still in my hands. The death of my worthy friend Mr. James Crawford at Rottm. having for sometime, viz. 'till his son was settled, deprived me of the opportunities I formerly had, and now again have, of geting things sent to Scotland by Shipmasters to be absolutely depended on, I thought 'twas better to delay sending your papers for sometime after I was favoured with yours.[1] Last Autumn I fell into a lingering distemper which held me for some months, and disabled me from thinking of any thing but my daily and necessary occupations, which are at present very numerous.[2] On my recovery I wrote you the letter above alluded to, in which I informed you that I would keep the papers 'till the spring, unless some sure hand should cast up sooner for carrying them over. Such an opportunity now actually offers. A son of Mr. Kinloch of Gilmertown who has lived with me these two winters past, is recalled to join his Regiment, sets out tomorrow, and takes your papers in his Cloakbag,[3] together with a Letter from you to Mr. De Zuylen, which he delivered me sometime ago, to transmitt to you.[4] As I could never expect to find a fitter occasion than this, unless I had delayed 'till July, when I might have been the bearer myself, I embraced it with pleasure; and I hope all will arrive safe, and to your satisfaction.[5] As for the Books, as soon as ever our Canals are again open I shall send them to Rottm. to be forwarded by the first ship for Leith. Johnson's Dictionary will not, probably, be of the number; for Miss de Zuylen having sometime ago applied to me for it, I made no scruple to let her have it; as knowing the proprietor would willingly homologate the deed. If that fair Lady is returned before the books are sent off, it shall be sent likewise, if not, when she does return. There is no getting, at present, all the Latin Gazett's of Cologne for the year 1763; but the Editor has promised to send me by the first occasion what of them he has been already been able to pick up, and to continue to do his best to get the remainder. Those of 1766 I shall have by the first opportunity and shall send you with the books.[6] The old Fencing Master was sensibly touched with your rememberance of him; but died suddenly soon after I communicated the contents of your Letter relative to him; so that I had no occasion of making him the present you mentioned; and indeed he stood in no need of it.[7]

And where then, you'll ask me, is Miss de Zuylen gone to? Had you received my letter you would have known that she has been in London these three months past. She is much pleased with the British Capital, and as you will easily beleive much admired there. She's lodged at Lt. Genl. Elliot's.[8] Won't you think of making a trip to see her on your own side the water?[9] Not a word more of the Marquis de Bellegarde. Mr. de Zuylen and his Lady are perfectly well, and seem to remember you with particular regard. Mr. de Tuyl, the eldest son is, as you know, returned long ago. The second, who is lately advanced in the navy, is here also at present. Both very pretty young Gentlemen. The third is at his Regimt.[10]— My family is indeed much more numerous than when you left us; but they are not of my begeting. I have had a house full of Dutch and English boarders, who have given me enough to do; tho' all very good Lads. Their number is at present diminished, which I am not sorry for, as we had rather too many. As for offspring, the Child at whose birth you was present, has, thank God! been hitherto preserved with us; and she is still all our stock.[11] Mrs. Brown and her sister desire their best Compliments, allways remembering Mr. Boswell in a very cordial manner; as do all your acquaintances here; hoping to have the pleasure of seeing you here again sometime or other. Mrs. Geelvink, the handsome rich widow of Amstm., and the great Companion of Miss De Zuylen, is to be married next month to the Marquis de Chatelaire a Nobleman of Lorrain, Chamberlain to Pr. Charles, a Widower with three Children, and as you can well conceive, Roman Catholick. This marriage has astonished all the world.[12]— I had almost forgot to tell you that your obligation to Mr. Peterson, duely discharged, is in my hands and shall be sent by Mr. Kinloch.[13] My paper is at an end, and I don't chuse to make you pay double postage; therefor conclude with subscribing myself with sincere regard, Dear Sir, your most affectionate, obliged, humble Servant,

ROBERT BROWN

P.S. I hope to have the pleasure of paying you my respects in Scotland in July next. Mr. Wishart, who is still with me, sets out from here in June to return by way of Paris; and if nothing falls out to prevent it, I propose to accompany him.[14]

[1] Three of Craufurd's sons, Patrick, James, and George, inherited their father's considerable business upon his death in July of the previous year. Patrick, who was appointed conservator of Scots privileges in Holland in 1769 (*Renfrew*, p. 367), remained at the head of the business until 1780, when he sold his interest to James (From Craufurd, 16 May 1766, n. 1).

[2] Brown was frequently not well and his health 'chancelante', according to Willem van Tuyll, writing to JB in the previous December (From Willem van Tuyll, 11 Nov.–4 Dec. 1766).

[3] Archibald Gordon Kinloch (d. 1800) was the second son of David Kinloch of Gilmerton, later (1778) Bt., and Mrs. Brown's first cousin (Henry Wagner, 'Descendants of Sir James Kinloch, Bt.', *The Genealogist* [1898] n.s. xiv. 200, 203). Ensign, lieutenant (26 Aug.), finally captain (3 June 1774) in the 65th Regiment of Foot (*Army List*, 1766–78), Archibald succeeded to the baronetcy in 1795 by shooting his elder brother Francis. He was adjudged insane and

confined to the Tolbooth for the rest of his life. See *Scots Mag.* (July–Aug. 1795) lvii. 477–79, 541–43 for a full account of the trial.

[4] In his letter of 16 Jan. 1766 to M. de Zuylen JB had asked him to return the letter at once if he considered that JB's proposal of marriage to Belle, contained in the letter, had no chance of success. A translation of JB's letter is printed in *Holland*, pp. 342–52.

[5] JB recorded in his journal for 28 Apr.: 'I received a Packet of papers brought from Holland by Captain Kinloch. But my Journal was amissing. I was much vexed.' JB's Dutch journal, a manuscript of over 500 pages, has never been recovered. For an account of the shipment of JB's papers from Holland and the loss of his journal, see *Holland*, pp. ix–x, 359 n. 5; From Brown, 22 Oct.

[6] The only Cologne newspaper published and printed in Latin at this time was the *Ordinaria relationis diariae continuatio*, founded in 1664, and by 1767 owned and edited by Balthasar Wilms

(Friedrich Kemmerling, *Studien zur Geschichte des älteren Kölner Zeitungswesens*, diss. Bonn, 1911, pp. 71–79). Information kindly supplied by Dr. W. Schmitz, University of Cologne Library.

[7] Frans Sircksen (c. 1668–1766—Death Register, Gemeente Archief, Utrecht), son of an Italian, according to JB, who was fencing instructor to William III. Young Sircksen travelled to England and Ireland with William and fought with his army at the Battle of the Boyne in 1690 (Dutch theme, c. 20 Feb. 1764, M 92). He returned to Utrecht in 1740 where, as drum major of a regiment garrisoned there, he was permitted to teach fencing (Gerhard W. Kernkamp, *Acta et decreta Senatus, Vroedschapsresolutiën en andere bescheiden betreffende de Utrechtsche Academie*, ii. 364, *Werken uitgegeven door het Historisch Genootschap gevestigd te Utrecht*, ser. 3. no. 68 [1938]). JB became his pupil in 1764 and found him 'as healthy and spry as a man of thirty [who] can fence with all the agility in the world' (Dutch theme, c. 20 Feb. 1764—*Holland*, p. 159).

[8] George Augustus Eliott (1717–90), general, defender of Gibraltar, later (1783) Kt. and (1787) Baron Heathfield of Gibraltar, after a long and distinguished army career, served as Governor of Gibraltar, 1776–90. Zélide remained in England for six months (From Willem van Tuyll, 11 Nov.–4 Dec. 1766, n. 6), spending most of her time in London with the Eliotts, whom she had come to know and like in 1765 (Godet i. 117, 127–34), and making at least one trip to Surrey to visit her Bentinck relations (Godet i. 131).

[9] JB wrote to Temple in March: 'Zelide has been in London this winter. I never hear from her. She is a strange Creature. Sir John Pringle attended her as a Physician. He wrote to my Father "She has too much vivacity. She talks of your Son without either resentment or attachment".... I am well rid of her' (To W. J. Temple, 1 Feb.–8 Mar.—MS. Pierpont Morgan).

[10] For the two older brothers, Willem and Diederik, see From Willem van Tuyll, 11 Nov.–4 Dec. 1766 and nn. 1, 6. Vincent Maximiliaan van Tuyll van Serooskerken (1747–94), was Belle's youngest brother. He had been an army officer since 1764 (Godet i. 54) and rose to the rank of lieutenant-colonel before dying of wounds received at the Battle of Charleroi (Polvliet, pp. 32–33, 40–41). JB had met Vincent at Zuylen and had been amused by his stories of the family (Notes, 19 Mar. 1764).

[11] The Browns' daughter (From Brown, 3 Mar. 1766, n. 7) remained their only child until the birth of their son on 2 June 1769 (From Brown, 25 Dec. 1769).

[12] Catharina Elisabeth (Hasselaer) Geelvinck (1738–92) became the close friend of Belle when she went to live with her sister in Utrecht on the death of her first husband in 1757 (Notes, 5 Feb. 1764; Walker, p. 123 n. 4.). JB was much taken with the 'young handsom amiable Widow with £4000 a year' (To Temple, 17 Apr. 1764), exclaiming after one successful card-party: 'For the first time in Holland, delicious love. *O la belle veuve*. . . . You took her hand to the coach and your frame thrilled' (Notes, 1 Feb. 1764; for an abridged translation of Zélide's character-sketch of Mme. Geelvinck, see *Holland*, p. 132 n. 9). Mme. Geelvinck's second marriage, on 22 Mar. 1767, to François-Gabriel-Joseph, Marquis du Chasteler et de Courcelles, whom Zélide characterized as 'un ridicule et despotique sot' (*Lettres Zélide* p. 310) was unhappy and lasted only until 1777 (*Biographie Nationale de Belgique*). Prince Charles was Governor-General of the Pays-Bas, a field marshal and Grand Master of the Teutonic Order (NBG).

[13] For this debt, see From Robert Brown, 3 Mar. 1766, n. 4.

[14] For Brown's trip to Scotland, see From Brown, 22 Oct.

From Count Antonio Rivarola, c. early February 1767

Not reported. See From Rivarola, 2 May: 'I received yesterday your most welcome letter of March 14th last, and I was disturbed to hear that you have not received the letter I sent you from here in response to yours in which you acknowledge receipt of the papers I sent you from Leghorn last September.'

To Pasquale Paoli, between early February and 8 April 1767

Not reported. See To Chatham, 8 Apr.: 'I have communicated to General Paoli the contents of your Lordship's letter, and I am perswaded He will think as I do.' The letter alluded to is From Chatham, 4 Feb.

From Lord Chatham, Wednesday 4 February 1767

MS. Yale (C 786).

ADDRESS: To James Boswell Esqr., at Lord Auchinleck's, at Edingburgh.

POSTMARKS: BATH; FREE; 7FE.

FRANK: Chatham.

Bath, Feb. the 4th, 1767

SIR: The honour of your letter found me here confined with a severe fit of the gout, and totally unable to write, or I shou'd sooner have acknowledged that favour. I now write with some difficulty, but can no longer deferr expressing the Sense I have of the great honour done me by the Sentiments contain'd in the Italian Passage of the letter you are so good to convey to me. I can assure You, Sir, I retain the same admiration of your Illustrious Friend, General Paoli, which I once express'd to you. But sincere as this admiration is, I must not, at the same time, forbear to acquaint you, (in answer to your desire to know my sentiments) that I see not the least ground, at present, for this Country to interfere, with any justice, in the Affairs of Corsica. As I think nothing more natural and commendable than the generous warmth you express for so striking a Character, as that able Cheif, so I doubt not you will approve the directness of my Opinion upon an occasion, which admits of no deliberation.

I am with great esteem and regard, Sir, your most obedient, humble Servant,

CHATHAM

From John Dick, Friday 6 February 1767

MS. Yale (C 1013).

ADDRESS: To James Boswell Esqr., to the Care of Messrs. Haries and Compy., London.

POSTMARK: FE 21.

Leghorn, 6th February 1767

DEAR SIR, I have now given up all thoughts of having the pleasure to hear from You, so have only to inclose You an Edict or rather Manifesto which I receiv'd yesterday, it seems well drawn up, and certainly will have concequences.[1]

I have receiv'd His Majesty's most gracious permission to return to England for one year.[2] I purpose setting out the beginning of April, if anything shall come for You, it will be carefully forwarded to You, as will any thing You may have to forward to the Island, by my Vice Consul,[3] who will have my particular directions about them. I have therefore only to add that I am always with the most perfect Regard, and true Esteem, My dear Sir, Your most Affectionate Friend and Assurd Servant,

JOHN DICK

[1] Paoli's manifesto of 27 Jan. addressed to the Corsican people chronicles the course of the war with Genoa up to the end of 1764, the straits to which the Genoese in Corsica had been brought by the Corsican blockade after 1764, and the attempts of the French to mediate a peace between the two countries. The manifesto makes clear the reason for the failure of the French effort: in accordance with the declaration of the General Consulta at Casinca of 1761, the Corsi-

cans had vowed never to accept a treaty with Genoa that did not have as its basis liberty and independence for the whole island. According to the manifesto, if the Corsicans wish to achieve independence once the French four-year period of occupation is over, they should choose their representatives to the General Consulta, to be held in May, with a view to resuming hostilities. JB sent the manifesto to *Lond. Chron.*; it appeared in the 18–21 Apr. issue (xxi. 383–84) and was reprinted in *Scots Mag.* (Apr. 1767) xxix. 215–16.

[2] Dick left Leghorn for London on 24 Mar. and did not return there until the end of August 1768 (*Daily Advertiser*, 20 Apr. 1767, 26 Aug. 1768).

[3] Richard Edwards (From Edwards, 26 June, n. 1).

From Sir John Pringle, Tuesday 10 February 1767

MS. Yale (C 2297).

London, 10 Febry. 1767

DEAR SIR, I received some time ago your kind and, I am[1] assured, sincere congratulations on the late honour conferred upon me by His Majesty.[2] I hope that You and my other friends will believe, that whatever good things befall me, either of that, or any other kind, one great part of the enjoyment to me will be the pleasure which they will testify on such occasions.

I continue to have the satisfaction of hearing from different hands of your application to business, and of the figure which You have made and are likely to make at the bar. I believe that I told you in a former letter, but I must repeat it, that my pleasure is the greater, as in this event I have had my vanity gratified, in thinking that I judged well when I told you, that Your genius, however differently it then appeared to You, was most calculated for that profession, which you seem now to have embraced in earnest. I will go further, since You must now give a little credit to my predictions, and tell you, that if you continue to give application, You will soon get the start of all our young men in the Parliament House, and will give the tone for a new eloquence very different from what prevailed there in my time. You have the advantage of possessing the English language and the accent in a greater degree than any of your rivals, and a turn for expressing yourself in a clear and energetic manner, without those hyperbolical modes of speech that were introduced long ago, and were still kept up during my youth, and which slipt from the bar to the teatables at Edinburgh.[3]

By letters, which I have since my return had from my worthy friend your father (for I have had more than one upon the subject) I have the comfort to find that you have made him very happy;[4] and I have the superstition to believe, that whilst you go on in this train, I mean in sobriety, diligence in your business, and attentions[5] to the best of parents, God will bless you, not only with conferring upon You his imperceptible favours, but will even condescend to gratify you with reputation and other worldly[6] enjoyments, which we may desire but never set our hearts upon. You may be assured that Your father's confidence in you and his affection will daily augment; for between our selves be it spoken, could you expect that after all that is passed, he should all at once consider You as arrived at the full maturity of your judgement. Permit me to predict once more. In a year, or two at furthest, if you persevere in this course, my[7] sage friend, so far will he be from seeing you in the light of a boy, that he will not only communicate to You all his most secret affairs, but will consult you upon them, and shew a regard to your judgement. In order to hasten this confidence, I will presume to suggest what may be the most proper means: that is I would advise you to look out for a wife, and to make such a match as he and the whole world shall approve of.[8] After examining that affair with some attention, I am much for early nuptials, and indeed so much, that if I were in your place I should set immediately about them.[9] I am persuaded that you would have a great deal of satisfaction in following that plan; for your temper is good, you would have joy in children; and I believe I may add that You have had too much experience of the vague[10] and vitious pleasures, not to relish the confined and virtuous ones, as soon as you will make the comparison. This would give great contentment to your father, and, as I said above, nothing would so much ripen that confidence which he is beginning to have in you as that very action. Your reconciled friend (and you may depend upon the sincerity of the reconciliation) is a married man, and I am persuaded happy in that state, altho' the match was made[11] upon prudential considerations only.[12]

With regard to your design of publishing an account of Corsica, I wrote to your father my thoughts on that subject. You may remember with what pleasure and approbation Sir And. Mitchell and I heard your natural account of those travels; but to relate and to print are two very different things.[13] If you had any encouragement from the Minister that would be another matter; but as he has not chosen to answer your letter on that subject, you may take it for granted, that the publication would give him no satisfaction. At present be You and Paoli private friends. Possibly the time may come when the Ministry here may find it their interest to support him; in which event they will probably apply to You. Mean while, I hope you have not omitted to take an opportunity of sending that brave man[14] the present which you proposed, as a just return for the civilities which he shewed you during your stay with him.[15] I am with great sincerity, Dear Sir, Your affectionate friend and humble Servant,

JOHN PRINGLE

[1] MS. 'I am' superimposed upon erased 'polite'; then comma added after 'and'

[2] Pringle was created baronet on 5 June 1766.

[3] Pringle had left Edinburgh in 1742. For a discussion of the varieties of colloquial Edinburgh speech between 1740 and 1760, see *Scotland and Scotsmen* ii. 542–45.

[4] These letters have not been reported.

[5] MS. 'and attentions' deleted before 'to'

[6] MS. 'worldly' not clear; superimposed upon an incompletely erased word, possibly 'things'

[7] MS. 'that' deleted before 'my'

[8] JB was still satisfied with his mistress Mrs. Dodds but was about to begin his unsuccessful pursuit of Catherine Blair.

[9] MS. 'them' superimposed upon 'it'

[10] Pringle preserves the Latin meaning, 'wandering' or 'inconstant'.

[11] MS. 'entered' written above partially deleted 'acted', both replaced by 'made'

[12] For this marriage, see To Mountstuart, 1 Jan. and n. 7.

[13] Sir Andrew Mitchell (1708–71), Under-Secretary of State for Scotland, 1742–46, M.P. for Aberdeenshire, 1747–54, and the Elgin Burghs, 1755–71. Appointed Envoy to Prussia just before the outbreak of the Seven Years' War, Mitchell became the close friend of Frederick the Great and accompanied him on many of his campaigns. He had a chequered career after the war, during which he angered Chatham and fell out with Frederick. His hopes for a lucrative post through the influence of his Whig friends in England came to nothing, and in Mar. 1766 he returned to Berlin and remained there until his death (Namier and Brooke iii. 143–44).

JB had known Mitchell in Berlin in 1764, finding him 'a knowing amiable easy man' (Journ. 8 July 1764); presumably the 'natural account' of his travels in Corsica was given to Mitchell and Pringle on 13 Feb. 1766 when they were all three together in London (Journ. 14 Feb. 1766).

[14] MS. 'that brave man' written above deleted 'him'

From Davies, 15 Oct.

From Lady Elizabeth Macfarlane, Friday ?13 February 1767

MS. Yale (C 812).

ADDRESS: Mr. Boswell.

[Edinburgh] Friday Even.

The honble. A. E. and the right honble. E. M. present their Compliments to Mr. Boswell.[1] They are engaged to Morrow to dine abroad, and to Morrow is the last Day of that Week in which he promised to exhibit his Friend.[2] But they hope, that the towering Oak Mr. Boswell, and that Scotch Fir the Laird of Grange, will be transplanted into their Parlour on Sunday or Monday next at furthest.

[1] The Hon. Andrew Erskine (1740–93—MS. Register of Births and Baptisms for the Parish of Carnbee, Fife, compiled 1742), Lady Elizabeth's younger brother, was JB's friend and literary collaborator in *Letters between the Honourable* *Andrew Erskine, and James Boswell, Esq.,* 1763. Erskine had recently returned from Gibraltar where he was serving as a lieutenant in the 24th Foot (From James Bruce, 23 Feb.; *Army List*).
[2] John Johnston of Grange.

From Lady Elizabeth Macfarlane, Saturday ?14 February 1767

MS. Yale (C 813).

ADDRESS: James Boswell Esqr.

[Edinburgh] Saturday

This Morning early was transmitted to your Desk a Card informing you of an unfortunate Engagement of the Captain's and mine to dine abroad this Day. But if the Laird of Grange and his pleasant Companion can make an Incursion on Sunday or Monday, they shall have a Dish after the Manner of Mary Queen of Scots. Dads and Blads from an original Receipt of Fergus the first and Scots collops at least as old as Malcolm Caenmore.[1]

[1] Dads and blads—often 'blads and dawds'— was the designation given to large leaves of greens boiled whole in a sort of broth. King Fergus I, according to legend first king of Scotland, is supposed to have flourished c. 330 B.C. The Scots collops as old as Malcolm Canmore (King Malcolm III—d. 1093) were thick slices of meat which were often minced before cooking.

From a friend of Robert Hay, Friday 20 February 1767

MS. Yale (C 1516).

Edinr. 20th Feby. 1767

Honourd Sir: The Sentanced Robert Hay, desaired me his Freend, to aquent you of his misarable Condition and of your goodnes in Coming to him on Thursday and of his own foolishnes in many ways, at last in not reviling his mind when you Desaired him if by any means his Life meight be lenthned by your means or any others Goodness in Recommending him to his Majesty's Cleamincy—As his Misfortoun is an Accidently Circumstance Ocasioned by Chance[1]—As your Honour meight be informed he cam that day from Irlland and had Letters to

Delaiver, being out at neight it may be Seposed he was in drink So as not to free himself from an un Seen Danger—As it undesinedly apears he had no Staf nor wepon for defence befor nor after the deed was Commited and who knows but both Pursuer and defender was drunk and in madness I mean the Sailer and the Soilders who atacked his youth 20 or 21 and Simplicty tels that he has not practised Robrey in Exposing the watch to Sale the day following[2]—he Says that he knocked not the man to the ground but got the watch to keep the Others Secret and not to revil his name, which made him not give him up to your Honour when desaired, But has told now that his name is John Buttersfield, that person that brought him A Clean Sheirt and drawers from ———— Totops hous in Cannongate[3] to the City Gaurd, but he is now fled to Ireland. He upon whom the deed was Comitted says he knows not if Hay was the man, but rather to his Judgment thinks it was an Other; his witness Cannot prove Hay to be the man if Theft was found in his hand it was restored, if not Suficent four Fold meight be restored, Or Scourged, Or Sold for his Theft. At the mouth of two or three witnesses—Shall he that is worthy of Death: be put to Death: but at the mouth of one witness he Shall not be put to Death DEUTERONOMY CHAP. XVII. 6 verse.—

> V. 18 And it Shall be when he Sitteth upon the thron of his Kingdom,
>   that he Shall write him a Copy of this Law in a Book, out of
>   that which is befor the priests the Levites.
> V. 19 And it Shall be with him, and he Shall read therein all the day
>   of his Life: that he may learn to fear the Lord his God, to
>   keep all the words of this law and these Statutes, to do them:

[1] Robert Hay (c. 1745–67), soldier in the 44th Foot, was accused of assaulting and robbing John Macaulay, sailor, of 40s. and a silver watch on 23 Dec. 1766. Apprehended the next day while trying to sell the watch, Hay at first tried to blame the robbery on another soldier. Only after JB's plea for him failed and he had been sentenced to death did he confess (via this letter) that he had been the accomplice of one John Butterfield, the principal attacker. Armed with this new evidence, JB petitioned the King for clemency, but Hay was hanged on 25 Mar. (printed Indictment, notes for JB's plea of 9 Feb., and a copy by James Brown, JB's clerk, of 'The Petition of Robert Hay', Lg 6; *Scots Mag.* 1767, xxix. 221; *Earlier Years*, pp. 310–11, 535).

[2] *Scots Mag.* gives Hay's age as twenty-two.

[3] Presumably Archibald Tudhope, tanner in Canongate, one of the witnesses (Lg 6:1).

From John Dick, Friday 6 March 1767

MS. Yale (C 1014).

NOTE in Dick's hand at foot of first page: James Boswell Esq.

Leghorn, 6th March 1767

MY DEAR SIR, Yesterday Mr. Ansley deliver'd me Your very kind and obliging Letter of the 9th of December last, which gave me great Satisfaction, for I could not help being very uneasy at your Silence, fearing that You had not receiv'd any of my Letters.[1] Your inclosed for the General came just in time to send him by two Capucines, of his Confidence,[2] who I believe sail to night for Sparta,[3] You may countermand the Chronicle, as I send him regularly mine, as also the Annual Registers, I mention this, because You say You purpose sending him books, so that You need not send these.[4]

I was pretty certain You would like Mr. Burnaby's Journal, this Gentleman is our worthy Pastor, and You have hit his Character and would like him still more, if You had been so fortunate as to make an acquaintance with him, when You was here, he was at Rome. I am very sure he will have a great pleasure in Corresponding with You provided it can afford You any Amusement, or be of use to the General, who he admires much, and with whom he Corresponds. I therefore shall beg the favour of You, to send him, any Letters that You may write to our Heroe, as I shall not have it in my power to obey Your Commands, the King having been graciously pleased to grant me leave to return to Britain, on account of my private Affairs,[5] Mrs. Dick and I purpose setting out from hence the latter end of this Month, and my good friend Mr. Burnaby is so obliging, as to take upon him the Charge of the Affairs of the Consulat in my Absence, so that, on the whole You will be a gainer by the change.

I wrote to You lately with the Corsican Manifesto dated the 27 January.[6] I hope it will have reached You, least it should not, I send You a French Translation of it, in the Leyden Gazette.[7] These brave people immediately prepaired to attack the Genoes, where they could come at them, without offending the French. On the 16 of last Month, they landed on the Island of Capraja, the last news we had from thence was, that, they had taken all the Towers, and were beseiging the Fortress[8] this day a Genoes fleett passed by going to the relief of the Place, said to consist in 3 Galleys, 2 Schiabecks,[9] 2 Barks, and the rest Feluccas, we are in pain for the poor Corsicans, You shall know the event of this affair. Indeed much will depend upon it.

The Person who was to procure me the Corsican Wine,[10] has been sick for some time, which is the reason that You have not had it, but it shall not be forgott don't think of sending us any Beer. I thank You for your kind intentions, perhaps we may come and drink some of it with You at Edenburg.

Your Letter for Count Reverola has been deliver'd to his Secretary,[11] he is still at Turin, but I believe is expected back here soon.

I have this day taken the Liberty to trouble our friend Ferguson,[12] with a Letter concerning my pretentions, to the Title, of the Braid Patent, which he will communicate to You, I have caused the Parish Registers in Northumberland to be search'd, and expect further information from thence, it gives me pleasure to hear, that my pretentions no ways interfere with worthy Sir Alexr. Dick, whose Character I much admire, and long to have the pleasure of paying my Respects to him, and of thanking him for his kindness in sending me the Historical Account of the Family.[13] Circumstanced as I am, without Children, the succeeding in making out my right to this Title, is of very little importance, save that in this Country You know it counts for something. And yet more so now than ever, since with the Court, we have imported all the Austrian Etiquette.[14] And I believe most of our people who come to Florence now without one, feel the difference. I beg You will present my most Respectfull Compliments to Sir Alexander, and tell him how much I think my self Obliged to him for his friendship in this Affair. I know I need not solicit yours, as I am convinc'd You will do every thing in your power. I hope to be in London about the latter end of next Month, and I shall hope for the pleasure of hearing from You there, You'l please to put your Letter under cover of my good friends Messs. And. Drummond and Compy.[15]

I shall write on Monday to Naples about your things, and lett You know what answer I receive.[16] Mrs. Dick begs leave to present You her kindest Compliments, and I ever am with the most perfect Regard, and Esteem, My dear Sir, Your much obliged, and Affectionate Friend,

JOHN DICK

I long to know Your answer from Lord C.[17]

[1] For Robert Ainslie, see To Sir Alexander Dick, 9 Dec. 1766, n. 2.

[2] Unidentified. Perhaps they were the two Capuchin professors at the University of Corte, Padre Angiolo Stefani da Venaco and Padre Gio. Battista Ferdinandi da Brando, one of whom JB had met in 1765 (Tommaseo I. xi. 66; Corsica p. 282).

[3] That is, Corsica. See From John Dick, 26 Sept. 1766, n. 2.

[4] MS. 'these' superimposed upon 'them'

[5] Specifically to file a claim to the dormant baronetcy of Braid.

[6] For the manifesto, see From John Dick, 6 Feb. and n. 1.

[7] The formal title of what Dick calls the 'Leyden Gazette' was Nouvelles extraordinaires de divers endroits. He enclosed with this letter a Supplement to that journal, dated 20 Feb., now preserved at Yale (P 35). An English translation of the manifesto appeared in Gent. Mag. (Apr. 1767), xxxvii. 186–87.

[8] For the attack on Capraia, see From Rivarola, 18 Mar. n. 2.

[9] For 'schiabecks', see From John Dick, 7 Jan. 1767, n. 4.

[10] Mentioned in From John Dick, 6 Oct. 1766.

[11] Giuseppe Balbi. See From John Dick, 30 May 1766, n. 4.

[12] James Ferguson. See From John Dick, 31 Oct. 1766, n. 3.

[13] Sir Alexander was descended from Alexan-der Dick (d. 1663), fourth son of Sir William Dick of Braid, but he inherited his baronetcy from his grandfather, Sir James Dick of Prestonfield (created 1677). In 1699 Sir James had entailed his estates on heirs male of his own body, which failing, to devolve upon the second and younger sons of his only surviving daughter, Janet. In 1707, under a baronet's patent granted him by Queen Anne, and again in 1710, he made entails to the same heirs and, on his death in 1728 without male heirs, the estates devolved upon his daughter Janet's sons successively. John Dick was descended from Louis, fifth son of Sir William Dick. Louis settled in England and was succeeded by his son Andrew Dick of West-Newton, Northumberland. The parish register of Kirk Newton, Northumberland, provided evidence of Andrew Dick's marriage in 1672 (Baronage, pp. 272–74). For a very different view of John Dick's claim to the baronetcy of Braid, see Stodart, pp. 265–67.

[14] Since 1765, the Grand Duke of Tuscany had been the Austrian-born Peter Leopold (1747–92), later (1790) Leopold II, Holy Roman Emperor.

[15] Andrew Drummond (d. 1769) was head of the bank in Charing Cross. His son John, M.P. for Thetford, 1768–74, succeeded him as head of the bank (Gent. Mag. 1769, xxxix. 110 ; Namier and Brooke ii. 343–44).

[16] Theodore Davel was soon to write to JB about this matter (From Davel, 7 Mar.).

[17] See from Lord Chatham, 4 Feb.

From Theodore Davel,[1] Saturday 7 March 1767

MS. Yale (C 892).

ADDRESS: Messieurs, Messieurs Herries Cochrane etc.[2] p[our] remettre à monsr. Boswell, G[entil]h[omme] Ecossois, à Londres.

Naples, Le 7e. mars 1767

MONSIEUR: Depuis V[otr]e depart de cette ville Jay sollicité bien des fois le Pere Antoine Piaggio de Portici,[3] de vous faire la feuille en Mignature[4] qu'il vous avoit promise, il me l'a faitte esperer plusieurs fois, mais en vain, et ayant perdû l'esperance de l'avoir, j'ay crû ne devoir retarder davantage l'expedition de la Caissette que vous me laissates contenant (m'avez vous dit) des coquillages, et autres curiosités naturelles.[5] Je l'ay chargée sous la marque B. No. 1. à bord du

Va[issea]u Salisbury Capn. Edmond Hawker anglois,[6] et p[our] economiser le frêt, je l'ay mise dans un même Connoissem[en]t avec un'autre Caisse p[our] Messrs. Loüis et David Bourgeois à Londres,[7] aux quels j'ordonne de s'en entendre avec Messrs. Herries Cochrane etc. p[our] la reception de cette ditte Caissette. Je souhaitte pouvoir vous etre plus essentiellem[en]t utile, et vous prouver la parfaitte Estime avec laquelle J'ay L'honneur d'Etre, Monsieur, Vôtre trés humble et trés Obeissant Serviteur,

THEOD. DAVEL

Monsieur Boswell, à Londres.

[1] Theodore Davel was a Neapolitan merchant. During JB's three-week tour of Naples in 1765 (Notes, 1–20 Mar. 1765), he purchased £20 of Davel's goods on his letter of credit (A 72, 'Torrazza, Paul & Pierre, bankers. Letter of Credit, 21 Janvier 1765').

[2] From John Dick, 30 May 1766, n. 1. Davel seems to have been unaware that Herries and Cochrane had parted ways and that 'Herries and Company' was the current name of the firm.

[3] Padre Antonio Piaggi or Piaggio (d. 1796), a Jesuit priest and engraver from Genoa, held the posts of Latin secretary and Curator of Miniatures in the Vatican, 1755–79 (Thieme-Becker xxvi. 561). Charles III of Naples hired Piaggi to restore charred scrolls recovered from the 'Villa of the Papyri' site at Herculaneum in 1752. Piaggi's workshop was housed in the Museum of Portici, located in the town of the same name at the foot of Mt. Vesuvius. Piaggi employed a 'macchina' of his own invention to recover the scrolls and managed, over a four-year period, to salvage segments of several documents including Philodemus of Gadara's Treatise on Music. JB visited the Portici Museum in 1765 to view the papyri and some recovered paintings, and spoke to 'Abbate Piazze' (Piaggi), who explained his techniques in detail (Notes, 7, 18–19 Mar. 1765).

For accounts of Piaggi and his method of recovering the papyri, see Domenico Bassi, 'Il P. Antonio Piaggio e i primi tentativi per lo avvolgimento dei papiri ercolanesi', Archivio Storico per le Province Napoletane, 1907, xxxii. 637–90; Joseph de LaLande, Voyage en Italie, 1770 ed. vii. 35–38; Egon C. C. Corti, The Destruction and Resurrection of Pompeii, 1951 trans., pp. 119–24.

[4] JB had asked Piaggi 'to have piece done for patria vestra [your country]' (Notes, 7 Mar. 1765); presumably this was to be a print of either a painting or a fragment of papyrus.

[5] Nothing further has been reported regarding the box containing shells and other natural curiosities.

[6] Perhaps the Edmund Hawker who became a lieutenant in the Navy in 1759 (Sea Officers ii. 419). If so, he was by this time captain of the merchantman Salisbury, listed in Lloyd's Register of Shipping, 1764–66 and 1768–71; where his name is given as 'E. Hauker' and 'Edm. Hucker'.

[7] Lewis and David Bourgeois were perfumers with a shop in St. James's, Haymarket. First listed in Kent's Directory 1769, they continued at 32 Haymarket at least until the end of the century (Universal British Directory, 1791, i. 81, 'Bourgeois, Amick, and Co.').

To Lord Marischal, Thursday 12 March 1767

MS. Yale (L 954). An excerpt from JB's Memorabilia for 1767 (M 175). The letter actually sent arrived c. early Apr. (From Lord Marischal, 14 Apr.).

[Edinburgh]

TO THE EARL MARISCHAL 12 March 1767. Your Lordship knows it is said that a Lawyer can never plead contrary to his conscience, because a Lawyer has no title to judge, so cannot say whether a cause be right or wrong.[1] This is specious, and may pass with understandings of a certain size. But to tell you the truth, My Lord, as we grow up, we become more callous, and our finer feelings and more generous sentiments insensibly decay. At least I feel it so, and taking it to be the general lot of humanity, I very quietly submit to it, like a pretty woman of good sense who perceives her charms fade: though I fear few pretty Women would resign their charms with as much serenity as I do my best qualitys. There is something real in what I am saying; for, in Spain or other happy climates one may enjoy perennial felicity but in this northern region one's mind contracts and grows cold very soon.

[1] On the subject of the lawyer's conscience, see From Lord Marischal, 2 Oct. 1766.

To John Dick, Saturday 14 March 1767

Not reported. See From Dick, 11 May, written from London: 'this day I have receiv'd from Leghorn, your kind Letter of the 14 March.'

To Count Antonio Rivarola, Saturday 14 March 1767

Not reported. See From Rivarola, 2 May: 'I received yesterday your most welcome letter of March 14th last'.

To Robert Strange, Monday 16 March 1767

Not reported. See From Strange, 16 May: 'The late hurry of my publication has prevented me the pleasure of acknowledging your agreeable letter of the 16th March.'

To George Muir, Wednesday 18 March 1767

Not reported. See From Muir, 23 Mar.: 'Your's of the 18th I had honour to receive this morning with the two memorials in the Douglas Cause.'

From Count Antonio Rivarola, Wednesday 18 March 1767

MS. Yale (C 2390).
ADDRESS: A Monsieur, Monsieur Boswell d'Auchinleck, à Edimbourg, Par Londres.
POSTMARKS: [London] MR 30; De Turin; P 2/6; M4N.

Torino, 18 Marzo 1767

MONSIEUR BOSWELL RIVERITISSIMO: Ricevo con questa posta da Livorno la gratma sua de' 9 di Dicembre scorso, la quale non so come abbia tardato tanto. Le sono ben tenuto dei ringraziamenti che mi fà, e vorrei essere al caso di servirla meglio sopra moltissime altre cose, delle quali me richiede.

Vedrò con piacer sommo la sua opera quando venga alla luce, la quale non puol essere che eccellente quando esce da così buona penna, e tanto più sarà gradita ed operativa nel pubblico, quanto che viene da persona imparziale.

Se la occupazioni che ho in abbondanza a questa Corte, ove sono stato chiamato espressamte. dopo il mio viaggio in Sardegna, mi dasser tempo, moltissimi materiali in ammasso potrei darle, che Ella saprebbe adattare a suo luogo; e ciò, di che mi vanto e mi preggio, si è, che non troverebbe cosa che non fosse più che certa, avend' Io troppo stima della verità, che soglio dire essere così bella da se, che non ha bisogno d'ornamenti: e sia ugualmte. certa che la passione non mi accieca, mentre ove la verità lo richiede non la perdono a me medmo. Per questo appunto mi sono acquistato fra chi mi conosce un credito di incapace ad ingannar chiunque, poichè prima lascerei la vita che perdere questo buon costume

125

che mi costa non poco studio. Crederebb' Ella che se la cause della mia Patria non fosse evidentissimamente giusta, io sarei il primo a condannarla? Ma che stò Io a perdermi ne' miei elogi che diventan sospetti dalla mia penna? Prenda ciò a puro fine di assicurarla su quanto da me sarà mai per sapere, e non per altro.

Avrà veduta la memoria che il n[ost]ro. degno Generale avea fatto al Re di Francia fin da Maggio dell' anno scorso, assieme al progetto d'accommodamto. colla Repca., qual progetto, essendo stato dai Genovesi rigettato, è uscito in seguito un Manifesto di esso Generale, che l'ha fatto seguitare dalla sorpresa di Capraja, ove i Corsi fanno l'assedie della Fortezza, avendo già prese le tre Torri, indi dall' assedio di Bonifazio. Non saprei dirlene fin quì il successo, che aspetto di sentire colle lettere de posdomane.

Vorrei che mi conoscesse abile in servirla perciò, che è di particolare suo servizio, mentre me trovera sempre quale con sentimenti di vera amicizia sono suo Devotissimo, Obbligantissimo Servitore,

RIVAROLA

[MOST RESPECTED MR. BOSWELL: I received your very welcome letter of 9 December last with the Leghorn post; I cannot think how it can have taken so long to reach me. I am very obliged to you for your thanks, and I should wish to serve you better in many other matters, in addition to your present requirements.

I look forward with the greatest pleasure to seeing your work in print; it can be nothing less than excellent, coming from so accomplished a pen, and will delight and persuade its public all the more for being the record of an impartial observer.

If I have time to spare from the many and various duties of this Court, to which I was expressly summoned after my visit to Sardinia, I could give you a mass of material I have gathered, which you would know best how to use.[1] I am proud to say that you would find nothing there to be otherwise than sure and reliable, as I have the highest respect for the truth, deeming it so lovely in itself that it needs no ornament. You may likewise rest assured that I have not been blinded by passion, for when the truth makes demands, I do not excuse it even in myself. It is exactly for this that I have gained a reputation, among those who know me, of being incapable of deception; for I should prefer to die rather than forfeit this good practice, which costs me no small effort. I would have you believe that I should be the first to condemn my country's cause, if it were not so transparently a just one! But what am I doing, singing my own praises, which can only be suspect when they come from my pen! Understand that I say this only to assure you of what I shall let you know, and for no other reason.

You will have seen the memorandum our worthy General sent to the King of France at the end of May last year, together with a proposal for a settlement with Genoa, which the Genoese rejected. There followed a manifesto from the General, and the surprise assault of Capraja. The Corsicans are laying siege to the citadel, and having already taken the three towers, are now besieging Bonifazio. I cannot tell you the outcome yet, as I am awaiting the news by the day after tomorrow's post.[2]

I hope you may find me worthy of rendering you what services you require; you will find me always to be your true friend, and most devoted and obliging servant,

RIVAROLA][3]

[1] Rivarola wrote biweekly reports for the King of Sardinia (From John Dick, 25 Feb. 1766, n. 2).

[2] On 18 May 1766 Paoli wrote to the King of France, as mediator between Genoa and Corsica, proposing that, in exchange for a guarantee of independence, Corsica would compensate Genoa for the loss of its Corsican ports. The Genoese could not accept what appeared to them a humiliating end to their sovereignty over Corsica and they rejected Paoli's offer out-of-hand. Following Genoa's rejection of the offer, Paoli issued a manifesto on 27 Jan. (see From John Dick, 6 Feb. n. 1) and, shortly afterwards, made a surprise attack on the island of Capraia, a Genoese garrison twenty-five miles east of the northern tip of Corsica (see From Burnaby, 10 Aug. n. 9). Despite repeated efforts on the part of the Genoese fleet to effect a landing, the commander of the garrison was forced to surrender to Paoli on 29 May (*Archivio Storica Italiano*, 1846, I. xi. 107–10, 115–17; P. A. Thrasher, *Pasquale Paoli*, 1970, pp. 105–09; *Gent. Mag.* 1767, xxxvii. 186–87).

[3] Translation by Caterina Bosio and Ian Duncan.

From Girolama Piccolomini, Friday 20 March 1767

MS. Yale (C 2259).

ADDRESS: à Monsieur, Monsr. Boswell, Gentilhomme Anglois, Chez Monsr. Waters Banquier, a Paris.[1]

POSTMARK: GENOVA.

Siena, 20 Marzo 1767

MONSIEUR: Voi siete quello, che mi giuravi ed in voce, e per mezzo di lettere, che mi avreste sempre scritto, *e che di qui a 20 anni avrei ricevute le vostre lettere con l'istesse espressioni.* Queste sono vostre parole, e ne conservo la memoria in carta, non per rapporto a me, che mi ricordo minutamente de tutte le vostre parole, ma per avere un'autentica di quanto dico, e per fare delle riflessioni di quanto poco si può contare sull'amicizia di un uomo, ancorchè si creda di buon carattere, e di buon cuore. Quando l'oggetto non è presente tutto svanisce. E vero, che questi riflessi non sono nuovi, ma mi rincresce che una funesta esperienza me le confermi in voi.

Io ricevetti una sola lettera al vostro arrivo in Iscozia, alla quale non mancaj di risponder subbito, e fare l'indirizzo come voi mi indicaste, e come farò in questa, ma temo che non vi pervenghino con questo indirizzo e non sò perchè non mi date l'indirizzo per il vostro Paese.

Io sto bene di salute, ed alla riserva di piccoli incomodi sono stata sempre bene; i miei consiglieri sono sempre gli medesimi ed in questo tempo non vi è stato altro di nuovo che un Cavaliere Tedesco, che è venuto da me; Il turno grosso (dicevi voi) e terminato e si sta ciascheduna da se; Il Paese non è molto allegro, per esservi della miseria, ed essere morta molta gente, ma nel maggio vengono i nostri Sovrani ed allora vi saranno gran feste e gran gente.

Ora ditemi voi le vostre nuove con esattezza. Come fate all'amore? Vi ricordate mai di me? Intendete la lingua italiana? Siete sempre incostante con le donne? Seguitate più l'amicizia con Russò, e con il Sigre. de Paoli? Vi prego di rispondermi sù tutte queste dimande, ed assicuratevi, che le vostre nuove mi faranno un vero piacere, tanto più doppo di aver disperato di averle. Vio mi avete promesso il vostro ritratto, ed io non sono in grado di rendervi la vostra parola, sicchè dovete eseguire la vostra promessa altrimenti me ne appellerò al vostra amico Russò, e sono sicura di averlo al mio partito per essere la causa troppo giusta, e per essere la promessa di troppo valore. Se posso obbedirvi comandatemi, e siate certo, che ne tempo ne lontananza mi farà cambiare di sentimento, e voi avrete vergogna di conoscere una Donna con tanta costanza senza poterla immitare, e senza potervi dire io sono senza riserva, come lo posso dire io, e come ve lo ratifico in lasciandovi con questa lettera.

Chi sa se verrà nelle vostre mani, ed in caso chi sa se potrete leggerla, ma qualchè volta bisogna azzardare come appunto segue nel mio caso. Devotissima ed Obbligatissima Amica,

GIROLAMA NINI PICCOLOMINI

[SIR: You are the man who swore to me in person and by letters that you would never stop writing to me, *and that twenty years from now I would still be receiving letters from you filled with the same expressions*. Those are your own words. I keep the written record of them, not for my own sake, for I remember in minute detail all you ever said, but for documentary proof of what I say, and for matter to reflect upon how little one can count on the friendship of a man, even though he is credited with a good character and a good heart. When the object is no longer present, everything disappears. It is true that these are not new thoughts, but it grieves me that my painful experience should have confirmed their truth in your case.

I received a single letter on your arrival in Scotland,[2] which I did not fail to answer immediately, addressing it according to your instructions, as I shall do with this one; but I am afraid they have not reached you with that address,[3] and I do not understand why you do not give me your address in your own country.

I am well so far as health is concerned, and except for some minor illnesses I always have been well. My counsellors are the same. The only new thing this season has been a German gentleman who has called on me. The turno grosso (as you called it)[4] is over, and everyone has gone back home. The country is not very cheerful, because of the sufferings of the poor and the deaths of many people, but in May our Sovereigns will come, and then there will be great celebrations and persons of quality.[5]

Now, give me news of yourself in detail. What are your love affairs? Do you ever think of me? Do you understand Italian? Are you as inconsistent as ever with women? Do you still keep up your friendship with Rousseau and with Signor de Paoli? I beg you to answer all these questions. You may be sure a letter from you will give me great pleasure, the more so because I have despaired of hearing from you. You promised me your portrait, and I am not going to release you from your promise. Therefore you must keep your word, or I shall appeal to your friend Rousseau; I am sure he will take my side because of the justice of my claim and the value of what you have promised. If I can serve you, I expect you to command me. Be assured that neither time nor distance will alter my feelings. You will be ashamed to know so faithful a lady without being able to imitate her example, and without being able to say to yourself, 'I have no reservations'—which I can say, and which I now set my name to, taking my leave of you with this letter.

Who knows whether it will come to your hands, and if it does, who knows whether you will be able to read it? But sometimes one must take risks, just as I am doing now. Your most devoted and obliged friend,

GIROLAMA NINI PICCOLOMINI][6]

[1] For Waters, see To John Waters, 10 May 1766. JB did not receive this letter until c. 11 Aug. (To W. J. Temple, 11 Aug.).

[2] Presumably this letter is the one JB noted in Reg. Let. as having been sent to her on 10 May 1766; in fact, this is a reply to the letter he had received from her on 9 Mar. (Reg. Let.).

[3] Her next letter to JB reached him on 11 May (Reg. Let.).

[4] Italian dictionaries do not give an English equivalent of *turno grosso*, but perhaps JB had something like 'the social round' or 'the season' in mind. Presumably he used that expression in one of the exercises he wrote in Siena while learning Italian.

[5] Sir Horace Mann (1706–86), Bt. wrote to Horace Walpole from Florence on 14 Feb.: 'We and all Italy have had a most cruel winter. . . . Many people in the country have literally died of hunger. . . . Notwithstanding this misery in the country, the Carnival in town is the gayest we have ever had' (*Corres. H.W.* xxii. 486). Peter Leopold, proclaimed Great Duke of Tuscany by order of his brother, the Holy Roman Emperor Joseph II, in Aug. 1765 (ibid. xxii. 328–29), made merry during the carnival in Florence, but we have found no evidence that either he or his wife, Maria Louisa (1745–92) paid a visit to Siena in May of that year.

[6] Translation by Frederick A. Pottle and Ian Duncan.

To Heer van Sommelsdyck, Saturday 21 March 1767

MS. Yale (L 1171).

HEADING: Extrait a M. De Sommelsdyck.

A Auchinleck, ce 21 de Mars 1767

Nous sommes á present á la Campagne de mes Ancêtres. Nous avons ici plusieurs Monuments de l'alliance que nous avons l'honneur de compter avec votre Famille. Nous avons le Contract de marriage entre My Lord Kincardine et Mademoiselle Veronica Van Aerssen van Sommelsdyck.[1] Nous avons beaucoup de lettres de Monsieur et Madame De Sommelsdyck le Pere et la Mere de My Lady Kincardine,[2] de My Lady Overkerk sa soeur,[3] et de ses soeurs pieuses qui se sont retirées á Rheinsburg.[4] Nous avons la toilette de My Lady, une varieté de Boetés faites en Hollande d'argent doré, le tout ayant couté 500 Livres Sterlings.[5] Nous avons aussi une quantité de lettres de My Lord et de My Lady Kincardine dont les Portraits ornent notre gallerie, aussi bien que ceux de M. et Madame De Sommelsdyck.[6] Et nous avons le Testament de Petronilla van Borre votre tres Ayeule ecrite de sa propre main, une grande curiosite qui etoit trouvée d'une manierre tres singulièrre.[7] La Femme de chambre d'un de mes Parents songeoit qu'il y avoit des Papiers de consequence en dedans la doublure d'un coffre qui etoit venu d'Hollande en Ecosse. Elle n'y fit pas attention: mais s'etant remise á dormir, elle eut la même reve. Elle le dit le matin, et on ouvrit la doublure de ce coffre, ou l'on trouvoit ce Testament. Il n'etoit pas un papier de consequence: mais on ne peut pas rendre raison de la rêve. Si vous souhaitez d'avoir une copie de ce Testament venerable, J'aurrois soin de vous l'envoyer. Tous ces Monuments nous font un grand plaisir. Nous les regardons comme quelque chose consacrée. Ils nous conservent la memoire d'un alliance avec des Gens d'une Famille distinguée en Hollande, des Gens sensés et aimables, et des Gens qui avoient la crainte de Dieu. Je me felicite, Mon Cher Monsieur, que J'ai eu le bonheur de renouveller notre anciênne amitié avec vous. Qu'elle ne s'oublie jamais. Que vos Descendants et les miens se regardent toujours comme des Parents.

[1] Alexander Bruce, second Earl of Kincardine (c. 1629–80), JB's great-grandfather, was a Scottish royalist in exile at The Hague when he married Veronica van Aerssen (1633–1701) in 1659.

Both the French original of the marriage contract (dated 6 June 1659) and a printed English translation of it survive at Yale (Boswell Collection, Box 102, folders 1879–88).

[2] The parents of Veronica (van Aerssen) Bruce, Countess of Kincardine, were Cornelius van Aerssen (1600–62), Heer van Sommelsdyck, born in Paris, privy councillor to Louis XIII, later colonel of a Dutch cavalry regiment, and his wife, Lucia (van Waltha—d. 1664) (van Epen iii. 168–69). The Boswell Collection (Box 101, folder 1850) contains 40 letters from Heer van Sommelsdyck and his wife to Lord Kincardine, 5 letters, written in French, from Lady Kincardine to her husband, and 1 letter from her to her daughter, Lady Elizabeth Bruce (later Boswell).

[3] Lady Kincardine's sister, JB's great-great aunt, was Françoise (van Aerssen—1642–1720), Countess van Nassau, Vrouwe van Ouwerkerk en Woudenberg, who, with her husband Hendrik, a follower of William III, settled in a house in St. James's Park, London, and remained there until her death (Abel Boyer et al., *Political State of Great Britain* [1720] xix. 116). The Boswell Collection (Box 104, folder 1914) contains 72 of her letters, the majority of them to her niece, Lady Elizabeth Boswell.

[4] Three of Lady Kincardine's eleven sisters, Anna (b. 1640), Maria (b. 1645), and Lucia (b. 1649), were converted to Labadism by the mystic, Pierre Poiret. Anna and Maria remained unmarried (one of them made an unsuccessful at-tempt to establish a Labadist community in Surinam before returning to the community at Rhynsburg, or Rijnsburg, near Leiden); Lucia married Pierre Yvon, the successor to Jean Labadie as leader of the sect, and settled at Wiewerd (NNBW; van Epen iii. 168–69). Lord Auchinleck wrote to JB c. 26 Oct. 1763 that the three sisters 'gave themselves up intirely to devotion even when full of Youth and Beauty'.

[5] The silver-gilt toilet set and boxes, given by Lady Kincardine to her daughter Lady Elizabeth Bruce (later Boswell), JB's paternal grandmother, remained at Auchinleck until dispersed in an auction on 2 Nov. 1886. Part of the set was purchased by the ninth Earl of Elgin and thirteenth Earl of Kincardine, a descendant of Lady Kincardine's.

[6] Two portraits of Lord Kincardine, inscribed 'De Witt pinxit', and one of Cornelius van Aerssen van Sommelsdyck, inscribed 'From van Dyke', both formerly at Auchinleck, are now owned by Mrs. Margaret Boswell Eliott of Redheugh, a descendant of JB's. Other portraits of Lord and Lady Kincardine now hang at Broomhall, the seat of the Earls of Elgin and Kincardine.

[7] Petronella (Borre) van Aerssen, Vrouwe van Sommelsdyck (b. 1578), was JB's great-great-great grandmother (van Epen iii. 166–68; NNBW). The testament, now in the Boswell Collection (Box 103, folder 1904) at Yale, is in Dutch, and in it, Petronella bequeaths her possessions to her husband and children.

From George Muir,[1] *Monday 23 March 1767*

MS. Yale (C 2063).

ADDRESS: To Mr. James Boswel, Younger of Auchinleck, Advocate, Ayr.

POSTMARK: Paisly.

Paisly, 23 March 1767

VERY DEAR SIR: Your's of the 18th I had the honour to receive this morning with the two memorials in the Douglas Cause.[2]— Such an honour and favour from any person of rank,[3] would have been great;—but, from a Gentleman of business— hurried with many important affairs, forgive me to say, they are doubly so.— Without guile I acknowledge the obligation, and beg youll accept of my heartiest thanks.

The papers beforehand I promise great entertainment from, as a display of eloquence and reasoning.— But the moral deducible from the whole Story I cannot help anticipating.— 'Vanity of Vanities, all is vanity.'[4]— The Treasure in dispute could not screen the proprietor from death;—nor will it be able to deliver either of the contending parties from the paw of that destroyer.— The rich—the celebrated, and the noble,—see how they're prostrate with their wealth, their names and their honours in the dust.— However distinguished among mortals, the poorest—the most obscure and ignoble, shall be raisd to a level with them in the world of spirits.— The DUREABLE Riches, Dear Sir, and righteousness, wherewith the Gospel of grace is fraughted are only worthy the ambition and pursuit of reasonable creatures. And I doubt not that one of the first lessons God hath taught you, from the possession and prospect of worldly plenty, is, That your rest is not in them. No — In the knowledge and enjoyment of Immanuel, there is infinitly more happiness, than the grovelling part of mankind can ever acquire or propose from the abundance of their corn—their wine and their oil.— 'Tis several years since I trusted that 'the unfeigned faith was in you, which dwelt first in Your Grandmother Lois and your mother Eunice.'[5] Nor can I help entertaining the agreeable hope, that the seeds sown in earlie life, will appear by their proper fruits through riper years.— Happy the man whose heart, and whose all, are devoted, without reserve, to a God in Christ!— Yea surely happy the person whose God the Lord is!

Begging youll make my dutiful Compliments acceptable to Lord Auchenleck, in which, and to you, my wife begs leave to join. And I am with all respect, Dear Sir, Your most obedient, humble Servant,

GEO. MUIR

[1] George Muir (or Mure) (1723–71), served as writer's clerk, came under the influence of the 1742 Cambuslang Revival, led by George Whitefield, studied for the ministry, and was finally ordained to Old Cumnock, Ayrshire, in 1752. In 1766 he removed to Paisley, and in 1768 was awarded an honorary D.D. by Princeton College, New Jersey, where John Witherspoon, one time colleague of Muir's (1757) at Paisley, was president of the college. Muir published *Christ's Cross* and *Crown: An Essay* as well as numerous sermons (*Fasti Scot.* iii. 172, 174–5; *General Cata-logue of Princeton University, 1746–1906*, 1908, p. 198).

[2] MS. 'Cause' written above deleted 'affair'. The Hamilton Memorial drawn up by Sir Adam Fergusson and the Douglas Memorial drawn up by Ilay Campbell had been submitted to the Court of Session on 24 Jan. (*Douglas Cause*, p. 19).

[3] MS. ?'hon[our]' deleted before 'rank'
[4] Ecclesiastes 1: 2.
[5] II Timothy 1: 5.

To Girolama Nini Piccolomini, Wednesday 25 March 1767

Not reported. See From Piccolomini, 3 May: 'This has been the first letter that I have received from you since your return to Scotland. I did not receive any of the others you mention in yours of 25 March.'

To John Tait, Saturday 28 March 1767

Not reported. See From Tait, 7 Apr.: 'My being out of Town a Little prevented my Answering yours of 28 Ulto. in Course.'

To Voltaire,[1] Sunday 29 March 1767

MS. Yale (L 1263). A copy, in JB's hand but unsigned.
HEADING: To M. De Voltaire

Auchinleck, 29 March 1767

SIR: The politeness with which you received me at Ferney, has never faded from my remembrance. I often recall it with the liveliest pleasure, and I am happy to think that I can boast of having had several conversations with M. De Voltaire.

After I left you, you was so good as to write me a letter in english, which I had the honour to receive at Naples. On my return to Rome, I sent you an answer. I know not if you received it.[2]

Since that time I have seen a great deal, and I think my travelling has done me great service. It has at least furnished me with a stock of ideas with which I can entertain my mind while I live; and to a man of keeness of thought that is very important. For, if He has not a good stock of ideas, He is apt to turn his keeness against himself, and You Philosophers know that the human mind cannot be nicely searched, without certain pain. My Philosophy appeared to you very gloomy; for, I confessed to you that misery seemed to me to be the principal portion of thinking Beings.[3]

I have visited the Island of Corsica, where I saw with enthusiasm a brave People who have vindicated their liberty with as much real spirit as was ever found in antiquity. General Paoli is a most extraordinary Man. His abilitys in Politics and in War, his learning, his eloquence, and his generous Sentiments render him truly illustrious. He has been now ten years the Commander of his Countrymen, from personal merit, a glorious distinction!

I am busy writing an Account of Corsica, with Memoirs of General Paoli, which will be published the beginning of next Winter. Mr. David Hume is so obliging as to take the charge of the Publication, as I cannot be at London myself.[4]

What does M. De Voltaire think of the Corsicans? I am perswaded He feels for them as I do. Why do you not write something in their behalf, to rouse the cold spirit of the times? Why does M. De Voltaire live in the same age with so gallant a Nation, and not compose a verse to their honour?[5]

After all my travels, I am now fixed in Scotland half the year as an Advocate, and the other half as a Country Gentleman. If it is not presuming too much on your former Goodness, I would beg to hear from you. I intreat you may make my best Compliments to Madame De Nis and to Père Adan.[6] I have the honour to be, Sir, your most obedient, humble Servant.

My Address is etc.

Je n'ai pas osé vous ecrire en françois. Je crois qu'il est mieux d'ecrire dans sa propre langue, même quand on sait bien une langue etrangêre; et á plus forte raison, quand on en sait três peu.

[1] Voltaire (1694–1778) had allowed JB three interviews at Ferney, 24–29 Dec. 1764, and had given JB permission to write to him in English (Journ.).

[2] Voltaire responded to JB's letter of 15 Jan. 1765 in English. JB received this letter on 15 Mar. 1765 (Reg. Let.) and answered it from Rome on 4 Apr. 1765 (Reg. Let.); JB's response has not been reported.

[3] There is no suggestion of pessimism in the account of his interviews with Voltaire that JB wrote to W. J. Temple on 28 Dec. 1764, nor in the notes that survive of his conversations with Voltaire. Presumably JB is referring here to his admission, after hearing Voltaire's unceremonious treatment of the soul (To Voltaire, 4 Apr. 1765), of his own need for reassurance: 'You must

forgive my Zeal for immortality. I am a Melancholy Man. . . . In this world my prospect is clouded. I cheer my hours of gloom with expectations of a brighter scene after death.'

[4] JB had written to Temple on 4 Mar.: 'David Hume told me sincerely He imagined my Account of Corsica would be a Book that will stand and He is obliging enough to transact the publication of it for me.'

[5] Writing to the Chevalier de Wargemont on 16 Jan. 1769 Voltaire described Corsica as 'un païs très misérable il en coûtera plus peut être pour le conserver que pour l'avoir conquis'. In Voltaire's opinion however, France, having already invaded Corsica, could hardly withdraw at that point without shame (Voltaire's Correspondence, ed. Theodore Besterman, 1953–65, lxxi. 43).

[6] Marie-Louise Mignot (1712–90), Voltaire's eldest niece, and Antoine Adam (1705–c. 1777), S.J., were members of Voltaire's household when JB visited Ferney in Dec. 1764. After a brief marriage (1738–1744) to a young army officer, Nicholas-Charles Denis, Mme. Denis joined Voltaire's household and, with the exception of a brief period following a quarrel in 1768, she remained with him until his death, becoming his hostess, mistress, and finally his heiress (DBF x. 1037–41). She arranged for JB to spend the nights of 27 and 28 Dec. 1764 at Ferney (*Earlier Years*, pp. 186–87). Père Adam was living in the neighbourhood of Ferney when the Jesuit order was suppressed in 1762. He sought, and finally gained, permission from the Jesuit authorities to remain in Ferney, and at that point (1764 or 1765) Voltaire provided him with a home. He was not well liked in the household: Mme. Denis called him 'un sot', 'une plate beste', while others thought of him as 'un espion de la Société' or 'un pauvre diable d'egoïste'. However, he remained with Voltaire until 1777, and gained some celebrity as a writer and theologian, though scholars, Condorcet among them, felt that Adam owed all his celebrity to his association with Voltaire (DBF i. 432–37). Voltaire had introduced Père Adam to JB on 24 Dec. 1764 as 'a broken Soldier of the Company of Jesus' (Journ.).

From Alexander Farquhar,[1] Monday 30 March 1767

MS. Yale (C 1239).

ADDRESS: To Mr. James Boswell Advocat, att Achenleck.

Gilmilscroft, 30th March 1767

DEAR SIR: I recaved yours with your fee returned which was not near Equal to the truble you have had in this process and the frendship you Express as Serving me as a Neighbour shall alway be kept in remembrance I doe not Intend you shal make a practice of this for by the Alter we Live.[2]— Archbald Steal is with me just now and he Says as to Smiths accknolegement of having no fault to the hors ther was non presant bot themselfs tuo at a Bottle of yal and this he Can Depon. I hope with what Information you have got we wil be Intituled to Expencess as I have no Doubt of your gaining the plea.[3]

My Wife and I joyns in Compliments to you and Lord Achenleck and Ever ame with Esteam, Dear Sir, your most Humble Servant,

ALEXR. FARQUHAR

P.S. I ame extreamly oblidged to Lord Achenleck for the favor he has Done me in granting the furrs. I Shall Send John murdoch on wendsy to Cut them.[4]

[1] Alexander Farquhar (d. c. 1779) had inherited Gilmillscroft, an estate three miles from Auchinleck House, in 1748 (*Ayrshire*, p. 295; *Ayr and Wigton* I. ii. 700). Gilmillscroft appears as one of the assize at the trial of the Garlieston rioters, whom JB defended in May (Lg 8:1).

[2] See, for example, the proverb, 'He that serves at the Altar, ought to live by the Altar', whose purport is that one ought to be paid for one's labour (W. G. Smith, *The Oxford Dictionary of English Proverbs*, 3rd ed. 1970, p. 12; T. Fuller, *Gnomologia: Adagies and Proverbs*, 1734, p. 94).

[3] In Feb. 1766 Farquhar of Gilmillscroft had employed Archibald Steel to sell a horse for him. After three months, John Smith, the buyer, claiming that the horse was defective, demanded a refund of his money (£10. 18s. 6d), and when Steel refused, took his cause before the Justices of the Peace for Ayrshire and won it. JB appealed for Steel on the grounds that Smith had not brought his action of redhibition promptly enough, and the Lord Ordinary (Kennet) reversed the decision of the Ayrshire Justices. Smith appealed and, after the presentation of additional evidence in Feb. 1768, Lord Kennet reversed himself and found for Smith. Steel appealed to the full Court of Session, which upheld Kennet's decision in July 1768 (Sidney Ives, 'Boswell Argues a Cause: Smith, Steel, and "Actio Redhibitoria"', *Eighteenth-Century Studies in Honor of Donald F. Hyde*, 1970, pp. 257–65).

[4] John Murdoch is not identified with certainty.

To Baroness von Spaen, before 31 March 1767

Not reported. See From Baroness von Spaen, 31 Mar. 1768: 'apres plus d'un an de silence vous devez douter si j'existe encor'.

To Pierre Loumeau Dupont, c. late March or early April 1767

Not reported. Acknowledged in From Dupont, 7 Apr., which indicates that this letter was addressed to the 'Reverend Père' Dupont.

To Robert Dundas, c. early April 1767

Not reported. See From Dundas, 10 Apr.: 'I had the favour of your Letter or Written Confession—which like a good Priest I shall treat as auricular only and never Communicate it'.

From James Gilkie,[1] Saturday 4 April 1767

MS. Yale (C 1373).
ADDRESS: To Mr. James Boswell, Advocate, at Auchinleck, by Air.
POSTMARK: ANNAN.

Annan, 4 Aprile 1767

SIR: Pardon me for being so presumptous as giveing you the trouble of this.— But I must humbly beg live to Remind you that Lord Kenet[2] ordained both parties to lodge informations in the Lords Boxes against the 25 Currant, That being a Box day.[3] When I had the Honour of seeing you in Edinr. you was so obligeing as to promise to draw my information and for that Effect I lodged with you a copy of my Proof which the Lord ordinary appointed to be adjected to the Information. I posest you also with a memoriall and other papers Relitive thereto.— Must now Entreate the favour of you to draw my Information and so soon as convenient for you to have it done. It will be mightly obligeing if you will transmitt the Information alone derect for me at Annan where my famely now stays and so soon as drawn by the first post thereafter. This favour shall be highly Esteemed alongst with the manny former ones Recived and so soon as I have the Honour of yours I shall go to Edinr. and get the Information printed the proof anext and put in the Lords Boxes as derect by the Lord ordinary and In the mean time accept of the most greatefull thanks of him who is with the outmost Esteem and[4] sentiments of Gratitude, Your very obleged Servant,

JAS. GILKIE

[1] James Gilkie (fl. 1749–78), who styled himself 'writer in Edinburgh' but may not actually have practised, was involved in litigation continually from 1749 to 1778. Since 1757 he had been engaged in litigation with William Wallace, the writer to whom he had once been apprenticed, but the Court of Session had thrown out his charges of defamation of character on 17 Dec. 1766 and 5 Feb. 1767 (Court of Session process, CS 235/G/3/9, SRO, Edinburgh). Gilkie's current lawsuit was against Wallace's son James who, he claimed, had attacked him with a knife—a charge supported by two witnesses, who had not, however, actually seen the knife. On 20 June James Wallace was sentenced to spend until 30 June in the Tolbooth, but the Court declined to assess damages because the 'complaint, as given in, was wrong laid, and contained false facts', and on account of 'very improper behaviour on the part of the complainer' (William Roughead, *Ras-*

cals Revived, 1940, pp. 144–51; *Acts of Sederunt of the Lords of Council and Session, 1553–1790*, 1790, pp. 562–63). JB was Gilkie's counsel in other litigation in 1773 and 1777 (Roughead, pp. 140, 156–58).

[2] Robert Bruce (1718–85), since 1759 Professor of the Law of Nature and Nations at the University of Edinburgh, and since 1764 Lord Kennet in the Court of Session (College of Justice, pp. 528–29).

[3] The day, usually a Saturday, on which boxes—one for each of the Lords of Session—lay upon a table in the waiting-room of the Inner House from three o'clock till six, 'that all who have bills to offer, may put them in these boxes, by a slit in the cover of them; whereby bills may be put in, and cannot be got out, till the Lords open their several boxes.' For a detailed account of The Order of Discussing Processes in the Court of Session, see James, Viscount of Stair, *Institutes of the Law of Scotland*, ed. D. M. Walker, 1981, bk. 4, pp. 802–11.

[4] MS. 'and and'

From Pierre Loumeau Dupont, Tuesday 7 April 1767

MS. Yale (C 1163).

ADDRESS: To Mr. James Boswell, Advocate at Auchinleck, To the Care of the Post Master of Air.

POSTMARK: [Edinburgh] AP 7.

A Edimbourg, le 7e. Avril 1767

MONSIEUR: Pour obeir a vos ordres jai eté chez Monsr. James Windram, et je l'apelle ainsi par anticipation, esperant quil aura cette grande somme d'argent pour la quelle il soupira depuis bien des années pour etre instruit[1] au sujet de lavertissement publié touchant la mort de David Cass.

Afin[2] de vous éclaircir la dessus je vous envoie la copie de ce que Windram m'a écrit. 'Sir Mr. Shaw read that Advertisement at London in the year sixty three, which he saïs that said advertisement spoke of David Cass who daied in the East Indies attested in the year forty six, Mr. Shaw read this in the dayly advortiser and that Mr. Janour was the Publisher of that paper. Mr. Janour lived in Fleet Street.'[3] Ainsi Monsieur vous pourrez quand vous trouverez a propos d'en écrire a votre Librair a Londres.[4]

Le pauvre Windram est fort tranquil, il attend l'evenement avec patience mais le mal est qu'il est pauvre, il y a bien du tems quil tire comme nous disons ordinairement dans le Stile familier le Diable par la queu.[5]

En lisant le commencement de votre lettre je n'ai pas pu m'empecher de sourire au titre que vous me donnez de Reverend Père[6] cela me fait penser aux Moines que l'on apelle en France les Pourceaux du bon Dieu,[7] on a celebré ces hommes venerables par ces magnifiques vers Latins

　　　　O Monachi Vestri Stomachi sunt amphora Bacchi
　　　　Vos estis, Deus est testis, teterrima pestis.[8]

Le fameux Rabelais le grand Panegeriste de l'ordre Monachale sexprimant sur un sujet si noble, dit que c'est une chose monstrueuse de voir un Moine savant,[9] et rapporte de cet auteur Satyrique que quand il lisoit les commandemens aux Cordeliers, il avoit eté autres fois de cet ordre au lieu de dire non *moechaberis* il lisoit non *monachaberis*.[10]

J'attends avec impatience votre livre sur L'Isle de Corse, et quand il sera imprime, on y voyagera avec plaisir sans courir risque de se casser le cou en grimpant ces hautes montagnes dont ce païs la abonde je suis sur que votre livre aura un bon debit[11] et quil faudra en donner une autre édition.

Monsieur Paris[12] que vous avez vu chez Madame Scott[13] est charmé de votre conversation, il regrette le malheur de n'avoir pas eu plutôt le bonheur de votre connoissance, cest un homme qui a bien etudié il a fréquenté les lescons de Theologie dans les academies de Geneve de Lausane et de Leiden, il est Precepteur des enfants de Mr. le Baron Mure, lesquels il a bien formes, ils savont bien pour leurs âges lhistoire ancienne et moderne, les jeunes filles parlent joliment le Francois, sans accent, Mr. le Baron, Madame son Epouse, les deux fils et Mr. Paris sont partis pour Londres, Mr. Mure a dessein de les mettre[14] dans une Ecolle,[15] ou ils aprendront a parler Anglois qui est fort en vogue a present, me voila privé de la conversation de notre Monsieur Francois dans la quelle je me plaisois infiniment, domage que nous n'avons pas parmi nos Francois des hommes de ce mérite, vous auriez occasion en les frequentant de vous entretenir dans la connoissance de cette langue.

Pour ce qui est de moi, je voyage toujours dans l'Arabie, je lis dans la Polyglotte le livre de job en Arabe, livre difficile, dans cette langue de même que dans l'original, pour ce qui est de cette version que l'on dit avoir eté faite dans le 9 Siecle par un Rabbin Saadias Aggaon n'est pas des meilleures,[16] mais j'y trouve plusieurs mots par[17] lesquels j'explique des formes en Italien, que Mr. le Professeur Maurice le Pére du Professeur d'aujourdhui que vous connoissez tres bien m'a dit que la langue Arabe est la langue Hébraïque vivante.[18] Madame Scott, et Mademoiselle[19] sa fille assurent My Lord Auchinlec et vous aussi de leurs trés humbles respects. Madame tousse beaucoup elle va par la maison, et nous esperons qu'avec la benediction de Dieu elle se rétablira quand il fera plus chaud, et nous irons a la Picardie pour y respirer le bon air.

Voila Monsieur une longue lettre qui sans doute a exercé votre patience, je vous demande la grace de me pardonner la grande faute que j'ai faite dans cette occasion et de me croire en même tems avec le plus parfait dévouement, Monsieur, Votre tres humble et tres obeissant Serviteur,

P. L. DUPONT

J'assure ici My Lord de mes plus profonds respects et je me reccommande a la continuation de l'honneur de Sa bienvoillance.

[1] MS. 'etre instruit' written above deleted 'savoir'

[2] MS. 'Afin' superimposed upon 'Pour'

[3] Matthew Jenour (1707–86), publisher since 1734 of the *Daily Advertiser* was, by 1763, established near St. Dunstan's Church in Fleet Street (*Dict. of Printers*, p. 140; Maxted).

[4] The affair of James Windram is a mystery in which all of the principals are obscure. It appears that Windram, who was perhaps a tailor (From Thomas Davies, 15 Oct.; Davies at one point seems to have thought he was JB's servant—From Davies, 18 June) had been told by one Mr. Shaw (unidentified) about a certain David Cass (also unidentified), who had died in the East Indies in 1746, and about an advertisement concerning his estate that had appeared in the *Daily Advertiser* in 1763. We do not know what the advertisement was supposed to have contained, but Shaw led Windram to believe that he could obtain a 'grande somme d'argent' as a legacy from Cass. On the basis of the information supplied by Dupont, JB asked Patrick Preston to search the records of the East India Company for any mention of David Cass (From Preston, 8 May), and asked Thomas Davies to have the *Daily Advertiser* searched for the advertisement Shaw had mentioned (From Davies, 18 June, 15 Oct., 12 Dec.). Neither search turned up anything. Preston wrote, 'I much fear Your Client has been imposed upon.'

[5] 'Tirer le diable par la queue' is a proverbial phrase meaning 'to have trouble making ends meet'.

[6] In France at this time, 'révérend père' was applied primarily to members of the regular clergy. Later, under English influence, it could be used of any Catholic priest (*Tresor de la langue*

francaise, 1971–, sv. père, révérend). Neither 'révérend père' nor 'Reverend Father' would have been appropriate for a Huguenot minister; presumably JB's applying the title to Dupont was a joke.

[7] John Calvin referred to monks as 'pourceaux' or 'porci' (*Institutio Christianae Religionis* IV. xiii. 15).

[8] 'O monks, your bellies are a wine-jug/ You are, God is witness, a terrible plague.' Verses unidentified.

[9] In Rabelais's *Gargantua* Friar John tells Gargantua: 'Nostre feu abbé disoit que c'est chose monstrueuse veoir un moyne sçavant' (ch. xxxix). Friar John emerges from the work both as a hero and as a butt for satire because of his worldliness and enormous capacity for food and wine.

[10] 'Non moechaberis' (Exodus 20: 14) means 'thou shalt not commit adultery'; 'non monachaberis' means 'thou shalt not become a monk'. A similar story is told in the 'Life of Dr. Francis Rabelais' prefixed to the popular translation by Sir Thomas Urquhart et al.: 'he is said not to have been able to refrain his Satyrical Temper, even while he was reading public Service; and instead of *Qui maechantur cum illâ*, as the Vulgate has it, to have said aloud, *Qui monachantur cum illâ*' (*The Whole Works of F. Rabelais*, 1708, i. xv). Here the allusion is to Apocalypse 2: 22, 'those who commit adultery with her'; the version attributed to Rabelais is 'those who become monks with her'. Rabelais belonged for a time to the Cordeliers, an order of Franciscan friars; his reputation for antifraternal and antimonastic humour caused many such stories to be ascribed to him (ibid. p. xi).

[11] MS. Dupont misspelled 'debit', drew a line through the 'b', then followed it with 'debits'

[12] Despite François Paris's admiration for him, JB thought him 'a secondrate man' whose violent anti-papism strained credulity (Journ. 17 Mar.—BP vii. 113). Nothing more is known about him.

[13] Magdalen Scott (From Dupont, 23 Apr. 1766, n. 4).

[14] MS. 'placer' deleted before 'mettre'

[15] William Mure (1718–76) of Caldwell, Ayr-shire, M.P. for Renfrewshire, 1742–61, and since 1761 a Baron of the Scots Exchequer, is chiefly remembered as a friend of Lord Bute's and of David Hume's (Sedgwick ii. 282–83). By his wife Katherine, daughter of James Graham, Lord Easdale of the Court of Session, he had six children, William, James, Katherine, Anne, Margaret, and Elizabeth (*Burke's Commoners* i. 457). It is not known where Mure sent his daughters to school; he sent his sons to a new academy at Norlands, near Kensington. This school, and in particular the deficiencies of its headmaster Graffigni, are the major topics of discussion in the correspondence of Mure and Hume for 1767 (*Selections from the Family Papers Preserved at Caldwell*, ed. William Mure, 1883–85, II. ii. 115-21; *Letters DH* ii. 148–49, 152–53, 155–57, 187–88).

[16] Possibly, Dupont used the polyglot Bible edited in ten volumes by Guy Michel LeJay and published in Paris, 1629–45. It was the first to add Arabic (as well as Samaritan) to the Hebrew, Latin, Greek, Syriac, and Chaldaic texts of other polyglot Bibles. An early Arabic translation of Job was made by Saadiah Ben Joseph (892–942), 'gaon, or head teacher, of the ancient academy of Sura', Palestine, who also translated the Pentateuch, Psalms, Canticles, and other parts of the Hebrew Bible into Arabic and made significant advances in textual criticism (*New Schaff-Herzog Encyclopedia of Religious Knowledge*, 1908–14, x. 130, ii. 168).

[17] MS. 'par' superimposed upon 'que'

[18] The elder Antoine Maurice (1677–1756) held professorships at Geneva first in belles-lettres and history in 1710, then in oriental languages in 1719, and finally in theology from 1724 until his death. His son, the younger Antoine Maurice (1716–95), succeeded his father in the chair of theology at Geneva (NBG). On 27 Dec. 1764 at Geneva JB described the younger Maurice as 'a man of knowledge, of rough sense, and of that sort of fancy which sound men have in abundance' (Journ.).

[19] MS. 'Madame' changed to 'Mademoiselle' before 'sa fille'

From John Tait,[1] Tuesday 7 April 1767

MS. Yale (C 2635).

ADDRESS: To James Boswell Esquire, at Auchinleck, by Air.

Edinr. 7th April 1767

SIR: My being out of Town a Little prevented my Answering yours of 28th Ulto. in Course.

I'm glad you have found time so soon to consider the Cause McKenzie v.

McKenzie.[2] There is no Day fixed for giving in the Informations, but the sooner they are ready the Better.

There was a Charter and sasine Expede[3] upon the Entail and by virtue thereof the late Sir Alexr. was Infeft in the Liferent and the present Sir Alexander in the Fee. And upon that Title he has possessed since his Father's Death, But as he Died only a Few months ago, or little more than a year since, His Answer will be that his present possession is as apparent Heir, and That he has recently after his Fathers Death, brot. the present Action for reducing the Deed of Entail. I fancy the Court will not willingly determine upon the General point, Therefore you will have double Trouble as you must Labour the Cause both upon that, and the Specialities.

I do not know of any Deeds granted by the present Gairloch, under the Character of Heir of Entail, Excepting his Marriage Contract with Redcastle's Daughter, His Marriage Contract with his present wife, and Liferent Deed granted by the late Sir Alexr. to One of his Mistresses to which the present Sir Alexr. is Consenter.[4]

I expect to have the pleasure of waiting of you at Auchinleck sometime in the beginning of May. My Wife Joins me in our Most respectful Compliments to My Lord Auchinleck. I am, Dear Sir, your Most Obedient, Humble Servant,

JOHN TAIT

[1] John Tait (d. 1800) of Harvieston, W.S., often employed JB as the advocate to plead his causes in court (*Scots Mag.* 1800, lxii. 215). Through his wife, Charles Murdoch, a cousin of JB's, Tait had family connections with members of the Boswell family of Auchinleck, and his sister was the wife of JB's client, Roderick Mackenzie of Redcastle (T. M. Fallow, *Short History of the Family of Murdoch of Cumloden*, 1905, pp. 53, 84, 87–88).

[2] The pursuer in this cause was Sir Alexander Mackenzie (c. 1730–70) of Gairloch, Bt., who had succeeded his father in 1766. The defenders were Roderick Mackenzie (d. 1785) of Redcastle, father of Sir Alexander's first wife Margaret (d. 1759), and Hector Mackenzie (1758–1826), Margaret's son and Sir Alexander's heir. To provide for the children of his second marriage, Sir Alexander wished to set aside an entail, executed by his father in 1752, that settled the estate of Gairloch on heirs-male and prohibited his selling it or burdening it with debt. Sir Alexander argued that under the terms of the marriage contract between his parents (1730), his father had bound himself to resign to his heir the fee (actual ownership of the estate), reserving to himself only the liferent (the right to income from the estate), and thus could not restrict his son's rights of ownership by a subsequent deed of entail. JB argued for the defenders that although Sir Alexander's father had bound himself by a marriage contract, he remained, for practical purposes, the estate's feuar, and had the right to make deeds (*Information for Hector Mackenzie*, 1 July 1767—Lg 10). On 4 Dec. the Court of Session decided in the defenders' favour; it confirmed its decision on 25 Nov. 1768 (Morison vii. 5665-69; Lord Hailes, *Decisions of the Lords of Council and Session, from 1766 to 1791*, 1826, pp. 252–53).

[3] Completed, and issued.

[4] In his *Information for Hector Mackenzie*, pp. 10–11, JB cited the marriage contract between Sir Alexander and Margaret Mackenzie, in which Sir Alexander had designated himself 'heir of tailzie', thus assenting to the entail.

To Lord Chatham, Wednesday 8 April 1767

MS. Chatham Papers, Public Record Office, London. The Yale MS. (L 368) is a draft in JB's hand, bearing the heading, 'To The Earl of Chatham'.

ENDORSEMENT: (in the hand of Lord Cardross): 1767 April 8th.

Auchinleck, 8 April 1767

MY LORD: I have had the honour to receive your Lordship's letter from Bath, and

I perfectly feel the sentiments which it contains. I only wish that circumstances were such that your Lordship could have an opportunity of shewing the interest you take in the fate of a People who well[1] deserve the favour of so illustrious a Patron of Liberty as your Lordship.— I have communicated to General Paoli the contents of your Lordship's letter, and I am perswaded He will think as I do.

Allow me to give your Lordship another quotation[2] from a letter of that Heroe.[3] It is addressed to a Friend of mine[4] at Leghorn.

'Essendo al Ministero il Conte di Chatham, voglio sperar tutto il buon successo alla generosa premura del Sigre. Boswell, per la rivocazione dell' ingiuriosa Proclama del 1763. Quel Sublime Genio della Gran Brettagna, e quell' Anima grande ne' propri sentimenti e nel Sistema della sua Politica, ritrovera i piu efficaci motivi per far uscir La sua Corte dello stato di indifferenza sopra gli affari di Corsica.'[5]

I leave with the Earl of Chatham,[6] these words of General Paoli, and I am perswaded Quell Anima Grande will not forget them.

Your Lordship applauds[7] my 'generous warmth[8] for so striking a Character as the able Chief.' Indeed My Lord I have the happiness of being capable to contemplate[9] with supreme delight those distinguished Spirits by whom God is sometimes pleased to honour humanity; And as I have no personal favour to ask of your Lordship, I will[10] tell you with the confidence of one who does not fear to be thought a Flatterer, that your character, My Lord, has filled many of my best hours with that noble admiration which a disinterested Soul can enjoy in the bower of Philosophy.

I think it my duty to inform your Lordship that I am preparing to publish an Account of Corsica. My Plan is First to give a Geographical and Physical Description of the Island. Secondly to exhibit a concise view of the Revolutions it has undergone from the earliest times till now. Thirdly to shew the present state of Corsica in every respect. And lastly I subjoin my Journal of a Tour to that Island, in which I relate a variety of Anecdotes, and treasure up many memoirs of the illustrious General of the Corsicans,—Memorabilia Paoli.

While I was in Corsica, I was carefull to write[11] down every thing that deserved attention;[12] and since my return home, I have received many materials from different People of that Country. I[13] hope my Book will be agreable, and may[14] do some service to the brave Islanders, by representing them in a proper light. General Paoli is very impatient for[15] my publishing it.

I beg to know what your Lordship thinks of my undertaking;[16] for, allthough I am so much engaged to the Island, that I must[17] at any rate go on with it, the approbation of My Lord Chatham would make me advance with double Spirit.

And I must intreat your Lordship's permission to take notice of your[18] noble sayings concerning Corsica and General Paoli. It will add[19] much dignity to the Subject, and to the Authour. I promise[20] to insert nothing that is[21] improper to be read by all the world. But[22] when[23] I record General Paoli's grand ideas of your Lordship, I would also record your Lordship's grand ideas of him, that Posterity[24] may see how[25] highly two such men thought of each other.[26]

As for myself, to please a worthy and respected Father one of our Scots Judges, I studied law, and am now fairly entered to the Bar.[27] I begin to like it. I can labour hard,[28] I feel myself coming forward, and I hope to be usefull[29] to[30] my Country.

Could your Lordship find time to honour me now and then[31] with a letter? I have been told how favourably your Lordship has spoke of me.[32] To correspond with a Paoli and with[33] a Chatham is enough to keep a young man ever ardent in the pursuit of virtuous Fame.[34] I ever am, My Lord, with the highest admiration your Lordship's Much obliged, Humble Servant,

JAMES BOSWELL

P.S. I beg to know if I may address my letters to your Lordship, by the public Post?

[1] Draft, 'well' inserted above the line.

[2] Draft, 'quotation' written above deleted 'Sentence'

[3] Draft, 'Heroe' written above deleted 'noble Chief'

[4] Draft, 'a friend of mine' written above deleted 'Mr. Dick the British Consul'

[5] The paragraph is quoted from Paoli's letter to John Dick of 6 Dec. 1766: 'Now that the Earl of Chatham is in the Ministry, I venture to hope for all good success to Mr. Boswell's generous concern in the revoking of the injurious Proclamation of 1763. That sublime Genius of Great Britain, and that great Spirit will find in his own sentiments and in his own political views the most efficacious motives for causing his Court to emerge from its state of indifference to the affairs of Corsica.' JB seems not to have known that Paoli had written to Chatham about the occupation by French troops of the fortresses in Corsica formerly held by the Genoese (Paoli to Chatham, 31 Jan. 1767, PRO, Chatham MSS., viii, 94, cited in *Boswell's Paoli*, p. 46, n. 5). On the same day, Paoli wrote to Louis XV and the Duc de Choiseul, and sent out a general 'Memoria del Governo di Corsica ai Sovrani di Europa.' The text of these three documents is printed in BSSC ('Correspondance du Général Paoli et du Duc de Choiseul', ed. L'Abbé Letteron, BSSC, 1886–87, fasc. 69. vi. 516–23).

[6] Draft, 'The Earl of Chatham' written above deleted 'your Lordship'

[7] Draft, 'is pleased' deleted before 'to applaud' and 's' added to 'applaud' ('to' left undeleted through oversight).

[8] Draft, 'my warmth' altered to 'my generous warmth'

[9] Draft, 'happiness of contemplating' altered to 'happiness of being capable to contemplate'

[10] Draft, 'will' superimposed upon 'can'

[11] Draft, 'kept an exact r' altered to 'was carefull to mark'; then 'mark' altered to 'write'

[12] Draft, 'attention' written above deleted 'any notice'

[13] Draft, '&' deleted before 'I'

[14] Draft, 'may' inserted above the line.

[15] Draft, 'till' deleted before 'for'

[16] Draft, 'schem' deleted before 'undertaking'

[17] Draft, 'allthough as I have engaged to the Island, I must'

[18] Draft, 'your' written above deleted 'the'

[19] Draft, 'go' deleted before 'add'

[20] Draft, 'Authour; and I give', with 'give' altered to 'promise'

[21] Draft, 'is' written above deleted 'would be'

[22] Draft, 'nothing but y' deleted before 'But'. JB deleted a reference to Chatham from the MS. of 'Corsica': 'With all deference to those who have had the guidance of the affairs of this nation I cannot conceive why We should in any respect give assistance to the Genoese; for, as I heard it observed by the greatest Minister whom Britain ever saw, Genoa is not only under the protection of France, but under the thumb of France' ('Corsica' MS., M 2, pp. 194–95).

[23] Draft, 'while'

[24] Draft, 'Posterity' written above deleted 'the world'

[25] Draft, 'with' deleted before 'how'

[26] For Chatham's and Paoli's stated opinions of each other, see To Sir Alexander Dick, 23 Oct. 1766 and n. 9 and To Lord Chatham, 3 Jan.

[27] Draft, 'business of the Northern Forum', with 'Northern Forum' altered to 'Bar'; then the whole phrase deleted and 'Bar' written above it.

[28] Draft, 'I can labour hard' inserted above the line.

[29] Draft, 'an' deleted before 'usefull'

[30] Draft, 'member' deleted before 'to'

[31] Draft, 'now & then' written above deleted 'sometimes'

[32] Chatham's praise has not been reported; presumably it was passed on to JB by Lord Cardross, Chatham's secretary and JB's distant cousin (From Pitt, 15 February 1766, n. 3).

[33] Draft, 'with' inserted above the line.

[34] Draft ends with 'fame.'

From Sir Alexander Dick, Friday 10 April 1767

MS. Yale (C 961).

ADDRESS: To James Boswell Esquire, Advocate, at Achinleck, Shire of Air.

POSTMARK: [Edinburgh] AP 10.

Prestonfield, April 10th, 1767

MY DEAR SIR: Since you left us I have been embarkt in the question about the great or small canal that is to be the Bond of Union betwixt your sea and ours.[1] Deeply embarkt before there is any sailing in it. They were pleasd to make me the praeses[2] of the great meeting held here by Lord presidents call which you woud see in the papers: by this means (for the Lord president declind the chair being to speak much in the debate) I am plungd into this matter with my best degrees of attention and Zeal. I fancy you have read in the papers all that the Glascow subscribers say we the dilatorians say for our selves. For my own self I think we are extreamly obligd to these adventurous Gentlemen of that City for attempting with their purses totis viribus any Canal;[3] but I cant help blaming them for their hurry: tho even that hurry has spurrd the stagnating humour of Government and rousd the true spirit of promotting this reall marriadge of the two Rivers Clyde and Forth.[4] John Swinton for the Glascow men as council sayd it put him in mind, the proposing a Delay, of the play where father foresight proposd to the young Couple a Delay a Delay they answerd with amourous Zeal that delays were alwise dangerous.[5] As I was in the chair I was only to collect the opinion of others and not be too lavish of my own: I thot he might have been properly answerd in this way which I subject to your consideration: 'Really Mr. Swinton what you say of marriadge is very true but on the other hand as this is a Virgin Scheme and a reall marriadge of the two Rivers is intended we were not for any long delay but were resolvd (as we hope it is not their[6] intention) that your Clients shoud be cleard of all suspicion of committing a Rape or in any shape ante nuptial fornication.'

But from Canals I come to Lochs for I am a very acquatic Being at present.[7] Our great Lord and neighbour has by a representation to Lord Gardenston[8] falln very heavy upon you for using him he says so rudely and abusively and seems to have lost all patience especially as he and his counsel have lost all argument: and calls you the witty Gentleman for offering the rediculum acri (Lord Shaftsbury's[9] test of truth) to the magnas res which affects his Nerves.[10] He says he waves his priviledge of a peer which he could do and has not at all digested the hint as to the perches suffering by it. He pretends he offerd me all friendly offers of arbitration as this will he thinks take of the claim of expences: but Mr. Tait sandy[11] I mean who read all the correspondence and this mighty Splendida Bilis[12] of my great neighbour, says the correspondence now shoud be laid fully before the Court and then[13] if there is any Scandalum Magnatum[14] his Lordship will have an action against himself for he will be found to be quite in a mistake I wont say worse.

I long to hear of every thing relates to you to My Lord your father to the great paoli and your works and to etc. etc. etc. you know tres fatiunt Collegium[15] and that is verbum Sapienti.[16] The good Consul of Leghorn has got your Letters and sends two friendly messages to me the 1st by Sieur Ferguson the 2d by young anzely[17] that he intends a Visit to see us here this summer. What shall we not learn

141

from so material a man in every Sense perhaps Dicks unborn shall bless the meeting of that day when he arrives. May Boswells unborn as well as born rejoice when friends meet for so good purposes and with so good hearts. May all black avarice spleen malice and Envy and distestable pride be buried in the deepest part of my Loch or in Acheron or wherever you will that it may never EMERGE Dear Councellor. Yours and my Lords Ever,

ALEXANDER DICK

P.S. Poor George Frazer has been almost killd with a violent fluxion on his Breast of sharp Rheum but your uncle and I have discust it and he at length gets an Issue in his arm.[18] He lay near 8 days will emerge soon and possibly we may get (tho I am tyd to the Committee on the Canal) to Kames at Blair Drummond the end of next week for 3 or 4 days. I beg I may hear[19] soon from you.

The House of Commons have put of the Canal till the Easter[20] holidays are over. Oswald and Elliot oppose the small canal and call it a monopoly of the most dangerous Natur.[21]

[1] The primary issue with which Sir Alexander was concerned was to determine which canal—the 'great' or the 'small'—should be constructed to form a link between the Rivers Clyde and Forth. Proponents of the 'small canal'—to be about four feet deep with draught enough for flat-bottomed barges only—wanted a cut from Glasgow to Carron-shore, Stirlingshire—i.e., from port to port; partisans of the 'great canal'—to be seven feet deep and able to accommodate coasting-trade sailing ships of up to forty or fifty tons, in addition to barges, advocated a cut from a point down the Clyde from Glasgow to a point about a mile above the mouth of the Carron River, at Grangemouth—i.e., from firth to firth. They pointed out that the great canal would open up trade to ships from other ports in both firths, such as Leith in the Forth and Greenock in the Clyde, commercial rivals of Grangemouth and Glasgow respectively. Glasgow merchants took the initiative and set about raising money for the small canal; Edinburgh citizens, on the other hand, tended to favour the deeper canal proposed by the engineer John Smeaton. At a meeting on 3 Apr., called by the Lord President of the Court of Session, it was agreed that the bill for the building of the canal previously put before the House of Commons should be delayed until the next session of Parliament to allow more time to decide whether the larger or smaller canal would better meet the needs of the country (Scots Mag., 1767, xxix. 129–38, 177–90). For the Parliamentary resolution of the Great Canal Bill, see below, n. 21.

[2] 'President' or 'chairman'.

[3] 'With all their strength'. By 18 Feb. the merchants of Glasgow had raised £40,000 (Scots Mag. 1767, xxix. 131).

[4] Sir Alexander alludes to the famous marriage of the Thames and the Medway in Book IV,

canto xi, of Spenser's Faerie Queene.

[5] John Swinton (d. 1799) of Swinton, whose family had been settled at Swinton, Berwickshire, since at least the 11th century, passed advocate in 1743, became sheriff-depute of Perth in 1754, and was raised to the bench as Lord Swinton in 1782 (College of Justice, p. 536). He was the author of several legal tracts. Presumably Swinton had in mind Congreve's Love for Love and the characters of Foresight and the two lovers Angelica and Valentine, but the line as given here does not occur in that play.

[6] MS. 'we hope it is not their' altered from 'is certainly not your'

[7] The dispute between Sir Alexander and James Hamilton (1712–89), eighth Earl of Abercorn, over Duddingston Loch, which lay between Prestonfield and Lord Abercorn's estate of Duddingston, lasted until 1769. By a charter of 1617, the loch belonged to the proprietor of Prestonfield, and an agreement of 1668 gave the proprietor of Duddingston the right to water his and his tenants' cattle in the loch. As a result of a boundary dispute that appears to have arisen because the loch's level had fallen, exposing dry land on the side of it that adjoined Lord Abercorn's estate, Sir Alexander brought suit, asking the court to confirm his ownership 'so far as the water now flows, or has flown on all the sides thereof'; he also asked that Lord Abercorn be forbidden 'to take any water from the foresaid lake for the use of his coal-mill' (Morison xv. 12813). We have few indications of what went on in this preliminary stage of the suit: Dick had asked that the court fix the boundary and mark it with stakes and posts; at some time before June 1768 the court agreed, and the Sheriff of Edinburgh visited the loch and marked the boundaries.

On 21 June 1768 the court ruled in Dick's favour. Abercorn appealed, arguing that Dick had a right to the loch only as a body of water, and not to the land under it; thus the legal boundary should shift with the shoreline. However, on 17 Feb. 1769 the Court ruled that Dick's property included the lake-bed, and that any land exposed by the falling of the waterline must be his. Abercorn obtained the right to water his cattle in the loch, even if that made it necessary to pasture his cattle on land not actually his; he was also granted the right to use the water from the loch for his coal-mill. Neither party was awarded expenses. Dick, apparently not entirely satisfied, appealed the decision, which the Court upheld on 13 July 1769. The printed record of the cause (Morison xv. 12813–17) ends here, but JB's legal notebook (Lg 5.5, pp. 49–53) shows that he argued the cause (presumably another appeal) before the Court of Session on 16 Nov. 1769. For further discussion of this cause, see From Sir A. Dick, c. 21 June 1768 and To Sir A. Dick, 12 Sept. 1769.

⁸ Francis Garden (1721-93), Lord Gardenstone (1764) in the Court of Session, was Lord Ordinary for this cause. His opinion of JB's use of humour in arguing this cause is not known; but on 6 Feb. he had complimented JB on his pleading of another cause (Journ.). On 4 Feb. 1775, arguing before Lord Gardenstone, JB 'threw out sallies of vivacity and humour'; when David Rae, who spoke after him, said, 'I have heard Mr. Boswell with great pleasure', Lord Gardenstone replied, 'and I dare say so has every body that heard him' (Journ.).

⁹ MS. 'Shaftsburs'

¹⁰ In his 'Letter Concerning Enthusiasm', (1671–1713), Shaftesbury quotes Horace's *Satires* I. x. 14–15: 'Ridiculum acri / Fortius & melius magnas plerumque secat res': 'Ridicule often decides great matters more forcefully and effectively than severity'. In '*Sensus Communis*: An Essay on the Freedom of Wit and Humour', he treats the concept more fully: 'Truth, 'tis suppos'd, may bear *all* Lights: and *one* of those principal Lights or natural Mediums, by which Things are to be view'd, in order to a thorow Recognition, is *Ridicule* it-self, or that Manner of Proof by which we

discern whatever is liable to just Raillery on any Subject' (*Characteristicks of Men, Manners, Opinions, Times*, 2nd ed. 1714, i. 13, 61).

¹¹ Alexander Tait (d. 1781), W.S., had been Principal Clerk to the Court of Session since 1760 (*Writers to the Signet*).

¹² 'Shining bile' or 'magnificent rage' (Horace, *Satires* II. iii. 141).

¹³ MS. 'there'

¹⁴ 'Dispute of nobles', a legal term describing an insult directed at a noble person, considered to merit a more severe punishment because of the injured party's rank (C. Du Cange, *Glossarium Mediae et Infimae Latinitatis*, 1883–87, *scandalum*, 1).

¹⁵ 'Three make an association', from Justinian: 'Neratius Priscus tres facere estimat "collegium" et hoc magis sequendum est', 'Neratius Priscus thinks that three make a "collegium" and this is rather to be followed' (*The Digest of Justinian*, ed. T. Mommsen et al., 1985, iv. 940).

¹⁶ 'A word to the wise'.

¹⁷ For James Ferguson, see From John Dick, 31 Oct. 1766, n. 3; for Robert Ainslie, see To Sir A. Dick, 9 Dec. 1766, n. 2.

¹⁸ For JB's uncle Dr. John Boswell, see From P. L. Dupont, 23 Apr. 1766, n. 5.

¹⁹ MS. 'I beg I may hear' altered from 'Shall I hear'

²⁰ MS. 'Easte'

²¹ Two opponents of the 'small canal' were James Oswald (1715–69), M.P. for Dysart Burghs, 1741–47, 1754–68, and for Fife, 1747–54, and Sir Gilbert Elliot (1722–77) of Minto, Bt., M.P. for Selkirkshire, 1753–65 and for Roxburghshire, 1765–77. Oswald subscribed £500 to the 'great canal' in May and became a member of the Company of Proprietors of the Forth and Clyde Navigation in Mar. 1768. Elliot is not mentioned in the many accounts of the canal in *Scots Mag.* and is not listed among the subscribers to it. Elliot, Oswald, and their allies prevailed with the House of Commons, Parliament approved the plan for the deeper canal, and the Great Canal Bill received the royal assent on 8 Mar. 1768 (*Scots Mag.* June 1768, xxx. 289–93; JHC, 1766–68, 1803, xxxi. 333, 360). Work was begun in March of that year, and the canal was completed in 1790 (*Scots Gazetteer*, pp. 613–14).

From Robert Dundas,¹ Friday 10 April 1767

MS. Yale (C 1155).

ADDRESS: To Mr. James Boswell, Advocate, at Achinleck, By Ayr.

POSTMARK: [Edinburgh] AP 14.

Arniston, Apr. 10, 1767

DEAR SIR: I had the favour of your Letter or Written Confession²—which like a good Priest I shall treat as auricular only and never Communicate it.— Nor do I think it necessary to Enjoin you any Penance because I Suppose you have already undergone that Sufficiently and does repent in Sackloth. However take a good Advice from an Old Man who was Once young like his Neighbours—Viz. As these Misfortunes are sometimes Incident to young men and Lawyers dum Spiritus hos regit artus[3]—Only Despise not your Chastening—but Be Carefull of your Health and in this Cold Country Hasten not your Cure more than it Ought to be—least Worse befall you.

As to Business my present Scheme is to See you and my good Friend in May.— But I will not promise any thing too Strongly[4]—as I really have not done much Business having found it necessary to take Exercise and mind my Farm etc. to Establish Health—and The Douglas Cause is Still on Hand.— But you Shall hear from me again about the Beginning of May.[5]— Make my Compliments and those of my Family[6] Acceptable the Good Old Trojan[7] and Believe me ever very Sincerly, Dear James, Your most obedient, humble Servant,

RO. DUNDAS

[1] Robert Dundas (1713–87) had served as Solicitor-General and Lord Advocate, and since 1760 had been Lord President of the Court of Session. An old friend of the Boswell family, he had last seen JB at Arniston, his estate near Edinburgh, on 10–12 Jan. (Journ.).

[2] Presumably JB had confessed to Dundas the gonorrhoea that he had contracted in early March and for which he was being treated as late as 16 Apr. (To Temple, 1 Feb.–8 Mar.; Journ. 2, 8, 16 Apr.).

[3] Aeneid iv. 335, translated by Dryden, 'While vital breath inspires this mortal frame'.

[4] Though JB again urged Dundas to join him and Lord Auchinleck on the circuit in May (To Dundas, 18 Apr.), there is no record of his having done so.

[5] MS. 'the' deleted before 'May'

[6] The Lord President's family included his second wife, Jean Grant, daughter of William Grant, Lord Prestongrange, their four sons, Robert, Francis, William, and Philip, two daughters of his present marriage, Grisel and Ann, and four daughters from his first marriage, Elisabeth, Henrietta, Margaret, and Ann (Baronage, p. 181).

[7] Lord Auchinleck; for the expression, see OED, Trojan, B. 2.

From Lord Marischal, Tuesday 14 April 1767

MS. Yale (C 1955). A leaf used as a wrapper and inscribed in JB's hand 'Earl Marischall' accompanied this letter and letters C 1957–61, 1966–68, and 1970–72, all found at Fettercairn House.

ADDRESS: To James Boswell Esqr., of Auchinleck, [Edenburg deleted; added in another hand] by Air, en Ecosse; par Londres, fr. Amsterdam [added].

POSTMARK: [London] MA 4.

Potsdam, 14 Aprile 1767

SIR: I have the honor of yours, and some days since had the pleasure to hear of you by your freind and acquaintance Sir Harry Eclin, who heard you plead at the bar with satisfaction; I have for you, lying at the custom house, a standish that you may have allways pen and ink ready on your table when folks come to consult you; make my best compliments to My Lord your father, I hope he has received a warm lining for a night gown, still in season, for the air continues rather cold, at least it is so to an old Spaniard.

The curst air of Africa has carried off pour Governor Lachlan,[1] I sent to Mr.

Forbes, cloath Merchant Covent garden,[2] a gun and a small present of 30ps., for Lachlan, it was too late; his brother may call for both, if he has not yet received them.[3]

As to what you say of generous sentiments decaying as men grow up, I grant in general, but deny it positively as to you, they will with you, I would venture my life, grow like old buildings which hardens by time.

I am much obliged and return my thanks for your good advice in my concerns, and your generous behavior, which I receive as a most kind mark of your freindship, but I hardly expect to see the determination of that afair, for I am *mui acabado much inded*, a strong Spanish expression.[4] I have not seen Sir Andrew nor Mr. Burnet but once of many months: I kept clos at home all winter, I shall make them your compliments by a note, for I sometimes hear from them.[5]

I am sorry for Mr. Rousseau's unjust quarrel with Mr. Hume, who certainly did all he possibly could to serve him with the best intention, tho ill interpreted by Mr. Rousseau, his persecutions have too much soured his mind.[6]

Mr. et Me. de Froment applyed by mutuall agreement for a divorce, easy here to be obtained; the marriage was declared, for good reason, null; she gave him a pension of 800 livres, during life, of her free accord; so that is setled, and he who had not a one farthing in the world, has to live tout doucement in Swisserland or where he pleases.[7]

I have no more memory, I can not say if it was the Prince d'Anhalt or Sir H. Eclin who heard you plead at Glasgow.[8] Your standish lay at the custom house till now waitin a boat for Hambourg, it now goes off.[9] Believe me ever with great regard, Sir, your most humble and obedient servant,

MARISCHALL

This lay by waiting the boat untill now, 24 Aprile.

[1] Perhaps Lauchlan Macpherson, the second son of Donald Macpherson of Breakachy, Inverness-shire, who was trained as a surgeon, served as an officer in the 78th Foot or Fraser's Highlanders, 1759–63, and then in a British independent company in Senegal from 1765 until his death (*Baronage*, p. 364; *Army List*, 1759–68). Marischal had taken a liking to Macpherson in Scotland and brought him to Berlin at his own expense. JB had found Macpherson 'a fine, honest, spirited fellow' and 'quite the man for me' (*Journ.* 5, 7, 14 July 1764). We have not ascertained why Lord Marischal might have called him 'Governor Lachlan'.

[2] George Forbes (fl. 1767–72), woollen draper, Bedford Street, Covent Garden (*Kent's Directory*, 1768; *London Directory*, 1772).

[3] If 'Governor Lachlan' was Lauchlan Macpherson, presumably the brother mentioned here is Duncan Macpherson (fl. 1759–1808), Lauchlan's older brother, who returned to Breakachy in 1766 after having served since 1759 as a captain in the 89th Highlanders. In 1773, after a vigorous court battle, Macpherson and his father were evicted from Breakachy, which the family had leased since at least 1735. Duncan

returned to active service with the 42nd (Royal Highland) Foot in 1775, gained his majority in the 71st (Highland) Foot in 1780, and a colonelcy in the army in 1782. Once the owner of several estates, Macpherson saw his holdings reduced to a single house in Kingussie, Inverness-shire, at the end of his life (*Army Lists*, 1761–83; *Sasines Index* no. 64, iii. 86; Charles Fraser-Mackintosh, *Antiquarian Notes*, 1897, pp. 361–63; *Scots Mag.* 1808, lxx. 880).

[4] A portion of JB's unreported letter of 12 Mar. presumably alluded to the 'afair', which had brought Marischal to the point of being 'muy acabado' or 'completely exhausted'. One likely candidate for this situation may be a protracted legal dispute which took place in the Court of Exchequer (Scotland), Court of Session, and House of Lords from 1766 to 1777. This dispute included the lawsuit, E. Marischal *v.* Y. B. Company, about which Alexander Keith, Marischal's agent, consulted JB on 9 Jan. (Consultation Book). After his attainder following the 1715 uprising, Marischal's estates were forfeited to the Crown and, as with those of many of his fellow Jacobites, subsequently sold to the York Buildings Company in 1719 and 1720. This Company—

chartered originally (in 1675) to erect a water-works on land surrounding York House in the Strand for the purpose of supplying neighbouring inhabitants with water at a reasonable rent—purchased a number of the forfeited Jacobite estates (Fifer, p. 109, n. 1). In 1759 Marischal was formally pardoned by George II and in 1763, soon after returning to Scotland almost a half-century after his attainder, he had a chance to buy back some of his ancestral estates from the now insolvent York Buildings Company (Cuthell ii. 68–75, 182–83). Having failed to make a profit from the Scottish estates and through involvement in other unsuccessful and questionable ventures, the Company was obliged to auction off a part of the estates it had purchased forty years ago. It was finally dissolved by Act of Parliament in 1829. For a detailed account of the York Buildings Company and its vicissitudes, see David Murray, *The York Buildings Company: a Chapter in Scotch History*, 1883. See also, *Scots Mag.* 1764, xxvi. 108–09 (auction); Court of Session Papers, no. 8, vol. 595, Signet Library, Edinburgh.

[5] For Andrew Mitchell, see From Pringle, 10 Feb. n. 13. Sir Andrew's secretary and chargé d'affaires in his absence was Alexander Burnett (1735–1802) who, on the death of his father George Burnett in 1780, inherited the estate of Kemnay, Aberdeenshire, near Keith Hall, one of Marischal's estates (*Scots Mag.* 1803, lxv. 72; *Burke's Landed Gentry*, 1937). JB had written, 'I found Burnet a sollid, clear-headed fellow, much better than myself' (Journ. 28 Aug. 1764).

[6] For the quarrel between Rousseau and Hume, see From Baroness von Spaen, 22 July 1766, n. 6.

[7] Emet-Ulla de Froment (c. 1725–1820), daughter of Sar Aly Oda Bachy, captain of janizaries in the Turkish army, was adopted by Marischal after his brother James found her orphaned at the Russian capture of Ochakov in 1737 (Archives de l'Etat, Neuchâtel; J.-H. Bonhôte, 'Note sur Emétulla', *Musée Neuchâtelois*, 1865, ii. 28; Cuthell ii. 176). In 1763 she converted from Islam to Calvinism, was baptized Marie, and married Denis-Daniel de Froment (d. 1810), a French officer in the Sardinian army (J.-H. Bonhôte, 'Un Gouverneur de Neuchâtel', *Musée Neuchâtelois*, 1864, i. 47; Ch. Berthoud, 'Les Quatre Petitpierre', *Musée Neuchâtelois*, 1873, x. 151; DBF xiv. 1350). The marriage was unhappy and childless, and ended in divorce on 18 Jan. 1765 (Certificate of Divorce, C 1324).

[8] Leopold III Friedrich Franz (1740–1817) had succeeded his father as reigning Prince of Anhalt-Dessau in 1751. The Prince travelled extensively during the years 1763–69 and in May 1767 returned from his second stay in England (ADB xviii. 356–59). So far, JB had travelled only once with the circuit court, which met at Glasgow on 11–16 Sept. 1766. Possibly Prince Leopold or Sir Harry had heard JB defend John Reid on 12 Sept. (From John Reid, 13 Nov. 1766, n. 1).

[9] JB received the standish on 11 May (Journ.).

To Jean-Jacques Rousseau, c. mid-April 1767

Not reported. See From William Fitzherbert, 17 Apr.: 'I deliver'd the Letter for Mr. Rousseau which you sent me to Mr. Davenport'.

To John Chalmer, c. mid-April 1767

Not reported. See From Chalmer, 22 Apr.: 'Your kind and obliding favour's I received'. At the same time as this letter JB sent a large bundle of legal papers.

To Sir Alexander Dick, Thursday 16 April 1767

MS. J. S. H. Fogg Collection, #420, Vol. 26, Maine Historical Society.

ADDRESS: To Sir Alexander Dick of Prestonfield, Baronet, near Edinburgh.

ENDORSEMENT: Sieur Boswell.

Auchinleck, 16 April 1767

MY DEAR SIR: Your favour of —— gave me much pleasure.[1] I was long of hearing from you, and began to think you waited for a letter from me, which you should not have wanted long. However, you have been better.

You are really an Aquatic Knight. As to the Earl, we may use the old Proverb, 'Let the galled Horse go wince'.[2] But we must not let him go till He[3] pays the Bill.

I have read many Essays in the News Papers about your Canal. No doubt the small one would be a dangerous Monopoly. But I confess I who can have no interest either way, am for the large one because of it's beauty and magnificence. We want such things in this northern Country, to keep a little ballance with our opulent neighbours. Let us improve this season of trade and riches and get some noble works done in Scotland which no Fanatics can have any pretence or even inclination to destroy.

I was made very happy by a long letter from Sir John Dick. He talks of you as if He had fished on your lake, drank your Curran Wine and enjoyed your classical conversation all his life. I have the merit of making You and him acquainted, and I flatter myself we shall have some elegant days with him, this summer. He is to be in London by the end of this month where I am to write to him. We must if possible contrive it so that when He returns to the court of Florence He may be Signor Cavaliere. He tells me a Title is now of some consequence there. For the Grand Duke has introduced all the Austrian Etiquette.

I have written a great part of my Account of Corsica. I am animated by the late accounts from my brave friends, who h⟨ave m⟩ade a descent on the Is⟨land o⟩f Capraia. It is a Min⟨orc⟩a to them.[4] I am very impatient for farther intelligence.

I go this forenoon to Cumnock, to bid at the sale of the Lands of Dalblair. If they are sold reasonably, I shall buy them. I want a sinking fund for my Consultation Guineas; and to follow your humour of punning, *Fundus* is certainly a fund, and as a great part of it is wet and mossy it may well be called a *sinking* fund.[5] With my best Compliments to Lady Dick and your good family,[6] I am ever, My Dear Sir, affectionately yours,

JAMES BOSWELL

We are much concerned for worthy Mr. Frazer. It is happy that he is so well. But I fear He will hardly be with us at Auchinleck.

My Father joins me in cordial salutations. He is also very happy to think of seeing our Leghorn Friend *Consul venit*.[7]

[1] JB forgot to fill in the gap in the MS. with '10 April'. Sir Alexander had written last on 17 Dec. 1766.

[2] Several proverbial expressions have to do with the 'wincing' or 'winching' ('kicking') of a 'galled' ('sore' or 'chafed') horse: see OED, 'Wince' v.[1] I. 1. and 'Winch' v.[1] 2. b. The closest analogue we have found to the proverb as given here is *Hamlet* III. ii. 242–43, 'Let the gall'd jade winch, our withers are unwrung', i.e., we do not care about pain that we do not feel ourselves.

[3] MS. 'He' superimposed upon 'the'

[4] Minorca had been ceded to Great Britain by the Treaty of Paris in 1763. Presumably the similarity between Capraia and Minorca JB has in mind is that both were strategically important islands in the Mediterranean.

[5] JB bought Dalblair for £2,410, a price he considered quite reasonable, as the bidding had started at £2,000 (Journ. 16 Apr.; *Earlier Years*, p. 325). A 'sinking fund' is 'a fund formed by periodically setting aside revenue to accumulate at interest', and 'sinking', applied to a piece of ground, means 'soft, yielding' (OED, 'sinking fund', 'sinking' ppl. a. 1. a). One of the senses of Latin *fundus* (from which English 'fund' is derived) is 'farm'.

[6] For Lady Dick, Sir Alexander's second wife, and Janet, the elder daughter of his first marriage, see From Sir A. Dick, 22 Aug. 1766, n. 2. Other children included Janet's younger sister Anne (now about 8) and the children of Sir Alexander's second marriage, William (4), Elizabeth (3), and Mary (11 months). John would be born in June, Margaret in 1771, and Robert-Keith in 1773 (*Scots Charta Chest*, p. 186; *Scots Mag.* 1764,

xxvi. 166, 1766, xxviii. 223, 1771, xxxiii. 53). Sir Alexander's nieces Janet and Catherine Douglas also lived at Prestonfield (From Sir A. Dick, 15 Aug. and n. 4).

[7] Cicero's *Orationes Philippicae* xi. 25: 'Quando enim veniet consul'. Hoping for one of the consuls to lead troops against Antony and Dolabella, Cicero asks: 'For when will a consul come?' JB uses the phrase again in his 21 Aug. letter to Sir Alexander.

From William Fitzherbert,[1] Friday 17 April 1767

MS. Yale (C 1265).

ADDRESS: To James Boswell Esqr. at Auchinleak, County of Ayr, N. Britain.

FRANK: Wm. Fitzherbert.

POSTMARKS: [London] 18 AP; FREE; JO.[2]

London, Ap'll. 17th, 1767

SIR: I deliver'd the Letter for Mr. Rousseau which you sent me to Mr. Davenport who will take care that He has it imediately.[3] I am, Sir, your most Obedient, Humble Servant,

WM. FITZHERBERT

[1] William Fitzherbert (1712–72), M.P. for Derby, 1762–72, and Commissioner of Trade and Plantations, 1765–72, had offered housing to Rousseau after his arrival in England with David Hume in Jan. 1766. When Hume told Rousseau that Fitzherbert's sister lived in the house offered him, Rousseau declined Fitzherbert's offer and, instead, accepted Richard Davenport's offer of his house at Wootton in Staffordshire (*New*

Hume Letters, pp. 132, 163–64; *Corres. Rousseau* xxix. 66–67).

[2] Partly illegible. Presumably the initials of the postal receiver, which would indicate where the letter was posted (Hendy, pp. 50–51, 58–60).

[3] Rousseau was still at Richard Davenport's estate in Staffordshire, but by 22 May he had fled England for France (*Corres. Rousseau* xxxiii. 75–78).

To Robert Dundas, Saturday 18 April 1767

MS. Yale (L 481).

HEADING: To My Lord President.

Auchinleck, 18 April 1767

MY DEAR LORD: I have had the honour of your Lordship's letter, and thankfully acknowledge the indulgence you have shewn me as a Father Confessor. I believe you would make as good a Pope as You do a President. You may be sure I shall carefully observe your Ghostly advices, which are perfectly sound.

I trust however that your Lordship will be with us. If you do not come, It will be a severer pennance than any you could have imposed upon me. You have allways been very carefull of my Father in matters of consequence. You must also contribute to his happiness upon this occasion. Recollect how distrest he was honest Man little more than a year ago, and how wonderfully he is now recovered, and rejoice his heart with your presence, when He holds his Circuit at his own County-Town.[1] He expects not only My Lady President, but also Miss Dundas, and it would divert You to see with what a hearty satisfaction He is taking care to provide you in good lodgings, good entertainment and good Company.[2] Pray then, do not dissappoint him.

Your Lordship does right to mind your health. The Douglas Cause lies heavy on this Vacation. Such *longa negotia* must follow you to Arniston, and disturb You in the enjoyment of your *venafra nos agros*.[3] My Father has been very busy with the Douglas Cause; and as a Relaxation has read Don Quixote. Whether there be any thing allegorical in this, or which of the Parties he takes to be fighting with Windmills, I leave to Your Lordship to judge.[4]

I have just now bought a little Estate of about £100 a year, to be a sinking fund for my Consultation-Guineas. What shall we say of this World? when an idle, dissipated, run-away fellow whom Your Lordship knows, will appear in the Charter Chest of his Family, to have been a sedate, diligent young Man, buying land before He had been a year an Advocate.[5] I shall not however be felonious enough to be a severe Father; especially if your Lordship lives to bear Witness against me.

I beg leave to offer my best Compliments to Mrs. Dundas and to the Young Ladies. I ever am with great respect and the warmest regard, My Dear Lord, Your Lordship's most obliged, humble Servant,

JAMES BOSWELL

[1] Lord Auchinleck was to go the Southern Circuit with Lord Kames. They were in Jedburgh on 6 May, in Dumfries on 13 May, and in Lord Auchinleck's 'own County-Town' of Ayr on 21 May (*Scots Mag.* 1767, xxix. 324).

[2] The oldest unmarried daughter was Henrietta (c. 1749–1832), daughter of the Lord President and his first wife Henrietta Carmichael Baillie (d. 1755), of Lamington. In 1777 Henrietta married Capt. Adam Duncan, who eventually earned flag rank and a peerage for his naval exploits (*Gent. Mag.* 1832, cii. 657; George W. T. Omond, *The Arniston Memoirs*, 1887, pp. 114–115, 189, 252). On 12 Jan. JB recorded his approval of and sympathy for Miss Dundas: 'Miss D. fine girl—lik'd her very well—was retenu for fear of appearing Lover—quite proper—was really sorry to think of her and her sister who might perhaps become maiden Aunts' (Journ.).

[3] Horace, *Odes* III. v. 53–56: 'quam si clientum longa negotia / diiudicata lite relinqueret, / tendens Venafranos in agros / aut Lacedaemonium Tarentum'; '[not otherwise] than if some case in court had been decided, and he were leaving the tedious business of his clients, speeding to Venafran fields, or to Lacedaemonian Tarentum' (Loeb ed. trans. C. E. Bennett). Venafrum (now Venafro) was a town in Campania. JB used the phrase again later (1782), to describe Burke's country estate of Gregories, near Beaconsfield (GBM, p. 125).

[4] On 27 Mar. while JB was working on *Corsica*, Lord Auchinleck studied the Memorials for the defendants in the Douglas Cause and at intervals read *Don Quixote*. He was 'much entertained' with the Don, and he called JB's *Corsica* 'Quixotism' (Journ.). Margaret Boswell's catalogue of the Auchinleck library (c. 1783–C 437.6) records a copy of *Don Quixote* in four volumes; this may be a printing of one of the popular eighteenth-century translations such as Charles Jervas's of 1742 or Tobias Smollett's of 1755. Since Lord Auchinleck took Archibald Douglas's side when the vote was taken on 14 July, he presumably would have thought of the Duke of Hamilton as Don Quixote.

[5] For JB's purchase of Dalblair, see To Sir Alexander Dick, 16 Apr. and n. 5.

To John Dick, Wednesday 22 April 1767

Not reported. See From Dick, 11 May: 'On my arrival here on Saturday last I found myself favour'd with your very kind, and oblig. Letter of the 22 April'.

From John Chalmer,[1] Wednesday 22 April 1767

MS. Yale (C 777).

ADDRESS: To James Boswell Esquire, Advocate, at Auchinleck House, Ayr.

POSTMARK: [Edinburgh] AP 22.

Edinr. 22 Aprile 1767

DEAR SIR: Your kind and oblidging favour's I received; The great Bundle containing Steele's Answer and Gilkies Information I only got from your Brother on Monday last which was sent to him under Commissioner Cochrane's Cover, in consequence of a Letter I wrote to John Boswell[2] on Thursday[3] last, after waiting with great impatience, and tribulation of mind; For if I had not received these papers at that very time—I could not have got them before the end of this week; by which a fine of Two pounds Str. on each would have been incurrd; And you know well that the President and Lord Auchinleck love to exact Fines for the sake of the Poor, a commendable Disposition I must own, Providing the Agent received no Rubs at the Barr. I dont mean the Lawier; for he always does his Duty, and which the Court are very sensible of.

Immediatly upon receiving yours I carried our answer to the Printing house and am just after writing this, going to read over the Proof Copy—I observe you have been a little merry in your Answer to the Petition;[4] I suppose we shall have a little Fun at the Barr at advising, particularly from Lords G. and M., who know the Nature of Horses particularly the last, who is a mighty Hunter.[5] As for the first he always rides on a Horse like Sancho Pancho's—But what will be the Countenance of Grave Claudius at advising; in short I beleive his Face will be an Ell long with laughing and Surprise—So much for Joacks.[6]

Gilkie being out of Town I carried his Bundle to the Printer, and gave him particular Instructions about the printing.

I would have been in the Countrey er this time, but have been confined with a most severe Cold. I hope Lord Auchinleck is well—Excuse haste. I am, Dear Sir, Your most obedient, humble Servant,

JOHN CHALMER

[1] John Muir Chalmer (1726–74), W.S., had succeeded to Gadgirth, Ayrshire, in 1764 (*Writers to the Signet*; *Ayr and Wigton* I. i. 237). JB's Consultation Book shows that Chalmer was the agent in Smith *v*. Steel; presumably he was also the agent in Gilkie *v*. Wallace (From Alexander Farquhar, 30 Mar. and n. 3; From James Gilkie, 4 Apr. and n. 1).

[2] 'Young Knockroon', writer in Ayr (To the Duchess of Douglas, 13 Oct. 1766, headnote and n. 2).

[3] MS. 'Saturday' deleted before 'Thursday'

[4] In his Answer to Smith's Petition, JB jokes about the names of the principals in the cause, finding it ironic that Steel should have the better of Smith, and quotes an epigram on Stephen the fiddler ('Stephen beat Time, / Now Time beats Stephen'). He characterizes Smith as 'a blade

now who rides you about . . . vapouring . . . having often with him a stoned horse [i.e. a stallion] . . . and never wanting a box of pepper in his pocket'. He lightheartedly compares the constitution of horses to that of men, and denounces 'the tricks of jockeys' (i.e. horse-dealers), who are notorious for practising fraud (Sidney Ives, 'Boswell Argues a Cause: Smith, Steel, and "Actio Redhibitoria"', *Eighteenth-Century Studies in Honor of Donald F. Hyde*, 1970, pp. 258–62).

[5] John Kay portrays Lord Gardenstone as 'a very timid horseman, mounted, moreover, on a jaded old hack, which he had selected for its want of spirit'. In contrast, James Burnett (1714–99), Lord Monboddo, is remembered for making his annual journeys to London on horseback and for scorning the carriage as 'an effete innovation of the Moderns' (J. Kay, *A Series of Original Portraits*,

ed. Hugh Paton, 1877, i. 20–22; *Later Years*, p. 46). Ramsay of Ochtertyre reports that Monboddo loved 'hunting and other manly exercises' (*Scotland and Scotsmen*, i. 351). Chalmer's description of Monboddo as 'a mighty Hunter' echoes Genesis 10: 9, 'Nimrod the mighty hunter'.

[6] Claud Boswell (From George Frazer, 4 Apr. 1766, n. 3) was 'a very good kind of man, but not particularly quick in the perception of the ludicrous' (*Original Portraits* i. 126).

From Richard Edwards, Friday 24 April 1767

Not reported. See From Edwards, 26 June: 'I had the Honour to write you the 24th April last'.

From Mrs. Dodds, c. Saturday 25 April 1767

Not reported. See Journ. 27 Apr.: 'after dinner I got a letter from —— that the *Black Boy* etc.' The remainder of the entry shows that Mrs. Dodds (JB's mistress in Edinburgh) was announcing her pregnancy.

To Robert Brown, Tuesday 28 April 1767

Not reported. See Journ. 28 Apr.: 'At night I received a Packet of papers brought from Holland by Captain Kinloch. But my Journal was amissing. . . . I wrote immediately to Mr. Brown at Utrecht, and to Mr. Kinloch of Gilmerton the Captain's Father.'

To David Kinloch, Tuesday 28 April 1767

Not reported. See To Robert Brown, 28 Apr. David Kinloch (c. 1710–95) of Gilmerton, Haddingtonshire, later (1778) Bt. was the father of Lt. Archibald Kinloch, who delivered the packet of papers from which JB's Dutch journal was missing (From Robert Brown, 27 Jan. and n. 3; Journ. 28 Apr.).

To John Wilkie, Tuesday 28 April 1767

Not reported. See From Wilkie, 7 May: 'I yesterday received your favor of the 28 last Month; and I hope you will accept my thanks for your promise of making use of me as your publisher.' On 24 Apr. the printer Robert Foulis had written with instructions to get 'Mr. Wilkie or Davies' to enter *Dorando* at Stationers' Hall. JB chose Wilkie as primary publisher of that work (*Lit. Car.* pp. 27–28).

From Thomas Davies, Tuesday 28 April 1767

MS. Yale (C 899).
ADDRESS: To James Boswell Esqr. of Auchenleck, at Edinburgh.
POSTMARK: [London] 28 AP; WM.[1]

London, April 28, 1767

DEAR SIR: I received the books from Glasgow and wait only for the Inscriptions that I may pack them up and send them away according to your order.[2] Dr. Johnson I hope I may venture to say will write to you very soon.[3] All your Friends are extremely happy to hear of your close application to business. One day we hope you will make a distinguished figure in the British Senate. May Your Country[4] join the name of Patriot to that of distinguish'd Orator and experienced Legislator.

I shall publish very soon the 2 first vols. of Hooles Translation of Metastasio.[5] I shall take the Liberty to send you them and should be glad to have your opinion. I hope you will find it a good Translation.

I am just now publishing a 3d Edition of the Idler with additional Essays.[6]

Your Freind Love's Brother has produced a very considerable picture on the subject of Timon of Athens[7] and is one of the most distinguished of those in our last Exhibition of the Artists.[8] Mrs. Davies desires her best respects. I am, Dear Sir, Your most obedient, humble Servant,

THOMAS DAVIES

[1] Probably the initials of the receiver; see From W. Fitzherbert, 17 Apr. n. 2.

[2] For JB's project of sending books to Paoli, see From Davies, 21 Aug. 1766 and n. 8.

[3] SJ did not write to JB until 23 Mar. 1768 (*Life* ii. 58).

[4] MS. 'Your Country will' altered to 'May Your Country'

[5] John Hoole (1727–1803), *The Works of Metastasio, Translated from the Italian*, 2 vols. 1767. No more of this edition was published, though an enlarged edition (3 vols.) appeared in 1800. SJ wrote the dedication of the 1767 edition (*Life* iv. 360, n. 1).

[6] *The Idler By the Author of The Rambler. . . . The Third Edition with Additional Essays*, 1767.

[7] MS. 'on the subject of Timon of Athens' written above deleted 'much approved'

[8] For James Love, see From Francis Gentleman, 26 Apr. 1766, n. 2. Nathaniel Dance (1735–1811) exhibited 'Timon of Athens' from Shakespeare's *Timon of Athens* IV. iv. for the Society of Artists. After a distinguished career as a painter he retired in 1790 and entered Parliament under the name of Dance-Holland. He was created Baronet in 1800 (*The Society of Artists of Great Britain 1760–1791*, ed. Algernon Graves, 1907, p. 70).

From Count Antonio Rivarola, Saturday 2 May 1767

MS. Yale (C 2391)

ADDRESS: A Monsieur, Monsieur Boswel d'Auchinlek, à Edimbourg, par Londres.

POSTMARK: DE TURIN.

Torino, 2 Maggio 1767

MONSIEUR BOSWEL RIVERITISSIMO: Ho ricevuta ieri la gratma. sua de' 14. Marzo scorso, e mi ha fatto specie riconoscere da essa, che Ella non abbia avuta la lettera che le ho già scritto da quì risponsiva all'altra sua in cui accusava i fogli che le mandai da Livorno nello scorso Settembre. Glie l'ho mandata per la Posta ugualmente che fò di questa, la quale se mi avvedo che non le pervenga, cambierò registro, e glie le farò passare per mano di un nostro Savojardo che è in codesta Città nominato M. Despines.

Le acchiusemi tanto allora che adesso, si incamminano da me puntualmte. a chi vanno; ed oggi stesso mando quella che ricevo per la via di Francia.

Ella saprà che i Corsi il dì 17. di Marzo anno sorpresa l'Isola de Capraja, e Padroni di tutto bloccavano la Fortezza, la quale agli avvisi che ho, deve essersi resa il dì 18. di Aprile, mentre sento che dal Capocorso si erano veduti due fuochi, che doveano essere il segno della resa della Fortezza, giacchè il mare tempestoso non lasciava partir bastimenti, nel tempo stesso che avea dispersi i Genovesi che vi erano attorno.

Credo che Mylord Chatham avrà avuta una memoria dal nostro Amico, che deve averne dirette a tutte le Corti: se Egli vuole, anche senza i torbidi puol giovare; pure almeno avesse memoria di chi pena a tempo proprio, che forse non avrebbe ad essere molto lontano.

Vorrei essere a luogo da poterla servire sulle richieste che mi fà; ma poichè ciò che me chiede dalla Corsica, bisogna farlo da colà venire, ne scrivo al medmo. Generale per vedere se Egli puol provvedermi tutto.

Sò che in Livorno vi è una moneta d'argento del Rè Teodoro, ma chi l'ha, non credo che voglia disfarsene per così poco. Io l'ho veduta ed è delle vere, benchè non è bene impressa a motivo che il conio vi è stato applicato doppiamente. Ne coniò Egli tanto poche, che andarono a volo per l'Europa, e si pagavano fino a quattro zecchini l'una. Da quì nacque che a Napoli, facendosene un traffico, vi fù chi ne fece battere, e col valore di due scelini di argento, ne ricavava d'ognuna venti volte più. Di queste pure coniate a Napoli ne è una in Livorno in un Museo, ma chi l'ha non la darebbe certamente via.

La distinzione che è fra queste due qualità di monete è, che le vere anno in una parte l'arme del Regno e della Casa di Newhof, e dall'altra la Concezione di Maria Vergine, e le fatte a Napoli anno le stesse armi da una parte, e dall'altra il busto di Teodoro.

Non so se partiro da qui in breve; ma o Ella diregga le sue quì, o le diregga a Livorno, le ricevero sempre, e con piacere gradirò l'onore de suoi commandi mentre mi troverà sempre Suo vero Amico e Servitore,

RIVAROLA

[MOST ESTEEMED MONSIEUR BOSWELL: Yesterday I received your most welcome letter of March 14th last, and I was distressed to learn that you have not received the letter I sent from here in response to your acknowledgement of the papers I sent you from Leghorn last September. I sent it to you by post just as I shall do with the present letter, so that if I find out that it hasn't reached you, I shall change course, and have my letters carried by one of our Savoyards, who goes in that city by the name of M. Despines.[1]

I have continued to be prompt in forwarding enclosed materials, and this very day I shall send on what I have received through France.[2] You probably know that on March 17th the Corsicans made a surprise attack on the island of Capraia, gained the upper hand and blockaded the Fortress. According to the news I have heard, it must have surrendered on April 18th. Two fires seen from the Capo Corso must have been the signal of the surrender of the Fortress, as the sea was so tempestuous that no ships were able to get away, and at the same time the Genoese in the area would have been scattered.[3]

I believe my Lord Chatham has received a report from our friend, who has no doubt circulated it among all the Courts. If he wishes, he can be of help without stirring things up; if only he would at least bear in mind, at the appropriate time, who is in difficulties, then perhaps he would not have to keep his distance.

I wish I were able to satisfy your request; but since what you ask me for must come from Corsica, I shall write to the General himself to see if he can get it for me. I know that there is a silver coin of King Theodore in Leghorn, but I don't think the owner would part with it for so little. I have seen it and it is genuine, but it is not well minted because the stamp has been applied twice. Very few of them were coined, and they circulated very quickly throughout Europe, fetching up to four sequins apiece. Because of this they started up a trade in these coins in Naples, minting them for a value of two silver Shillings, and thus making a twentyfold profit. There is one of these Neapolitan coins in a museum in Leghorn, but the owner would certainly not give it away.

The distinction that can be made between these two coins is that the genuine ones have on one side the arms of the Kingdom and of the House of Newhoff, and on the other the Conception of the Virgin Mary. The Neapolitan coins have the same coats of arms on one side and on the other a bust of Theodore.[5]

I do not know whether I shall be leaving here soon, but whether you address your letters to me here or to Leghorn I shall get them all the same. I will honour your commands with pleasure, and remain, as ever, your faithful friend and servant.][6]

[1] Possibly Joseph Despine (1737–1830), born at Le Châtelard, Savoy, who received a doctorate from the University of Turin in 1769 and embarked upon a distinguished medical career that included service as physician to the royal family of Savoy (DBF).

[2] Not reported; presumably Corsican Gazettes being sent to JB's banker in Paris to be forwarded to Edinburgh or Auchinleck.

[3] The citadel did not fall until 28 May (Gent. Mag. 1767, xxxvii. 326).

[4] Rivarola presumably refers to Paoli's general 'Memoria del Governo de Corsica ai Sovrani di Europa,' dated 31 Jan. He may not have known that Chatham had received a personal letter, also dated 31 Jan., from Paoli addressing the same grievances (To Chatham, 8 Apr. n. 5).

[5] JB was much interested in coins. In Gotha, 20 Oct. 1764, he had written: 'I am somewhat of a Virtuoso. Wherever I am, I make a collection of the silver specie struck the year in which I have

been in the country' (Journ.). JB used much of Rivarola's information about King Theodore's silver coins in Corsica (p. 103), and he mentioned that he himself owned one of Theodore's copper coins. Theodore's mint was headed by a forger named 'Seven Brains', who made only two or three silver coins but a number of copper ones. The Naples type far exceeded in number the original coins minted in Corsica (Valerie Pirie, His Majesty of Corsica, 1939, pp. 316–18). Both the originals and the Naples type are pictured in André Le Glay, Théodore de Neuhoff, 1907, opposite p. 88. In Corsica (pp. 101–08) JB also describes the reign of Théodore von Neuhoff, the adventurer who persuaded the Corsicans to make him their king in 1736 (Le Glay, pp. 16, 43, 55). His tenure was brief, and he died shortly after his release from debtors' prison in England. His epitaph was composed by Horace Walpole.

[6] Translation by Caterina Bosio and Ian Duncan.

From Francis Ashbury,[1] Sunday 3 May 1767

MS. Yale (C 42).

ADDRESS: To James Boswell Esq., at [Edinburgh deleted; added in another hand] by Air.

[London] May 3d, 1767

SIR: An address to a Gentleman wholly unknown to me will I fear appear abrupt if not impertinent but Mr. Boswells known politeness flatters me with his pardon when I acquaint him with the reason for takeing this liberty. The public has been inform'd Sir, long ago of your travels into Italy and your reception in the Island of Corsica by the heroic General of that brave people. Before I add any thing farther Sir permit me to inform you that I am a Lieutt. in the Royal Navy without hopes of preferment or employment.[2] In such a situation Sir I am in a manner sold to the government (for better I cannot consider myself whilst the most active part of my life is likely to be spun out in a scanty pittance of half pay).[3] You percieve I doubt not Sir, by this time that I aim at offering my service to his excellency General

Paoli as a sea Officer but am totaly unacquainted as to the mode of application. To your goodness Sir my inexperience directs me for information how to apply. I am aware Sir of a proclamation to the contrary but believe that might be obviated as the government seems tacitly to favor the noble struggle those brave Islanders have made this thirty years past for their liberty. Unacquainted as I am with Mr. Boswell how shall I hope for his advice and assistance other than from his known politeness. Your address, Sir, I am furnish'd with from St. Pauls Church Yard.[4] Any the least information or assistance will be most gratefully acknowledg'd address'd to Lieut. Francis Ashbury at Major McDonald's in Lawrence Street Chelsea.[5] Allow me Sir to add to you that I have serv'd in the Royal Navy fifteen years ten of which as Midshipman and Mate the rest in the Rank I at present hold best part of which to my excessive mortification has been spent in a sordid retirement on the scanty appointments of half pay. It will perhaps be necessary to add Sir that I am now twenty nine Years of Age. I am, Sir, with the most perfect respect Your Obedient, Humble Servant,

FRANS. ASHBURY

[1] Francis Ashbury (b. c. 1738) received his lieutenant's commission in the Royal Navy on 27 Dec. 1762 (Sea Officers i. 21). He appears in the navy lists of the Royal Kalendar and the Court and City Register from 1763 to 1770.
[2] Promotion in the Royal Navy depended on a combination of patronage, seniority, and talent (N. A. M. Rodger, The Wooden World: An Anatomy of the Georgian Navy, 1986, pp. 273–302). The Seven Years' War had produced a large crop of lieutenants who ranked both in wartime experience and seniority above those, like Ashbury, who had been commissioned after the peace preliminaries of Oct. 1762. Preferment within this group was not impossible, however. Of the thirty lieutenants commissioned between Nov. 1762 and Dec. 1763 (Court and City Register, 1766, p. 218), eleven reached the rank of commander, six became captains, one was pensioned off as a Rear Admiral, and one reached the rank of Vice-Admiral of the White. Eighteen never attained a rank above lieutenant (Sea Officers, vols.

i–iii, s.v. names listed in Court and City Register).
[3] The daily wage for a lieutenant on active service in 1766 ranged from 4s. to 5s. (Court and City Register, 1766, p. 223). The Admiralty recognized the inadequacy of half-pay and allowed officers on half-pay to join civilian ships' crews. By the end of 1764, a total of 120 lieutenants had gone to sea on merchant ships and other trading vessels. The Admiralty also allowed officers on half-pay to serve in the navies of foreign powers friendly to Britain (Rodger, p. 269).
[4] JB was writing numerous articles on Corsica for Lond. Chron., published in St. Paul's Churchyard by John Wilkie (Lit. Car. pp. 237–39; Earlier Years, pp. 266–68, 304–08).
[5] Presumably James McDonald (d. 1773) of Chelsea, whose obituaries describe him as 'formerly an officer in the Scots Greys', i.e. the Second Regiment of Dragoons (Gent. Mag. 1773, xliii. 255; Scots Mag. 1773, xxxv. 278). An obituary of his widow, Jemima, describes him as 'Major M. late of Chelsea' (Gent. Mag. 1790, lx. 376).

From Girolama Piccolomini, Sunday 3 May 1767

MS. Yale (C 2260).

ADDRESS: James Boswell Esqr., at Edimburg, by London; [added] by Air, From Wakefield.

POSTMARKS: WAKEFIELD: [London] MA 22, 29 MA.

Siena, 3 Maggio 1767

MONSIEUR: Questa è la prima lettera che ricevo da voi doppo che siete in Iscozia, e non ho ricevute altre lettere come mi accennate nella vostra del 25 di marzo, della quale vi rendo mille grazie per avermi assicurata della vostra carissima amicizia, e per avermi cavata da una grand'impazienza di saper le vostre nuove; tantochè doppo di avere aspettate per lungo tempo vostre lettere, mi risolvetti di scrivervi che sarà un mese e l'indirizzai al vostro Banchiere di Parigi; Eccoci dunque giustificati per rapporto alla nostra amicizia, ed io potrei egualmente giustificarmi in genere di galanteria, poichè passo il mio tempo sens'avere un attacco di cuore e molto meno amo la debosche, ma tutto questo a voi non importa nulla, mentre per vostra confessione voi siete immerso nel vizio, ed il piacere del senso vi trasporta, senza lasciarvi gustare quei sentimenti di delicatezza che convengono e che sono il condimento di tutti i piaceri; ma io non voglio fare la predicante, perchè tanto non vi persuaderei credendomi troppo interessata nel persuadervi.

Le mie nuove sono buone per la mia salute, riguardo alla compagnia ci viene sempre la stessa, alla riserva di Placidi, che mi lascio doppo la vostra partenza di Siena. In questo inverno vi è stato un Baron Tedesco, il quale veniva sempre da me, ma non vi è stato che un principio di galanteria. Il nostro Turno grosso si mantiene nell'istesso piede, e la Porzia è gravida; voi venè maraviglierete come se ne maraviglia tutto il mondo ma il fatto è questo.

Mercoledi vengono i nostri Sovrani, chè si tratterranno fino al 18, ed in questi giorni avremo gran Forestieri, e gran feste per quello, che può fare la nostra Città. Sicuramente voglio il vostro ritratto, e con me non si promette sensa mantenerlo, così potessi farvi mantere la parola di amarmi? Ma gli assenti anno sempre torto, e con voi forse anno torto anche i presenti. Mi sono molto meravigliata di vedere, che voi scrivete italiano ed anche meglio di quando partiste; questo mi fa credere, che voi abbiate di doppo studiato, ò pure che siate in commercio con qualchè italiana, sicchè vi prego di schiarirmi su questo punto. Mandai all'Abaté Crocchi il vostro indirizzo accio me lo facesse in un foglio per non essere sicura di farlo bene da me; egli lo copiò e emendò dove gli pareva che non fosse esatto, e m'impose di farvi mille complimenti da sua parte; Tiburzio ancora vi rende grazie della memoria che tenete di esso, e spesse volte si parla di voi con Tiburzio, come ancora fanno tutti gli miei amici, che si recordano di voi con tutto il piacere, giacchè è impossibile l'avervi conosciuto sensa conservarne una vivissima memoria.

La vostra lettera mi pervenne con sicurezza però potete conservare lo stesso metodo per farmele recapitare, ma non rammentate le cose con tanta chiarezza poichè si potrebbero perdere, e seguire ancora molti casi, che per mancanza di carta tralascio. Ricordatevi di me, e comandatemi se volete che lo creda.

[Sir: This has been the first letter I have received from you since your return to Scotland. I did not receive any of the others you mention in yours of 25 March. I give you a thousand thanks for assuring me of your friendship which is so dear to me, and for having freed me from a great impatience to hear from you. After having waited for letters from you for a long time, I decided to write to you about a month ago, and addressed the letter to your banker at Paris.[1]

So here we are, both justified in regard to our friendship. I am equally justified in regard to gallantry, for I lead my life without any tender attachment, and still less do I care for casual encounters. But all this will mean nothing to you, since by your own confession you are sunk in vice, transported by sensual pleasure, unable to taste those feelings of delicacy which are seemly and which are the spice of all pleasures.[2] But I do not wish to play the preacher, and in any case I could not persuade you, for you think me too interested in the result.

I can give good reports of myself so far as my health is concerned. As to the company that comes here, it is always the same, except for Placidi, who left me after your departure from Siena.[3] Last winter a German baron, who was visiting here, came to see me all the time, but the gallantry between us did not go beyond the preliminaries. Our *turno grosso* continues on the same footing. Porzia is pregnant; this will surprise you as it surprises everyone, but it is a fact.[4]

Our sovereigns arrive on Wednesday and will stay until the 18th. During that time we expect to have important foreign visitors and the most splendid festivities that our city can arrange.[5]

Certainly I wish for your portrait. One does not promise, as far as I am concerned, without keeping one's word. If only in like manner I could make you keep your promise to love me! But he who is absent is always wrong, and with you perhaps, he who is present is wrong, too. I am greatly surprised to see that you write Italian, and even write it better than when you left. This makes me suspect that you have studied the language further, or that you are carrying on an intrigue with some Italian girl. I beg you to enlighten me on this point. I sent your address to Abbé Crocchi so that he could write it out for me on a piece of paper, as I was not sure I had done it correctly by myself. He copied it and corrected it where he thought it inaccurate, and asked me to send you his very best regards. Tiburzio thanks you again for remembering him, and very often we talk of you with Tiburzio, as do all my friends, who remember you with much pleasure.[6] It is impossible to have known you without remembering you vividly.

Your letter came safely to my hands, so you can continue to use the same method for getting future letters delivered to me. But do not recall things so openly, for the letters might get lost, and many other accidents might follow, which I do not mention for lack of space. Remember me, and write, if you wish me to believe that you do.][7]

[1] See To John Waters, 10 May 1766.

[2] Presumably JB had confessed his relationship with Mrs. Dodds, his mistress in Moffat, for whom he had taken a house in Edinburgh (To Temple, 1 Feb.–8 Mar., 30 Mar.).

[3] Placido Placidi (b. 1729) was the son of Cavaliere Girolamo di Luzio Placidi and Teresa di Stefano Dei ('Nati e Battezzati, Maschi e Femmine di Famiglie Nobili Senesi', MS. Biblioteca Communale, Siena). He had been a member of Moma's circle of admirers in 1765, but on 12 Dec. of that year she wrote to JB: 'Placido comes very seldom, and I do not bother myself with winning him back' (From Piccolomini, 12 Dec. 1765, translation *Grand Tour II*, pp. 264–66).

[4] Porzia Sansedoni (1726–90), daughter of a nobleman, Niccolo Gori-Pannellini, had been married to Giovanni Ambrogio Sansedoni since 1746. In 1765, when JB attempted to seduce her, she was a mother of three. In Aug. 1767 she gave birth to twin boys, Ambroglio and Orazio ('Nati e Battezzati'; Death records, Archivio di Stato, Siena; To Sansedoni, various dates, Aug.–Sept. 1765, and From Sansedoni, 21 Sept. 1765, all

translated *Grand Tour II*, pp. 117–37).

[5] For this visit, see From Piccolomini, 20 Mar., n. 5.

[6] Tiburzio has not been identified with certainty. The name appears in JB's list of Siena acquaintances (M 110) just after that of Pandolfo Spannocchi, indicating, perhaps, that Tiburzio's family name was also Spannocchi. The only Tiburzio Spannocchi found in Siena records of the time is Pandolfo's first cousin (1707–80), the record of whose death reads 'nob. Sig. Abbate' ('Nati e Battezzati'; Death records, Siena). It is possible that this is the Tiburzio who appears in JB's 'Scena Sanese' (M 109; translated in *Grand Tour II*, pp. 122–23) and in the list of acquaintances, and the possibility is raised to likelihood by the apparent completeness of the Siena birth records. But if Tiburzio was a cleric in 1765, JB almost certainly would have said so, for he rarely omitted titles. It may be that the Tiburzio Spannocchi JB knew in Siena escaped mention in the birth records (being born elsewhere); or perhaps he became a cleric late in life.

[7] Translation by F. A. Pottle and Ian Duncan.

From John Wilkie, Thursday 7 May 1767

MS. Yale (C 3111).

ADDRESS: To James Boswell Esqr., at Auchenleck, County of Ayr, Scotland.

POSTMARK: [London] 7 MA.

London, May 7, 1767

SIR: I yesterday received your favor of the 28 last Month; and hope you will accept my thanks for your promise of making use of me as your publisher.

The method of entering Books at Stationers hall is as follows. Before one single Copy of your book is sold you must send Nine Copies to the Hall and give the Clerk 6d. for entering them on the Companys Book. This is the whole matter which I will execute for you as soon as I receive the Books—but great Care must be taken that not a Single Book is sold before the entry is made, for if upon any Litigation at law that coud be proved the whole woud be invalid.[1]

I communicated the Contents of your last letter to me on the Subject of the Corsican Gazzettes to the proprietors of the L. Chronicle at our last meeting, they desired me to thank you for Your several favors, and to accept of the Offer you make them of paying half the expence of the Corsican Papers. But wish at the same time you woud order them to be directed to me, here, which woud (I suppose) give[2] us an opportunity of having the Corsican News at least fourteen or fifteen days sooner than at present. And as Our Translater is always at hand, he coud make of them, and you might have them forwarded[3] to you the same day or the following for certainty.[4] I am, Sir, Your most Obedient, humble Servant,

JOHN WILKIE

[1] The printing of *Dorando* was now nearing completion; the Foulis brothers expected to have the whole set in type by 8 May (From Robert Foulis, 8 May). On 26 May 300 copies were shipped to Wilkie by sea; the nine copies for Stationers' Hall were shipped by land, presumably on or before that date (From Robert Foulis, 29 June). On 6 June Wilkie entered *Dorando* at Stationers' Hall, and on 15 June the book was published in Scotland. The advertisement in the *Caledonian Mercury* read, 'N. B. This tale is entered in Stationers-hall, so that whoever shall presume to reprint it, without license of the proprietor, shall be prosecuted with the utmost rigour of the laws' (*Lit. Car.* p. 35). Foulis's letter of 8 May shows his anxiety about securing the copyright of *Dorando*: 'There is a great chance of its being put into News-papers and Magazeens, and even of its being pirated'. However, no pirated editions were issued. See further From John Wilkie, 28 July.

[2] MS. 'gives'

[3] MS. 'forwarded' superimposed upon 'sent'

[4] In response to this request, JB asked John Dick to have Andrew Burnaby in Leghorn send the gazettes directly to Wilkie (From Dick, 17 June). But Wilkie later found that his editor did not know Italian sufficiently well to translate them, and asked JB to send them himself as before (From Wilkie, 28 July.)

From Patrick Preston,[1] Friday 8 May 1767

MS. Yale (C 2284).

NOTE at foot of page 2 of MS.: James Boswell Esqr.

London, 8th May 1767

MY DEAR JAMES: I did not neglect, immediatly after my Arrivall Here, to take the proper Steps to gett certain Information with regard to the Memorandum You gave me; this I found cou'd be done in no other way, than by examining[2] the Books of the East India House, where an Exact Register is kept, not only of the Names of every Person employed in their Service, or who resides in any of their Settlements, but of the Wills they make.

This Search cou'd not be made till lately, on Accot. of the great Struggles, which have been about the Choice of new Directors Gen. but is now done,[3] and as no such Name as that of Davd. Cass can be found, nor any Accot. of such a Will, I much fear Your Client has been imposed upon.[4]

I am in Hopes soon to have the Pleasure of seeing You in Scotland, in the mean Time beg You'll offer my best Respects to Your Father, and that You'll believe me ever very truely to be, My Dear Sir, Your most faithfull and most affectionate, Humble Servant,

P. PRESTON

[1] Patrick Preston (d. 1776) had been promoted to the rank of major in the 57th Foot on 6 May; he had held the army rank of major since 1762 (*Army List*, 1768). The eldest son of Sir George Preston of Valleyfield, Bt., and Anne, sister of JB's maternal grandmother Euphemia (Cochrane) Erskine, he was JB's first cousin once removed. Preston was trying to locate information for JB's client, James Windram.

[2] MS. 'examinining'

[3] The major issues in this election of directors were the East India Company's payment to the Government and the size of its dividend. Encouraged by the optimistic projections of increased revenue that followed Clive's assumption of the dewani (or chief financial office) of Bengal, the company faction led by Laurence Sulivan, M.P., had succeeded the year before in forcing an increase in dividend from 6% to 10%. Despite the backing of Chatham, however, Sulivan in March had failed to make the company raise the dividend another 4% and pay the Government £800,000 in return for the renewal of its charter and various trade concessions. In the hotly contested election of directors on 9 Apr. Sulivan's slate of candidates failed to oust the sitting directors, but the challenge had its effect: in June the company agreed to pay the Government £400,000 a year for two years, but won a statutory limitation of the dividend to 10% (Lucy S. Sutherland, *The East India Company in Eighteenth-Century Politics*, 1952, pp. 138–39).

[4] An extensive search of the East India Company records by Sally Hofmann in London (indexes of the Minutes of the Court of Directors, 1744–68, and of Home Letters Received, 1745–67) turned up no mention of a David Cass or any account of a legacy for JB's client. See From P. L. Dupont, 7 Apr. n. 4.

From John Dick, Monday 11 May 1767

MS. Yale (C 1015).

ADDRESS: To James Boswell Esqr. of Auchinleck, [Edenburgh *deleted, added in another hand*] by Air.

POSTMARK: [London] 12 M ⟨A⟩ .

London, 11th May 1767

MY DEAR SIR, On my arrival here on Saturday last I found myself favour'd with your very kind, and oblig. Letter of the 22 April, and this day I have receiv'd from Leghorn, your kind Letter of the 14 March.—Mr. Edwards my Vice Consul acquaints me, that he has taken proper care of your Packett for Count Reverola.

I am sorry that, I cannot yet send You an account of the Surrender of the Fortress of Capraia, The Revd. Mr. Andrew Burnaby, our worthy Chaplain, and Chargé[1] des Affaires of the Consulat, writes me the 24 of last Month, that the Blockade still continued.—I hope however that we shall soon hear of its' falling.

I have not faild to throw out several hints about a free Communication with the Island, and of the advantage it might be to our Trade, and I hope that I shall be able to do something. If I succeed I shall lett You know it.

I long much to see Your book publish'd,[2] I am certain it will take, You have one advantage that is, that every one is much prejudiced in favour of our Heroe—and pitty the poor people.

I am much obliged to Sir Alexr. for his goodness, pray present him, my most Respectfull Compliments. Make also my most friendly Compliments to our worthy friend Mr. Ferguson.[3] I wish I knew what methods are used, and where, to claim the Title, I have had some Registers from Northumberland, but one is yet wanting, I have wrote about it, but I am not certain if I shall be able to procure it, as they told me in a former Letter, that at the Place I orderd them to Search, there were no Registrs. further back than 40 years.—However, if our friend the good Bart. has no objection to it, I should imagine, that this difficulty may be gott over, expecially, as it is of little concequence, seeing I have no Children to Succeed to it.

You may talk this matter over as from your self, and lett me hear from You; I mean with Sir Alex. and Mr. Ferguson. I verily beleive there are several who have resumed titles of this nature who have not so good a right to them as I have to this. I cannot possitively say if I shall be able to make an excursion to You, but I will endeavour to do it, I shall have great pleasure in paying my Respects to You and our friend Ferguson, and of making a Personal Acquaintance with Sir Alexander, whose Charactr. I much admire.

Mrs. Dick Salutes You very kindly, and I have only time to repeat to You, what I hope You already know, that is that I ever am with unalterable Regard and Esteem, My dear Sir, Your most Obliged and Faithfull Servant,

JOHN DICK

[1] MS. 'my' deleted before 'Chargé'
[2] MS. 'publish'd' superimposed upon 'out'

[3] For James Ferguson, see From John Dick, 31 Oct. 1766, n. 3.

From Alexander Montgomerie-Cuninghame, Monday 11 May 1767

MS. Yale (C 2048).

ADDRESS: To James Boswell Esqr., Auchenleck.

Lainshaw, May 11, 1767

DEAR SIR: The bearer Currie—Can not loose his half Pay—he had better be hanged—the whole of them Says that they have Something more to Say for them selves—if You have Patience to hear them it will be Verrie Obligeing—and I am Certain You will do them all the good You Can.[1]

Best wishes to my good freind Lord Auchenleck and am, Dear Sir, Your Verrie humble Servant,

ALEXR. MONTGOMERY CUNINGHAM

[1] James Currie, out-pensioner of Chelsea Hospital, and five others were charged with leading a mob that had forced several Stewarton mealmongers to sell their meal, which had been

intended for export, locally. According to defence documents in the hand of the writer William Brown, the inhabitants of Stewarton had asked James Barclay, bailie of the town, 'to grant a warrant for bringing meal to the market place'. Barclay had passed the request on to the Justice of the Peace, Sir David Cuninghame of Corsehill, the neighbouring estate, who had agreed to grant it only if Captain Montgomerie-Cuninghame, his son and heir, would cosign. The riot broke out when Montgomerie-Cuninghame declined to act before obtaining legal advice (Papers relating to the case of the Stewarton Rioters—Lg 9). Two of the rioters absconded and were outlawed. JB represented the remaining four, who were tried before the Circuit Court of Justiciary at Ayr on 23 May; the jury found the charge against them 'not proven' (Court of Justiciary Records: South Circuit Minute Book, no. 12).

From Anne Mackintosh,[1] Tuesday 12 May 1767

MS. Yale (C 1845).

ADDRESS: To James Boswell Esquire, Advocate, at Auchinleck, by Edinburgh.

POSTMARK: INVERNESS.

Moyhall, May 12, 1767

DEAR SIR: I have not forgot ane Old Correspondent. And it was with Pleasure I hard of your Safe return to your Country wher I Sincerely wish you a happy and long life.

Your kind Enquiry about McIntosh is most Obligeing, Sorry am I to Say he is not so well as his friends could wish, The Numbness and Coldness still Continues in his Right Seed And Cold Sweets that has made him very Weak, God Preserve him to his Poor family and friends, I am much affraid of him.

The Good Siason comeing on is my only Comfort and hopes, hapy I am to hear your Worthy father is well. Real is the Meeting he has in McIntosh Affection and Mine.

He was So Good as Allow McIntosh to Name him to take Some Concern in the Affairs of the little that is left, of ane Old Opresed family.[2] And in your Absence your Nam was put in as a Real friend, As for how long may it be or we want your Assistance, But when we doe McIntosh desires me to tell you that he hope you will be the same to his Poor family As your Grand father:[3] And Father was, his own word: is, A Sincere Adviser; it will make McIntosh and me happy to See you in this House, what is it but a little jant to you. McIntosh joins me in Respects to my Lord and best wishes to you. And I am, Dear Sir, Your Most Obedient Servant,

A. MCINTOSH

You will not Read this scral, but I never have a Moment to write since McIntosh was hurt.[4] A. M.

[1] Anne Mackintosh (c. 1725–84), daughter of John Farquharson of Invercauld and Margaret Murray (granddaughter of John Murray, first Marquess of Atholl) in 1741 married Aeneas (or Angus) Mackintosh (d. 1770), twenty-second Chief of Clan Chattan. As the wife of a Highland chief, she was known as Lady Mackintosh (Scots Mag. 1770, xxxii. 398; 1784, xlvi. 167). In Aug. 1761 JB had written her a verse-epistle recalling their dancing together at the circuit ball in Inverness that spring and praising her husband's plainspoken honesty and his hospitality. She had replied on 22 Sept. 1761 with spirited verses of her own (Boswell's Book of Bad Verse, ed. Jack Werner, 1974, pp. 128–31, 199–200). This story is told in F. A. Pottle, 'Bozzy Was a Bold Young Blade: The Story of His Lady Mackintosh Episode', New York Times Book Review, 23 Aug. 1925, pp. 1, 13, which reproduces a portrait of Lady Mackintosh attributed to Allan Ramsay. An engraving of her is printed in Charles Fraser-Mackintosh, An Account of the Confederation of

Clan Chattan, 1898, p. 154.

[2] Though Aeneas Mackintosh, a captain in the 42nd Foot, remained loyal to the Hanoverian monarchy during the Jacobite rising of 1745, his clan took part in the rebellion and suffered accordingly. Lady Mackintosh housed Prince Charles Edward at Moy Hall, Inverness-shire, in Feb. 1746; her active participation in his defence earned her the soubriquet 'Colonel Anne' and led to her imprisonment briefly after the battle of Culloden (Robert Forbes, *The Lyon in Mourning*, ed. Henry Paton, 1895–96, ii. 134–37, 189). Mackintosh was an interested party in the cause of the Macdonell brothers, whom JB was representing at this time (From Alexander Macdonell, 26 Aug. 1766, n. 3). After the attainder of Evan Macpherson in 1746, Mackintosh claimed to hold the right of redemption of the Clunie estate, and in 1761 and 1763 the Court of Session up-

held his claim. On the strength of this ruling and of Mackintosh's promise that he would not remove the Clunie tenants, the Macdonells and others made improvements to their lands. On 27 Feb. 1766, however, the House of Lords reversed the Court of Session's ruling on Mackintosh's claim. Soon afterwards, the Barons of the Scots Exchequer leased Clunie to the Rev. Robert Macpherson and, through their factor Henry Butter, began proceedings to remove the tenants (Charles Fraser-Mackintosh, 'The Depopulation of Aberarder in Badenoch, 1770', *Celtic Magazine*, 1876–77, ii. 418–26; JHL (1760–64), xxx. 445, (1765–67), xxxi. 287).

[3] For JB's grandfather, see From John Dun, 29 July 1766, n. 4. If any Boswell served the Mackintoshes as more than 'A Sincere Adviser', his legal services have not been reported.

[4] MS. 'hu' ending in a flourish.

From Robert Strange,[1] Saturday 16 May 1767

MS. Yale (C 2587).

ADDRESS: To James Boswell Esqr., at Edinr.

London, May 16th, 1767

DEAR SIR: The late hurry of my publication has prevented me the pleasure of acknowledging your agreeable letter of the 16th March. I have had occasion to send a parcel to Edinr. and have transmitted to Mr. Esplins care four impressions of my late works which you'll do me the favour to accept of—they will recal to your remembrance certain pictures you must have admired when in Italy.[2] I have been three months in London and have during that time had no letter from our friend at Rome, but I have reason to believe he is well. The Death of his late Master, and the ruin'd affairs of that family, faling entirely upon him, has renderd him, I may say, almost a slave since that period—he may from necessity have ommitted writing his friends, but you must know as well as I that he is incapable of forgetting them—I am in the same Situation with yourself, he has several things of mine he should have sent me, but as yet I have no accounts of them.[3] In my first letter I shall write him particularly with regard to you, and you need not question of hearing from him soon. He has belonging to me certain works of piranesi which he has occasion to consult, and which he must have been retarded in from his late hurry.[4] I beg my respectfull Compliments to Sir Allexr. Dick,[5] and am, Dear Sir, Your most obedient, humble Servant,

ROBT. STRANGE

[1] Robert Strange (1721–92), later (1787) Kt., fought with the Young Pretender in 1745, and during his years of exile (1747–50) gained a reputation as an engraver of the first rank. He had befriended JB in Paris in 1766 (Journ. 20–30 Jan. 1766).

[2] The Mr. Esplins who received the prints was perhaps a London postal clerk; Sir John Dick also

saw Esplins in London about a package he expected from Scotland (see From Dick, 12 Aug. 1768). The publications that had kept Strange busy lately were prints of Abraham dismissing Hagar and Esther before Ahasuerus, both after the Italian master Giovanni Francesco Barbieri (Guercino) (Dennistoun, ii. 56–59; Charles Le Blanc, *Catalogue de l'oeuvre de Robert Strange*,

1848, pp. 3–4, 67). This year or the year before he had executed prints of the Sleeping Cupid and the Offspring of Love, both after Guido Reni (Dennistoun ii. 287; Le Blanc, pp. 9–10, 33–34, 67). These four prints were issued together (Dennistoun ii. 55); presumably they were the 'four impressions' that Strange was sending JB.

[3] Andrew Lumisden (1720–1801), brother of Strange's wife, had been secretary to the Young Pretender in 1745–46 and secretary to the Old Pretender from 1757. After the Old Pretender's death in 1766 the Young Pretender kept him on, but with menial duties: in 1767 Lumisden wrote to his sister, 'I have lived for many years in a sort of bondage; but I may name these past months a mere slavery' (Dennistoun ii. 107). In 1768 he parted with the Young Pretender after a quarrel

(*Lyon in Mourning* iii. 222–23, 231–32). JB and Lumisden became friends in Rome in 1765 (Journ. 27 Mar.–29 May; see *Grand Tour* II, pp. 61–85, especially the medallion portrait facing p. 84). It is not known what things Lumisden was to have sent JB from Rome; see further From Isabella Strange, 28 Dec. 1768 and 24 Jan. 1769.

[4] Presumably Lumisden was using the engravings of Giovanni Battista Piranesi (1720–78) in researching his *Remarks on the Antiquities of Rome and Its Environs*, 1797, which cites them frequently.

[5] Strange's wife Isabella was Sir Alexander Dick's second cousin: Dick's grandmother was Anne Paterson of Dunmure, Fife; Isabella Strange's grandmother was Anne's sister Isabel (Dennistoun i. 74–75).

From Sir Alexander Dick, Sunday 17 May 1767

MS. Yale (C 962).

ADDRESS: To James Boswell Esquire, Advocate, at affleck, air Shire.

POSTMARK: [Ayr] MY 19.

Prestonfield, May 17, 1767

Tho I cannot tell where my worthy friend and Councellor is I write this short line to catch you if it can at affleck.[1] You have in your excursions I dare say savd the Life of many a miserable sinner and object of the human *charming Virtue* Compassion.

You made me extreamly happy by the Information you gave me that our friend Sir John Dick intended us soon a Visit. To show you how much I like him from the description you give me of my namesake I am determind if my little Wife brings me a Son to give him the name of John after him and as he is the great paolis friend and yours I coud almost add that illustrious name of Liberty to my friends if it was not like too much presumtion;[2] but of de quo est deliberandum[3] and you may possibly be at the christning as well as the Ilustrissimo Sig. Cavaliere. May you soon my dear Friend get a Son to bear that name which can not fail to blaze in posterity and perhaps be the sourse of recovery of the Liberties of Italy. In my old Age I am much given to the prophetic spirit and I think I see often in my dreams such charming Visions before me as nascent Brutus's and Ciceros of the times to come: the fall of the Jesuits is a prodigious acquisition to these times: if they dont like Samson pull the old Fabricks of Empires along with them.[4]

When shall I see you here to communicate all I know of our Victories relative to the greater Navigation betwixt Forth and Clyde another happy Event I hope for Brittain: we have got now what your Father my Lord was afraid we shoud not get is plenty of money and I hope that will enable us likewise to make or get another requisite his Lordship was in concern for viz. plenty of Water. The compromise is on the tapis.[5] I long for next post and expect the meeting of the friends of both seas and friths and rivers will make a glorious marriadge of it at length and dignify our Country our Island and our times. Dont you think it deserves an Obelisk half way: you shall write the Inscription and let 50 marriadges on each side of the seas be made by crossing the families and mixing the Interests the best of Hecatombs for this poor Country to give on so great an occasion. Much more you are to have at meeting. Till then my best compliments affections and regards from all this family to My Lord and you and all friends, Dear Councellor and friend, yours, Adieu,

ALEXANDER DICK

[1] JB was at Dumfries, where the Circuit Court for the south district was in session (Journ. 12–18 May).

[2] Sir Alexander's second son John Dick (1767–1812) was born on 10 June; he succeeded to the baronetcy in 1808.

[3] 'That must be pondered'; Sir Alexander wrote 'of that' before 'de quo' (intending to write this phrase in English), then deleted 'that' but forgot to delete 'of'.

[4] The reference here is to Judges 16: 20–31. For the fall of the Jesuits, see From John Dick, 17 June, n. 7.

[5] The Edinburgh advocates of the large canal won out on 13 May, and a sum of £99,500 was quickly subscribed. The Glasgow group dropped its petition for a small canal when its conditions were met: (1) that the group would be reimbursed £1,500 for its expenses; (2) that the canal would be 'at least as deep and wide as that proposed by Mr. Smeaton'; (3) that a cut would 'be made between Glasgow and the most proper part of the great canal'; (4) that boats of fifteen tons would be allowed to pass at all times; (5) that landowners would be allowed to make cuts from the canal (*Scots Mag.* 1767, xxix. 236, 252–54).

To William Brown, c. Monday 18 May 1767

Not reported. Acknowledged in From Brown, 18 May. As Brown was in Kilmarnock, this exchange of letters could easily have taken place in a single day; but the date of a day or two earlier is not unlikely for this letter.

To Basil Cochrane, Monday 18 May 1767

Not reported. See From Cochrane, 20 May: 'Since writeing the above I have your's of the 18th'.

From William Brown,[1] Monday 18 May 1767

MS. Yale (C 597).

ADDRESS: To James Boswell Esqr., Advocate, at Auchinleck House.

Kilmarnock, 18 May 1767

SIR: The bearer and this will inform you, that the Stewartoun Rioters have determined to stand trial. They look on a voluntary banishment to be as bad as a legal one, and by a trial, think there's a chance for their being acquitted. The moment I received yours an account of it was sent to them, but it seems the best advice will not perswade. I am sorry for it, and shall be sorrier still if their Obstinacy occasions a greater punishment than their absence for a short time from their Wives, Children, Friends, and connections in business might prove. The last would be most severely felt by Robt. Reyburn, whose occupation of Bonnetmaker knits him to this Country.[2] They have all great hopes, more from the eloquence of their Counsel than their own innocence.

To Petition my Lord Your Father for a warrant to Summon Witnesses is part of the bearers errand.[3] The facts are fairly represented, and I hope my ⟨Lor⟩d will be under no difficulty to grant it.

Would you be so good as inform Whether it is necessary to cite all the Witnesses mentioned in my Notes.[4] Every one of them, it is said, will depose that the meal was sold at the ordinary rate of the Market.

But after all, Is there no possibility of getting the Trial put off? Nothing more could be done to get Letters of Exculpation.[5] I had a second letter from Edr. on Sunday night telling it was impossible; and latter end of last week the Petition was sent to Glasgow, in expectation of finding Lord Coalston there, and getting a warrant from him, without effect.[6]

I must trouble you, at Capt. Montgomrie Cuninghame's desire, with another Stewartoun affair. You'll receive with this, Copy of a Precognition taken here this day against one John Dunlop, for your perusal, and advice how to proceed against him. The Captains Letter to Mr. Pater⟨son⟩, and his Baron officer's information that the Capt. had already mentioned this to you is the only apology I can make for sending it in this manner.[7] A Copy of the Letter is also herewith sent. I am, Sir, with the greatest respect, Your most obedient Servant,

WILLM. BROWN

[1] William Brown (fl. 1767–c. 1794), writer in Kilmarnock, was the brother of JB's law clerk James Brown. Between 1776 and 1780 he and JB conducted an extensive correspondence, mostly concerning the affairs of JB's impecunious cousin Sir Walter Montgomerie-Cuningham of Lainshaw, for whom William Brown was factor (Reg. Let.). By 1779 JB and Brown were meeting socially as well as on business (Journ. 12 Apr., 3 June 1779). Brown was the agent in the cause of the Stewarton rioters (From Alexander Montgomerie-Cuninghame, 11 May, n. 1).

[2] Robert Reyburn in Goosehill, one of the six rioters charged in the Criminal Letters (Lg 9:1). Stewarton's principal trade was bonnet-making, and the 'bonnets' (soft, flat, rimless caps worn by men and boys—CSD) were sold locally and in the Highlands as well as exported in large quantities (Stat. Acct. Scot. vi. 622).

[3] The cause was to be tried before Lord Auchinleck (Court of Justiciary Records: South Circuit Minute Book No. 12). This petition has not been reported.

[4] Brown's 'Notes for Stewarton Rioters' lists twenty witnesses for the panels (Lg 9:4).

[5] A warrant given to defendants for citing witnesses in their own defence (Bell i. 291).

[6] George Brown (d. 1776), since 1756 Lord Coalston of the Court of Session and since 1765 a Lord of Justiciary, was assigned to the Western Circuit that sat at Glasgow beginning on 8 May (College of Justice, p. 522; Scots Mag. 1767, xxix. 324). The documents mentioned in this paragraph have not been reported.

[7] Capt. Alexander Montgomerie-Cuninghame was married to the elder sister of Margaret Montgomerie, JB's future wife (Hist. Ayr ii. 454–55). We do not know why he was proceeding against John Dunlop, who, presumably, was a tenant or minor heritor in Stewarton parish. Dunlop is a common name in Ayrshire, and we cannot be more precise. 'Mr. Paterson' is almost certainly William Paterson, a writer who was Town Clerk of Kilmarnock from 1769 to c. 1790 (Ayrshire, pp. 87, 133, 278), and Cuninghame's 'baron officer' is James Barclay, baron baillie (magistrate) of Stewarton and father of the James Barclay charged as one of the rioters in the Criminal Letters (Lg 9:1, 2).

From James Maitland,[1] Monday 18 May 1767

MS. Yale (C 1887); enclosed in Maitland's letter to Lord Auchinleck, 18 May 1767
ADDRESS: For Mr. Boswel Junr. of Auchinleck.

[Sorbie, Wigtonshire]

Facts Serving to Shew the Scarsity of Meal at the time of the Mob and the facts may be proven by the witnesses Cited against the pannels.[2]
1. In Wigtown and Whithorn there Could not be Meal Got for money—So that

the Magistrats were obliged to buy in some quantity, and become retailers of it to the poor.

2. In Whithorn the Magistrats were obliged to buy up Corn and become Meal Makers as well as Meal Sellers.

3. In Newton Stewart the people could Not get Meal at any rate till by their Clamor the proprietor of the place was forced to Make his own Corn and Send it to them.

4. The Military who Came to Suppress the Mutinous Buyers of Meal Could not Get Meal from the Sellers, Whom[3] they were supporting and defending, till they were obliged to apply to the Gentlemen of[4] the Countrey to see them provided.

5. There was an universal Clamour of Want in the Countrey, and meetings of people Concerting to leave the Countrey for want, this happned at Wigtown.

[1] The Rev. James Maitland (1712–74) had been minister in Sorbie parish, Wigtownshire, since 1738 (*Fasti Scot.* ii. 377). This note to JB was enclosed in a letter Maitland addressed to Lord Auchinleck on behalf of the two Garliestoun residents who were to come before him in the Circuit Court of Ayr on a charge of riotous behaviour. In his letter Maitland stressed the point that 'the Unlucky people assembled on that occasion used no violence no force, Neither stole nor Robd nor Embezled any part of the Victual'.

[2] On 21 Apr. two residents of Garliestoun— George Guthrie, carpenter, and James Cready, sailor—and three residents of the neighbouring town of Whithorn—Robert Johnstone, excise officer, Patrick Conning and Keith Birnie, merchants—were indicted for having formed part of a mob. Johnstone was also charged with having written the letter which incited the mob to ac-

tion: a much more serious offence but one for which there was no firm evidence in this case. The inhabitants of Garliestoun 'being in greate destress For their want of Meall since the begining of febr. 1767', the five rioters boarded two ships that were loading meal on the shore of Glasserton parish and forced them to sail to Garliestoun, where they unloaded the meal, intending to sell it. JB represented four of the defendants (Conning had absconded and was outlawed) on 22 May at the Circuit Court in Ayr. The jury found the charges against Johnstone and Cready not proven; Guthrie and Birnie were convicted and sentenced to twenty-one days in the Tolbooth of Ayr (Papers relating to the case of the Garlieston Rioters, Lg 8; Court of Justiciary Records: South Circuit Minute Book, No. 12).

[3] MS. ?'It' deleted before 'Whom'

[4] MS. 'of of '

To William Brown, Between Monday 18 May and Friday 22 May 1767[1]

MS. Yale (L 273). In an unidentified hand, with comments and answers to JB's queries written by William Brown in the wide right-hand margin (printed in the annotation).

ENDORSEMENT in the hand of James Brown, JB's clerk: Excerpts from Mr. Boswell's Letter and Answers, 1767.

[Auchinleck]

Excerpts from Mr. Boswells letter

I think we may be the better of all you have mentioned in the notes except those who will swear that meal was secreted on the day of the riot which as you very well observe may be considered as a consequence of the riot and indeed it might give it a more formidable air.

Pray ask Wyllie and Cameron who helped Wallace to secrete the meal if they did it before or after the riot.[2] If they should only say in general that it was that day I can argue that it was before the riot. But the Advocate Depute Will most probably Interrogate them specially.[3] You may however enquire if they or if Gemmill and Caldwell the other two Witnesses to meal being secreted did not know of it's having been done at some prior period.[4] And if they can swear so it will be of use. You may at any rate cite two of these and when at Ayr I can determine whether it will be proper to Examine them.[5]

Is Jean Currie spouse to Bryce Caldwell a near relation of Currie the pannel.[6] If she is you need not cite her as we have two other Witnesses on the same head. If she is not she will be a good Witness. The Circumstance of 7 Children wanting bread may be turned to our purpose very much. You mention only John Montgomerie as lifting on a load of meal.[7] I know they all did as much, and I suppose it will be proved. If not I shall be very well pleased. The Blows given by some of the pannals must be made appear as a Battery distinct from the meal Riot. Let us have as full a prooff as possible that Russel was required to sell the meal he was carrying away and let us also have all the evidence we can that they to whom the meal belonged acquiesced in the sale.[8]

[1] This letter is a reply to From William Brown, 18 May. The last possible date for it is 22 May, the day of the trial (Lg 9:4).

[2] John Wallace, mealman and carrier, claimed to have been attacked by the rioters and robbed of six bolls of meal. William Cameron, farmer in Tapperfall, and Gavin Wyllie, stocking-weaver and baker, carried sackfuls of meal from the kitchen to the stable and concealed it (Lg 9:2). Brown's answer: 'After the riot was begun. Therefore not cited.'

[3] William Nairne (c. 1731–1811), Advocate-Depute, later (1786) Lord Dunsinnan on the Court of Session and (1790) baronet.

[4] Peter Gemmill, wright, and James Caldwell, cooper, witnesses for the defence (Lg 9:4). Brown's answer: 'Gemmil and Caldwal did not know of Wyllie and Cameron having assisted to secrete the Meal—They suspected Wallace had Meal concealed, searched his Houses, and found it in the stable-Byre under litter.'

[5] Brown's comment: 'They are cited. But should not be examined too minutely. See Interrogatorys page 15.' Brown refers to his bound MS. 'Notes for Stewartoun Rioters', in which he lays out questions to ask the various witnesses. On p. 15, under the heading 'Concealing of Meal', are the following questions to be asked of Gemmill and Caldwell: 'Do you know if meal was ever found secreted about the house of John Wallace? Did you ever see any meal so secreted? When? And in what manner?' (Lg 9:4).

[6] Brown's answer: 'She is a Sister consanguin and was therefore scored out of the List sent over to Stewartoun. But the Pannels caused the Messr. cite her notwithstanding. It is a hardship that the other Pannels should be deprived of her evidence, because related to one.'

[7] John Montgomerie, mason in Stewarton, one of the accused.

[8] William Russel, one of the mealmongers whose meal was forcibly sold.

From Basil Cochrane, Wednesday 20 May 1767

MS. Yale (C 802).

ADDRESS: To James Boswel, advocate, Esqr., att Auchenleck house, per Air.

POSTMARK: [Edinburgh] MY 20.

Edinburgh, May 20th, 1767

DEAR JAMES: The weather was Rainy and[1] I now Grown very Lazzie prevented me goeing to Drumfreis.[2] When you come to my Age you will likewise find out Manny excuses to Stay att Hom.

About three weeks hence your Father and you will be looking towards Edinburgh where you will have Work Enough upon your hand to pay off your Debts otherwise Dalblair most certainly goe to the Markate again[3] You have nothing for it but by the Sweat of your Brow to Save Dalblair from being Sold and your Self from a Gaol[4] So Labour for your Bread or goe to the Devil either the one or the other most be your Fate.[5]

Since writeing the above I have your's of the 18th and shall Send the letter you Inclose to me to your Brother David. Inclosed you[6] have a letter which came under Cover to me.[7] My Compliments to your Father. I am, Dear James, Your's,

BASIL COCHRANE

[1] MS. 'and and'
[2] Presumably Cochrane was to have met JB and his father on 13 May in Dumfries, where Lord Auchinleck was presiding over the Southern Circuit (*Scots Mag.* 1767, xxix. 324).
[3] JB's Consultation Book records that between the rising of the Court at the end of the spring session on 12 Mar. and at the end of the summer session on 11 Aug., he received seventy-three guineas, nine of them earned during the spring vacation (*Edin. Almanack*, 1767, pp. 15,

20). For JB's purchase of Dalblair, see To Sir Alexander Dick, 16 Apr. and n. 5.
[4] MS. 'Goal'
[5] JB and his granduncle frequently engaged in what JB called 'rough jokes' (Journ. 18 Oct. 1775).
[6] MS. ?'receive' deleted before 'you'
[7] JB's letters to Cochrane and David Boswell have not been reported. We do not know what letter Cochrane was forwarding to JB.

To William Drummond, Saturday 30 May 1767

Not reported. See From Drummond, 1 June: 'I am this moment favored with your letter of the 30th of May'.

To James Montgomery, Saturday 30 May 1767

Not reported. See From Montgomery, 4 June: 'Yesterday I considered a very long Precognition about the Affair mentioned in Your Letter of the 30th May.'

To Lady Grizel Cochrane, Saturday 31 May 1767

Not reported. Sent 31 May 1767 (Reg. Let.). Lady Grizel Cochrane (b. 1727) was the daughter of Thomas Cochrane, eighth Earl of Dundonald, and his wife, Elizabeth Ker of Moriestoun (*Scots Peer.* iii. 360); thus she was JB's first cousin once removed.

To Giuseppe Baretti, between May and October 1767

Not reported. See From Baretti, 7 Nov.: 'You inclosed your last in one to Mr. Johnson, which has been the reason of its not coming to hand, as he stay'd many months at Lichfield, and his letters were never sent him there by the person that received them here.' Johnson was away from London, in Oxford and Lichfield, from May to October (*Life* iii. 452).

From William Drummond,[1] Monday 1 June 1767

MS. Yale (C 1114).

ADDRESS: To James Boswell Esquire, at Auchinleck, by Ayr.
POSTMARK: [Edinburgh] IU 1.

Edinb. Monday June 1st, 1767

SIR: I am this moment favored with your letter of the 30th of May, and will be proud to do any thing in the way of my business which may in the least or in the greatest be obliging to you. I suppose you have taken measures to have the object of my trust put into my hand stitched and ready, or otherways that it will be done in such time as that they may be stitched by the day of the Session's first sitting. I shall be glad to know whether you incline to have it advertised in the News papers, or if you think it sufficient that I send it about, as a publication to be had at my shop, to all whom I may know to have a taste for that kind of writing. As no one knows of your letter, you may with confidence rely upon me, that no one shall know whence I have the pamphlet, till the Author is not onely pleased to own it, but till he shall please to give me in charge to say who he is.[2] I have the honor to be with great respect, Sir, Your most obedient and most humble servant,

WILL. DRUMMOND

[1] William Drummond (c. 1708–74), bookseller at the Cross in Edinburgh and a friend of SJ's (*Edinburgh Directory*, 1774–75; *Dict. of Printers*; *Letters SJ* i. 112–13; *Life* ii. 26–31).

[2] Drummond refers to *Dorando*, of which he was to be the principal Edinburgh bookseller. The book had already been printed and 300 copies shipped to John Wilkie in London (From Wilkie, 7 May, n. 1), and yet from this letter it appears that JB had asked Drummond to handle the Edinburgh sale only on 30 May. Presumably JB delayed contacting the Scottish booksellers so as to insure secrecy. The Court of Session sat down on 12 June (*Edinburgh Almanack*, 1767, p. 18), and *Dorando* was first advertised in Edinburgh on 15 June (*Lit. Car.* p. 35). As far as we know, JB never did authorize Drummond to disclose his authorship of the book. On 29 June Robert Foulis wrote from Glasgow that people were 'at a loss about the Author of Dorando' and recommended that 'The Curiousity of the Public on that subject should not be satisfied'. JB never acknowledged *Dorando* publicly, though he may have let the information slip once, indirectly (*Lit. Car.* p. 235). Ramsay of Ochtertyre knew about it, however, as did Henry Mackenzie; Robert Hunting speculates that it 'was as ill-kept a secret as was Swift's authorship of *The Drapier Letters*' (*Scotland and Scotsmen*, i. 172–73; *Anecdotes and Egotisms of Henry Mackenzie*, ed. Harold William Thompson, 1927, p. 106; *Dorando*, ed. Robert Hunting, 1974, p. xxi).

From Lord Marischal, c. Monday 1 June 1767

MS. Yale (C 1956).

ADDRESS: To James Boswell Esqre., of Auchenleck, Edenbourg, en Ecosse; Fr. Amsterdam, par Londres [*in other hands*].

POSTMARK: [London] IV 12.

Potsdam

MONSIEUR: Ce billet vous porte les assurances de mon amitié et de celle de Madame de Froment, elle me prie de vous dire qu'elle á envoyé a Hambourg a Mrs. Stephen et Renny pour garder a votre ordre, un fusil, une pair de pistolets, et une épée a la prussienne, telle que porte le Roy et tous les officiers d'Infanterie ici.[1] Elle souhaiteroit pouvoir envoyer, 6000 Arnauts, 12 mil Janisaires, et 4. mil Spahis,[2] avec une bone armée Navalle, car elle ne se contente pas que le General Paoli rend sa patrie Libre, elle voudroit qu'il fisse la Conquete de Genes; vous aurez donc, Monsieur, la bonté delui envoyer cet petit present de sa part. La vertu se fait admirer depuis la *ultima Thule*[3] au bords de la mer noire. J'ay l'honeur d'etre avec une consideration distinguée, Monsieur, Votre tres humble et tres obeissant serviteur,

MARISCHAL

Vous souvenez, peutetre, que l'Inscription sur les lames d'epée ici est, *Pro Patria et Gloria*. C'est Emetulla qui á fait mettre, *Pro Libertate*, disante qu'elle seule est au dessu de tout.

[1] Messrs. Stephen and Renny were merchants in Hamburg. They often handled shipments to Great Britain for Lord Marischal, who mentions Stephen as late as 1772 (From Lord Marischal, 4 Feb. 1772).

[2] An Arnaut is an Albanian serving in the Turkish army. A janizary is a Turkish infantryman, and a spahi a Turkish cavalryman (OED, 'Janizary', 'Spahi'; OED *Supplement*, 'Arnaut').

[3] 'Farthest Thule' (Virgil, *Georgics* i. 30), proverbially, the ends of the earth.

To Francis Ashbury, Thursday, 4 June 1767

MS. Yale (L 18). A draft in JB's hand. The original date in the heading, 'Ayr 31 May 1767', has been deleted.

HEADING: To Lieutenant Ashbury.

Auchinleck, 4 June 1767

SIR: I have had the honour to receive your letter, and should have answered it sooner, had I not been much hurried with my business as a Lawyer upon the Circuit.

Your letter did not surprise me; for you must know I had the pleasure of seeing your friend Mr. Maitland, at Dumfries, who gave me a note you had written as a Memorandum to him.[1]

I greatly admire the generous spirit which you shew in wishing to be employed in the service of Corsica, and I heartily wish that it could answer your views, and that I could be of any use to you.

But as far as I can judge the Corsican service would not be very advantageous.[2] They are very poor, and can afford little pay to a foreign officer. Their war is confined as they have no ennemy but their old oppressors the Genoese. I would hope indeed that the French troops will soon be removed from the Island, and then a[3] Gentleman of your skill and experience might assist them in reducing the fortified towns, by[4] attacks either from the land, or from[5] the Sea, while they at the same time could[6] have a sufficient number of vessels to cruise about and prevent the arrival of succours from Genoa, and if your pay should not be great you would at least live very reasonably.[7]

In the situation you are in no doubt a Service where you could have[8] an opportunity of acquiring[9] reputation would be preferable to remaining[10] in a total inactivity provided your future hopes should not suffer by it. I am affraid if the Genoese Minister[11] should remonstrate against it the Lords of the Admiralty could not well overlook a British Sea Officer's going contrary to an express Proclamation. However you are to judge of that after being properly informed. And with regard to the measures you should take in order to get into the service of Corsica I would recommend you to my worthy friend Mr. Dick His Majesty's Consul at Leghorn who is now in London and to be heard of at Mr. Drummond's Banker at Charing Cross.[12] You will please shew him this letter and I am perswaded He will give you his best advice. Make no apology for applying to me, but be assured that I shall with the greatest pleasure do any thing you can desire of me to forward your views.[13] I am, Sir, Your most obedient, humble Servant,

JAMES BOSWELL

[1] Possibly David Maitland, who, like Ashbury, was a lieutenant of long service without hope of promotion (*Court and City Kalendar*, 1767, p. 201; *Sea Officers* ii. 592).

[2] Draft, 'to you' deleted after 'advantageous'

[3] Draft, 'indeed' deleted before 'a'

[4] Draft, 'either' deleted before 'by' and added before 'from'

[5] Draft, 'cannonading them' deleted before 'from'

[6] Draft, 'you could' deleted before 'could'

[7] Draft, 'and if your pay . . . reasonably' is a later interlinear addition.

[8] Draft, 'at least' deleted before 'have'

[9] Draft, 'acquiring' written above deleted 'gaining'

[10] Draft, 'remaining' written above deleted 'living'

[11] Francesco Maria Ageno, Genoese Minister to Great Britain 1760–89 (*Court and City Kalendar*, 1761–89; F. Hausmann, *Repertorium der diplomatischen Vertreter aller Länder*, 1936–50, ii. 138).

[12] Andrew Drummond (c. 1687–1769), banker at Charing Cross (*Kent's Directory*, 1768; *Gent. Mag.* 1769, xxxix. 110; Sir William Musgrave, *Obituary Prior to 1800*, 1899–1901, ii. 215).

[13] Draft, 'Pray tell Mr. Dick' deleted before the complimentary close of the letter.

From James Montgomery,[1] Thursday 4 June 1767

MS. Yale (C 2051).

Edinbr. 4th June 1767

SIR: I arrived here upon saturday last, and Yesterday I considered a very long Precognition about the Affair mentioned in Your Letter of the 30th May. As things stand circumstanced I do not think it is my Duty to bring Your Clients to Tryal at present, and as that is the Case, I can have no Objection to their being liberated without delay and will concur in any measure necessary for that purpose, unless in answer to a Letter to be wrote this day, I get some fresh information which may alter my Opinion, but which I[2] do not expect.[3]

The spiriting away McMurtrie, and other Circumstances give a conviction to my mind, that Persons of some consideration have[4] been concerned in the Wicked Conspiracy;[5]—It is Your Duty to defend Your Clients, and I observe Your Zeal in doing so upon every occasion with great pleasure and satisfaction, But it is both your Duty and Mine to wish a detection of the Persons guilty of so foul a Crime, and that the punishment of their guilt may not be prevented by illegal means; It is my Duty in those Matters to do more then merely to wish, and I shall endeavour to do what the Publick has reason to expect of me, with impartiality and without using any unnecessary severity. I beg You will offer my most respectfull Compliments to Lord Auchinleck; And believe that I am with great regard, Sir, Your most Obedient and Most humble Servant,

JAS. MONTGOMERY

[1] For James Montgomery, Lord Advocate, see To the Duchess of Douglas, 13 Oct. 1766, n. 6.

[2] MS. 'at present' deleted before 'I'

[3] Matthew Hay (d. 1780), farmer in Plewlands, and one McClure, probably John (b. 1722), brother of David McClure of Shawwood (From David McClure, 13 June) had been arrested on 25 Mar. and charged with firing shots at William Harris, merchant in Ayr, killing his horse. It was alleged that Hay had met with Harris and two others, Alexander Gordon, Collector of Customs at Ayr, and John McMurtrie, extraordinary tide-waiter (or customs official) at Ayr, on the road between Irvine and Ayr; later Hay and three others (one of them presumably McClure) had attacked Harris, thinking he was Gordon. The government regarded the affair as a conspiracy to assassinate a customs officer and offered a reward of £200 and a pardon to any one of the conspirators who would give evidence against the others (Ayr Burgh Records, Register of Incarcerations and Arrestments, 25 Mar.; *Scots Mag.* 1767, xxix. 222, 325). JB visited Hay and McClure in prison on 22 and 25 May (Journ.), and

he had a further consultation about their case on 2 July (Consultation Book), but court records list no prosecution, the case having never come to trial.

[4] MS. 'have' superimposed upon 'were'

[5] Montgomery's strong hint that JB had something to do with 'spiriting away McMurtrie' (see *Earlier Years*, p. 329) would seem to be contradicted by David McClure's protestations of his own innocence in his letter of 13 June, which at least shows that McClure did not suspect JB of having had anything to do with McMurtrie's disappearance.

From Godfrey Bosville, Friday 5 June 1767

MS. Yale (C 175).

ADDRESS: To James Boswell Esqr., at Lord Auchinlecks House in [Edinburgh *deleted, added in another hand*] by Air.

POSTMARK: WAKEFIELD.

Gunthwait, 5th June 1767

DEAR SIR: I am now got into my Old Habitation at Gunthwait again, Tommy to his great Satisfaction is here too and Miss Julia to help him to do Mischief, Di is in London with her Aunt Annabella, and is to come down with her Uncle, they have been so kind as to take the Trouble of her: Billy is turnd a drift in Town till the Grand Review on the 19th, and then I shall expect him soon after, but without Prior Notice, the first News I shall have of him will be His Appearance here.[1] Mrs. Bosville and I came down by Nottingham which is a Place she had never seen, and indeed the Castle commands a Noble View and there is something extraordinary in the Cellars of the Town being cut out of the Rock it stands on, and Cottages like Fox Denns made the Same way.[2] We saw too the Duke of Bedfords at Woburne, the Park is a large Lawn and strikes one something like the Entrance from Woodstock into the Duke Marlboroughs Park, but there seems to be no Variety either in that of the Gardens,[3] as to the House we were much more pleasd the week before with one of Mr. Walpoles at Twickenham which is built in the Gothic Manner, there is a Gallery and a Library exceedingly well contrivd, and an odd Octagon Chappel.[4] I wish you had seen it. I protest if we were to build a House now I am sure it woud be Gothic. I am very glad you are writing the History of Corsica, and I will get the[5] Book as soon as ever it comes out, I love Historys more than any other reading, and it will be a particular Pleasure to have one by a Person of my own name and family: we have interested our selves much in behalf of Paschal Paoli ever since we had the pleasure of seeing his Letter to you,[6] as far as our good wishes coud go, and been very attentive to every thing relating to the Corsicans. I have bot. Observations on The Statutes[7] from Magna Charta and I think you woud be pleasd with it, I am sure I was, it is wrote by Lord Barringtons Brother a Welsh Judge.[8] We that ride round the Sun know very little of the Motions of the Vehicle that carrys us, though Philosophers pretend they know the road through the Skies as exact as the Man knows his road upon Earth that drives the Machine from London to Edinburgh, but I am sure the Poles are movd a little out of their former Direction, by the Alteration in the Seasons, for it is Winter in June: yesterday a good deal of Snow fell upon the Moors about two Miles of, and to day it rains as hard as it can: The Track may be the same, because we expect to receive the Fruits of the Earth at the Usual times.[9] I am much pleasd with the hopes you give me of seeing Lord Auchinleck and yourself this Summer,[10] I should be glad to talk to his Lordship to see if we coud not settle togather the time when our familys seperated, and if[11] this Old house be no matter of Beauty it is Matter[12] of Curiosity to one of the Family.[13] Mrs. Bosville desires her Compliments and please to present our Compliments to Lord Auchinleck. I am, Dear Sir, Your Kinsman and most Humble Servant,

GODFREY BOSVILLE

Miss Julia desires her Compliments.

[1] The persons mentioned here are (in order) Bosville's children Thomas, Julia, and Diana; his sister- and brother-in-law Annabella and Thomas Wentworth; and Bosville's son William (From Bosville, 24 June 1766, nn. 3, 5, 6; 12 Aug. 1766, n. 15).

[2] A tourist in Nottingham and its environs in 1772 remarked upon the row of dwellings cut out of precipices and the Castle 'placed on the highest of these rocks; it is a very large structure, with one ornamented front; Corinthian columns on a rustic ground; a grand flight of steps, forming a central entrance.... The prospect from the castle is very extensive, and the Trent meandering through the vale very beautiful', but he concluded that he had seen views which pleased him better (Gent. Mag. 1774, xliv. 355).

[3] Woburn Abbey was the seat of John Russell, fourth Duke of Bedford. A Cistercian abbey until the dissolution of the monasteries under Henry VIII, it had been granted to the Russell family by Edward VI in 1549. The present house had been rebuilt in 1747 for the fourth Duke (Howard Colvin, Biographical Dictionary of British Architects, 1600–1840, 1978, p. 312). Bosville compares Woburn Abbey with Blenheim Palace, the great house near Woodstock, Oxfordshire, built for John Churchill, first Duke of Marlborough, by Queen Anne in gratitude for his victory at Blenheim in 1704.

[4] Strawberry Hill, Horace Walpole's (1717–97) estate in Twickenham, had been under construction more or less continuously since 1750. Two of the latest projects, the gallery and cabinet, later called the chapel and tribune, had been completed in 1763 (Corres. HW i. 11, n. 1). The 'chapel', actually a kind of museum, was square with a rounded alcove on each side, giving Bosville the impression of an octagon.

[5] MS. 'will get the' superimposed upon two erased words, perhaps 'assure you'

[6] Presumably Paoli's letter of 23 Dec. 1765, which JB printed and translated in Corsica, pp. 376–81.

[7] MS. 'The Statutes' superimposed upon erased 'Magna Char'

[8] Observations on the Statutes, Chiefly the More Ancient, from Magna Charta to the Twenty-first of James the First, ch. xxvii, 1766. The author of the work, Daines Barrington (1727–1800), barrister and naturalist, was a younger brother of William Wildman Barrington (1717–93), second Viscount Barrington. He was appointed justice of the counties of Merioneth, Carnarvon, and Anglesey in 1766.

[9] A report from neighbouring Derbyshire in Gent. Mag. (1767) xxxvii. 327 states that it snowed all day on 3 June and most of the day on 4 June, and that the snow 'was above half a yard deep'.

[10] JB did not visit Bosville until 25 Mar. 1768 in London (Journ.) and Lord Auchinleck and Bosville did not meet until Bosville visited Auchinleck in early September 1777 (Journ. 31 Aug., 4 Sept. 1777).

[11] MS. 'and' altered to 'and if '

[12] MS. 'is Matter' superimposed upon erased words, perhaps 'some of C'

[13] For the house, see From Bosville, 24 June 1766, n. 7.

To David McClure, Saturday 6 June 1767

Not reported. See From McClure, 13 June: 'I had the honour of Receiveing Your letters of the 6th and 9th Inst.'

To John Dick, 6–13 June 1767

Not reported. See From Dick, 17 June: 'A thousand thanks wait on You my dear Sir for your very kind and obliging Letter of the 6 and 13 Inst.'

To David McClure, Tuesday 9 June 1767

Not reported. See To McClure, 6 June.

To Andrew Burnaby, c. Saturday 13 June 1767

Not reported. Enclosed in To John Dick, 6–13 June; see From Dick, 17 June: 'The inclosed which You sent me for Mr. Burnaby shall go forward the next post.'

From David McClure,[1] Saturday 13 June 1767

MS. Yale (C 1820).

Air, 13th June 1767

SIR: I had the honour of Receiveing Your letters of the 6th and 9th Inst. the Last Incloseing My Lord Advocate's letter to You concerning Your Clients Mr. Hay and my Brother, which I communicated to them, and have obeyed your directions in Shewing it to but few, and those only particular freinds.[2] I Return you my Sencear[3] thanks for the favour of Seeing Lord Advocate's letter, Whereby Those concerned are made Accquaint with his Lordships Sentements on that Subject, and Agreeable to your Desire I Return you it Inclosed. The proper Application has been made for the Leberation of the Prisoners, in Consequence Whereof Letters of Leberation Came up Thursday night, and they were Set at Liberty immediatly. As Lord Advocate Seems to hint in his letter that they Still Stand exposed to his prosecution, and that it may be his duty to Bring them to tryal in Some after period, Should any Such prosecution be intended or Set on foot Against them hereafter, I beg You'll Continue to espouse their Intrest, and order What may be needfull to be done for them, It appears by my Lord Advocate's letter, that it has been Represented to his Lordship that McMurtrie has been Sent out of the Way by Some freinds or Conexions of the Prisoners, Which by all that Has every been heard or Known, appears to be a most Groundless and Fallashouss aspersion, (thought by many) to be propigated by a Certaint party to answer Some purposes which they are not able to Carry on by fair means, and that after they Seeing themselves Baff'd[4] in Getting their Intentions Carried into execution they have thought of this last Resource in order to through an odium and suspiteon on Peoples Carecters, this may appear from the Result of the last Precognition, which Concerned McMurtrie's goung away which Pre[c]ognition I immaigen they will not lay before my Lord Advocate for his opinion, althought upwards of thirty persons were Deposed on that head, but I have been Informed that McMurtrie has left behind him Writings of his own hand that dos throw a different light on matters and unvail Some mens Carecters and Actions, but whither these Writings Can be obtained I cannot Say. If they Shall be come at I Shall let you Know thier Contents. I am with due Regard, Sir, Your Most Obedient and most Humble Servant,

DAVID MCCLURE

[1] David McClure (1733–99) of Shawwood, Ayrshire, merchant, was a Burgess and Guild Brother of the Royal Burgh of Ayr (1759) and had served on the Ayr Town Council, 1761–63, 1764–65 (Genealogical Papers Relating to the McClure Family, collected by Arnold McJannet

and R. M. Hogg, Irvine Burns Club, Wellwood, Irvine, Ayrshire; Ayr Town Council Records, Ayr Carnegie Library). McClure was a partner in several firms, including Alexander Oliphant and Company, wine importers, founded in 1766 (Sir James Fergusson, 'A Wine Merchant's Letter Book', *Ayrshire Collections*, 1958, iv); the Oliphant Company has been identified as 'a front for organising the growing smuggling trade on the Ayrshire coast' (L. M. Cullen, 'Smuggling in the North Channel in the 18th Century', *Scottish Economic and Social History*, 1987, vii. 17). McClure had two elder brothers, John and James; according to the McClure Genealogical Papers, John was connected with the Oliphant Company, making it probable that he was the brother arrested for attacking Alexander Gordon, whom he mistook for a customs officer (From James

Montgomery, 4 June, n. 3). The Genealogical Papers identify Matthew Hay, arrested with John McClure, as having been connected with another group of Ayrshire smugglers. David McClure, whose farm at Lochlea was tenanted by Robert Burns's father from 1777 to 1784, lost heavily in the Ayr bank crash of 1772; after selling Shawwood in 1788 he moved to Liverpool, where he remained until his death (*Ayrshire*, pp. 112, 143, 312, 340; *Liverpool General Advertiser*, 17 Oct. 1799). The information and references in this note were kindly supplied by John Strawhorn.

[2] For the Lord Advocate's letter, see From James Montgomery, 4 June.

[3] MS. 'senecar'

[4] 'Beaten' (*Scot. Nat. Dict.* 'Baff' 2. 1).

From John Dick, Wednesday 17 June 1767

MS. Yale (C 1016).

ADDRESS: To James Boswell Esqr. of Auchinleck, Edenburgh.

NOTE in Dick's hand at foot of first page: James Boswell Esquire.

London, 17 June 1767

A thousand thanks wait on You my dear Sir for your very kind and obliging Letter of the 6 and 13 Inst. The inclosed which You sent me for Mr. Burnaby shall go forward the next post, and I shall write him about sending the Corsican Gazette to Mr. Wilkie and particularly mention to him, that none of your Letters be sent that way. Mr. Davies has not yet sent me the books, but has promised me to send them on fryday morning, when I shall carry them to the City with me, and deliver them to a Capt. who is on the point of Sailing, the watch keys shall be put into the box.

I have this day receiv'd a Letter from Mr. Burnaby, he says they have nothing new from Capraja that can be depended on. When I receive any notices worthy your attention, You may depend on being informed of them.

I am glad to perceive that You are return'd to Edenburg, and that you were going to Sir Alexanders. I therefore shall hope to have the pleasure of hearing from you in concequence of any discourse You may have had with the worthy Knight, and Mr. Ferguson. Sir William certainly was a Knight Bart. and altho' I fear some of the proofs may be difficult to make out, yet if Sir Alexander could be induced to give his Consent, I should think, that all the other difficultys might be gott over, especially if it depends on the Kings acknowledging me, as I have the Honour to be well with the King, nay by much more so, than I dare venture to mention, least it should look like Vanity. His Majesty takes every opportunity of being very Gracious to us both, and I know from a person of very great distinction, that the other day he said many handsome things of me, and how much he was Satisfied with my Services.[1] I have also the good fortune to be well with his Ministers, so that if I was even to ask to be created a Bart. I should immediately have it, but that is not the thing, I should like much better, if I could be allow'd to resume the old title of the family, for many reasons and I verily believe, I know of some Scots titles which are now allow'd, who have not so good a right to them as I have to this. If application is to be made to the King about this Affair, I must beg of You my dear Sir, after You have seen my last letter to our worthy friend Mr. Ferguson, and obtained Sir Alexanders Consent, to draw up such a paper as may be thought Sufficient, and proper to present either to the King, or his Ministers for his Majesty's information, if such a Step is necessary. You see I take You at your word, and employ you freely. I have done all I can to find out further registers in Northumberland, but cannot come at them, so that conclude they have been destroy'd, indeed they are to me so. Thus am I at a loss to know if Lewis Dick was married there, or in Scotland, and then came and Setled there[2]—at all events, whether you think there is a possibility or not of my Succeeding, I shall hope for the pleasure of hearing from You soon. We leave Town on Monday for a short time on a Visset to Mr. Hans Stanley in Hampshire,[3] and from thence to Lord Hallifax's in Sussex,[4] but your Letters directed as usual to Messs. Drummonds, will always find me.[5] I am afterwards engaged on a Visset to Mr. Ansons in Staffordshire,[6] but shall be in Town for a few days in my way thither, so that, I cannot possibly pay my Respects to Sir Alexander and You, as yet, but shall endeavour to do it, before the end of Summer, as I long for an Opportunity to tell You, how much I think myself Obliged to You, and wish much to pay my Court to the good Knight, and shake honest Ferguson by the hand, pray present our most Respectfull Congratulations to Sir Alexander on the Birth of his Son, my name Sake, who I hope to be acquainted with, and say every thing that's kind, and proper to Lady Dick from my Wife and me. If You ever meet with Capt. Napier present him our kindest Compliments.

The Pope has refused to receive the Spanish Jesuits, and the Cannon were pointed at Civitavechia, in order to prevent their landing, if they should attempt it. The Genoese agreed to receive 2500 of them, in the Presidj. at Corsica, but Count Marbeuf will not admit them; and the Genoese will not receive them upon the Continent, so that two Cargoes of them consisting together of more than a thousand, which went to Civita Vechia, have made sail again, and no body can conjecture where they are gone to. Some say to Orbitello, but that place is not capable of receiving them; besides it belongs to the King of Naples. In short they seem to be denied Fire, and Water by all the Italian Powers.[7]

I will not entertain You with dull Polliticks, they are what they always were, and what they always will be, those out of Employments rail at the measures of those that are in, in order to have their places.

I long to see Your book, I endeavour all I can to prejudice people in favour of our friend, Addio mi Volia bene. Yours very Affectionately,

JOHN DICK

---

[1] It is perhaps evidence of Dick's being 'well' with the King and his ministers that in 1780 Lord North asked him to head his prospective Commission of Accounts and held out 'future honors' as an inducement. Dick declined this post, but in 1781 was made one of two Comptrollers of Army Accounts at a salary of £750 (*Scots Charta Chest*, pp. 263, 286; *Roy. Kal.*, 1782, p. 169).

[2] Citing Sir Alexander Dick's records, the *Baronage* account notes that Louis Dick married Margaret, daughter of Sir James Foulis of Colington, Bt. It does not say where the marriage took place, but indicates only that Louis Dick settled in England, where he died in 1649 (p. 274).

[3] Hans Stanley (c. 1720–80), M.P. for Southampton since 1754, had served as a Lord of the Admiralty and as Governor of the Isle of Wight.

176

In Aug. 1765 he had visited Florence and Leghorn, where he presumably met Dick (*Corres. HW* xxii. 326–27). His Hampshire estate was Paultons, near Romsey, a market town some ten miles north-west of Southampton and an equal distance south-west of Winchester.

[4] George Montagu Dunk (1716–71), Earl of Halifax, had been Lord Lieutenant of Ireland and first Lord of the Admiralty. As Secretary of State for the South, 1763–65, he had been Dick's superior. Lord Halifax had estates in Kent and Northamptonshire, but we have found no record of his owning land in Sussex.

[5] See To Ashbury, 4 June, n.12.

[6] Thomas Anson (c. 1695–1773) of Shugborough Hall, Staffordshire, M.P. for Lichfield, 1747–70, and brother of Admiral George Anson, had lived many years abroad in his youth (Namier and Brooke i. 23). JB wrote that he had at his estate 'a rich assemblage of what is curious in nature, as well as of what is elegant in art', including two Corsican muffoli, or wild sheep (*Corsica*, p. 41). Presumably Dick supplied this information, since JB did not meet Anson until 14 Apr. 1772, when they were together with Paoli at a dinner at Mrs. Montagu's (Journ).

[7] On 31 Mar. and the days following, the Jesuits were expelled from Spain and placed on ships bound for Città Vecchia in the Papal States. The accounts reaching Britain of what happened to them after their arrival there closely match Dick's (e.g. *Scots Mag.* 1767, xxix. 217, 274–75, 316, 381, 493; *Ann. Reg.* 1767, pp. 27–34). Modern commentators differ as to the Pope's motives for refusing the Jesuits, some saying he was concerned that to accept them would encourage Naples and Parma to follow the Spanish example, others that Città Vecchia was already crowded with refugees (J. C. H. Aveling, *The Jesuits*, 1982, pp. 282–83; Christopher Hollis, *A History of the Jesuits*, 1968, p. 150). The motives of Louis-Charles-René, Comte de Marbeuf (1712–86), commanding general of the French troops in Corsica, are also unclear. According to one commentator, Marbeuf believed that the barren island could not support thousands of new inhabitants (Alexis de Saint-Priest, *History of the Fall of the Jesuits*, 1845, p. 38); but also significant is the fact that France had recently (1764) proscribed its own Jesuits, and was pursuing a policy of increasing assertiveness with respect to Corsican affairs. The Jesuits remained on their ships off Bastia for about a month while more ships arrived and negotiations went on among France, Genoa, and Spain. Negotiations were concluded in early July, the Jesuits disembarked in various Corsican ports, and Paoli is said to have received them with great hospitality (*Scots Mag.* 1767, xxix. 316), although most of them were lodged in spartan accommodations such as barns, stables, and old chapels (W. V. Bangert, *A History of the Society of Jesus*, 1972, p. 388).

To Pasquale Paoli, c. Thursday 18 June 1767

Not reported. See From John Dick, 29 July: 'Before I left Town, I forwarded Your Letter for the General to Mr. Burnaby'. Dick left London on Monday, 22 June, so the letter for Paoli must have been written by 18 June at latest.

From Thomas Davies, Thursday 18 June 1767

MS. Yale (C 900).

ADDRESS: To James Boswell Esqr. of Auchinleck, at Edinburgh.

POSTMARKS: 18 JV, WM.[1]

London, June 18, 1767

DEAR SIR: Your Friend Mr. Dick omitted to give me any notice of his being in Town till yesterday: when all on a sudden he[2] sent his Servant to desire one of my Shopmen might call on him directly. Upon this I sent immediately to know his pleasure, He acquainted my Servant that the books must be packed up and ready in[3] two days, for the ship would sail in that time. This has prevented my being able to get the Inscriptions written[4] so well as I could wish, nor know I now if I can possibly get all the Vols. of the English books finished in time. On the other side you have a bad specimen of the Writing; for I assure All the Classicks are much better done. The English are[5] not begun yet: I have been so hurried with business that I have had no time to apply about your Servants Estate. Have you not all the Gazetts and News papers at Edinburgh? If you have it will answer the purpose as well and save me a great deal of trouble. If you have not I will imploy a proper person.[6] Mr. Johnson promised faithfully to write to Mr. Boswell I hope he has kept his word.[7]

I have orders to purchase 6 Watch keyes to send with the General's books, we are all hands[8] at work upon this business. I have made bold to add Mr. Addison Miscellaneous Works to the Spectators etc. Octo. Twou'd be allmost a sin to send Addison without Cato and the Charming Letter from Italy to Lord Halifax etc. I am, Dear Sir, Your most obedient, humble Servant,

THOMAS DAVIES

*

Academiae De Corte doctissimae
CORSORUM
Vim insitam promoventi
Cives optimos
Heroas fortissimos erudienti
Jacobus Boswell de Auchinleck
SCOTUS
In Animi venerantis memoriam[9]
D.
*

[1] Probably the initials of a receiver.
[2] MS. 'yesterday' inserted before 'he', then deleted.
[3] MS. 'the' and an illegible word—perhaps '20'—deleted before 'in'
[4] MS. 'd' (for ?'done') deleted before 'written'
[5] MS. 'are are'
[6] Davies refers to the affair of James Windram; see From P. L. Dupont, 7 Apr. n. 4.

[7] SJ's next reported letter to JB is dated 23 Mar. 1768 (*Life* ii. 58).
[8] MS. 'at' deleted before 'hands'
[9] 'To the most learned academy of Corte of the Corsicans, for increasing innate worth and teaching the best citizens and the strongest heroes, James Boswell of Auchinleck, a Scot, gives [this book] in memory of a revered spirit.'

From Francis Gentleman, Tuesday 23 June 1767

MS. Yale (C 1367).

ADDRESS: To James Boswell Esqr. of Auchinleck, Edinburgh.'

POSTMARK: MALTON.

NOTE in Gentleman's hand at foot of second page: James Boswell Esqr.

New Malton, Yorkshire, June the 23d, 1767

SIR: Every fresh instance of my living in Mr. Boswell's remembrance must afford me very delicate and great satisfaction; wherefore[1] I should much sooner have acknowledged the last Honour you indulged me with; had I any thing to say which might compensate an intrusion upon Time so importantly devoted as yours is at present; however lest silence should bear any mark of disrespect or cold esteem, I have seized the Pen and rush with more sincerity than decorum into your Presence.

I most heartily rejoice that the happy Union of a Good Head and Gen'rous Heart is applied to the study of Law; which when made a proper use of must be esteemed the noblest application of the Human Mind; perhaps my regard may be too sanguine; else I could flatter myself with the Idea of seeing, with equal opportunities of action, a rival to our celebrated Camden, in the Person of one who has vouchsafed me some notice;[2] rest satisfied, sir, that every addition to Mr. Boswell's Public character and private happiness will create very pleasing sensations in my Breast; nor can I avoid drawing the most agreeable let me say glorious expectations from that truly amiable attachment you have shewn to Liberty in the Corsican cause; I own my curiosity for your intended publication is very impatient; and I most sincerely wish that so suitable a Subject may be properly attended to by the Sons of Britain.

The approbation you vouchsafe my Fables has pleased me more than any other point of Praise; notwithstanding I have received a considerable deal from diff'rent Quarters; indeed all my Publications have been kindly received by many Persons of Learning and Taste; yet as to emolument they have answered little or no end, except obtaining me some connections which may be and I believe will be of considerable use—this last remark I insert to give your benevolent feelings satisfaction for I have always presumed to think you wish me well.

When in Scotland I proposed publishing some Pieces by Subscription, and received from Some Persons the first payments; yet various circumstances concurred to prevent my design taking effect, and remoteness of situation having rendered it impossible to return such small Sums; I have perhaps appeared to less advantage in point of character than I could wish; but a similar scheme being now on Foot countenanced by Many very leading characters I[3] intend to insert the names of my Scots patrons and order Books when Published to be delivered both in Edinburgh and Glasgow.[4] With what sincere joy does Mr. Hamilton's situation affect me; shall I request to convey thro' your favour as I know not his address; my warmest congratulations[5]—by meer accident I heard of the Act for enabling his Majesty to Grant a Patent for the Edinburgh Theatre, had I known it in Time I think I have Interest that would have obtained it.[6] I very much want a Copy of my Oroonoko and the two Musical pieces which were done at Glasgow; I did myself the Honour to present them bound together to Lord Auchinleck; there is a person going from here to Edinburgh in a Month who would convey them to[7] my hands if I knew where to direct him for them; and they should be duly returned.[8]

Believe me to be, Sir, with warm attachment and infinite respect, Your most obliged and very obedient Servant,

FRANCIS GENTLEMAN

When leisure and inclination concur to make me happy with a line directions to *New Malton* will find me.

[1] MS. 'theref' deleted before 'wherefore'

[2] Charles Pratt (1714–94), Baron, later (1786) Earl, Camden, had been Lord Chancellor since 1766.

[3] MS. 'to' deleted before 'I'

[4] We have no contemporary record of Gentleman's having collected subscriptions during his stay in Scotland, 1758–c. 1760, but he men-

tioned having done so in a letter to William Julius Mickle of 12 Oct. 1766, where he described his current project as the publication of 'a Play of mine and several other poetical pieces', for which he already had more than a hundred subscribers, 'above fifty of them people of consequence'. On 7 Dec. 1766 he reported to Mickle that he had seventy subscribers for an edition 'on Royal Paper at half a Guinea each' and a hundred subscribers for the edition on 'common Paper' at 5s. He expected to print '100 Royals and 300 Common Copies', each adorned with 'four copper plates elegantly engraved'. On 14 Mar., in answer to Mickle's enquiry about the book's progress, he wrote that he would shortly publish 'some proposals on an improved plan' (MSS. Mickle Papers, Osborn Collection). We have no further report of this project until Jan. 1770, when Gentleman published *The Sultan: or, Love and Fame. A New Tragedy*, in which this notice appeared on the back of the title-page: 'The SUBSCRIBERS to an Octavo Volume of POEMS by the AUTHOR of this TRAGEDY; are respectfully requested to take Notice, that the said Volume will certainly be delivered on or before the 1st of next *June*.' No such book of poems has been attributed to Gentleman (*Biog. Dict. Actors* vi. 147).

[5] For John Hamilton of Sundrum, see From Gentleman, c. late July 1766, n. 3. No salutary change in Sundrum's life for 1767 has been reported. JB had last seen him on 16 Apr. (Journ.).

[6] The King signed the act on 20 May granting a patent to the proprietors of the Theatre Royal (*Scots Mag.* 1767, xxix. 322; Dibdin, p. 144). See From Thomas Davies, 12 Dec. n. 7, for the opening of the theatre.

[7] MS. illegible deletion before 'to'

[8] No doubt Gentleman, who often revived or published works he had written long before, was chiefly interested in recovering the two 'Musical pieces' for performance or publication. He asked for them again in a letter of 6 Feb. 1770. We have found no record of a copy of *Oroonoko* in the Auchinleck library, and the two musical pieces are unidentified. Some of Gentleman's comedies (e.g. *Cupid's Revenge*, 1772) were accompanied by music, but it is unlikely that he would call such a play a 'Musical piece'. Perhaps he was thinking of works he called 'interludes', such as 'The Scarborough Lass' and 'The Fairy Court', both written in the early 1760s after he had left Glasgow, and both unpublished (*Biog. Dict. Actors* vi. 143–44, 150). Possibly, however, these pieces were simply songs that he wished to include in his projected book of poems.

From Richard Edwards,[1] Friday 26 June 1767

MS. Yale (C 1176).

Leghorn, the 26th June 1767

SIR, I had the Honour to write you the 24th April last, and now have that to trouble You with this to enclose You Your Papers, which the Revd. Mr. Burnaby has just received from Corsica.

It will always give me great Pleasure to obey Your Commands, having the Honour to be with great Truth and Regard, Sir, Your most obedient, Humble Servant,

RICHARD EDWARDS

[1] Richard Edwards was presumably deputed by John Dick to forward papers for JB while Dick was in England (From John Dick, 6 Feb.). Nothing more is known about him.

From Lady Grizel Cochrane, Saturday 27 June 1767

MS. Yale (C 807).

ADDRESS: To James Boswell Esqr., Advocate, at Lord Auchenlecks, Parliament Closs, In Edinburgh.

Culross-Abby,[1] June 27, 1767

Will Mr. Boswell take the Trouble to read a few Lines from an Old Friend? It will be great Condescension, If he does—As I hear all his hours are fully Employ'd.

Dayly the Guineas are Coming In. Bliss Me how rich You will Be—pray will you Lend an Old Acquaintance a hundred or So? But honnestly I'll tell You the Security Won't be such as Mr. John Stobie will advise You take.

Well how do you do? And how does Worthy Lord Auchenleck keep his Health? None Can Esteem or respect his Lordship more than I Do and a Gratefull Sense and remembrance I have of his Friendship. Many, Very Many happy days may Mr. Boswell and his Lordship Live together.

Compliments to Mr. David Boswell. I hope Doctor Boswell and his family are Well? Where Is Mrs. Montgomery your Cousine Staying Now—does any of the Miss Montgomerys stay with her?[2] I offer my respectfull humble Compliments to Lord Auchenleck and I trouble You with Compliments to Mr. Claud Boswell. He Is a great favourite of Mine as I Esteem him to Be Worthy.

Now will You write Me two or three Lines and tell Me how the Douglass Cause Is Determin'd.[3] How Cruel You are to make the Quallity Ladies Ly In at the Cross. Sure You Won't Oblige Lady Betty Mc——to do So[4] —Adeiu Mr. Boswell may You Be as Happy and fortunate as I and Some Other of Your Good Friends Wishes You to Be.

Yours etc.,

G. COCHRANE

[1] Culross Abbey, Fife, belonged to Lady Grizel's father Lord Dundonald.

[2] Mary and Margaret Montgomerie lived at Lainshaw with their elder sister, Elizabeth Montgomerie-Cuninghame, who had succeeded to the estate on the death of her brother the previous December (From Mary Montgomerie, 27 Mar. 1766, nn. 1–3).

[3] The Douglas Cause was not yet decided. The Court of Session would come down against Douglas on 15 July (*Scots Mag.* 1767, xxix. 387).

[4] Although the Cross of Edinburgh had been torn down in 1756, the site was still a popular meeting place for public proclamations, the conduct of business, and the exchange of news (Hugo Arnot, *The History of Edinburgh*, 1788, pp. 302–04). Lady Grizel refers to JB's ballad *The Douglas Cause*, composed on 20 May and circulated as a broadside (Journ.; *Lit. Car.* p. 27; see also F. A. Pottle, 'Three New Legal Ballads by James Boswell', *The Juridical Review*, 1925, xxxvii. 209–11, where the ballad is printed in full). Stanzas 3 and 4 ridicule the Hamilton argument that there were few witnesses of Archibald Douglas's birth:

No birth must henceforth be believ'd,
Unless proclaim'd by sound of trumpet;
And ev'ry Dame of high degree
Become as brazen as a strumpet.

The Cross of Edinburgh must be made
A perfect hospital in-lying;
Nor will the music-bells be heard,
For Female Quality a-crying.

'Lady Betty Mc——' is JB's friend Lady Elizabeth Macfarlane; we do not know why Lady Grizel mentions her in this connection.

From John Dick, Sunday 28 June 1767

MS. Yale (C 1017).

NOTE in Dick's hand at foot of first page: James Boswell Esq.

Winchester,[1] 28th June 1767

MY DEAR FRIEND, I had the pleasure to write You about ten days ago, before I left Town, and as I have this moment receiv'd advice that Capraja surrenderd to the Corsicans the 28th past, I would not defer a moment to send You news which I knew would afford You so much pleasure, and at the same time to Congratulate You most sincerely thereon. Inclosed I send You the Capitulation and Copy of a Letter that was wrote to Capt. Santi with it.

We shall remain in this Country about ten or twelve days, but when You have Occasion to favour me with a Letter you may always direct for me at Mess. Drummonds.

Mrs. Dick begs your acceptance of her kindest Compliments and pray present hers, and mine at Priestfield,[2] and to our friend Mr. Ferguson—and believe me to be always with the most unalterable Regard and true Esteem, My dear Sir, Your much obliged and Affectionate friend,

JOHN DICK

[1] Dick was visiting Hans Stanley at Paultons. See From Dick, 17 June and n. 3.

[2] Prestonfield, Sir Alexander Dick's estate, built upon land that had belonged to the Cistercian monastery of Harehope or Holm Cultram in the thirteenth century (William Baird, *Annals of Duddingston and Portobello*, 1898, p. 91), had formerly been called Priestfield and was still so called in some eighteenth-century documents (e.g. the records of the lawsuit between Dick and Lord Abercorn—From Dick, 10 Apr. and n. 7).

From Robert Brown, c. late June or early July, 1767[1]

MS. Yale (C 592)

ADDRESS: To James Boswel Esquire, Advocate in Edinburgh.

Edinr. 6th July 1767

DEAR SIR: You will no doubt have thought me very much to blame in not having made some return before now to your last favour. I have been extremely faulty, I must acknowledge, in having delayed so long to do it; and it is the design of this to sollicite your forgiveness for that ommission. However, I must in justice to myself observe that my silence is to be considered in a point of light very different from what it ought to be if it had proceeded from mere neglect or indifference; which 'tis impossible I can ever entertain towards a Person I have such a high value for as I sincerly and deservedly have for You. To have barely acknowledged the receipt of yours would have answered no purpose; and to have told you I put up the papers you want along with the others, would have been equally insignificant, since I had mentioned this to you very expressly in my preceding letter.[2] I resolved to wait a return from Mr. Kinloch; and this I had not 'till two days before I set out from Utrecht. That Gentleman having informed me that not having been allowed to go himself to Scotland, he had left these papers with a careful hand in London, to be forwarded to his father, and had left them in the same order I had delivered them to him (which was such that they might be inspected at the Customhouse and at the same time could not be read) I made particular enquiry in London as to this packet, and find it was sent just in such a way as Capt. Kinloch had left it. I am exceedingly sorry any part of the contents should have miscarried; and that it has surprises me much: insomuch that I cannot help flattering myself that the mistake is already rectified, and that the strayed parcel is now come to rights. I could think of no surer method of transmitting these papers to you; as Mr. Kinloch was one I could absolutely depend on, and when he left Utrecht was resolved to go directly to Edinr. I propose to set out for that city in a very few days, and in my way will spend an evening at Gilmerton, when I shall inform myself particularly from Mr. Kinloch as to the fate of these papers; but this will rather be to satisfy so much the sooner my own curiosity than to procure you any new satisfaction about them; for he has certainly told you long ago all he knows—and indeed, as I have already mentioned, I persuade myself that Gentleman has been able to send you the ipsissima desiderata.³ I repeat that it has given me great pain that these papers, which I had all along kept with so much care, and which I congratulated myself on having sent you by so promising an occasion, did not reach you entire.

I hope you will give me leave when in Edinr. to pay you my respects, and to assure you once more by word of mouth of the sincere esteem and regard with which I have the honour to be, Dear Sir, Your most obedient, humble Servant,

ROBERT BROWN

My intention was to have sent this by post, because at the writing of it, I did not exactly know what time I could be in Scotland; but having afterwards resolved to set out directly, I thought best to be the bearer myself. We unluckily passed Mr. Kinloch of Gilmerton on the road—(He is gone to London) so that tho I lodged last night at his house, I have not had the pleasure of seeing him, and consequently know nothing more than before of the papers; for nobody at Gilmerton could give me any information about them. I'm extremely mortified at not having it [in] my power to wait upon you at this time, being obliged to hasten with the utmost dispatch to Dundee—but in a fortnight or perhaps ten days hence, I shall certainly be again in Edinr.;⁴ and then will have nothing more material on hand than to renew acquaintance with a Gentleman I so highly value.

¹ The date of this letter and the place of its writing are uncertain. The dateline 'Edinr. 6th July 1767' applies to the postscript, which Brown wrote on the inside of the cover. From his phrasing ('I made particular enquiry in London', not 'I have made' and not 'here'), it appears that he may have written this letter after leaving London. Brown's statement that he plans to set out for Edinburgh 'in a very few days' combines with the three or four days it would take to travel from the south of England to Edinburgh to make possible a date in the last few days of June; but if the letter was written in Scotland or the north of England, a date in early July is likely.

² From Brown, 27 Jan.

³ 'The missing things themselves'.

⁴ JB's journal lapses for this period, and we have no other record of Brown's having visited him in Edinburgh. Presumably he did, however, for he received from JB a letter to carry to Zélide (From Brown, 22 Oct.).

From Thomas Smith,¹ Wednesday 1 July 1767

MS. Yale (C 2499).

ADDRESS: To Mr. James Boswell, Advocate, Edr.

POSTMARK: IRVINE.

Irvine, July 1st, 1767

SIR: Some weeks ago My friend Mr. Kidd in Wearsdale Informed me that according to my desire he had Sent you the Spar directed to The Reverd Mr. Aitkines Care in N. Castle.² It would give me pleasure to hear you had rec'd it Safe and pleased, if So lucky. You Shall have more, as I am well accquanted with Many of the Stuards over the Lead Mines.

I am Just now with my Good friend Lady Boninton who I understand is one of your Clients. She thinks her Self happy that She has Such an able and worthy

Advocate (as She Calls you) to plead her Cause, She is Impatient to hear from Mr. Ore her Agent if he has laid the Memorial before you and Got your opinion; all the Gentlemen in this place that I am acquaint with Condemns Mr. Cochran for the bad usage he has Given Lady Bonninton, However he may Impose upon people to Give Credit to his Storries, yet I am Sure he Cannot justify himself before any Impartial Judge. If Sir you Know how he has treat her it would make your tender heart weep! as She would Gladly have the whole affair Speedily ended. I presume to Implore and beseach you my best of friends to be active in this Cause of the distressed widow, and make the heart of the widow Sing for joy.[3] I Can assure you She is beloved and respected by all who has the happiness of her acquaintance, (except her oponent) who has not paid her a farthing Sinc Bonintons Death and was obliged to Borrow Money to Suport her family. I hope your Goodness will forgive this freedom and what favour you Shew by Getting her Speedily releaved from her distresses I'le take as done my Self.[4] I return to Cumbertrees to Morrow. Lady Bonninton joins me In respectfull Compliments to you. I ever am, Dear Sir, your much obliged and most obedient, Humble Servant,

THOS. SMITH

[1] The Rev. Thomas Smith (c. 1718–99) had been minister at Cummertrees, Annan, Dumfriesshire, since 1760. Earlier, he had served as tutor at Mountstuart, Dumfriesshire, and as minister at Alston Moor, Cumberland (*Fasti Scot.* ii. 244). He was a dinner guest at Lord Auchinleck's in Edinburgh on 28 May 1780 (Journ.).

[2] Parish registers show that Kidd was a common name in the neighbourhood of Wearsdale, Durham; this Mr. Kidd has not been identified further (*Registers of Stanhope, in the County of Durham. Marriages, 1613–1812*, Durham and Northumberland Parish Register Society, 1900). The Rev. Edward Aitken (c. 1695–1771) had been chaplain to JB's grandfather James Boswell and tutor to Lord Auchinleck (Charter recording the sale of Bassiesyke, 2 Nov. 1730, MS. Boswell Collection, series XV, Box 115, folder 2088; Journ. 18 Mar. 1768). Since 1736 Aitken had been minister at Castlegarth, Newcastle (*Fasti Scot.* vii. 516; *Scots Mag.* 1771, xxxiii. 559). Lt.

John Boswell, Boswell's younger brother, had boarded with Aitken in early 1766 (From Mary Montgomerie, 27 Mar. 1766); he was now living at Lavrick Hall near Monkton, Durham, but occasionally walked to Newcastle to call on Aitken (Lt. John Boswell's Journal, C 404:2, 22 Apr., 6, 19 May, 27 June). It is not known why JB wanted spar from the Durham lead mines.

[3] Job 29: 13, 'I caused the widow's heart to sing for joy'.

[4] 'Lady Boninton' was the widow of John Chalmers of Bonnyton or Bonnington, Ayrshire, who had died in 1766; nothing more is known about her (Ayr and Wigton I. ii. 618, 633; Ayrshire, p. 277). Alexander Orr (d. 1774) of Waterside, W.S., is listed in JB's Consultation Book as agent for several causes during the period Dec. 1766–Dec. 1767; but this cause is not among them. The 'Mr. Cochran' who was oppressing Mrs. Chalmers has not been identified, and the details of this cause have not been reported.

To Edward Dilly, c. early July 1767

Not reported. JB asked Edward Dilly (1732–79) and his brother Charles (1739–1807), booksellers at the Rose and Crown, 22 Poultry, to publish his *Corsica* (Maxted, pp. 66–67). For the answer, see From Edward Dilly, 28 July. This letter initiated a lifelong friendship between JB and the brothers Dilly, despite the political and religious differences between them (the Dillys were Dissenters and Whigs). Their firm brought out not only *Corsica*, but also the *Journal of a Tour to the Hebrides*, 1785, and the *Life of Johnson*, 1791. Nichols says of them, 'Though neither of them had much pretensions to Literature, they were zealous in cultivating the friendship of the Literati', including SJ. He also notes that JB in his later years substituted as host when Charles Dilly was unable to meet with visitors (*Lit. Anec.* iii. 191–192 nn.). Their numerous publications are detailed in the unpublished Yale dissertation of S. H. Bingham, 'Publishing in the Eighteenth Century with Special Reference to the Firm of Edward and Charles Dilly', 1938.

From Marie de Froment, Thursday 9 July 1767

Ms. Yale (C 1325). The letter was enclosed in From Lord Marischal, 10 July.
NOTE at bottom of page: mr. bosvell.

de potsdam, ce 9 juillet 1767

MONSIEUR: Quoique depuis votre dépar de ce pays je n'ay eu ocune relation avec vous peutetre suis entierement eface de votre memoire, je veus m'y renouveller, de plus j'ay meme une faveur a vous demander, j'aspere que vous ne voudrier pas me refuser, persuadé de lamitie que vous aves pour mylord et ceux pour qu'il s'interesse, c'est jai aplacé 500 ll. sterlig ver jenvier prochen je voudrai bien que sa soit en Écosse, si vous voulie bien m'aider en cette affaire vous vous obligeres infiniment, mosieur, votres tres humble servant,

MARIE DE FROMENT NEE EMETE

From Lord Marischal, Friday 10 July 1767

MS. Yale (C 1957).
ADDRESS: To James Boswell Esqr.

Potsdam, 10 July 1767

SIR: Madame de Froment has writ to you that soon she will have 500, ps. St., or thereabout, to place on good security; she has taken the liberty to adresse herself to you from the entire confidence she has in your honor and probity, as I have also, and therefor allow me to recommend to you her business; she wants to have her money placed surely for the regular payment of interest at 4.pr. cent, without hasard of law suit, the money on land security. She will ere long have about six thousand Thalers, about 1000, ps. St., of my furniture etc. here, for I grow not only old, but infirm, tho without pain or sickness;[1] which also she will place in Scotland, for she intends to leave what she has to my neices, but this only between you and me.[2]

Let me know how you and My Lord your Father are, I hope well, and believe me ever with the greatest regard your most humble and obedient servant,

MARISCHALL

Is it true that Mr. Rousseau wrote to the Chancellor demanding a messenger to conduct him to Dover?[3] There was here lately the Comte de Guines, who affirms that Paoli did not write to R. to have a Code of laws, but that it was positively a trick of Voltaire.[4]

We drink dayly *Success to the arms of Emetulla*, they are in Hamburg, at your orders in the hands of Mss. Stephen and Renny.[5] I am told that money lent in good security in Scotland at five per cent is payable only in two years, and at four per cent is payable yearly, is it so?[6]

[1] Lord Marischal lived for another eleven years, dying on 23 May 1778. His age has been variously given as 84 and 86.

[2] Emet-Ulla may have included Marischal's only niece Lady Clementina Fleming, daughter of his sister Mary, Countess of Wigton, in her proposed bequest, but since Emet-Ulla and Clementina were of the same generation, it seems

more likely that Marischal's *grandnieces*, Mary, Eleanora, Primrose, and Clementina, the four surviving daughters of his niece and her husband Charles Elphinstone, 10th Lord Elphinstone, were to be the beneficiaries (*Scots Peer*. iii. 545–49). See also Sir William Fraser, *The Elphinstone Family Book*, 1897, i. 245–68.

[3] On 5 May Rousseau had written from Spalding, Lincolnshire, to the Lord Chancellor about his ill treatment in England and the dangers posed by his many enemies; he asked for 'un guide autorisé' to conduct him to Dover (*Corres. Rousseau* xxxiii. 44).

[4] Adrien-Louis de Bonnières (1735–1806), Comte de Guines, as a brigadier had been sent by the King of France to Frederick the Great in 1766 to assist with troop manoeuvres. In 1768 he became the French ambassador to Berlin and in 1770 ambassador to Great Britain (NBG). On the story that the Corsican invitation to Rousseau was Voltaire's trick, see From Lord Marischal, 30 Apr. 1766, n. 4.

[5] See From Lord Marischal, 29 May 1768, for Paoli's acknowledgement of Emet-Ulla's arms; their arrival in Corsica was reported in *Lond. Chron*. 28–30 Jan. 1768, xxiii. 98.

[6] Marischal may perhaps have been remembering the 1730s, when a clause was inserted in the bank notes of two of the major Scottish banks (The Royal Bank and The Bank of Scotland), which made repayment of the notes (after the usual term of six months) an option of the bank, though it was stipulated that in such circumstances, the interest should accrue at the rate of 5%. This clause remained in effect until the bank regulating Act prohibiting the insertion of such clauses was passed in 1765 (Andrew W. Kerr, *A History of Banking in Scotland*, 4th ed. 1926, pp. 47, 73–79). In 1762, before the Act was passed, Edinburgh banks were paying 5% on deposits for six months or longer and 4% on deposits payable on demand (Kerr, pp. 69–70).

To Isabella van Tuyll van Serooskerken, c. mid to late July 1767

Not reported. See From Robert Brown, 22 Oct.: 'You must have received a letter lately from a very fair hand, in answer to one you sent by me; in which you will remember you propose and desire a renewal of Correspondence.' In a postscript, dated 6 July, to his letter of c. late June or early July, Brown stated that he expected to see JB in Edinburgh 'in a fortnight or perhaps ten days'; that is the only time he could have been the bearer of a letter for Zélide.

To John Dick, 18–20 July 1767

Not reported. See From Dick, 29 July: 'On tuesday morning . . . I had the pleasure to receive your very kind, and obliging Letter of the 18/20 Inst. which brought me one likewise from good Sir Alexander, for which, I am greatly obliged to You.'

To Lord Marischal, Monday 20 July 1767

Not reported. See From Marischal, 1 Sept.: 'I delayed some posts answering your favor of July 20th'.

To John Wilkie, c. Tuesday 21 July 1767

Not reported. See From Wilkie, 28 July: 'I had the favor of your letter last Saturday, with the Corsican papers for the Chronicle.'

From Alexander Mitchell,[1] Saturday 25 July 1767

MS. Yale (C 2034).

ADDRESS: To James Bosswell Esqr., Advocate, att Ednr.

Ayr, July 25th, 1767

DEAR SIR: According to your Desire I went to Dalblair this day tho it was very wet

I got two Brace of fowls and browgt them to Adamton and gave them to mis Blair[2] who was very Kind and insted that I would Stay all night but I beged to bie Excused as I was obledged to be att Ayr but befor She wowld Let me go I was to promise to Com and See her as Soon a[s] I cowld, and if posibl Shall Send you a Brace or two with Simcott[3] and I am, dear Sir, your Humble Servant,

ALEXR. MITCHELL

[1] Alexander Mitchell (fl. 1760–80) was a distant cousin of JB's, being descended from John Boswell, third laird of Auchinleck (*Ominous Years*, Gen. chart II, p. 375). He had held the estate of Hallglenmuir in Auchinleck parish since before 1760, but in 1780 was forced to flee abroad to escape his creditors, and the estate was sold to Hugh Logan of Logan (*Ayr and Wigton* I. i. 204; *Ayrshire*, p. 297; Journ. 18 Apr., 28 May 1780). JB and 'honest Hallglenmuir' had been together frequently in the spring (Journ. 23 Mar., 10 Apr., 5, 11, 23 May). In early June, JB and Mitchell, with some others, had stopped in Auchinleck village for 'Twopenny with *Cap* and *Stoup*' and had drunk to 'agriculture Trade mines and minerals Coal and lime etc. and Miss Blair in all manner of ways' (Journ. 3 June).

[2] Catherine Blair (c. 1749–98) was a distant cousin of JB's, being descended from David Boswell, fifth laird of Auchinleck, through his daughter Margaret, who had married David Blair of Adamton (*Ominous Years*, Gen. Chart II, p. 375). JB was now campaigning for her hand. He had written to Temple on 30 Mar., 'There is a young Lady in the Neighbourhood here, who has an estate of her own between two and three hundred a year, just eighteen, a genteel Person, an agreeable face, of a good family, sensible, good tempered, chearful, pious'. JB competed for her affections with William Fullarton, 'the Nabob', until Feb. 1768, when she rejected them both (Journ. 8 Feb. 1768; *Earlier Years*, pp. 322, 329–30, 336–37, 343–51). In 1776 she married Sir William Maxwell of Monreith, Bt. (*Comp. Bar.* iv. 311).

[3] Unidentified.

From Edward Dilly, Tuesday 28 July 1767

MS. Yale (C 1061).

ADDRESS: To James Boswell Esqr., at Lord Auchenlecks, Edinburgh.

London, July 28th, 1767

SIR: I arrived in London on Friday last, and have had only a few Moments leisure to look over the Specimens you sent me. I approve of what I have seen, and do agree to your Proposal.

1. To Pay Mr. Boswell One Hundred Guineas for the Copyright of his Account of Corsica etc., the Money to be due three Months after the Publication of the Work in London.

2. That the Book be Printed in Scotland, Viz. the first Edition, under Mr. Boswell's direction.

3. That a Map of Corsica be Engraved for the said Work at the Expence of E. and C. Dilly. There is a Map of Corsica lately Printed in London. I intend to send you a Copy of it in a few days, and you may possibly make some amendments, and I believe it will be better Engraved in London than at Edinr.[1]

I shall take the first opportunity of transmittg. the Specimens to you at Edinr., there are some inaccuricis of Style which I make no doubt you will correct. As this is the best Season of the Year for Printing, the sooner you send the Work to Press the better, for I would by all means have it ready for Publication the latter End of November. Mr. Foulis, I presume you intend to be the Printer, if the Copy is quite finishd.[2] I shall be glad if he will Cast it off, and let me know what it will make, in Pica Octavo; and likewise English Octavo, and I will send Paper Accordingly.[3]

The favour of an answer Your first opportunity will Oblige, Sir, Your most Obedient Servant,

EDWD. DILLY

[1] Two maps had been published in London since 1760. 'A New Map of the Island of Corsica Divided into Cantons, Called Pieves', by Thomas Kitchin, appeared in the early part of the decade (c. 1760–62) and was reprinted by *Lond. Mag.* (1768) xxxvii. 128. 'An Accurate Map of the Island of Corsica' by George Rollos appeared in the *Royal Magazine* (1762) vi. facing p. 272, accompanying 'A Succinct Account of the Island of *Corsica*', pp. 273–76. The map issued with Corsica was engraved by Thomas Phinn in Edinburgh. Phinn was an engraver, not a cartographer (Thieme-Becker xxvi. 557), so it is unlikely that the map was his own work; but it is not copied from either Kitchin's or Rollos's map, and its source has not been identified.

[2] The three chapters of the 'Account of Corsica' (*Corsica*, pp. 1–239) were delivered to the Foulis Press 21 Aug. (From Foulis, 21 Aug.). Nevertheless, the 'Journal of a Tour to Corsica' (*Corsica*, pp. 261–382) was delayed until November, partly because JB solicited opinions of it from Temple and others (To Temple, 8 and 9 Nov.). The book stood 'compleat' by 18 Dec. (To Temple, 18 Dec.), Foulis finished printing it around the end of December (From Foulis, 30 Dec.), and it was published on 18 Feb. 1768 (Journ.).

[3] Around the middle of August JB received specimens of the *Corsica* text printed in different types. He preferred the 'large Type' to the 'English' (To Foulis, c. middle of August). These specimens have not been reported, and conjecture about them is made difficult by JB's vague uses of typographical terminology. Philip Gaskell suggests that the specimens were in two styles of 'English Roman': the 'large Type' was presumably what Gaskell designates 'RE 3', a font with a large and rounded look; the 'English' was presumably 'RE 2', a type that appeared much smaller, although technically it was the same size. Foulis printed the main text of *Corsica* in RE 2, and the Preface in RE 3 (Philip Gaskell, *Bibliography of the Foulis Press*, 1964, pp. 41–2, 278–9, 399–400).

From John Wilkie, Tuesday 28 July 1767

MS. Yale (C 3112).

ADDRESS: To James Boswell Esqr. at Edinburgh.

POSTMARK: [LONDON] 28 IY.

London, July 28, 1767

SIR: I had the favor of your letter last Saturday, with the Corsican papers for the Chronicle. In my last letter I belive I mentioned that the Proprietors of the Chronicle wished to have the Corsican Gazets directed to me rather than wait their return from Scotland—but I believe I must now beg the favor of you to continue them in the same Channell as heretofore because I find our Editor does not sufficiently understand Italian to translate the papers with that expedition as is necessary. If therefore Sir you will please to favor us as usual[1] it will be most agreeable and half the Expence I have orders to pay, for the proprietors.

I did not receive the 300 Dorando till some days after you expected I shoud have had them, however I believe every part of your directions about them[2] has been attended to. Of the 300 there remains now in my hands 79 what Mr. Davies may have remaining of the 25 I sent him I do not know. By this account you will see Sir that the sale is not very rapid here. If I had seen the least signs of wanting another Edition I shoud have wrote to you but I really think it will not answer reprinting here, especially as the Douglas Cause is now over. If you have more printed than you think will sell in Scotland—you can reprint the title—and send me any Number more you please which by an Advertisment or two may carry them off.[3] I am, Sir, Your most Obedient, humble Servant,

JOHN WILKIE

¹ MS. 'usal'
² MS. 'am' altered to 'them'
³ We have no further information about the twenty-five copies that Wilkie had sent to Davies

(who appears on the title-page as one of the publishers). In Scotland, *Dorando* had gone through three editions (*Lit. Car.* p. 35).

From John Dick, Wednesday 29 July 1767

MS. Yale (C 1018).

NOTE in Dick's hand at foot of first page: James Boswell Esquire.

Shugborough, 29 July 1767

MY DEAR SIR, On tuesday morning, (just as I was setting out from London for this place on a Visit to my worthy friend Mr. Anson) I had the pleasure to receive your very kind, and obliging letter of the 18/20 Inst. which brought me one likewise from good Sir Alexander, for which, I am greatly obliged to You, Had You favour'd me with it before, I should er'e this, have had the pleasure to be with You, as I should have made other arrangements, and taken this place in my way from Scotland to Bath, where I must be, the beginning of Septr. in order to drink the Waters for a Billious disorder which I am troubled with, however, as Sir Alexander and You are so extreemly obliging, I shall endeavour to excuse myself here, as soon as possible and make a Scappata¹ to Edenburgh, and pay my Respects to You, and the good Baronet, indeed I long to have an opportunity to thank you both, for your readiness to serve me, but as I shall be pressed for time, I shall not have it in my power to make any long stay with You. I shall however have the Satisfaction to make a personal acquaintance with Sir Alexander, and perhaps we may find means of being of mutual advantage to each other.

Our friend Ferguson had not acquaintd me with the method which You have in Scotland called a *Service*.² I like this method much, and wish that You may be able to manage it Successfully for me, during the few days, that I may be able to stay with You, the Circumstance of the impossibility of its' being of any prejudice to any one what ever, may perhaps be a great facility. I shall stop at Newcastle, and endeavour to find out some of my Fathers Cotemporarys (in case any such are living) and obtain what You call a *habit*, and *repute* that my Grand Father Andrew Dick came from Scotland, which was certainly the Case, as he was married in Northumberland, the 2 July 1672, and no register can be found in all the County, of his Birth, from whence it is clear, that he must be of an other Country, and I have often when a child heard my father say, that his Father was a Scotsman, and as there were many Arms, and Officers Accutraments in the family, it looks as if my great Grandfather had been the Captain Lewis, which Sir Alexr. mentions, but in either case, whether he was this person, or the Lewis 4th. Son of Sir William it is one and the same thing in Effect, as to the Title.³

The printed paper which You sent me certainly merits serious Consideration, we must talk of this matter, it may be of concequence to the worthy Knights family, and me, and I shall be happy in having it in my power to shew the very great Regard, and Esteem, which I have for him, but of this more when we meett.⁴ As soon as I can fix the time of my setting out from hence, I shall lett you know, in the mean while may I beg the favour of You to send me a form of such a Certificate as you may think will by the Jury be considered as a Habit and Repute. You may send me one Copy of it here directed to me, and put your Letter for me, under a blank cover directed to Thomas Anson Esqr. Member of Parliament, at Shugborough, near Litchfield Staffordshire, and a duplicate of it, and your Letter directed for me, to be left at the Post Office at Durham, least I should be set out from hence before your answer reaches me, which I think very probable. I will not make any Apology for giving You all this Trouble, as you are so very kind, and ready to serve me, but I cannot help adding, that, I shall always have a pleasure in convincing You of my gratitude.

Before I left Town, I forwarded Your Letter for the General to Mr. Burnaby, who I am sure will take care of it, as also of Lord Marshalls kind presents when they reach him, the directions which You have given about them are quite sufficient.[5]

I have the pleasure to acquaint You, that, I have this day receiv'd a Letter from my friend Rutherfurd dated the 10 Inst.,[6] who says, that the French Troops are evacuating all the Sea Port Towns in Corsica, to make room for the Spanish Jesuits, and only a Garrison of them, will perhaps remain in Bastia, so that our Heroe will likely soon be in possession of the Towns evacuated, which I am sure will give You very great pleasure.[7]

Pray present my very kind Compliments to our friend Ferguson, I have this day taken the Liberty to write a few lines to good Sir Alexander, Mrs. Dick Salutes You very Kindly, and I ever am with the most perfect Regard, and unalterable Esteem, My dear Sir, Your most Obliged and Affectionate Friend,

JOHN DICK

[1] From the Italian verb 'scappare', 'to fly away', 'to escape to or from'. Cf. 'scarper', a slang word with the same meaning and derivation, commonly used in Cockney London (OED, 2nd ed. 1989, xiv).

[2] 'Before an heir can regularly acquire a right to the estate of the ancestor, he ought to be served heir, which is one of the old forms of the law of Scotland proceeding upon a brieve, and including in it the decision of a jury, fixing the right and character of the heir to the estate of the ancestor' (Bell ii. 688). A brieve or writ for serving a person heir was issued from Chancery to a judge-ordinary, then proclaimed and published in the jurisdiction where the heir was to be served. Fifteen days later the service proceeded before the judge-ordinary and a jury of fifteen persons. If the jury was satisfied by the claimant's evidence, they served him heir. Finally, the Chancery prepared a certified copy of the decision (Bell ii. 690–91).

[3] The birthplace and birthdate of John Dick's grandfather Andrew are not known, and it is not certain that he was from Scotland. Dick's difficulty was to prove that Andrew's father was either Capt. Lewis Dick (d. 1649), son of Sir William Dick of Braid, or Capt. Lewis Dick, Sir William's grandson by his second son, Sir Andrew Dick of Craighouse, Kt. (Baronage, p. 274, says that John Dick was descended from Sir

William's son). 'Habit and repute' are Scots legal terms that 'express whatever is generally understood and believed to have happened' (Bell i. 330). John Dick hoped to show that his grandfather was by habit and repute a Scotsman; thence he hoped it would be surmised that he was descended from one of the Capt. Lewis Dicks.

[4] Not reported. The paper may have concerned the money owed to Sir Andrew Dick of Craighouse, whose only living descendants were Sir Alexander Dick's two daughters by his first wife (From Sir Alexander Dick, 1 Sept. n. 7 and To Sir Alexander Dick, 2 Sept.).

[5] JB's letter to Paoli has not been reported. By 'Lord Marshall's kind presents' Dick means Emet-Ulla's gift of arms (From Lord Marischal, c. 1 June).

[6] Robert Rutherford (d. 1794) had been a merchant in Leghorn for many years. Through Sir John Dick's efforts he was appointed agent to the Empress of Russia for the Mediterranean area (1771) and was later made a Baron of the Russian Empire. In 1777 Rutherford returned to Scotland a wealthy man and repurchased the ancestral estate of Fairnington, Roxburghshire (Gent. Mag. 1794, lxiv. 276; Burke's Landed Gentry, 1851; Scots Charta Chest, p. 239). JB had met Rutherford in Leghorn (Notes, 9 Oct. 1765).

[7] For the situation of the Jesuits, see From John Dick, 17 June, n. 7.

To John Dick, c. late July or early August 1767

Not reported. See From Dick, 26 Sept.: 'You say that You had wrote me an other letter to Shugborough, I assure You that I never receiv'd it. I hope that it contained nothing material.' Dick wrote from Shugborough on 29 July and 10 Aug.: JB would not have written to him there after receiving the letter of 10 Aug., which announced that Dick was leaving for Durham the next day.

To Alexandre Deleyre, Thursday 30 July 1767

Not reported. For a reply to this letter, see From Deleyre, 25 Sept.

From Heer van Sommelsdyck, c. July or August 1767

Not reported. See From Patrick Preston, 19 Sept.: 'I return inclosed Monsr. de Sommersdycks Letter, which I shewed Lord Cochrane, useing at the same Time such Arguments as I immagined were sufficient to convince Him of the Absurdity of His Father's Ideas'. Apparently Sommelsdyck wrote concerning the matter of Lord Dundonald (of which we know little): JB sent the letter to Preston to show to Lord Cochrane. The evidence does not allow us to date Sommelsdyck's letter very closely, but a date a month or so before Preston returned the letter seems most likely.

To Archibald Stewart, c. summer 1767

Not reported. In his reply of 8 Jan. 1768, Stewart wrote that this letter had arrived while he was away and that, upon his return, he had asked an acquaintance to search for JB's lost journal, but had received no answer for 'near four Months'. Thus this letter could have been written, at latest, around the end of August.

To Godfrey Bosville, c. August 1767

Not reported. See From Bosville, 4 Oct.: 'I am sorry to hear of your being so much out of Order, but I hope you are now perfectly restord to your former good State of health.' Bosville alludes to JB's bout of gonorrhoea, which kept him confined for the month of August.

To Sir John Pringle, c. August 1767

Not reported. See From Pringle, 4 Dec., which apologizes for the long delay in answering this letter, the date of which is indicated by Pringle's allusion to JB's having asked for advice concerning his gonorrhoea.

From Edward Dilly, Saturday 1 August 1767

MS. Yale (C 1062).

ADDRESS: To James Boswell Esqr., Advocate, Edinr.

London, Augt. 1st, 1767

SIR: I sent you a Letter a few Days ago intimating my agreement to your Proposal for the Purchase of the Copy right of your History of Corsica. It is necessary on your Part to send me something Counter to that, of your acceptance of the same.

191

I here send you inclos'd the Introduction, and as the Summer is somewhat advanc'd, it is highly expedient to send the Work immediately to the Press, that so the Book may be finish'd at the meeting of Parliament,[1] if [2] Mr. Foulis is the Printer. You will find that he will not do more than two Sheets a Week; which will make it[3] about 10 or 12 weeks before it is finish'd; and Packing up, and sending to London will take up about a Month longer. The Map of Corsica and the Third Chapter of the History: I shall either send by a Private Hand or under Covers by Post, but as there is no immediate hurry for either of these, a fortnight hence will be Time enough. You will please let me know if the Printer has cast off the Copy and what Number of Pages it will make.

Almon in Piccadilly has advertised to be Publish'd in a few Days, an acct. of the Hamilton and Douglas Cause, with the Speeches of the Lords on the Occasion.[4] I am at a loss to guess, who could send the speeches to Almon, I am apprehensive what he has sent, will be very deficient, for the only Person in Edinr.[5] who Wrote out the Speeches the most Complete, Promised that if his Copy was to go to the Press, it should be transmitted to me, and moreover added, that he apprehended some of the Lords would revise their own Speeches and prepare them for the Press. This indeed would be the only means of preventing a Spurious Edition gaining ground. If you can procure any intelligence upon this Matter I shall take it as a particular favour if you will inform me. I have sent a Cover, that you may inclose whatever you may have occasion to send to, Sir, Your most Obedient Servant,

E. DILLY

[1] This year's session of Parliament opened on 24 Nov. (*Parl. Hist.* xvi. 379); traditionally, the theatrical and social seasons opened at the same time. Booksellers timed their publications to coincide with the 'London Season' and the return of the country gentry to the city (Lawrence Stone and J. C. F. Stone, *An Open Elite?: England 1540–1880*, 1984, pp. 35, 253).

[2] MS. 'if' superimposed upon 'as'

[3] MS. 'make it' deleted after 'make it'

[4] John Almon (1737–1805) printer and bookseller at 178 Piccadilly, 1763–81; 183 Fleet Street, 1784–89 (Maxted, pp. 3–4). In August,

Almon published A *Summary of the Speeches, Arguments, and Determinations . . . upon that Important Cause, Wherein His Grace the Duke of Hamilton and Others Were Plaintiffs, and Archibald Douglas of Douglas, Esq; Defendant.* A review of the work warned that the speeches were 'imperfectly taken' but also maintained that they contained 'nothing but what was said, though not ALL that was delivered on this important cause' (*Scots Mag.* 1767, xxix. 427–28).

[5] William Anderson (From Dilly, 10 Aug. n. 12).

From Edward Dilly, Tuesday 4 August 1767

MS. Yale (C 1063).

ADDRESS: To James Boswell Esqr., at Edinburgh.

London, Augt. 4th, 1767

SIR: I sent you the Introductory Part of the Histy. of Corsica, by Saturday's Post. I now take the opportunity of sending you by a private Hand, the Other Part of the Copy you sent me, together with a Map of Corsica, there is another Island in the same Map, which is not to be inserted.[1] The Names of the Towns etc. are in French. It is requisite to have them translated into English. And when that is done, I think the Map will[2] be much better Engraved in London, it should be done on a Quarto Scale, to make it convenient to Bind up with the Book.

I shall be glad to hear from you in answer to my two former Letters Your first opportunity. As the Summer is pretty far advanc'd, no Time should be lost in sending the Work to the Press, that so it may be Publish'd about the Meeting of Parliament. I am, Sir, Your most Obedient Servant,

EDWD. DILLY

[1] On maps of Corsica, see From John Dick, 30 May 1766 and From Dilly, 28 July, n. 1.

[2] MS. 'which' deleted before 'will'

To Edward Dilly, Thursday 6 August 1767

MS. Houghton Library.

ADDRESS: To Mr. Dilly, Bookseller, London.

ENDORSEMENTS: [in Dilly's hand] Mr. Boswell. Agreement for the Copy. [in an unidentified hand] Jas Boswell.

NOTE in JB's hand at foot of page: To Mr. Dilly, Bookseller, London.

Edinburgh, 6 August 1767

SIR: I have received your letter agreeing to pay me One Hundred Guineas for the Copy-Right of my *Account of Corsica* etc., the money to be due three months after the publication of the Work in London, and also agreeing that the first Edition shall be printed in Scotland, under my direction, and a map of Corsica be engraved for the work at your Expence.[1]

In return to which, I do hereby agree that you shall have the sole Property of the said Work. Our Bargain therefore is now concluded, and I heartily wish that it may be of advantage to you. I am, Sir, Your most humble Servant,

JAMES BOSWELL

[1] JB and Dilly used this letter to record payment of the 100 guineas. On the back of the letter is a receipt: 'London 8 June 1768. Received one hundred guineas in full of the within agreement. James Boswell.' On the wrapper in an unidentified hand is written: '*June 8th, 1768* Boswell's Corsica £105.'

To Edward Dilly, c. early August 1767

Not reported. See From Dilly, 10 Aug. 'I received your Letter by this Day's Post, and am very sorry to hear of your Indisposition.'

To Edward Dilly, Sunday 9 August 1767

Not reported. See From Dilly, 15 Aug.: 'The favour of Yours of the 9th Instant, came to Hand this Day'.

From Andrew Burnaby, Monday 10 August 1767

MS. Yale (C 699).

ADDRESS: To James Boswell Esqre. at Auchinleck, North Britain, By London.
POSTMARK: [LONDON] AV 26.

Leghorn, Augt. 10th, 1767

SIR, The letter You honoured me with, did not arrive till long after the time it was due; otherwise I should have answered it sooner. I now beg leave, Sir, to return You my very sincere thanks for it; and for the honour you are so good as to confer upon me by your correspondence.

You are extremely obliging in speaking so favourably of my journal.[1] I am conscious Myself that nothing but your generosity could induce You to it; for it is very superficial and incorrect. Indeed some parts of it I doubt may not be exact; particularly I have some difficulties concerning the Anecdote I have related of the attempt to assassinate de' Paoli. I have since heard that affair variously related; and the Accounts do not coincide.[2] In general however the journal I believe is true, and your own discernment and knowledge of the State of the Island, will enable You to distinguish what is so, and what is not.

Mr. Symonds has just made a tour to Corte,[3] and is returned full of the Generals praises. He says he thinks him one of the greatest Characters that the World has ever produced. I believe he intends to write to you.

You will have heard without doubt that De Paoli immediately took possession of Algaiola upon the French's retiring: he was in hopes of getting Calvi and Ajaccio also, but he was not able to succeed, as Genoese Succours arrived before the French were departed. He is now making great preparations for war, and is beseiging the two places above mentioned.[4] The Jesuits are really to be pitied, they are cooped up in the Presidio[5] and suffer the greatest distress. Whatever their crime may have been, nothing can justify the King of Spain in an act of so much cruelty. Some of them are of the first families of Spain. They are all in the same deplorable State, and draw tears[6] from every one who see's them lying upon the ground in Company's together, perishing with fatigue, with Sickness and affliction. Paoli has permitted 300 to be at Algajola.[7]

I will take the first occasion of procuring You some information about Capraja, but I apprehend it will not be an object sufficiently interesting to the Publick, to merit a sett relation. About 200 years ago it belonged to o⟨ne⟩ of the Fiefs upon Cape Corse, and on the Extinction of the Family to whom the fief belonged, was seized upon by the Genoese. The Smallness and Sterility of it[8] must have hindered it at all times from being a place of consequence. I will not fail however to inform myself more particularly about it.[9] I am with very great regard, Sir, your most Obedient and most humble Servant,

ANDREW BURNABY

P.S. When You favour me with any letters, be so good as to direct, For the Revend. Mr. Burnaby Chaplain to the British Factory at Leghorn at John Dick's Esqre. Consul to his Britanque. Majesty.

Il Cannonico Rostino is now with me, and desires me to present his respects to You.[10]

¹ From John Dick, 24 Oct. 1766. Burnaby's *Journal of a Tour to Corsica in the Year 1766* was published in 1804. The printed volume contains only thirty-two pages of journal text, and was intended as an Introduction to the major part of the volume—a series of sixty-three letters, in Italian without translations and ranging in date from 1766 to 1802, from Paoli to Burnaby. Burnaby annotated some of the letters in English. In his Preface to *Corsica* (p. xiv) JB acknowledges that he took much of the material for his *Account* from Burnaby's journal: 'As Mr. Burnaby was so obliging as to allow me to make what use I pleased of his Journal, I have freely interwoven it into my work'; according to Foladare, over half of Burnaby's work 'was copied almost verbatim into the *Account*, and several more pages . . . were used as sources for other remarks by Boswell' (Joseph Foladare, 'James Boswell and Corsica', Yale diss. 1936, i. 72).

² Burnaby's journal does not mention any attempt to assassinate Paoli; the anecdote Burnaby refers to is recounted in his note to a letter he received from Paoli, dated 22 Dec. 1768 (Burnaby, pp. 64–65). It describes an attempt on Paoli's life by his secretary Giuseppe Maria Massesi—all the more distressing for Paoli because Massesi's father was his 'Great Chancellor' (*Corsica*, p. 281)—and his ultimate execution. Burnaby goes on to relate Paoli's reluctance to accept the sentence until, other assassination attempts having come to light, he was obliged to have it carried out, if only to prevent similar attempts in the future.

Smollett gives an account of an earlier but similar incident involving Paoli. During negotiations for the Treaty of Compiègne in 1764, 'some of the Corsican officers had been bribed by the enemies of Paoli . . . to assassinate him. The plot was discovered, and the conspirators were carried before the . . . chief, who behaved towards them with amazing magnaminity. He told them, tho' they had forfeited their lives by conspiracy against him, yet they were at liberty to depart and to examine themselves, whether from that moment he deserved their enmity; and that, if they could prove a single article of a criminal charge against him, he was ready to submit' (Tobias Smollett, *Continuation of the Complete History of England*, 5 vols. numbered 'xii–xvi', 1760–65).

³ A report in *Lond. Chron.* dated 'Corte, Aug. 4' notes that John Symonds had left Corsica 'with very high ideas of Paoli, and of our island'. In the margin of his own copy of the paper JB wrote, 'materials Mr. Burnaby. Expression my own' (*Lond. Chron.* 19–22 Sept. 1767, xxii. 288; *Lit. Car.* p. 240). The report was reprinted in *Pub. Adv.* 23 Sept.

⁴ These events were reported under the date of 4 Aug. in *Gent. Mag.* (1767), xxxvii. 474.

⁵ MS. 'Presidj'. Presumably, Burnaby means the castle or citadel of Corte, which served among other functions as a prison (*Corsica*, pp. 282–83).

⁶ MS. 'tears' superimposed upon 'them'

⁷ Though the Jesuits had few friends in Britain (cf. From Sir Alexander Dick, 17 May), several writers, like Burnaby, responded to their plight with sympathy. Burnaby's long note to a letter, dated 5 July, that he received from Paoli concerning the Jesuits, describes their desperate plight after their expulsion from Spain and his own efforts to help them while acting as Proconsul at Leghorn (Burnaby, pp. 91–92). And the author (Burke?) of the 'History of Europe' in *Ann. Reg.* 1767, p. 32, wrote, 'Without considering the religious or political tenets of this society (which appear to have been dangerous, from the general persecution raised against them in so many countries of their own persuasion) we are obliged, as men, to sympathize with them in the miseries which they underwent in their exile'. Horace Mann expressed similar sentiments in a letter of 11 July to Horace Walpole (*Corres.* HW xxii. 535–36).

⁸ MS. 'hindered' deleted before 'it'

⁹ Burnaby's information on Capraia arrived after the printing of *Corsica* was finished (From Burnaby, 17 Jan. 1768; From Edward Dilly, 28 July, n. 2). JB added several pages on Capraia after he had completed the 'Account of Corsica', writing in the margin of the MS., 'The taking of Capraja to be here introduced', but the 'Paper Apart' mentioned in this MS. and relating to Capraia has not been reported (M 2, p. 226); see *Corsica*, pp. 231–35. JB's account of the ownership of Capraia differs from Burnaby's: JB tells that Capraia belonged to 'the noble family of Damari who were deprived of it by the Genoese' (*Corsica*, p. 231). A historian writing a few years later gives more details: the da Mare family of Cap Corse held Capraia until 1507, when, at the entreaty of the oppressed residents, the Genoese Bank of San Giorgio, which ruled Corsica, deposed them ([François-René-Jean de Pommereul], *Histoire de l'isle de Corse*, 1779, ii. 94–95).

¹⁰ The Abbé Carlo Rostini (1710–73) had been chaplain of the Royal Corsican regiment in the French army, 1742–62, before embracing the Corsican cause and becoming Paoli's treasurer. JB had met Rostini in Oct. 1765, and in *Corsica* praised his 'literature' and 'the excellency of his heart' (G. P. Borghetti, 'L'abbé Rostini', BSSC, 1881, fasc. i, pp. i–vii; Louis Campi, 'Notice . . . de Rostini', BSSC, 1882, fasc. xxii, p. lv; *Corsica*, p. 315).

From John Dick, Monday 10 August 1767

MS. Yale (C 1019).

ADDRESS, in the hand of John Offley:[1] To James Boswell Esqr. at Auchinleck, Edenburgh.

POSTMARK: STON.[2]

FRANK: Free J. Offley.

NOTE in Dick's hand at foot of first page: James Boswell Esqr.

Shugborough, 10 August 1767

MY DEAR SIR, I had the pleasure to write You the 29 of last Month. I now trouble You again to acquaint You, that I shall sett out from hence tomorrow morning, and shall stop about two days at Durham, and as many at Newcastle, and then proceed to Edenburgh, but I hope I shall have the pleasure of finding a Letter from You at Durham. If not, I shall wait there untill it arrives, as I shall not know how to proceed without it. I shall also call on my friend Mr. John Askew at Pallinsburne House near Berwick,[3] pray be so kind, as to lett me find there a Letter from You, and acquaint me in it, which is the best Inn to put up at, in[4] Edenburgh.[5] You are so good, that I am sure You will excuse all this trouble which I am giving You.

Pray present my most Respectfull Compliments to Sir Alexander, and Mr. Ferguson, and believe me always with the most unalterable Regard, and true Esteem, My dear Sir, Your most Obliged and Affectionate Friend,

JOHN DICK

[1] John Offley (c. 1717–84), of Wichnor, Staffs., M.P. for Bedford, 1747–54, Orford, 1754–68, and East Retford, 1768–74 (Namier and Brooke iii. 223).

[2] Stone, about twenty miles north-west of Lichfield, Staffs.

[3] John Askew (1732–94—*Burke's Landed Gentry*, 1937), of Pallinsburn, was at various times deputy lieutenant of Durham, Northumberland, and Berwick upon Tweed, and High Sheriff of Northumberland (*Gent. Mag.* 1794, lxiv. 1059).

[4] MS. 'in' superimposed upon 'att'

[5] JB recommended Peter Ramsay's Red Lyon Inn (To Sir Alexander Dick, 15 Aug. and n. 1).

From Edward Dilly, Monday 10 August 1767

MS. Yale (C 1064).

ADDRESS: To James Boswell Esqr., Advocate, Edinburgh.

London, Augt. 10th, 1767

SIR: I sent you the remaining Part of the MSS. Copy together with a Map of Corsica, by a private Gentleman, who set off for Edinr. last Wednesday in a Post Chaise: and hope long before this Time they will have come safe to Hand.

I received your Letter by this Day's Post, and am very sorry to hear of your Indisposition.[1] I hope you are now upon the recovery and will soon be restored to perfect Health. I was perfectly accurate in regard to my Expression for Mr. Foulis to Cast off the Copy, and any Printer would immediately understand it. Casting off signifies no more than looking over the Whole MSS. and having one Page Composed of English, or Pica Letter; and from that, they can Calculate nearly what the Whole will make.[2] I have not yet heard from Mr. Foulis, and therefore cannot send the Paper. I should not have the least objection against Mr. Foulis

196

supplying the Paper, but I apprehend he has got nothing by him that will answer the Purpose so well as what I can get in London, if he has that Sort which he thinks will do, he[3] may send me a Sheet by Way of Sample by Post, and if I approve of it, he may begin to Print directly[4] the Sooner the Book is finishd the better, as I would willingly have them in London, the beginning of October before the bad Weather comes on, and that I may Publish at the Meeting of Parliament. The Map of Corsica I will submit entirely to your Care, but you will observe to have it done upon as Small a Scale as possible, or otherwise it will not conveniently Bind up with the Book. I can't hear of any Map of Corsica with an English Title.[5] The Arms of Corsica to Embelish the Title Page I would by all means have done at Mr. Foulis Academy,[6] and Workt off there, something in the Manner of Lord Littleton's in his *Histy. of Henry the 2d*; but I would have it neater done than that, and a little ornamented, it must not be too large or otherwise it will look preposterous for an Octavo Volume,[7] a proper Medium must be observed, though the Book is Printed at Glasgow I would have it said in the Title Page London Printd for Edward and Charles Dilly in the Poultry 1768, after Michaelmass is turn'd we generally put in the ensuing Year, at the back of the Title Page I would also have Printed in Old English Black Letters, *Entered at Stationer's Hall, Agreeable to Act of Parliament.*[8] This will deter the Scotch Booksellers from Pirating the Book,[9]—the Title and Preface will be the last that is Printed, a Spirited Dedication to Paoli perhaps would be of Service.[10] Almon has not yet Publish'd the Speeches etc. there is another person Started up with an advertisement of the same Nature, to be Publish'd in a few Days.[11] I am apprehensive that both of them will be very imperfect, for there was only one Person, who had got any thing tolerably complete of the Speeches and that is Mr. Anderson of Bristol Port, and he Promised that if ever he committed them to the Press, I should have the first offer, the Agents for Hamilton and Douglass have both applied to him for a Copy of the Speeches, which is a plain indication that they suppose what he has taken down to be the most perfect. The observation you make, may possibly prove true, that the Lords of Session Seeing a very imperfect or rather Mangled Account of the Speeches Publish'd, may be induced to give a Correct Copy of their own Speeches, if that should be the Case no Person will have an opportunity of knowing sooner than Mr. Boswell, and I shall esteem it as a particular favour if he would Interest himself on my behalf, and whoever furnishes me with a Copy I hope to shew a generous Spirit in recompencing him for the same. If it is possible to Obtain such a Copy with the approbation of the Lords, the sooner an advertisement is put in the London Papers the better, as that will be a means of Stoping the Sale of the Spurious Editions which are now in the Press.[12] The favour of an Answer to this, and the particulars Abovemention'd, will much Oblige, Sir, Your most humble Servant,

EDWD. DILLY

[1] JB had gonorrhoea again (To W. J. Temple, 29 July).

[2] JB had very likely confused 'cast off', 'To estimate how much printed matter will correspond to (a piece of MS. copy)' with 'throw off', 'To print off' (*OED* Supplement, Cast, v. 79. j.; *OED*, Throw, v.1 42. i). For another example of 'throw off' that antedates the earliest citation in *OED* (1803), see To Edmond Malone, 30–31 Oct. 1785 (Baker, p. 259).

[3] MS. 'he' superimposed upon ?'one'

[4] The source of the paper used for *Corsica* is not known with certainty. The paper used was a medium-quality Printing Demy, an unusual paper

for the Foulises, who generally used Foolscap (Gaskell, *Bibliography of the Foulis Press*, 1964, pp. 23–27, 278–79).

[5] For the map used, see From Dilly, 28 July, n. 1.

[6] The Academy of Fine Arts, founded in 1753 by Robert Foulis under the auspices of the University of Glasgow and closed after the death of Andrew Foulis in 1775 ([William James Duncan], *Notices and Documents Illustrative of the Literary History of Glasgow*, 1831, repr. 1886, pp. 81–90; David Murray, *Robert & Andrew Foulis and the Glasgow Press, with Some Account of the Glasgow Academy of the Fine Arts*, 1913, pp. 57–114). We do not know if the engravings for Corsica were actually done by artists from the Foulis Academy, as Dilly had suggested.

[7] Lord Lyttelton's *History of the Life of King Henry the Second, and of the Age in which He Lived*, 1767. The engraved device of the arms of Corsica on the title page is as large as the coat of arms on the title-page of Lord Lyttelton's book, even though the latter work is quarto and JB's octavo. The engravers 'ornamented' the arms by adding a rugged landscape as a background.

[8] The title-page of the first edition reads, 'GLASGOW, PRINTED BY ROBERT AND ANDREW FOULIS FOR EDWARD AND CHARLES DILLY IN THE POULTRY, LONDON; M DCC LXVIII'. The title-page of the second edition mentions only the Dillys. On the half-title page of the first edition is printed, in the manner Dilly requested, 'Entered in Stationers Hall according to Act of Parliament'.

[9] The work was not pirated by Scottish booksellers, but there were three Irish reprints, 1768–69 (*Lit. Car.* pp. 58–59).

[10] The 'Dedication to Pascal Paoli General of the Corsicans' appears on pp. v–viii.

[11] On 10 Aug. Almon's edition of the *Speeches* was still being advertised as to be published 'In a few days' (*Pub. Adv.* 10 Aug. p. [1]). It was published on 13 Aug. (*Pub. Adv.* 13 Aug. p. [1]; *Lond. Chron.* 11–13 Aug. xxii. 147; *St. James's Chron.* 11–13 Aug. p. [3]). On 6 Aug. the bookseller

William Griffin published *A Concise Narrative of the Proceedings in the Douglas Cause*; between 8 and 11 Aug. advertisements for that book carried a notice that 'in a few days' Griffin would publish 'The Speeches, Arguments, and Determinations, of the Right Hon. the fifteen Lords of Council and Session in Scotland, upon the above important Cause' (*Pub. Adv.* 8 Aug. p. [1], 10 Aug. p. [1]; *Gazetteer* 8 Aug. p. [1], 11 Aug. p. [1]). Griffin stopped advertising after 11 Aug., and the projected volume never appeared.

[12] Dilly had no hand in the publication of *The Speeches and Judgement of the Right Honourable The Lords of Council and Session in Scotland, upon the Important Cause, His Grace George-James Duke of Hamilton and Others, Pursuers; against Archibald Douglas, Esq; Defender*, 1768, reported by William Anderson, on the title-page styled 'Writer in Edinburgh'. In a conversation with Lord Mansfield of 20 May 1768, JB calls him 'a Writer's Clerk' (Journ.); presumably he became a writer in 1767 or 1768. Dilly's 'Bristol Port' is a mistaken rendition of 'Bristo Port', an area around one of the gates of the old walled city, near the Greyfriars Church and in the same general area as the premises—at the Cowgate Head, at the Head of the Pleasance, in the West Bow—variously occupied by one of two William Andersons listed as writers in the *Edinburgh Directory* for 1773–76. This William Anderson apparently did not practise after 1776, and nothing more is known about him.

JB considered Anderson's report to be the most accurate one, stating that he had 'sent each Judge his own speech to look over and make what corrections he pleased' (Journ. 20 May 1768). Unaware of this circumstance, Robert Richardson, in *A State of the Evidence in the Cause between His Grace the Duke of Hamilton . . . and Archibald Douglas*, 1769, attacked Anderson's accuracy (*Douglas Cause*, p. 189); influenced in part by Richardson's criticism, Francis Steuart reprinted in *Douglas Cause* the version published by Almon.

To John Dick, c. Tuesday 11 August 1767

Not reported. Acknowledged in From Dick, 20 Aug. For the date, see To Sir Alexander Dick, 15 Aug.: 'He [John Dick] was to set out from Mr. Anson's on Tuesday, the 11, was to stay two days in Durham, and as many at Newcastle. We may suppose him then at Durham by this time. He will there have found my letter informing him of my unlucky situation.'

To Basil Cochrane, c. Friday 14 August 1767

Not reported. See From Cochrane, 14 Aug.: 'What you Say in your letter anent John's going into the Customs I much approve off'.

From Basil Cochrane, Friday 14 August 1767

MS. Yale (C 803).

ADDRESS: James Boswel Esqr., Edinburgh.

Pinkie,[1] Fryday August 14th, 1767

DEAR JAMES: What you Say in your letter anent John's going in to the Customs I much Approve off but for goeing to London I am greatly Against. You must be Sencible he can't Live in London upon Sixty pounds a year. New Castle is the only proper place for him. There are good Masters to Learn Arithmetic and there is a Custom house where he easiely can gett Access to See the Method and Manner bussiness is Carryed on in that Bransh of bussiness and So Qualify himself for that affair. Besides it will give him a Notion how he likes that bussiness.[2] I am Your's,

BASIL COCHRANE

[1] JB's granduncle lived in Pinkie House, near Musselburgh, Midlothian, some five miles east by south of Edinburgh.

[2] Lt. John Boswell, who was living in Newcastle during this period, had been visiting Scotland since 6 Aug., staying mostly at Pinkie House. On 13 Aug. he visited Edinburgh, drank tea with JB, and returned to Pinkie 'resolved now to go up to London by sea'. The next day he visited JB again and then went to Leith, where he 'called on the Ship Master with whom I proposed going to London'. The next morning, however, he changed his mind and 'resolved to return directly to Newcastle'. He set out on 17 Aug. (John Boswell's Journal, C 404:2, 6–17 Aug.). His journal does not mention his scheme of becoming a customs officer; apparently nothing came of it.

To Sir Alexander Dick, Saturday 15 August 1767

MS. Mrs. Janet Dick-Cunyngham.

ADDRESS: To Sir Alexander Dick Baronet, Prestonfield.

Edinburgh, Saturday 15 August 1767

MY DEAR SIR: I had last night a letter from our worthy Consul. He was to set out from Mr. Anson's on Tuesday the 11, was to stay two days at Durham, and as many at Newcastle. We may suppose him then at Durham by this time. He will there have found my letter informing him of my unlucky situation. He is to proceed to Mr. John Askew's at Palinsburne House near Berwick and there He is to wait for a letter from me. He desires to know the best Inn at Edinburgh. I will recommend him to Peter Ramsay's.[1] But I will get him to notify the day of his arrival, that you may be ready at Ramsay's to receive him, and bring him to this house that we may all embrace with joy, on the commencement of so valuable a friendship, I may say on the reunion of so near Relations brought together by a mutual friend. My Dear Sir such Scenes are infinitely above interested schemes. They are the best things that such men as Sir John Dick and you and I find in this world.

I wish much to see you here today, before I write to the Consul. But as that may not be the case, I beg you may give me any instructions you think necessary.

In the mean time please return me by the Bearer what you have of Corsica as I am going to send it to My Lord Hales.[2] Ever yours with affection,

JAMES BOSWELL

[1] Peter Ramsay (d. 1794) was proprietor of the Red Lyon Inn at the foot of St. Mary's Wynd near Cowgate Port from at least 1760 until he sold it in 1785 (Grant i. 299, where the inn is erroneously called the 'White Horse'; James H. Jamieson, 'Some Inns of the Eighteenth Century', *The Book of the Old Edinburgh Club*, 1925, xiv. 134–37; Robert Chambers, *Traditions of Edinburgh*, 1825, ii. 295–96). In 1776 Ramsay advertised that he had 'a good house for entertainment, good stables for above 100 horses, coach houses and shades for above twenty carriages' (Jamieson, p. 136).

[2] Sir Alexander was one of the readers of the 'Corsica' manuscript. JB does not acknowledge Sir Alexander's help in his preface, but he does report his observation that the scarcity of roads in Corsica had helped the islanders defend their freedom against regular troops (*Corsica*, p. 39). Sir David Dalrymple, Bt. (1726–92), a judge in the Court of Session styled Lord Hailes, also read the manuscript. He was Lord Auchinleck's colleague and one of JB's oldest friends and trusted advisers. JB wrote in the preface to *Corsica*, 'I am principally indebted to the indulgence and friendly attention of My Lord Hailes, who under the name of Sir David Dalrymple, has been long known to the world as an able Antiquarian, and an elegant and humourous Essayist' (pp. xvi–xvii).

From Sir Alexander Dick, Saturday [15 August 1767]

MS. Yale (C 963).

ADDRESS: To James Boswell Esqr., Advocate, Edr.

prest., Saturday

MY DEAR FRIEND: By some unhappy blunder when 3 days agoe I returnd your papers they sent me answer you was gone to affleck and not to return till the winte[r] Session. You may believe I was struck but sent in all to day supposing a blunder.

You regale me with nectar and ambrosia by your Lette[r] saying the good Consul approaches.

This year is one of my white years for

No. 1st   The male family Head of the Dicks recoverd.[1]

2d   Ratter my near friend by my father Earl of Caithnes.[2]

3d   Are you not surprizd! My Niece Jenny Douglass to be well married in a few days out of my house! to Mr. Irwine of Bonshaw with a good fortune a good[3] Man.

4th   Still I surprize you! Miss Katty her youngest sister to Dr. Butter of Derby a thriving physician.[4]

All this going on like clock work and Lastly your getting quite well and Corsica shown to Mankind and gloriously!

Strichen and the clan Frazer and Sinclar dine here to day. Woud to God you had been able to be of the party.

I approve of Ramsays to be the landing place but shall expect to be made certain of the arrival and that he must make his head quarters here after seeing you. My best affections to the Consul from us all. I dedicate my self to him and you. Dear friend, yours in vast hurry,

ALEXANDER DICK

[1] Sir Alexander considered John Dick to be the male head of the family because the baronetcy of Braid was more ancient than that of Prestonfield.

[2] William Sinclair (1727–79) of Ratter was cousin to Sir Alexander, whose father was grandson of John Cunningham of Geiss and Brownhill and Elizabeth Sinclair of Ratter (*Comp. Bar.* iv. 273–74). On the death in Dec. 1765 of Alexander Sinclair, ninth Earl of Caithness, William Sinclair, descended from the fourth Earl, sued to have himself served heir to the title. He was opposed by James Sinclair (later a captain in the East India Company), who was descended from a

brother of the eighth Earl. William charged that James's father was illegitimate, a circumstance that barred James from the succession. On 28 Nov. 1768 a jury served William heir-male of the ninth Earl. James's appeal to the Court of Session was denied in 1770, and William's title was confirmed by the House of Lords in 1772 (*Scots Peer.* ii. 349–50; John Riddell, *Inquiry into the Law and Practice in Scottish Peerages*, 1842, ii. 610–20).

³ MS. 'godd'

⁴ Janet Douglas (d. 1806) and her sister Catherine were daughters of Sir Alexander's sister Christian and Sir John Douglas of Kelhead, Bt. Because of financial difficulties that followed

Sir John's imprisonment for Jacobite activities, 1746–48, Janet and Catherine lived at Prestonfield (*Scots Charta Chest*, pp. 223–24). Janet was to be married to William Irving (d. 1779) of Bonshaw (*Burke's Landed Gentry*, 1886). William Butter (1726–1805), distinguished physician and writer on medical topics, had courted Janet Dick, but, being refused by her, acquiesced in Sir Alexander's arranging a marriage for him with Catherine (*Life* iii. 467–68; *Scots Charta Chest*, pp. 224–26). Janet and Catherine were married at Prestonfield on the same day, 13 Nov. (Robert Douglas, *Peerage of Scotland*, 1813, ii. 388).

From Edward Dilly, Saturday 15 August 1767

MS. Yale (C 1065).

ADDRESS: To James Boswell Esqr. at Edinburgh.

London, Augt. 15, 1767

SIR: The favour of yours of the 9th Instant, came to Hand this Day, I Wrote an answer to your former Letter, last Week, and sent it by a private Gentleman, at the same Time I inclosd the remainder of the Mss Copy. I also sent you this Week by another Gentleman a Copy of Almon's Publication of the Speeches etc., and likewise one for Mr. Anderson to compare with what he has taken down, I believe you will have them come to Hand, before any Bookseller in Edinr. can possibly have them, you will please to inform me if both the Parcels come¹ to Hand.

The Arms of Corsica I would by all means have neatly Engravd at Glasgow to adorn the Title Page.

I have left Mr. Foulis Letter Open which will inform you fully of my Opinion in regard to the Printing.² You will please to Seal it up and send it with the Specimens of Paper by the first Opportunity, and as you are upon the Spot at Edinr. if you please, you may Call on Mr. Fleming and desire him to Show you a Ream of the fine Printing Demy Paper which he gave me a Specimen of: and to inform you what Quantity he has already made; and if he has not a sufficiency at this Time, how soon he can get a Quantity finished.³ And you may send Mr. Foulis a clean Sheet of the same with these Specimens. It is not customary (when an Author is Paid a Consideration for the Copy) to give a Number of Books, nevertheless, half a Dozen Copies of the Common Paper, together with two Copies more on Royal Paper, is at Mr. Boswell's Service, to give to any of his Friends, and he may order Mr. Foulis to Print off the same accordingly.

As for sending the Sheets to a Gentleman Abroad,⁴ it is a little dangerous unless You can place great Confidence in the Friend, that no Other Person shall See the Sheets, and that only a translation shall be Printed, and indeed when that is the Case the great advantage arising to the Person Abroad in having the Sheets from the Press, before the Publication is in England, is of peculiar benefit, for in that Case he gets the Start of every Other Person in the Market. For Instance suppose a Book by Voltaire or Rousseau was now Printing in Paris of a very Popular Nature. I would give the Proprietor of that Book a very handsome Consideration to transmit the Sheets to me, as they are Workt off from the Press, that so I might have the Translation finish'd, and Printed in London almost as soon as it is Publish'd in Paris.

However in the present Case, as your Friend at Parma in Italy, is a Gentleman you can place Confidence in, I have no objection against your sending the Sheets as they are Workt off from the Press, and if the Translation should answer his expectation, I shall leave it to his Honor, either to send me a Number of the Printed Copies, or if any thing should offer at Parma of a Popular kind, to convey the Sheets to me in the same Manner.

There will be no occasion to advertise immediately in the Scots Papers till we See how Mr. Foulis goes on, and then we may judge what Time the Book will be finish'd, in the mean Time you may send me the Title and Motto,[5] and I will draw up a proper advertisement, at the Meeting of Parliament. I believe such Steps will be taken by the Trade in London as to Obtain an Act of Parliament to Secure our Property from being Pirated in Great Britain, and to prevent the Sale of such Copies as are Printed in Ireland, from being Sold in Scotland, this is a Matter which concerns every Author in the Kingdom, as well as the Booksellers in London, for it is a Discouragement to Literature, and an injury to the fair Trader,[6] an answer to this, and my former Letters will oblige, Sir, Your most Obedient Servant,

EDW. DILLY

[1] MS. 'came' changed to 'come'

[2] Not reported.

[3] Robert Fleming (d. 1778), bookseller and printer in Edinburgh, published *Edin. Eve. Cour.* in partnership with Alexander Kincaid, and also the *Edinburgh Almanack*. He and his father Robert (now retired) were among the booksellers summoned before the Court of Session on 30 June and rebuked by the Lord President on 28 July for publishing stories about *Dorando* and the Douglas Cause (M. E. Craig, *The Scottish Periodical Press, 1750–1789*, 1931, p. 25, where it is erroneously stated that Fleming published *Edin. Eve. Cour.* until 1785 instead of until his death in 1778; *Dict. of Printers*; *Scots Mag.* 1767, xxix, 338–44, 1778, xl. 511). For the type and quality of the paper used by the Foulis brothers for *Corsica*, see From Edward Dilly, 10 Aug. and n. 4.

[4] Alexandre Deleyre (From Deleyre, 8 Dec. 1766 and n. 8).

[5] Among JB's outlines and notes for *Corsica* are four drafts of the title-page (M 6, pp. 5, 6, 12, 20). The title as printed in an advance advertisement resembles one of them (M 6, p. 5): 'AN ACCOUNT OF CORSICA, its Situation, Extent, Air, Soil, and Productions. A concise View of its Revolutions from earliest Times. Its present State, with respect to Government, Religion, Arms, Commerce, Learning, the Genius and Character of its Inhabitants. With the JOURNAL of a TOUR to that ISLAND, and MEM-OIRS of PASCAL PAOLI. Also an Original Letter from the General of the Nation; and an Appendix, containing Corsican State Papers' (*Lond. Chron.* 6–8 Oct. 1767, xxii. 339).

The advertisement of 8 Oct. did not print a motto. JB tried out several mottos and settled on a quotation from a letter of the Scottish Parliament to Pope John XXII, 6 Apr. 1320: 'Non enim propter gloriam, divitias aut honores pugnamus, sed propter libertatem solummodo, quam nemo bonus nisi simul cum vita amittit', 'We fight not for glory, wealth, or honour, but for liberty alone, which no good man loses except with his life' (Lord Hailes, *Annals of Scotland*, 1776–79, ii. 92–95; Journ. 6 Oct. 1764).

[6] Because the copyright act of 1710 did not apply to Ireland, booksellers there could reprint books cheaply, a practice that not only closed Ireland as a market for English and Scottish booksellers, but also enabled the Irish to undersell legitimate books in London and Edinburgh. A bill introduced in the English Parliament in 1737 would have prohibited the reprinting of English books in Ireland, but it did not pass (A. S. Collins, *Authorship in the Days of Johnson*, 1927, pp. 60–64). The Commons had last considered the issue in 1754 (JHC xxvi. 958). We know of no bill such as the one described by Dilly: the next petition to the Commons by the booksellers for protection of their trade was not presented until 28 Feb. 1774 (*Parl. Hist.* xvii. 1078–1110).

To Lord Marischal, c. mid August 1767

Not reported. See From Marischal, 12 Sept., which JB endorsed, 'My Lord Marischal in Answer to Book p. 4.'

To John Dick, c. Saturday 15 August 1767

Not reported. Acknowledged in From Dick, 20 Aug. JB wrote to Sir Alexander Dick (15 Aug.) that he intended to ask John Dick about the date of his arrival in Edinburgh and recommend an inn.

From John Dick, Thursday 20 August 1767

MS. Yale (C 1020).

ADDRESS: To James Boswell Esqr. of Auchinleck, Edenburgh.

Newcastle, 20 August 1767

My DEAR SIR, Many thanks wait on you for your obliging Letters, which I have receiv'd, and I am extremely Sorry to learn that you are indisposed, the more so, as I am so much pressed for time, and cannot possibly stay above two or three days with You, having business of Concequence which calls me back to the South. Indeed I ought to have return'd directly from hence, but cannot resolve to omit paying my Respects to Sir Alexander, and You. I therefore shall sett out tomorrow morning, and I hope to be at Edenburgh on Saturday at noon. In the meanwhile pray present my Respects to the worthy Baronet, and our friend Mr. Ferguson. Adieu. Yours most Affectionately,

JOHN DICK

To Edward Dilly, Thursday 20 August 1767

Not reported. See From Dilly, 31 Aug.: 'I received yours of the 20th Instant with a Specimen of Douglasiana'.

From James Brown,[1] Friday 21 August 1767

MS. Yale (C 586).

ADDRESS: To James Boswell Esqr., Advocate, Edinburgh.

Glasgow,[2] 21 August 1767

DEAR SIR: You have prefixed Mr. Foulis's Receipt for the first three Chapters of Your Corsica.[3] Mr. Foulis would have given Receipt for the Book also had you not mentioned sending it to Mr. Dilly. He will write himself and acknowledge the receipt then.[4] I arrived here precisely at four oClock, and intend to set off immediately for Kilmarnock.[5] I am, Dear Sir, Your Most Obedient Servant,

JAS. BROWN

[1] James Brown (d. 1788) was JB's law clerk from c. 1766 to c. 1770 (Journ. 28–30 Mar. 1767; 17, 18 July 1769). He signed on as a cadet in the Bengal Army in 1771 and by 1784 had risen to

the rank of captain (V. C. P. Hodson, *List of the Officers of the Bengal Army, 1758–1834*, 1927, i. 224). JB and Brown exchanged letters during the period 1770–78 (Reg. Let.), but none of these has been reported. Brown died in Monghyr, India, in Sept. 1788 (From William Brown, 1 Feb. 1790).

[2] MS. 'Edinr.' deleted before 'Glasgow'

[3] The receipt is written at the top of the page in Robert Foulis's hand: 'Glasgow 21st. August 1767. Received from James Boswell Esquire, Advocate by the hands of James Brown his Clerk A Packet containing Three Chapters of his Account of Corsica. Robert Foulis.'

[4] It is uncertain what book Brown refers to; the most likely possibility is that it is all or part of the copy for *Letters of the Right Honourable Lady Jane Douglas*, 1767. On 31 Aug. Dilly acknowl-edged receipt of JB's letter (To Dilly, 20 Aug.) and 'a Specimen of Douglasiana' – a phrase that best describes the *Letters*, though it may possibly be *The Essence of the Douglas Cause*, 1767. We do not have copy for either *Letters* or *Essence*, but 'a Specimen' of *Letters* is likely to have consisted of a marked copy of the printed Douglas *Service* or *Proof* from which the letters were taken (*Lit. Car.* p. 48)—hence Brown's phrase 'the Book'. JB may have sent copy for the *Letters* to the Foulises to have it 'cast off' (though they did not in fact print the book), or simply because they could arrange to have a hefty volume cheaply transported to London. Presumably they forwarded To Dilly, 20 Aug. together with the book.

[5] James Brown's brother William lived in Kilmarnock (From William Brown, 18 May).

From John Dick, Friday 21 August 1767

MS. Yale (C 1021).

ADDRESS: To James Boswell Esqr. of Auchinleck[1]

at Ramsays [Edinburgh], ¼ before nine

MY DEAR SIR, I wrote you yesterday morning from Newcastle, which place I left this morning, but as I am so pressed for time, I push'd on, and am just arriv'd, and going to refresh my self, and go to bed, for I am realy Tired —but I want to know how You do. As soon as I can gett up in the morning, I shall have the pleasure to wait on you. Adieu. Yours affectionately,

J. DICK

[1] MS. 'Au' superimposed upon 'Aff'

To Sir Alexander Dick, Friday 21 August 1767

MS. Mrs. Janet Dick-Cunyngham.

ADDRESS: To Sir Alexander Dick, Baronet, Prestonfield.

[Edinburgh], Augt. 1767

MY DEAR FRIEND: I this afternoon received a letter *Consul venit*,[1] telling me He would be here tomorrow at noon. I was to have sent to you early tomorrow morning; but Behold the Consul is arrived. Being pressed for time, He has pushed on, and is now at Ramsay's. Being a good deal fatigued, He goes to bed immediatly. I have wellcomed him by a few cordial lines and told him that as soon after nine o clock tomorrow morning as He pleases I shall be ready to receive him here, where He will find the worthy Baronet. Therefore My most excellent Knight let me beg of you to be here before nine. I insist that you come here first. My servant will go for the Consul, and I shall have the joy of bringing you together. We will drink Chocolate which I have got from my charming Miss Blair, and feel ourselves friends as if We had been together for years. Then in the warmth of the Noonday Sun we will repair to your Villa. In the mean time pray be kind enough to keep a constant fire in a snug room for the friend of Paoli, and prepare your good family to see a man *slowly recovering from a fever*.[2] Let me have a line in answer. Adieu till we meet, ever yours,

JAMES BOSWELL

Friday 21 August 1767

I pay the Nuncio.[3] So no disputes.

I enclose our friend's letter and Note for your satisfaction.[4]

You will return me them tomorrow.

[1] 'That the consul is coming'. The classical allusion is explained in To Sir Alexander Dick, 16 Apr. n. 7.

[2] JB's latest bout of gonorrhoea had been made worse by both a cold and a fever (To W. J. Temple, 29 July and 11 Aug.).

[3] 'Messenger', i.e. the bearer of this letter.

[4] From John Dick, 20 Aug. and 21 Aug.

From John Widdrington, between 24 and 29 August 1767

Not reported. See To Sir Alexander Dick, 31 Aug.: 'As for old Aesculapius, Mr. Widdrington wrote me last week that He left Newcastle this day senight'. John Widdrington (d. 1797), merchant in Newcastle-upon-Tyne and J.P. for Northumberland, had gone abroad 'for his improvement' in 1753, while an apprentice (*Extracts from the Records of the Merchant Adventurers of Newcastle-upon-Tyne*, ed. F. W. Dendy, 1895–99, ii. 362; *Scots Mag.* 1797, lix. 931); perhaps he had met John Dick during that period. For the seal of Aesculapius, see From John Dick, 27 Aug., 1 Sept.; To Sir Alexander Dick, 31 Aug. and n. 4, 2 Sept. and n. 5; From Sir Alexander Dick, 3 Sept.

From Sir Alexander Dick, c. Thursday 27 August 1767

MS. Yale (C 964).

ADDRESS: To Mr. James Boswell, advocate, Edr., Lord afflecks, with a packet and Large Letter for the Consul.

[Prestonfield]

Our Consul my friend must have been greatly occupied for Lo! another Immense packet comes to you by James which I suppose you will forward and place to his accompt of sundries.[1]

The journal you gave me yesterday is now returnd.[2] It engagd my fancy so much that after my usual time of looking at the Rising Sun I took up your papers to read only 3 or 4 pages but such is your fascinating manner[3] of writting that I never rested till I had gone through the whole packet.

I approve of Lord Hales s notes especially the prudential. I knew his hand and his arch remark on the Lady of Brodiguiath made me laugh a gorge deployee.[4] You must know I fancyd you (when you had got your Sienna Innamorata into the Journal)[5] a young Hercules (as in the famd Table of Cebes which poussen has nobly exprest) balancing betwixt the soft endearments of Sienna and the Rude virtuous paths to paoli at Corsica: it will strike many as it did me and will the more so as you dont hint the least of it, espesally the wise old parents of the debaucht youth of Brittain.[6] Addio Stimabissimo e Caro amico,[7]

A. DICK

P. S. I am now on my Search for papers for the Consul and have got some but not yet sufficient for a Bundle fit for your perusal. Expect me soon in Town as I shall expect you soon in the Country.

[1] John Dick must have left some of his belongings at Prestonfield on 22 Aug. By Dick's 'accompt of sundries' Sir Alexander presumably means the expenses he incurred as British consul for the 'Postage of Letters' between Leghorn and London. The postal records among the Home Office Papers (P.R.O. SP44/328 3210, pp. 205, 241) are unfortunately not itemized, but one can get a fairly good idea of the high cost of postage and shipping between England and Italy in the mid-eighteenth century. From 1 July 1766 to 30 June 1767, Dick paid out, for postage and franking at Leghorn, Florence, Genoa, and Gibraltar, 2,948. 12. 0 livres 'making £112. 1. 6 sterling.'

In letters to Joseph Spence in 1762, Sir Alexander mentions two servants named James: one a gardener and the other a cook (Joseph Spence, *Anecdotes, Observations, and Characters of Books and Men*, ed. S. W. Singer, 1820, pp. 459, 466).

[2] The journal section of *Corsica*, of which only a few pages survive in manuscript.

[3] MS. 'manner manner'

[4] The MSS. of the 'Account of Corsica' and materials for the 'Account' survive with several examples of Lord Hailes's marginal notes (M 2, 6), but unfortunately, his 'arch remark' on the Lady Brodiguiath is not among them and she remains unidentified. Sir Alexander uses the French idiom, 'Rire à gorge deployée': 'to split one's sides, to roar with laughter'.

[5] Girolama Piccolomini.

[6] Presumably, Sir Alexander was aware that the *Table* (properly *Tabula*) of *Cebes* was regarded as an elaboration of themes found in Xenophon's 'Choice of Hercules', a dialogue between Socrates and Aristippus on the relative benefits of a life of ease and pleasure versus a life of strenuous virtue (*Memoirs of Socrates*, trans. Sarah Fielding, 1762, II. i. 93–101). Some 18th-century adaptations of the myth of Hercules include Reynolds's portrait, 'Garrick Between Tragedy and Comedy' and Handel's 'Choice of Hercules,' his 'musical interlude' (P. H. Lang, *George Frideric Handel* (1966, pp. 501–05). Only a fragment of the Greek manuscript of the *Tabula* survives. It is a dialogue between a group of young strangers and an old man, who agrees to explain the allegorical characters and landscapes portrayed on a picture deposited in a temple as a votive offering. Richard Parsons's introduction to his *Cebes' Tablet* (1887, pp. 5–18), discusses the problems of assigning a date to the *Tabula* and the difficulties of determining the authorship.

The painting by Nicolas Poussin (1594–1665), 'Hercule entre le Vice et la Vertu', portrays Hercules between two female figures, one with a small child (cf. Reynolds's portrait, 'Garrick Between Tragedy and Comedy'). Sir Alexander may have seen the painting itself at Stourhead, Wilts., the seat of the Hoare family, or the engraving done in 1759 by Sir Robert Strange, his relative by marriage (Musée du Louvre, *Exposition, Nicolas Poussin*, 1960, No. 69; Dennistoun i. 267). The painting remains at Stourhead, now part of the National Trust.

[7] 'Farewell, most esteemed and dear friend'.

From John Dick, Thursday 27 August 1767

MS. Yale (C 1022).

NOTE in Dick's hand at foot of first page: James Boswell Esq.

Alnwick Castle,[1] Thursday morning

MY DEAR SIR, Give me leave to return You my very sincere thanks for all your goodness, to me while at Edenburgh— and I beg You will say every thing that's kind, and proper for me to worthy Sir Alexander and his Amiable Family.

The morning I left Prestonfield, I took the Liberty to write the inclosed note to Sir Alexander and meant to leave it on the Table, but to my great surprise, I found it amongst my papers which my man had put up in the Chaise Seat— I shall contrive to send the Seal to You, and must beg the favour of You to prevail on Sir Alexander to accept of it.[2] When You see our friend Ferguson,[3] say every thing that's kind for me. I shall long to have the pleasure of hearing that You are quite reinstated, being with unalterable Regard, and true Esteem, My dear Sir, Your most Obliged and Affectionate friend,

JOHN DICK

P. S. I shall also hope to have the pleasure of hearing from you about what I recommended to You.[4]

[1] Alnwick Castle was the seat of the Dukes of Northumberland. The current Duke was Hugh Percy (Sedgwick ii. 428–29; *Comp. Peer.* ix. 743–44), but we do not know whether Dick was acquainted with him.

[2] For the seal, see To Sir Alexander Dick, 31 Aug. n. 4.

[3] James Ferguson, younger of Pitfour, advocate and mutual friend of JB and John Dick (*Fac. Adv.* p. 69; From John Dick, 31 Oct. 1766, n. 3). Since 6 Mar. Ferguson, like JB, had been 'troubled' by Dick with requests for legal assistance in his pursuit of the Braid baronetcy (From John Dick, 6 Mar., 17 June, 29 July).

[4] It is not known what Dick had recommended to JB.

To Sir Alexander Dick, 31 August 1767

MS. Pierpont Morgan Library, New York.

ADDRESS: To My honoured and worthy friend Sir Alexander Dick Baronet at his Seat of Prestonfield.

Monday, Noon.

MY DEAR SIR, You cannot conceive how much I regret your having been here yesterday, when there was no admittance.[1] *Abroad* did you think? Yes I was abroad as poor John Reid would be when you knock at the prison door when the Turnkey is absent.[2] In short as yet *non ego sum vates.*[3] However a few days more will I hope waft me to the amenity of Prestonfield. As for old Aesculapius, Mr. Widdrington wrote me last week that He left Newcastle this day senight But I have not yet seen him though I have much ⟨n⟩eed of him.[4] Pray let me know when I shall have the pleasure of seeing you⟨.⟩ The Press is prolifick.[5] Adieu, ever yours,

J. B.

[1] JB was confined to his rooms because of his continuing bout of gonorrhoea.

[2] For John Reid and his trial for sheep-stealing, see From John Reid, 13 Nov. 1766.

[3] Literally, 'I am not a prophet'. Presumably JB means he is uncertain as to exactly when he will be cured and able to visit his friends.

[4] The 'old Aesculapius' referred to was a seal bearing the likeness of the Roman god of healing and medicine (OCD); John Dick intended it as a gift for Sir Alexander (From John Dick, 1 and 26 Sept.). For 'Mr. Widdrington', see From John Widdrington, between 24 and 29 Aug.

[5] That is, the printing of Corsica by the Foulis brothers was continuing apace.

From Edward Dilly, Monday 31 August 1767

MS. Yale (C 1066).

ADDRESS: To James Boswell Esqr., Advocate, Parliament Closs, Edinburgh.

London, Augt. 31t. 1767

SIR: I received yours of the 20th Instant with a Specimen of Douglasiana, I do not think it quite proper for to have my Name Printed to this Piece, as I am now about Publishing your Histy. of Corsica, you may send up a Number to Wilkie in St. Pauls Church Yard, and I make no doubt a Number will be sold.[1] The sooner they are sent the better, for though the Douglass Cause has made a great noise, yet it is only of a Temporary nature, and will soon Dye away; which makes me apprehend that any future Publication upon the Subject, will be very uncertain in regard to its Sale. The Map of Corsica, I presume is already in Hand. I do not know any Person more proper to have it inscribed too, than Mr. Boswell, you will take Care to have it brought into as small a Compass as possible, that it may fold up conveniently in the Book,—you may Work off 500 Maps for Scotland; and the plate may then be sent up to me, and I can Work them off, as I have Occasion for them. I hope long before this Time, you have two or three Sheets of the Work from Foulis, and that he will get at least that Number of Sheets done every Week, I shall be glad to know how he goes on, and Whether you have fixt on Fleming's Paper; I think it very good, and even better than the Specimens I sent.[2] The Appendix I would by no means have Paged apart from the History, but let the Pages be continued; for many Purchasers judge of the Price, and Quantity, by the Number of Pages,—the Appendix will begin on a fresh Page, and the Printing it in English Letter will make but very little diffirence, than if it was Printed in Pica.[3] I enquird of Corbet, for the Author of an Acct. of Corsica Printed in 1739, but he can give me no information concerning him.[4]—I shall be glad to have the Title and Motto as soon as you can, that I may give orders about advertising in the Scots Papers. I saw a Letter in the London Chronocle of last Thursday, relative to the Publication, it is Dated from Oxford and signd B. M. I here send it to you inclos'd; from what I can judge of the Letter, I apprehend that this Oxonian is now upon a visit at Edinburgh, and Lodges, in, or near the Parliament Closs;[5] possibly Mr. Boswell may know him, and if he should be happy in his acquaintance, please to inform him, that I am well pleased with the Letter, and shall esteem it as a favour, if he will now and then send a Letter to the Printers of the different London Papers, and likewise of the Scots Papers, upon the same Subject, and I would have you by all means shew him the Printed Sheets, and he will then be able to give a better account of the Publication, if you will send me the Title and Contents of the Work, I will Write something on the Occasion, and send it to our London Papers, this will be a means of making the History a Subject of Conversation, Wet the appetite of the Public, and make them very anxious of Seeing it. I shall expect to hear from you soon, that I may know what Progress you make, the Work should be finished if possible by the latter End of October, that I may have them in London by the middle of November. I am, Sir, Your most Obedient Servant,

EDWD. DILLY

[1] It is likely that the 'Specimen of Douglasiana' Dilly received from JB was a part of *Letters of the Right Honourable Lady Jane Douglas*, advertised for sale on 28 Nov.: JB was one of the editors of this work (*Lit. Car.* pp. 48–50). For other possibilities, see From James Brown, 21 Aug. n. 4.

[2] For the paper to be used for Corsica, see From Edward Dilly, 10 Aug. n. 4.

[3] The Appendix, which contains Corsican state papers, appears between the Account section and the Journal section of *Corsica* and is numbered pp. 241–58. The typographical distinctions between English Letter and Pica are explained in From Dilly,

28 July 1767, n. 3.

[4] Charles Corbett the younger (1732 or 1734–1808) succeeded his father as bookseller at Addison's Head, Fleet Street, in 1752. He published the *Whitehall Evening Post*, which his father had founded, and later ran a lottery office (Maxted, p. 52). In 1739 Charles Corbett the elder printed *A New Description, Geographical and Historical, of the Island of Corsica*; the author remains unknown.

[5] MS. 'Closs' superimposed upon ?'Hou'. JB marked this piece as his own in his file of *Lond. Chron.*; it was signed 'B. M., Oxford' (*Lit. Car.* p. 240).

From Sir Alexander Dick, Tuesday 1 September 1767

MS. Yale (C 965).

ADDRESS: To Mr. James Boswell, Advocate, Edr., Lord afflecks, with a packet. [Notation on address side:] Return Dr. Walke[r']s Letter by the Bearer.

Prestonfield, Septr. 1, 1767

I am dissapointed to day, I thot to have regald my self with seeing you in your Camera obscura,[1] but I know you will rejoice with me, for my relief, when I inform you that your Cousins Jenny and Katy Douglasses marriadges which warm a pace, have occupied me all this forenoon.[2] Kate tho the youngest (by my Letter from Derby to day) goes of in the end of this month, and Jenny, with more deliberation by my Letter from Kelhead to day goes of next October out of my House. You must Stay and dance and be⟨el⟩ectrify'd of Course for La Bella Bl⟨ond⟩a's sake—the best of virgin's![3]

You can't imagine how deep I just now am in Schemes for population. A Letter comes this moment piping hot from Moffat from one of my choice Spirits and Correspondents, the Holy man, of God of the place, Dr. Walker. I send it for your perusal, it is all Gospel by the Evangalists![4]

The packet I send by James[5] is all I have as yet found relative to Consul Dick's view and the orkney Debt which is deeper and better founded than I at first imagind: at your leisure look at the whole. The Geneaology and a State of Sir Wm. Dicks affairs 1642[6] I send enclosd as they happend to fall in my way after the packet was made up.[7]

We long to see you well eneough to be regald with very ripe apricots, in your Camera piu aperta, here.[8] Adieu, Yours,

ALEXR. DICK

P. S. I write to your Father next post as Uncle to the[9] two marrying Nieces, Jenny and Kate for his approbation.[10]

P. S. The Revd. Mr. Weyvill and his father are just now arrivd[11] or[12] else I had sent you a vast packet of other news viz. my Interview with Lord Morton about our Consul and his vast desire to see us a week at Dalmahoy[13] and Sir Laurence Dundas's keen wishes expesst to see me often.[14] Does not this point at good things from the orkney's, after so much misery of our fore fathers!

[1] Dick is alluding to JB's confinement to his rooms with gonorrhoea (To Sir Alexander Dick, 31 Aug. and n. 1).

[2] Janet and Catherine Douglas (From Sir Alexander Dick, 15 Aug. n. 3). The Douglas sisters were tangentially related to JB through a common ancestor, Lt.-Col. John Erskine (Ominous Years, Gen. Chart iv., p. 377). Although the names of Janet and Catherine do not appear on the chart, their position in the lineage is indicated by that of their father, Sir John Douglas of Kelhead.

[3] Presumably Janet Dick, Sir Alexander Dick's older daughter (From Sir Alexander Dick, 22 Aug. 1766, n. 2), whose fair, blue-eyed beauty

is referred to in letters addressed to her by Lady Elizabeth Lindsay (Scots Charta Chest, pp. 185–86, 289–95, 300–02).

[4] John Walker (1731–1803), M.D., D.D., botanist, had been minister at Moffat since 1762, and in 1779 became Professor of Natural History at Edinburgh (Fasti Scot. i. 4, 322). In 1764, at Lord Kames's instigation, Walker undertook to make an 'economical survey' of the Hebrides and Highlands, which was not published till 1808, after his death (I. S. Ross, Lord Kames and the Scotland of His Day, 1972, pp. 320–21). Walker also wrote a 'Report to the General Assembly, 1772, concerning the State of the Highlands and Islands' (Scots Mag. 1772, xxxiv. 289–93). A new

scholarly edition of the Report, entitled *The Rev. John Walker's Report on the Hebrides of 1764 and 1771*, ed. M. M. McKay, was produced in 1980.

[5] One of Sir Alexander's servants (From Sir Alexander Dick, c. 27 Aug., n. 1).

[6] MS. '1742' changed to '1642'

[7] Sir Alexander's comments relate to the Dick family's claims on loans dating back to the mid-seventeenth century. See Appendix I for the Dick genealogy, and From John Dick, 6 Mar. n. 13 for the basis of John Dick's claim to the baronetcy of Braid. Sir William Dick, (?1580–1655), supposed baronet of Braid, was a merchant-banker who served as Provost of Edinburgh, 1638–39, and as a Member of the Committee of Estates, 1645–46. He owned extensive properties in the Orkneys, but was ruined by a series of ill-advised loans (around 500,000 merks' worth) to the Covenanters (1639), to Charles I (1641), and to Charles II (1650). The last of these loans incurred him a fine as a malignant against the Commonwealth and pushed him into bankruptcy. Nevertheless, he was able before his ruin to make provision for his five sons (*Baronage*, pp. 269–74).

His second son, Sir Andrew Dick of Craighouse (d. 1687), owned lands in the Orkneys and served as Sheriff there after his brother's death. Sir Andrew lent 100,274 merks, the aforementioned 'Orkney Debt', to William Douglas, eighth Earl of Morton, on the security of a 1662 Orkneys land grant. Due to a 1669 revocation of Morton's rights to the land, Sir Andrew was never repaid. As a token of gratitude, however, Charles II awarded Dick a pension of £132 (Stodart, pp. 260, 262). In 1777, the Treasury ordered a lifetime annuity of £100 to be paid jointly to Janet and Ann Dick as a final settlement of this Orkney debt (Stodart, p. 263; *Scots Charta Chest*, p. 268).

[8] 'More open chamber'. Dick expresses his hope that JB will soon be well enough to receive visitors.

[9] MS. 'the the' with 'our' superimposed upon second 'the'.

[10] Lord Auchinleck sent his approval on 9 Sept., along with his regrets that he could not attend the weddings (*Scots Charta Chest*, pp. 226–27).

[11] The Rev. Christopher Wyvill (1740–1822), LL.B., LL.D., later a noted Parliamentary reformer, was one of the readers of the manuscript of JB's *Corsica* (From Wyvill, 3 Oct. nn. 1 and 6). His father, Edward Wyvill (c. 1710–91), was general supervisor of excise at Edinburgh (*Scots Mag.*, 1791, p. 154).

[12] MS. 'to'

[13] James Douglas (c. 1702–68), K.T., P.R.S., thirteenth Earl of Morton, astronomer and archivist, had been Lord Clerk Register since 1760 and a Representative Peer for Scotland since 1739. His estate, Dalmahoy, lay about seven miles south-west of Edinburgh. After an Act of Parliament in 1742 confirmed his rights to Orkney and Shetland, Morton sold these islands to Sir Lawrence Dundas in 1766 for £63,000 (*Scots. Peer.* vi. 381–82).

[14] Sir Lawrence Dundas (c. 1710–81), Bt., M.P. for Newcastle-under-Lyme, 1762–68, Vice-Admiral of Shetland and Orkney (*Comp. Bar.* v. 124). Dundas made his fortune as a contractor and commissary to the Hanoverians. He invested this wealth in the purchase of various estates, thereby controlling their associated Parliamentary seats, and by the time of this letter was termed 'Nabob of the North' (Shelburne to Henry Fox, 19 Aug. 1762, in Henry Fox MSS.). By 1767, Dundas was known to influence around eight or nine seats via his Scottish empire; his purchase of Orkney and Shetland from the Earl of Morton (see above, n. 13) brought him control over their county representation and a leading interest in Tain Burghs (Namier and Brooke ii. 359).

When JB and Dundas met for the first time on 20 Sept. 1780, JB found him 'a comely, jovial scotch Gentleman of good address but not bright parts' and was satisfied at having added 'a new distinguished character to my collection' (Journ.).

From John Dick, Tuesday 1 September 1767

MS. Yale (C 1023).

ADDRESS (In Thomas Anson's hand): To James Boswell Esqr., at Lord Auchinleck's, Edenburgh.

FRANK: Free T. Anson.

NOTE in Dick's hand at foot of first page: James Boswell Esq.

Shugborough,[1] Tuesday 1st Septr. 1767

MY DEAR SIR, I had the pleasure to write You a few lines from Alnwick Castle, where I was obliged to stay untill Saturday. I then told You of the mistake which my servant had made in packing up the note which I had wrote to worthy Sir Alexander: when at N. Castle, I deliver'd the Seal to Mr. John Witherington who promised me to send it to You. I hope er'e this You have receiv'd it, and that You have prevaild on the good Bart. to accept of it, and that he will wear it, as from one who is greatly his obliged humble Servant— pray present my most Respectfull, and Affectionate Compliments to all the family, as also Mrs. Dick's.

I expect Letters to know if my presence is necessary in Town. If it is, I shall make but a[2] very short stay, therefore at all events, you may when you favor me with an Answer to this, direct your Letter to me, to the Care of Benj. Price Esqr. at Bath.[3]

Our Heroe immediately took possession of Algaiola upon the departure of the French; and was at the Gates of Ajaccio, and Calvi with the Cannon which he took at Capraja.[4] *Viva i Corsi.* I long to have the pleasure of hearing that You are quite recover'd, pray say every thing that's kind for me to our Honest friend Ferguson, and accept of my Wife's best Compliments—and believe me ever truely and Affectionately Your Obliged Friend,

JOHN DICK

[1] Dick wrote from Shugborough Hall, estate of Thomas Anson (From John Dick, 17 June n. 6), who franked this letter.

[2] MS. 'a a'

[3] Unidentified.

[4] Algaiola, Ajaccio, and Calvi were among five garrisoned Corsican towns placed under French protection by the Genoese at the Second Treaty of Compiègne in 1764. In July the French troops were pulled out of the towns. This movement was ostensibly to protest the Genoese offer of Corsica as an asylum to Jesuits expelled from Spain; France had expelled its own Jesuits in 1764. It is more likely that the withdrawal was a political move by Choiseul to point up Genoese weakness on the island (Thrasher, pp. 111–12).

The temporary evacuation of French troops allowed Paoli a long-awaited opportunity to conquer Genoese garrisons without damaging his policy of appeasing the French. At the siege of Capraia in June Paoli had captured four pieces of brass battery cannon, seven smaller pieces, and a large quantity of bullets and powder (*Gent. Mag.* 1767, xxxvii. 326; F. Girolami-Cortona, *Histoire de la Corse*, 1971, p. 361). For an account of Paoli's campaign to reduce the three fortresses, see *Gent. Mag.* 1767, xxxvii. 474; 1768, xxxviii. 41–42; *Scots Mag.* 1767, xxix. 438.

From Lord Marischal, Tuesday 1 September 1767

MS. Yale (C 1958).

ADDRESS: Monsieur, Monsieur Boswell d'Auchenleck, à Edenbourg en Ecosse; par Londres; fr. amsterdam.

POSTMARK: [London] SE 15.

Potsdam, ce 1r Sept.[1] 1767

SIR: I delayed some posts answering your favor of July 20th, expecting every post a return to mine concerning the placing of 500, ps. for Emetulla,[2] which I think may be done as follows, she gives 'me here some money she has scraped together, about 400 guineas, I make over to her 500 ps. part of money owing to me on good security by al. Keith of Revelston,[3] and that sum of 500 ps. in the hands of said Mr. Keith is reimbursed by 500 of my rents of last year and which therefor I shall not draw from him.' But she and I will wait your better advice.

George Keith Boswell will I hope soon arrive in good health, and I hope he shall be as good a man as his father;[4] you ask what country man he is to be, were it not on account of his religion, I should advise his being *Espanol*, because in that country the natural son of a gentleman is reputed such, and does naturally by birthright inherit as a lawfull son; for in Spain they make a just difference betwixt a bastard the offspring of folks marryed either one or both, or a natural son born of two free unmarryed.[5] We drink at our table here soberly as you know, only one toast, Succés aux armes d'Emetulla, she has received compliments on the retreat of the Gavachos, and hopes to make a compleat conquest of the Republick of Genova, for an exemple to all Princes to governe mildly and justly.[6]

I have seen in the English newspaper that Mr. Rousseau with my directions and assistance has writ a Romance, Dorando I think it is called, they tell me that it has given offence, and that it is a history of the Douglas's unlucky law suit,[7] I wish you would send it me by one of the oyster boats coming to Hamburg, adress to Mrs. Stephen and Renny.[8] My best compliments to my Lord your father, believe me ever to you both a faithfull humble servant,

MARISCHALL

mit compliments de Madame de Froment.

I intend to send you some turnip seed,[9] of which some to Sir James Stuart and some to Baron Muir, I believe they are both your neighbours,[10] some also to my Niece at Cumbernald.[11] It shall be sent to Captain James Ogilvie of Leith, a very honest Killymuir man, when you go one day to Lieth make him my compliments.[12] Bon soir.

[1] MS. '1r Aout', probably written in error for 1 Sept.

[2] For the money, see From Marie de Froment, 9 July, and From Marischal, 10 July.

[3] Alexander Keith of Ravelston and Dunottar (d. 1792), writer in Edinburgh and Depute-Clerk of the Court of Session, was descended from the fourth son of William Keith, third Earl Marischal, and was thus a distant kinsman of the present Earl. He bought the estate of Dunottar, Kincardineshire, from Marischal in 1766, and was thought to have been generally accepted by him as his rightful heir (Comp. Peer. viii. 477 n. 'd', 749; Cuthell ii. 307).

[4] After learning of Mrs. Dodds's pregnancy on 27 Apr., JB presumably informed Marischal that the child, if a son, would be named for him. The child, born in late November or early December, was named Sally (To W. J. Temple, 24 Dec.; Earlier Years, p. 345).

[5] Marischal's knowledge of Spanish law was first-hand; he had spent about twenty years of his exile in Valencia and Madrid (From Lord Marischal, 30 Apr. 1766, n. 1). Spanish inheritance law made a distinction between naturales, the offspring of two unmarried persons, and bastardos who, although they were conceived in an act of adultery, nevertheless carried rights to inherit. Their qualification to inherit depended on the father's recognition of the child as his own, and also on an absence of legitimate heirs (D. Joaquin Escriche, Diccionario razonado de legislacion y jurisprudencia, 1875, s.v. hijo natural, hijo illegitimo,

hijo adulterino).

[6] From Marischal, c. 1 June, 10 July, and n. 5. 'Gavachos' was an epithet given to foreigners in Spain who did menial work (Sebastian de Covarrubias, Tesoro de la lengua Castellana o Espanola, ed. Martin de Riquer, 1943, pp. 633–34); in Dorando JB applies the term 'Gavaccios' to French supporters of the Duke of Hamilton (Dorando, A Spanish Tale, ed. Robert Hunting, 1974, p. 31).

[7] The anonymous reviewer of the tale, actually JB himself, observed 'that if the hand of M. Rousseau guided by my Lord Marischal of Scotland is not here, Dorando is at least the production of no less ordinary Genius' (Lond. Chron. 30 June–2 July, xxii. 5). In writing this pamphlet, a vigorously partisan allegory of the Douglas Cause thinly disguised as a Spanish tale, JB was influenced by Walpole's Castle of Otranto and by notions of Spain imbibed from Lord Marischal. See further, Earlier Years, pp. 323–25, 330–34; Lit. Car. pp. 32–38.

[8] For Stephen and Renny, see From Lord Marischal, c. 1 June, n. 1.

[9] Turnips played a leading role in Britain's agricultural revolution and were valued by 'improvers' because of the flexibility they introduced into crop rotation and their serviceability as winter fodder. North European turnips such as swedes were hardy, and therefore much sought after (James E. Handley, Scottish Farming in the Eighteenth Century, 1953, pp. 203–04).

[10] Sir James Steuart (1713–80) of Goodtrees,

Bt., later (1776) Steuart-Denham, advocate and political economist (*Comp. Bar.* iv. 377; *Fac. Adv.* p. 199), whom JB thought 'most lively and full of expression' (Journ. 8 Feb.). Steuart joined the Jacobite uprising of 1745 and remained in exile on the Continent until 1763; he was formally pardoned in 1771. He returned to Scotland and retired to his estate of Coltness, Lanarkshire, about twenty miles north-east of Auchinleck, where he set about preparing his major work, *An Enquiry into the Principles of Political Economy*, 1767, the first systematic and complete treatise on the subject in English. For the controversy over this book's mention of Corsica, see To Steuart, c. mid-September.

The other of JB's neighbours to receive a gift

of turnip seed was William Mure of Caldwell, Renfrewshire. Mure's principal interest lay in agricultural improvements, a field in which he was an acknowledged authority. For details of Mure's career, see From P. L. Dupont, 7 Apr. n. 15.

[11] Clementina, Lady Elphinstone (From Lord Marischal, 10 July n. 2).

[12] Captain James Ogilvie (d. 1791), ship's master in Precious's Close, Leith, until his death (*Scots Mag.*, 1791, p. 50); *Edinburgh Directory*, 1774–91). Kirriemuir, commonly pronounced 'Kellamuir' or 'Killymuir', was a parish in Forfarshire where the Ogilvies of Inverquharity and others of that Ilk had long been resident (*Stat. Acct. Scot.* xiii. 354; xiv. 65–66 n.; *Baronage*, pp. 49–52).

To Sir Alexander Dick, Wednesday 2 September 1767

MS. Mrs. Janet Dick-Cunyngham.

ADDRESS: To Sir Alexander Dick Baronet, Prestonfield

Edinburgh, 2 Septr. 1767

MY DEAR KNIGHT AND FRIEND: I have received all your papers which I have allready looked over in a cursory manner. It would seem your Orkney claim may be a sollid affair. It also appears to me that Sir Andrew Dick's son Lewis has either been dead or been supposed to be so without heirs at the time of Dunbar's claims. But that supposition may be false.

What I *desiderate*, as we Lawyers say, is some authentic documents either written or traditional as to the peri[o]d that either[1] of the two Lewiss went to England.[2] You will please search your Hogshead and if you find there what will make our friend a Baronet, we will fill it to the brim with generous wine to drink his health.[3] I shall peruse your papers at more leisure and we shall talk every thing over fully together. In the mean time avoid saying any thing as to the Consul's Pretentions. I send you a letter from him to me, with a card to you which will please you much.[4] As I am charged by the Consul to obtain your acceptance of his most elegant present, I insist on your doing so with the frankness of a friend who is perfectly sure that He is made heartily welcome to it. The image of the God of Physic will be a suitable Signet for the President of the Royal College.[5]

What is become of the Genalogy of Dick which I took the liberty to correct? Is this a copy of it?[6] When we meet, I will talk to you of the manner in which the Consul must be mentioned. I congratulate with you on the Nuptials in view. Dr. Walker's Letter is substantial like the fences of which He writes but like them too wants neatness. What think you of his *Congeries of Trumpery?*[7] Adieu Dear Sir Alexander, ever yours,

JAMES BOSWELL

I have this morning received a Corsican *Proof*. The Press *sudat*.[8] Bravo.

[1] MS. 'either' written above deleted 'any'

[2] Lewis (or Louis) Dick (fl. 1683–1727), second son and eventual heir of Sir Andrew Dick of

Craighouse, was an officer in the Royal Scots Fusiliers, served in the War of the Spanish Succession, and rose to the rank of Captain-Lieutenant in 1727 (Charles Dalton, ed., *English Army Lists and Commission Registers, 1661–1714*, 1960, vi. 340 n. 15). He was said to have married an English lady (*Baronage*, p. 271), but we have no evidence that he ever went to England. James Dunbar was the second husband of Lewis's stepsister Elizabeth, whose first husband was Thomas Boyd of Pinkell (ibid.). On 27 Jan. 1709, Dunbar brought suit against Elizabeth Boyd in an attempt to gain control of the fortune she had inherited from her first husband. In the record of the lawsuit Dunbar is referred to as 'head of the family', suggesting that Lewis Dick was presumed dead and without heirs in 1709 (Morison, p. 5999). The second Lewis (or Louis) Dick (d. 1649) was the youngest son of Sir William Dick of Braid. He became commander of a frigate of war in the coasting service and settled in Northumberland after his marriage, which took place in 1644 (*Baronage*, p. 274; Stodart, pp. 261, 265).

³ 'Sir Alexander preserved his large correspondence in a barrel, or hogshead, in his library,

into which everything of interest was dropped' (*Scots Charta Chest*, p. 219 n. 2). Sir Alexander had materials in his hogshead on the Dicks of Craighouse because his first wife, Janet, was granddaughter of the younger Lewis Dick and heir-general of that line.

⁴ Presumably From John Dick, 27 Aug. The card has not survived.

⁵ For the 'elegant present', see To Sir Alexander Dick, 31 Aug. n. 4. Sir Alexander had been president of the Royal College of Physicians in Edinburgh from 1756 to 1763.

⁶ JB's corrected genealogy has not been reported. Presumably it was among the papers he received that day.

⁷ Presumably quoted from Dr. Walker's letter, which has not been reported. See From Sir Alexander Dick, 1 Sept. n. 4. There is no record of Walker's having written a work of this title, and the phrase does not appear in his *Economical History*.

⁸ 'sweats' or 'labours hard'

To Sir Alexander Dick, Thursday 3 September 1767

MS. Mrs. Janet Dick-Cunyngham.

ADDRESS: To Sir Alexander Dick, Baronet, at Prestonfield.

ENDORSEMENT (in another hand): Mr. Boswell Corst. 1767.

Edinburgh, Thursday morning

MY DEAR SIR: I had an application last night from the Reverend Mr. Robert Colvill youngest minister of Dysart to beg that you would present him to the Parish of Corstorphine.¹ He is an old Schoolfellow of mine.² His stipend is but £55 a year without either manse or Glebe. He is married, and has three Children, and his Wife is big with another. He is a very worthy lad. He is Son to Mr. Walter Colvill the best macer in the Court of Session.³ With so many circumstances to plead for him, I dare say He will have a good chance for your favour, unless you are engaged. I shall be very happy if it is in your power to do what will really be a complication of good actions. I beg an answer from you by the Bearer, explicit as to a friend who is ever most cordially yours,

JAMES BOSWELL

¹ The Rev. Robert Colvill or Colville (1732–1788) had been minister at Dysart, Fife, since 1758. In 1784 he was suspended after he confessed to an unspecified 'libel' (charge) brought against him (*Fasti Scot.* v. 89–90). Colvill was also a minor poet (J. C. Robertson, *Lives of the Scottish Poets*, 3 vols., 1822, pt. vi. 116); his *Poetical Works* were published in 1789. He devoted twenty lines of his panegyric on Paoli to celebrating JB's adventures in Corsica, followed by six lines equating Paoli with Addison's Cato and JB with Juba; all this was accompanied by a lengthy

footnote (*The Cyrnean Hero*, 2nd ed., 1772, pp. 10–12; *Earlier Years*, pp. 364–65). JB and Colvill had both contributed to *A Collection of Original Poems by the Rev. Mr. Blacklock and Other Scotch Gentlemen* (pp. 184–203 of the first volume, 1760, for Colvill, thirty poems in the second volume, 1762, for JB). JB's Register of Letters lists thirteen letters between Colvill and himself, but none has been reported. For a recent treatment of Colvill's poetry, and the relationship between him and JB, see R. C. Cole, 'James Boswell and Robert Colvill', *Studies in Scottish Literature*,

1981, xvi. 110–121; for facsimile reproductions of two of Colvill's poems, see Robert Colvill, *Atalanta (1777) and Savannah (1780)*, ed. R. C. Cole, 1987, pp. 7–15.
[2] Colvill and JB both attended Mundell's School. Although Colvill entered in 1739 and JB in 1746, they might well have met at one of the school's annual reunions (*List of Scholars Educated by the Late Mr. James Mundell*, 1789, pp. 2, 6, 10).
[3] Walter Colvill (or Colville) (fl. 1731–74), baker, had been a burgess of Edinburgh since

1731 (*Roll of Edinburgh Burgesses and Guild Brethren, 1701–1760*, SRS, v. 3, 1930). In the years 1763 and 1765–68 he was one of four macers in the Court of Session (*Universal Scots Almanack* 1763; *Edinburgh Almanack* 1765–68). His shop 'opposite foot of Nidderys Wynd' is listed in the *Edinburgh Directory* for 1774–75, but according to the next issue Mrs. Colvill (presumably his widow) was the shop's proprietor. Robert Colvill became a burgess of Edinburgh by his father's right on 16 Feb. 1774 (*Roll of Edinburgh Burgesses, 1761–1841*, SRS, v. 68).

From Sir Alexander Dick, Thursday 3 September 1767

MS. Yale (C 966).
ADDRESS: To James Boswell Esqr., Advocate, Edr.

Prest., Thursday noon

MY DEAR SIR, I have yours by your servant. It gives me great concern that on the vacancy lately happend in Corstorphine I am so far engagd as to have my self tyd down in prudence and friendship to make choice of one of 3 persons warmly and greatly reccomended by 3 different persons I shall name to you at meeting.[1] It is needless then to say more till I see you perhaps to morrow before 12. I thot to have been with you to day but Mr. Bennet is just going with me to Corstorphine to attend the funeral of our ancient preist.[2]

Our Consul by yours of yesterday has overpowr'd me with his gentile and really magnificent present[3] but it is like himself to do every thing with a good grace. I burn with Zeal to find out proofs of such a Treasure as his propinquity to me and my family. More papers I certainly have and shall fish again for your desiderata. Pray write to the Consul my hearty thanks for his noble present and bid him be assurd he is to be constantly in our memory and in the affections of all my family, I shall write my Self after we meet.

I return you the Consuls Letter. Till[4] we meet, yours affectionately,

ALEXR. DICK

P. S. The Genealogy etc. was put together from Scraps by Mr. Cummyng and Sir R. Douglass,[5] and I believeave must all suffer a close revisal and correct the language by you and my Cousin Lord Hales, if you please also to whom I am related by the Roucheads of Innerlieth.[6]

[1] On the death of the Rev. George Fordyce, incumbent minister of Corstorphine (*Fasti Scot.* i. 7), Sir Alexander chose the Rev. John Chiesley or Cheislie (ibid. i. 7–8, v. 179) to fill the vacancy. Chiesley later gave offence to some of his congregation by introducing the *Paraphrases* into public worship. The man who recommended Chiesley was Robert Alexander of Clermiston, who did so as a reward for Chiesley's assistance in his attempt to win the Parliamentary seat for Anstruther Easter Burghs (*Fasti Scot.*, 1866 ed. i. pt. 1. 137; Namier and Brooke i. 498–500). The

other two candidates and their patrons are unknown.
[2] The Rev. William Bennet (1707–85) had been minister of Duddingston since 1746 (*Fasti Scot.* iv. 304, i. 20). JB describes him as 'worthy' (Journ. 25 Aug. 1776) and 'apostolick' (Journ. 22 Aug. 1779). Fordyce (n. 1), the 'ancient preist', lived to be eighty-four.
[3] For the 'magnificent present', see To Sir Alexander Dick, 31 Aug. n. 4.
[4] MS. '&' deleted before 'Till'
[5] James Cummyng (d. 1793), herald-painter

and Lyon Clerk Depute from 1770, later held the posts of Keeper of the Lyon Records (1774), and Secretary to the Society of Scottish Antiquaries (1780) (SRS *Publications* vol. 77, *Court of the Lord Lyon*, ed. Sir Francis Grant, 1945, p. 14; *Edinburgh Almanack* 1774–93). JB was impressed by Cummyng's 'curious variety of knowledge' of both genealogy and antiquities (Journ. 17 Feb. 1784).

Sir Robert Douglas of Glenbervie and Ardit (1694–1770), Bt., genealogist (*Comp. Bar.* ii. 284–85) had already published his two-volume *Peerage of Scotland* (1764). He announced his *Baronage of Scotland* in September 1767, but the text was left unfinished at his death and published posthumously in one volume in 1798. In a 'manuscript' dated 1 July 1778 Cummyng indicated which families had warrants for Arms alone and which for Arms and Supporters (*Baronage*, p.

ix n.). The original 'Genealogy etc.' put together 'from Scraps' to which Dick refers is no longer extant; presumably, it formed the basis for the accounts of the Dick family claims in the published text.

[6] Sir Alexander Dick and Sir David Dalrymple, Lord Hailes, were related through common ancestors in the Rochead of Inverleith family. Sir Alexander was the great-grandson of Alexander Dick of Heugh by his wife Helen, daughter of Sir James Rochead of Inverleith, Kt. (*Comp. Bar.* iv. 306; Stodart, p. 264). Lord Hailes was the grandson of the Hon. David Dalrymple of Hailes (c. 1665–1721), who married (1691), as her second husband, Janet Rochead, one of four sisters and co-heirs of Sir James Rochead, 1st Bt. [1704], (who died unmarried in 1737) and daughter of Sir James Rochead, Kt. (*Comp. Bar.*, iv. 397, 427 and n. d., 454).

To Thomas Davies, Friday 4 September 1767

Not reported. Enclosed in To Edward Dilly, 4 Sept.; in his reply to that letter Dilly wrote, 'The Letter you enclosed for Mr. Davies, was sent soon after it came to Hand' (From Dilly, 10 Sept.).

To Edward Dilly, Friday 4 September 1767

Not reported. See From Dilly, 10 Sept.: 'I had wrote you about Douglasiana, before Yours of the 4th Instant came to Hand.'

From Edward Dilly, Thursday 10 September 1767

MS. Yale (C 1067).

London, Sept. 10th 1767

SIR: I had Wrote to you about Douglasiana, before Yours of the 4th Instant came to Hand. I am a little apprehensive it will not do for me to Publish, as I am now about Publishing your History of Corsica, but when you have finishd the Whole of Douglasiana and will send up the Mss. to me, I can then better Judge whether it will be proper for me to Print, if it is not, I will then endeavour to make the best bargain I can with some Other Bookseller, the sooner it is sent, the better. I am glad to find Mr. Foulis is fairly set a going. I hope he will not exceed the latter End of November before he finishes.[1] On the back of the Title Page, he must say, *Entered at Stationer's Hall agreeable to Act of Parliament*, Printed in the Old black English Letter. Shoud be glad if you would send me under Cover the first Sheet that is Workt off, the very first opportunity, with the Title Page you intend to give, and the Motto. The Map of Corsica I presume will be done this Month. You will please to send me a Specimen of that also. As for Mr. Anderson's Speeches of the Lords, I do not apprehend there would be any great demand for them now, as Almon's Publication has in a great measure satisfied the Curiosity of the Public.[2] If you have got the Whole of Lord Auchinleck's Speech correct, and intend to put it in some of the Papers, you had better send it to one of the Daily Papers, for the Printers of the Evening Papers, generally take every thing that is entertaining from the Daily Papers, the best Daily Paper is Printed by Mr. Woodfall[3] in Paternoster Row, as that Paper is taken in by all the Polite People as it contains all the advertisements of the Polite Places of resort, Play-Houses, Ranelaygh, Vauxhall, etc. etc., and these advertisements are confined to this Paper only, if you confine your Correspondence to that Paper you may always depend upon having every thing inserted, that is Curious or entertaining, within a few Days after your Letters are received.[4] The Letter you enclosed for Mr. Davies, was sent soon after it came to Hand. I am, Sir, Your most Obedient Servant,

EDWD. DILLY

[1] Dilly appears to have revised his original timetable: on 10 Aug. he had hoped to see the books in London by the beginning of October (From Dilly, 1 Aug. n. 1; 4 Aug.; 10 Aug.).

[2] For Almon's and Anderson's editions of the speeches in the Douglas Cause, see From Dilly, 1 Aug. n. 4; 10 Aug., nn. 11–12. Lord Auchinleck's speech appears on pp. 134–49 of the Almon edition and pp. 63–86 of the Anderson edition.

[3] Henry Sampson Woodfall (1739–1805), editor of the *Pub. Adv.* from age 19 until his retirement in 1793, succeeded to ownership of his father Henry Woodfall's printing business in 1769 (*Maxted*, pp. xxxv, 252). JB later called Woodfall 'an old publishing acquaintance, and a fine hearty fellow, and one who loves a bottle'

(Journ. 26 Mar. 1783); JB once 'drank too freely—just to drink with Woodfall' (Journ. 26 Apr. 1773).

[4] JB could 'depend upon having every thing inserted' within a few days of Woodfall's receipt of the letter on account of Woodfall's well-known policy of printing everything he received, even when he disagreed with it. According to Nichols, the *Pub. Adv.* dealt with its unpaid correspondents in a 'strictly impartial' fashion (*Lit. Anec.* i. 300–02). As Woodfall stated, 'The printer looks upon himself only as a purveyor . . . and the "Public Advertiser" is, in short, what its correspondents please to make it' (*Pub. Adv.* 2 Sept. 1769, quoted in DNB).

From Lord Marischal, Saturday 12 September 1767

MS. Yale (C 1959).

ADDRESS: To James Boswell Esqr., of Auchenleck, Edenburgh, en Ecosse; [added] fr. Amsterdam; par Londres.

POSTMARK: [LONDON] SE 25.

ENDORSEMENT: My Lord Marischal in Answer to Book p. 4.[1]

Potsdam, 12 Sep. 1767

Bonny wark, Colonel,[2] getting the lassys wi bairns, and worse to your sel; what sais Mes. John?[3] whats done is done; get well; take care of Keith Boswell; who in time I hope shall become a Nabob; there is a fine country for such adventurers and Knights errant: he slays[4] a Nabob, gets upon his Elephant, and becomes himself Nabob; amen.[5]

I have writ to Mr. Keith of Revelstone that Madame de Froment expects from your goodness and friendship your assistance in placing her 500,ps.; that she has somewhat more than 100, guineas in the hands of Mr. charles smith;[6] that he Mr. Keith shall give you at Martimass what is wanting to make up 500, ps. she gives me here near to that sum, so that I shall not draw on him any more of a long time.[7]

I can not oblige any one, (neither need I) to fix what they have but as they please, but I know that it is done (not by my advice but by her free will) allready by testament. What I have is fixed in the channel you advise,[8] and I thank you for your advice; this by my will before I left Scotland: since, I have given to the two young adventurers Elphingstons now in china 800, ps. and have lent them 4000 without interest, which 4000, I have given to their four sisters at their return.[9] Is not this right, and agreable to your wish. Mr. Keith made an objection, that a marryed woman could not lend to her own account. Her marriage was declared nul and void by a lawfull Sentence of the proper Juges at Berlin, and this without opposition of the husband or wife; and they since have made a renunciation of all demands of any kind one to other, which declaration is in the publick register at Neufchatel;[10] so that I should think there can be no doubt that she can dispose freely of what she has. If it should be otherwise, you will inform us.

Rousseau is in Auvergne, herbolising, and (as I am told) writing against Voltaire;[11] I wish he do not realise so his own opinions as to give them for evident proofs, as he did to Mrs. Hume, Walpole, and Davenport.[12]

As to what you mention of certain things to be left you, such are not entirely the property of the possessor, another has a right allways to demand them, this will probably happen; if it does not, I shall leave such directions as will show the confidence I have in your honor and discretion; there are many things I would say which I do not choose to write on this occasion.[13]

My best compliments and respects to your father. I protest against your giving the standish, and shall send you to redeem it a porringer, to serve caudle towards the end of next year.[14] Please offer to the young Lady my respects, and tell her this from me, who ever am your most obedient servant,

MARISCHALL

Send me the names of my neices Elphingstone.

Here inclosed two receits from Me. de Froment, which send to Mr. Seton of Touch.[15] Mr. Keith will furnish against martimass the rest.

[1] Presumably a book of drafts or copies of JB's letters to Marischal. This letter is number four in JB's folder of Marischal's letters (From Marischal, 14 Apr. headnote).

[2] For the nickname 'Colonel', see From Marischal, 30 Apr. 1766, n. 3.

[3] 'Mes (or Mess) John', a Scotticism used as a jocular name for a Presbyterian minister or for ministers as a class (CSD, s.v. 'Mes; Mess').

[4] MS. 'slays' superimposed upon 'stays'

[5] Already by the 1760s 'nabob' had come to mean a person who returned from India with a fortune (nawab was the Urdu name for a governor or nobleman of India). In telling JB he wants the career of nabob for Keith Boswell, Marischal alludes to 'Nabob' Clive's crushing defeat of the Moghul forces at Plassey (1757), where the opposing general, mounted on a war-elephant, was shot and killed. Though it was not Clive but his ally Mir Jafar who gained the title of nawab after the victory, Clive's Indian riches would have justified Marischal's allusion to him as a nabob.

[6] Charles Smith (d. 1768), for many years a Scots merchant and a Jacobite agent in

Boulogne, had worked with Marischal in 1744 to help organize the abortive French scheme of landing a small Franco-Scottish force in Scotland. Marischal visited him in Scotland in 1763, at which time Smith was evidently visiting or residing in Britain (Scots Mag. 1768, xxx. 447; Cuthell ii. 175–76, 308).

[7] From Marischal, 1 Sept. n. 3. Martinmas was one of two legal term days when payments were due. Half of the year's rent came due at the end of seed-time, on Whitsunday (fixed at 15 May in Scotland), and the other half at the conclusion of the harvest, on Martinmas (11 Nov.) (Bell ii. 734).

[8] In an unreported letter, To Marischal, c. mid-August.

[9] William Fullerton (1740–1834) and George Keith (1746–1823), named for Marischal, were the third and fifth sons of Charles, tenth Lord Elphinstone, and Clementina, Marischal's niece. William, a sailor from the age of fifteen, joined the East India Company sea-service in 1757, eventually became a director, and finally chairman of the Company (Sir William Fraser, The

Elphinstone Family Book, 1897, ii. 1–48). George (1746–1823) had a brilliant career in the Royal Navy, serving with distinction in the American and Napoleonic wars; he was created Baron Keith in 1801 and Viscount Keith in 1814. In 1808 he married Hester Maria Thrale ('Queeney'), daughter of Hester Lynch Thrale (later Piozzi) (Fraser i. 269–74; *Scots Peer.* iii 546–49). For an account of the Elphinstone brothers' voyage to China, see Fraser ii. 6–7 (where Marischal's interest-free loan of £2,000 to each of them is erroneously described as a gift). The five (not four) Elphinstone sisters were Mary (1741–1825), Eleanor (1747–1800), Primrose (1748–1802), Clementina (1749–1822), and Charlotte (1759–81) (*Scots Peer.* iii. 549; Fraser i. 163–68).

[10] For Emet-Ulla's marriage and divorce, see From Marischal, 14 Apr. and n. 7.

[11] Rousseau had actually been staying since 21 June at Trye-le-Château, near Gisors, thirty miles north-west of Paris, as the guest of the Prince de Conti (*Corres. Rousseau* xxxiii. 166). Rousseau was an amateur botanist, and on 12 Sept. sent some specimens to his fellow herbalist the Duchess of Portland, accompanied by a letter signed 'Votre . . . Herboriste' (*Corres. Rousseau* xxxiv. 95–97). The antagonism between Voltaire and Rousseau continued, and in *La Guerre civile de Genève* (1768, pp. 45–47) Voltaire accused Rousseau of burning down the comic theatre in Geneva. Rousseau chose not to respond to Voltaire's poem (*Corres. Rousseau* xxxv. 264–65).

[12] For Rousseau's quarrel with Hume and Walpole's part in it, see From Baroness von Spaen, 22 July 1766, n. 6; for his relationship with Davenport, his host at Wooton, and his abrupt departure from there, see From Rousseau, 4 Aug. 1766, n. 2; *New Hume Letters*, Appendix A, pp. 213–35.

[13] It is not known what 'things' JB asked Marischal to leave to him or what other person would have had the right to demand them.

[14] JB appears to have given the inkstand to Catherine Blair. Marischal's proposal to exchange a porringer for it perhaps suggests that he is anticipating JB's becoming a husband and father within the year and needing a vessel to hold the caudle—warm gruel with sugar and wine—typically given to women in childbed.

[15] Hugh Seton (d. 1795) of Touch, was the son of Marischal's old friend Charles Smith (n. 6, above). On his marriage to Elizabeth Seton, heiress of Touch, Hugh Smith was granted the right by the Court of Session to the name, lands, and titles of his wife's family (*Baronage*, pp. 169–70). Marischal visited the Setons at Touch in 1763 and remained in lifelong communication with Hugh Seton, who managed his financial affairs and also those of Emet-Ulla (Cuthell ii. 175–77, 246–48, 252–53, 256, 308–10).

To John Dick, Tuesday 15 September 1767

Not reported. See From John Dick, 26 Sept.: 'I return You a thousand thanks for your very kind, and obliging Letter of the 15th Inst. but am concerned to hear You was not quite recover'd.'

To Edward Dilly, c. mid-September 1767

Not reported. See From Dilly, 24 Sept.: 'I received the favour of yours by Yesterday's Post, and am glad to find Messrs. Foulis are making some little Progress'.

To Sir James Steuart, c. mid-September 1767

Not reported. See To W. J. Temple, 22 Sept.: 'I have received a most polite letter from Sir James Stewart, in answer to one I wrote to him with regard to a passage in his *Political Oeconomy* which is injurious to the Corsicans.' The offending passage was as follows: 'The Corsicans have exported, that is, sold the best part of their island to Genoa; and now, after having spent the price in wearing the damask and velvet, they want to bring it back, by confiscating the property of the Genoese, who have both paid for the island, and drawn back the price of it, by the balance of their trade against these islanders' (quoted in *Corsica*, pp. 235–36). JB's answer in *Corsica* (likely to resemble the content of his letter) is as follows: 'With this respectable writer's permission, it was not a balance of trade, but a balance of bad fortune, which subjected Corsica to the Genoese; and the greatest part, if not all the property of the nobles of the republick in that island, was acquired only by force or by fraud.'

The expensiveness of the Corsicans in wearing damask and velvet, is merely ideal. Corsica is perhaps the only country upon the face of the globe, where luxury has never once been introduced. The Genoese cannot pretend to have made themselves masters of Corsica, by commercial superiority; for those republicans have been supplied from that fertile island, with a great many of the necessities of life, which their own narrow dominions could not furnish in sufficient quantities' (p. 236).

From Sir James Steuart, c. mid-September 1767

Not reported. See reply To Steuart, c. mid-Sept. 1767.

To Christopher Wyvill, c. mid-September 1767

Not reported. See From Wyvill, 3 Oct.: 'On my return to this place from York, last night, I received the favor of your letter. It must have lain here a fortnight'.

From Elizabeth Montgomerie-Cuninghame, Friday 18 September 1767

MS. Yale (C 2049).
ADDRESS: To James Boswell Esqr. of Auchinleck, Parliament Closs, Edinburgh.
POSTMARK: STEWARTTON.

Lainshaw, Sept. 18, 1767

MY DEAR SIR: I thought to have had the Pleasure of seeing you when in Edinr. but was Dissapointed. Now it will give great Pleasure to all hear if you will Fly west some Day and let me know the Day you Can Come and the Chais shall meet you at Glasgow. Lord Auchinleck past a night with uss on his way to the Circuite and expects you hear at his Return[1]. I have been very ill of a Fever near a Fourtnight and thiss is the first of my writeings so must make it very short all hear give their Love to you and be shure you Come soon. I am, my Dear Jamie, Your affectionate Cousen,

E. MONTGOMERY CUNINGHAM

[1] The High Court of Justiciary assigned Lords Auchinleck and Coalston to the Northern Circuit. The Court was to sit at Perth 10 Sept., at Aberdeen 17 Sept., and at Inverness 25 Sept. (Scots Mag. 1767, xxix. 497).

From Patrick Preston, Saturday 19 September 1767

MS. Yale (C 2285).

Valleyfield, 19th Septr. 1767

MY DEAR SIR: I return inclosed Monsr. de Sommerdyks Letter, which I shewed Lord Cochrane,[1] useing at the same Time such Arguments as I immagined were sufficient to convince Him of the Absurdity of His Fathers Ideas; how far I have succeeded I shall not say, but sure I am, enough is done, to convince any Unprejudiced Person; I neither spoke to the Earl,[2] nor to Mi Lady,[3] on the Subject, as I immagined that wou'd be doing more than was necessary, and as I thought it better they shou'd hear of it, from *their Son*, which I am sure they did.[4]

John Stobies telling me that Lord Auchinleck was to be in this Country, prevented my waiting upon Him at Perth, which I regrett extremly, as He did not come, and as I shall not now have any Oportunity of receiveing His Commands before I leave Scotland, which I am obludged to do, about the End next Week, so must beg You'll assure Him of my most respectfull Compliments and that nobody can be more truely gratefull than I am, for the very uncommon Freindship which He has ever shewen Our Familly.

I trust that You will be so good, as to take the Trouble of examineing the Affair of the Thirladge, which is really of very great Importance to me, and if possible gett Your Fathers Opinion, as I shou'd not like to engage in a Law Suit, without His Aprobation;[5] beleive me ever most truely to be, My Dear James, Your most Affectionate and most faithfull, Humble Servant,

P. Preston

P.S. Make my best Compliments to my Freind David and assure Him that I am very sincerely rejoiced, to hear of the Conclusion of His Affair.[6]

[1] Archibald Cochrane (1748–1831), styled Lord Cochrane, later (1778) ninth Earl of Dundonald, JB's first cousin once removed (*Ominous Years*, gen. chart V). A gifted inventor and engineer, he was actively engaged throughout his life in chemical and manufactory experiments. Among his many discoveries relating to coal products, the prevention of the ravages of worms by the application of coal-tar to ships' bottoms and the illuminating power of gas were among the most important. For an account of his wide scientific and agricultural interests, see the *Dictionary of Scientific Biography*, 1970–80, s.v. Dundonald. Despite the theoretical soundness of his discoveries, Dundonald lacked business sense, failed to recoup either the costs of his experiments or the debts inherited from his father, and died in poverty in Paris (*Scots Peer.* iii. 361).

[2] Thomas Cochrane (1691–1778), 8th Earl Dundonald, brother of Euphemia Cochrane, JB's grandmother, and Ann Preston, Patrick's mother (Sedgwick, i. 561–62; *Scots Peer.* iii. 358–60; *Ominous Years*, gen. chart V.). Lord Bute considered Dundonald to have been 'an entertaining Man' and 'a bold Man at a pretty advanced age to marry a beautiful young woman', but at the same time regretted that the ninth Earl 'had project [a speculative tendency—OED, 'project' 2.] from his Father' (Journ. 13 May 1781), a heritage which explains the debts and financial difficulties with which Archibald Cochrane was burdened.

[3] Lord Dundonald's second wife was Jean

Stuart, then forty-five years old (*Scots Peer.* iii. 359). A woman of parts, she consulted JB as to how to persuade Lord Eglinton to assist her son by subscribing for a share of his forest, managed the family's accounts (Journ. 29 Dec. 1780), and took a keen interest in planting and linen manufactory. In her long widowhood she divided her time between the two Dundonald estates: La Mancha, in Peeblesshire, and Belleville, near Edinburgh.

[4] We know nothing about this matter. There is no clue to the nature of the Earl's absurd ideas in the letter JB received from Sommelsdyck on 1 July 1766 or the letter JB wrote to him on 21 Mar. JB's own relations with the Cochranes were less than amicable in late 1767. As he later put it, 'There had been a coldness between that family and me, and I had not seen them of a long time' (Journ. 20 Feb. 1768).

[5] Thirlage was the obligation of a tenant farmer to carry his grain to the landowner's mill, where he was obliged to pay as a fee to the miller anywhere from 1/30 up to 1/12 of the flour produced thereby (Bell ii. 743–44). Lord Auchinleck's opinion on these matters, if indeed he ever gave one, has not been reported, nor does any case in the Court of Session involving tenants of the Prestons appear to deal with a dispute over thirlage.

[6] David Boswell was preparing to leave the Coutts bank in Edinburgh for Valencia, Spain, where he was to join the trading firm of Honorious Dalliot and Company (Walker, p. 235 n. 7).

From Andrew Burnaby, Monday 21 September 1767

MS. Yale (C 700).

NOTE in Burnaby's hand at foot of first page: —Boswell Esqr.

Leghorn, Septr. 21st, 1767

SIR, I have just recieved the inclosed for You from Corsica, and could not prevail upon Myself to forward it, without accompanying it with a few lines, to inform you of my having recieved the books which you sent through Mr. Dicks hands for the General. I hope they are by this time safe in his Library.[1]

I really grow impatient for a sight of Your book, as I don't doubt of its doing our Hero great honour. Indeed I have other reasons; there are so many People now go to Corsica, that I fear something may come out before yours, which I should be sorry for, on many accounts; chiefly however as I dare say, none of them will be so deserving of the publick Attention, or do the General such strict justice as Yours. Sigr Raimondo Cocchi[2] of Florence is just gone there, and from what I could discover, has certainly intentions of writing his remarks. Indeed he is very capable, and has been long preparing himself for his Expedition.

I mention these particulars to you merely as hints, and therefore you will make no other use of them.

The General at present does not seem happy; he is surrounded with difficulties; and so little Spartan Virtue remains now in the World, that Oppressed liberty finds few Avengers.[3]

I shall be happy to recieve your commands upon all occasions, being with true esteem, Sir, Your most Obedient and most humble Servant,

A. BURNABY

P.S. I have not yet been able to learn anything of consequence about Capraja.[4]

[1] For the books, see From Thomas Davies, 15 Oct. Burnaby notified John Dick on 1 Oct. that the books for Paoli had arrived in Leghorn (From John Dick, 29 Oct.).

[2] Raimondo Cocchi (1735–75), M.D., antiquarian and writer, had inherited posts as professor of anatomy and as Antiquary to the Granducal Collections in Florence from his father in 1758 (*Letters HW* xxi. 194; *Dizionario Biografico Degli Italiani*, 1982–). Both Horace Walpole and Sir Horace Mann knew Cocchi through his father and through his series of essays, called 'Canneto', in imitation of the *Spectator* (*Letters HW* xxii. 73 and n. 33). Cocchi aided the Paolist cause by keeping the General informed of British news he heard from his friend Mann (*Boswell's Paoli*, p. 56). Paoli's letters to Burnaby during the autumn of 1767 mention Cocchi's visit to Corsica, and note that Cocchi returned to Florence on 1 Nov. to write his account (Andrew Burnaby, *Journal of a Tour to Corsica in the Year* 1766, 1804, pp. 47–51). Some scholars have attributed *Osservazzioni d'un viaggiatore inglese sopra l'isola di Corsica* (1768) to Cocchi, but the present consensus seems to be that John Symonds is the true author (From Symonds, 3 Oct. n. 5).

[3] Paoli had just (12 Sept.) learned from the Duc de Choiseul, French foreign minister, that France, presumably encouraged by the breakdown of the Chatham ministry in the second half of 1767 and the lessening of the threat of British intervention, intended to retain permanent control over two strategic ports of their own choosing in Corsica. Paoli was forced to accept that the French were not neutral, as they had claimed to be, but had designs on Corsica (*Boswell's Paoli*, pp. 48–49; Tommaseo, I. xi. 118–20).

[4] News arrived only sporadically from Corsica and Capraia because of successive blockades by Genoa and other Italian states (From John Dick, 11 May; From Burnaby, 17 Jan. 1768).

From Robert Scott,[1] Monday 21 September 1767

MS. Yale (C 2437).

ADDRESS: To James Boswell Esqre., Advocate in Edinburgh.

London, Sept. 21, 1767

SIR: It is more from the Knowledge I have of your Character, than our too small personal Acquaintance, that I take the Liberty I now do, of writing to you in this Manner: a Liberty which, I am afraid, may seem hardly excuseable. Shall I plead Similarity of Taste, and those transient Devoirs We have formerly paid to the Pierian Ladies,[2] on which, I believe, neither You nor I ever bestowed much Pains? Shall I plead that social Tranquillity We have long enjoyed together in the calm recess of Donaldsons Collection?[3] Or as

One moral, or one mere well natur'd Deed
Does all Desert in Sciences exceed,[4]

Shall I refer You to our common and intimate Friend, Mr. Erskine,[5] who might perhaps have good nature enough to tell You that if You knew Me better, You would find me not altogether unworthy of your good Wishes. This is the Vanity of my Heart: pray excuse it: and now to my Subject.

From bestriding Pegasus, I have some Time since descended to tread the sordid Earth, and follow the humble Practice of Physick, in Hopes of doing some good to Society and Myself. The Difficulties of getting once established in such a Place as London are many, especially when One has not an extensive Acquaintance, or many Friends. I am settled in Park street Grosvenor Square,[6] and as I imagine You are acquainted with many Scotch Families, in that Neighbourhood, or about the West End of the Town, if you would be so good as to mention Me to some of them, as you may have Opportunity, it might be of great Service to Me. I am the more encouraged to ask this Favour of You as I have some Reason to hope my Character will be found to justify your Recommendation, and my Education greatly above the common Run of London Apothecaries.[7] We have many Scotch Families in our Neighbourhood; I see in particular that Gl. Murray has taken a House just by Us, in Portman Square,[8] and, I am told, Lord Archibald Hamilton.[9] The Duke of Buccleugh is to live in Grosvenor Square against Winter, and as He never had a Family in Town, is probably disengaged.[10] It will be a valuable Family, whoever gets it. I wish some Body would persuade Him that I am a Bastard of his Grandfather's.[11] If Mr. Erskine is in Edr. I beg You will present my compliments to Him, and communicate this Letter.

And now, Sir, I have done the most impudent Thing I ever did in my Life. I have been told Impudence was what I greatly wanted: surely that Objection is removed. In Hopes You will forgive Me this Freedom, I am, Sir, Your most Obedient, humble Servant,

ROB. SCOTT

---

[1] Presumably Robert Scott (d. c. 1813) was the man of that name who earned his M.D. in 1767 (*List of the Graduates in Medicine at the University of Edinburgh*, 1867, p. 9). Scott's letter suggests that he was self-employed as an apoth- ecary after his arrival in London (see n. 7). In 1769, he enlisted in the army as a surgeon and continued on active service until 1797 when he went on half pay (*Army Lists*, 1769–1813). Scott published a volume of *Elegies* in 1764, containing

five poems from Donaldson's Collection (see n. 3) and three new ones. A collection of his poems was published in 1765 in London (*Eighteenth-Century Short Title Catalogue*). Two poems from this collection were printed in *Lond. Chron.* 10–12 Apr. and 15–17 Apr. 1766, xix. 352, 361.

[2] The Muses.

[3] Alexander Donaldson's *A Collection of Original Poems By the Rev. Mr. Blacklock and Other Scotch Gentlemen*, 1760, and *A Collection of Original Poems by Scotch Gentlemen*, 1762, bound JB and Scott together only in the bibliographical sense that poems by both men appeared in the second volume of that series. Scott produced fourteen poems for the first volume (pp. 40–75), and one, 'Solitude', for the second (pp. 180–85). For details of JB's contributions to the second volume, see *Lit. Car.* pp. 13–14; for Donaldson, see To Alexander Donaldson, 24 Apr. 1766, To Lord Mountstuart, 1 Jan. n. 1.

[4] Quotation unidentified.

[5] This claim to 'intimate' friendship with Andrew Erskine may be an exaggeration; Scott is not mentioned in the extant correspondence between JB and Erskine.

[6] Park Street was one of the less fashionable areas adjacent to Grosvenor Square, 'populated by shopkeepers and persons of no social importance in 1750' (Hugh Phillips, *Mid-Georgian London*, 1964, p. 258; *S. of L.*, 1980, xl. 251, 256).

[7] Scott's eagerness to set himself above the 'common Run of London Apothecaries' suggests he was somewhat ashamed of following a profession beneath his 'Education'. Yet as Thomas Mortimer remarked, 'In by far the greatest number of families, the Apothecary now acts in the threefold capacity of Physician, Surgeon, and Apothecary' (*The Universal Director*, 1763, p. 57).

[8] The Hon. James Murray, (?1719–94), youngest son of Alexander, fourth Lord Elibank (*Scots Peer.* iii. 512), was lt.-colonel in the 15th Foot by 1746 (*Peerage of Scotland* i. 528). He distinguished himself in Canada, serving under Wolfe at the siege of Quebec (1759), and being appointed Governor-in-Chief of all Canadian troops in 1763 (*Peerage of Scotland* i. 528–29). Accused by British settlers of putting French interests before British ones, Murray was recalled to London in 1766, but the House of Lords absolved him. He was promoted to the army rank of lt.-general in 1772 and made Governor of Minorca

in 1774. In 1781 Minorca was attacked by Spain, and in spite of a heroic defence on the part of Murray and his troops, the island was forced to capitulate after a long-drawn-out siege. Charges were brought against Murray after the defeat, but he was acquitted by the House of Commons (*Scots Peer.* iii. 515–16). In his last years he was promoted to general (1783), made colonel of the 21st Royal Scots Fusiliers (1789) and, shortly before his death, appointed Governor of Hull.

Portman Square was built on the outskirts of the town between 1764 and 1784, and at this period was much less well established than the much larger and older Grosvenor Square, situated slightly to the south-east.

[9] Lord Archibald Hamilton (1740–1819), later (1799) ninth Duke of Hamilton, was the son of the fifth Duke of Hamilton and uncle of the seventh Duke, who lost the rights to the Douglas and Angus estates in the Douglas Cause. Lord Archibald was elected M.P. for the county of Lancaster in 1768 and succeeded his nephew in the dukedom in 1799 (*Scots Peer.* iv. 392–94). Presumably his Portman Square residence was no. 12, 'the Duke of Hamilton's' (Wheatley and Cunningham iii. 111.

[10] Henry Scott (1746–1812), third Duke of Buccleuch, succeeded his grandfather in 1751 (*Scots Peer.* ii. 242–43). At the time of this letter, Buccleuch was still in Scotland, but he set out for London in November (*Scots Mag.* 1767, xxix. 556). In 1766, he bought the lease of no. 20 Grosvenor Square, one of the square's most highly-rated houses, for £9,000 and kept his London residence from 1768 to 1791 (A. I. Dasent, *A History of Grosvenor Square*, 1935, pp. 69, 202; *S. of L.*, 1980, xl. 137).

[11] Francis Scott, second Duke of Buccleuch, had died sixteen years previously. A grandson of James Scott, Duke of Monmouth, the only illegitimate son of Charles II, he was characterized by Lady Louisa Stuart as 'a man of mean understanding and meaner habits', who, after his first wife's death, 'plunged into such low amours, and lived so entirely with the lowest company, that . . . his character fell into utter contempt' (*Comp. Peer.* ii. 367–68, 368n. d). However, we have found no record of his having fathered bastard children. The second Duke was a resident of no. 1 Grosvenor Square from 1743 to 1751 (Dasent, pp. 42–43, 185; *S. of L.*, 1980, xl. 118).

From Edward Dilly, Thursday 24 September 1767

MS. Yale (C 1068).

ADDRESS: For James Boswell Esqr., Parliament Closs, Edinburgh

London, Sept. 24, 1767

SIR: I received the favour of yours by Yesterday's Post, and am glad to find Messrs. Foulis are making some little Progress, but unless you spur them on, I am afraid they will be too long before they get to their Journey's End.[1] I acknowledge that I am a Friend to Punctuality and dispatch, and have Often Wish'd that I had more of both. In Yesterday's Public Advertiser, there appeared a little Anecdote relative to Corsica.[2] I have Cut it out, and send it you inclosed, and likewise the Day's Paper which contains the short Extract of a Letter about the Douglass Cause:[3] the Public advertiser is the best Printed Paper in London and the most entertaining; and as the Play Bills are inserted in that Paper, it is consequently taken in by more Polite Families than any one Paper in London. A Person has therefore a great advantage in keeping up a Correspondence with this Paper,[4] and if you would, now and then, together with your Friends send an Entertaining Letter to the Printer, I shall esteem it a particular favour, and I have got the Promise of every Day's Paper being sent to you (Gratis) the preceeding Night before the Publication, so that you would have the London News one Day sooner than what any Evening Paper can possibly reach you, and the Printers of all the Evening Papers make it a constant Rule if any Entertaining Letters appear in the Daily Papers they insert them in their own, so that a Double advantage arises to any Correspondent who wants to have a thing made Public. The Speech which you intend to send up, if it was inserted in the *Public*, the Evening Papers would immediately Copy it, if it is not already sent to the London Chronocle shall be glad to have it convey'd to me, and you shall see it appear in a very handsome Manner[5]—if you have Permission from any Friend of yours a Member of P. at Edinr. to Direct the Covers too, the Papers will then come to you free of all Expence of Postage etc. if you approve of what I have now Mention'd, favour me with a proper Direction, and I will take care to have it strictly Obey'd.[6] I beg pardon for this long digression from our own particular affair, but now I proceed to Corsica. I have drawn out a Sketch of a Title Page with some little additions and alterations from yours, which I think material: but no Person can be a proper Judge till the Printer has set up the Page, and then he must Alter it, till it looks handsome and appears beautiful to the Eye. I purpose to advertise about the 6th or 8th of October which will be full soon enough; and perhaps too soon for Mr. Foulis.[7] As the Map is Dedicated to you, your Arms should by all means be inserted. The Book I think should be inscribed to Paoli. You cannot well flatter him, for he is deserving of the highest Praise. Entered at Stationers Hall Agreeable to Act of Parliament may be Printed in Roman Letter at the back of the Title Page, and though you seem to think it superfluous, as every Body will suppose it, I am of a very contrary opinion, for a recent Instance appeared a few Months[8] ago, owing to the negligence of the Publisher not Entering Dr. Fordyce's Sermons to young Women the Consequence was, two Pirated Editions were Printed immediately at Edinr., and in Fact the London Booksellers have been too negligent in this respect.[9] It will not be amiss if the Oxonian now and then drops a hint; and a little before a Publication it is of great service, as well as afterwards.[10] I own I am no friend to what is called *Puffing* in the common acceptation of the Word; but surely Sir when the Truth is spoken of anything that is deserving of Praise, it cannot be call'd by that Name. Merit deserves applause and Justice requires it to be given.

I shall be very ready to do any thing in my Power to promote the Sale of Dorando, but as it [is] a small affair, and has all along been in one Booksellers Hand, My having any to sell, would look as interfering with him, and indeed as that Work was only a Temporary thing, the Sale is now almost over, and there would be but a small probability of selling them.[11]

Yesterday I calld on Flexney, and got two Dozen Copies of the Letters between Capt. Erskine and Yourself:[12] I have Orderd[13] them to be Packt up in a Parcel, Directed for Mr. John Wood Bookseller at Edinr.,[14] and the Parcel is shipt this Day on Board The Exchange Capt. Beatson who will sail in a few Days.[15] I have desired Mr. Wood to send the small Parcel to you, as soon as it comes to Hand. You will favour me with a Line in about 10 or 12 Days, and inform me when you think the Work will be finished. I am, Sir, Your most Obedient Servant,

EDWD. DILLY

P.S. The Extract of your Friend's Letter is inserted in this Day's Papers among the London News which makes it more conspicuous, at the End of the Extract you will see a small addition, relative to the Ladies Delivery in Scotland, since the Decision of the Douglass Cause.[16]

[1] JB had seen the first proof of the 'Account' section of *Corsica* on 2 Sept.; the 'Journal' section was still in manuscript as of 2 Oct. (*Lit. Car.* p. 61).

[2] For the anecdote, see From Andrew Burnaby, 10 Aug. n. 2.

[3] *Pub. Adv.* 25 Sept. p. 2, prints a letter in French from 'A Gentleman of Scotland . . . to a French Friend', accompanied by a translation: 'The great Douglas Cause has been decided here in an astonishing Manner. . . . It is imagined that the Decision will not be of great Consequence; every body is persuaded that the House of Peers will reverse the hard Sentence of the Court of Session'. An item following this letter reports that Scottish ladies in childbed have begun to crowd their delivery rooms 'with as many Persons of both Sexes as they conveniently can hold; the Intention of which is, that there may always be Witnesses enough alive to authenticate the Birth of any Child whose Title to any Estate or Legacy shall be litigated on that Account.' *Lit. Car.* p. 255 suggests that JB wrote the letter; for a sentiment similar to the one expressed in the paragraph that follows it, see From Lady Grizel Cochrane, 27 June, n. 4.

[4] Dilly had previously advised JB to correspond with Woodfall, the editor of *Pub. Adv.* (From Dilly, 10 Sept.). Amateur correspondents were a major source of the news reported in the London press (Jeremy Black, *The English Press in the Eighteenth Century*, 1987, p. 970).

[5] *Pub. Adv.* was a morning paper; *Lond. Chron.* an evening one (R. S. Crane and F. B. Kaye, *A Census of British Newspapers and Periodicals, 1620–1800*, 1927, 54–55). The greater part of Lord Auchinleck's speech before the Court of Session in the Douglas Cause, which Dilly had advised JB to send to *Pub. Adv.* (From Dilly, 10 Sept.) was printed in *Lond. Chron.* for August (xxii. 156, 164, 172), but JB did not mark these passages as his own (*Lit. Car.* pp. 93–94).

[6] Two of JB's Edinburgh friends with franking privileges as M.P.s were George Dempster and Archibald Montgomerie (From Dilly, 13 Oct.).

[7] For Dilly's revisions of JB's draft title page, see From Dilly, 10 Aug. nn. 7 and 8; 15 Aug. n. 5. JB's advance advertisements for *Corsica* appeared according to Dilly's plan in *Lond. Chron.* for 8 Oct. They indeed came out 'too soon for Mr. Foulis': his press did not have the book ready for sale until Feb. 1768 (*Lit. Car.* p. 61–62).

[8] MS. 'Months' superimposed upon ?'weeks'

[9] The importance of the phrase, 'Entered at Stationer's Hall' in early attempts to protect books against literary piracy is discussed in From Dilly, 10 Aug. n. 8; 15 Aug. n. 6. The Rev. James Fordyce (1720–1796), D.D., Scottish divine, served as pastor to the Presbyterian Congregation in Monkwell Street, London, 1760–1782. A

prolific author of sermons and tracts and famed for his preaching, he was a friend of SJ, whom he eulogized in his *Addresses to the Deity*, 1785, pp. 209–32 (*Fasti Scot.* iv. 293). The *Life* notes SJ's 'long and uninterrupted social connection' with him (iv. 411). Fordyce's *Sermons To Young Women* (2 vols.) was published in 1766 and had already gone through four editions. Early editions appear to have been printed in London, and neither of the pirated Edinburgh editions have been reported. JB read one of the sermons to Lord and Lady Auchinleck and recorded his own reaction on 26 Dec. 1779: 'I was quite disgusted with the affected, theatrical style. I left out many superfluous words in many sentences. Yet they were still florid' (*Journ.*).'

[10] For the 'Oxonian', see From Edward Dilly, 31 Aug. n. 5.

[11] Cf. From John Wilkie, 28 July.

[12] William Flexney (c. 1730–1808), bookseller in London c. 1760–1808, with premises at 319, corner of Southampton Buildings, Holborn, from 1760 to 1792, was best known as the original publisher of Churchill's poems (Maxted, p. 82).

On the strength of that, JB and Erskine took their pamphlet, *Critical Strictures on Elvira*, to him. They found him 'a fine lively affable little man' who 'readily undertook' their business (*Journ.* 20 Jan. 1763). Later in the same year (12 Apr. 1763), JB prevailed upon a reluctant Flexney (*Elvira* had not sold well) to bring out *Letters between the Honourable Andrew Erskine and James Boswell, Esq.* (*Lond. Journ.* pp. 238–39 and n. 5).

[13] MS. 'Ordered' superimposed upon 'had'

[14] John Wood (d. 1781) was a bookbinder and bookseller in Edinburgh, 1744–78, with a shop in South West Kirk Parish from 1745. In 1774 Wood was named in the action brought against Alexander Donaldson, of which JB published the decision (*Dict. Printers*, p. 369; *Scots Mag.* 1781, xliii. 446).

[15] The earliest *Edinburgh Directory* (1773) lists a Captain William Beatson, located on Queenstreet, Coal-Hill, Leith. *Pub. Adv.* for 2 Oct. p. 4, in its 'Ship News' for the Port of London reports that Captain William Beatson's ship *Exchange* was cleared outwards for return to Leith on 1 Oct.

[16] See n. 3 above.

From Alexandre Deleyre, Friday 25 September 1767

MS. Yale (C 928).

à 12 milles de Parme, ce 25 septembre 1767

Votre Lettre du 30 juillet, cher Ecossois, m'a trouvé dans les larmes sur la mort de mon fils. Ce pauvre enfant, aprés une fievre de huit mois, a été emporté en deux jours par une inflammation de poitrine, et je l'ai perdu le 15 du mois dernier. Je reçûs de vos cheres nouvelles, dix ou douze jours aprés, et c'est beaucoup que je puisse vous écrire aujourd'hui. Ah! mon cher ami, puissiés-vous n'èprouver jamais une semblable douleur, et si la nature et l'amour vous destinent à être pere, soyés-le au moins plus heureusement que moi! C'est un cruel déchirement d'entrailles que de se sentir arracher ainsi le premier et le plus tendre objet de l'affection paternelle.[1] Je le vois bien à mes dépends que l'amour descend toujours vers l'avenir et s'accroît plus des soins rendus que des bienfaits reçûs. Cet enfant que vous avés vû disgracié de la nature, ne m'en étoit devenu que plûs cher par les peines qu'il m'avoit couté. J'allois peut être recüeillir quelque douceur de mes sacrifices et mes attentions, quand il est mort dans mes embrassemens. La tombe le dévore, et je vis pour le pleurer avec sa mere. Je scais qu'il ne souffre pas; toutes les douleurs qu'il ne sent plus, sont pour moi.[2] Et qui m'en consolera? Deux filles qui me restent, ne me semblent rien pour me dédommager de cette perte. Je n'aurai plus de fils, je n'en veux plus, et le souvenir amer de celui que j'aimai, que j'aimerai toujours, me suivra jusqu'au tombeau, où je serois peut être dejà couché sans ma femme qui me soutient dans cette misérable vie.

J'ay pourtant lû votre Lettre avec ces sentiments d'amitié que la tristesse rend plus profonds, lors même qu'elle semble nous y laisser moins accessibles.[3] J'y vois que vous avés toujours une ame belle, quoique rarement heureuse.[4] C'est votre sort et le mien, cher ami, d'acheter la vertu au prix de peines continuelles. Quand on a le coeur droit et sensible, on souffre également de ses foiblesses et de ses lumieres. Tous nos panchans et nos goûts, honnêtes ou vicieux, nous tourmentent. Pardon, si je vous parle de moi, vous trouverés peut être dans ce que j'en dirai, les conseils que vous me demandés. Je me suis marié non seulement par amour, mais par un principe d'honnêteté. Honteux et las du dérangement inséparable d'une vie célibataire, et d'abandonner à la débauche ce que la nature destinoit au maintien de la société, je sentis qu'on ne pouvoit goûter les pures joüissances de l'amour sans l'hymen. Je me mariai pour être plus honnête homme et meilleur citoyen.⁵ J'eus le bonheur de trouver la femme la plus heureusement née que je connûsse, qui étoit naturellement vertueuse et qui sans besoin d'aucun homme étoit capable de faire les délices et la félicité de celui auquel elle attacheroit son coeur encore plus que sa main. Aprés deux ans, nous eumes⁶ un fils dont la naissance ne nous causa que des chagrins. Un défaut de conformation dans les pieds nous fit craindre qu'il ne demeurât estropié toute sa vie. Cependant la tendresse nous familiarisa avec sa disgrace qui sembloit diminuer à mesure qu'il prenait des forces. Aprés l'avoir veillé jour et nuit pendant quatre ans, et suivi la méthode qui nous paroissoit la meilleure pour lui former le corps et l'esprit, malgré les murmures et la desapprobation des cagots du païs et des bavards de la cour, nous l'avons perdu par tous les moyens peut-être que nous avions pris pour le conserver. Il a souffert longtems, à notre insçû; sans que nous ayons pû soupconner ni son mal, ni la cause d'où il provenoit, ni les remédes qu'on pouvoit y apporter. Une mauvaise humeur continuelle qui nous en donnoit souvent à nous-mêmes, étoit ce qu'il y avoit de plus visible dans l'altération de sa santé. Joignés à cette source de peines et d'inquiétudes, mon peu de succes dans une cour où l'espérance d'etre utile à ma famille en la devenant au Prince que je servois, m'avoit attiré;⁷ une diminution considérable et subite du tiers de mes appointemens au moment où mes besoins s'ètoient accrûs. Mais ces deux sujets de chagrin n'ont pas troublé mon repos un quart d'heure. Je n'ai jamais assez connu le prix de l'argent pour en desirer ni en regretter. Enfin aprés sept ans de mariage et de traverses, je songe à me retirer en France avec la pension qu'on voudra bien m'accorder gratuitement: car on ne m'a pas laissé ni mis à portée de mériter des bienfaits par mes services.⁸ J'as quarante deux ans, ma femme en a trente neuf; elle est d'une santé délicate et moi je me sens altéré par le travail. Nous sommes à l'age de la force pour la raison, mais de la foiblesse pour les douleurs. La tems des maux succéde à celui des passions, et voilà la vie humaine, mon cher ami. Vous avés une perspective plus agréable sans doute; mais la fortune qui met à l'abris des besoins, vous expose à bien des fautes, en vous donnant des desirs avec les moyens de les satisfaire. Si l'ambition vous prend, vous serés encore plus malheureux que moi, qui n'en ai jamais eu. Réüssissés, vous aurés plus d'ennemis; manqués votre but, vous serés abandonné au dépit secret d'avoir échoüé. Cependant mariés vous, mon cher ami: c'est votre devoir, quelque mal qu'il vous en puisse arriver. Mais prenés une femme qui ait de la santé, de la raison, peu de vanité, qui ne soit tourmentée ni par les idées de la religion, ni par les erreurs et les folies du monde.⁹ Elle vous aimera sans doute; mais surtout qu'elle vous estime pour vos vertus autant que pour vos talens. Consultés son caractere et le votre, avant de vous resoudre à vivre avec elle dans la maison paternelle. L'incompatibilité des humeurs est une source journaliere de contradictions et d'amertume. Connoissés la bien et pratiqués la longtems avant de vous unir, afin de vous voir l'un et l'autre tous les côtés favorables et desavantageux. Montrés lui vos défauts et tâchéz de pénétrer les siens. J'espere que votre mélancolie se dissipera d'elle-même par les plaisirs et les soins du mariage. Je crois que cette humeur tient un peu à un certain tems de fermentation du sang: depuis vingt ans jusqu'à trente six je[10] l'ai sentie augmenter en moi. Maintenant elle diminüe, soit pour la force ou la fréquence des accez. Les bons médecins devroient mieux étudier qu'ils ne font, les rapports de l'etat du corps avec celui de l'ame, ils guériroient bien plus de maladies de toute espéce. Vous ai-je dit qu'un de mes freres dont je vous avois parlé à Parme, est retourné à la Trappe entraîné par cette mélancolie qui le rendoit incapable de rien faire dans le monde?[11] Eh bien, son humeur vient encore du principe et des sources de l'amour sensuel. Mais je vais finir ma Lettre, dans la résolution de vous en écrire une autre dans quelques jours; car je n'ai point à la campagne où je suis, le morceau que vous me demandés d'une Lettre, de M. Rousseau au sujet des corses.[12] Je vous l'envoierai incessamment avec quelque autre chose peut-être. Je vous remercie de la Brochure qui concerne M. Douglas.[13] Mais je ne connoissais point assez son Histoire pour y prendre un certain intérêt. Vous pouvés adresser vos Lettres à M. Charay par la poste, pourvû qu'elles soient affranchies jusqu'à Calais.[14] Ma femme vous en souhaitte une meilleure et surtout plus heureuse qu'elle. Tout à vous,

DELEYRE

[1] Although he had always been prone to melancholy (Notes, 1 Feb.), Deleyre was plunged into a state of permanent depression by the death of his five-year-old son, who had admired JB and once asked his father if a letter from JB contained anything for him (DBF x. 818; From Deleyre, 28 Dec. 1765).

[2] Deleyre, a professed atheist, had argued with JB about the immortality of the soul. JB noted that Deleyre was convinced that death led only to a 'long mere *aneanti*' (Notes, 3 Aug. 1765).

[3] MS. 'laisser' and 'accessibles' superimposed upon illegible words.

[4] Deleyre had observed to JB, 'Vous etes fait d'être malheureux' (Notes, 4 Aug. 1765).

[5] Deleyre's opinions on the ideal of virtue in marriage as expressed in this letter form a sharp contrast to the libertine attitudes he had flaunted to JB two years before. Deleyre had remarked to JB at that time, 'Je ne sens aucun gout pour la vertu. . . . Vous perdrez la vertu, et vous ne reviendrez jamais' (Notes, 6 Aug. 1765).

[6] MS. 'deux ans nous eumes' superimposed upon illegible words.

[7] Don Ferdinand succeeded his father as Duke of Parma in 1765; he ruled until Napoleon's conquest (*Dict. Nob.* xv. 476; Robert Warnock, 'Boswell in Italy 1765', Yale Diss. 1933, p. 145). The sixteen-year-old enlightened despot had benefited from his father's having employed *philosophes*, the most eminent of whom was Etienne Bonnot de Condillac, as his tutors (Warnock, p. 151). However, the disappoint-

ments Deleyre suggests in this letter and the completion of the prince's education presumably led him to leave his post as Ferdinand's court librarian in 1768. Deleyre later became prominent as an enthusiastic supporter of the French Revolution, serving as a Girondin deputy (voting for the death of Louis XVI), and in 1794 as commissioner, of the Convention (DBF).

[8] Deleyre received a pension of 2,000 livres from Don Ferdinand on the completion of the young Duke's education (BU x. 670).

[9] In his unreported letter of 30 July JB presumably asked Deleyre's advice about what qualities to look for in a potential wife. Catherine Blair was still his choice at this time.

[10] MS. 'ans' deleted before 'je'. Deleyre's own 'fermentation' took place between 1746 and 1762, before he met JB.

[11] Deleyre's brother had returned to the primitive Cistercian monastery at La Trappe, Normandy. Deleyre was educated by Jesuits, but had long been staunchly anti-clerical by the time he met JB (DBF). He was sceptical of his brother's chances of remaining a monk, and had earlier remarked to JB, 'For 3 weeks he will apply himself; then all as if never seen' (Notes, 3 Aug. 1765).

[12] In Parma JB had seen several of the letters between Rousseau and Deleyre (Notes, 6 Aug. 1765). He made a copy of at least one of them, Rousseau's letter of 20 Dec. 1764 (*Corr. Rousseau* xxii. 253–55), and quoted two sentences from it in *Corsica* (p. 138).

[13] Presumably *Dorando*, since *Essence of the Douglas Cause* and *Letters of Lady Jane Douglas* were not published until November.

[14] For François Charray, see From Deleyre, 1 Mar. 1766, n. 20.

From John Dick, Saturday 26 September 1767

MS. Yale (C 1024).

ADDRESS: To James Boswell Esqe. of Auchinleck, Edenburgh, North Britain.

POSTMARKS: ⟨B⟩ATH, [London] 29 SE, 29 SE

NOTE in Dick's hand at foot of first page: James Boswell Er.

Bath, 26th Septr. 1767

MY DEAR SIR, I return You a thousand thanks for your very kind, and obliging Letter of the 15 Inst. but am concerned to hear that You was not quite recover'd. I assure You, that I long very much to have the Satisfaction of hearing that You are abroad, and well, as can not but interest myself greatly in what ever concerns You.

You say that You had wrote me an other letter to Shugborough,[1] I assure You that I never receiv'd it. I hope it contained nothing material.

I am glad You approved of the Liberty which I took in presenting the worthy Baronet with my Esculapius, which I hope is ere this safe arriv'd, I durst not have ventur'd, had it not been the Propriety of the thing tempted me, and it is the Seal he ought to have.[2]

I have receiv'd many Letters which You was so good as to forward to me. Mr. Drummonds Clerk[3] made a mistake in sending them to Edenburgh. Pray be so good as to reimbourse Sir Alexander the Postage which he has paid—and sett it down, that I may account with You for it, I love exactness even in[4] triffles.

I never doubted that You would like my friend Mr. Burnaby. I hope You will some time or other meett.[5] I have not yet seen Mrs. Mcauleys book, neither do I beleive that the General ever heard of it.[6]

The Trees for Masts which the French wanted to cutt in Corsica are at Aitone seven Miles from Ajaccio—and the Ship timber is near Porto Vechio.[7] But my dear Sir, pray reflect a little before You mention these particulars—perhaps the General would not like to have this affair told, it might hurt him with the French, for altho' he may not like them, it is necessary for him to keep on good terms. And the publishing this might be of great prejudice to him, for it was told me in confidence. If You do mention it, pray do it so as it cannot hurt him with the French ministry. Don't lett your zeal to serve him, carry You too far.[8]

I presume Your Father will be return'd ere this, so that I shall hope soon for the pleasure of hearing from You.[9]

Pray present my kindest Compliments to Sir Alexander, and Lady Dick, and all the good family at Prestonfield. And accept of Mrs. Dick's yourself. I ever am with true Regard and Esteem, My dear Sir, Your much Obliged and Affectionate Friend,

JOHN DICK

The moment Your book is out—lett me know it. It is long'd for. We shall stay here untill the latter end of next Month—pray present my best and kindest Compliments to honest Ferguson.

[1] Not reported. Dick had been at Shugborough around the first of the month (From John Dick, 1 Sept.).

[2] For the seal, see To Sir Alexander Dick, 31 Aug., n. 4.

[3] Before arriving in London in April, Dick had put his mail under the care of the London banking firm of Andrew Drummond and Co. (From John Dick, 6 Mar. and n. 15). The errant 'Clerk' is unidentified.

[4] MS. 'in in'. Postage at this time was paid by the addressee rather than the sender.

[5] JB had spoken favourably of Burnaby's journal (From Burnaby, 10 Aug. and n. 1), and the two men had already exchanged several amicable letters. Nevertheless, they did not meet face to face until 22 Sept. 1769, and upon their meeting JB was disappointed with his correspondent: 'He seemed a worthy, sensible and knowing man. But he had a curious lank countenance, and a reserve and closeness, that I sometimes laughed at, and sometimes was angry at' (Journ.).

[6] Catharine Sawbridge Macaulay (1731–91), historian, published this year the third volume of her eight-volume *History of England* (completed 1783). She also published anonymously in 1767 *Loose Remarks on . . . Mr. Hobbes's Philosophical Rudiments. . . . With a Short Sketch of a Democratical Form of Government, in a Letter to Signior Paoli*, a work which offered Paoli her suggestions for constructing a 'democratic republic' in Corsica. The book was one of the works Davies sent to Paoli at JB's request (From Davies, 15 Oct.). JB finally met the 'celebrated female histo-rian', in 1768: 'She was very complimentative to me; but formal and affected; and she whined about liberty as an old Puritan would whine about Grace. In short, I was rather disgusted with her' (Journ. 30 Mar. 1768). He later handled legal matters for Mrs. Macaulay (Journ. 12 Apr. 1773), but she remained a constant butt of his and SJ's jests. Recent work on her includes B. B. Schnorrenberg, 'The Brood Hen of Faction: Mrs. Macaulay and Radical Politics, 1765–1775', *Albion* (1979) xi. 33–45; and Bridget Hill, *The Republican Virago: The Life and Times of Catharine Macaulay*, 1992.

[7] Corsica 'is principally adorned with pines of different kinds, oaks, and chestnut trees. All of these are to be found of a great size. . . . There are extensive forrests in different places. That of Vico is most remarkable. There is in Corsica, timber sufficient to maintain a very large fleet' (*Corsica*, p. 45). Two of JB's sources, Jean-François Goury de Champgrand, *Histoire de l'Isle de Corse*, 1749, p. 236, and Burnaby's manuscript journal (p. 8 of the 1804 edition), also remark on the size of the forests of Vico. Paul W. Bamford's *Forests and French Sea Power, 1660–1789* (1956) gives a detailed account of the provenance and importance of French naval timber in this era.

[8] The increasingly strained relations between Paoli and the French are detailed in *Boswell's Paoli*, pp. 48–49, 56–57.

[9] Lord Auchinleck had gone on the Northern Circuit; it had ended at Inverness on 25 Sept. (*Scots Mag.* 1767, xxix. 497).

To Robert Brown, c. early October 1767

Not reported. See From Brown, 22 Oct.: 'Honest François, as you term him, arrived safe, and with him your Letter, for which receive my thanks.'

To Lord Marischal, c. early October 1767

Not reported. See From Marischal, 24 Oct.: 'I have yours and expect dayly Dorando'.

From John Symonds, Saturday 3 October 1767

MS. Yale (C 2634).

Venice, Oct. 3, 1767

DEAR SIR: Agreeably to Your Desire, I wrote to You last Year, and gave You an Account of my Journey into Calabria,[1] and I am afraid, that the Letter has not come safe to Your Hands, as I have not had the Pleasure of hearing from You. I am now on the Point of leaving Italy, where I have spent two Years with the utmost Satisfaction, and in no Part with more Happiness, than at Venice, as Sir James Wright has shewed me more Favours and Civilities, than could be expected from the longest Friendship.[2] When I was at Leghorn, I could not resist going to Corsica—and every Thing answered to me, as You foretold—I never found a Person of a more liberal improved Conversation, than the General—and this prompted me to write down a few Particulars, which he imparted to me. I have reduced these into the Form of a Letter, which I have sent to a Lawyer, one of my most intimate Friends, Mr. Cole of the Inner Temple, and have desired him to wait upon You with it.[3] I am informed of Your Design to write an Account of Corsica, and it would give me the greatest Pleasure in the World to contribute my Mite towards it—but I am afraid, I can promise nothing new, as the Materials are contracted, and common to all, and as You have been very industrious in informing Yourself. But however if mine has no other Use, it will at least convince You of the Goodness of my Intention—it is what one owes to the Arts, and to Friendship—and You will be so good, I am sure, as to deliver it back to Mr. Cole, as soon as You have examined[4] it.[5]

The General told me, that he had given You Permission to print a Letter that he sent You. This is a very great Favour, and will convince the World of what You would be glad to have known, that You do not write without his Approbation. But to be free with You, I think it is a very delicate Point—His Letters are written generally in a common familiar Style—He is above thinking much, when he dictates, and indeed would not have Time, if he was inclined to it; Else how would it be possible to dictate from twenty to sixty Letters in a Day, as he actually did, when I was at Corte? I know the Genius of the English is such, that they will not bear a Letter, that is not written with some Degree of Elegance, and I should be very sorry, that the General's Character which stands on so superior a Footing, should be vulnerable in any Part.[6]

I hope this will find You in good Health—Believe me to be with great Regard, Your obedient, humble Servant,

J. SYMONDS

[1] Not reported. The bibliography in the standard account of Symonds's works (Mauro Ambrosoli, *John Symonds: Agricoltura e Politica in Corsica e in Italia, 1765–1770*, 1974, pp. 141–143) does not mention any published version of the Calabrian journey.

[2] Sir James Wright (d. 1803), Kt., later (1772) Bt., was Resident at Venice, 1766–74 (Horn, pp. 85–86).

[3] The letter containing the 'few Particulars' about Paoli has not been reported; presumably it was the letter enclosed in From Cole, 7 Nov. 1767. Symonds's manuscript arrived too late for JB to incorporate anything from it into *Corsica*. Charles Nalson Cole (1723–1804), lawyer and editor, was a member of the Inner Temple who also served as a Commissioner of Bankruptcy (*Court and City Kalendar*, 1767, p. 128). He was a long-time friend of Symonds's (From Cole, 7 Nov.) and shared his interest in agricultural in-

novations (Ambrosoli, pp. 44–45, n. 12). Upon their meeting in London, JB found Cole 'a sensible sound man', and learned some 'good facts' from him, as well as a bawdy joke (Notes, 29 Apr. 1768). In 1790 Cole published an edition of *The Works of Soame Jenyns, Esq.* (4 vols.).

[4] MS. 'examined' superimposed upon another word, probably 'read'

[5] The Italian manuscript version of Symonds's draft of his book on Corsica, 'Osservazioni sopra lo stato presente dell'isola di Corsica . . . da Mr. S——', was edited by C. A. Vianello ('Una relazione sulla Corsica del 1767', *Archivio Storico di Corsica*, 1940, ii. 178–201). In 1768, it was printed in London as *Osservazioni d'un viaggiatore inglese sopra l'isola di Corsica*. Ambrosoli (see n. 1) gives a full account of the circumstances surrounding its composition, and also reviews the scholarly debate over whether its author was Symonds or his travelling com-

panion Raimondo Cocchi (Ambrosoli, p. 45 n. 13; p. 43 n. 11).

[6] In *Corsica* (p. 376) JB quotes Paoli's granting him permission to print the letter he had written to JB on 23 Dec. 1765: 'I do not remember the contents of the letter; but I have such a confidence in Mr. Boswell, that I am sure, he would not publish it, if there was any thing in it improper for publick view'. JB praises the letter as demonstrating 'the firmness of an heroick mind' and 'a gallant pleasantry' (*Corsica*, p. 381).

Though Symonds is apologetic about Paoli's supposed lack of elegance in his style of letter-writing, Joseph Foladare is of the opinion that Paoli's letters of this period need no defence (*Boswell's Paoli*, p. 115). He consciously adopted a plain style in his letters and explained to Burnaby that it had been his inviolable custom to 'speak of things as I see them, to express my opinions with simplicity and frankness' (ibid. p. 17).

From Christopher Wyvill,[1] Saturday 3 October 1767

MS. Yale (C 3155).
ADDRESS: To James Boswell Esq., Advocate at Edinburgh.
POSTMARK: BURTON.
FRANK: North.[2]

Constable Burton,[3] Oct. 3d, 1767

DEAR SIR: On my return to this place from York, last night, I received the favor of your letter. It must have lain here a fortnight; entirely owing to the negligence of the servants; with whom I left directions to send my[4] letters after me. By this disappointment so much time has been lost, that I fear little can be done with your journal. If I understand You right, it will be wanted at the press by the end of this month.[5] Your friend Temple, Lord Hales, and Lord Auchinleck are in their turns to revise it.[6] If you send it to Burton, there seems hardly to be time for all. However, if You are still desirous, that I should look it over, be assured of the utmost readiness on my part, to serve You. In that case, send what You can in[7] franks, the rest without. The other manner of conveyance is too dilatory and uncertain; and you need have no scruples about the trifling expence of this.[8] I fancy I shall leave this place about the 18th but when I receive your papers I shall soon dispatch them. You judge rightly of my attachment to Corsica. But be just to yourself and to me, believe You have on[9] your own account a sufficient title to command me. Be assured of my wishes for your success,[10] on this and every other occasion. I am, Dear Sir, Your faithful, humble Servant,

C. WYVILL

I have since determined to stay till the 22d of this month.

[1] Rev. Christopher Wyvill (1740–1822) was born in Edinburgh, where he met JB and Temple when they were fellow students at the University in 1757. Wyvill went on to Cambridge, where in 1764 he was awarded the honorary degree of LL.D. and in 1766 was presented to the living of Black Notley in Essex. He managed the parish through a curate until 1806. Best known as a Parliamentary reformer, he served later in life as Secretary, then Chairman, of the Yorkshire As-

sociation for shortening Parliaments and equalizing representation (Bettany, pp. 28, 98).

[2] Frederick North (1732–92), styled Lord North, later (1790) second Earl of Guilford, served as M.P. for Banbury, 1754–90, and as First Lord of the Treasury, 1770–82. Little is known of North's relations with Wyvill during this period; from 1779 to 1782 Wyvill's reformist activities allied him with the Opposition to North's Ministry.

[3] Constable Burton, near Bedale in the north riding of Yorkshire, had been the seat of the Wyvills since the early seventeenth century, though the family dated from Norman times. According to T. D. Whitaker's *History of Richmondshire*, 1823, i. 322, the mansion 'appears to have been designed by Inigo Jones.' Descended from a cadet branch of the family, Wyvill married (1773) his cousin Elizabeth, heiress to the extensive estates of her uncle, Sir Marmaduke Wyvill, Bt. On the death of the uncle the following year, Wyvill succeeded, through his wife, to the Yorkshire estates and set about renovating the manor house, but his usual address was that of his rectory at Black Notley (To Temple, 2 Oct.).

[4] MS. 'my' superimposed upon 'any'

[5] Dilly was still insisting that JB speed up revisions so that the manuscript might arrive at the Foulis Press in time to be published in late November (From Edward Dilly, 10 Sept. and n. 1).

[6] Temple and Lord Hailes were two of the five readers who assisted JB in revising *Corsica*, the other three being Sir Alexander Dick, Lord Monboddo, and Wyvill himself. JB had previously described Wyvill as 'an admirable Critic on my Account of Corsica' (To Temple, 25 Aug.), and he had asked Temple to write down his criticisms and then send the manuscript to Wyvill (To Temple, 2 Oct.). Wyvill perhaps wrote 'Lord Auchinleck' for 'Lord Monboddo': in light of Lord Auchinleck's generally negative attitude towards JB's publications, it is unlikely he would have approved of the endeavour (*Earlier Years*, pp. 339, 342).

[7] MS. 'in' altered from 'if'

[8] Presumably 'the other manner of conveyance' was by private courier. The maximum weight allowed for franked letters was 2 oz. (Kenneth Ellis, *The Post Office in the Eighteenth Century*, 1958, p. 39); paid postage varied with the weight of the packet and the distance sent. For rates, see *Roy. Kal.* 126–30, and 'On the Post and Postage of Letters', *Gent. Mag.* 1784, liv. 644–49.

[9] MS. 'on' altered from 'in'

[10] MS. 'behalf' deleted before 'success'

From Godfrey Bosville, Sunday 4 October 1767

MS. Yale (C 176).
ADDRESS: To James Boswell Esqr., at Lord Auchinlecks in Edinburough, Scotland.
POSTMARK: WAKEFIELD.

Gunthwait, Octr. 4th, 1767

Dear Sir: I am sorry to hear of your being so much out of Order, but I hope you are now perfectly restord to your former good State of health. I shall be very desirous to see your History of Corsica, and think it will be more Valuable to Futurity than many other Historys, for it will give a true Account of the beginning of the Corsican State, whereas the Romans coud give but a fabulous Account of the beginning of their own, and the Corsicans as they have shown so much Valour in the present may make a very great[1] figure in future times: But I am apt to believe, though you do not say so, that your too great Application both to Law and History has brought on this Distemper. I am sure you have been very assiduous, for you have not had time to see the fair flowers of Edinburough, by the Compliments you are so kind as to pay my daughter, We have had some of them that have strayd into Yorksh. This very Summer a young Lady from the Highlands greatly surpassd our Yorkshire females, I heard much of her though I was not at any of our Public Places, she is one of the Laird of MacLeods daughters, the rest they say are very handsome, and notwithstanding what you say of my daughter if you will lay Pascal Paoli and the Law aside till you have reconnoitred them a little you will soon see that there is no occasion to pass over the Tweed.[2] In this County we are very Quiet in regard to the approaching Election,[3] but in Westmoreland and Cumberland there is a general Motion, they are opposing Sir James Lowther every where both in Countys and Burroughs.[4] I have not heard that there is any Contest in your Country except about the Douglas Estate which had made A very great noise over England too, and I have like other people puzzled my Pate a good deal about it:

There are two Speeches for and against that I was much entertaind with Lord Auchinlecks and Lord Aylmers:[5] I am most enclind to wish for Douglas, and the more so as it is your fathers Opinion, and likewise they[6] say the Opinion of my Old Acquaintance Sir Fletcher Norton.[7] I shall be very glad to see you in Great Russel Street[8] and shall hope for your Company there whenever you have any time to spare: My Compliments to Lord Auchinleck and shall think it an honor to see him here and if my Old Habitation can afford any Amusement to his Lordship it will give me great Pleasure, it may for its Antiquity though not for its Beauty for it is above four hundred years old.[9] William desires his Compliments, he is to be back before the 20th, Mrs. and Miss Bosville and Miss Julia desire their Compliments and I am, Dear Sir, Your most Obedient Servant,

GODFREY BOSVILLE

[1] MS. 'great' superimposed upon 'good'

[2] Norman MacLeod of MacLeod (1706–72), 22nd Chief of Clan MacLeod, whose seat was Dunvegan Castle in Skye, had inherited one of the wealthiest estates in Inverness-shire. Always kind and generous towards his numerous step-brothers and -sisters and beloved of his tacksmen, he took a personal interest in improving Dunvegan and in agricultural reform, but towards the end of his life, economic difficulties after the 1745 uprising and the extravagance of his two wives brought the estate to the brink of ruin (I. F. Grant, *The MacLeods: The History of a Clan, 1200–1956*, 1959, pp. 391–400, 494–98). The closest friend of MacLeod's youth was Sir Alexander Macdonald of Sleat, Bt., father-in-law of Bosville's elder daughter Elizabeth Diana (From Bosville, 24 June 1766, n. 3) and father of the Sir Alexander Macdonald whom JB and SJ visited in Skye in 1773 (*Hebrides*, pp. 113–19). MacLeod had a daughter Emelia by his first wife, who married some time after his second marriage in 1748 (*Burke's Landed Gentry*, 1937). By his second wife he had three daughters, but the dates of their marriages are unknown except for that of Elizabeth, who on 11 Sept. wed James Pringle of Stichell, later (1779) Bt. Presumably the charming 'young Lady' was one of the two remaining marriageable daughters, Anne or Rich Mary (*Burke's Landed Gentry*, 1937).

[3] Sir George Savile, Bt. and Edwin Lascelles were returned uncontested for Yorkshire as independents backed by Rockingham in the 1768 General Election (Namier and Brooke iii. 405–09, 22–23).

[4] Sir James Lowther (1736–1802) of Lowther, Bt., Lord Lieutenant of Westmorland and Cumberland, later (1784) first Earl of Lonsdale, was reputed to be worth over £2,000,000. While still a youth he had set out to control the representation of Cumberland and Westmorland, and with that in mind he married the daughter of the third Earl of Bute; at the 1761 General Election

he secured the return of eight Members. Despite his underhanded tactics, Lowther lost several seats in the General Election of 1768, including his own (Namier and Brooke iii. 56–60). For JB's connection with Lonsdale in the 1780s, after he had recouped his losses and again controlled nine seats in the area, see *Pol. Car.* pp. 131–63; for a study of Lowther's political career, see Brian Bonsall, *Sir James Lowther and Cumberland and Westmorland Elections, 1754–1775*, 1960.

[5] Andrew Pringle (d. 1776) of Alemore, Lord Alemore, was known for his 'easy flow of eloquence' and 'dignity of expression' during his years on the bench (*College of Justice*, p. 523). His speech against Douglas's claims and Lord Auchinleck's in favour of them were reprinted by John Almon in his *Summary of the Speeches . . . of the Right Honourable the Lords of Council and Session in Scotland, upon that Important Cause*, 1767, pp. 134–49, 181–204.

[6] MS. 'they' superimposed upon 'that'

[7] Sir Fletcher Norton (1716–89), Kt., later (1782) Baron Grantley, jurist, held the posts of solicitor-general and attorney-general in the 1760s. He served as M.P. for Wigan, 1761–68, later (1770–80) as Speaker of the Commons; he was a formidable orator, although occasionally coarse and brutal in debate. He had had numerous opportunities to cultivate his 'Old Acquaintance' with Bosville: both were Yorkshiremen and students at St. John's College, Cambridge, in the 1730's, and Norton had studied at the Middle Temple around the time Bosville trained at the Inner Temple (From Bosville, 24 June 1766, n. 4).

[8] Bosville owned a house in Great Russell Street, where JB and other wits often dined with him. In the eighteenth century this street was 'graced with the best buildings in all Bloomsbury, and the best inhabited by the nobility and gentry' (*Old and New London*, iv. 489).

[9] For the manor house at Gunthwaite, see From Bosville, 24 June 1766, n. 7.

From Lord Cardross, Sunday 4 October 1767

MS. Yale (C 673).

Excise Office [Edinburgh],[1] Octob. 4th, 1767

Lord Cardross's kind Compliments to Mr. Boswell, he hears, with pleasure that the Account of Corsica is now in the Press; and as he is just now Stepping into his Chaise to move Southwards, if Mr. Boswell is to present that Book to Lord Chatham Mrs. Macauly or any other friends of Liberty Lord C. will take the charge of any Copies Mr. Boswell thinks proper to destine to such purposes, which may be sent to the care of Mr. Craig at the Stamp Office London.[2] Lord Cardross supposes Mr. Boswell intends to dedicate that work to Lord Chatham and if he had not imagined so would laid in a ⟨c⟩laim long ago for that honor to him.[3]

[1] The Excise Office was in the Cowgate (*Old and New Edinburgh*, i. 217).
[2] Robert Craig served as warehouse-keeper of unstamped goods in the Stamp Office, Lincoln's Inn, 1751–78 (*Court and City Kalendar*, 1767, p. 147).
[3] JB dedicated *Corsica* to Paoli.

To Edward Dilly, Monday 5 October 1767

Not reported. See From Dilly, 13 Oct.: 'I received the favour of Yours of the 5th Instant, and transmitted the inclosed to the P. A. and the Proprietors (of which I am one) are much oblig'd to you for the same'.

From Edward Dilly, Tuesday 13 October 1767

MS. Yale (C 1069).

ADDRESS: To James Boswell Esqr., Edinr.

London, Oct. 13th 1767

Sir: I received the favour of Yours of the 5th Instant, and transmitted the inclosed to the P. A. and the Proprietors (of which I am one) are much oblig'd to you for the same, and will think themselves happy with your Correspondence.[1] A Paper is order'd by this Nights Post to be sent to you agreeable to the Direction. Whatever curious Anecdote may happen either on this, or the Other side of the Water, will be thankfully received. Early Intelligence is the very Life of a News Paper, and now and then an Entertaining Essay is Like a Cordial that recruits the Spirits and gives Vigour to the Whole Animal Frame, every one reads with Pleasure the Appetite is Quickned, and kindled with desire for what is to come. You may expect to have the Papers regularly sent you, in this Day's Paper is the Song, and to my great Surprize every London Paper of this Day contains an Extract of a Letter from Coupar of Fife relative to Mr. Dempster, which I am fearful will hurt his Interest.[2] The Song Speaks against Bribes and Mr. D. is charg'd with the very Crime. How far the Alligation is just I know not. I heartily Wish it may prove false.[3]

I call'd on Mr. Wilkie and gave him Direction how to send the London Chronocle—I send this under Cover to a Friend at Edinr. Could you conveniently procure 3 or 4 Covers Directd for me from Mr. Dempster or Col. Montgomery,[4] and send to Mr. Adam Neill at Mr. Fleming's the Printer.[5] He is Printing a large

Work for me, and has occasion to send a Proof Sheet now and then,[6] if you can do this without any inconvenience, I shall be much Oblig'd to you. Whatever Essays you send to me, you may depend upon Secrecy.

I am glad to find our Work is going on Well though deliberately, I would make no more haste than good Speed, yet upon occasions it is necessary to be a little Expert.[7] You will see in the Chronocle I have advertised, and likewise in some other Papers.[8] By all means reprint the two leaves, I would have the Work as perfect as possible—range the Matter in what manner you please, but I think the State Papers should be translated for the benefit of English Readers, if they are not too long.[9] I shall endeavour to procure Theodore 1st K. of Corsica and whatever other Books relate to Corsica that is not in your List.[10] As you cannot send the Judges Speeches, and Some Gent. are about Publishing a Complete Editn. shall be obligd to you (if they are not particularly Engaged) to have them Sold by me in London,[11] I will use my best endeavours to promote the Sale. I hope to have the pleasure of hearing from you soon, with the first Sheet of our Work inclos'd. I am, Sir, Your most Obedient Servant,

EDWD. DILLY

[1] The piece for *Pub. Adv.*, enclosed in To Dilly, 5 Oct., was presumably 'DEMPSTER's BOROUGHS: A *Constitutional* BALLAD,' which, as mentioned below, appeared in the issue for 13 Oct. (p. 2). The song, introduced by a letter signed 'Your constant Reader,' raises a toast to Dempster and his incorruptible supporters, and accuses his opponent, Robert Mackintosh of Ashintully (*Fac. Adv.* p. 133), referred to as 'Bob,' of bribery.

[2] Cupar was one of the Perth Burghs, which Dempster represented in the Commons. The report of the charge of bribery against Dempster appeared on the same page of *Pub. Adv.* as JB's ballad in praise of him; JB responded to the charge, brought by Robert Mackintosh, in an 'invention' for *Lond. Chron.*, an extract from a supposed 'letter from Cupar' expressing 'surprise and indignation' (13–15 Oct., xxii. 362). In Aug. 1768 the charges were dismissed on technical grounds, and Mackintosh's appeal of the case to the Lords also failed. The litigious campaign proved fatal to Mackintosh's political hopes; Dempster also suffered, as he spent most of his fortune on his defence and the election, but by Apr. 1769 he was once again M.P. for Perth Burghs (*Letters of George Dempster to Sir Adam Fergusson, 1756–1813*, ed. James Fergusson, 1934, pp. 65–68). JB, who had been 'very keen against' Mackintosh at this time (Journ. 26 Feb. 1783), preserved a set of pamphlets relating to the case among his legal papers (Lg 11).

[3] Dilly's concern that the song could be interpreted as satirizing Dempster as well as Mackintosh was astute: Dempster also had East India investments, and was, of course, the candidate *officially* charged with bribery at the time. The

allegation of bribery was probably true. In 1774 the Perth Burghs were said to be 'open, venal, and expensive' (Namier and Brooke i. 509). Furthermore, Dempster's advocate, Henry Dundas, did not attempt to deny the charges, arguing instead that bribery was no crime in Common Law, and defending it as a typical method of canvassing and solicitation (Lg 11:4, p. 7, 'Information for George Dempster . . . against Robert Geddie', June 2, 1768).

[4] The Hon. Archibald Montgomerie (1726–96), later (1769) eleventh Earl of Eglinton, Colonel of the 51st Foot, 1767–95. Colonel Montgomerie served as M.P. for Ayrshire, 1761–68.

[5] Adam Neill (d. 1812) printer in Edinburgh, 1766–1812. His firm was in the College buildings, 1766–69, in Old Fishmarket Close until 1812. He and his brother Patrick were partners until 1769 when Patrick retired and was succeeded by Robert Fleming (d. 1779). Neill and Fleming may have parted company by 1776 (Journ. 4 Jan 1776), but Neill later published JB's *Letter to Lord Braxfield* (Journ. 28 Apr. 1780).

[6] Presumably the two-volume *Travels through Germany* by Thomas Nugent, published 1 Mar. 1768. The other works published by Dilly for the year 1768 were either single volumes, reprints, or collaborations among Dilly and other booksellers (S. H. Bingham, 'Publishing in the Eighteenth Century with Special Reference to the Firm of Edward and Charles Dilly', Yale diss., 1937, items 213–76 of bibliography).

[7] A non-standard use of 'expert': Dilly may be thinking of Latin *experiens* 'active, industrious'.

[8] *Lond. Chron.* (6–8 Oct.) xxii. 339; (10–13 Oct.) xxii. 359.

[9] The state papers in Italian appear in an appendix (pp. 241–58) to the 'Account' section of *Corsica*. JB provided no translation.

[10] Presumably the *History of Theodore I, King of Corsica* (London, 1743).
[11] Presumably W. Anderson's edition.

From Thomas Davies, Thursday 15 October 1767

MS. Yale (C 901).

ADDRESS: To James Boswell Esqr. of Auchenleck, at Edinburgh (deleted).[1]

POSTMARKS: 15 ⟨OC⟩, WM.

London, Octr. 15th

DEAR SIR: I received yours—And tho' I took all the pains in the world to obey your Commission I could only procure Revolutions de Genes which I will take care to send in some booksellers parcel. All imaginable dilegence has been employed with respect to your poor Taylor, but all in vain.[2]

Dr. Johnson is still at his beloved Litchfield, the place of his birth, I had a letter from him very lately, he has been ill all the Summer, is[3] at last become Sick of the place for want of proper amusemt. and yet cannot assume resolution enough to break his fetters and come away to his Friends.[4] The Lady who enslaves him is his Daughter in law, very rich, and very fond of Dr. Johnson:[5] on the other side is I believe a just account of what you commisioned—if you can favour me with that trifle it will be extreamly acceptable to, Dear Sir, Your most obedient and very humble Servant,

THOMAS DAVIES

P.S. I sent the inclosed in your last to Wilkie.

Jas. Boswell Esqr. Bot. of T. Davies
1766

Feb. 14	Johnson's Shakespear 8 Vol	2. 8.0
	Traveller[6]	0. 1.6
	Erasmus de Conscrib. Epist.[7]	0. 1.6
	Lowth's Letter to Warburton[8]	0. 1.6
25	Ancient Poetry 3 Vol[9]	0.10.6

1767 May 29 for Genl. Paoli

Addison's Works 19 Vol. 8vo. gilt[10]	4. 5.6
Harrington's Works Do.[11]	1. 1.0
Sidney on Govt. 4to.[12]	1. 1.0
Cato's Letters 4 Vol[13]	0.14.0
Rambler 4 Vol	0.14.0
Idler 2 Vol.	0. 7.0
Rasselas 2 Vol	0. 6.0
Johnson's Dicty. 2 V. 8vo.	0.10.6
Gordon's Tacitus 4 V. 8vo.[14]	1. 4.0
Barretti's Dict. 2 V. 4vo.[15]	1.18.0
2 Remarks on Hobbes[16]	0. 2.0

	Box for Packing the above Books	0.	2.6
	Writing 46 Inscriptions	1.	1.0
Sep. 15	Remarks on Hobbes – by Post	0.	1.0
	Revolutions de Genes 2 Vol[17]	0.	7.0

£16.17.6

[1] MS. 'Edinburgh' deleted; 'by Air' added, presumably by a postal clerk.

[2] For 'poor Taylor' see From P. L. Dupont, 7 April, n. 4.

[3] MS. 'he' deleted before 'is'

[4] SJ wrote to Mrs. Thrale from Lichfield on 3 Oct.: 'I have felt in this place something like the shackles of destiny. There has not been one day of pleasure, and yet I cannot get away.' He told Robert Chambers (c. 8 Oct.) that he had passed the summer 'very uneasily. My old melancholy has laid hold upon me to a degree sometimes not easily supportable.' SJ left Lichfield on 17 Oct. (*Letters SJ* i. 199–202).

[5] Lucy Porter, SJ's fifty-two year old step-daughter, lived on a fortune of £10,000 inherited from her brother (*Life* ii. 462 and n. 1). SJ wrote to Mrs. Thrale from Lichfield on 20 July that 'Miss Lucy is more kind and civil than I expected, and has raised my esteem by many excellencies very noble and resplendent, though a little discoloured by hoary virginity' (*Letters SJ* i. 198). JB met this 'good maiden Lady with much simplicity of manner' in Lichfield later, and learned that she had never been in London (*Journ.* 23 Mar. 1776).

[6] Goldsmith's *The Traveller: Or a Prospect of Society*, first published in 1765.

[7] The most recent editions of Erasmus's manual on the composition of letters, *De Conscribendis Epistolis*, were those of Nuremberg, 1732 and 1745 (*Bibliotheca Erasmiana, Répertoire des oeuvres d'Erasme*, 1893, p. 59).

[8] Robert Lowth, *A Letter to the Right Reverend Author of 'The Divine Legation of Moses Demonstrated'*, 4th ed. 1766.

[9] Probably Thomas Percy, *Reliques of Ancient English Poetry*, 1765; the second edition appeared in 1767.

[10] We have found no nineteen-volume edition of Joseph Addison's works; perhaps Davies composed this set from various editions of individual works. In *Corsica*, JB wrote that he had sent Paoli the works of Addison and 'a compleat set of the Spectatour, Tatler and Guardian' (p. 298, n.).

[11] Almost certainly *The Oceana and Other Works of James Harrington, Esq.*; but the three editions thus far published (1700, 1737, 1747) were in folio, not duodecimo. For the contribution of Harrington's disciples to eighteenth-century political discourse, see J. G. A. Pocock, *The Machiavellian Moment* (1974). The utopian scheme of *Oceana* had been proposed as a model for the new Corsican government in *Lond. Chron.* (10–12 Apr. 1766) xix. 352.

[12] Millar's quarto edition of Algernon Sidney's republican *Discourses concerning Government* (1698) appeared in London in 1763.

[13] The latest edition of *Cato's Letters*, the essays of Commonwealth philosophers John Trenchard and Thomas Gordon, appeared in 1755 (J. A. R. Séguin, *A Bibliography of John Trenchard*, 1965, p. 31).

[14] Thomas Gordon's translation of the *Works of Tacitus*, 2nd ed. 1737. Other editions had appeared, but these do not match Davies's description.

[15] Giuseppe Baretti's *Dictionary of the English and Italian Languages*, 1760.

[16] For Catharine Macaulay's *Loose Remarks*, see From John Dick, 26 Sept. n. 6. Except for SJ and Baretti, all the authors in the set of 'English books' JB is sending to Paoli may be categorized as commonwealthman or whig political theorists. As JB himself noted, he deliberately chose 'writers in favour of liberty', although he does balance out the list with 'some of our best books of morality and entertainment' (*Corsica*, p. 298, n.).

[17] Louis-Georges Oudart Feudrix de Bréquigny, *Histoire des révolutions de Gênes* had appeared in three volumes, not two, in 1750 and 1752. An English translation, also in three volumes, appeared in 1751.

To Girolama Nini Piccolomini, c. mid October 1767

Not reported. See From Piccolomini, 16 Nov.: 'It has been some days since I received your dearest letter, but as I was in the country and had not carried your address with me I could not reply immediately, as I should have liked to do.'

To Andrew Burnaby, Friday 16 October 1767

Not reported. See From Burnaby, 17 Jan. 1768: 'I am afraid You will think I have been very dilatory, in not acknowledging the favour of Your letter of the 16 of Octr. last sooner'.

From John Dick, between 18 and 24 October 1767

Not reported. See From Dick, 29 Oct.: 'I had the pleasure to write to You last week, when I told You that Sir William was in the list of Scots Baronets, and that he was created the 28 May 1623'.

From Robert Brown, Thursday 22 October 1767

MS. Yale (C 593).

ADDRESS: To James Boswel Esquire, At the Honourable The Lord Auchinleck's, Edinburgh [*deleted*; Air *added*].

POSTMARK: [LONDON] OC 30.

NOTE in Brown's hand at foot of first page: James Boswel Esqre

Utrecht, 22d October 1767

DEAR SIR: Honest François, as you term him, arrived safe, and with him your Letter, for which receive my thanks.[1] I had a very agreeable journey home, not without some adventures really amusing; and to crown all found my dear concerns here in perfect health.[2] I can hardly say that this is my own case at present. My Stomatical complaints are indeed much abated; but the weakness I have had ever since last winter in my left side, and particularly in the thigh and leg, seems to encrease daily.[3] Patience, patience is my only resource. I am already reduced to walk not only with, but upon a Stick, as we say in our part of the world, and shall be very happy if I can keep at this pass; being afraid I shall be obliged 'ere long to cause myself be hurled about in a wheel barrow[4]—But of this enough.

Your books are certainly arrived at Leith several weeks ago. They are in a small chest, and were addressed to Mr. Gilbert Meason at Leith,[5] or to Mr. Alexander Ogilvy of the Ropework.[6] The reason of this alternative, which will appear strange to you, is that a Chest of Books belonging to Mr. Wishart was sent at the same time with yours, addressed to Mr. Ogilvy, and I am not certain but Mr. Craufurd sent both to the same hand.[7] Please therefor to cause make enquiry at both these Gentlemen; nay the shortest way will perhaps be to enquire at the Customhouse, where very likely the Chests may still be lying. If they are, please make the smallest be broke open, and take out your own books, which are at the top, and distinguished from the others by a stratum of brown paper. Those below are for my Brother at St. Andrew's.[8] Mr. Ogilvy, I hope, will be so good as either forward them by the St. Andrew's Carrier, or give them house room 'till called for. All expences will be refunded by my Brother, whom I have already advised on that head. Of your books, you will find wanting Johnson's Diction. which I lent with your approbation to Miss De Zuylen, and could not get back before the others were sent to Rottm., which was in May last; Salmon's Geogr. Grammar[9] and Tooke's Pantheon,[10] which not being to be had here, I made free to keep, for the use of a

240

young Gentleman who lives with me, and shall give orders that they be immediately furnished you, for my accott., at Edinr. L'Anglois à Bourdeau was claimed by Mr. Wishart as his property, and as such seized upon by his two Claws.[11] If in this, the Laird of Carsboddie was badly founded; you are a man of Law, and a man of weight in the Parlt. House, and so can bring him to account. But please remember that if you call me over to give evidence, you must bear my charges; and I can neither walk afoot nor ride a horseback. Le Comte de Warwick I myself lost;[12] and therefor in the place of it send Tancrede.[13] You'll find a Copy of the Letters I foolishly published concerning Geneva, according to the 3d. and last Edition, bound.[14] This volume contains several other pieces than those you have seen. Should any of your Acquaintances who read French, have the curiosity to desire to look into these Letters etc. please indulge them with a loan of the Book. Had I weighed all circumstances as maturely as I might have done, I would not have been the midwife of this performance; however there's certainly a number of very good things in it, and things that ought to be known. I sent a parcel of Cologn Gazettes in the Chest.[15] Those for the year 1763 'twas impossible to find; but my Correspondent has promised to lose no opportunity of procuring them. Your orders shall be strictly followed with regard to these papers, as also to whatever pieces this Country affords relative to Corsica. I have wrote to an intelligent and active Bookseller at Amstm. to make a collection of all such Tracts, which he has promised to do. For the future I shall send whatever I have to transmitt to you to your friend Mr. Stewart at Rottm., who I dare say will take particular care of it.[16]

I made the strictest enquiry everywhere concerning the packet of papers lost by Capt. Kinloch, but all to no purpose. I hope he will be able to recollect something about it himself; otherwise shall begin to fear it gone for ever. 'Tis extremely unlucky that I had not kept these things still a few months longer, and carried them over myself; but when Mr. Kinloch left Utrecht, I had very little view of being in Scotland last summer.[17]

Knowing how zealous you are in Douglas's Cause, I send you inclosed, notwithstanding 'twill put you to the expence of double postage, a letter I lately received from our friend at the Hague, to whom I had sent all the memorials which both parties had furnished me with at Edinr.; and which by the bye, took up a great deal of room in my Trunk.[18] I don't pretend for my own part, to form any definitive judgement on that intricate affair, which I cannot spare the time I find necessary to examine and weigh all the circumstances of, with that attention they deserve. I have been obliged to tell the story perhaps to fifty people since I came home; and every time I must tell it, the mystery appears deeper. However, I am certainly more inclinable to Douglas than the other party; which is generally the case of those I have conversed with on the matter abroad. In short, I have met with few people who did not make the same reflection that I myself have often done viz. that all the suspicions raised against Douglas's descent, allowing them to be sufficient to make private people doubt, are not enough to authorize a Judge, in qualitate qua,[19] to decide against him.

You flatter me with the hopes of seeing you here next Summer.[20] A visit from you will I dare say be highly acceptable to more of your acquaintances at Utrecht than those of my family. You must have received a letter lately from a very fair hand, in answer to one you sent by me; in which you will remember you propose and desire a renewal of Correspondence. Such matters are too delicate for me to meddle in; however without meddling, I believe one might say (in his private judgement) that a Correspondence between you and a very close one too, might be abundantly suitable to both parties. Should you push the question farther, and ask if it would be agreeable to the party on this side the water, I could make no answer but from pure conjecture. And what, then, are your conjectures? perhaps you'll ask—Why, Sir, maids, you know, are shy, and I have been so long out of the practice of unraveling female hearts (for thanks to providence! my wife whose heart is the only one I give a fig for, is as sincere as her infant offspring) that I may be mistaken; but if I am not egregiously so, the Lady in question would be sufficiently disposed to follow good advice on the occasion. What mean else those particular and impatient enquiries concerning Mr. B————?—Scotland is certainly a Country which according to the description of it, and what one sees of the Scotch who come abroad, one might live much more *à son gré* than in England; and Edinburgh by all accounts abounds with polite clever sensible people. A Scotch Gentleman of Character and Fortune is greatly preferable to half a Score of Savoyard Marquises,[21] German Counts[22] or Jutland Baron's.[23] Sed satis superque dixi; nam verbum sapienti sat est.[24]

Shall I beg the favour of You to offer my Compliments to my worthy friend Mr. Constable, when you meet him in the parliament-House with his load of Hornings, adjudications, and Sub poena's under his arm.[25] I intend to write him next week, if possible, desiring among other things that he will take the trouble of sending me by the first Leith ship for Rottm. a barrel of Bell's best Ale, which of all the good Creatures that have entered my poor Stomach these six months past, is, I think the most comforting and delectable.[26] In case an opportunity should cast up before I write him, I beg he'll be so good as dispatch it without further advice. Mr. Constable is one of the worthiest men I know, and I have reason to think very capable in his business. If it should fall in your way to wish him to a good fat Cause now and then, your doing so would be extremely obliging to me.

We talk of nothing here at present but the grand parade we are to make next Friday, on occasion of the Prince's return with his Royal Consort.[27] Oh! what fine doings there are to be at the Hague! When we Dutchmen take it into our heads to cut a figure, I can assure you we cut a long one, and a large one, and a broad one. The Princess is extremely well spoke of; and the prince they say is passionately fond of her—which I pray God may continue to their latest breath! Mrs. Brown and her Sister join me in the very kindest Compliments to you. We often remember and speak of you with pleasure.

I long much to see your History of Corsica. 'Twill make its way here, I suppose, early in the spring. I propose to engage Miss de Z———— to translate it. What do you think of this project?[28] I shall not fail to send you all the journals where mention is made of it; nor do I doubt but they will all concurr in commending it to the publick.

Shall I beg my most respectful Compliments to my Lord your Father? Beleive me ever with the truest regard, Dear Sir, Your most faithful, humble Servant,

ROBERT BROWNE

[1] François Mazerac, JB's former valet, now in the employ of William T. Wishart (From Robert Brown, 3 Mar. 1766, n. 5); Wishart, Mazerac, and Brown had been touring Scotland and France together.

[2] For Brown's family, see From Brown, 3 Mar. 1766 and nn. 6–7.

[3] It is clear from a later statement in this letter that Brown suffered from a 'poor Stomach'; presumably he was one of many in the era who confused the term 'stomatical', which applies to diseases of the mouth, with 'stomachical', which applies to diseases of the stomach (OED).

[4] In addition to its modern sense, in the eighteenth century the word also connoted a light one-horse carriage (OED).

[5] Gilbert Meason or Mason (d. 1808) of St. Andrew Square, Edinburgh, was a burgess of that city (*Edinburgh Directory, 1773–96*; SRS, *Roll of Edinburgh Burgesses and Guild-Brethren, 1701–1760*, ed. C. B. B. Watson, 1930). Meason was sufficiently prosperous as a merchant to acquire the estate of Moredun, Midlothian, and two plots of land in the Orkneys (*Scots Mag.* 1808, lxx. 958; SRS, *A Directory of Landownership in Scotland* c. 1770, ed. Loretta Timperley, 1976, pp. 245–46).

[6] Alexander Ogilvy or Ogilvie (d. 1789), merchant in Leith and by 1775 manager of the New Ropery, Saw-Mill, Leith (*Scots Mag.* 1789, li. 259; *Edinburgh Directory*, 1773–89).

[7] Patrick, eldest son of the late James Craufurd. Brown had not been able to send the books until after 27 Jan. because of delays resulting from the elder Craufurd's death in July 1766 (From Brown, 27 Jan. and n. 1).

[8] The Rev. William Brown (1719–1791), D.D., was Professor of Divinity and Ecclesiastical History at St. Andrews University; before that he preceded his brother as minister of the English Presbyterian Church of Utrecht, 1748–57 (*Fasti Scot.* v. 280, vii. 432, 555).

[9] Thomas Salmon, *A New Geographical and Historical Grammar* (1749). Brown apparently kept his word to replace the purloined copy, for the book (in the 1767 Edinburgh edition) is listed in JB's 1770 catalogue of his library (Cat. of JB's Books, 1770—MS. NLS).

[10] François-Antoine Pomey, *The Pantheon, Representing the Fabulous Histories of the Heathen Gods*, in the 1694 translation by Andrew Tooke. JB must have received the promised replacement copy of this book too, since the 1770 catalogue notes his owning the 1767 London edition of 'Tooke's Pantheon'.

[11] Charles-Simon Favart's one-act comedy, *L'Anglois à Bordeaux* (1763); Wishart appears never to have returned the book.

[12] Jean-François de la Harpe's five-act tragedy, *Le Comte de Warwik* (1764).

[13] Voltaire's five-act tragedy, *Tancrède* (1761).

[14] Jean-Jacob Vernet (1698–1789), Swiss theologian, was the true author of *Lettres critiques d'un voyageur anglois sur l'article Genève du Dictionnaire encyclopédique* (1761), which defended Calvinist Geneva against the ridicule to which it had been exposed in the *Encyclopédie*. JB owned the third edition (1766) of this work (Cat. of JB's Books). Brown was the book's 'midwife' inasmuch as Vernet initially passed him off as the book's author, although Brown had only written its preface. Both were ridiculed by Voltaire in *La Guerre civile de Genève* (1768).

[15] For the 'Cologne Gazette,' see From Robert Brown, 27 Jan., n. 6.

[16] Archibald Stewart.

[17] JB's Dutch journal was never found (From Brown, 27 Jan. n. 5).

[18] The Rev. Robert Richardson (1731–81), D.D., who at that time was composing *A State of the Evidence in the [Douglas] Cause*, published in London in 1769. Richardson spent several years as chaplain to Sir Joseph Yorke, British Minister at The Hague, 1751–80 (Horn, p. 166), was rector of St. Anne's, Westminster, and prebenbary of Lincoln (*Alum. Cantab.* I. iii. 454; *Fasti Eccl. Angl.* ii. 235). JB was often in Richardson's company when at The Hague during the first half of 1764, and found him a 'genteel amiable, church of england Clergyman' (To Johnston, 20 Jan. 1764). He enjoyed discussing morality with him (Journ. 2 June 1764), and was entertained by his 'sound hard knowledge' (Journ. 12 June 1764). The 'inclosed' letter is not reported. The *Memorials* for each side in the Cause were sizeable books: Fergusson's *Memorial* for Hamilton (1767) alone runs to some one thousand 7 1/2'x 10' pages.

[19] 'In his specific capacity as such'.

[20] JB never returned to Holland, although he wrote to W. J. Temple on 24 Mar. 1768 that he hoped to get his father's permission to visit Utrecht.

[21] The reference is to François-Eugène-Robert, Comte de Bellegarde, Marquis des Marches et de Cursinge, one of Belle de Zuylen's suitors. See From Baroness von Spaen, 22 July 1766, n. 8.

[22] One 'German Count' prominent among Belle's suitors was Count Friedrich von Anhalt, aide-de-camp to Frederick the Great. Although von Anhalt never met Belle, he was so enchanted by accounts of her charm that he sent formal proposals to her in 1764 (ADB; Godet i. 68, 102–03; Journ. 3 July 1764; Geoffrey Scott, *The Portrait of Zélide*, p. 29). JB met von Anhalt at Frederick's court on 3 July 1764 (Journ.).

[23] Presumably Christian Frederik, Baron of Holstein, who was also a suitor of Belle's in 1764 (*Dansk Biografisk Leksikon*, 1933–44, x. 508–09; Godet i. 68, 102).

[24] 'But I have said enough and more; for a word to the wise is sufficient': a gloss on the Roman proverb, 'dictum sapienti sat est', which appears in Terence's *Phormio* (III. iii. 541) and Plautus's *Persa* (IV. vii. 729).

[25] This must be George Constable, 'writer admitted by the Court of Session,' who resided first in Canongate-Head, thereafter in Advocates' Close (*Edinburgh Directory*, 1773–79). Letters of horning, or 'hornings', were documents by which the Court of Session or a magistrate could command someone to pay a debt (Bell i. 344–45; for a full explanation of 'horning', see *An Introduction to Scottish Legal History*, 1958, pp. 235–36).

[26] Bell's Brewery, famous for its ale, was located on The Pleasance in Edinburgh (Grant i.

382).

[27] On 30 October, the newly wed Stadtholder Willem V, Prince of Orange, and his consort Princess Frederica Sophia Wilhelmina of Prussia were greeted enthusiastically by the populace of Utrecht, where they stopped on their way from Germany to The Hague (NNBW i. 1536, 1556). Zélide's father, Baron van Tuyll, represented the nobility on the welcoming committee (*Gazette d'Utrecht*, 3 Nov.). See also From Robert Brown, 3 Mar. 1766, n. 10.

[28] Zélide began the translation of *Corsica* enthusiastically (From Zélide, 27 Mar. 1768) but had abandoned it by June 1768 because JB would not allow her to alter it to suit her literary tastes (*Oeuvres Zélide* ii. 186–88).

From Lord Marischal, Saturday 24 October 1767

MS. Yale (C 1960).

ADDRESS: To James Boswell Esqr., of Auchenleck, Edenbourg, en Ecosse; par Londres; [inserted between lines] fr. Amsterdam.

POSTMARK: [LONDON] NO 18.

Potsdam, 24 Oct. 1767

SIR: I have yours and expect dayly Dorando, I learn by the English prints, that you are threatned to be murdered in the dark for writing it;[1] this is a new way of confuting a book, for the spanish Inquisition when they put one to death do it in day light.

The Standish is Berlin ware, earthen ware.[2] I am going to pack up the Cawdle cup, that it may be ready for the Lady, when she has fairly win it, not before; she is only to see it untill that time. I write to Mr. Keith to give you 400, pounds at martimass, if he can, for my money is not payed in untill the end of December.[3] You will secure it as you think best for Emetulla; therefor I must tell you that whatever I have in Great Brittain is by will disposed that she can have none of it, so that if you give me a bond, which I make over to her, perhaps she cannot have it as being in Scotland, you know better than I how to do, and I trust you as I do my self, and more in a case of law.[4] Before the sentence annulling the marriage Mr. and Me. de Froment made a convention of which I send you a copy: since, at Neufchatel they made a new convention, stipulating a fund par payment of the pension to the ex husband, I have writ to Neufchatel to have a copy to send you also.[5] However in the mean time take into your hands the 400, ps. and keep it as belonging to Emetulla, and am very glad to have any small occasion to serve you, and shall allways be while I live.

The law suit grieved me from the respect I allways had for Lady Jean, whom I knew from her being a child, and also from the respect I have for the family, it hurts me to see Duglasses against Duglasses, for the Hamiltons are Duglasses, and I have heard that the estate if adjuged not belonging to young Duglas will be torn to peices by many, perhaps I have as good a claim as others, for my grand mother was a daughter of the family:[6] the news papers say there is commenced an other such law suit in England; this may be of dangerous consequence to many.[7] Receive the compliments of Emetulla, present mine to my Lord your father and believe ever with great regard, Sir, your most humble and obedient servant,

MARISCHALL

I enclose a note of transfer to Me. de Froment of the 400, ps., will such a note suffice.[8] I think it should, since my will only mentions what at my death I may have, but not what I have allready given.[9] Bon jour.

[1] The death threat was JB's 'invention' to promote sales of his book: 'a threatening incendiary letter has been lately sent to the Author of Dorando, a Spanish Tale, declaring with horrid imprecations, that if he does not retract the speeches and arguments therein contained ... he shall be stabbed in the dark' (*Lond. Chron.* 6–8 Oct. 1767, xxii. 344).

[2] Frederick the Great actively encouraged the Prussian potteries, and bought Johann Gotzkowsky's Berlin factory in 1763. This royal manufactory became known for its porcelain of a 'creamy tone' and 'eminently restrained Rococo style' (John Fleming and Hugh Honour, *A Dictionary of the Decorative Arts*, 1986, p. 80). Warren E. Cox notes that although the 'useful wares' made in Berlin were not worse than those of other European factories, 'Berlin was never a very popular ware and never commanded high prices' (*The Book of Pottery and Porcelain*, 1944, 2 vols. ii. 661–64). For the standish, see From Marischal, 14 Apr. and n. 9.

[3] Marischal apparently received payment of rents and debts owed him in Prussia later than the traditional Scots payment period of Martinmas (From Marischal, 12 Sept. n. 7). The letter to Alexander Keith, his lawyer in Scotland, presumably incorporated the note of transfer described in n. 8, below.

[4] Marischal's British estates were entailed on his cousin, Anthony Adrian Falconer, seventh Lord Falconer of Halkertoun (*Comp. Peer.* v. 238); the provisions Marischal made in his will for Emet-Ulla had therefore to come from his European houses and funds (Cuthell ii. 307–08). In Scots law, a bond was defined as a document of indebtedness, functioning much like moveable property, which in certain cases could be bequeathed to a designated heir (Bell i. 94–97).

[5] A copy of the agreement was enclosed in Marischal's letter. Mme. de Froment agreed to give M. de Froment an annual pension of £800, on condition that M. de Froment renounce all other claims on her property (C 1324, 'Certificate of Divorce, Marie de Froment and Denis-Daniel de Froment').

[6] Marischal's grandmother was the daughter of William Douglas, first Marquess of Douglas. James Hamilton, seventh Duke of Hamilton, the challenger in the Douglas Cause, was descended from the same Marquess of Douglas (*Scots Peer.* i. 202–06, iv. 381–94, vi. 61, vii. 51–53). The 'many' whose rival claims threatened to tear the estate into pieces included Lord Douglas Hamilton (the seventh Duke's younger brother), the Earl of Selkirk, and Sir Hew Dalrymple of North Berwick, Bt.: the other heirs of line chose not to press their claims in the courts (*Douglas Cause*, pp. 14–15).

[7] 'We hear a Law-Suit is like to be commenced between two opulent Families in the West of England, in the Case of a supposititious Birth, similar to that of the Douglas Cause' (*Pub. Adv.* 16 Oct. p. 2b). However, either this report was unfounded or the lawsuit went nowhere.

[8] The note, in Lord Marischal's hand, orders Alexander Keith of Ravelstoun to lend JB the money on behalf of Mme. de Froment, with the £400 to be repaid to her (see From Marischal, 1 and 12 Sept.). JB wanted the loan to help pay for his new estate of Dalblair. Emet-Ulla's demand in her letter of 16 July 1779 that he repay it immediately forced him to borrow from elsewhere (A 52, 'State of my Affairs', 1 Sept. 1782).

[9] Marischal was known for his generosity in his declining years, and made certain to include his dependents and friends in his will (Cuthell ii. 289–90).

From Andrew Burnaby, Sunday 25 October 1767

MS. Yale (C 701).

NOTE in Burnaby's hand at foot of page: —— Boswell Esqre.

Leghorn, Octr. 25th, 1767

SIR, I have just recieved the inclosed Pamphlet from Dr. Cocchi who is in Corsica;

and as I imagine the sight of it may not be unacceptable to You, have transmitted it to You; hoping it may arrive in time for you to peruse it, before your Book shall have made its Appearance.[1]

Paoli is much embarrassed I believe at the strange and changeable Conduct of the French,[2] and has summon'd the secret Congress, which I believe is either met, or will meet to-morrow.[3] I remain with great esteem and regard, Sir, Your most Obedient and Most humble servant,

ANDREW BURNABY

[1] For Cocchi's activities in Corsica, see From Andrew Burnaby, 21 Sept. n. 2. The pamphlet sent from Corsica is not reported.

[2] In contrast to his former pose of neutrality, Choiseul now defiantly informed Paoli that France would choose two Corsican port cities to be used as naval bases and would control them outright (From Burnaby, 21 Sept. n. 3).

[3] A Corsican *Gazette* from Vescovato on 15 Nov. noted that Paoli had summoned 'an assembly of all those who have ever held the office of counsellors of state in the supreme government of this nation' (*Scots Mag.* 1768, xxx. 44) to discuss the impending crisis. For a description of the Supreme Council and Paoli's formation of a Constitution, see Thrasher, pp. 83–86.

From John Dick, Thursday 29 October 1767

MS. Yale (C 1025).

NOTE in Dick's hand at foot of first page: James Boswell Esq.

Bath, 29th October 1767

MY DEAR SIR, I had the pleasure to write to You last week, when I told You that Sir William was in the list of Scots Baronets, and that his was created the 28 May 1623—but in looking accidently into the Book again I find it 1625—which has occasioned You the Trouble of this Letter, pray excuse it, for I fear that I am become very troublesome.[1]

We continue our resolution of leaving this place the 1st of next Month, so that I shall hope to have the pleasure of hearing from You soon after my arrival in Town.[2]

I cannot send You any news from this place worthy your notice, if You have never seen it, You ought to come, but pray don't be so indiscreet, as to bring a young Wife here, all is amusements and dissipation, and a young woman will never relish any other place after this.[3]

I have a letter from Burnaby dated the 1st Instant, he says that he has receiv'd the box of books for the General, but that the Arms have not appear'd.[4]

Mrs. Dick's best Compliments attend You, and pray say every thing that's kind for us to good Sir Alexander, and the whole family, and beleive me ever with the most unalterable Esteem, and true Regard, My dear Sir, Your much Obliged and Affectionate Friend,

JOHN DICK

[1] It is uncertain to which book or list Dick is referring, as there were no baronets created on 28 May in either 1623 or 1625. Douglas's *Baronage* (p. 270), then in manuscript, cited *Chamberlain's State of Britain* as proof of Sir William Dick's elevation to the baronetage in 1642 (see To Sir Alexander Dick, 28 Apr. 1768). According to *Comp. Bar.* ii. 448, the creation took place in 1638, 1642, or 1646, if at all.

[2] Dick spent about a year living in Park Lane, London, before his return to Leghorn (*Scots Charta Chest*, pp. 220, 236–37).

[3] Dick's own wife, forty-seven-year-old Anne Bragg (*Comp. Bar.* ii. 449), was neither young nor seduced by the amusements of Bath. Quite the opposite: she became ill after drinking the Bath waters 'while in perfect health', and was confined to bed for a month (*Scots Charta Chest*, p. 220).
[4] For the books, see From Thomas Davies,15 Oct; for the arms, see From Marischal, c.1 June.

To Edward Dilly, c. late October 1767

Not reported. See From Dilly, 4 Nov.: 'I receiv'd the favour of Yours, with a Letter inclosed for Wilkie, which I deliver'd'.

From Isabella van Tuyll van Serooskerken, c. late October 1767

Not reported. See To W. J. Temple, 8 Nov.: 'Do you know I had a letter from *Zélide* the other day, written in english, and shewing that an old flame is easily rekindled.'

To John Wilkie, c. late October 1767

Not reported. Enclosed in To Edward Dilly, c. late October.

To Sir Alexander Dick, Saturday 3 November 1767

MS. New York Public Library.

ADDRESS: To Sir Alexander Dick of Prestonfield, Baronet, near Edinburgh.

Auchinleck, 3 Nov.[1] 1767

DEAR SIR: I am perfectly well.[2] There is not any foundation for the east indian attacks.[3] I wrote to her and wished her joy, but she told me I had no occasion. Her silence which you well know is I fear not to be excused, and so much am I the grand Turk, that I have not seen her yet. I shall however pay her a visit before I leave the country.[4] I wish all joy to the Brides.[5] I shall have the happiness of seeing you next week, so need not expatiate in letter. I am much obliged to you for your admirable *folio*.[6] Trust me the Consul shall be *served* this winter.[7] I have it now. With my best compliments to all in your *Templum Concordiae* I am, Dear Sir, your very affectionate friend and faithful servant,[8]

JAMES BOSWELL

[1] MS. 'Octr'. JB was still in Edinburgh on 3 Oct. He set out for Auchinleck on 13 Oct. and seems to have stayed there until he made his visit to Adamton around 5 Nov. He returned to Edinburgh on 9 Nov. in time for the opening of the Winter Session (*Earlier Years*, pp. 341–44).
[2] JB wrote to Johnston on 9 Oct., 'I am now, I may say, perfectly recovered' (Walker, p. 233).
[3] JB had feared that Catherine Blair ('the Princess') had acceded to the proposal of his rival, William Fullarton, whom JB described as 'the formal Nabob' (To Temple, 29 July) and whom he had recently maligned as a 'man of copper' (To Temple, 11 Aug.). Fullarton, now on a visit from India, returned to Scotland permanently in 1770 to manage the family estate of Rosemount, Ayr-

shire, and put his Indian fortune into improvements (*Ayr and Wigton* I. ii. 747). JB and Fullarton finally met on 7 Feb. 1768, and JB decided that he 'liked the man'. The two rivals agreed upon rules by which they would regulate their competition for Miss Blair's hand (Journ.). The following day, the Nabob was rejected. JB remarked that in his consolation of his jilted rival, 'I relieved him from serious love by my vivacity' (Journ. 8 Feb. 1768). Fullarton later married a distant cousin of JB's, Anabella Craufurd.
[4] JB arrived at the Blair estate of Adamton around 5 Nov. (To Temple); his courtship of Catherine Blair continued to waver between love and a mixture of affronted pride and irritation

247

(*Earlier Years*, pp. 343–44).

[5] Janet and Catherine Douglas; see From Sir Alexander Dick, 15 Aug. n. 4.

[6] Presumably records sent by Sir Alexander substantiating John Dick's claim to a baronetcy (From Sir Alexander Dick, 3 Sept. and nn. 5–6).

[7] Dick was served heir on 14 Mar. 1768 (*Baronage*, p. 274).

[8] Lord Auchinleck also had used this image to describe Sir Alexander's household (Alexander Boswell to Sir Alexander Dick, 9 Sept., *Scots Charta Chest*, p. 227); the phrase was apt in light of the two weddings about to take place there (n. 5). 'Concordia' was the Roman goddess of contracts among citizens. Her oldest and principal temple stood near the Forum (OCD).

From Edward Dilly, Wednesday 4 November 1767

MS. Yale (C 1070).

ADDRESS: To James Boswell Esqr., Parliament Closs, Edinr.

London, Novr. 4th 1767

SIR: I receiv'd the favour of Yours, with a Letter inclos'd for Wilkie, which I deliver'd, and inform'd him at the same Time of the Clerk's Franking the Papers, which he will rectify. Mr. Woodfall will also take care for the future in sending his Paper, and he will be glad to hear from you as Often as you can, and likewise from any of your Friends—the two Letters I presume you Saw in last Week's Papers.[1] Last Saturday I was inform'd by a Friend, that there is now Printing in London a concise History of Corsica in one volume Octavo,[2] it is Wrote by a private Gentleman and has been in the Press some Months, in what Manner it is executed I know not, the Work is Printing at Richardson's in Salisbury Court Fleet street.[3] You therefore See the necessity of Publishing your Work as fast as possible, that we may have the Start of Publication—you will please to hasten Foulis for it is absolutely requisite to have it finish'd the latter End of this Month or beginning of next. I hope the Map will be done in due Time.

Almon is now Publishing a Political Register which is Read by many of the Nobility etc, if you was to send a Letter addrest to Almon, relative to the Hist. of Corsica, I make no doubt he will insert it in the Political Register for next month.[4] I sent you by Capt. Beatson, The History of Theodore the first, King of Corsica, and Voyages and Travels relating to Corsica, hope they are come safe to Hand.[5] The Speeches of the Judges I find are now Printing; if the Person who is employ'd in the Undertaking, has not fixt upon a Bookseller in London, I would engage to Promote the Sale in Town. Please to let me hear from you soon. I am, Sir, Your most humble Servant,

EDWD. DILLY

P.S. I desired Mr. Neill to send a Sheet of a New Work he is Printing for me, to your Care, be so obliging to inclose it in the first Cover you send to me.

[1] JB marked as his own work a letter by 'Probus' in defence of Lady Jane Douglas in his copy of *Lond. Chron.* for 29–31 Oct. He had used the pseudonym 'Probus' while defending Lady Jane in the July and Sept. issues. On the same page as this 'Probus' letter is an extract from a letter concerning the cousin of Signor Romanzo, the fictitious Corsican courier whose diplomatic adventures JB invented to raise flagging British interest in Corsica. He had been detailing this courier's travels since the 22–24 Jan. number (*Lit. Car.* pp. 238–41).

[2] All that is known about this book is contained in this letter and in From Dilly, 19 Nov. The compiler, a Scottish gentleman who had served in the Seven Years' War, apparently never

finished the work.

[3] William Richardson (1701–88), was the nephew and heir of Samuel Richardson. Partner with Samuel Clarke until 1768, his shops were located at Salisbury Court and 76 Fleet Street (Maxted, pp. 187–188; *Dict. of Printers*).

[4] John Almon (From Dilly, 1 Aug. n. 4), the client and friend of John Wilkes, began his *Political Register* in May of this year under the patronage of Richard Grenville, Earl Temple (Lucyle Werkmeister, *The London Daily Press, 1772–1792*, 1963, pp. 111–112). The *Political Register* ran for eleven volumes, 1767–72; the first volume, containing the eight numbers for 1767, does not include a letter concerning *Corsica*.

[5] The first book was *The History of Theodore I, King of Corsica* (1743). We have found no book whose title resembles 'Voyages and Travels relating to Corsica'; perhaps Dilly sent R. P. de Singlande's *Mémoires et voyages* (1765).

To Edward Dilly, c. early November 1767

Not reported. See From Edward Dilly, 10 Nov.: 'Yesterday I received the favour of yours with Letters for Wilkie and Woodfall, which are deliver'd.'

To John Wilkie, c. early November 1767

Not reported. Enclosed in To Edward Dilly, c. early November.

To Henry Woodfall, c. early November 1767

Not reported. Enclosed in To Edward Dilly, c. early November.

From Giuseppe Marc'Antonio Baretti, Saturday 7 November 1767

MS. Yale (C 76).

London, Novr. 7th 1767

DEAR SIR, do not think me so unmannerly as to neglect answering my Correspondents' letters. But you inclosed your last in one to Mr. Johnson, which has been the reason of its not coming to hand, as he stay'd many months at Litchfield, and his letters were never sent him there by the person that received them here.[1]

I am pleased to see you pleased with the course of life you have engaged in, and wish you success in it with all my heart. Great is my impatience to see your account of Corsica. A good narrative of the customs and manners of that little kingdom cannot fail of being acceptable to the Inhabitants of this great Island, and from an acquaintance of Johnson I expect a very good one. I am likewise printing an account of Italy in two small volumes, and am handling pretty roughly some of your British travellers and their Italian Itineraries.[2] The impertinence of these people has of late exceeded all bounds, and I will endeavour to put a stop to it for the future, by vindicating my Country, and proving that they are but silly liars when they say, that there is nothing in Italy but ignorance and folly, vice and poverty.[3]

Our friend Johnson has not been well all this summer at Litchfield, and his spirits seem still very low.[4] I have past a whole day with him this week, and could scarcely make him speak. He is now gone to one Mrs. Thrail, a fine and learned Lady of his acquaintance, who lives a few miles from town.[5] I hope her liveliness and beauty will revive him a little, and recruit his mind with chearful ideas. London is still a desart, as all our men of note are still in the country about their new parlamenteering.[6] We have a very dull Opera, but the Play-managers make us some amends with the briskness of their operations at Drury-lane and Covent-garden.[7] They are to give us some new plays this season, and amongst others one by Doctor Goldsmith, which I have heard read by the authour, and hope will meet with success.[8] See what a good Correspondent I might prove to a Lady, as I can talk pretty glibly of plays and operas, and the emptiness of the Town. But when are we to see you here? I am afraid it will not be so soon, as you hint nothing of that in your last; and yet I should be very glad to see you again, and have some such chat again with you, as we had one night on the Rialto-bridge.[9] Vale, Boswell, vale. Your most humble Servant and affectionate Friend,

JOSEPH BARETTI

[1] JB's letters to SJ and Baretti are not reported; neither do we know the identity of the Londoner responsible for forwarding SJ's mail. SJ was away from London, in Oxford and Lichfield, for nearly six months (May–Oct.). He was back in London by 24 Oct. (*Letters SJ* i. 196–202; *Life* iii. 452).

[2] Baretti had begun composing his two volumes in April 1767; T. Davies and L. Davis published them in February 1768 under the title, *An Account of the Manners and Customs of Italy; with Observations on the Mistakes of some Travellers with Regard to that Country*. The initial run of 800 copies sold out, and a second edition followed in 1769. Baretti's book attacked views about Italy promulgated by Roger Ascham's *Scholemaster* and Richard Steele's *The Conscious Lovers* (2nd ed. i. 294, ii. 138–42), but his main target was Dr. Samuel Sharp's acerbic *Letters from Italy, Describing the Customs and Manners of that Country, in the Years 1765 and 1766* (1766).

[3] Sharp's *Letters* had disparaged the Italian aristocracy as dissipated, the Italian plebeians as benighted, and the entire nationas superstitious and bloodthirsty. Baretti sought to prove that Sharp's inadequate Italian, lack of acquaintance with Italian aristocrats and etiquette, illness during his travels, and superficial knowledge of Italian life made him ill-qualified to criticize Italian mores. The ensuing pamphlet war pitted Sharp's *A View of the Customs, Manners, Drama, &c. of Italy* (1768) against Baretti's *An Appendix to the Account of Italy, in Answer to Samuel Sharp, Esq.* (1768).

[4] SJ had written from Lichfield to George Colman on 19 Aug. about his poor health (*Letters SJ* i. 198–99). See also From Thomas Davies, 15 Oct. and n. 4.

[5] On 10 Oct. SJ had written to Hester Thrale (1741–1821) that he would 'see Streatham with great delight' after his 'return from exile' in Lichfield (*Letters SJ* i. 201). Streatham Place or Park lay some six miles from London. SJ had been

a frequent guest there since 1765; he had written of Streatham as his home in a letter of 20 July to Mrs. Thrale (*Letters SJ* i. 198).

[6] Candidates standing for Parliament were already busy campaigning for the General Election of 1768 (Namier and Brooke i. 67–73).

[7] The 'dull Opera' was *Tigrane*, which had opened the season on 27 Oct. at the King's Theatre (*Lond. Stage* IV. iii. 1286). *Tigrane* was advertised as 'A new serious Opera; music by several celebrated Composers', and was compiled and conducted by Pietro Alessandro Guglielmi (*New Grove's Dictionary of Music and Musicians* ed. Stanley Sadie, 1980, vii. 797). Drury Lane had begun its season of 189 performances on 12 Sept. and Covent Garden its season of 192 performances on 14 Sept. (*Lond. Stage* IV. iii. 1267, 1272, 1274).

[8] Drury Lane had scheduled three new mainpieces and four new farce-afterpieces; Covent Garden projected two new mainpieces and three new afterpieces (*Lond. Stage* IV. iii. 1267, 1272). One of the new plays had already opened. Garrick's theatrical burlesque 'A Peep Behind the Curtain' had its first performance at Drury Lane on 23 Oct., and George Colman introduced his afterpiece 'The Oxonian in Town' at Covent Garden on this evening (*Lond. Stage* IV. iii. 1285, 1289). Goldsmith's sentimental comedy *The Good Natured Man* opened on 29 Jan. 1768 at Covent Garden to lukewarm reviews. Indeed, one scene of the play was hissed, which so unnerved Goldsmith that he later burst into tears and swore to SJ that he would never write again (G. B. Hill, *Johnsonian Miscellanies*, 1897, i. 311). However, the offending scene was dropped, and the production ran for nine more nights in February and one in March (*Lond. Stage* IV. iii. 1308–10, 1319).

[9] Boswell's Notes for 13 July 1765 mention his meeting Baretti on the Rialto Bridge but do not report their conversation.

From Charles Nalson Cole,[1] Saturday 7 November 1767

MS. Yale (C 810).

Tanfield Court,[2] Temple, Nov. 7. 1767

SIR: Tho' I have not the Honor of being known to you, yet it is with great pleasure I obey Mr. Symonds's commands in transmitting the inclos'd to you—A friendship with him from the morning of life, convinces me that those to whom he pays a particular attention att his noon of life, deserve the esteem of all good men. It is on this principle that I have expressd myself in the manner I have, att this address to you without knowing you.

When you come to Town I shall be much pleasd in paying my respects to you att this place[3]—Mr. Symonds's friends will allways finde me desirous of shewing them in General, and you in particular, that I am their Faithfull, Humble Servant,

CHARLES NALSON COLE

[1] For Cole and the information he was forwarding, see From John Symonds, 3 Oct.

[2] Tanfield Court, formerly known as Bradshaw's Rents, was a set of lodgings in the Temple named for an early seventeenth-century Baron of the Exchequer.

[3] Cole called on JB in London on 29 Apr. 1768 (Notes).

From Edward Dilly, Tuesday 10 November 1767

MS. Yale (C 1071).

ADDRESS: To James Boswell Esqr., Parliament Closs, Edinburgh.

London, Novr. 10th, 1767

SIR: I Wrote to you a few Days ago, informing you at the same Time, that a Work similar to yours is now in the Press at Richardson's in Salisbury Court, and that we cannot Use too much dispatch in geting ours Published, the Map of Corsica I Presume is done, or at least will be finished in a few Days.

Yesterday I received the favour of Yours with Letters for Wilkie and Woodfall, which are deliver'd. I am glad you find Mr. W. judg'd right in not inserting one of the Essays.[1] You will please to Observe that the Printers have often Smarted for their inadvertency[2]—it therefore behoves them to take care, and I am confident Mr. Boswell can't blame them for being cautious, all is now well and Mr. W. will be very glad to hear from you upon every occasion. You inform me that a long Essay has been sent to him since you Wrote me last, and in this Day's Public Advertiser, I See a Letter relative to the Corsicans, Sign'd a Real Friend to Liberty and Dated Grosvenor[3] Square. Is that Wrote by Mr. B. or not?[4]

I sent you about 3 Weeks ago, the Hist. of Theodore 1st King of Corsica, and another Vol. of Travels etc. by Capt. Beatson, which I hope are come safe to Hand. As you request Mr. Foulis's Names should be in the Title Page. I give my full Consent, (though I acknowledge a London Title might be more beneficial to the Sale) and you will please to Print it thus

Glasgow
Printed by R. and A. Foulis
for Edward and Charles Dilly in the Poultry London
MDCCLXVIII.

251

I make no doubt but Mr. Fouliss will exert themselves on this occasion, and make the Book appear very neat, and I shall be glad, if this Publication recommends the Glasgow Press. You will reprint the Leaf You mention in the fifth Sheet, for I would have the Work appear as Correct as possible.[5]

I hope your next Letter will inform me that you are very near upon that Emphatical Word finis. As this Season of the Year is pretty boisterous, I would not have all Shipt on Board the same Vessel, but put 500 on Board one Vessel and 500 on Board Another, so that if any misfortune happens, I may receive One; the other 500 may be left to supply Edinburgh and Glasgow, as I am in hopes Scotland will take off that Number. I am, Sir, Your most Obedient Servant,

EDWD. DILLY

P.S. On the back of the Title say, Entered at Stationers-Hall.[6]

Thursday Evening 7 oClock. This Day I had the pleasure of Seeing your Brother,[7] and Mr. Cullen,[8] and I expect them to spend the Evening with me, with a Select Number of Friends: our Party consists of both Sexes, which renders it the more agreeable, as the Sprightliness of the Female enlivens Conversation, and gives a relish to every Enjoyment. As your Brother is a Stranger in Town, I shall think myself happy to have it in my Power to serve him in any respect, I will take an opportunity of introdu⟨cing hi⟩m to my Friends, and shall be ready to shew him any Part of the T⟨own that⟩ he has an inclination of Seeing.[9]

[1] Presumably Dilly refers to an essay on the Douglas Cause that Woodfall found too controversial for inclusion in the *Pub. Adv.*, though he was generally not afraid to publish controversial material. From 1770 to 1784 he was prosecuted for libel five times—'fined by the House of Lords; confined by the House of Commons; fined and confined by the Court of King's Bench, and indicted at the Old Bailey' (*Lit. Anec.* i. 301; Maxted, p. 252).

[2] In June the court of Session cited four Edinburgh newspaper publishers for contempt of court for their reporting of the Douglas Cause. JB, who had composed many of the offending articles, including those interpreting *Dorando* as an allegory of the Cause (*Lit. Car.* pp. 240–41, 251), served as counsel for the *Edin. Adv.* (*Earlier Years*, pp. 330–34) in 'the most impudent act of a life not unremarkable for impudent actions' (ibid. p. 333). The publishers escaped with a rebuke, but it was common knowledge that even when defences against charges of libel were successful, they were costly and could ruin a printer's finances (C. R. Kropf, 'Libel and Satire in the Eighteenth Century', *Eighteenth-Century Studies*, 1974–75, viii. 153–58).

[3] MS. 'Groversnor'

[4] The letter, which appeared in *Pub. Adv.* 10 Nov. p. [2], is dated 7 Nov. and mentions the writer's pleasure at the prospect of reading *Corsica. Lit. Car.* does not attribute the article to JB.

[5] For an account of the cancel of leaf E₂ (pp. 67–68), see *Lit. Car.* pp. 51–52. We have no copy

of the original leaf, but this letter suggests that it was cancelled merely to correct a misprint; apparently Z₃ (pp. 357–58) was cancelled for that very reason.

[6] The phrase is actually on the half-title page preceding: the reverse of the title page is blank.

[7] David Boswell wrote to JB from London on 16 Nov.: 'Dilly has been very civil to me I supp'd with him one night, and I never see him, but what he invites me to dine or supp.'

[8] Presumably one of the six younger sons of Dr. William Cullen F.R.S., noted physician and Professor of Medicine, later president of the Edinburgh College of Physicians (the eldest son, Robert, a friend of JB's, was an advocate and it is likely that he was back in Edinburgh when the Court of Session sat down on 12 Nov.). For Cullen's sons, see John Thompson's *Account of the Life, Lectures, and Writings of William Cullen, M.D.*, 1859, ii. 506–12, 681–86.

[9] This was David Boswell's first visit to London: he was in Glasgow preparing for his journey to Spain on 30 Oct., in London at least by this date, and in Paris by 3 Dec. In a letter to JB of 16 Nov., he gives his initial impressions of 'this astonishing place: I am certainly lost in amazement and wonder. at the grandeur and magnificence, the hurry and confusion amidst which I here find myself . . . and I frequently cannot help crying out as loud as I possibly can "this is london the mistress of the world".' He also noted the confusion he suffered as a stranger trying to find his way through the tangled streets of the metropolis.

From the Accademia Cyrnaea,[1] Friday 13 November 1767

MS. Yale (C 825). A copy in the hand of JB's clerk, James Brown.

Dat Curiae[2] ex Aedibus Accademiae Idib. Novembris Aerae Vulg. MDCCLXVII[3]

Accademia Cyrnaea Jacobo Boswelio
Viro Erudito. S. P. D.[4]

Accepimus, Jacobe Bosweli doctissime, nonnullos Gentilium scriptorum Libros, quos Tu nostrae huic accademiae dono mittere voluisti, eosque membranis adeo magnifice et ornate involutos, formis praeterea, et charta tam nitide, tamque eleganter impressos, ut nihil supra. Equidem non mediocre hoc est tui in Literas amoris argumentum, tum maxime in hanc Accademiam; quam Tu omnium primus dignatus es insigni munere eorum voluminum: quibus primum veluti Lapidem ei, quae excitanda[5] est, Bibliothecae posuisse videaris.

Verum[6] quod judiciis eam tuis et probaveris, et ornaveris: iisque, primo cujusque voluminum folio scriptis, affirmes: vim insitam Cyrnaeae Juventutis ad sublime quoddam, et excelsum Natura conformatae, excitari[7] Maxime ab hac Accademia, et provehi ad omnem sapientiae Laudem, et Christianae Virtutis, hoc inquam, judicium tanti est, ut nihil ei accidere possit ad splendorem illustrius. Non enim tanti illud est probari, ornarique tam gravi judicio: Sed illud maximum, ornari, eo, et probari a Jacobo Boswelio, illo nimirum tam severo honestatis cultore, tantarumque praedito Luminibus doctrinarum, ut non ille ferat vel minimam aspergi Labem, veritati. Hanc enim[8] Tibi Laudem Cyrnaea Gens tribuit universa.—- Equidem Tu annis ab hinc duobus cum peragrares hoc Regnum, ubi tua ex consuetudine, et colloquiis advertit eam, qua summopere flores, integritatem morum et elegantiam cum tanta sapientiae[9] Luce conjunctam, non Te modo suspicere coepit, et Laudibus in Coelum efferte,[10] sed mirabiles sibi sensit adversum Te amores excitari. Nunc vero ubi hanc Accademiam, nostramque Iuventutem judiciis tuis ornasti: vix dici potest, quantum quisque Tibi sit animo devinctus,[11] quasve habeat gratias. Utinam, Bosweli dulcissime possemus referre. Sed qui possumus paria paribus? Maximas certe Tibi habemus et agimus: verum,[12] ut apud summos viros fieri solet, sentiendo copiosius, quam loquendo. Deum precamur Tibi ut favens sit, et propitium eius numen divinum. Vale.

[Dispatched from the Senate House of the University, the ides of November, in the common era 1767.

The University of Corsica sends its warmest greetings to the distinguished scholar, James Boswell.

We received, most learned James Boswell, a considerable number of volumes of the classical authors that you were gracious enough to send as a gift to this University of ours, books so magnificently and handsomely bound in parchment, moreover of such beautiful design and paper and so elegantly printed, that they are unsurpassed.[13] Now this is no mean proof of your love both of learning and, most of all, of this University, which you beyond anyone have deemed worthy of the exceptional gift of these books, by which you may be regarded as having laid the first stone of the library which must be built up.

But further, the fact that in your judgements you have singled out this University for your approbation and have honoured it and in the words you have written on the first leaf of every one of those volumes, you affirm that the inborn power of Corsican youth, which is shaped by Nature for something lofty and sublime, is chiefly inspired by this University and advanced by it to every distinction of wisdom and Christian virtue; this judgement of yours I say is so momentous that nothing hereafter can shed greater lustre on the University. For the importance is not merely in the receipt of approbation and benefaction resulting from so weighty a judgement; but the matter of prime importance is that the approbation and benefaction are those of James Boswell, so strict a devotee of rectitude and endowed with such brilliance of learning that he could not endure even the slightest stain to be cast on truth. For it is this distinction that the entire people of Corsica has presented to you. In fact, two years ago, when you were travelling in this Nation, when the people from your demeanour and conversation marked that integrity of character and elegance of manners for which you are outstandingly noted, joined with so great a brilliance of wisdom, they began not only to admire you and praise you to the skies but felt within themselves the awakening of great affection for you. But now that you have become the benefactor of the University and our young men, it is impossible to say how each one of us is bound to you in affection or how grateful he feels. Would that we could have returned adequate thanks to you, dearest Boswell. But how can we find adequate expression? Our gratitude to you is enormous, but, as is the case with even the greatest of men, we are giving our thanks more fully in our feelings than in what we can say. We pray that God may show you His favour, and that His divine power may be propitious to you. Farewell.[14]]

[1] The University at Corte was authorized in 1763 and opened in 1765 (F. Girolami-Cortona, *Histoire de la Corse*, 1971, p. 351). Paoli's Enlightenment views on the civic value of education were its chief inspiration: as Paoli himself noted, 'Education should aim, not at producing a race of scholars, but a society composed of educated men' (Thrasher, p. 95). Seven chairs were created in the foundation of the University: theology and ecclesiastical history (to create a generation of priests educated in Corsica), moral theology, civil and case law, ethics, philosophy and mathematics, rhetoric, and civil and commercial practice. Later, instruction became available in Latin, Greek, French, English, and drawing (Thrasher, p. 96; Tommaseo, pp. 66–67). By the time of Burnaby's visit to Corsica in 1766, twelve chairs had been established, and there were 'more than 150 students' (Burnaby, p. 16). In Oct. 1765 JB had visited the university, where he met four members of the faculty. Of this letter, possibly written by the Rector, R. P. Francesco Antonio Mariani da Corbara (From Robert Foulis, 30 Dec.; Tammaseo, p. 66), JB wrote to Temple on 24 Dec., 'I have this day received a large packet from Paoli, with a letter in elegant latin from the University of Corte, and also an extract of an oration pronounced this year at the opening of the University, in which oration I am celebrated in a manner which does me the greatest honour.' The originals of the letter and the extract of the oration have not been reported; the manuscripts by James Brown appear to be inaccurate. For Brown's transcript of the extract, see Appendix C.

[2] Copy, 'Curiis'

[3] Copy, 'MDCCLXXVII'

[4] Salutem Plurimam Dicit.

[5] Copy, 'excilanda'

[6] Copy, 'Rerum'

[7] Copy, 'excilari'

[8] Copy, 'enin'

[9] Copy, 'sapientae'

[10] Copy, 'effere'

[11] Copy, 'devinetus'

[12] Copy, 'rerum'

[13] For the books and inscription, see From Thomas Davies, 18 June, 15 Oct.

[14] Translation by Edmund T. Silk and Gordon Williams.

From Pasquale Paoli, c. Friday 13 November 1767

Not reported. Enclosed with From the Corsican Academy, 13 Nov., in 'a large packet from Paoli' (To W. J. Temple, 24 Dec.). JB appears to have reported part of the content of this letter when he informed Catherine Macaulay that Paoli agreed with her views on a constitution for Corsica (From Macaulay, 17 Feb. 1768).

To Edward Dilly, c. mid-November 1767

Not reported. See From Dilly, 19 Nov.: 'I wrote to you about 10 Days ago, pretty fully, and in some particulars, have answer'd, what you require in the Letter which I received by Yesterday's Post.'

From Girolama Nini Piccolomini, Monday 16 November 1767

MS. Yale (C 2261)

ADDRESS: To James Bossuell Esqr., at Edinburg, by London.

POSTMARK: [LONDON] DE 14.

Siena, 16. 9bre 1767

Sono qualchè giorno che ricevetti la vostra lettera Carissima, ma siccome mi ritrovavo in Campagna, e non avevo portato il vostro indirizzo non potei rispondervi subbito come avrei desiderato di fare. Sempre più vi sono obbligata della premura che conservate per me nello scrivermi e pare che prendiate interesse nelle più piccole cose che mi riguardano; e per rispondervi minutamente a tutte le vostre dimande vi dirò, che la mia piccola servitù e tutta cambiata per motivo di un rubbamento seguito in Casa. Il turno grosso è riprincipiato se non tutte le sere almeno spesso. La Porzia partorì felicemente due maschi, ma l'anno rovinata, ed era meglio mostrar meno i segni di gioventù con ingravidare, che doventare tanto disfatta. Le mie nuove sono buone rispetto alla salute ed intorno alla compagnia la conservo numerosa, ma placidi non ci viene più doppo la vostra partenza da Siena, ed io vivo molto tranquilla in genere di galanteria, ed ora mai credo che lo sarò finchè vivo; perche non fate lo stesso ancora voi? Vi pare una bella cosa il passare ogni momento ad uno ogetto nuovo, che non diverte che la materia sensa dar pascolo al cuore, il quale alimento e necessario ad una persona ben nata, ed a una persona del vostro talento. Non dubito che voi non siate per guadagnare la Sigra. che vorreste per moglie, perche basta conoscervi per crederlo, ma temo solamente, che anche con una moglie accanto vi piacerà qualchè ragazzetta, ed allora non sola voi ne pagherete la pena, ma sarete due a soffrire, ed in conseguenza ne nascono le dissenzioni, e di una vita piacevole diventa insoffribile, pero non saprei dirvi se sarete felice con prendere una moglie, solo posso dirvi che avete tutte le qualità per essere amabile, e per fare la felicità altrui, e con tutte queste buone disposizioni temo che avrete l'abilità di dare de dispiaceri ad una moglie; ma dove azzardo di dare delle ragioni? Non mi ricordavo più che io parlo con un avvocato che mi troverà mille ragioni per ritorcere il mio argomento, e bisognerà lasciarsi sedurre con argumenti falsi, e forse me persuaderete ancora, e crederò che voi avete ragione, però vi prego per l'avvenire di darmi fedelmente le vostre nuove, ma non di interpellare più il mio giudizio, per non avere la temerità di dare delle ragioni ad un *Giurisconsulto*; e se prima vi stimavo, ora vi stimo e temo. Perche non avete più a corrispondenza con Rousseau? Mi pare più a proposito per voi de quella di Paoli. Aspetto il vostro ritratto con ansietà, ed indirizzatelo al Sigre. Crocchi acciò me lo dia con segretezza; ma fatevi dipingere quando siete guarito da i vostri incomodi, altrimenti sareste troppo pallido.

Mi maraviglio come possiate far de i progressi nella lingua italiana sensa parlare con qualcheduno, ma in voi mi fa maraviglia il vostro buona come il vostro cattivo. Volevo farvi una lettera scempia e sensa avvedermene lo fatta doppia; però abbiate pazzienza e date un calcio all'avarizia giacchè mi confessaste una volta che vi sentivi portato all'avarizia; il che non conviene quando eccede la giusta economia, io poi sono essente da questo vizio perche per possederlo bisogna essere ricchi; vedete se anche nella miseria vi si cava il suo buon partito, ma con tutto questo non mi soddisfo in questa morale, se non pensasse che vi è chi manca della necessità per sussistere. Mantenetemi la vostra amicizia, e se vi fa piacere il sapere che siete corrisposto con usura ne potete essere persuaso, come lo doveti essere che mi farete una grazia di comandarmi.

[It has been some days since I received your dearest letter, but as I was in the country and had not taken your address with me I could not reply immediately, as I should have liked to do. I am ever more and more obliged for the solicitude you continue to show in writing to me; it appears that you take an interest in even the smallest things which concern me.

To give detailed replies to all your questions: my small retinue of servants is completely changed because of a burglary that occurred in our house.[1] The *turno grosso* has begun again, if not every night, at least often. Porzia was safely delivered of twin boys, but they have ruined her, and it would have been better for her not to have appeared so youthful, getting herself pregnant into the bargain, than to have suffered such a fall.[2] My own news is good, so far as my health is concerned. My circle of friends remains numerous, but Placidi visited me no more after your departure from Siena.[3] I live very quietly as far as gallantry is concerned, and think I shall continue to do so as long as I live. Why do you not follow my example? Does it seem so fine to you to flit every moment to a new object of passion, amusing your body without nourishing your heart—a kind of sustenance necessary for a man of birth and talent like yourself?

I have no doubt that you are on the point of winning the lady whom you wish to marry:[4] it is enough to have known you to believe it. I only fear that when you have a wife some wench will take your fancy. Then it will not merely be you who will pay the penalty, but there will be two to suffer; quarrels will follow, and a peaceful life will be changed into an intolerable one. So I cannot say whether or not a wife will make you happy. I can only tell you that you have all the qualities necessary to be loved and to make another's happiness, but, with all these fine attributes, I fear you also have it in you to make a wife miserable. But to whom am I presuming to give reasons? I forgot that I was speaking to a lawyer who will find a thousand ways to turn my argument against me. False arguments may be irresistible; perhaps you will persuade me yet, and I will believe that you are right. So I beg you for the future to be faithful in letting me hear from you, but not to ask me again for my opinion, as I do not have the temerity to argue with a *jurisconsult*; and if I esteemed you before, now I esteem and tremble before you too.

Why do you no longer exchange letters with Rousseau? It seems to me that it would be more appropriate for you to correspond with him than with Paoli.[5]

I await your portrait anxiously. Address it to Signor Crocchi so that he can give it to me privately; but have it painted after you have recovered from your illness. Otherwise you will be too pale.[6]

I am amazed how you can make progress in Italian without speaking it with anyone, but the good in you amazes me as much as the bad.

I intended to write you a letter only one sheet long, and without realizing it I have made it two. But have patience, and give your avarice the boot—you once confessed to me that you were inclined to avarice, which is unbecoming when it exceeds just economy.[7] I, now, am free from this vice, for one must be rich to have it. You see that even from poverty one draws some advantages. But for all that, I should get no comfort from that adage if I did not know that there are those who lack the very necessities of life.

Keep up your friendship with me, and if it gives you pleasure to know that it is returned with interest, rest assured of it, as you must be if you will oblige me by the honour of your commands.[8]]

[1] Nothing is known about the servants of Orazio Piccolomini or the burglary which had recently occurred at his house.

[2] For Porzia's pregnancy, see From Girolama Piccolomini, 3 May and n. 4.

[3] The members of Moma's *conversazione* or salon are listed in *Grand Tour* II, p. 122; in From Piccolomini 7 Oct. and 12 Dec. 1765, she mentions the addition of a Sienese gentleman, Sgr. Bianconi, to her group. As JB explains in his letter to Rousseau of 3 Oct. 1765, Italian ladies were customarily surrounded by admirers called *cavalieri serventi*, of whom JB claimed every lady had one or two. Moma, writing to JB on 14 Feb. 1766, referred to these gallants as her 'consiglieri'.

[4] Catherine Blair.

[5] JB had been disenchanted with Rousseau for nearly a year. See F. A. Pottle, 'The Part Played by Horace Walpole and James Boswell in the quarrel between Rousseau and Hume: A Recon-

sideration', in W. H. Smith, ed., *Horace Walpole: Writer, Politician, and Connoisseur*, 1967, pp. 255–91; *Grand Tour* II, pp. 299–301. JB told Rousseau in a letter of 3 Oct. 1765 that Girolama admired his works, though, in scolding JB for his hypocritical views on adultery, she equated him with Rousseau himself (printed in *Grand Tour* II, pp. 3–20; this reference p. 18). She had mentioned Paoli by name only once in previous extant correspondence (12 Dec. 1765); there she expressed pleasure that JB's Corsican trip has been a success and that Paoli had appreciated JB's merits.

[6] When he had written to Moma in October, JB was still recovering from gonorrhoea, which would presumably have made him pallid.

[7] As the receiver of the letter, JB was obliged to pay the postage. The journal does not record his having spoken to her of what he called his 'sheer love of coin' (Journ. 9 Feb. 1763).

[8] Translation by F. A. Pottle and Ian Duncan.

From Edward Dilly, Thursday 19 November 1767

MS. Yale (C 1072).

ADDRESS: To James Boswell Esqr., Advocate, Edinburgh.

ENDORSEMENT: Letters from Mr. Edward Dilly concerning the first Edition of my Account of Corsica.

London, Novr. 19, 1767

SIR: I Wrote to you about 10 Days ago, pretty fully, and in some particulars, have answer'd, what you require in the Letter which I received by Yesterday's Post. I have been this Day to a Friend of mine who is intimately acquainted with Richardson's Partner[1] in the Printing House, and by his means, I am thoroughly acquainted of what is going forward—the Hist of Corsica, which I inform'd you is Printing in Salisbury Court; A small Part of the M.S. was sent about 15 months ago and there is now only about one fourth Part of the Work Printed, and they have had no Copy sent them for above four Months past, so that at present the Work lies dormant, the Author, or rather Compiler, I cannot get his Name, but he is a Scotch Gent. who was in the Army last War, and is now dismissed the Service. The Compilation is bad, chiefly collected from News Papers and Magazines, and the Printer imagines the Work will not be finished, so that we need not fear any danger from that Quarter, though I must acknowledge when I first heard it, I was a little Alarm'd. But as the Case now Stands, we had much better omit the advertisemt. for the present, for by inserting it the author might be awakned out of his Lethargy, Whereas he now lies dormant, and as soon as we are ripe for Publication then I will advertise very briskly. The Map of Corsica I think may easily be finish'd by the latter End of this Month—or Otherwise the Engraver is a very slow hand, make that as complete as possible. I Wrote in my last, that you have full Liberty to say, Glasgow-Printed etc. and that I imagined Edinr. and Glasgow would take off 500 Copies, in that Case 1000 must be sent to me 500 by one ship and 500 by another, and when they are shiptd information being sent to me with the Captains Receipt. I would insure the Value in London; for this Season of the year many Vessels are cast away. If you Work off 500 Maps for Scotland, the Plate may be immediately sent to me and I can get the 1000 Workt off in London which perhaps may be better done, than at Edinr., as we can suit ourselves much better with Paper, proper for the purpose. If the Books are well Packt up, by Foulis, they may be sent Directed to Mr.[2] Neill Printer at Edinr. who will take Care to ship them by the first Leith Ship, and Foulis may send 500 by a Carron Ship.[3] You will inform me as near the Time as you can, when You think it will be finished, and I will Write then to Mr. Neill, how to dispose of the Copies which may be sent to Edinr. for sale. The Books I sent by Beatson I hope are come safe to Hand[4]—Mr. Woodfall received the Essay on Travelling, and is well pleased with the Answer you sent.[5] I wish the Oxonian woud send a Letter to the *Political Register*, and the Publisher of that Work may hear from another Quarter likewise.[6] I shall not be wanting in my endeavours—I have just Parted with your Brother, he is in good Health, and is perfectly well pleased, with what he has seen in Town. I am, Sir, Your most Obedient Servant,

EDWD. DILLY

[1] Dilly's friend is unidentified. Richardson's partner until 1768 was Samuel Clarke, then aged forty-two, a Quaker who occupied rooms in Bread Street, Cheapside, from 1765–89 (Maxted, p. 45, *Gent. Mag.* lix. 178).

[2] MS. 'Pri' deleted before 'Mr'

[3] Leith was the seaport for Edinburgh. The shipping firm of Francis Garbett and Co., an offshoot of the Carron ironworks, was situated at Carronshore on the Forth, about twenty-five miles from Glasgow (R. H. Campbell, *Carron Company*, 1961, pp. 114–17).

[4] For the books, see From Dilly, 4 Nov. and n. 5.

[5] JB's essay, signed 'Britannus', appeared in *Pub. Adv.* 20 Nov. p. 1. It was subsequently reprinted in *Cal. Merc.*, 28 Nov. and *Lond. Mag.* xxxvi. 582. Yale has a marked leaf with JB's own notations, which indicate that he wrote the piece at Auchinleck and later added the title 'An Essay on Travelling' (P 114:1). The essay suggests that the world needs fewer 'Catalogues' of travels, and more books detailing 'the Effect of Travelling after it is over'. JB devotes the bulk of it to

satirizing the deleterious effects of the Grand Tour on the national character of 'True Britons'. We do not know what the 'Answer' Dilly mentions refers to.

⁶ For 'the Oxonian', see From Dilly, 31 Aug.

and n. 5. Neither *Lit. Car.* nor NCBEL suggests that JB ever published as the Oxonian or B.M. in Almon's *Political Register*. The 'other Quarter' is unidentified: the following line suggests that it means Dilly himself.

From Lord Leven,¹ Monday 23 November 1767

MS. Yale (C 1737).

ADDRESS: To James Boswell Esqr., Edinburgh.

Melvill,² Novr. 23d, 1767

SIR: Alexr. Grig One of my Tenan[ts] in Markinch, and who I recommended to you for Your Assistance in the Summer Session, has been with me just now and seems to be so much satisfied with the Attention you have given to his Cause, that he will not leave me till I return you thanks for it and by the Continuance of your good Offices.³ This I do with the greater Readiness as I really beleive, from what I have heard of the Cause, that the man has been oppressed, and at the same time ask Your pardon for taking this Liberty, as I dare say you want no Spur to do all in your power to serve your Clients. I beg leave to offer My best Respects to Lord Auchinleck, and am with great Regard, Sir, Your most Obedient and most humble Servant,

LEVEN

¹ David Melville (1722–1802), sixth Earl of Leven and fifth Earl of Melville, attended the Univ. of Edinburgh, briefly served as an ensign in the Army (1742–c.46), and had been Grand Master Mason of Scotland (1759–61). He later (1773–82) held office as Lord of Police and (1783–1801) Lord High Commissioner to the General Assembly. An account of his life may be found in Sir William Fraser, *The Melvilles, Earls of Melville and the Leslies, Earls of Leven*, 3 vols., 1890, i. 337–352. JB called on Lord Leven in Edinburgh 7 Jan. 1768 and on 2 March 1778 (Journ.), but the journals and correspondence indicate no more than a social acquaintance.

² Leven's seat, Melville House, was situated about seven miles from Markinch, in the parish of

Monimail, of which the Earl was patron (A. H. Millar, *Fife: Pictorial and Historical*, 1895, 2 vols. i. 203, ii. 63–73). Melville House was Leven's most valuable property: the rent-roll was valued at £3,590 Scots—about half the total worth of his Fife estates (L. R. Timperley, *A Directory of Landownership in Scotland* c. 1770, SRS New Series, 1976, v. 151, 153). The best account of the tenantry of Markinch is to be found in *Stat. Acct. Scot.* (new edition, eds. I. R. Grant and D. J. Witherington, 1978, x. 624–25, 648–50); the area was notable for its many resident heritors, or landlords.

³ JB's Consultation Book lists the cause of Greig *v.* Heggie brought before the Court of Session 16 July. No more is known about the cause.

From Richard Edwards, Monday 30 November 1767

MS. Yale (C 1177).

NOTE at foot of page: James Boswell, Esq. Lyer.

Leghorn, the 30th November 1767

SIR, I have the Honour to enclose You a Packet which is just come to hand from Corsica, and also to acquaint You that I this Night forward to Your Bankers, Bill of Loading for a Case containing a Gun and a Pair of Pistols; and also a Dogg, which I have likewise received for You from Corsica.¹

I have the Honour to be on all Your Commands with great Truth of Respect,

Sir, Your most obliged and most obedient Servant,

RICHARD EDWARDS

[1] Paoli had written to the Rev. Andrew Burnaby on 1 Nov. that he was sending firearms and a dog to JB (Burnaby, pp. 49–50). He had given JB a brace of pistols in Corsica in 1765 (*Corsica*, p. 317) and had added a gun barrel to a shipment of goods, including books and gun barrels, sent to JB by John Dick in the following year (From James Craufurd, 16 May 1766, n. 2). This was to be the second dog JB received from Paoli: for the first dog, Jachone, see *Earlier Years*, pp. 264–65, 525. The second dog, unnamed, was lost in London. When JB went with Robert Herries and Sir William Forbes to see the guns and claim the dog, he found that the dog, 'had broken loose, and was running about the town'. They searched but did not find him (Journ. 23 Mar. 1768).

To Godfrey Bosville, c. late November or early December 1767

Not reported. See From Bosville, 19 Dec.: 'Your Letter found me in Yorkshire, since that we have passed through Staffordshire in our way to visit an Old Lady of our own Name.'

To Thomas Davies, c. early December 1767

Not reported. See From Davies, 12 Dec.: 'I excuse your joke of Metropolitan Bookseller'; it appears that JB had intimated that Davies, a London bookseller, was too busy to answer his request for his client James Windram.

To Alexander Maconochie, c. early to mid-December 1767

Not reported. See From Maconochie, 25 Dec.: 'I had the pleasure of receiving yours some time ago and am very happy you have forgiven the libertys we took for the good of the Cause (as we thought) upon the publication if your *Essence*'.

From Sir John Pringle, Friday 4 December 1767

MS. Yale (C 2298).

ADDRESS: To James Boswell Esqr.

London, 4 Decr. 1767

DEAR SIR, By this time You will probably have heard, that I have been abroad once more, for my health, and that it is not long since I returned.[1] This will partly apologise for my long silence, after having received so obliging a letter from You, and one too that made a demand upon me for speedy advice. In effect Your letter came and lay sometime here during my absence; for as I wanted to be free from all business, and especially writing, I left orders that no letters, except such as came from certain quarters, should be sent after me. Since I returned I have had so much to do during my writing hours I mean from the time I get up till dinner that I have not yet half answered those letters which lay for me at my arrival.

I should have the more regretted, and[2] apologised for my unmannerly silence, had I been persuaded that I could have influenced your judgement with regard to most of those articles which were the subject of your letter. Not that I consider You as more wilful or tenacious to Your own opinion than others are, in general; but because the determination was to be about such things, as a man, after asking the opinion of twenty friends, will either do or omit doing just as if he had no friends at all. I will therefore not pretend to give you my advice, but I will amuse You with my opinion. In the first place (as I am assured by Mr. F. that you have got intirely free from your disorder)[3] I should think that Miss B. would be a very proper match, if she has all those good qualities which You mention, and which I am the more inclined to believe she has, as You seem not to be blinded by love when You recite her good qualities, and especially as You are likely to have Your father's approbation. How far You yourself are qualified for entering into the holy bonds and fitted for Miss B. is another question, notwithstanding that point, about which You were doubtful, was settled fully to my satisfaction by Mr. F. I should hope that principles of honour as well as prudence would engage You to keep those solemn vows, which too many make too lightly of. I was amused, as I have been before, on the like occasion, with your confidence about your success. I have commonly observed, that vanity is for the most part punished by mortifying the person in the very thing in which he most prides himself; and upon that principle, I could lay a bett that in this very affair you will meet with a disappointment. But we shall see.

You have had, it seems, too much success, upon less honourable terms, with a weak one of the sex. I hope You have as sincerely repented of that action, as You must have done of that act, which brought You into the condition in which Mr. Forbes saw you. If You have not repented, and with great compunction too, be assured that your misfortunes are not at an end, and that Providence, for your amendment will not cease to chastise You till you cry *peccavi*.[4] Is it nothing to render ashamed and unhappy for life a poor silly creature whom you have catched off her guard? The damage is irreparable, but since the thing is done, you ought to make amends, as much as you can, by money.[5] In the first place, I hope You will apply that sum which you tell me you are to receive for the copy of your book. Not that I approve of that merchandise, but since you have made the bargain, I take the liberty to tell you, what my opinion is with regard to the disposal of the money.

I have always, You will know, used great freedom with you, not only when You have asked my opinion, but likewise, whenever You afforded me matter to form opinions relating to your conduct and character.[6] On the occasion of the book, I must therefore tell you, that since, contrary to my advice, you have written it, and will publish it, you have done I am afraid rather ungenteelly in selling the copy (before the publication) to a Bookseller. This has too much the air of writing for gain, I mean for money, which is below a gentleman. I know this was not your only motive, nay I will do you the justice, as to say that I believe that this circumstance did not at first enter into the consideration at all: but you ought to have avoided the appearance of it. I shall keep your secret, but will your bookseller do it; or have you done it yourself? Were I the Heiress of A. be assured I should never listen to a lover who had been capable of so doing. See the consequences. Your bookseller, in order to indemnify himself must puff your work with a pompous title-page and advertisements in the news-papers. He must tell that You give not only the political but the *natural history* of that island. Now surely, You could never call your self a Naturalist; or, if you had had[7] any genius, or education for that branch of science, had you time to make any observations that could claim an article in such a book. If it be not too late, I would advise you to change that at least.[8] You see I take great liberties. I shall conclude with telling you that with regard to separate houses in case of marriage, Your father is too reasonable not to consent to it. But remember that by leaving him lonely, he may be tempted to take a companion likewise. Perhaps the best for you both would be for each to have to have a good one. I am most affectionately yours,

J. P.

¹ Pringle was given six weeks' leave from his post as Queen's physician for travel to France with Benjamin Franklin. The journey lasted from 28 Aug. to 8 Oct.; Franklin describes their tour in a letter to Mary Stevenson of 14 Sept. (*Franklin Papers*, xiv. 250–55). The exact nature of Pringle's illness is unknown.
² MS. 'and' superimposed upon erased 'my'
³ JB's latest bout of gonorrhoea (To Sir Alexander Dick, 21 Aug., n. 2) had been treated by 'Mr. F.', Duncan Forbes (d. 1779), an Edinburgh surgeon and medical officer for the Second Troop of Horse Guards, 1756–78 (*Scots Mag.* 1779, xli. 110; *Army List*; William Ober, *Boswell's Clap and Other Essays*, 1979, pp. 14–15). JB was subsequently treated by Forbes in Apr. 1768 and Oct. 1769 (To Temple, 26 Apr. 1768; Notes, 16 Oct. 1769).
⁴ The word occurs in the confessional in the

Roman Catholic Mass: 'I confess to Almighty God ... that I have sinned (Lat. *peccavi*) exceedingly in thought, word, and deed'.
⁵ JB continued to send money to Mrs. Dodds, who bore him a daughter later this month (To Temple, 24 Dec.) until at least Mar.1769, but it is uncertain what financial arrangments he may have made for her after that (*Earlier Years*, 347–354).
⁶ JB notes in Journ. for 2 Sept. 1769, 'As Sir John has witnessed many of my weaknesses and follies, and been allways like a Parent to me, I cannot help standing much in awe of him'.
⁷ MS. 'if you had had' written above deleted 'had you had'
⁸ JB did not take Pringle's advice. He entitled the first chapter 'Of the Situation, Extent, Air, Soil, and Productions, of CORSICA'.

From Thomas Davies, Saturday 12 December 1767

MS. Yale (C 902).
ADDRESS: To James Boswell Esqr. of Auchenleck, at Edinburgh.
POSTMARK: [London] DE 12; WM.

London, Decr. 12th, 1767

DEAR SIR: I excuse your joke of Metropolitan Bookseller,¹ but beg leave to assure Mr. Boswell [I] am² not so taken up with any business as to neglect the least request of my Friends—To convince you that I have not neglected your Clients affair I here Transcribe the words of the careful and exact person I employed to examine into the business. This person is Mr. Wilkie's Clerk.

'I have again turned over the Daily Advertizer for the year 1763 from end to end, and cannot for the Soul of me see any such article as Mr. Boswell mentions, or any thing like it—*I not only examined the news part of the paper very circumspectly, but ran my eye once more over the Advertisements and assure you Sir, I can see no such thing.*'³

Now Sir, I hope you will allow that I have not neglected your commands.

The watch keys were paid for by your Friend⁴—You affront me when you desire⁵ me to charge the postage of letters—I am always happy to be favour'd with a line⁶ from Mr. Boswell.

Pray tell me which of the Candidates is most likely to succeed Lee or Ross⁷—We have various reports here notwithstanding the letter signed David Ross in the newspaper. I⁸ really concluded he had fairly got the Victory.⁹ Which of these two Heroes do you espouse?¹⁰ I cou'd send you some Theatrical news but fear you will term me impertinent for giving you disturbance when you are so much better employed before the Lords of Session. I have not seen your Brother yet.[11] I am, Dear Sir, Your most obedient, humble Servant,

THOMAS DAVIES

[1] Presumably JB made this jest in a letter of early December, which has not been reported.

[2] MS. 'I ha' deleted before 'am', and 'Mr. Boswell' written above the line. Davies deleted 'I' by mistake.

[3] For an account of this matter, see From Pierre Loumeau Dupont, 7 Apr. n. 4.

[4] John Dick. See From Davies, 18 June.

[5] MS. 'desire' written above deleted 'ask'

[6] MS. 'Mr. Boswells' deleted before 'a line'

[7] Davies is referring to the competitors for the patent of the Edinburgh Theatre Royal. John Lee (1725–81), veteran player in London (Drury Lane) and Dublin, had managed the Canongate Concert Hall in Edinburgh, 1752–56, and was considered by theatregoers to be the first manager to raise the status and morale of the Edinburgh theatre. He was successful in instituting reforms, notably his refusal to allow members of the audience to occupy seats on the stage or 'gentlemen' to be admitted behind the scenes, but his successes were soon followed by a period of difficulties. He ran into debt, the 'gentlemen' proprietors of the Canongate Playhouse (all prominent Edinburgh citizens, among them several judges on the bench of the Court of Session) deserted him, and he spent two months in gaol (Dibdin, pp. 70, 72, 75–81). On 2 Sept. a royal patent had been granted to the Canongate Theatre, and in Nov. David Ross (1728–90) acquired the patent. The

theatre opened on 9 Dec. as the Theatre Royal with Ross performing in *The Earl of Essex* and reciting a prologue composed by JB (Baker, p. 25; Dibdin, pp. 145–48).

[8] MS. Abbreviation for 'which' deleted before 'I'

[9] Ross made an appeal to the public in the papers of 29 Nov., begging their indulgence because he was not as well known as Lee. He promised that he would give up the Theatre in two years if his work was not satisfactory (*Scots Mag.* 1767, xxix. 613–14).

[10] The Edinburgh theatrical world had been split into two rival camps over the Lee-Ross patent battle. The 'public party' supported Lee. On 28 Nov. they held a meeting at Fortune's to force the proprietors to respect the 'public's' wish for Lee, and to express their outrage that the proprietors would try to impose Ross upon them. Although Lee was the public favourite, his decade-old squabbles with the proprietors hurt his already poor chances of winning the patent. The ensuing paper war between supporters of the two 'Heroes' is covered by Dibdin, pp. 144–148. JB espoused Ross's claim; for Ross's career and JB's relationship with him, see Baker, pp. 25, 63–64.

[11] Davies had missed his chance, as David Boswell was in Paris, on his way to Spain, by 3 Dec. (From David Boswell, 3 Dec.).

From Godfrey Bosville, Saturday 19 December 1767

MS. Yale (C 177).

ADDRESS: To James Boswell Esqr., at Lord Auchinlecks, in Edinburgh.

POSTMARKS: 19 DE, JJ.[1]

London, Decr. 19th, 1767

DEAR SIR, Your Letter found me in Yorkshire, since that we have passd through Staffordshire in our way to visit an Old Lady of our own Name.[2] You will be surprizd when I tell you that Billy is going to see Paschal Paoli your Old friend, but so it is.[3] When he got here from Yorkshire Major Hawke the Admirals Son who had been with him when they were Ensigns together on a Six weeks Expedition into France,[4] and who had often desird to go with him upon another Expedition desird him to ask for a twelve months Leave of Absence to go with the Tripoli Embassador[5] home again, Captain Bennet who commands the Eolus[6] is a Particular friend of the Admls. and very desirous of their Company: Billy was averse to ask my Lord Tyrawley because he had refusd sevl Officers leave to go to France;[7] but Hawke insisted upon his asking and went along with him: Lord Tyrawley receivd them with great Good Humour as he always has done, said it was a very rational Scheme: that he shoud have Leave and has got him the Kings Leave, they are to touch at Lisbon Gibraltar Tripoli[8] Corsica and other Places, Lord Tyrawley gave him some Good Advice such as to observe the Works at Gibraltar see Paschal Paoli bring an account what kind of a man he is and what sort of Troops the Corsicans are; I wish they coud have carryd a Letter from you but now it is too late for they have sayld from Portsmouth and are now at Falmouth whither the Tripoli Embassador is gone by Land: they will have an excellent Opportunity of seeing that Country as the Embassadors Brother is Dey of Tripoli.[9] Lord Tyrawley says it will be an Improvement to Billy, but he knows nothing of Williams going to Prussia without being sent and it is well for him he dos not.[10] You commend the Scotch Laws, but in one particular we have greatly the advantage of you in our Evidence being deliverd Viva Voce,[11] Cross Examinations very often gets out the truth and the Craftiest Witnesses will hesitate when they know that they are to be sifted: but people upon depositions can be easily brought to swear streight forwards, for which reason here I shoud prefer our Common Law Courts to our Chancery. But I suppose if the Douglas Cause comes into the House of Lords their Method is by Depositions.[12] I shall like very much to hear you explain these things yourself for I am not as you may perceive a Sufficient Judge of them. Our Compliments to Lord Auchinleck and I am sorry we coud not have the pleasure of seeing his Lordship and yourself at our old habitation but I hope we shall see you in Great Russell Street. At Stafford the Members made a Compromise Lord Chetwynd[14] and Mr. Mennil[15] who the last time had joynd two others and opposd one another and Mr. Mennil very imprudently went out at Back door from a house he was visiting at and when his Post Chaise drove of empty the People who expected mony were in a rage. Mr. Whitworth another gentleman has offerd himself and they say stands a good Chance, he can give them nothing but treats and now the Old Members give ten Guineas a man and what is very provoking the more they give the more the people thank Mr. Whitworth, in short if they cannot bind them by notes they will probably bring him in.[16] I cannot say but I wish for Whitworth for he is the only Candidate[17] I know. I am, Dear [Sir], Your most Obedient Servant,

GODFREY BOSVILLE

[1] Probably the initials of a postal receiver.

[2] Bosville succeeded to Biana, a house and estate in Eccleshall parish, Staffordshire, in 1762 upon the death of the house's previous owner, Charles Bosville. The two were distantly related through a common ancestor, Sir Robert Bosville, uncle of Godfrey's great-great-grandfather (*Fortunes of a Family*, pp. 100–01, 232–34). The 'Old Lady' is unidentified.

[3] Although William Bosville got as far as Lisbon, Gibraltar, Morocco, and presumably Tripoli, the trip to Corsica does not seem to have taken place (Alexander Stephens, *Memoirs of John Horne Tooke*, 1813, reprt. 1968, ii. 309–311).

[4] Edward Hawke (1746–73), son of the Admiral of the same name, and William Bosville

were ensigns together in the Coldstream Guards between Mar. 1762 and Sept. 1765. Hawke left the Coldstreams in 1765, moved to the Fifth Foot, had recently (17 June) been raised to the rank of Major in the Buffs (Third Foot), and by the time he died, 2 Oct. 1773, was Lt.-Colonel of the Sixty-second Foot (*Army Lists*, 1761–72; *Ann. Reg.* 1773, p. 174). Bosville remained in the Coldstreams as an ensign until 1769, when he was promoted to lieutenant—the rank he retained until he retired from the army in 1777 (Frank MacKinnon, *Origin and Services of the Coldstream Guards*, ii. 488). The two men must have taken the first 'Expedition into France' during the period when they were ensigns together; on the second, in 1767–68, they formed part of an English embassy sent to Africa to congratulate the Emperor of Morocco on his accession to the throne (*Fortunes of a Family*, p. 187).

[5] Ambassador Hamet Aga (or Hamed Agen) Joya Effendi—the titles 'Aga' and 'Effendi' suggest that he was both a senior military officer and a government official—had arrived in London in July bearing a present for George III. He left London on 14 Dec., and on 23 Dec. embarked from Portsmouth aboard the *Aeolus* (*Court and City Register*, 1768, p. 111; *Lond. Chron.* 1767, xxii. 91, 570, 606; *Annual Register*, 1767, x. 155). As Seton Dearden recounts, 'a series of Tripoline ambassadors, usually relatives or friends of the Karamanli Bashaws, had descended on London with large trains of servants, had overstayed the statutory period of six months, and had then departed leaving heavy debts behind them'. The British government hoped that Hamet Aga would be the last of these 'ambassadors': and sent Consul Barker to Tripoli in 1768 with specific instructions to persuade the Bashaw to send no more emissaries to London (*A Nest of Corsairs: The Fighting Karamanlis of Tripoli*, 1976, pp. 88–89).

[6] Captain William Bennet (d. 1790), a naval officer since 1741, had been a captain for seven years (*Sea Officers*, i. 61). The *Aeolus*, a thirty-two-gun ship of the fifth-rate size and strength, had recently been returned to Mediterranean duty after service in Portsmouth (*Court and City Register*, 1767–68).

[7] For Lord Tyrawley, see From Bosville, 12 Aug. 1766, n. 6. Absenteeism and a casual attitude towards leaving one's post characterized the junior officers of the British army in this period. Major R. Money Barnes notes that 'desertions were fairly common as the result of harsh treatment by N.C.O's or boredom with the routine, the lack of amusements or variety, and the generally vile conditions regarding rations and quarters' (*A History of the Regiments and Uniforms of the British Army*, 1962, p. 63).

[8] MS. 'Triopoli'

[9] 'Dey', lit. 'Uncle', was a Turkish title given by the janissaries to their own leaders. Since 1711, when the Karamanli family, aided by the native Kuloghli cavalry, had massacred the Turkish janissaries and assumed power, they had been styled 'Bashaws' (or 'Pashas'), an Ottoman term meaning 'head man'. The current Pasha was the indolent and dissolute Ali, who ruled from 1754 to 1793 (Dearden, pp. 36, 81–138, 322–23).

[10] For William's absence in Prussia, see From Bosville, 12 Aug. 1766 and n. 5.

[11] 'Orally.' Proceedings in both the Court of Session and the Court of Justiciary were carried on largely in writing and often in printed form.

[12] The English Common Law courts relied heavily upon *viva voce* cross-examination; the Chancery Court which, like the Scottish system, had its origins in Roman civil law, depended more upon written testimony. The Douglas verdict, delivered 7 July, had been appealed to the House of Lords, which would review the written evidence in the cause.

[13] Where Bosville's London house was situated (From Bosville, 4 Oct. n. 8).

[14] William Richard Chetwynd (c. 1683–1770), third Viscount Chetwynd, M.P. for Stafford, 1715–22, Plymouth, 1722–27, Stafford 1734–70, Master of the Mint, 1744–69. Chetwynd came from an old Staffordshire family—he was the representative of the most powerful family interest in the borough—that had traditionally held one seat at Stafford. His political career seems to have been uneventful after 1754; he was a regular supporter of the Administration (Namier and Brooke ii. 211).

[15] Hugo Meynell (1735–1808), M.P. for Lichfield, 1762–68, Lymington, 1769–74, and Stafford, 1774–80. A gambler like his father, he founded the Quorn Hunt, and was 'long esteemed as the first foxhunter in the kingdom'. He was a close friend of the Duke of Grafton's and followed his lead in politics, opposing the Grenville administration and supporting those of Rockingham and Chatham (Namier and Brooke ii. 134–35). He was currently acting as Grafton's intermediary in negotiations with the Bedfords (*Corres. HW* xxii. 569 and nn. 5–6).

[16] Richard Whitworth (?1734–1811), an aspiring M.P., stood on his own interest for Stafford, an 'expensive and difficult constituency, with an electorate composed mostly of tradesmen' (Namier and Brooke i. 375) against Lord Chetwynd (see n. 14), and Hugo Meynell (see n. 15). *The Univ. Brit. Directory* (1798, iv. 437) suggests that when the Chetwynd estates became the property of the Talbot family (on the death of the second Viscount in 1767), the burgesses of Stafford controlled the 400 voters of the borough. Whitworth was optimistic of success: on 6 Jan. 1768 he wrote to Lord Grosvenor, 'Everyone says I am sure to be first upon the poll, notwithstanding the high price my opponents give I have grately the majority. . . . Many people wonder how I dare attack two such powerful men. I did at first wonder at it myself but my success has made me forget those thoughts. . . . I have carried the whole at my own expense and paid my way, and I think about £900 or £1,000 will settle me there for life.' On the election day (18 Mar. 1768) Whitworth had a majority of 15 over Chetwynd and 31 over Meynell (Namier and Brooke ii. 634).

[17] MS. 'Canditate'

To the Duke of Queensberry, Saturday 19 December 1767

Not reported. See From Queensberry, 5 Jan. 1768.: 'Your letter of the 19th of Decr. did not come to my hands till yesterday'.

From Alexander Maconochie,[1] Friday 25 December 1767

MS. Yale (C 1867).

ADDRESS: To James Boswell Esqr., Advocate, Edinburgh

London, 25 Decr. 1767

MY DEAR SIR: I had the pleasure of receiving yours some time ago and am very happy you have forgiven the libertys we took for the good of the Cause (as we thought) upon the publication of your *Essence*. The observations upon the *Considerations* are not I am very sensible a Sufficient answer to that infamous performance nor was it possible to answer it in the time.[2] The *Considerations* did not come out till late on the Saturday night and there was no thought of making any observations upon them at all till the Duke of Queensberry read them and said he thought it would be necessary to take the Sting a little from the *Considerations* by contradicting some of the grossest misrepresentations contained in them, this was all we had in view and all we had time to do as the Appeal you know was to be entered next day.[3]

As to employing some person here still to answer them it is in the first place impossible to print any thing here without being most Severely fined and otherways punished by the house of Lords.But my notion and design is this, after our Case is finished by Mr. Thurlow who is Just now bussy at it,[4] and seing his Ideas of the Cause, ⟨to c⟩ause some person of remarkible parts to write something ⟨for the⟩ publick upon the Cause and take occasion to refute the ⟨Considerations misrep⟩res⟨entings⟩ and to have it translated into French published at Paris and many Copies of it may be brought to Britain and there Circulated, this I imagine the Parliament could not take hold of and it would answer the purpose as well as if printed in English as every mortal can read French and after so much English has been read in the Cause any thing in the French language would be more eagerly read than if the same thing was in English. I should be glad to have your oppinion of this project which I have as yet communicated to nobody, only something of this kind was Suggested by Mr. Stuart McKenzie to the Duke of Queensberry some days ago.[5]

You have no doubt heard that the Cause cannot be heard this winter which is no doubt a very great loss to us but for which there is no help. I really am fully and absolutly convinced that Mr. Douglas will prevail and this is the universall oppinion of every person whatever. It is true the Law Lords[6] will not say to us expressly that they have read the Cause and that they are of that oppinion, but from every thing that passes they seem to point strongly our way. For instance the Chancellor said Mr. Douglas ought not to be uneasy for he had nothing to fear[7] Mansfield said that tho he had not read the Cause many of the Judges of Westminster hall had and that they were Clear for us and that it had been lucky for Mr. Douglas if his Cause had depended in Westminster hall.[8] And most Certainly if the Law Lords were to differ in the house of Peers and a division of the house to happen we would have Six to one.[9] In these Circumstances how is it possible for us to be in bad Spirits and I beg Youl banish fears far from you for we will prevail and Mr. Douglas will live to thank as he ought those who have so generously and with so m⟨uch⟩ Spirit stood by him in his time of need—if the Decisi⟨on⟩ of the Court of Session had not been as it is he never would have Sufficiently known the extent of some persons friendship which I am Certain he has a heart to acknowledge as he ought. He and the Dutchess[10] are perfectly well and send their most respectfull Compliments to good Lord Auchenleck and to You and I have the honour to be with the utmost esteem and respect, My Dear Sir, Your most oblidged, humble Servant,

ALEXR. MCKONOCHIE

P. S. You need not take any notice of what I have said of the Chall. or Mansfield to any except to Lords A——— or M———o.[11]

[1] Alexander Maconochie or McKonochie (c. 1736–96), writer in Edinburgh, was one of Archibald Douglas's chief legal agents. JB described him as 'a little man of admirable common sense observation, activity and really a good share of neat taste, from having seen so much of the world' (Journ. 8 July 1769; Proof, in the Conjoined Processes, George-James Duke of Hamilton . . . against the Person Pretending to be Archibald Stewart, alias Douglas [1766] p. 435; Scots Mag. 1796, lviii. 289; Douglas Cause, p. 19).

[2] JB's Essence of the Douglas Cause was first advertised in the Lond. Chron. for 24 Nov. Three days earlier a pamphlet entitled Considerations on the Douglas Cause—a violently pro-Hamilton tract purporting to be written by an impartial gentleman who had examined the facts of the case—had appeared simultaneously in Edinburgh and London. An ardent supporter of Douglas's hastily wrote an 18-page response to the Considerations, entitled Some Observations on a Pamphlet Lately Published (i.e, The Considerations). Wilkie, without consulting JB, printed the Observations with JB's Essence, giving equal mention to both on the title-page. JB was outraged and demanded that Wilkie print an advertisement disclaiming the Observations (Lond. Chron. 3–5 Dec., xxii. 543; Lit. Car. pp. 39–41).

[3] For the Duke of Queensberry's connection with Archibald Douglas, see To the Duchess of Douglas, 13 Oct. 1766, n. 10.

[4] Edward Thurlow (1731–1806), barrister and Bedfordite M.P. for Tamworth, 1765–78, later (1778) Baron Thurlow, was already known for his bluff and common-sense manner of speaking. The Douglas party retained him for their Appeal after he had been overheard speaking in favour of Douglas in Nando's coffee-house (Lillywhite, p. 383). The legal skills he demonstrated in the Douglas Cause aided his eventual rise to the post of Lord Chancellor (Namier and Brooke iii. 529–31).

[5] The Hon. James Stuart Mackenzie (?1719–1800) of Rosehaugh, brother of the third Earl of Bute. He stood as M.P. for Argyllshire, 1742–47, for Buteshire, 1747–54, for Ayr Burghs, 1754–61, and for Ross-shire, 1761–80, and he was Lord Privy Seal for Scotland, 1763–65, 1766–1800. A man of strict honour, he disliked jobbery, and only rarely gave way to political pressure (Namier and Brooke iii. 503–07).

[6] MS. 'Lord'

[7] Camden was one of the two 'Law Lords'. This letter appears to furnish the only account of his pre-trial opinion of the cause (see Earlier Years, pp. 398, 554).

[8] William Murray (1705–93), M.P. for Boroughbridge, 1764–56, raised to the House of Lords as Lord Mansfield in 1756, and later (1776) created Earl of Mansfield (Namier and Brooke iii. 189). He was appointed Lord Chief Justice of the King's Bench in 1756, and was the other 'Law Lord' in the Douglas Cause Appeal (Earlier Years, pp. 398, 554). Mansfield's opinions as reported by Maconochie agree with those he expressed to JB on 20 May 1768. Speaking of the decision of the Court of Session, Mansfield said that he was 'sorry for the manner in which that cause was decided; so much time employed in a question of fact, when I should have decided it at a sitting. And such a division. It makes one suspect there was something more in that cause than the cause itself.' Yet Mansfield added that there were 'very respectable opinions on both sides', and reminded JB that he had not read the record of the cause (Journ.).

[9] Maconochie's estimate seems to be little more than a guess. As the decree of the Court of Session was reversed without a division of the House of Lords, the actual proportions are unknown.

[10] Margaret Douglas, Dowager Duchess of Douglas.

[11] Lords Auchinleck and Monboddo, who had voted for Douglas in the Court of Session.

To Lord Marischal, c. late December 1767 or early January 1768

Not reported. See From Lord Marischal, 26 Jan. 1768: 'I have put off from post to post wishing you and yours many happy new years, untill I should receive a letter from you. . . . I now have yours'.

Appendix A

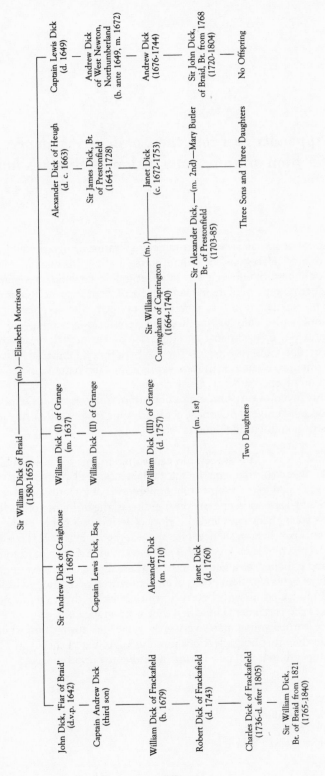

PARTIAL GENEALOGY OF THE DESCENDANTS OF SIR WILLIAM DICK OF BRAID,
WITH SPECIAL REFERENCE TO THE CONTROVERSY OVER THE 'BARONETCY' OF BRAID c. 1766-69.

269

Appendix B: From the Corsican Academy, extract from oration, copy in James Brown's hand.

Atque in hunc Locum, cum Me rapuerit impetus Orationis, ingrati equidem animi arguendus viderer, si Jacobum Boswelium, quo sane alius a Me numquam est viscis[1] Aut tenacior honestatis cultor, aut moribus, et indole amabilior, aut praestantior luminibus doctrinarum, Si illum inquam, juvenem, Scotorum, et literarum decus, ac cum primis nobilem decus, ac cum primis nobilem silentio praeterirem. Qui duobus abhinc annis, cum ad hoc Regnum venisset, tanto hujus Accademiae Amore captus est, ut ei ornadae, et augendae ab utrimis[2] florentissimi Regni Scotorum oris dono miserit egregios veterum Scriptorum Libros, ad historiam, et Poesim pertinentes, eosque Scotorum Typis, et membranarum quibus innoluti[3] sunt, concinnitate et ornamentis elegantissimos.

Quae tanta juvenis Lectissimi in nos liberalitas, cum erit intimis sensibus, non nostrum modo, sed universae Cyrneae gentis in omne tempus infixa, tum perpetuo illa erit nostris hominibus incitamento etc.

And since the thrust of my speech has carried me to this place, I would indeed seem to be convicted of an ungrateful spirit if James Boswell, than whom surely no one else ever seemed to me a more stubborn observer of integrity or more lovable in character and disposition or more outstanding in the brilliance of his learning, if, I say, this young Scotsman and the glory of letters and noble in the highest degree, I should pass over in silence. He, two years ago, when he had come to this kingdom, was taken by such love of this academy that he sent to it, needing to be enhanced and enriched, as a gift from the farthest shores of the most prosperous kingdom of the Scots excellent books of ancient writers pertaining to history and poetry, and most elegant with Scottish printing and with the refinement and decorations of the parchments in which they were wrapped.

The most learned young man's very great generosity towards us, when it has been fixed in the innermost affections not only of us, but of the entire Corsican race for all time, then it will be a lasting incentive to our people, etc.[4]

---

1. For 'viscis', read 'visus'
2. For 'utrimis', read 'ultimis'
3. For 'innoluti', read 'involuti'
4. Translation by Michael Behen.

Index

This is a simplified index (a fully analysed index will accompany Volume II) of proper names and places, but includes a few subject headings (e.g. London, Edinburgh). Sovereigns and British royal families are entered under their first names, and all others under their surnames with cross-references to their titles. A hyphen between page numbers (e.g. Burnaby, 154-57) does not necessarily indicate continuous discussion, but just that Burnaby is mentioned on all four pages. The Introduction is only lightly indexed. The following abbreviations are used: D. (Duke), M. (Marquess), E. (Earl), V. (Viscount), B. (Baron), Bt. (Baronet), P. (Prince), C. (Comte, Count), W.S. (Writer to the Signet), JB (James Boswell), MM (Margaret Montgomerie Boswell), SJ (Samuel Johnson).

The index was compiled mainly by Rachel McClellan with the assistance of Heather Barkley, Jessica Branch, and Marion Wells. Richard Cole composed the Boswell entry.

Accademia Cyrnaea, 253-54
Account of Corsica, JB presents, to Academy of Corte, 178
Addison, Joseph, 239, *Remarks . . . on Italy*, 104
Adie, Peter, Edinburgh surgeon, 76
Aesculapius, seal of, 205-06, 207, 211, 230-31
Agnew, Alexander, Judge Advocate, 35
Ainslie, George, of Pilton, later Bt., 94
Ainslie, John, of Newbottle, great-grandfather of preceding, 94
Ainslie, Robert, merchant in Bordeaux, son of George Ainslie, 93-94, 121, 123
Aitken, Rev. Edward, clergyman in Newcastle, 15, 50, 51, 184
Alderton, Maj. William, 55
Alembert, Jean d', mathematician and philosopher, 47, 52
Alemore, Lord. *See* Pringle, Andrew
Alexander, Robert, of Clermiston, 215
Almon, John, bookseller, *Speeches* [Douglas Cause], 192, 197-98, 201-02; *Parliamentary Register*, 248-49
Alnwick Castle, Northumberland, 207, 211
Anderson, Janet, aunt of Janet Graham, 34
Anderson, William, writer in Edinburgh, 192, 197-98, 201
Anhalt, Count Friedrich von, 242-43
Anhalt-Dessau, Leopold III Friedrich Franz, P. of, 145-46

Anson, Thomas, of Shugborough Hall, M.P. for Lichfield, 176-77, 189, 199
Armstrong, John, M.D., *Art of Preserving Health*, 60; *A Day: An Epistle to John Wilkes*, 103-04
Ashbury, Francis, naval officer, 154-55, 170-71
Askew, John, of Pallinsburn, 196, 199
Athlone, 5th E. of. *See* Reede-Ginckel, Frederik van
Auchinleck House, 85, 163

Bacon, Francis, 7, 8
Bagnall Clarke, Godfrey, M.P., 16
Balbi, Giuseppe, Vice-Consul in Leghorn, 32, 66, 123
Barbieri, Giovanni Francesco, painter, 162
Barclay, James, bailie, 161
Baretti, Giuseppe Marc'Antonio, critic and writer, 40, 86-87, 108-09, 111-13, 238-39, 249-50
Barrington, Daines, barrister, *Observations on the Statutes . . . from Magna Carta*, 172-73
Barrington, William Wildman, 2nd V. Barrington, 173
Beatson, Capt. William, seaman, 226-27, 248, 251
Béchameil, Madeleine, 22
Bell's Brewery, Edinburgh, 242, 244
Bellegarde, François-Eugène-Robert, C. de, 47,

81, 115, 242-43

Bellevue, Clèves, country estate, 47

Bennet, Capt. William, naval officer, 263-65

Bennet, Rev. William, minister of Duddingston, 215

Besoyen, Maria Philippina Jacoba (Pieck) van, wife of following, 43

Besoyen, Daniel A. le Leu de Wilhelm de Bantousel, Heer van, 43

Bianconi, Sgr., Sienese gentleman, 257

Black, Joseph, chemist, 21

Blair, Catherine ('the Princess', 'the Heiress'), xxxix, xliii, 187, 204, 219, 247-48, 261

Boninton, Bonnington, Lady, 184-85

Bonnières, Adrien-Louis de, Comte de Guines, 186

Bosville family, history of, 56

Bosville, Charles, 264

Bosville, Diana (Wentworth), wife of Godfrey, 38, 172-73

Bosville, Elizabeth Diana ('Di'), dau. of following, 38, 54-55

Bosville, Godfrey, of Gunthwaite Hall, xxxv-xxxvi, 16, 24, 37-39, 44, 54-56, 172-73, 191, 234-35, 260, 263-66

Bosville, Julia, dau. of preceding, 38-39, 54, 172-73

Bosville, Robert, Constable of Pontefract Castle, 100

Bosville, Thomas, army officer, younger son of Godfrey, 55-56, 172-73

Bosville, Capt. William, bro. of preceding, 38-39, 54-55, 172-73, 264-65

Boswell, Alexander, Lord Auchinleck, xliii, xlvii, 5, 11-15, 17, 19, 21, 24-25, 27, 31; suffers from strangury, 35; 53, 67, 84-85, 98, 106, 133, 144, 148-49, 163, 167-68; his speech on Douglas Cause, 216-17; 221, 248, 261-62, 267

Boswell, Claud Irvine, of Balmuto, 17, 61, 71, 89, 96, 151

Boswell, David, 2nd Laird of Auchinleck, 102

Boswell, David, later Thomas David, bro. of JB, 15, 35, 63, 73, 76, 105-06, 168, 221, 252, 262-63

Boswell, Lady Elizabeth (Bruce), JB's grand-mother, 129-130

Boswell, Euphemia (Erskine), 1st Lady Auchinleck, mother of JB, 4-5, 8, 11-12, 14

Boswell, James, 'Old James', grandfather of JB, 48-49

BOSWELL, JAMES

General: and Corsica: campaign to get government support for, 1, 2, 3, 5, 9, 31, 36, 64-66, 68-69, 107-08, 117-19, 139-40; books for, 57-8, 110-11, 119-20, 151-52, 175-78, 222, 238-41, 246, 253; return from Grand Tour, 1, 3-5, 9-10, 12-13, 50; death of mother, 6-15, 12-13,

18, 31, 45; depression, 4, 73, 90, 132, 227-29; and father, 12-14, 25, 34-35, 44-45, 53, 67, 91-92, 116, 149, 235; and brothers, 15, 35, 50, 56, 61-62, 73, 105, 199, 221, 252; values heart over head, 25; in Moffat for waters, 27, 29-30, 33-35; oddities of, 30, 104-05; interest in genealogy, 42-43, 56, 100-02, 129; courts Zélide, 46-47, 81, 114-16, 183, 186, 247; suffers from malaria, 48-49, 75-76; mistress of, 63, 66-67, and child by, 151, 156-57, 211-12, 217, 261-62; researches Braid Baronetcy, 69-70, 93-96, 122-23, 147, 160, 175-77, 189-90, 200-01, 203, 204, 206-10, 213-16, 246-48; venereal disease, 88-89, 144, 148, 191, 193, 196-97, 205, 209, 211, 230, 234, 257, 261-62; and Douglas Cause, 125, 130-31, 181, 197-98, 216-17, 241, 243; has stock of ideas, 132; buys Dalblair, 147-49, 167-68, 245; courts Catherine Blair, 187, 218-19, 228-29, 247-48, 255-57, 260-62

Law Practice: studying Scots law with father, 12-15, 17, 24, 29, 34-35, 42-43, 98-99; admitted to Faculty of Advocates, 42-43, 45, 48-51, 76-77; attitude towards law, 53; criminal causes: James Haddow, 71-72, John Reid, 76, 79, 82-83, 86, 88, 93-96, 207, Garlieston rioters, 84-85, 133, 165-67, Robert Hay, 120-21, Stewarton rioters, 160-61, 164-65, Matthew Hay and John McClure, 171-75; civil causes: Macdonells, 61-62, 162, Archibald Steel, 133, 150, James Gilkie, 134-35, Mackenzies, 137-38, Sir Alexander Dick, 141-43, 146-47; success as advocate, 106, 118, 144, 151; happiness as advocate, 108-39

Writings:

Account of Corsica, research for, 31-33, 64-70, 76-77, 94, 102, 110-13, 116-17, 122-27, 139, 152-55, 194-95, 231-32; quoted, 32-33, 67, 70, 195, 231, 233, 239; writing, 75, 78, 132, 139, 147, 172; translations of, 92; advertisements for, 101, 110-11, 226-27; describes to Lord Chatham, 139; advises publisher of, 180, 184, 187-89, 191-93, 196-97, 201-02, 216-17, 219, 231, 236-37, 247-49, 255; proof-reads, 213, revises, 216-17, 233-34

Collection of Original Poems by Scotch Gentlemen, vol. 2, 18, 102, 214

Critical Strictures on Elvira, 227

Disputatio Juridica Ad Tit. X. Lib. XXXIII. Pand. De Supellectile Legata, 39-40, 52-53, 57, 104-05

Dorando, A Spanish Tale, 16, 151, 158, 169, 188-89, 212, 229-30, 244-45

The Douglas Cause, 181

Essence of the Douglas Cause, 16, 204, 216-17, 260, 266-67
Letters Between the Honourable Andrew Erskine and James Boswell, Esq., 18, 36, 120, 227
Letters of the Right Honourable Lady Jane Douglas, 16, 204, 208, 216
Newspaper articles: on Corsica, 16, 24, 94, 101, 155, 195, 208, on Douglas Cause, 16, 212, 225-26, 248, 252, on travelling, 258-59
Boswell, John, 3rd Laird of Auchinleck, 71
Boswell, John, M.D., bro. of Lord Auchinleck, 21, 43
Boswell, John, of Balmuto, father of Claud Boswell, 17
Boswell, Lt. John, bro. of JB, 15, 35, 56, 184, 199
Boswell, John, 'young Knockroon', writer in Ayr, 70-71, 150
Boswell, Margaret (Montgomerie) (MM), xxxix, xlvii, 15, 17, 19, 81, 149, 165
Bourgeois, Lewis and David, perfumers, 124
Bristol, 15
Brown, Ann Elizabeth, dau. of Robert, 9, 10, 115-16
Brown, Catharine (Kinloch), wife of Robert, 9, 10, 115
Brown, Charles, defender of James Haddow, 71
Brown, George, Lord Coalston, 17, 27, 165
Brown, James, law clerk to JB, bro. of William, 165, 166, 203-04
Brown, Rev. Robert, 9-11, 114-16, 240-43
Brown, William, later Principal Aberdeen Univ., 10
Brown, William, writer in Kilmarnock, 161, 164-65, 204
Brown, Rev. William, D.D., bro. of Robert, 240, 243
Bruce, Alexander, 2nd E. of Kincardine, JB's great-grandfather, 12, 129
Bruce, Charles, glazier in Edinburgh, 79
Bruce, Lady Elizabeth, dau. of Alexander Bruce, wife of 'Old James', 12, 49, 130
Bruce, Robert, Lord Kennet, 133-35
Bruce, Veronica (van Aerssen), C. of Kincardine, wife of 2nd E., 12, 129-30
Buccleuch, 2nd D. of. *See* Scott, Francis
Buchan, 10th E. of. *See* Erskine, Henry David
Buchanan, George, Scots historian and poet, 57-58; *Franciscanus et Fratres*, 102
Burchard, Cuno, Baron von Pless, 85
Burke, Edmund, statesman, his estate at Gregories, 149
Burnaby, Rev. Andrew, chargé d'affaires, Leghorn, 101, 122, 158-59, 174, 222, 230-31, 240, 245-46; *Journal of a Tour to Corsica*, 65-66, 68, 194-95
Burnett, Alexander, secretary to Sir Andrew Mitchell, 145-46

Burnett, James, Lord Monboddo, 150-51, 235, 267-68
Burney, Fanny, 82
Bute, 3rd. E. of. *See* Stuart, John
Buttafoco, Col. Matteo, Corsican soldier, 22, 24
Butter, Henry, factor of Clunie estates, 62, 162
Butter, William, physician, 200-01
Butterfield, John, felon, 121
Buxton, Derbyshire, 55-56

Cairncross *v.* Heatly, 93-94
Cairncross, Hugh, mason in Galashiels, 94
Cairncross, William, 94
Caithness, 9th E. of. *See* Sinclair, William
Calas, Jean, trial of, and aftermath, 21
Calvin, John, 137
Campbell, James, of Treesbank, 15
Campbell, Jean (or Jane), cousin of Lord Auchinleck. *See* Reid, Jean
Campbell, John, *Present State of Europe*, 32
Capraia, Corsica, 122-23, 126-27, 147, 159-60, 175, 194-95, 211
Capuchins at Corte, Corsica, 121, 123
Cardross, Lord. *See* Erskine, David Steuart
Carmontelle, Louis, engraver, 21
Carruthers, Christopher, friend of JB and Johnston, 34
Cass, David, 135-36, 159
Castillon, J. F. Salvemini de, mathematician in Utrecht, 9-11
Cebes, Table of, 205-06
Cervantes, *Don Quixote*, 149
Chais, Rev. Charles, Swiss theologian, 19-21
Chalmer, John Muir, W.S., 146, 150
Chalmers, John, of Bonnyton or Bonnington, 184
Chambers, Sir William, architect, 41
Champgrand, J. F. Goury de, mapmaker, 32
Chandler, Samuel, *Life of King David*, 38
Charles Edward, Prince, 'Young Pretender', 24, 27, 61, 94, 162-63
Charles III, King of Naples, 124
Charles, Prince, Gov.-Gen. of Pays-Bas, 116
Charlotte, Queen of George III, King of Great Britain and Ireland, 82
Charray, François, clerk, foreign affairs office, Versailles, 73, 229-30
Charrière, Charles-Emmanuel de, husband of Belle de Zuylen, 47
Chasteler et de Courcelles, Marquis de, 116
Chatham, E. of. *See* Pitt, William
Chetwynd, William Richard, 3rd V. Chetwynd, 264-65
Chiesley, Rev. John, 214-15
Choiseul, Etienne-François, Duc de, 246
Churchill, Charles, *Rosciad*, 58
Chéron de Boismorand, Claude-Jean, 8
Cicero, *Cato Maior, De Senectute*, 12-13
Clarke, Samuel, printer, 258
Cleriheugh, tavern keeper, Edinburgh, 95

Clive, Robert, B. Clive of Plassey, ('Nabob Clive'), 159, 217-18

Clomfort, ?farmer, 96-97

Clyde-Forth Canal, 141-42, 163-64

Coalston, Lord. *See* Brown, George

Cocchi, Raimondo, antiquarian and writer, 222, 245-46

Cochrane, Archibald, Lord Cochrane, inventor, later 9th E. of Dundonald, 220-21

Cochrane, Basil, bro. of 8th E. of Dundonald, JB's great uncle, 16-17, 22, 26-27, 45, 56-57, 167-68, 198-99

Cochrane, Euphemia, JB's grandmother, 74

Cochrane, Lady Grizel, dau. of 8th E. of Dundonald, 33, 180-81

Cochrane, Thomas, 8th E. of Dundonald, bro. of JB's grandmother, 98-99, 220-21

Cochrane, William, 1st E. of Dundonald, 99

Cochrane, William, partner in Coutts' London bank, 32

Cole, Charles Nalson, lawyer, 232, 251

Cologne, Latin Gazettes of, 114-15

Coltellini, Marco, publisher and librettist, 32

Colvill, Rev. Robert, poet, 214-15

Colvill, Walter, baker, 214-15

Colville, Alexander, 7th Lord Colville, 44

Condillac, Etienne Bonnot de, 229

Constable Burton, Yorkshire, 233-34

Constable, George, writer in Edinburgh, 242, 244

Conway, Lt.-Gen. Henry Seymour, 2

Corbett, Charles, the younger, bookseller, 208

Cornaro, Luigi, 75-76, *Discorsi della vita sobria,* 76

Corsica: xxxvi-xxxvii, 1763 Proclamation, 1; climate, daily life, 8; Corte, Univ. of, 32; Paoli's Manifesto of 1767, 117-18

Coutts, John, and Co., bankers, 15

Covington, Lord. *See* Lockhart, Alexander

Craufurd, George, son of following, 115

Craufurd, James, merchant in Rotterdam, 28, 114, 243

Craufurd, James, son of preceding, 28, 115

Craufurd, Patrick, son of James, 28, 115, 240, 243

Craufurd, Patrick, of Auchenames, M.P., bro. of James the elder, 28

Crawford, 19th E. of. *See* Lindsay, John

Crawford, James, merchant in Dundee, 89-90

Crocchi, Pietro, Abate, 4-5, 156-57, 256-57

Croker, John Wilson, 109

Cullen, William, M.D., F.R.S., 29-30, 252

Culross Abbey, Fife, 180-81

Cummyng, James, herald-painter, 215-16

Cuninghame, Sir David, of Corsehill, 15, 161

Cunningham, Sir John, of Caprington, Bt., 78-79

Cunningham, Sir William, of Caprington, Bt., father of Sir Alexander Dick, 59, 79

Currie, James, outpensioner of Chelsea Hospital, 160-61

Currie, Jean, witness, 167

Dalblair, Auchinleck estate, 147, 149, 167-68, 186

Dalmahoy, estate near Edinburgh, 209-10

Dalrymple, Sir David, Lord Hailes, 199-200, 205-06, 215-16, 233-34

Dance, James. *See* Love, James

Dance-Holland, Nathaniel, painter, 152

Darfield, Yorkshire, Bosville family estate, 99

Davel, Theodore, Neapolitan merchant, 123-24

Davenport, Richard, from Derbyshire, 52, 73, 148, 218-19

Davies, Susannah (Yarrow), wife of Thomas, 58, 111

Davies, Thomas, bookseller, xxxvii-xxxviii, 53-54, 57-58, 70, 83-84, 86, 101, 110-11, 136, 151-52, 216, 238-39, 260, 262-63

Deffand, Mme. du, 47, 92

Degenfeld-Schomburg, Friedrich Christoph, C. von, 42-43, 46

Degenfeld-Schomburg, Louise Susannah, C. von, wife of preceding, 43, 47

DeLeyre, Alexandre, 5-9, 73, 90-93, 191, 227-30; *Analyse de la philosophie de . . . Bacon,* 9

Deleyre, Caroline-Alexandrine (Loiseau) 7-8

Dempster, George, M.P., 11, 15, 16, 18, 33, 54, 63, 70, 89, 101-02, 226, 236-37

Denis, Marie-Louise (Mignot), niece of Voltaire, 132-33

Denis, Nicholas-Charles, husband of preceding, 133

Despine, Joseph, Savoyard, 154

Dick, family of, xxxviii-xxxix, 93-94

Dick, Sir Alexander, of Prestonfield, Bt., xxxviii, xlv-xlvi, 58-60, 70, 74-76, 78-79, 95-96, and Clyde-Forth Canal, 141-42, 147; dispute over Duddingston Loch, 141-43; family by second wife, 147; 160, 163-64, 175-76, 189-90, 199-201, 204-07; and Orkney claim/debt, 209-10, 213-16; 235, 243, 247

Dick, Andrew, of West Newton, son of Louis Dick, 123

Dick, Andrew, grandfather of John Dick, 189-90

Dick, Sir Andrew, of Craighouse, 190, 210, 213

Dick, Anne (Bragg), wife of John Dick, 33, 66, 69, 110, 230, 246-47

Dick, Anne, younger dau. of Sir Alexander's 1st marriage, 147

Dick, Sir James, of Prestonfield, grandfather of Sir Alexander, 59, 79, 123

Dick, Janet, dau. of Sir James Dick, 123

Dick, Janet, elder dau. of Sir Alexander's 1st marriage, 58-59, 147, 209

Dick, John, son of Sir Alexander's 2nd marriage, 163-64

Dick, Sir John, British Consul in Leghorn,

xxxviii-xxxix, 5, 18, 22, 28, 31, 36, 63, 66,68, 76-77, 94, 109-10, 113, in England for a year, 117, 121, 125, 147, 158-60, 163; in London, 169, 173, 175-76, 181-82, 186, 189-91; in Durham and Newcastle, 196, 198; 'male family Head', 200, 203-04, 215, 230-31, 246-48

Dick, Lewis (or Louis), son of Sir Andrew Dick of Craighouse, 189-190, 213

Dick, Lewis (or Louis), son of Sir Wm. Dick of Braid, 69, 123, 189-190

Dick, (Mary Butler), Lady, 2nd wife of Sir Alexander Dick, 59, 147, 230

Dick, Sir William, of Braid, xxxviii, 69-70, 94, 123, 190, 209-10, 214, 246

Dick, William, son of Sir Alexander, 93-94

Dilly, Charles, bookseller, bro. of following, xxxvii-xxxviii, 58, 111, 197

Dilly, Edward, bookseller, xxxvi-xxxviii, 58, 111, 184, to publish *Corsica*, 187-88, 191-93, 196-98, 201-02, 207-08; 219, 225-27, 231, 234, 236-37, 247, 248-49, 251-52, 255, 257-59

Dodds, Mrs. JB's mistress, 57, 63, 66, 212, 261-62

Donaldson, Alexander, bookseller, 22, 105, *Original Poems By ... Scotch Gentlemen*, 223-24

Donaldson, John, bookseller, 104-05

Douglas, Archibald James Edward Douglas, 1st B., 149

Douglas, Archibald Douglas, 1st D. of Douglas, 70-71

Douglas, Catherine, niece of Sir Alexander Dick, 148, 200-01, 209

Douglas, Charles, 3rd D. of Queensberry, Lord Justice General, 72, 266-67

Douglas, Heron, and Co. (Ayr Bank), 30

Douglas, James, 13th E. of Morton, astronomer and architect, 210

Douglas, Janet, niece of Sir Alexander Dick, 148, 200-01, 209

Douglas, Margaret, Dowager Duchess of Douglas, 70-72, 267

Douglas, Sir Robert, of Glenbervie and Ardit, Bt., 216

Douglas, William, 1st M. of Douglas, 72

Douglas, William, 8th E. of Morton, 209

Douglas Cause, 72, 149, 181, 197-98, 224, 241, 243, 245, 251-52, 264, 267, Almon and Anderson editions of speeches, 216-17

Drongan, Ayrshire, 85

Drummond, Andrew, and Co., bankers in Charing Cross, 123, 169-70, 175-76, 182, 231

Drummond, John, son of Andrew Drummond, 123

Drummond, William, bookseller, 168-69

Duddingston Loch, 75

Dudley, Sir Robert, agriculturalist, 32-33

Dun, Elizabeth, dau. of John Dun, 97

Dun, Isabella, sis. of preceding, 97

Dun, Rev. John, minister of Auchinleck parish, 13, 14, 33, 44, 48, 84, 96-97

Dun, Mary (Wilson), wife of preceding, 12, 13

Dunbar, James, 214

Duncan, Capt. Adam, naval officer, 149

Duncan, Henrietta (Dundas), wife of preceding, 149

Duncan, James, burgess of Moffat, 97

Dundas, Henry, *later* V. Melville, 237

Dundas, Jean (Grant), wife of Robert Dundas, 148

Dundas, Sir Lawrence, Bt., M.P. for Newcastle-under-Lyme, 209-10

Dundas, Robert, Lord President of the Court of Session, 95-96, 134, 143-44, 148-49

Dundonald, E. of. *See* Cochrane, Thomas

Dunk, George Montagu, E. of Halifax, 176-78

Dunlop, John, 165

Dunsinnan, Lord. See Nairne, William

Dupont, Rev. Pierre Loumeau, Huguenot minister in Edinburgh, 19-22, 134-37

Dupré de Sainte-Maur, Nicolas-François, 8

Dutens, Louis, on Grand Tour, 30

Duyn, Adam François van der, son of Heer van Maasdam, Dutch cavalry officer, 43

Duyn, Willem Hendrik van der, bro. of preceding, 43

Echlin, Sir Henry, Bt., 103-104

EDINBURGH: Prestonfield House, 59, 79, 93, 182, 200-01; Arthur's Seat; 59, 78-79, Bell's Brewery, 242, 244; Brucehill (Belmont), 78-79; Clermiston, 78-79; Corstorphine, 78-79; Court of Session, 94; North Loch, New Town, 95-96; Star and Garter Tavern, 95; Tolbooth, 115; Theatre Royal, 179-80, 262-63; The Cross, 181; Peter Ramsay's Red Lyon Inn, 196, 199-200, 204; Pinkie House, 199; Mundell's School, 215

Edwards, Richard, Vice-Consul, Leghorn, 151, 159, 180, 259-60

Eglinton, 10th E. of. *See* Montgomerie, Alexander

Eglinton, 11 E. of. *See* Montgomerie, Archibald

Elibank, Lord. *See* Murray, Alexander

Eliott, George Augustus, General, 115-16

Elliot, Sir Gilbert, Lord Minto, 19, 21, 142-43

Ellis, Henry, explorer, 113

Elphinstone sisters, 218-19

Elphinstone, Charles, 10th Lord Elphinstone, 218

Elphinstone, Clementina (Fleming), Lady, wife of preceding, 212-13, 218

Elphinstone, George Keith, naval officer, 217-19

Elphinstone, William Fullerton, East India Sea Service, 217-19

Erasmus, 57

Erskine, Alexander, 5th E. of Kellie, 18

Erskine, Hon. Andrew, son of preceding, 18, 26, 33, 120, 223-24

Erskine, David Steuart, Lord Cardross, *later* 11th E. of Buchan, 1, 3, 37, 109, 138, 140, 236

Erskine, Euphemia (Cochrane), JB's grandmother, 159

Erskine, Henry David, 10th E. of Buchan, 37

Erskine, John, 7th E. of Mar, 1

Eskgrove, Lord. *See* Rae, David

Esplins, Mr., ?postal clerk, 162

Falconer, Anthony Adrian, 7th Lord Falconer, 245

Farquhar, Alexander, of Gilmillscroft, 133

Fauconnerie, Nicolas de Catinat de la, marshal of France, 67-68

Favart, Charles-Simon, playwright, 241, 243

Ferdinand, Don, Prince of Parma, 228-29

Ferguson, James, younger of Pitfour, 77, 122-23, 160, 175-76, 189, 190, 206-07

Fergusson, Sir Adam, of Kilkerran, Bt., 131

Fergusson, Alexander, of Caitlock, 93

Fergusson, Joseph, tutor to Boswell children, 26, 68, 98-99

Ferney, France, 132-33

Fitzherbert, William, M.P. for Derby, 148

Fleming, Robert, printer in Edinburgh, 237

Flexney, William, bookseller, 36, 226-27

Foley, Robert-Ralph, banker in Paris, 25-26, 106

Forbes, Duncan, surgeon, 261-62

Forbes, George, woollen draper, 144-45

Fordyce, Rev. George, 215

Fordyce, Rev. James, D.D., Scottish divine, 225-27

Fort William, 62

Foulis, Robert and Andrew, printers in Glasgow, 58, 110-11, 151, 169, 187-88, 192, 196-98, 201-02, 203-04, 251-52

Fraser, Alexander, Lord Strichen, 60, 200

Frazer, George, in the excise, 15, 17, 142-43

Frederick II, King of Prussia ('the Great'), 24-25, 39, 55, 245

Freeman, Robert, publisher, 38

Froment, Denis-Daniel de, Sardinian army officer, 145-46

Froment, Emet-Ulla, Mme. de, wife of preceding, 145-46, 169, 185, 211-12, 217-19, 244-45

Fullarton, William, ('the nabob'), 187, 247-48

Garden, Francis, Lord Gardenstone, 141-43

Garlieston rioters, 84-85, 133, 165-67

Garrick, David, *Cymon*, 41, 111

Gayot, Mme., wife of Félix-Louis, 104

Gayot, François-Marie, Royal Praetor of Strasbourg, 102

Gayot, Félix-Louis, son of preceding, 102

Geelvinck, Catharina Elisabeth (Hasselaer), 115-16

Geneva, 8

Gentleman, Francis, 23, 40, 101, 178-80, *Royal Fables*, 23; *Characters*, 41; *Oroonoko*, 180

George III, King of Great Britain and Ireland, 40-41, 73, 175-76

Gili, l'Abate, secretary to Paoli, 69-70

Gilkie v. Wallace, 150

Gilkie, James, ?writer in Edinburgh, 134-35

Goldsmith, Oliver, 57-58; *The Traveller*, 238-39; *The Good Natured Man*, 250

Gondi, François-Paul de, Cardinal de Retz, 75-76

Gordon, mail carrier, 74

Gordon, Alexander, Customs officer, 171-72

Gordon, Rev. John, Principal of College for Scots Catholics, 26-27

Gorkum, Holland, 42-43

Graffigni, headmaster of Norlands Academy, 137

Graham, James, 1st M. of Montrose, 75-76

Graham, Janet, poet, 33-34

Graham, John, burgess of Moffat, 98

Graham, Margaret, sis. of Janet, 34

Graham, Nicol, of Gartmore, 21

Graham, William, of Gartmore, son of preceding, 21, 85

Graham, William, of Shaw, Dumfriesshire, 27, 34, 68

Gray, Thomas, poet, 1

Gregories, Burke's estate, 149

Grimaldi da Campoloro, Leonardo, mapmaker, 32

Grimm, Friedrich Melchior von, journalist and critic, and subscription for Calas, 21

Guiffardière, Charles de, French reader to Queen Charlotte, 81-82

Guines, Comte de. *See* Bonnières, Adrien-Louis de

Gunthwaite Hall, Yorkshire, 39

Haddow, James, 71

Haddow, James, son of preceding, felon, 71, 76

Hailes, Lord. *See* Dalrymple, Sir David, Bt.

Halifax, E. of. *See* Dunk, George Montagu

Hamilton, Lord Archibald, son of 5th D. of Hamilton, 223-24

Hamilton, James George Hamilton, 6th D. of, 149

Hamilton, James, 8th E. of Abercorn, 75, 142

Hamilton, John, of Sundrum, 49-50, 179-80

Harpe, Jean-François de la, *Le Comte de Warwik*, 241, 243

Harris, William, merchant in Ayr, 171-72

Hawke, Edward, army officer, 263-65

Hawker, Edmund, naval officer, 124

Hay, Matthew, farmer, 171-72, 174-75

Hay, Robert, accused of assault, 120-21

Hayes Place, Chatham's estate, 2

Heatly, William, in Cairncross v. Heatly, 94

Hennert, Johan Frederik, Professor of Mathematics, Utrecht, 9-10

Herculanium, 'Villa of the Papyri', 124

Heron, Jean (Home-Drummond), dau. of Lord Kames, wife of following, 30

Heron, Patrick, of Kirroughtree, 29-30·

Herries and Co., bankers, 123-24

Herries, Robert, partner in Coutts' London bank, 32

Hervey, Rev. Frederick Augustus, later 4th E. of Bristol, 65-66, 113

History of the Man after God's Own Heart, 37-38

Holdford, James, British consul in Genoa, 32, 113

Holstein, Christian Frederik, B. of, 242-43

Home, Agatha (Drummond), wife of Lord Kames, 27, 29

Home, George, of Blair Drummond, son of following, 30

Home, Henry, Lord Kames, 29, 209

Hoole, John, translator, *Metastasio*, 152

Horace: *Epistles*, 73, 105; *Odes*, 92; *Satires*, 109, 143

Howard, Frederick, 5th E. of Carlisle, 50

Huet, Daniel-Théodore, 81-82

Hume, David, 8, 41, 46-47, 51-52, 73, 91-93, 96-97, 101, 132, 136-37, 218-19; *History of England*, 80-82

Hunter, James, M.D., 29-30, 35

Hunter, Mrs. James, wife of preceding, 29, 35, 68

Inverwidden, Macdonell farm, 62

Irving, William, of Bonshaw, 200-01

Isleworth, Surrey, 40-41

Jafar, Mir, nawab, 218

James Francis Edward Stuart, 'Old Pretender', 163

Jaussin, Louis-Amand, *Mémoires historiques*, 62, 113

Jenour, Matthew, publisher, 135-36

Jesuits, expelled from Spain, 163-64, 176-77, 190, 194-95, 211

Johnson, Samuel (SJ), xl, 40, 53, 57-58, 68, 84, his degrees, 110-11; 169, 178, 249-50; *Dictionary*, 114; *Idler*, 152

Johnston, Archibald, 68

Johnston, Daniel, 88-89

Johnston, John, of Grange, 13, 21, 33-34, 43, 98, 113

Johnstoun, John, writer in Glasgow, 79, 82-83, 86

Joseph II, Holy Roman Emperor, 129

Kames, Lady. *See* Home, Agatha

Kames, Lord. *See* Home, Henry

Kay, John, portaitist, 150-51

Keith, Alexander, of Dunottar and Ravelston, W.S., antiquarian, 145, 211-12, 217-18, 245

Keith, George, 10th E. Marischal of Scotland, xl, xlvi, 24-25, 47, 57, 67-68, 124-25, 144-46, 169-70, 185-86, 203, 211-12, 217-19, 231, 244-45, 268

Keith, Margaret (Dick), wife of following, 79

Keith, Robert, 'Ambassador' Keith, 79

Kellie, 5th E. of. *See* Erskine, Alexander

Kemnay, Aberdeenshire, 146

Kincardine, 2nd E. of. *See* Bruce, Alexander

Kinloch, Lt. Archibald Gordon, son of following, 114-15, 151, 182-83, 241

Kinloch, David, of Gilmerton, 115, 151

Kinloch, Francis, son of preceding, 115

Kinloch, Sir James, Bt., expatriate, 10

Kinloch, Marguerite Susanne, dau. of preceding, 10, 115

Kircheisen, Caroline, 92

Kitchin, Thomas, mapmaker, 188

La Trappe, Cistercian monastery, Normandy, 229

Labadie, Jean, leader of Labadist sect, 130

Laidlaw, Robert, 83

Lascelles, Edwin, 235

Le Vasseur, Marie-Thérèse, mistress of Rousseau, 6, 8, 14, 51-52, 54

Lee, John, actor, 262-63

LeJay, Guy Michel, polyglot Bible, 137

Leoni, Francesco, gunsmith, 28

Leyden Gazette, 122-23

Leven, 6th E. of. *See* Melville, David

Linder, Mr., tutor to Willem von Spaen, 46-47

Lindsay, John, 19th E. of Crawford, 60

Little, Elizabeth, wife of following, 98

Little, James, vintner, 97-98

Lockhart, Alexander, Lord Covington, 50-51

Logan, Hugh, 'Laird of Logan', 85

LONDON: 'The London Season', 192

    Buildings and Institutions: Drury Lane Theatre, 23, 111, 250, Covent Garden Theatre, 250, King's Theatre, Haymarket, 250; Beefsteak Club, 25, the Temple, 99, Westminster School, 38

    Churches and Chapels: Portland Chapel, 87

    Taverns, Coffee-houses: Prince of Orange, 86-87

    Streets and Squares: Gt. Russell St., 38, 99, 235, Queen Anne St., 87, Haymarket, 124, 250, St. James's Park, 130, Grosvenor Sq., 223-24; Portman Sq., 223-24

    Miscellaneous: Kensington, 137, Chelsea, 155

Lord Chancellor. *See* Pratt, Charles

Lord President. *See* Dundas, Robert

Louis XV, King of France, 104, 127

Love, Mrs. James (née Hooper), 23

Love, James, actor and theatre manager, 23, 40-41, 152

Lowth, Martha, dau. of Robert, 60

Lowth, Mary, wife of following, 59-60

Lowth, Robert, D.D., prebendary of Durham Cathedral, 59-60, 239
Lowth, Robert, son of preceding, 60
Lowther, Sir James, later 1st E. of Lonsdale, 234-35
Lumisden, Andrew, secretary to Pretenders, 162-63

Maasdam, Aarnout Joost, B. van der Duyn, Heer van, Dutch general, 42-43
Maasdam, Anna Margaretha (van Aerssen), B. van der Duyn, wife of preceding, 43
Maasdam children, 42-44
Macaulay, Catharine Sawbridge, historian, 230-31, 236, 239
Macdonald, Lady, wife of following. See Bosville, Elizabeth Diana
Macdonald, Sir Alexander, of Sleat, Bt., later 1st B. 100, 235
Macdonald, Jessie, of Keppoch, 2nd wife of following, 61
Macdonell, Alexander, Highlander, 61, 162
Macdonell, Ranald, bro. of preceding, Jacobite, 61, 162
Macfarlane, Lady Elizabeth (Erskine), dau. of 5th E. of Kellie, 44, 45, 51, 56, 120, 181
Mackenzie, Sir Alexander, of Gairloch, 137-38
Mackenzie, Hector, Mackenzie v. Mackenzie, 138
Mackenzie, Hon. James Stuart, bro. of 3rd E. of Bute, 266-67
Mackenzie, Roderick, of Redcastle, 137-38
Mackintosh, Aeneas (Angus), 22nd Chief of Clan Chattan, 161-62
Mackintosh, Anne (Lady Mackintosh), wife of preceding, 161-62
Mackintosh, Grisel, 1st wife of Alexander Macdonnell, 61
Mackintosh, Robert, of Ashintully, advocate, 237
MacLeod, Bannatyne, 83
MacLeod, Norman, of MacLeod, 22nd Chief of Clan MacLeod, 234-35
Maconochie, Alexander, writer in Edinburgh, 260, 266-68
Macpherson, Donald, of Breakachy, 145
Macpherson, Duncan, bro. of Lauchlan, 145
Macpherson, Duncan, son of following, 62
Macpherson, Evan, of Clunie (or Cluny), 62, 162
Macpherson, James, Fingal; Works of Ossian, 79
Macpherson, Lauchlan, son of Donald, of Breakachy, 144-45
Macpherson, Rev. Robert, 62, 162
Maillebois, Jean-Baptiste-François Desmarets, Seigneur de, 20-22
Maillebois (Marie-Emmanuelle d'Algère), Madame la Maréchale de, widow of preceding, 20, 22
Maitland, ?David, naval officer, 170-71

Maitland, Rev. James, 165-66
Malton, Yorkshire, 23
Mann, Sir Horace, Bt., 129
Mansfield, 5th E. of. See Murray, William
Mante, Thomas, British/French double agent, 40-41
Maria Frederica, B. van Reede-Ginckel, 80-81
Maria Louisa, Grand Duchess of Tuscany, 129
Maria Theresa, Empress of Austria, 39
Maria of Braganza, Portuguese Infanta, 24
Maryburgh, 62
Massesi, Giuseppe Maria, Paoli's secretary; assassin, 195
Maurice, Antoine, Professor of Theology at Geneva, 136-37
Maurice, Antoine, the younger, succeeded father, 136-37
Maxwell, Beatrix, 36
Mazerac, François, valet to JB, 9-10, 240, 243
McClure, David, of Shawwood, conspirator, 171-72, 173-75
McClure, John, bro. of preceding, conspirator, 171, 174-75
MoClure, James, ?Ayrshire smuggler, 175
McDonald, James, army officer, 155
McMurtrie, John, tide-waiter (customs officer), 171-72
McQuhae, Rev. William, tutor to Boswell sons, 44, 48, 70
Meason (or Mason), Gilbert, Edinburgh merchant, 240, 243
Melville, David, 6th E. of Leven and 5th E. of Melville, 259
Meynell, Hugo, M.P. for Lichfield, 264-65
Mickle, William Julius, translator and writer, 179-80
Miller, Thomas, of Barskimming, Lord Justice Clerk, 19, 21, 71-72
Milton, John, Paradise Lost, 7, 8
Mitchell, Alexander, of Hallglenmuir, 186-87
Mitchell, Sir Andrew, Under-Secretary of State for Scotland, 119, 145-46
Moffat, Dumfriesshire, 27, 29-30
Monboddo, Lord. See Burnett, James
Monnet, Jean, director of the Opéra-Comique, Paris, 41
Montagu, Edward Wortley, husband of following, 56
Montagu, Lady Mary Wortley, mother of Lady Bute, 56
Montgomerie, Margaret. See Boswell, Margaret (Montgomerie) (MM)
Montgomerie, Alexander, 10th E. of Eglinton, 11, 15
Montgomerie, Hon. Archibald, later 11th E. of Eglinton, 225-26, 236-37
Montgomerie, David, of Lainshaw, father of MM, 15
Montgomerie, James, bro. of MM, cousin of JB, 15, 36

Montgomerie, Jean (Maxwell), wife of preceding, 15, 36

Montgomerie, Mary, sis. of MM, later 2nd wife of James Campbell of Treesbank, 14, 15, 18, 19, 181

Montgomerie, Veronica (Boswell), sis. of Lord Auchinleck, mother of MM, 15

Montgomerie-Cuninghame, Capt. Alexander, 15, 160-61, 165

Montgomerie-Cuninghame, Elizabeth, wife of preceding, 15, 181, 220

Montgomerie-Cuninghame, Sir Walter, of Lainshaw, Bt., 15, 165

Montgomery, James, Lord Advocate, 71-72, 82-83, 171-72, 174-75

Morton, 8th E. of. See Douglas, William

Morton, 13th E. of. See Douglas, James

Morton, Andrew, stonemason, 44

Morton, Hugh, stonemason, 44, 48

Mountstuart, Lord. See Stuart, John

Moy Hall, Inverness-shire, 162

Muir, George, writer's clerk, 125, 130-31

Mure, William, of Caldwell, M.P., agricultural improver, 136-37, 213

Murphy, Arthur, playwright, School for Guardians, 110-11

Murray, Alexander, 4th Lord Elibank, 224

Murray, Hon. James, son of preceding, 223-24

Murray, Patrick, advocate depute, 71

Murray, William, M.P., later 5th E. of Mansfield, 267

Nairne, William, later Lord Dunsinnan, 166-67

Nani, Monsieur, of Bruxelles, 36

Napier, Hon. Charles, 77

Napier, Francis, 5th Lord Napier, 77

Nassau, Louise Susanna, C. van. See Degenfeld-Schomburg, Louise Susanna

Neill, Adam, printer in Edinburgh, 258

Newall, Adam Craufurd, of Polquhairn, 34

Newall, John, of Barskeoch, 34

Newhall, Yorkshire, Bosville estate, 99

North, Frederick, styled Lord North, later 2nd E. of Guilford, 233

Northumberland, 1st D. of. See Smithson, Hugh

Norton, Sir Fletcher, Attorney-General, 235

Nottingham, description of, 172-73

Nugent, Thomas, Travels Through Germany, 237

Offley, John, M.P. for Bedford, 196

Orford, 4th E. of. See Walpole, Horace

Ogilvie, Capt. James, ship's master, 212-13

Ogilvy (Ogilvie), Alexander, merchant in Leith, 240, 243

Oglethorpe, Gen. James Edward, 47

O'Hara, James, 2nd B. Tyrawley, Field Marshal, 55, 264-65

Orr, Alexander, W.S., legal agent, 184

Oswald, James Townshend, son of following, 30

Oswald, James, of Dunnikier, M.P., 30, 142-43

Oswald, Richard, London merchant, 44-45

Paoli, Giacinto, father of following, 69-70

Paoli, Pasquale, Corsican, General of the Nation, 1, 2, 5, 23, 31, 33, 68-70, 74, 75-77, 94, 101, 107-08, 110-111, 113, 116, 117, 126-28, 132, 139-40, 153, 160, 169, 177, and Code of Laws for Corsica, 185; and assassination attempts on, 194-95, 205; captures Capraia, 211; 222, 230, 246, 255,

Paris, François, 136-37

Parliament, House of Lords, 93-94

Parma, 8, 73

Paterson, William, writer and Town Clerk, Kilmarnock, 165

Paultons, estate of Hans Stanley, 176-77, 182

Percy, Algernon, son of Hugh Percy, 1st. D. of Northumberland, 29-30

Percy, Thomas, Bp. of Dromore, ed., Reliques of Ancient English Poetry, 239

Peter Leopold, Great Duke of Tuscany, 129

Peterson, Henry, bookkeeper in Utrecht, 9, 10, 115

Philip, King of Macedon, anecdote about, 13

Phinn, Thomas, engraver, 32, 52-53, 188

Piaggi, Padre Antonio, S.J., 123-24

Piccolomini, Girolama ('Moma'), wife of following, 3, 16, 127-28, 205, 239, 255-257

Piccolomini, Orazio, 4, 257

Pieck, Willem Hendrik. See Zoelen

Pieck, Anne Francis Willem. See Zoelen

Piranesi, Giovanni Battista, engraver, 162-63

Pitt, William, 1st E. of Chatham, 1-3, 31-32, 36, 63-64, 66, 69, 75-76, 106-07, 117, 138-40, 153, 236

Placidi, Placido, from Siena, 156-57

Pless, B. von. See Burchard, Cuno

Plutarch, 75-76

Poiret, Pierre, mystic, 130

Pomey, François-Antoine, The Pantheon, ('Tooke's Pantheon'), 240, 243

Pope, Alexander, Essay on Man, 103-04

Porter, Lucy, stepdaughter of SJ, 238-39

Portici, Museum of, 124

Poussin, Nicolas, painter, 205-06

Pratt, Charles, B. Camden, later 1st E., Lord Chancellor, 179, 266-67

Preston, Agnes, dau. of following, 74

Preston (Anne Cochrane), Lady, wife of following, 70, 74

Preston, Sir George, of Valleyfield, Bt., 74, 159

Preston, Patrick, son of preceding, East India Co., 136, 158-59, 220-21

Pringle, Andrew, Lord Alemore, 235

Pringle, Sir John, Bt., M.D., P.R.S., xliii, xlv, xlvii, 16, 31, 34-35, 41, 81, 101, 106, 110, 118-19, 260-62

Pérez, C. Jean-Baptiste de, 109-10

Queensberry, 3rd D. of. See Douglas, Charles

Rabaut, Paul, Protestant pastor, 22
Rabelais, François, Gargantua, 135, 137
Racine, Louis, Life of Milton, 8
Rae, David, Lord Eskgrove, 143
Rambonnet, Jean-Jacques, 81-82
Ramsay, Allan, poet, 79
Ramsay, John, of Ochtertyre, 151
Ramsay, Peter, innkeeper, Red Lyon Inn, 196, 199-200, 204
Ramsay, Robert, M.D., 54
Reede-Ginckel, Frederik van, 5th E. of Athlone, 81
Reid, Benjamin, son of John Reid, 83
Reid, Rev. George, Lord Auchinleck's tutor, 44-45, 48,
Reid, Janet, wife of John Reid, 83
Reid, Jean or Jane (Campbell), wife of Rev. George, 44
Reid, Janet, dau. of following, 83
Reid, John, sheepstealer, 82-83, 88, 93, 95, 146
Reni, Guido, painter, 163
Reyburn, Robert, bonnet-maker, 164-65
Reynst, Jean Lucas, Dutch army officer, 46-47
Richardson, Rev. Robert, D.D., 241, 243
Richardson, William, bookseller, 248-49, 251
Richmond, Surrey, 41
Rivarola, Count Antonio, Sardinian chargé d'affaires, 5, 23, 31, 36, 64-66, 68, 94, 116, 125, 152-54
Rochead of Inverleith, family of, 215-16
Rochefoucauld de Roye, Jean-Baptiste-Louis-Frédéric de la, 21-22
Rochefoucauld, Marie-Louise-Nicole de la, Duchesse d'Anville, 20-22
Ross, David, manager, Theatre Royal, Edinburgh, 262-63
Rostini, Abbé Carlo, Paoli's treasurer, 194-95
Rousseau, Jean-Jacques, 6, 8, 13-14, 22, 24-25, 41, 46-47, 49, 51-52, 73, 91-93, 96-97, 128, 146, 148, 185, 218-19, 257; Emile, 8; Lettres écrites de la montagne, 8; Second Discourse, 73
Rowand, John, gaoler, 88
Rutherford, Robert, merchant in Leghorn, 190

Salmon, Thomas, New Geographical and Historical Grammar, 240, 243
Sansedoni, Giovanni Ambrogio, 157
Sansedoni, Porzia, wife of preceding, 156-57
Santi, Captain, in Leghorn, 36, 68, 181
Sardinia, King of, 127
Savile, Sir George, Bt., 235
Schoepflin, Jean-Daniel, historiographer, Historia Zoeringo-Badensis, 103-04
Schoonhaven, Holland, 43
Schouwen, Schelde estuary, 43
Scott, Francis, 2nd D. of Buccleuch, 223-24
Scott, Magdalen (Le Mercier), 2nd wife of

William Scott, 19-21, 136-37
Scott, Magdalen, dau. of preceding, 19-21, 136
Scott, Robert, M.D. and apothecary, 223-24
Seton, Elizabeth, of Touch, 219
Seton, Hugh, of Touch, son of Charles Smith, 218-19
Sharp, Samuel, Letters, 249-50
Siena, Italy, 3-5
Sinclair, William, of Ratter, later 10th E. of Caithness, 200-01
Smith, Rev. Andrew, 16
Smith, Charles, Scots merchant and Jacobite agent, 217-18
Smith, James, writer in Edinburgh, JB's schoolfellow, 18, 63
Smith, John, horse buyer, 133
Smith, John, of Drongan, 85
Smith, Mungo, of Drongan, son of preceding, 84-85
Smith, Rev. Thomas, 183-84
Smith v. Steel, 150
Smithson, Hugh, 1st D. of Northumberland, 99
Smollett, Tobias, 195
Sommelsdyck, Cornelius, Heer van (d. 1662), 130
Sommelsdyck, Everdina Petronella, wife of following, 11, 12, 42
Sommelsdyck, François Cornelius van Aerssen, Heer van, 11, 12, 17, 26, 42-44, 129-30, 191
Sommelsdyck, François Johan, son of preceding, 11-12
Sommelsdyck, Lucia (van Waltha) (d. 1664), wife of Cornelius, Heer van, 130
Sommelsdyck, Petronella (Borre) van Aerssen, Vrouwe van (b. 1578), 130
Spaen, Alexander Sweder, B. von Spaen, 47
Spaen, Elisabeth Agnes Jacoba, B. von, wife of preceding, 18, 45-47, 134
Spaen, Willem Anne, son of B. von Spaen, Dutch official, 47
Sparta, i.e., Corsica, 121-23
Spence, Rev. Joseph, anecdotist and writer, 58-60, 75
Spencer, John, of Cannon Hall, Cawthorne, 55, 264
Stanley, Hans, M.P. for Southampton, 176-77, 182
Steel, Archibald, cause of Steel v. Smith, 13
Stefanopoli, Dr., 77
Stephen and Renny, merchants in Hamburg, 169-70, 185
Steuart, Sir James, Bt., later Steuart-Denham, advocate and economist, 212-13, 219-20
Stewart, Archibald, merchant in Rotterdam, 54, 63, 89-90, 191
Stewart, Sir Michael, of Blackhall, Bt., 90
Stewarton rioters, 160-61, 164-65
Stobie, John, factor, 70, 221
Strafford, 2nd E. of. See Wentworth, William

Strange, Isabella, wife of following, 163

Strange, Robert, engraver, 125, 162, 206

Strawberry Hill, Twickenham, estate of Horace Walpole, 172-73

Strichen, Lord. *See* Fraser, Alexander

Stuart, Charlotte Jane (Windsor), V. Mountstuart, 105

Stuart, Jean, C. of Dundonald, 2nd wife of 9th E., 220-21

Stuart, John, Lord Mountstuart, *later* 4th E and 1st M. of Bute, 13-14, 30-31, 36, 39-40, 52-53, 88, 102, 104-05

Stuart, John, 3rd E. of Bute, Prime Minister, 14, 137

Stuart, Mary (Wortley-Montagu), C. of Bute, wife of 3rd E. of Bute, 55-56

Sulivan, Laurence, M.P., director, East India Company, 159

Symonds, John, historian 1, 194-95, 231-32, 251

Tait, Alexander, W.S., 141, 143

Tait, John, W.S., 131, 137

Talbot, William, 1st E. Talbot, Steward of Royal Household, 100

Temple, Rev. William Johnson, 3, 30, 64, 132, 234

Theodore, King of Corsica, 153-54, 248-49, 251

Thomson, James, poet, *The Castle of Indolence*, 59-60

Thorpe Hall, Yorkshire, 39

Thrale, Hester Lynch (Salusbury), later Mrs. Piozzi, 239, 249-50

Thurlow, Edward, barrister, *later* B. Thurlow, and Lord Chancellor, 266-67

Tissot, Simon-André, M.D., 82

Tod, Capt. George, shipmaster, 28

Trotz, Christian Heinrich, Professor of Law, Utrecht, 10-11

Tullochrom, Inverness-shire, 61

Tyrawley, 2nd B. *See* O'Hara, James

Urquhart, Sir Thomas, translator of Rabelais, 137

Valleyfield, Fife, 74, 220

Van Tuyll van Serooskerken, Diederik Jacob. *See* Zuylen, Heer van

Van Tuyll van Serooskerken, Diederik, ('Ditie'), bro. of following, 81, 116

Van Tuyll van Serooskerken, Isabella Agneta Elisabeth. *See* Zuylen, Belle de (Zélide)

Van Tuyll van Serooskerken, Vincent Maximilaan, bro. of preceding, 116

Van Tuyll van Serooskerken, Willem, bro. of Belle de Zuylen, 74, 79, 81, 115-16

Vasco, Padre Pio Clemente, Dominican, 8

Vernet, Jean-Jacob, Swiss theologian, 241, 243

Villegas, Gen. de, Dutch general, 43

Virgil: *Aeneid*, iv, 144; *Eclogues*, 75; *Georgics*, 75, 169

Voltaire, 24-25, 131-32, 219, *Sentiment des citoyens*, 8; *Tancrède*, 241, 243

Walker, Rev. John, botanist, 209

Walkinshaw, Clementina, 27

Wallace, William, writer, 134

Wallace, William, of Cairnhill, advocate, 62

Walpole, Horace, *later* 4th E. of Orford, 129, 172-73

Ward, Julia (Bosville), V. Dudley and Ward, 39, 54

Ward, William, 3rd V. Dudley and Ward, 39

Wargemont, Chevalier de, 132

Waters, George, bro. of following, 27

Waters, John, JB's banker in Paris, 5, 27, 156-57

Wemyss, Lady Catherine (Lindsay), wife of following, 60

Wemyss, John, Lt.-Governor of Edinburgh Castle, 60

Wentworth families, 55

Wentworth, Annabella, sis. of Sir Thomas, 38, 56, 99, 172-73

Wentworth, John, Governor of New Hampshire, 99-100

Wentworth, Sir Thomas, bro. of Diana Bosville, 38, 54, 99, 172-73

Wentworth, William, 2nd E. of Strafford, 55

Westphalia, Treaty of, 107-08

Whitworth, Richard, aspiring M.P., 264-65

Widdrington, John, merchant in Newcastle, 205, 207, 211

Wilkes, John, 5, 25-26, 100

Wilkie, John, publisher of *Lond. Chron.*, 16, 24, 63-64, 75, 100, 101, 151, 158, 169, 249, 251

Willem V, Prince of Orange, Stadtholder, 11-12, 43, 242, 244

Willison, George, portrait of JB, 101-02

Windram, James, JB's client, 135-36, 159

Windsor, Herbert Hickman Windsor, V., 105

Wishart, William Thomas, 10

Witherspoon, John, President of Princeton College, 131

Woburn Abbey, seat of D. of Bedford, 172-3

Wood, Adam, London merchant, 62-63

Wood, John, bookbinder and bookseller, 227

Woodfall, Henry Sampson, editor of *Pub. Adv.*, 217, 249, 251

Wooton, Staffordshire, 148

Woulfe, George, nephew of John Waters, 27

Woulfe, Laurent, bro. of preceding, 27

Wright, Sir James, Resident at Venice, 232

Wyvill, Edward, father of following, 209-11

Wyvill, Rev. Christopher, Parliamentary reformer, 209-10, 220, 233-4

York Buildings Co., 145-46

Yvon, Pierre, Labadist leader, 130

Zoelen, Anne Frans Willem Pieck, Heer van, Dutch wastrel, 43-44

Zoelen, Willem Hendrik Pieck, Heer van, 43
Zoelen children, 43
Zuylen, Belle de, dau. of following, 47, 81, 114, 116, 186, 240-44, 247
Zuylen, Diederik Jacob van Tuyll van

Serooskerken, Heer van, 26, 81, 115, 244
Zuylen, Helena Jacoba (de Vicq) van, wife of preceding, 80-81
Zélide. *See* Zuylen, Belle de